D0021345

Inner Circles

Inner Circles

HOW AMERICA CHANGED THE WORLD

A MEMOIR

ALEXANDER M. HAIG, Jr.

with Charles McCarry

WARNER BOOKS

A Time Warner Company

Copyright © 1992 by Worldwide Associates, Inc.
All rights reserved.

Warner Books, Inc., 1271 Avenue of the Americas, New York, NY 10020

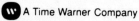 A Time Warner Company

Printed in the United States of America
First Printing: September 1992
10 9 8 7 6 5 4 3 2 1

Library of Congress Cataloging-in-Publication Data

Haig, Alexander Meigs, 1924–
    Inner circles : how America changed the world : a memoir /
Alexander M. Haig, Jr.
        p.   cm.
    Includes bibliographical references and index.
    ISBN 0-446-51571-X
    1. United States—Foreign relations—1945–1989. 2. United States—
Foreign relations—1989– 3. Haig, Alexander, 1924– . I. Title.
E840.H335   1992
973.927'092—dc20
[B]   91-50409
                                                             CIP

Book design by Giorgetta Bell McRee

To all who served the cause of freedom in the Cold War,
and especially to the 113,000 Americans who laid down
their lives for humanity in Korea and Indochina.

Non omnis moriar.

CONTENTS

ACKNOWLEDGMENTS ix

I. A MILITARY CALLING

1. Haigs and Murphys 3
2. Councils of War 19
3. Meeting the Enemy 38
4. "Fierce Actions" 52

II. VERSIONS OF PEACE

5. Army Life 73
6. A Trip to Iran 84
7. Missiles and Mythology 93
8. Covert Actions 106
9. The Gulf of Tonkin 117
10. Vietnam: The Illusion 125
11. Vietnam: The Chemistry 140
12. Vietnam: The Reality 155

III. NIXON'S WORLD

13. Homecoming 183
14. Nixon and Kissinger 192

15. National Security 210
16. Steel and Mush 224
17. Cambodia 233
18. Two Confrontations 241
19. Mission to China 256
20. The Art of the Possible 267
21. Biting the Bullet 281
22. A Parting of the Ways 291
23. Persuasive Force 304
24. Aftermath 315

IV. WATERGATE

25. "Deep Throat" 321
26. On Virtue 327
27. The Worst Happens 332
28. Shadow of a Coup 350
29. A Question of Innocence 371
30. Blindman's Buff 382
31. The Middle East Crisis 409
32. The Burden of Proof 418
33. The Tale of the Tapes 435
34. Hail and Farewell 457
35. The Smoking Gun 466
36. The Final Paradox 487

V. ABROAD AND AT LARGE

37. Ford's White House 509
38. The Western Alliance 520
39. Carter Abroad 531
40. Politics 544
41. Afterword: America, the Future, the World 553

A NOTE ON SOURCES 569
NOTES 570
INDEX 599

ACKNOWLEDGMENTS

My wife, Patricia Fox Haig, has been my companion in every detail of this book, as in the life on which it is based. Our children, Alexander, Brian, and Barbara, offered many valuable suggestions, as did my sister, Regina Haig Meredith, and my brother, the Reverend Francis Haig, S.J. Marjorie E. Rynas and Nancy Stanford McCarry performed with admirable efficiency and unfailing cheerfulness the difficult jobs of researching and checking facts for a work that covers nearly half a century of American history and personal experience. Their task was made easier by the generous cooperation of the staff of the Library of Congress, where my personal papers are stored, and especially by the Librarian of Congress, Dr. James Billington; by Dr. James H. Hutson, chief of the Manuscript Division, and his staff; and in the main library by Victoria Hill, assistant chief of the Humanities and Social Sciences Division; Bruce Martin, head of research facilities; and the Library's dedicated research librarians, especially David Kelly and Arthur Emerson. At the Nixon Presidential Materials Project of the National Archives, Clarence Lyons, Jr., and Walter Owen were unfailingly helpful, as were Gene Keating and Donald Smith of the Archives' Center for Electronic Records. At Warner Books, I have benefited from the enthusiasm and professional advice of my editor, Nanscy Neiman, and at the William Morris Agency from the sagacity of Norman Brokaw and Owen Laster. My longtime associates

Sherwood D. Goldberg, Harvey Sicherman, Richard Sinnreich, and Loyd Williams reviewed portions of the manuscript and provided valuable counsel. I benefited also from the comments of Charles Alan Wright, DeWitt Smith, Joseph A. Califano, Jr., John M. Buck, Fritz Kraemer, and Generals William DePuy, George Joulwan, Robert Schweitzer, and Hamilton Twitchell.

A. M. H.

It is excellent
To have a giant's strength; but it is tyrannous
To use it like a giant.

WILLIAM SHAKESPEARE,
Measure for Measure, II, ii.

Korea 1950-1951

Map by Hildegard B. Groves

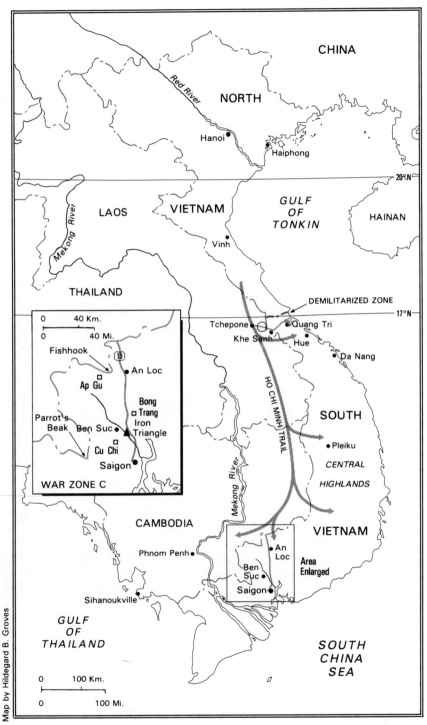

Indochina during the Vietnam War

Map by Hildegard B. Groves

I

A MILITARY CALLING

Commanders should be counseled, chiefly, by persons of known talent; by those . . . whose knowledge is gained from experience; by those who are present at the scene of action, who see the country, who see the enemy; who see the advantages that occasions offer, and who, like people embarked in the same ship, are sharers of the danger. If, therefore, anyone thinks himself qualified to give advice respecting the war which I am to conduct . . . let him come with me into Macedonia.

LUCIUS ÆMELIUS PAULUS,
as quoted in Titus Livius's *History of Rome*
(Copied from the framed translation on the wall
of General MacArthur's office in Tokyo.)

1

Haigs and Murphys

My father, who died five days after my ninth birthday, was commissioned a first lieutenant in the infantry after finishing his studies at the University of Pennsylvania Law School in the spring of 1917. He became a machine-gun instructor in various stateside training camps, but World War I ended before he could be sent to France. His uniform and equipment were stored in the attic of his parents' house in Merchantville, New Jersey. I was still a very small boy, no more than six or seven, when I found them there—the rakish Anglo-American steel helmet, the gas mask in its canvas pouch marked U.S., the web belt with canteen, first-aid kit, and pistol holster suspended on hooks from the brass grommets, and the scratchy khaki uniform itself with my father's silver bars pinned to the shoulder straps of the high-necked tunic.

Thereafter, on our Sunday visits to my Haig grandparents, I crept upstairs as soon as I could slip away after the midday dinner and quietly played soldier, all alone in that vast, shadowy attic. No adult interfered, least of all my long-suffering Grandmother Haig. I was a rambunctious child who had formerly spent my Sundays racing wildly around the broad Victorian porches of the house with my older sister, Regina. Although Regina was, at that time, a bit of a tomboy, she took no interest in helmets and gas masks, and could not understand my fascination with these wonderful objects. Thereafter, she stayed downstairs in the parlor, where

3

under my mother's resolute example and my grandmother's withering eye she became noticeably more ladylike.

As time passed I carried my father's military kit home with me, item by item, to our house in Bala Cynwyd, Pennsylvania, on the Philadelphia main line. My father condoned this pilferage by never remarking on it when I climbed into the car at the end of the day with the stolen goods. I think he may even have got a kick out of it, but it was difficult to tell. Alexander Meigs Haig was an aloof father who neither punished nor conversed with his children, and although his death was, and remains, the critical event of my life, I remember the uniform I never saw him wear better than I remember him.

My younger brother, Frank, is said to resemble our father; the family agrees that I look like my mother, whose assertive temperament I also inherited. As a child, naturally, my father seemed tall to me, slender (though with the beginnings of a lawyer's paunch), impeccably dressed in a high starched collar, snowy shirt, and dark suit as for an appearance in court, always with his pince-nez strung around his neck on a gold chain. It is impossible to imagine him in old clothes and a baseball cap. Even in his relaxed moments he seemed to be dressed for an exotic life in a world apart: he was an amateur cricket player and sometimes appeared in grass-stained knee pads with a strange, foreign paddlelike bat in his hands.

In retrospect, it seems to me that he always behaved the way he dressed, a little too formally, a little too correctly. This memory of paternal severity does not, however, accord with the facts of my childhood. Father had a merry side, especially when he was near my mother, and I remember the two of them skylarking and him singing popular songs from sheet music while she played the piano by ear. He himself was an accomplished pianist who, on more formal social occasions, was often coaxed into playing something by Bach or Brahms, peering at the score through his pince-nez while Mother turned the pages. Certainly he was good to us children, even if he was not a roughhousing father who got down on the floor with us. When I cried one Labor Day because we were leaving the New Jersey shore after a golden summer in a rented cottage, he said, "Don't worry, Alex—we'll take the beach home with us!" And, pince-nez swinging, he shoveled a huge washtub full of sand and wrestled it into the trunk of our car. In fact, whatever we wanted as children, as long as he lived, we got—or perhaps it only seemed that way in the less carefree years that followed his death.

He died without life insurance, his savings eaten up by medical bills and the cost of supporting his family during his illness. He lingered for more than a year, with many stays in the hospital. He died at home. The agonizing disease that killed him—not merely cancer but cancer of the colon—was then considered a shameful cause of death, and we children were sworn to silence about it by my mother, who herself kept the secret until the day she died. He had been a rising young lawyer, and each big case he won was like a ship coming in. It is true that he left his family in dramatically reduced circumstances, but how could he possibly have known that he was going to die before he was forty? The sense of optimism that came with success caused him to spend what he earned, in the expectation that more money would come, as it had always done before. After he died, the Packard and Studebaker cars, the rented summer cottages on the Jersey shore, the maid and the nanny, the private schools, and the other luxuries he had provided for his wife and family, and which seemed to us to be the normal paraphernalia of middle-class life, were suddenly revealed as ruinous extravagances.

My mother, to whom my father had refused nothing, was devastated by this change in fortune. Married when barely out of her teens, she had had a brief career as an English teacher in the days before teachers were required to have a college degree, but that had changed, and now she had no trade or profession, no earning power. How would she keep the family together? How would we survive? The year was 1933, the very bottom of the Great Depression. Regina and I talked of working after school, and in time we both did so, but we could not earn enough between us in a week to feed the family for a day. Seven-year-old Frank, though already recognized as an intellectual prodigy, was a calamity kid who seemed to catch every contagious disease that passed by the door. His more or less constant need for Mother's bedside care made it unlikely that she could ever work outside the house. She tried selling cosmetics and, later, religious articles; she tried any number of schemes to earn money at a time when almost no one was earning enough of it. For the remainder of her life, I think, she hoped continually for a way out of the situation into which God had put her. None ever materialized, but she never abandoned hope, and, as the years passed, her struggle against adversity transformed itself into a burning ambition for her children. She wanted all of us, including her daughter, to succeed in school, to enter the professions, to know the satisfactions that our hardworking father had known in his own career. In my case, she saw some natural aptitude for my father's old profession that never revealed itself to me, and the leitmotiv of her motherly advice was composed of three oft-repeated words:

Study the law. Writing down the phrase even now, I hear her voice again and smile at the recollection.

My father's friends, and he had many of them from his own world, disappeared almost as soon as he was buried. They had little in common with my mother, born Regina Anne Murphy in a house with lace curtains in northeast Philadelphia. How this high-church Episcopalian lawyer and high-spirited Irish Catholic maiden met and fell in love, let alone married and produced children, in the socially stratified Philadelphia of the early twentieth century remains a mystery. Although she was full of stories about her life with my father, Mother seldom spoke of their courtship except to say that another man, a fellow Irishman who subsequently became a judge in Pittsburgh, had already proposed marriage to her when she met my father, but it must have been a tempestuous one to overcome the differences between them. My father had gone to the William Penn Charter School and the University of Pennsylvania, where he played piano in productions of the theatrical society, Mask and Wig. He came from a Scots-English family that shared the same bloodlines as the Haigs of Bemerside, Scotland, distillers of the well-known Scotch whisky, and Field Marshal Douglas Earl Haig, commander in chief of the British Expeditionary Force in France and Flanders during World War I. (When I met the British Haigs many years later, I discovered that they knew all about the American Haigs and that the stories of the two branches of the family matched quite closely.) Although my mother's uncle John Murphy was a Pennsylvania state senator and all her brothers were members of the learned professions, her chief credentials, from the Haigs' point of view, were her extraordinary beauty—which never faded to the end of her long life—and the charm of her joyful personality. From a very early age, I was aware that my Grandmother Haig looked down her lorgnette on my mother. I think it is possible that the impulsive and romantic marriage my mother and father contracted—he adored her and made no effort to conceal his feelings—must have been seen by his parents as a repudiation of the conventions of his upbringing. Certainly his conversion to Roman Catholicism and the deep sincerity with which he embraced his adopted faith were sore points in a family that regarded its Anglicanism as a social credential as well as a religious affiliation. The Haigs believed that they owned the finest house in Merchantville; the original American Haig emigrated to the New World just after the Revolutionary War and made his fortune in pottery, and all of his descendants had made their livings in equally respectable ways. On the other hand, my Irish grandfather, Edward Murphy, had owned a tobacco factory, which failed in the

1890s, and then opened a saloon for workingmen. He sent two of his four sons to law school and two to medical school on the profits. He got little credit from the other side of my family for this admirable American accomplishment: "Blood money," Grandmother Haig (momentarily forgetting the label on the Haig & Haig bottle) called the sinful proceeds from Murphy's saloon.

My Grandmother Haig, already widowed, died soon after my father did. By then, the Great Crash and Depression had turned whatever remained of "the Haig fortune" into a memory. The Haigs did not desert us. My uncle Chester Haig, an Army surgeon who had been General of the Army John J. Pershing's personal physician, and who at one time held a high post at Walter Reed Hospital, was very kind to my mother, often calling on us and keeping tabs on the family. He was a lively conversationalist, a former Rhodes scholar, and the first grown-up to speak to me about the world and my future in it as if I were an intellectual equal. Another uncle, Howard Haig, a dentist who sported a spiffy waxed mustache, something like Mandrake the Magician's in the funny papers, took care of our teeth free of charge.

The Murphys rallied round in typical Irish style with affection and advice and assistance, but they all had large families of their own to worry about. It was my mother's older sister, my Aunt Mame, and her kindly and good-hearted husband, John H. Neeson, who came to our rescue in a practical way. This remarkable couple had taken my mother into their home when she was orphaned as a young girl, and now they stepped forward at another tragic moment to help her raise her own family. Uncle John, a graduate of Notre Dame University and an enthusiastic football fan who was a close friend of Knute Rockne and of all Four Horsemen, was for many years the head of public works for the city of Philadelphia. He contributed twenty-five dollars a week toward our support and paid the rent on our house in Bala Cynwyd from the month my father died until we children were grown. These were considerable sums for the time, but the money John Neeson gave us was only a small part of the unfailing, unstinting support, moral and material, that he and Aunt Mame extended to us every day of our lives. We frequently visited them in their large, dignified house in North Philadelphia, and never a weekend went by when they did not visit us in Bala Cynwyd, always arriving in a long chauffeured limousine of the old type, in which the liveried driver sat in an open compartment and received his orders from the "cabin" over a voice tube. Aunt Mame and Uncle John always came bearing gifts and exuding cheerful affection. Aunt Mame loved her beautiful younger sister dearly; she was altogether a motherly, practical, humorous, down-to-earth woman—in the Irish phrase, the rock to which my mother clung. She and Uncle John saved our family, and the passage of more than half a century has served to make the example of their Christian behavior only brighter and more admirable in my memory and estimation.

Whether Uncle John imagined that his financial obligation would last as long as, in fact, it did, I do not know. It would have been reasonable to suppose that a woman in her early thirties who was as famous for her beauty as my mother would marry again. And indeed she had many suitors in the years just following my father's death, but with my sister's enthusiastic help I contrived ways to make conversation with these gentleman callers impossible and drove them out the door one after the other. It seemed to me from the beginning of our life as a fatherless family that I was the man in the house. I loved my mother, but in my stern opinion she was too inclined to let herself be carried away by frivolity, and was too much impressed by appearances. I thought she needed protection. I should have known that memories of my father, who died so untimely, and her complete dedication to her children eliminated any possibility of a new marriage. My mother tolerated my presumptuousness and patiently went on loving me and my siblings, giving a sense of direction and an emotional and ethical center to a family that in the end, I hope, lived up to her hopes for it: My sister became a lawyer as well as a wife and mother; and my brother, a Jesuit priest and university president. Mother left me in no doubt, however, that my own failure to heed her advice to follow in my father's legal footsteps was a bit of unfinished business between us. When, in 1979, I was informed that the doctors had given her only a short time to live, I rushed home from Europe, where I was stationed as NATO commander, and went directly from the airport to her hospital room without changing out of my uniform. Mother looked up at me as I stood over her with four stars on my shoulders and ribbons on my chest, smiled forgivingly, and said, "Oh, Alex, if you had only studied the law, you might have made something of yourself." Those were virtually her last words to me.

There was never the slightest chance, after I discovered that uniform in the attic, that I would be anything but a soldier. For a long time, no doubt, the intention was unconscious, but it was always foremost: I felt the pull of the adventure and excitement of the military life from the very first. Also, like my mother, I suppose I was looking for some way to escape the humdrum circumstances of my life, and even as a child I understood that I had to break out of Philadelphia in order to do that. My father's social credentials were not inheritable; the Haigs had passed on; I had to make my own way. From early boyhood, my heart was set on West Point. Idealistically (but accurately, as it turned out), I saw the Army as a just system in which a young man could rise according to his ability and his willingness to work. And then, of course, there was the uniform itself and everything it symbolized to an eager young mind in terms of the Military Academy's noble motto: Duty, Honor, Country.

Life as a fatherless boy in the Great Depression was hard, and I made it harder by taking it so seriously. As in D. H. Lawrence's short story "The Rocking Horse Winner," the family's haunting need for more money was in the air I breathed. The pittance I could contribute helped very little, but I always had several jobs and money-making schemes. I mowed lawns, shoveled walks, delivered those two great Philadelphia publications, *The Saturday Evening Post* and the *Evening Bulletin*. The parish priest, aware of our family's circumstances, made sure that I served as altar boy at more than my share of weddings and funerals, and this brought in a small but steady income in tips. Later on, dreaming of greater riches (say, a hundred dollars), I organized a number of short-term business schemes, such as distributing programs at football games, and hired other boys to help me.

Most of my neighborhood friends were older than I was, and most were hell-raisers. Many would not have been welcome in "the best house in Merchantville, New Jersey." Mother didn't really approve, either, but she understood why I liked my rough-and-ready friends, and she made them welcome when I brought them to the house. They loved her. She had the Irish gifts of gab and hospitality and could make any stranger feel at home. Mother had the gift of happiness, too, and, better than anyone I've ever known, she knew how to make others happy; my father's joy in their marriage is still a vivid memory to me. In spite of all obstacles raised by his premature death and the collapse of the economy, we were a close and contented family. Mother wasn't one to dwell on misfortunes of the past; it was the glories of the future that occupied her imagination in our daily councils around the kitchen table. After dinner (with help in English from Mother, who was a true expert in grammar and a true lover of the inexhaustible felicities of the language), we did our homework around that table, and there we discussed our finances, our problems, our doubts and disappointments and hopes, and, most of all, our futures. Mother was a great believer in the basic American proposition that in our country any young person can make a fortunate future come to pass through a combination of hard work and upright behavior. At times, when I was young, I doubted this, but of course she was right and I was—well, young.

I got by better as a student at Saint Mathias parochial school than most of my pals. The "interesting subjects"—that is to say, anything but arithmetic and science—came easily to me, and I ranked first among the boys academically on graduation from eighth grade. I was well up in class rank in mischief, too, but I suffered no serious consequences. The nuns who were my teachers liked me (even my sister says I made an angelic appearance in altar-boy togs) and tolerated behavior that they shouldn't have tolerated. I always liked them, too; they were good and kindly women who loved children and wanted nothing more than to help each one of their pupils live up to God's expectations for them.

In my last year at Saint Mathias, I had a stroke of good fortune when I entered a citywide spelling bee and against all expectations, including my own (I have always been a very poor speller), became a finalist. There were only three or four of us still standing when I stumbled on the word *trafficking*. The prize was a partial scholarship to Saint Joseph's Preparatory School, a Jesuit institution in Philadelphia, and I stayed there for two profitable years, working hard on the subjects I hoped would get me into West Point, before the burden of paying even partial tuition became too much to bear and I transferred to public high school.

By then, it was 1940 and World War II was almost upon us, and as I devoured the newspaper and watched the fall of France and the Battle of Britain in the newsreels, a life in uniform seemed more appealing than ever. It was clear even to a sixteen-year-old that the military was going to play an important role in the American future. At the same time, I was beginning to develop intellectual interests, even political opinions. My sister was now attending Temple University in Philadelphia, though of course she lived at home as an economy measure. Among her courses was one in Marxist economics. Apparently, the subject was taught with enthusiasm by a persuasive professor, because Regina brought it home with her, starting a colossal, and wildly enjoyable, argument with me that went on nearly every evening until she won a full three-year scholarship to the University of Pennsylvania Law School and had less time to bait me. Those kitchen-table debates, juvenile as they no doubt were, forced me to read with an independent mind in order to collect information with which to outflank Regina (no easy task then or now), and the experience left me with convictions about Marxism-Leninism as a political philosophy, and about the U.S.S.R. as a society, that persist to this day. These convictions are, in brief, that the former was a manifest fraud and the latter a vile tyranny. Early though these beliefs may have formed, they were intellectual rather than visceral; it just seemed obvious to me, as George F. Kennan was to write in a famous essay years afterward, that "lacking wide popular support for their choice of bloody revolution as a means of social betterment, these revolutionaries found in Marxist theory a highly convenient rationalization for their own instinctive desires."[1]

In public school, I gave up some of the rigors of study imposed by the Jesuits for the joys of the football field and the after-school camaraderie that was such a happy feature of adolescent life in America. It is also true that the presence of girls in the halls and classrooms of Lower Merion High School in Ardmore, Pennsylvania, was a distraction. Nevertheless, I maintained a respectable $B+$ average and continued to hope for an appointment to West Point. In a way, such an appointment was my only hope. When I graduated in 1942, I had no money for college and no realistic prospects for a scholarship to a civilian university. My uncle John Neeson, who had political connections, arranged an appointment as a third alternate candidate for appointment to the United States Military Academy. This meant that I was good enough to be noticed but not good enough to be singled out. I was not selected.

My mother advised me to swallow my disappointment and believe that my chance would come again; secretly, no doubt, she hoped that I would come to my senses and start thinking about law school. But my mind was firmly made up in favor of the military life: I investigated the flight-training programs of the Army Air Force and the Navy, but at seventeen I was too young to be accepted. To Mother's relief, I was so intent on being an officer, as my father had been, that I did not seriously consider enlistment in the Marines or the Navy; you had to be eighteen to join the Army. Uncle John, who among his many other distinctions was a trustee of Notre Dame University, made a deal with me: He would underwrite my tuition at Notre Dame if I would earn the first year's tuition myself. I gave up the dream of West Point—I thought forever—and got a job as a floorwalker at John Wanamaker Department Store in Philadelphia, later transferring to much better-paying war work at the Atlantic Refining Company. By January, I had saved enough money to keep my bargain with Uncle John, and on arrival in South Bend I landed a job in the Notre Dame dining hall to pay for my food.

Somewhat to my surprise, I loved Notre Dame. The campus with its famous golden dome, stately buildings, and magnificent tree-shaded lawns was, and remains, the architectural realization of a dream of college life. I came to South Bend hoping to have a rollicking good time, and instead discovered the life of the mind. I learned to study, and as I studied I developed the gift of curiosity. My teachers then showed me how to satisfy that curiosity, or sharpen it further, by directing me to the great works that they already knew by heart. Thanks to them, I became aware of the universe of knowledge and excited by its limitless potential to describe, examine, and explain the human condition. My grades skyrocketed. Even the pedagogical resources of Notre Dame could not, however, persuade me to apply myself to mathematics and science. These subjects were too abstract; my interests were history, philosophy, literature, politics, and the social sciences. This was, of course, a peculiar concentration of studies for a young man who still hoped against hope to get into the United States Military Academy, where math and science were the lifeblood of the academic program and every cadet either graduated with a degree in engineering or did not graduate at all.

I began to wonder whether West Point was what I really wanted and whether a life in the military would be the best way to play a role in what I already perceived as the great cause of the postwar era, the struggle between democracy and evangelistic totalitarianism for the future of humanity. This was, however, a passing fancy. The magnetic pull of military life remained very strong. It was wartime, and I wanted to serve in uniform as so many of my high school friends were already doing. I hedged my bets by applying for an accelerated course that led in two academic years to a reserve commission as an ensign in the Navy and the opportunity to return to Notre Dame after the war to complete work on a bachelor's degree. I was interested in PT boats, partly because they were the most personal, and therefore the most soldierly, way of fighting the enemy on water and partly because even very young and junior officers were eligible for command.

Then, in the first semester of my sophomore year at South Bend, Uncle John Neeson stepped forward, as he had done so many times before, to make my chosen future possible. Through his connections, I was awarded a congressional appointment to the West Point class of 1947, and this time, thanks to my intellectual awakening at Notre Dame and the string of A's that were its result, I was good enough to be accepted. Mine was the last of the World War II classes that completed the Academy's course of study and training in three years instead of four. This accelerated schedule suited my impatient mood, and like nearly every other member of the class of 1947 I believed and hoped that the war would still be on when I graduated.

* * *

I had, of course, heard about West Point's famous discipline, which in those days included the hazing—that is, the systematic bullying and humiliation—of plebes by upperclassmen. It is one thing to read about hazing or see it acted out in the movies and another to undergo it in reality. In my case, it represented my first exposure to real, inescapable discipline, and it was a very rude awakening for a young man who had never before had to answer to an authority figure of any kind. In the first shock of being insulted, shouted at, and forced into ridiculous physical postures and even sillier verbal exchanges, I literally could not believe what was happening. Among my classmates were men who had been selected from the Army and who had given up wartime commissions as captains and majors and even, in a one case, as a lieutenant colonel in order to start all over again at West Point. The rest of us, though young and inexperienced, were intelligent human beings. I thought the whole process was childish, stupid, and petty (an opinion in which I have never wavered), and at first I made a joke of it. On one occasion, anticipating that the inspecting officer, a lieutenant colonel, would reach into a secret compartment in my bookcase in search of dust and contraband (crackers! cheese! peanut butter!), I poured an entire jar of honey inside. When he retrieved the sleeve of his magnificent melton greatcoat, it, and the yellow glove he wore in hopes of detecting dust, dripped with the sticky stuff. Not surprisingly, such pranks against the gods infuriated the designated bullies of the yearling (sophomore) class and drove them on to more imaginative outrages.

In a second stage of rebellion, I opposed the system by outwitting it in ways designed to make my contempt for it absolutely plain. In the dining hall, plebes who could not bellow out on command any one of the countless definitions and quotations we were all required to memorize could not get anything to eat. Some who had especially bad memories went for days without sustenance. I avoided malnutrition by going out for the boxing and football teams, which had training tables exempted from this nonsense, but found myself hoist on my own petard when I discovered that I had to diet in order to stay in my weight class: One or two extra pounds put me in the ring with bigger men capable of knocking my block off. At the same time, I was scrimmaging against the most famous varsity football team ever to play for the Academy. When called upon to try to tackle all-American fullback "Doc" Blanchard or absorb a block thrown by all-American tackle "Tex" Coulter, I could have used more meat on my rattling bones.

My attempts at fancy footwork, naturally, infuriated my tormentors even more, and the turning point came when one of the yearlings called me a draft dodger (a mortal insult in that day and age) while I was "braced" in the contorted parody of the military position of attention invented for such occasions. I stepped out of ranks and aimed a punch toward his eye. The hazing system was, of course, designed to break just such stubborn fools as I, and after that episode the whole weight of its accumulated lore came down on my close-cropped skull like a ton of sandbags. Few year-lings passed me by that fall and winter without bracing me while scream-ing an imprecation into my face with a shower of saliva or imposing some demeaning physical task. By night, when I should have been studying, I was subjected to "shower sessions" in which relays of upperclassmen forgathered in the shower room required me to perform marathon push-ups. The objective was to "pass you out"—that is, to render the plebe unconscious through overexertion. With each push-up (and thanks to my yearling friends I was eventually able to perform dozens at a session), I repeated a silent oath to myself: No son of a bitch is going to pass me out!

None ever did by the established methods, but one puckish yearling nearly succeeded in doing so by trickery. He ordered me to perform a time-honored West Point exercise in which the plebe, wearing a gas mask and holding a rifle at arm's length, performs the deep knee bends called "squats" in cadet jargon. This ingenious fellow, standing behind me, put the gas mask canister into a desk drawer and shut the drawer on the hose so I couldn't breathe. Just before passing out, I discovered what he had done and ripped off the gas mask. He laughed hilariously, and, when I caught my breath, so did I. Eventually, hazing came to an end, except at the hands of the fellow I had socked in the eye. Understandably, he had taken a special interest in me, coming into my room every hour on the hour throughout the night to dump my locker, so that I got no sleep for weeks, and inventing other ways too numerous to catalog to make my life miserable. Gradually, I realized that he was dedicated to driving me out of the Academy. As his activities made it almost impossible for me to study, it became clear that he might succeed. I was saved in the end by a first classman, a member of the varsity eleven, who had befriended me on the football field. As a football hero and senior, his word was law. He took my nemesis aside and told him to lay off; my troubles ceased.

By the time I began my second year as a cadet, the war was ending, and the West Point faculty began to receive an infusion of World War II heroes, youthful battalion and regimental commanders who had been wounded in the campaigns in Africa, Europe, and the Pacific. They had seen discipline tested on the battlefield, and under their influence the teaching of the military arts flourished and the ferocity of hazing moderated, though the practice itself persisted for years. Maj. Gen. Maxwell D. Taylor, fresh from battlefield commands in Europe, became Superintendent, and an exhilarating sense that the Academy was in the hands of a new generation of battle-hardened soldiers spread through the Corps of Cadets.

Nevertheless, I continued to throw myself against the thorny hedgerow of rules and regulations, with the result that I spend many hours "walking the area," as solitary drill while carrying a weapon was called. Instead of spending the time thus lost from my studies pounding the books, I got into the habit on weekends of slipping away after "Taps" to enjoy a convivial hour or two at Benny Haven's Tavern in nearby Highland Falls—and who knows but what I was beckoned thither by the sociable ghost of Grandfather Murphy? In any case, being out after "Taps" was a most serious offense, for which supernatural excuses were not accepted. When, inevitably, I got caught, I fully expected to be drummed out of the Corps. Instead, I was sentenced to six months' confinement. A cadet subjected to this punishment spent all his time when he wasn't in class either in his room or walking the area, forbidden recreation of any kind. That meant no movies, no football games, no pep rallies, no social punctuation of any kind in the long gray succession of days in that place of gray stone walls, gray skies, gray uniforms, and black and white rules of conduct.

So heinous was my crime, in fact, that the Commandant of Cadets himself, Brig. Gen. Gerald Higgins, summoned me to his office. Needless to say, this was our first face-to-face meeting, and as I fully expected him to upgrade my sentence to the maximum, it seemed likely that it would be our last. Higgins, famous for his humorless demeanor, began asking grimly whether I was guilty as charged. I admitted that I was. "Haig," he said, "how often have you done this?" We both knew he wasn't supposed to ask this question—I was in enough trouble on the basis of the single offense that had so far been proved. But I had no other choice but to answer truthfully; in the United States Army, every cadet and officer is always under oath. "Almost every weekend, sir!" I replied. Higgins nodded inscrutably. He held my future in his hands, and we both knew this, too. By what he said next, he showed that he knew it better than I did. "Haig, this is a serious matter; it has come to the attention of General Taylor himself and a decision has been made," the Commandant said. "You're not going on summer leave with the rest of your class in June.

Instead, I'm going to send you to Camp Buckner. There's an open slot
on the camp commander's staff. You're going to fill that slot for the
summer; then we'll decide what to do with you. That's all."

Higgins didn't tell me what the job was; Camp Buckner is the installation in New York State where West Point cadets spend the summer after
plebe (freshman) year in military training, so I knew it well. A few days
later, I reported to the commanding officer of Camp Buckner, Col.
Russell T. ("Red") Reeder, who had lost a leg in action against the
Wehrmacht. Reeder, a gifted writer who had published many popular
books and stories about the old Army, seemed to know all about my case.
(Years later, I learned that he had, in fact, discussed it with his friend
Maxwell Taylor, and probably with some of the other brass who visited
West Point for commencement ceremonies. With my usual unerring
timing, I had got caught in June Week, assuring maximum visibility and
gossip among visiting alumni, including many generals, who may or may
not, in their own youthful high spirits, have paid a visit to Benny Haven's
place. "I remember you, Haig," Taylor said when we met in line of duty
years later. "You were *some cadet*.")

Wasting no time on small talk, Reeder said, "I'm making you S-4 for
the entire camp. That's a lieutenant colonel's job." This meant that I, a
mere cadet, would be in charge of all logistics for Camp Buckner—and
not only that. Reeder continued: "You'll also be in charge of all punishment for this installation." My heart soared. I don't know whether Reeder
and Taylor cooked up this assignment between them, or whether Reeder
just gave me the one job he thought I was qualified by experience to do,
but the decision was Solomonic in its wisdom. This was the chance I had
been waiting for, to show the system how mistaken it was in its disciplinary
methods. "Sir, walking the area is stupid," I said. "Why not put these
men to constructive work?" Reeder told me to go right ahead; he didn't
care how I did my job as long as I got the right results. For the rest of the
summer, the erring yearling cadets of Camp Buckner (usually about 10
percent of the class on any given day) painted, raked, planted, weeded,
carpentered, and generally refurbished the camp. By September, the old
summertime post sparkled, its barracks covered with fresh paint, its lawns
trimmed, its walks graveled, its trees pruned, its sports fields rebuilt, its
flower beds geometric and weedless. It would be going too far to say that
the cadets who accomplished these wonders enjoyed the experience, but
they could at least see that they had accomplished something positive,
and I considered that an improvement over the tens of thousands of

invisible footprints I had left while walking the concrete area at West Point.

At summer's end, Colonel Reeder gave me the highest possible efficiency rating—remember, this was a lieutenant colonel's job I had been doing—and when I returned to the Academy I was pardoned by the Superintendent from completing the remainder of my six months of confinement. Whether I ever again visited Benny Haven's Tavern after "Taps" is a matter between me and my Irish great-grandfather, but thanks to Higgins and Taylor and Reeder, whose example of sagacious leadership guided me for the rest of my Army career, my life as a soldier began. I decided that I liked the Army, after all, and the Army began to show some sign that it liked me, too. I seemed to rise in the estimation of my superiors from near the bottom of the Corps to somewhere around the top. More responsibility came my way; I did well and was seen to do well; in due course I became a cadet officer (but lost my stripes temporarily for cutting a lecture—I wasn't completely rehabilitated). Nevertheless, like many a young man before me, I found myself motivated by golden opinions. I began to study harder, which enabled me at the end of the three-year course to graduate 214th in a class of 310. This was nothing to boast about, but it was better than I might have done, and better than George Armstrong Custer and George E. Patton had done before me. As I headed for my first assignment as a second lieutenant of cavalry, wearing, at last, the same insignia that my father had worn, I thought that I had as good a chance as any of my classmates to rise through the system. I had no hope of riches: General of the Army Douglas MacArthur, the most senior general in the service, was then being paid $18,761 a year.[2]

The prospects of promotion seemed fair: Men only three or four years older than I and my classmates were returning from combat with oak leaves and eagles on their shoulders. The war was over, it was true, but the United States remained the greatest military power in history, and the whole world understood that American primacy and lasting peace were indivisible. The tactical wartime pretense of a community of interests between the Soviet Union and the West was already being abandoned by Moscow. The Red Army, under the guise of liberation, had effectively annexed the ill-fated nations of Eastern Europe to the Soviet Union; Russian agents in Greece, Turkey, and Iran were plotting to do the same; a heavily armed Communist regime was being installed by Moscow in North Korea; leftist insurgencies were forming in Malaya and Indochina; the struggle between Mao Zedong's Communists and Chiang

Kai-shek's Kuomintang for control of China presented one third of the world's people with appalling alternatives in regard to their future.

As a plebe, I had written a theme arguing that the geopolitical factors (Russian national interest, the defeat of Germany and Japan, the exhaustion of Britain, the weakness of the rest of Europe, the humiliation of China, and what Kennan was later to call the Soviet leaders' belief in an ideological "duty eventually to overthrow the political forces beyond their borders"[3]) suggested that America's likeliest postwar enemy would be its wartime ally, the Soviet Union. At the time, this paper puzzled some of my instructors in its unorthodox, not to say unfashionable, treatment of the evidence. But as the reality of these factors revealed themselves in one crisis after another, it seemed inconceivable to me that the United States, having stumbled unprepared into two world wars in the space of twenty-five years, and now facing the undiminished military power of a hostile Soviet Union, would be so blind to its own national interests and so deaf to the lessons of history as to rush into virtual unilateral disarmament. But that is exactly what the Truman administration did. By the time I made first lieutenant, three years after graduation, the mighty American Army that had played the decisive role in destroying the Axis powers in the greatest war ever fought had turned into a memory.

First from the vantage point of Gen. Douglas MacArthur's headquarters in Tokyo, and then upon the battlefields of Korea, I was to witness the consequences of this baffling policy as many of my West Point classmates, together with many other young Americans, died in action as they led undertrained, underequipped, understrength American formations in a brave but often suicidal attempt to slow down an invading North Korean army that was equipped with Soviet tanks and Soviet guns, advised by Soviet officers, and set in motion for Soviet purposes.

Alexander M. Haig, Jr.,
as West Point "yearling,"
1946.

First Lieutenant Haig and his bride, the former Patricia Fox,
Tokyo, May 24, 1950.

Regina Murphy Haig (*seated*) in 1973 with (*left to right*) Pat and Gen. Alexander M. Haig, Jr., Regina Haig Meredith and Edward Meredith, and the Reverend Francis R. Haig, S.J. (*U.S. Army photo*)

Captain Haig with Maj. Gen. Edward M. Almond (*center*), commander of X Corps, and Almond's pilot, 1st Lt. Robert J. St. Aubin, at Wonju, Korea, January 25, 1951. (*U.S. Army photo*)

ROK (South Korean) troops awaiting transport south from Hungnam, North Korea, December 16, 1950. (*U.S. Army photo*)

Gen. Douglas MacArthur with Almond (*left*) and the author's father-in-law, Maj. Gen. Alonzo P. Fox, at Kimpo Air Base, Korea, 1950. (*U.S. Army photo*)

Captain Haig as Company Executive Officer at the Naval Academy, 1955. (*U.S. Navy photo*)

2

Councils of War

Soon after dawn on Sunday morning, June 25, 1950, I arrived at the Dai Ichi Building, the headquarters of the Supreme Commander for the Allied Powers in Japan (SCAP) in downtown Tokyo, to take my turn as duty officer for Gen. Douglas MacArthur's chief of staff. My bride, the former Patricia Fox, and I had returned from our honeymoon at a seaside hotel only a few days before. Though we both begrudged losing a summer Sunday that we might have spent together, "we" were in the Army, as wives and husbands used to say, and I reported as ordered without giving the matter a second thought. That is how I happened to be the first military officer in Tokyo to learn that the Korean War had begun.

One of the chief responsibilities of the duty officer was to answer the telephone and decide when a call was important enough to warrant disturbing MacArthur's brilliant but irascible chief of staff, Maj. Gen. Edward M. Almond. Only Almond, to whom I was an aide-de-camp, was empowered to approach MacArthur. Later in the morning—I did not record the exact time—the telephone rang, and when I picked it up I heard the faraway voice of John J. Muccio, the American ambassador to the Republic of South Korea. Over a line crackling with static, he told me that very large formations of North Korean infantry, supported by tanks and aircraft, had crossed the 38th parallel at around 4:00 A.M.

19

and were streaming toward Seoul, the capital, on the main north-south highway. South Korean forces were offering little effective resistance.

"Lieutenant," Muccio said, "this is not a false alarm."

"Understood, Mr. Ambassador. Your message will be passed to SCAP immediately."

I called the volcanic Almond. U.S. intelligence had warned of an imminent Communist invasion of South Korea no fewer than fifteen hundred times since June 1949,[1] and, as I expected, he was in no mood for another cry of wolf.

He demanded details, and the sobering facts of Muccio's report seemed to impress him. "Muccio called this operation an invasion, quote unquote?"

"Sir, the ambassador said, 'This is not a false alarm.' "

Almond hung up on me and called MacArthur. On hearing Muccio's report, the latter replied, "Very well, Ned. Assemble the staff and prepare your recommendations. I will be in at seven o'clock."

In his memoirs, MacArthur wrote that he was so staggered by the news that he believed, after answering the telephone, that he was still asleep and having a nightmare. At the time, my own belief in his imperturbability was such that I imagined him carrying on with his usual Sunday routine: prayers with his wife, Jean, and his young son, Arthur, luncheon followed by a nap, perhaps an hour or two with Arthur watching movies of a West Point football game, a form of entertainment of which he seemed never to tire (the films were flown out to him during the season as soon as they could be developed). MacArthur was a man of very regular habits, designed, as he once told me, to conserve every atom of energy in his seventy-year-old body.

In any case, as I have since reflected, he was probably the last American commander in the field who was, in similar circumstances, safe from the telephone operators at the White House and the Pentagon. The four or five hours in which MacArthur was able to listen to himself think may well have been the reason for the brilliant military victories he would win soon afterward, against all odds and most predictions.

In a matter of minutes, headquarters filled up with generals and colonels and majors. Secure teletype communications were established with Washington and with the American military and intelligence people in Seoul, and by the time MacArthur arrived, wearing his usual unadorned uniform with an open shirt collar and with his customary air of calm self-possession, Almond and the commanders of the Far East ground, air, and naval forces were able to report to him in authoritative detail that the situation was desperate. At least six North Korean infantry divisions and three border constabulary brigades, totaling some 135,000 troops, supported by a brigade of 150 Soviet-made T-34 medium tanks, ample heavy artillery, and about 100 World War II–vintage Yak war planes, had struck across the 38th parallel in at least three different places and were thought to be carrying out an amphibious landing. Although we did not know all these details at the time, about one-third of the soldiers in the North Korean People's Army were battle-tested veterans who had fought in all-Korean units with the Chinese Communists in World War II and against Nationalist forces in the postwar campaign in Manchuria; in the six months before the invasion about 40,000 of these had been repatriated from China, usually in regimental-size units, and integrated into the North Korean army. Others had served in Soviet combat units during World War II. Soviet officers had been attached to the invading force as advisers down to battalion level,[2] but, according to Nikita Khrushchev, Stalin "gave orders to recall all our advisers . . . [perhaps] because he was afraid that one of our officers would be taken prisoner and it would provide an opportunity for the United States to accuse us of participating in the war."[3]

The Republic of Korea army (ROK), trained as constabulary, numbered fewer than 100,000 men; it had no officers or noncoms with combat experience, no tanks, no combat aircraft, almost no artillery, and only a few days' supply of ammunition. Some units put up a stiff fight at certain points along the front. But there was small hope that it could last very long as an organized fighting force. The enemy, moving with amazing speed and chewing up everything in his path, was already approaching the Han River, which runs west and south of Seoul but north of Seoul's industrial suburb, Yongdungpo, key to the country's road and rail networks. It seemed inevitable that the capital would fall in a matter of days, likely that the entire Korean peninsula would be conquered by the invader in little more than a week.

One of my jobs was to keep the situation map in Almond's office up-to-date. This map was the focal point of subsequent discussions between MacArthur and his subordinate commanders. There was no atmosphere of crisis. Not only MacArthur but all the other senior officers had recently passed through the fire of World War II; MacArthur had been a general officer in World War I, and some of the others, including Almond, had led troops as junior officers on the Western Front. MacArthur's detractors have suggested that he surrounded himself with sycophants, and General of the Army George C. Marshall is supposed to have told him, during a World War II conference in the Pacific, "General, you don't have a staff, you have a court."[4]

It was true that with some notable exceptions—first of all Almond, who bowed his head only to the Almighty—many around MacArthur seemed to me to be sycophants. MacArthur knew this and compensated for it by filling up the second echelon, which did the work, with the brightest colonels, lieutenant colonels, and majors in the Army; all were battle-tested veterans.

The true nature of the military situation in Korea, with all its dramatic political import, was clear from the first moment. No one at Supreme Headquarters, least of all MacArthur, doubted that the choice facing Washington was to commit American troops to the battle or lose Korea, an outcome that would place the entire Pacific littoral of Asia from the Arctic to the northern frontier of French Indochina in Communist hands. It is fair to say, however, that there was considerable doubt, especially in MacArthur's mind, whether this might not be a result that Washington was willing to accept.

Six months before, Secretary of State Dean Acheson had given a speech before the National Press Club in Washington in which he appeared to exclude Korea and Taiwan from the Pacific line of defense;[5] among its many other effects, this speech had sent spasms of anxiety coursing through the fledgling Japanese government, which, then as now, regarded Korea as "a dagger pointed at the heart of Japan." American foreign policy, as conducted by Truman and Acheson, was obsessed with Europe to what seemed to MacArthur (who during the war had suffered the torments of playing second fiddle in the Pacific while Eisenhower enjoyed first priority in Europe) to be the near-demented neglect of Asia. MacArthur was hardly less single-minded, believing that Europe was "a dying system, worn out and run down" and incapable of protecting itself from conquest by Soviet Russia, and that "the lands touching the Pacific with their billions of inhabitants will determine the course of history for the next ten thousand years." His exasperation with Washington's one-dimensional foreign policy was never far below the surface. "The inertia that exists!" MacArthur was to exclaim later, at the Senate hearing on his dismissal from command. "There is no policy! There is nothing, I tell you, no plan, no anything."[6]

In this judgment, as it turned out, MacArthur had been mistaken; the administration was about to stumble into a policy that would paralyze American power, to the dismay of her friends and the puzzlement of her enemies, for nearly two generations to come. This policy was to be called "limited war." This was a misnomer: It was, in fact, a policy of war without victory. But as MacArthur put it in an enduring phrase, "War's very object is victory." Throughout history, great nations had fought limited wars—the Caesars against the Gauls, the British against the Americans in 1812, the Americans against the Spaniards in 1898. But they had fought to win, to destroy the military capability of their enemy to carry on the war, or else, in another of MacArthur's phrases, they "suffer[ed] all the consequences of defeat."[7] To MacArthur, war without victory was an immoral waste of lives, a concept so self-contradictory, so alien to everything he knew about warfare and believed about the nature of the United States and its role in the world, that he went down to personal ruin rather than accept it.

MacArthur reported on the military situation to the Joint Chiefs of Staff and to the President himself in a series of lengthy two-way conversations in which words dictated to a typist would be exchanged over the secure teletype. Sometimes, I was in the communications room when this happened. It was obvious to me, listening to him dictate his flawless sentences to the teletypist, that he assumed that the United States must intervene in Korea in defense of its own national interests and the peace of the world. Many agreed. A future Secretary of State, John Foster Dulles, then in Tokyo as the State Department's representative on the negotiating team for the peace treaty with Japan, sent a cable to Washington saying that U.S. forces should be used in Korea as a means of averting a world war. Acheson showed this communication to the President[8] but apparently neglected to furnish MacArthur with a copy.[9]

On Sunday (Monday, June 26, in Tokyo) the United Nations Security Council, taking advantage of the absence of Jacob Malik, the Soviet representative, adopted a resolution condemning the North Korean invasion and calling on member nations to render assistance to the Republic of Korea. This opened the way for American intervention, and the next day Truman ordered MacArthur to support South Korean forces with United States air and naval action (confining such action to areas below the 38th parallel) and to evacuate all Americans from Korea. At the same time, committing a fundamental error of strategic judgment from which great misfortunes would flow, Truman ordered the Seventh Fleet into the Formosa Strait to "repel any attack on Formosa and [to ensure] that no attacks should be made from Formosa on the mainland."[10] This made a strong impression on the world, but it also linked the Formosa question to the Korean War although the two had little or nothing to do with each

other, and very likely led, as we shall see, to the intervention of the
Chinese Communist armies in Korea.

For the moment, Truman's orders presented MacArthur with certain
practical difficulties: U.S. Air Force fighter-bombers flying from airfields
in Japan carried only enough fuel to stay over Korean targets for an
average of fifteen minutes;[11] the Far East Air Force, in theory, consisted
of some twelve hundred aircraft of all types, but many of these were in
storage on Okinawa or under repair or in the process of being salvaged.
Naval forces under MacArthur's command were one cruiser, the *Juneau*,
and four destroyers, while the Seventh Fleet, deployed partly in Okinawa,
partly in the Philippines, consisted of one aircraft carrier, the *Valley
Forge*, one heavy cruiser, the *Rochester*, eight destroyers, and three submarines.[12]

Budgetary cuts pushed through as a matter of administration policy by
Truman's first Secretary of Defense, Louis A. Johnson, had reduced
defense expenditures from $45.2 billion in 1946 to $12.3 billion in
1950.[13] MacArthur adjusted to these policies but did not conceal his
opinion that they would lead the country into difficulties. In the spring
of 1950, shortly before the war in Korea began, Secretary of Defense
Johnson came to Tokyo and invited MacArthur to dinner. MacArthur
lunched but did not dine with visiting dignitaries. In fact, he never went
out in the evening at all; this was part of his regimen to conserve his
physical and intellectual energies. He asked me to visit the Secretary in
his suite at the old Imperial Hotel and explain this long-standing policy
to him. I found Johnson, a hairy man, lounging in his undershirt, with
an open bottle of bourbon whiskey on the table before him. "Lieutenant,"
he said after I delivered MacArthur's message, "I want you to go back to
the General and tell him that the Secretary of Defense is giving him a
direct order to report for dinner at 1900 hours."

I said, "Yes, sir!" then returned to headquarters and delivered Johnson's
command verbatim.

On hearing it, MacArthur threw back his head and fixed me with a
glittering eye. "B-u-l-l*shit!*" he guffawed.

"Does the General wish me to deliver a reply?" I asked.

"That won't be necessary, son."

MacArthur did not show up for Johnson's dinner party. This was,
incidentally, the only time I ever heard him use a cussword.

As a result of the dramatic postwar reduction in U.S. military power,
North Korean ground forces on the day of the invasion were not signifi-
cantly inferior in numerical strength to the combat forces of the entire

United States Army, and they were better equipped. Our Army in June 1950 consisted of eleven divisions, plus nine regimental combat teams, but nearly all infantry, tank, and artillery battalions had been reduced to two, rather than the regulation three companies or batteries. The divisions stationed in Japan (the First Cavalry, and Seventh, Twenty-fourth, and Twenty-fifth Infantry divisions) were, in the aggregate, at about 70 percent of strength;[14] the total number of effectives was probably slightly more than fifty thousand. All were short of divisional tanks and artillery and operated with shortages of mortars, recoilless rifles, and other small-unit heavy weapons.[15] Corps artillery and armor units were virtually nonexistent. In contrast to the high quality of headquarters staff, officers commanding down to regimental level tended to be overage and overtime in rank and below their peak physical condition; the troops were young, with a high percentage of teenagers, and, because of the budget constraints and the nature of occupation duty, they were undertrained and in many cases physically soft. A small but troublesome minority were young criminals to whom civilian judges, as was then the practice, had given the choice of going to jail or joining the Army; as a platoon leader in the First Cavalry, I was detailed to defend several who renewed their criminal careers with such enthusiasm after enlisting that they were court-martialed for capital offenses.

These negative factors did not daunt MacArthur, who figured that the Army, Navy, and Air Force were capable of anything so long as the fundamental system was intact. He envisaged it as any old soldier would: Reinforcements and supplies would flow over a maritime bridge from the homeland, units would be brought up to strength, officers and NCOs would lead, and American soldiers would fight. Victory would follow. He behaved from the first as if it was a foregone conclusion that the armed forces of United States would overwhelm the enemy. The question was, How best to accomplish this? I vividly remember MacArthur tapping the map in Almond's office and describing his plan. Our troops would fall back on the deep-water port of Pusan, establish a defensive perimeter, build up strength by feeding divisions and matériel into the perimeter, and then, when the time was right, turn the enemy's flank and cut his lines of supply with an amphibious landing.

"We will take Seoul, break out from Pusan, and crack the North Korean army like a walnut between the jaws of an American pincers," he said.

We lacked the troops, the equipment, the supplies, and maybe the political will in Washington to do this. But never for a moment did I doubt that MacArthur would make it happen. Older heads present clearly felt the same. To me, at twenty-five, MacArthur seemed venerable, a figure like Pompey or Wellington out of the pages of history. The fact that he knew my name and personal background, as he knew those of every other officer under his command, only added to the mystique. But he was also a soldier among soldiers, giving off sparks of humor and camaraderie, and no one else I ever knew in military or civilian life was remotely his equal in the ability to summon the best from other men. They seemed more intelligent, more confident, more daring when they were with him than at other moments; to me, who worked with all of them every day, the difference was palpable. I never noticed that any honest officer was afraid to speak his mind in MacArthur's presence, or that anyone was penalized for doing so.

MacArthur's plan was brilliant but risky—as he himself said, a gambler's plan at five-thousand-to-one odds.[16] In order for it to work, he needed to buy time. The South Korean army no longer existed as a fighting force; Americans must do the job. Elements of the Twenty-fourth Infantry Division enplaned almost immediately for the battlefield. The first U.S. units to go into action fought against suicidal odds, and paid a heavy price.

To me and his other aide, Capt. Fred Ladd, Almond assigned the job of going over action reports and casualty lists with MacArthur at the end of each day. This was somber duty. There has been in the character of every true military leader I have met a strain of deep emotion with regard to the men he sends into combat. This is not sentimentality but something more complicated, a mixture of pride, patriotism, love for soldiering and all who have ever practiced it, an awareness of the price that men must be prepared to pay on the field of battle, and the powerful psychological undertow of knowing young men with their lives before them have died carrying out your orders.

In MacArthur's case, because his service was so long, because he had himself narrowly escaped death in battle on so many occasions, and perhaps because his sensibility was so literary, the anguish he registered on hearing the names of the dead can only be called paternal. Around nine or ten o'clock, after the nighttime hush settled over the ruins of Tokyo, MacArthur would come into Almond's office, which adjoined his own smaller and more plainly furnished room, and I would stand with pointer in hand beside the maps and recite the details of the combat engagements that had been fought during the preceding twenty-four hours. Daily, the casualties mounted as American and South Korean forces fell back, fighting for every foot of terrain, toward Pusan. MacArthur would listen to terse descriptions of small unit actions fought, more often than not with scarcely believable courage, at such places as Pyongtaek or Chonan or Chochiwon, and on hearing the identity of the company or battery or squadron engaged, would remember the name of the captain or lieutenant in command.

"Is ———— all right?" he would ask.

Nearly every day, it would be my duty to answer, "No, sir. He was killed."

MacArthur would look as if he had lost his own son. When Tom Lombardo, who had played quarterback for West Point on the famous Davis-Blanchard team, was killed, the general could scarcely contain his emotion. I, too, was deeply affected. Lombardo had coached our own First Cavalry Division team, and many of the other dead and wounded were, as I have said, men I had known as cadets at West Point or with whom I had soldiered.

By mid-July, elements of three divisions (Twenty-fourth and Twenty-fifth Infantry, First Cavalry) based in Japan were at the front as the Eighth Army, under the command of Lt. Gen. Walton H. ("Johnny") Walker. On July 15, the Twenty-fourth Division was hit from three sides by a massive enemy attack. Reports from inside the Pusan perimeter were grim and defeatist. Maj. Gen. William F. Dean, the division commander, was captured. General Walker called every day to talk to MacArthur or Almond, and I was often ordered to listen to these conversations on another telephone and take notes.

Walker was a stouthearted man, and the way in which he commanded the Eighth Army was an epic of leadership that has never been given its due. Like all American officers, however, he had been trained to think of and plan for every contingency. MacArthur visited Walker's headquarters inside the perimeter on July 27 and was briefed on detailed plans for incremental retreats that could result, in the end, only in ignominious evacuation. Similar ideas were being discussed in Washington and in the press. MacArthur would not tolerate such talk.

"These plans will be scrapped at once," he ordered. "The present line must be held at all costs." Over the following days, battered American units attacked all along the line and by August 11 drove the enemy back some fifteen miles.[17] Over the teletype, MacArthur, choosing his words with care, told Truman, "The enemy's plan and great opportunity depended upon the speed with which he could overrun South Korea . . . this chance he has now lost through the extraordinary speed with which the Eighth Army has been deployed."[18]

On July 23, he had informed the Joint Chiefs of Staff, who did not immediately reply, that he intended to carry out an amphibious landing at Inchon in September, using a force of two divisions.[19] Within five days in early July, he had twice asked Washington for the First Marine Division and was twice refused. Reinforcements from the stateside Army arrived, in his phrase, "in a trickle." Washington explained that these men were needed in Europe, where the administration was preoccupied with possible Soviet threats against Berlin as it prepared the ground for bringing a rearmed West Germany into the Western alliance. As MacArthur pointed out, there was no war in Europe; the order of strategic priorities touched a nerve in the old war eagle, and all could see this.[20]

In the absence of reinforcement, MacArthur innovated. He mustered his troops where he could find them, making riflemen of clerks and cooks and bringing some eight thousand South Korean soldiers to Japan and integrating them into the U.S. Seventh Infantry Division as a means of filling up empty American ranks and at the same time seasoning the Koreans who would form the core of a rebuilt ROK army. The acute shortage of trained officers and noncoms, MacArthur thought, was the chief reason for the poor showing, sometimes amounting to panic, made by the ROK divisions in the earliest phases of the war. Training and fighting beside American professionals, he thought, would remedy these shortcomings.

Stripping Japan of American troops was exceedingly risky from a strategic point of view in that it involved the possibility of losing all of Japan, the most important nation in Asia, in order to save half of Korea, a divided, backward country that only a year before had seemed so unimportant to Washington that the U.S. government had removed all American troops from its soil. In theory, the United States could drop atomic bombs, in which it still enjoyed a monopoly, on an approaching Soviet armada, but there was reason to doubt, as MacArthur did, that any American President would resort to these weapons except in extremis—that is to say, in defense of Europe.

In my own mind, I questioned our technical ability to deliver nuclear weapons. On the morrow of the North Korean invasion, I had watched while Lt. Gen. George E. Stratemeyer, the dapper commander of the Far East Air Forces, tapped the map of Korea with his silver-headed swagger stick and told MacArthur, "General, give me the targets and my bombers will isolate the battlefield right across the waist of Korea in forty-eight hours."

Under the best of circumstances, this seemed an ambitious project. But the Air Force had its own shortages, and it did not get a B-29 off the ground for days. For a long time afterward, the battlefield was far from being isolated. Even less, as Washington imposed one political restraint after another on the use of air power for military purposes, was it ever isolated.

MacArthur dealt with the problem of defending the Japanese home islands by first persuading and then authorizing the Japanese, on July 8, 1950, to form an internal security force, or "national police reserve," of 75,000 men and to increase the coast guard by 8,000 men. This force formed the basis of the subsequent Self Defense Force, which soon consisted of five regular divisions equipped with artillery, tanks, and other heavy weapons.[21] In retrospect the speed and efficiency with which he made things happen in the crisis seems dazzling, and his ability to move mountains was, of course, the major element in his subsequent brilliant military successes. All the while, it should be remembered, he continued to function as the virtual shogun of Japan at one of the most sensitive hours in that nation's history.

On evenings when I drew late duty, I sometimes ushered Prime Minister Shigeru Yoshida into MacArthur's presence. He was a small, dignified, deferential man in striped trousers and frock coat who always bowed very deeply when he entered MacArthur's presence. The formality was all the more noticeable because of the extreme simplicity of MacArthur's office, which was barely large enough for his desk and a pair of straight-back chairs for visitors. When receiving the prime minister, MacArthur dressed in the casual, open-collar uniforms he had designed for himself. He never wore decorations or campaign ribbons, not even the Medal of Honor he had been awarded for his defense of the Philippines in 1942 (and perhaps felt was inappropriate after having been twice recommended for the decoration in personal combat).

Their long conversations took place behind the closed door between MacArthur's office and mine. They spoke in English and sometimes, though I made a dutiful effort not to listen, I would overhear a word or a sentence. MacArthur's tone was generally kindly, but sometimes it was imperious. Yoshida's voice was always a murmur. The creation of a democratic Japan was being decided between the two of them, and the concept of democracy was so difficult for a Japanese of Yoshida's generation and background to grasp that he frequently emerged from these conversations with tears in his eyes. It was my impression that the tears were an expression of admiration and gratitude, as well as a sign of bafflement and frustration. In his book *Reminiscences*, MacArthur quotes as follows from a letter written to him by Yoshida some fourteen years later: "Fondly and gratefully I cherish the memories of those years of our intimate contact—you as Supreme Commander for the Allied Powers and I as executor of your directives. You were so good to me, so kind and gracious, that I was able to perform my duty to the best of my ability, and therefore contribute my mite to the making of the new Japan."[22]

Despite every innovation, the manpower shortage at the front remained acute—some would have said desperate. Less than a week after the war began, Generalissimo Chiang Kai-shek informed the American government that Nationalist China, as a member of the United Nations, was willing to contribute as many as 33,000 troops, or three infantry divisions, to fight in Korea. The offer was transmitted to MacArthur, as the UN commander, by General Ho Shai-lai, the worldly Kuomintang officer who headed the Chinese Nationalist Mission in Tokyo. From a strategic point of view, it made little or no sense to accept Chiang's offer. As MacArthur pointed out to the staff, and later to General Ho and Chiang himself, this was not the moment to draw down the garrison of Taiwan (then called Formosa).[23] Moreover, the Nationalist troops had no sea or air transportation with which to get themselves to Korea, little or no armor or artillery, and were in an unknown state of training and supply. The political effect on Beijing (then called Peiping or Peking) of placing three divisions of Kuomintang troops across the border from Manchuria was unknowable. MacArthur teletyped his advice home but thought that Washington must decide.[24] President Truman was at first disposed to accept Chiang's offer but then, on Acheson's advice, said no, on grounds that "the situation of Nationalist China was different from that of other U.N. members."[25]

MacArthur flew to Taiwan on July 31 to explain matters to his old friend Chiang Kai-shek. This journey caused consternation in the State Department, which regarded it (with some reason) as a military invasion of diplomatic prerogatives. In responding to such criticism, MacArthur always maintained that his discussions with Chiang Kai-shek during his visit to Taiwan were strictly military. In his opening remarks at the formal conference between the two sides on August 1, MacArthur stated, according to the declassified secret record,[26] that this group was "purely professional and has nothing to do with political matters. It is concerned with defense only. . . ." But it proved difficult to discuss military matters without flirting with political questions. When the chief of the Nationalist joint staff, General Chou Chi-jou, asked MacArthur's opinion about the advisability of holding the offshore island of Kin Men (Quemoy), MacArthur replied, "Until I know more, I can't advise you on that. My instinct is to fight anywhere!" Chou replied that he wanted to know "if the U.S. will hinder the mainland effort. If not, Kin Men will be held as springboard for an invasion. . . . If we can bomb the mainland there is some purpose in holding the island." MacArthur replied, "What [Chou] has said is sound and true. This is being discussed in Washington now. In Tokyo there is no disagreement with his views. Soon we may expect an extension of President Truman's recent statement. I sincerely hope this extension is in accord with General Chou's view." Did he mean, Chou asked, that his question would be clarified? MacArthur replied, "That's my belief." Chiang and MacArthur spent about an hour alone together in a car during a tour of Taipei en route to the airport, but the record does not show what, if anything, they said to each other.[27]

The chief business of the mission was to determine whether the Nationalist forces were capable of defending Taiwan from invasion. The two sides agreed that an American military team would be sent from Tokyo to study the situation in detail. On August 4, the Joint Chiefs ordered MacArthur (in support of the decision taken on July 27 by the National Security Council) to "initiate without delay a survey of the needs and extent of the military assistance required to enable the Chinese Nationalist forces to . . . prevent the capture of Taiwan by the Communists."[28] MacArthur appointed his chief of staff for SCAP, or occupation matters, Maj. Gen. Alonzo P. Fox, to carry out this mission, and with Almond's grudging consent (Fox was my father-in-law) I was included as the most junior of approximately thirty officers on the team.

On Taiwan, I encountered Mandarins and warlords for the first time, sometimes in one and the same person, and was impressed by the well-tailored hauteur of the former and the elbow-in-the-ribs worldliness of the latter. By far the most impressive figure I met was Madame Chiang; as many have reported before me, she was a woman of great beauty and charm who fairly crackled with intelligence and aristocratic self-confidence. It was she who carried the conversation (in fluent English) at social occasions, introducing topics of interest, asking subtle questions, and controlling the tone and atmosphere of any social encounter while her much older husband sat by in a state of somnolent detachment.

Chiang's army was organized on feudal lines. His general staff consisted of a group of leaders, each of whom controlled a body of troops large enough to be called a division or corps. Some of these generals seemed to be philosophers who lived and led troops according to the maxims of the ancient Chinese military sages; others gave the impression of being merchants in uniform; still others were right out of the comic strip "Terry and the Pirates." The Nationalist Chinese army, as I first saw it, operated as a sort of barter economy, in which the soldiers' loyalty to the generals, and the generals' loyalty to the generalissimo, depended on what they got in return in the way of pay, weapons, uniforms, supplies, and so on. Evidently, Chiang had examined this stew of irreconcilable interests and decided that he would deal with it by treating everyone exactly alike. All categories of equipment were divided equally, regardless of military need. In practice, this meant that if Chiang came into the possession of, say, twenty-five miles of barbed wire, a general whose division was charged with defending twenty-five miles of beach facing the mainland would be issued one mile of the wire, the same amount as twenty-four other generals who were unlikely to need it in any conceivable set of military circumstances.

According to Chiang's intelligence officers, twenty Communist armies, or about sixty divisions of regulars, roughly 635,000 men, were positioned on the mainland opposite Taiwan and the Pescadores. We were to hear more of these troops later, in another time and place. Meanwhile, the Communists possessed enough boats to transport nineteen divisions across the strait but had only scanty naval and air forces to protect them; it was assumed that they would be supported, in case of an actual operation, by Soviet warplanes and submarines disguised as Chinese. Opposing this formidable foe, the Nationalists on Taiwan had, in theory, thirty-one divisions, or about 360,000 men. These divisions were inadequately and, as a result of the spoils system, often illogically equipped. There was a disproportionately high ratio of officers to enlisted men.[29] As to their state of readiness, an early report of the Fox mission read, in part, as follows: "One division of approximately 8,000 men defends [forty kilometers] of coastline. About one man in three has a personal weapon, which may be of several types and calibers, and the ammunition is in such critical short supply that many of the men have never fired a single round from their weapons."[30] There was no artillery, no transportation, and severe shortages of automatic weapons, mortars, and ammunition, but the armored contingent had about four hundred tanks. On the positive side, the troops seemed to be in excellent physical condition, training methods were sound if inefficiently carried out, and morale was high.

It was a formidable task to inventory this force that had so much in common with the armies of Genghis and Tamerlane. I recall a blur of impressions: mostly the cheerful, patient Chinese troops who stared at our pink skin and peculiar uniforms with the intense childlike curiosity that is so easy for the Westerner to mistake for hostility and rudeness. We had no time to be offended. But I remember also the hubbub and stench of Taipei; the rough humorous manners of the Chinese, and what a contrast they seemed to the sober, remote Japanese; the poverty of the ragged Taiwanese, who had been turned into bystanders to history by the arrival of the Kuomintang, and their air of puzzlement over the bustling Americans who had dropped from the sky; the wild beauty and amazing fecundity of the island's interior and the kidney-punching surface of the roads. Taiwan is one of the most fertile places on the planet, blessed by a climate in which nearly anything can be grown.

We were all greatly impressed by the innumerable banana trees—bananas were a rare treat in Japan—and loaded up the plane with huge stalks of them when we left at the end of the fortnight. There was a mountain at the end of the runway and the overloaded C-47 could not climb above it. While the plane shuddered upward inch by inch with both engines at full power, we flung open the door and threw out the bananas. As I kicked the last stalk overboard, I looked down on green treetops that seemed to be brushing the belly of the aircraft.

The Fox mission departed Taiwan on August 26. Its final report was transmitted to the Joint Chiefs of Staff on September 11. This document, every line reflecting the clearheaded intelligence and military expertise of its author, General Fox, consisted of a complete report in plain early-twentieth-century English on the ground, air, and naval forces and needs of the Nationalists, a comprehensive intelligence report from Nationalist sources on Communist forces threatening the island, a detailed plan for defense of the island in case of attack, an estimate of the goals and plans of the leadership of the Kuomintang, and recommendations for the reorganization and reequipment of the Nationalist army, navy, and air force that, when put into effect, transformed it from a medieval horde into a modern military establishment. In one generation, under the protection (and sometimes the repression) of these armed forces, Taiwan, a single province of China, was transformed from a poverty-stricken, backward island into the sixth largest trading partner of the United States of America.

At the time, the work we did in such a short time, starting from what would now be called a zero data base, seemed routine. We handed it in and went on to the next assignment. The better part of a lifetime later, this accomplishment seems to me little short of miraculous. Maybe the fact that it was all written with stubs of pencils on foolscap and then typed by corporals and privates first class on cantankerous typewriters that were already antiques had something to do with it; we didn't have time to do anything but get it right on the first try.

General of the Army Omar N. Bradley, chairman of the Joint Chiefs of Staff, said on the eve of Inchon that the day of the amphibious landing had gone by. "Bradley is a farmer," said MacArthur.[31] He himself was convinced that Inchon was the key to victory and would not give an inch to his critics. "Like Montcalm," he explained, "the North Koreans [will] regard the Inchon Landing as impossible. Like Wolfe I [can] take them by surprise."[32] Others have attributed his tenacity to some sort of mystical belief in his own luck or destiny. It was my impression that he understood the difficulties better than anyone else but believed that they could be overcome by the arrangements he had made, reinforced by the power of surprise. Nothing in my experience since has given me reason to change my opinion. This was no haphazard operation. MacArthur had made more careful provisions for the landing than his critics acknowledged. Two months before the war, in April 1950, he had arranged for a Marine Corps training team headed by a brilliant officer, Col. Edward H. Forney, USMC, to school Army units in Japan in amphibious tactics; Forney subsequently played a leading role in the planning of the Inchon operation.

On hearing MacArthur's analogy to Wolfe's victory on the Plains of Abraham, some may have thought that the North Koreans were right about the impossibility of the landing. MacArthur intended to attack with a two-division corps under Almond's command. Christened "X Corps," it would consist of a heavy Marine division made up of the First Marine Brigade, which was already fighting inside the Pusan perimeter, plus two green Marine regiments from the United States, and the Seventh Infantry Division, a mixed American–South Korean unit composed largely of unblooded troops, and some ROK units, or about seventy thousand men in all. North Korean trained reserves on the day the North invaded the South had been estimated at more than 100,000.[33] About fifty landing craft for troops were required, but the Navy could provide only seventeen; the rest were requisitioned from former U.S. Navy ships on loan to the Japanese for interisland shipping.[34] We had practically no intelligence about Inchon harbor and were relying on Japanese tide tables and charts.

(These turned out to be scrupulously accurate, but no one could have been sure of that at the time.)

As to the natural difficulties presented by water and terrain, to Lt. Comdr. Arlie G. Capps, gunnery officer on the amphibious staff of Rear Adm. James H. Doyle, the flag officer who commanded the naval phase of the Inchon landing, summarized them in a memorable phrase: "We drew up a list of every natural and geographic handicap—and Inchon had them all."[35]

To begin with, the landing could only take place on September 15. Inchon has one of the highest tides in the world; when the tide is out, the only approach to the port is over mud flats that are two miles wide in some places. The extreme high tide at 6:59 A.M. on September 15 would reach 31.2 feet. Not until October 11, a very late date for operations in Korea, where winter comes early, would there again be thirty feet of water, the minimum needed to float the landing craft to the base of the seawall, which was itself sixteen feet high. MacArthur was undaunted. When, at the meeting in Tokyo with the Joint Chiefs, someone objected that it would be foolhardy to maneuver a warship in darkness up the narrow, winding Flying Fish Channel that was the best approach to the harbor, Adm. Forrest Sherman, the chief of naval operations, retorted that he would not hesitate to do so.

"Spoken like a Farragut!" said MacArthur.[36]

The meeting with the Joint Chiefs took place in a conference room of the sixth floor of the Dai Ichi Building at 5:30 P.M. on August 23. Besides MacArthur and Admiral Sherman, those present were Gen. J. Lawton Collins, the Army chief of staff, together with Almond and a small group of generals and admirals from MacArthur's command. The Air Force chief of staff was represented by Lt. Gen. Idwal H. Edwards, the deputy chief for operations. Fred Ladd took notes. I put the pads and pencils and water glasses on the conference table, then sat down on a straight chair outside the door in case I was needed. I could hear quite clearly everything that was said inside the conference room. The participants who have recorded their recollections of this meeting differ on many small points (and some large ones, including the month in which it was held). Although I took no notes, I knew that I was privy to a historic encounter and that I might be called upon by Almond to remember something that had been said; therefore, I paid attention.

All agree with my recollection that Collins had come to deliver a message from on high. He was strongly opposed to the landing, calling it a shoestring operation and pointing out that the consequences in case of failure would be calamitous: Even if he got ashore, MacArthur might not be able to link up with Walker to the south; he might be trapped around Seoul by a superior enemy force and destroyed.

Collins, supported by Edwards, argued for landing instead at Kunsan, a less difficult site farther down the west coast. Even I knew that a landing at Kunsan would not have accomplished the primary objectives, which were to cut the enemy's lines of communication to his rear and capture Seoul, through which passed all important roads, railways, and wires to the north. In MacArthur's words, Kunsan represented "an attempted envelopment that would not envelop."[37]

Sherman supported Collins, in the sense that he had similar reservations about the military feasibility of the Inchon operation, but he said that if MacArthur was determined to go ahead, the Navy would support him. More than once, the President's name was brought into the discussion; no one found it necessary to say aloud that Truman's party would face a hard-fought midterm election scarcely six weeks after the proposed landing, but it was clear that MacArthur was alone in wanting to go ahead with an operation that was so pregnant with many-headed disaster.

MacArthur listened in silence to all the arguments against him. He later wrote, "I could almost hear my father telling me as he had so many years ago, 'Doug, councils of war breed timidity and defeatism.' "[38] Others, including MacArthur, have reported that he then defended his plan in a forty-five-minute extemporaneous speech that impressed everyone present with the brilliance of the argument and the theatricality of the presentation. For some reason—maybe because I was already so familiar with the argument—I do not remember this.

The way I recollect it (after refreshing my memory by comparing it to Fred Ladd's), MacArthur, puffing on a pipe (not his ceremonial corncob but one of the well-charred briars he usually smoked), listened to all the arguments against him. A brief silence followed.

Then the old warrior said, "Gentlemen, we will land at Inchon on September 15 or you will have a new Supreme Commander in the Far East."

He then knocked the ashes out of his pipe, making the glass ashtray ring, and stalked out of the room. The opposition collapsed, and with no further discussion the generals and admirals filed out after him in silence.

It was an extraordinary moment. Even as it was happening, I realized that I had witnessed something that would go down in history, a Cincinnatian act of moral courage. Some years passed before I fully understood the lesson it contained: That when you are in a position of trust and a course you know to be right is questioned for political reasons, you must act on your own convictions based on your own experience, because that is your duty to the American people. It was not vainglory but wisdom that motivated MacArthur. He believed that the Inchon landing would succeed, and that it would save 100,000 lives.[39]

As events were to prove, he was right when everyone else was wrong.

3

Meeting the Enemy

Victory at Inchon was achieved at 7:30 on the morning of the second day, September 16, 1950, when the Fifth and First Marines made contact with each other on the outskirts of the city, effectively trapping inside what remained of the enemy. Success had been assured almost exactly twenty-four hours earlier when the Fifth Marines secured the fortified island of Wolmi-do after a fight that lasted one hour and fifteen minutes.

The Marines' landing was preceded by a naval bombardment, the first I had ever witnessed in a war situation, by American and allied warships and aircraft. The barrage was astounding in its power and efficiency: For long moments, the entire island seemed to have been converted into a hellish garden of exploding napalm, shrapnel, and high explosive. It was not a one-sided battle. The approach to the beach up the infamous Flying Fish Channel was made in pitch-darkness, and Navy lookouts spotted Soviet mines lying on the mud of Inchon harbor. Although no vessel actually struck a mine (thousands of Soviet mines were available in Korea, but the Soviets had omitted to include some vital part without which they could not be deployed), this incident added to the nervous tension of the occasion.

Some of the ships, maneuvering in treacherous waters, took hits from enemy shore batteries, and men were killed. When the barrage lifted, the Fifth Marines, who had been in close combat on the Pusan perimeter

38

only ten days before, went ashore. The water was calm, the day clear and cool. The Marines, meeting little resistance at first, attacked up the steep slopes of Wolmi-do. Half an hour later, they raised the Stars and Stripes on the island's 335-foot summit.[1] From the command ship, USS *Mount McKinley*, MacArthur signaled the fleet: "The Navy and Marines have never shone more brightly than this morning."[2]

It was an astonishing performance. That we were there at all was due to equally astonishing feats of seamanship en route. The invasion task force, 230 ships, including many rusty civilian merchantmen chartered for the occasion, had sailed from Japanese ports and from Pusan just ahead of an approaching typhoon named Kezia. The Navy reported that the winds generated by the typhoon were measured at ninety knots (103 mph) and the waves were forty feet high; I can well believe it. Fortunately, the storm veered away and went up the opposite coast of Korea, giving everyone, including some of the admirals, a chance to recover from bad cases of seasickness. Nevertheless, Admiral Doyle, commander of the amphibious assault, remarked later that Kezia's mountainous seas were the worst he had ever encountered in a ship as small as the *Mount McKinley*.[3]

I made the journey aboard a vessel so small that it had a number instead of a name. Such glimpses as I caught of the bombardment and landing, I captured from the deck of this craft, where I was seeing to the off-loading of General Almond's mobile command post—or what was left of it: Two of the five Jeeps that composed it had been blown overboard during the typhoon. Almond was aboard the *Mount McKinley* with the rest of MacArthur's staff. MacArthur had named him commanding general of X Corps, and despite my pleas to be transferred back to the First Cavalry, or to any line division as a platoon leader, I was still his aide.

Around six o'clock in the evening, I took the remaining equipment ashore. Fifteen minutes later, Almond came ashore on Blue Beach, on the mainland to the south of Wolmi-do, with the ninth assault wave of the First Marines.[4] He immediately asked whether I had managed to get his baggage ashore without getting it wet; fortunately, I was able to answer, "Yes, sir!"

The Marines were still mopping up. Almond hurried forward, with me at his side, in search of the point man in the lead squad, his preferred position in any combat situation. As I was to rediscover on an almost daily basis in the hair-raising months ahead, Almond believed in getting as close as possible to the action.

This was my first glimpse of a battleground. The city was on fire. Corsair fighter-bombers pounced out of the smoke-filled sky; musketry rattled; mortar rounds whumped into the earth; a foul-smelling flame-thrower tank rumbled by. North Korean corpses lay underfoot on the bloodstained pavement. I was surprised by the appearance of the enemy dead: Their weapons and uniforms, which I had studied in pictures, were familiar yet unfamiliar, and the fallen soldiers themselves, unexpectedly, were young, like myself. Almond, interested in every detail, paused to inspect their equipment and state of nourishment.

"Makes notes for the war journal!" he commanded. Automatic fire rattled on a nearby hillside as the Marines cleared an enemy bunker. I scribbled in my notebook as he dictated his observations. No detail was so small as to escape his notice. This was only the beginning. Almond inspected everything: a Navy hospital in a beached LST, every Marine and Army command post he could visit, a prisoner-of-war camp, the LSTs unloading supplies on the beaches. When a Navy fighter plane crashed in the harbor as Almond was returning to the *Mount McKinley* for a conference with MacArthur, he rushed to the scene in his launch but was beaten to the rescue by a helicopter; the pilot lived.[5] Even before the Corps command post became fully operational, Admiral Doyle came ashore in the evenings and had a drink with Almond, who had brought along a supply of spirits in his baggage; then as now, American naval wardrooms were as dry as Carry Nation's front parlor. We lower ranks were always glad to see Doyle coming; he was a convivial Irishman with a bulbous nose who never hesitated to offer us a glass of Almond's bourbon.

Doyle and his sailors performed prodigies in bringing troops and maté-riel ashore. By the evening of September 18, the Thirty-second Infantry Regiment of the Seventh Division had landed and by the next day had taken over the First Marines' responsibility for the area south of the Inchon-Seoul Road,[6] freeing the Marines, who had taken Kimpo airfield on the morning of eighteenth, for the attack on the capital. Seoul was the primary objective of the Inchon operation, and Almond had personal as well as military reasons for wanting to take this objective in the shortest time possible. That day, the Eighth Army had begun its breakout from the Pusan perimeter, and Almond wanted to get there before General Walker.

To use a word that does not begin to describe their contentious relation-ship, Almond and Walker were competitors, and this had a greater effect on the way the war was fought than is generally realized. Many theories have been advanced to explain MacArthur's decision to split his command into two forces, Eighth Army in the west of the Korean peninsula and X Corps in the east, each operating independently and each reporting directly to headquarters in Tokyo.

MacArthur explained that the mountainous spine of Korea divided it naturally into two lanes for military advance and that communications between the two forces would have been difficult or impossible.[7] There is truth and logic in that, but it is also true that MacArthur's decision was influenced by the fact that Almond and Walker did not enjoy each other's company. MacArthur solved the problem by giving each general half of Korea. According to the operational plan, "Eighth Army and X Corps were . . . to meet in the north, when the united command would pass to General Walker."[8]

Meanwhile, Almond remained MacArthur's chief of staff (which gave him organizational precedence over Walker even though he wore only two stars to Walker's three) as well as being commander of X Corps. The prospect of falling under Walker's command consternated Almond as much as it must have captivated Walker, and, as we shall see, Almond found a way to forestall this outcome.

Seoul was eighteen miles from Inchon. On September 20, the Fifth Marines crossed the Han River west of Seoul; and by the evening of the twenty-first, they were at the gates of the city.[9] Under the original plan of operation, the work and honor of capturing the capital was to go to the First Marine Division. But after reaching the outskirts, the Marines were held up for three days by strong enemy resistance. No military force has ever fought more heroically or successfully than the U.S. Marines in Korea. Almond appreciated this, but like other Army commanders he was perplexed by Marine Corps tactical doctrine, which most often seemed to involve identifying the enemy's strong point and overwhelming it by frontal assault. Almond believed with Napoleon and MacArthur in fixing the enemy's center in place and then enveloping it by maneuvering to its flanks and rear under cover of heavy bombardment. In this particular case, he believed, with greater and more outspoken conviction as the days wore on, that the North Koreans holding Seoul could be routed by an envelopment from south of the Han River.

Maj. Gen. O. P. Smith, commanding the Marine division, was loath to make this maneuver because, as he explained to Almond, he did not wish to have the First and Fifth Marine regiments on opposite sides of the Han River. Almond, with the curtness that was his hallmark, told Smith that he had twenty-four hours to take the city; if he failed, Almond would forthwith carry out the envelopment maneuver with the Thirty-second Infantry of the Seventh Division.[10] This was a bitter pill. The Marines had done most of the hard fighting in this campaign, and now they were faced with the prospect of being deprived of its chief prize. Worse, it might look as if they were being extricated from a failure by the Army.

Although no one said so then, and military courtesy has generally prevailed in official accounts of the campaign, the reader should understand that the Marines' respect for the Seventh Division at this stage of the war was ostentatiously low. There was some reason for the Marines to feel as they did: The Seventh was, at that time, a ragtag outfit with troops drawn, as we have noted, from many sources; one-third of these were South Koreans, many of whom, only a few weeks before, had been terrified, ill-clothed, half-nourished civilians. Many others, such as the school troops from the Infantry School at Fort Benning, Georgia, and the Artillery School at Fort Sill, Oklahoma, were the very best that the Army had to offer. But in general, this was a division that was faced with the bloody job of learning its trade and building its esprit while fighting and dying. Interservice emotions had been exacerbated on September 21 when troops of the Seventh Division and the First Marine Division fired on each other by mistake along the boundary between the two; Almond intervened personally to straighten out the problem.[11]

Almond was not oblivious to this rivalry or its potential for damaging consequences. In his ceaseless rush around the battlefield, he was constantly ordering small corrections in the behavior of his subordinates to minimize it, but he could hardly let himself be influenced by it where his military judgment was concerned. As a practical matter, he probably was incapable of letting himself be influenced by it.

It is sometimes said of a singular man that he belongs to the pages of fiction. Edward Mallory ("Ned") Almond was far too powerful a personality to be contained by any novel or movie; he had to be experienced in real life to be believed. When I knew Almond, he was approaching sixty, a gray-haired man with a weathered, expressive face and frosty blue eyes in which there was a perpetual glint of skepticism. You felt that you had to prove yourself to him every day. He was medium in size and slightly stooped, but with the athletic physique of a soldier who kept himself in shape for any duty he might be called upon to perform. In June 1950, Almond probably could have climbed the Matterhorn if ordered to do so.

He was a Virginian and a graduate of Virginia Military Institute. This credential was not an advantage in the old Army, but, like his fellow VMI alumnus George Catlett Marshall, Almond achieved great things in spite of the West Pointers. In World War I, he served with the Fourth Division in France and was wounded and won the Silver Star for heroism, the first of many decorations for bravery (including the Distinguished Service Cross for his actions in the Inchon-Seoul campaign). During World War II, in Italy, he commanded the Ninety-second Infantry Division, whose enlisted men were Negroes and whose officers were mostly white. The performance of the Ninety-second Division never came up to Almond's uncompromising expectations. It was commonly said by his peers that he would have been a four-star general instead of a two-star one at the end of the war if he had been given command of one of the regular divisions in the beginning, and it is possible that Almond himself believed that this was true.

In any case, he was not a believer in the racial integration of the Army and thought that those who were, such as myself, were in need of education, or perhaps something stronger, to wake us up to reality. I disagreed with him then, sometimes more vocally then he liked, and I disagree now with those who continue to express similar ideas. But wrong as Almond was about the spirit and quality of black soldiers, he was far from being alone in his attitude in the Army or in any other part of American society in 1950. The Army, in its innate realism and justice, overcame these biases and provided a model of a color-blind environment that the rest of American society has yet to equal. This could not have happened if commanders such as Almond had not submerged their own biases and followed the order to integrate as they would have followed any other order, with loyalty and efficiency and in the knowledge that it was their duty to set an example.

The important fact about Almond is that he was a phenomenally gifted soldier. Like MacArthur, who admired him almost without reservation and regarded him as his right arm at headquarters and in the field, Almond was blessed with an intuitive gift for understanding the possibilities of terrain. He could glance at a battlefield and know at once where to place his troops and guns, how to maneuver them, how to take advantage of the mistakes that he seemed to know in advance the enemy would make. He took this talent for granted and was annoyed when others could not perceive through earnest study what he saw, as a great painter must see a picture he has not yet painted, by means of inborn genius.

He drove his subordinates unmercifully—my head nods even now as I remember trying to stay awake to draft his war diary in the early hours of the morning after having kept up with him since dawn the day before. In combat situations, he exposed himself to mortal risk several times a day, and, if you happened to be his aide, he exposed you to the same dangers with the same insouciance. On the other hand, he hated to see men fall in battle, and he safeguarded the lives and welfare of his troops with a single-minded concentration that often broke into fury. He had, remember, lived through the slaughter of World War I, and his only son and his son-in-law had both been killed in action in World War II. He understood what death on the battlefield means to the bereaved. His insistence on proper artillery and mortar preparation and on other tactics that preserved lives were part of this pattern. His affection for his men was genuine and, again resembling MacArthur, fatherly: He called most soldiers and officers, including other generals, "son," but he usually called me only Haig, possibly because I was too close to him for intimacy to work. Almond was continually turning up at forward command posts demanding to know whether the men had dry socks, whether they had eaten a hot meal, and whether they were keeping proper discipline on the line in order to protect one another. He also liked to check on the personal courage of his commanders. Often these interviews were conducted while standing up in the open beside white-faced commanding officers while small-arms fire crackled around their heads and mortar rounds burst at their feet; good-bye salutes were usually fervent.

In regard to his own safety, Almond was the most reckless person I have ever known—and the luckiest. As far as I could tell, he was utterly without fear: I know that this is supposed by psychologists to be impossible, but I am reporting what I observed (and his was not the only case I saw firsthand among American soldiers). Like his model, Gen. George S. Patton, Jr., he thought that the men should be able to recognize him, and he designed his own uniforms to this end. But if American troops realized, on spotting him in his dramatic furry parka or his leather belt with the big brass medallion for a buckle, that they were looking at their commanding general, so did the enemy. While I was with him, his Jeep, his helicopter, the light plane he used to observe the battlefield, all were hit by enemy fire.

In a typical incident, while the two of us were riding on the deck of the lead tank of the lead platoon, the tank came under machine-gun attack. The crew buttoned up, leaving Almond and me clinging to the hull while enemy rounds rang the armor like a bell. I persuaded the general, who was, of course, wearing his usual distinctive clothes, to get under the tank, which was returning fire with its .50-caliber machine guns. Peering between the treads, Almond cried, "The stupid bastards are shooting the wrong way! Get up there and direct their fire, Haig!" I crawled back up on top, banged on the hatch with my steel helmet, and, when it was opened, pointed out the position of the enemy machine gun to the tank commander, who silenced it. On another, even less enjoyable occasion, Almond invited a general officer to accompany him to an exposed forward position. The enemy soon spotted them. With machine-gun and rifle bullets swarming round his head and that of his unfortunate companion, Almond stood at ease, chatting about the terrain as if nothing out of the ordinary was happening, meanwhile gazing searchingly into the other man's eyes. Finally, the other man quailed and hit the dirt. For a prolonged moment, Almond stared downward at him as if wondering how he had got himself into such a strange posture. Finally, as much to save myself as to preserve the commanding general's life, I tackled Almond. Apparently, Almond had regarded this episode as a test of the other man's mettle; later that day he relieved him of his command. He never mentioned the flying tackle to me.

Outside Seoul, despite courageous assaults against enemy positions, General Smith and his Marines missed Almond's deadline for conquest of the city. The latter's war diary notes that "previous day's casualties suffered by Second Battalion, First Marines, some 116, were a result of aggressive forward movement without the required artillery preparation." The Marine officer in charge explained that he had been worried about shelling Seventh Division troops operating in the same area.[12] In the early afternoon of September 24, Almond called a meeting of Army and Marine commanders and told them that the Thirty-second Infantry, with the ROK Seventeenth Regiment attached, would attack across the Han River at first light the following morning. General Smith argued vehemently against this order; he wanted to try yet another attack against the enemy's strength. Icily, Almond ignored Smith's arguments and explained the operation in classroom detail. The Seventh Division troops would take South Mountain, the dominant terrain feature in the area, thus placing themselves at the enemy's rear and relieving the pressure on the Fifth and First Marines. He inventoried the artillery, air, and armor available and then ended the conference without troubling to repeat the orders he had given at the beginning.

On leaving the others, Almond drove, characteristically, to an observation point overlooking the site of the next day's action in order to reconnoiter the ground in person. The spot he chose was on the forward slope of a hill overlooking the Han. His war diary notes, "This outpost extended beyond the then-existing friendly lines." He returned to the same place at 4:00 A.M. the next day to observe the actual operation. An enemy mortar round fell about one hundred yards from Almond and his party. When, after the detonation, someone suggested the group should move back, Almond, absorbed by the martial spectacle below, said, "What the hell for?" The rest of the group did fall back, as the war diary notes, "slightly, to a position offering more defilade."[13] After a moment or two, Almond, left with no one to talk to, joined the rest.

On that morning, Almond had ordered me to accompany the leading elements of the Thirty-second Infantry in the river crossing. This was an important operation for him, since he had overruled the Marines, and he wanted to be sure that all the elements of the attack—the artillery barrage, the mortar barrage, the concentration of firepower, the tactical maneuver of the infantry and tanks—went by the books. I crossed the Han in an amphibious vehicle borrowed from the Marines and observed the action from ground level, radioing back observations to Almond in his aerie and relaying his orders to the commanders on the ground. Although the troops I was with were in direct contact with the enemy, this duty seemed relaxing compared to tramping around with Almond.

To his great satisfaction, the envelopment by the American and ROK troops succeeded brilliantly, with every element of the attack falling into place with clockwork efficiency—the artillery barrage was a work of art— and, as Almond had foreseen, the possession of South Mountain proved to be the key to the final capitulation of Seoul on September 26.

The remnants of the enemy forces defending Seoul retreated swiftly across the 38th parallel, fading into the mountainous and near-trackless and -roadless interior of North Korea. In the Inchon-Seoul campaign, some 7,000 prisoners were taken; the number of enemy dead was estimated by the U.S. Army's official history at 14,000. There were 3,500 United Nations casualties, of which the First Marine Division suffered 2,383, or 68 percent of the total; 364 Marines and 106 members of the Seventh Infantry Division were killed in action. The Seventh Division reported 466 wounded and missing.[14]

These were not the only casualties. In the three months they controlled the country, the North Korean security police executed an estimated 26,000 South Koreans for political reasons; these systematic murders continued even after the Inchon landing.[15] Large numbers of American prisoners of war were found by the advancing Eighth Army, shot through the head, with their hands tied behind their backs.[16] This I did not witness, but I did see a large group of Koreans whose spines had been broken by blows delivered with rifle butts; the victims had been lying in the open for days, but some were still alive. When, after the fall of Seoul, we reconnoitered the leading hotel, which had been used by Soviet advisers as a headquarters, we discovered that the former occupants had defecated in every room before retreating; the same was true in other buildings that might be of use to us. This bestial insult made a lasting impression on me.

With the liberation of Seoul, the sovereignty and territory of the Republic of Korea had, as a practical matter, been restored. Within the administration and in Congress, there were doubts about the democratic instincts of President Syngman Rhee, whose police had enthusiastically suppressed the opposition, Communist and otherwise, during South Korea's brief prewar existence. The Joint Chiefs of Staff cautioned MacArthur that he "must have the approval of higher authority" to restore Rhee's government in Seoul. MacArthur replied, "Your message is not understood," and restored it on September 29 by intoning the Lord's Prayer before a large crowd at a ceremony in the war-damaged National Assembly building.[17]

Because I accompanied Almond, I was standing quite close to MacArthur. As he spoke, distant explosions shook loose Damoclean shards of broken glass from the plate-glass roof and these plunged down, shattering on the floor among the audience. Like most of the people around me, I hastily put on my helmet. MacArthur, uncovered and undismayed, finished the prayer and added a brief remark: "Mr. President, my officers and I will now resume our military duties and leave you and your government to the discharge of the civil responsibility." Weeping openly, President Rhee replied, "We admire you. We love you as the savior of our race."[18] Remembering the tears I had seen in Prime Minister Yoshida's eyes back in Tokyo, I wondered with youthful irreverence what there was about MacArthur that produced this lachrymose reaction in his elderly friends. I did not then realize how rare it is to know a great man who is also a good man.

During planning sessions in Tokyo, MacArthur had told Almond and the rest of the staff that he would take Seoul in five days. Almond demurred that it would require two weeks to liberate the capital, and he was correct. In either case, the operation was historic in its military brilliance and in its political implications, and the whole world knew this. Nikita Khrushchev tells us that this swift victory terrified Kim Il-sung, the North Korean ruler: "He was crying and kept repeating that 'there is no way out. The Americans are sure to come and occupy North

Korea.' "[19] According to Khrushchev, Stalin then and there decided that Soviet troops would not intervene in Korea no matter what happened to Kim or the North Korean People's Republic. "[Stalin] was afraid of the United States," Khrushchev states. "He developed fear, literally fear, of the United States."[20]

Khrushchev states that it was the Chinese who "saved the situation" for the Communist bloc. Mao Zedong sent Zhou Enlai to southern Russia to meet with Stalin and inform him that Beijing was prepared to throw half a million Chinese troops, already massed in Manchuria, into Korea. Khrushchev says that Stalin acquiesced in the Chinese intervention but gave the Chinese no promises beyond this. Stalin repeated to his own ministers that the Soviet Union would take no direct part in the war: "Stalin said, 'So what? If Kim Il-sung fails, we are not going to participate with our troops. Let it be. Let the Americans now be our neighbors in the Far East.' Such was his inner reconciliation. Stalin already believed it was inevitable." Khrushchev regarded this decision as a sign of "cowardice" on Stalin's part.[21]

This is a provocative glimpse into the enemy camp. Some twenty-two years after these events took place, I met Zhou Enlai for the first time during a mission to China to arrange the advance details of President Nixon's historic visit to Beijing in February 1972. He told me that the Chinese had entered the war because they believed, in the wake of MacArthur's shattering victory, that they were confronted by a pincers movement in which the American armies would advance on Beijing from Korea while Chiang Kai-shek's reequipped and retrained Nationalist forces would invade the mainland across the Strait of Formosa under the protection of the U.S. Seventh Fleet and strike for the capital.*

It would be a mistake to dismiss this as mere paranoia. Geographically and militarily, an operation of this kind was by no means impossible: Beijing is only four hundred air miles from the North Korean frontier, less than the distance from Pusan to the Yalu River. The United States certainly possessed the power to carry out a successful attack from Korea; Chiang had half a million troops, recently rearmed and retrained by the Americans, on Formosa; and, as a result of the very first order issued by President Truman after the North Korean invasion of the South, the Seventh Fleet was on station in the Formosa Strait. To the Communist

---

*A secret 1950 cable from Mao to Stalin, summarized in the *New York Times* on February 26, 1992, confirms that "Mao became convinced that a significant American presence in Korea might lead to an American backed offensive by . . . the Nationalists, who had been expelled from the Mainland but still posed a threat from Taiwan."

regime in Beijing, which had been in power for less than nine months, these factors may very well have added up to something that looked like a mortal threat.

Against this background of mutual ignorance and paranoia, each side misjudged the other's intentions very badly. In light of later events, one may wonder whether hearing these facts would have made any difference in Washington. For one thing, they describe behavior in Stalin and Kim Il-sung that would have been regarded then, and for a long time afterward, as inconceivable in Communist dictators, who were supposed by many Kremlinologists to have been immunized by Marxism-Leninism against the human frailties common among leaders of capitalist countries: What point would there have been in appeasing an adversary that was not afraid of us?

Meanwhile, a debate raged in Washington and allied capitals as to whether the United Nations forces should cross the 38th parallel* in pursuit of the retreating enemy. From a military point of view, no other course made sense; if Walker and Almond failed to pursue and destroy what remained of the North Korean army, they would be repeating the mistake Meade made after Gettysburg, and this would surely prolong the war. But the question was not merely military; it was also profoundly political. As early as 1948, in a speech at Seoul, MacArthur, calling the 38th parallel one of the "greatest tragedies of contemporary history," had assured the South Koreans that "the barrier must and will be torn down."[22]

In Washington, there was a tendency to regard this imaginary line as one the Soviets had drawn on the earth as some sort of primitive warning sign, or symbolic likeness of the Iron Curtain, which the United States would ignore at its peril. The Communists had done the same, Acheson noted, in Germany, Berlin, and Iran.[23] What did this shamanistic exercise

---

*The 38th parallel, which came to form the border between the two Koreas, was adopted after the Japanese surrender in 1945 as a convenient and purely temporary line on the map designed to divide those Japanese troops in Korea who would surrender to the Soviet forces north of the line (the Red Army invaded Korea on August 9, three days after the atomic bomb was dropped on Hiroshima) and to the Americans south of the line. The line was drawn a little later in August, in haste, and apparently with no reference to historical precedents, by a young wartime staff colonel just transferred to the Pentagon from China—Dean Rusk, afterward Secretary of State under Presidents Kennedy and Johnson, and his fellow Rhodes scholar, Col. Charles H. Bonesteel. (*See* Warren I. Cohen, *Dean Rusk* [Cooper Square Publishers, Totowa, NJ: 1980]). It appears that neither Rusk nor Bonesteel nor anyone on the General Staff realized that the 38th parallel had been invoked before as a sort of informal demarcation line between Czarist and Japanese spheres of influence in Korea. As Dean Acheson notes in *Present at the Creation* (p. 449): "We soon found that the Soviet Union considered the 38th parallel not as a line of military administrative convenience but as a wall around their preserve." This is a sobering lesson in the importance of scholarship to diplomacy.

mean? No one in the West was sure; none wished to make a misjudgment that might result in a wider war, especially since many believed that the United States lacked the means even to fight a limited war in Korea to an unequivocal conclusion while still defending Europe.

Oddly, the most significant bit of evidence that crossing the 38th parallel might lead to serious consequences was ignored. On October 1, in a speech in Beijing, Zhou said that China "will not tolerate foreign aggression and will not stand aside should the imperialists wantonly invade the territory of their neighbor."[24]

Two days later, the State Department received word from the Indian government that Zhou Enlai had called in the Indian ambassador to Beijing, K. M. Panikkar, and told him that if UN forces crossed the 38th parallel, China would send in troops.[25] Panikkar was regarded in Washington as unduly sympathetic to the Communist Chinese; so, indeed, was the Indian government itself. Acheson regarded Zhou's message as "a warning, not to be disregarded, but, on the other hand, not an authoritative statement of policy."[26] Perhaps not, but Zhou was the premier of China, and if he did not speak authoritatively on his government's policy to a foreign ambassador, then who did? Evidently, no attempt was made to answer Zhou's message in order to measure its seriousness—or to reassure the Chinese about American intentions.

General Marshall, who a few days before Inchon had succeeded Louis Johnson[27] as Secretary of Defense, sent General MacArthur a telegram saying, "We want you to feel unhampered tactically and strategically to proceed north of the 38th parallel."

MacArthur decided to drive to the Chinese border along the Yalu River, if necessary, for the purpose of destroying the North Korean armies. He understood the military risk involved. "This decision," as he wrote in *Reminiscences* (and said to his staff at the time), "immediately raised the shadow of Red Chinese intervention."

Maj. Gen. Charles A. Willoughby, his chief of military intelligence, told him that the "transfer [toward Manchuria] of Lin Piao's Fourth Field Army, aggregating 500,000 men alone, from South China, from Hainan, and offshore Formosan areas, was trailed from one railroad terminal to the next."[28] These were the troops the Nationalists had told us about when the Fox mission visited Formosa the month before.

But what were the *intentions* of the Chinese? On this point, confusion reigned. Zhou Enlai's clear warning had been disregarded. The Central Intelligence Agency, which had taken over the gathering of strategic intelligence less than a year before, reported on November 24, the day the Eighth Army launched its drive to the Yalu River (X Corps having arrived there on November 21): "There is no evidence that the Chinese Communists plan major offensive operations in Korea."[29] The Joint Chiefs of Staff decided to wait and see what the Chinese actually did instead of adapting allied plans to the mere possibility of intervention.

Because our Air Force and Navy controlled the skies, MacArthur himself believed that no Chinese military commander would hazard an invasion.[30] But if the Chinese did attempt to attack across the Manchurian border, he told a journalist, "our air will turn the Yalu River into the bloodiest stream in all history."[31] But when, on November 6, MacArthur ordered the Far East Air Force to bomb the Yalu bridges with ninety B-29s, his order was countermanded by Secretary Marshall after Acheson protested to the President.[32]

Finally, MacArthur was authorized by Washington to bomb only the Korean end of the bridges. If we began to attack Communist China, Truman now figured, we had to anticipate Soviet intervention,[33] and any confrontation between the United States and the Soviet Union risked a third world war. MacArthur was forbidden to bomb beyond the Yalu even after the Chinese had crossed it in force, the administration having decided that the Yalu River was a line that the Chinese could violate at will but one that United Nations aircraft could not cross, even for reconnaissance purposes. The decision concerning the Yalu bridges was, MacArthur told his staff, "the first time in military history a commander has been denied the use of his military power to safeguard the lives of his soldiers and the safety of his army. . . . It will cost the lives of thousands of American soldiers and place in jeopardy the entire army."[34]

When he made a similar statement publicly, it was derided as bombast. I doubt that any American soldier or Marine who retreated from the Yalu that winter through chains of mountains held by the hundreds of thousands of brave, disciplined Chinese regulars who had marched with impunity into Korea would have called it that. To us, it seemed to be the simple truth.

4

"Fierce Actions"

After the fall of Seoul, MacArthur ordered Almond to reembark X Corps, sail around the Korean peninsula, and bring his forces ashore at Wonsan, a deep-water port on the east coast with a good airfield 110 miles north of the 38th parallel. Wonsan, the principal port of entry for supplies and equipment transported by sea from the Soviet port of Vladivostok, was still in enemy hands.

According to MacArthur's plan, X Corps, once ashore, would join up with the South Korean Capital and Third divisions and attack along the only east-west highway in North Korea with the intention of entering Pyongyang, the North Korean capital, from the east while Eighth Army hit it from the west and south. In the event, to quote the words of the official history, "The flanking operation originally conceived by General MacArthur for the X Corps after it had landed on the east coast at Wonsan had, in fact, been carried out by ROK army units under Eighth Army control before a single soldier of X Corps landed in the east."[1] On October 20, the 187th U.S. Airborne Regiment dropped on two highway and railroad centers, Sukchon and Sunchon, some thirty miles north of Pyongyang, cutting off the enemy's retreat. The enemy capital fell, Kim Il-sung vanished, and for all intents and purposes the North Korean regime ceased to exist.

Meanwhile, to Almond's intense frustration, X Corps was unable to land at Wonsan. The North Koreans had sown about three thousand Soviet mines in the approaches to Wonsan. Two U.S. Navy minesweepers and several South Korean vessels had already been sunk after hitting mines in the channel. Admiral Doyle, again in command of the assault force, ordered that the mines be swept before any landing was attempted. Some of the troops had been living in LSTs for more than a week as they cruised back and forth outside the harbor; their name for this choppy voyage to nowhere was "Operation Yo-yo."

Almond and I flew up and down the coast in a helicopter, searching for alternative landing sites and finding one at Iwon, more than one hundred miles north of Wonsan, where he would eventually land the Seventh Division,[2] overcoming great difficulties caused by the rough surf. The First Marine Division did not come ashore through Wonsan harbor until October 26.

A day or so before that, Almond's patience ran out. He decided to go ashore by helicopter and set up his command post. He sent me on ahead with his gear in a small boat operated by a Navy coxswain, with orders to have everything in full operation by the time he arrived. There were no other Americans in Wonsan. As Almond put it with no hint of a smile, "Haig, I'm giving you the honor of being the first member of X Corps to make an amphibious landing in Wonsan."

Taking a chance with his temper, I said, "Thank you, sir. I won't forget the General's confidence in me."

The day was cold, with a wind out of Siberia, and the windchill factor was probably below zero. The anchored ship rolled and pitched dramatically in the surf. The Navy coxswain asked whether I was sure I wanted to try a run for the beach. Desire had nothing to do with the situation. We embarked, and the coxswain immediately encountered difficulties. The big offshore swell took the small craft up and down like an elevator, and, after several narrow escapes, the boat capsized several yards from shore, dumping me and the coxswain into water over our heads.

It was impossible to swim and save Almond's gear as well as myself, so I marched underwater toward shore, holding the general's bedroll at arm's length above my head in the vain hope of keeping it dry. When my head broke water, the water on my face turned instantaneously to ice, and soon after I emerged onto dry land my clothes froze, too. I spotted a large bonfire fifty yards or so down the beach, and, shuddering with cold, ran toward it, ripping off garments as I went.

That evening, coughing, nursing a temperature of 104 degrees, and worrying about pneumonia, I was summoned into Almond's presence. "Damn it, Haig," he thundered, "you got my bedroll wet! Can't you do anything right?"

MacArthur called the Korean War "this savage and terrific conflict, the most savage I ever fought in."[3] Although I had no other war to compare it to, I was deeply affected by the scenes that I witnessed. The poverty of the people intensified the impression of appalling suffering caused by the savagery of the fighting and the harshness of the climate. Before the landing, from Almond's helicopter and while on the ground among South Korean troops, we had seen rivers of refugees all along the coast. Many families seemed to have moved with all their possessions onto small rock islands in the sea; since there was no fresh water on these sea-lashed outcroppings, we speculated that they collected and drank the cold rain that poured almost ceaselessly from the sky.

Wonsan city officials told Almond that the city's population had dropped from about 150,000 to an estimated 90,000 since the war had begun, but the people we had seen laboring along muddy, rutted roads were returning home.[4] Almond issued orders to South Korean commanders that all food commandeered from civilians must be paid for; city officials asked whether they might be paid in South Korean *won* rather than in what they called "Red money"; before withdrawing, the North Korean army had stripped the local population of as much North Korean currency as its soldiers had been able to find.[5]

I doubt that anyone could have comprehended the whole of the war's horror. The most brutal outrages were discovered in a perfectly casual way. During my first moments ashore, while I was warming myself by the bonfire on the beach, I heard a number of explosions off to one side and wondered whether the area was somehow under mortar attack, until I realized that the noise was being created by North Korean prisoners of war who were being marched through a mine field by South Korean troops as a means of clearing it. It was a surrealistic scene, with men stepping on mines and being blown to bits and the others closing the interval and marching stolidly onward.

Somewhat later, in Hamhung, I encountered a very intelligent young boy, no more than ten years old, who asked me in English to come with him to his school.

I was suspicious. "What for?"

"All teachers dead." He mimed the throes of several people being shot to death.

I followed him through the twisting streets to the courtyard of a Roman Catholic school and found the decomposing bodies of a priest and several nuns who had been executed in front of their pupils.

"Communists come, shoot all, then run away," he explained. "Students run away, too."

He made me understand that he wanted to give the dead a decent burial. He himself had nowhere to go, no warm clothes, nothing to eat except what he could beg in a starving city. Against standing orders forbidding fraternization with North Korean civilians, I "adopted" him, giving him food and GI clothes and cigarettes, which he could trade for necessities on the black market.

After the fall of Pyongyang, the North Korean Army, which had suffered 200,000 dead and wounded and had 135,000 of its soldiers taken prisoner,[6] was supposed to be virtually destroyed. Yet it continued to fight all across northern Korea both as organized units and in large-scale guerrilla actions. On October 28, American troops near Kojo were attacked in sufficient strength for one battalion commander to request either to be reinforced or be granted permission to withdraw; Almond issued outraged orders that there would be no withdrawal.[7]

On our side, the ROK troops were ill-clothed and ill-fed. Each soldier had half a blanket; most had no winter coats and many wore worn-out boots or none at all. Nevertheless, they had recently defeated large North Korean forces in a series of major engagements. Their officers were as serious as the troops were brave: I saw a South Korean corps commander pistol-whip one of his division commanders in Almond's presence because he had failed to carry out a mission; he used a .45 Colt automatic, which weighs two and a half pounds. I feared that he would kill the man, but he remained at attention through it all, his face covered with blood.

The troops speculated constantly about the Chinese. Were they going to come in? Were they already here? By mid-October, the South Koreans had had many contacts with troops they said were Chinese. In late October, an X Corps intelligence officer, flying in an L-5 observation airplane over the barren wasteland of northeastern Korea, spotted a patrol of half a dozen soldiers mounted on small, shaggy horses.

He came back to headquarters in a state of excitement. "These guys wore tall fur hats and long overcoats with bright yellow sashes across the chest," he said. "They carried sabers on their belts as well as carbines slung across their backs. It was like spotting the Mongol horde."

We looked up these colorful uniforms in the intelligence manuals on the Chinese order of battle and discovered that they were worn by a cavalry unit that accompanied only army groups—that is, a formation of at least three field armies. This information was reported to headquarters in Tokyo, but, like earlier identifications of Chinese troops, it was insufficiently interesting to MacArthur's intelligence people to elicit a reply.

On October 31, seven more Chinese soldiers were taken prisoner. On the basis of information they provided, X Corps intelligence officers concluded that elements of two Chinese divisions were in place just north of the reservoirs.[8] The correctness of the analysis was demonstrated on November 2, when the Seventh Marines were engaged by a large Chinese force at the approaches to the Koto-ri Plateau; this proved to be the opening fight of a six-day battle in which the Marines, especially Marine air, inflicted very heavy casualties on the 124th Division of the Chinese Army and captured fifty-eight prisoners, including four from the 126th Division.[9]

I saw Chinese troops close up for the first time on October 30, at Hamhung, when Almond inspected sixteen enemy prisoners of war who had been captured near the Chosin Reservoir by South Korean units. We were surprised by their appearance, if not by their presence: These men, who were clearly Han Chinese, were young, well fed, and showed every sign of good training and excellent morale. They wore new quilted goose-down uniforms and fleece-lined hats—but no gloves or overcoats—and, instead of boots, a sort of rubber sneaker. The military significance of these omissions in their winter gear would become evident only later, when they attacked our positions in snow and subzero temperatures. They were simple fellows, and, in return for food (they said they hadn't eaten in three days), they spoke openly. They were, for the most part, former members of Nationalist units that had defected to the Chinese Communist army. Some had belonged to an artillery unit, others to a heavy-mortar company. They had crossed the Yalu River at Manpojin in October 16 and then marched southeast with their equipment packed on horses and mules. That evening, as soon as he reached X Corps command post at Wonsan, Almond sent a personal message to MacArthur by radio, summarizing this information.[10] Once again, Tokyo took no notice.

While these sightings were being reported in late October, X Corps, with the two-division South Korean I Corps attached, was advancing steadily northward through the hills and valleys of eastern Korea in the direction of Manchuria. Eighth Army was also advancing on the Yalu River, but as a separate force far to the west, beyond the Taebaeck Range, which MacArthur had called the spine of the peninsula.[11] Neither force had any plan to cross the frontier with China. On October 18, MacArthur had issued an order restricting operations by United Nations forces (but not South Korean units) to territory south of a buffer zone twenty to thirty miles from the frontier of China. This restriction was later lifted.

On November 6, while the battle between the Marines and Chinese regulars was still in progress, General Willoughby visited X Corps headquarters, accompanied by several other generals from Tokyo. They were briefed on the presence of Chinese troops[12] but demonstrated no great concern despite the fact that MacArthur had told the Joint Chiefs only the week before that the Chinese order of battle in Manchuria consisted of at least fifty-six regular army divisions—a total of 868,000 men, including support troops—and that additional People's Liberation Army (PLA) forces were en route from central China.[13]

Certainly there was no suggestion that the Chinese encountered by X Corps were the vanguard of a large invasion force. On October 15, the day before the prisoners we had captured said they had crossed the Yalu, General MacArthur, during a meeting with President Truman on Wake Island, had said that "my own local intelligence, which I regarded as unsurpassed anywhere, reported heavy concentration near the Yalu border in Manchuria whose movements were indeterminate; that my own military estimate was that with our largely unopposed air forces with their potential capable of destroying, at will, bases of attack and lines of supply *north as well as south of the Yalu* [emphasis added], no Chinese military commander would hazard [it]."[14]

The movement of Chinese troops across the Yalu had begun in October and was virtually complete by November 6. On November 25, Eighth Army intelligence estimated that there were no more than 54,000 Chinese troops inside North Korea.[15] No voice in the national intelligence community was raised in disagreement. In fact, there were nearly six times that many.

During World War I, MacArthur tells us, he and his fellow officers "had often dreamed and boasted . . . of 'watering our horses in the Rhine.' "[16] This is a soldierly euphemism. During World War II, General Patton had urinated into the river when his Third Army reached the Rhine. In Korea, Almond wished to do the same in the Yalu, and when, just before 10:00 A.M. on November 21, 1950, the First Battalion of the Seventeenth Infantry entered Hyesanjin,[17] a Korean town on the banks of that river, he accomplished his purpose, to the enthusiastic emulation of several other generals and staff officers. The Yalu was no broader than a football field here, and it was frozen except for a narrow channel of running water in the middle. On the other side, we could see Chinese sentries walking their rounds and other soldiers coming and going. Their breath vaporized in the frigid air, and I suppose they could see what our generals and colonels were doing from where they were. This seemed a poignant sign of the common humanity of men who had already begun to kill one another and would soon be doing so on a much larger scale. I did not join the boyish celebration by the riverside: "Now that we were there, the exaltation seemed to have disappeared."[18]

Hyesanjin, completely deserted, had been almost entirely destroyed by U.S. air action, but diagonally across the river in Manchuria stood an intact Chinese village that may have resembled it. A bridge connecting the two sides had also been destroyed in the bombing despite the stern ban on such targets, and I remember reflecting that this would make little difference to the Chinese. The temperature fell below zero every night, and the Yalu would be frozen solid in a matter of days.

The Chinese across the river made no effort to fire on us. Yet other elements of the Seventh Division had defeated Chinese troops in small but fierce actions in this area only six days earlier,[19] but we had seen little or nothing of Chinese troops since. After the series of sharp attacks in the first couple of weeks in November, the Chinese simply disappeared. The reader may wonder how so large a force could hide itself so successfully, and I can only answer that the hill country of northeastern Korea had to be seen to be appreciated. Not even the Japanese had attempted to control this empty country with its innumerable valleys, caves, riverbeds, and other natural hiding places. Large sections lacked roads, or even tracks, entirely; some units of X Corps used ox carts (and when the snows came, which was soon, ox-drawn sleds) to transport supplies and ammunition and evacuate the wounded.

Almond was not content to move at such a pace. Wishing to inspect an isolated Marine unit in the reservoir area and receiving little encouragement from the unit (the Marines were hardly ever glad to see him), he sent me to their position with orders to build a landing strip for his plane. "I'll be there at 1600 hours this date, Haig; have the strip ready."

Traveling by Jeep through a blizzard, I arrived at the Marines' position with about three hours to spare. As I noticed while approaching, a firefight was raging on all sides, but in spite of the confusion I managed to find the gruff lieutenant colonel commanding the Marine engineers.

He knew who I was and offered no very warm welcome. I said, "Sir, General Almond's compliments. He wants a landing strip constructed so he can land here at 1600 hours."

"He wants a *what?*"

I repeated the order. The Marine lieutenant colonel told me what I could tell General Almond to do with his order.

"Sir, if there's no landing strip built by 1600 hours, it won't be General Almond's anatomy that will suffer. It will be yours and mine, sir."

The Marine, his helmet and field jacket rimmed with snow and ice, drew my attention to the howling blizzard and the sounds of small-arms and mortar fire. "It can't be done," he said.

"If there is no landing strip, let me point out to the Colonel that General Almond will land, anyway. That will bust up his airplane and he won't be able to take off again. It looks like you're snowed in here, sir. The Marines could be stuck with him for days."

The lieutenant colonel understood. He gave some orders. Equipment rolled. Just as the sound of the general's airplane came into hearing, the bulldozers completed a rude runway in the half-frozen dirt. Almond had a bumpy landing, bullets kicking up the snow around his plane. After conferring with the Marine commander, he flew away. I returned to headquarters by Jeep.

From mid-November onward, our troops reported numerous cases of frostbite, especially among units operating at higher altitudes—the terrain in general lay above three thousand feet, and some of the higher peaks were around five thousand feet. Almond fussed and stormed and managed to obtain some pup tents and oil heaters for the troops, together with warmer clothes for both South Koreans and Americans. Most of our own men were still wearing World War II–issue cotton field jackets and un-lined combat boots. Not until later were all American troops issued parkas, arctic boots, and other winter clothes.

In retrospect, I suppose the sudden suspension of Chinese activity ought to have seemed eerie to X Corps staff. Instead it was merely puzzling. Afterward, it was explained by some analysts as a tactical pause while the Chinese brought the rest of their forces across the Yalu. It seems possible to me now, knowing the Chinese a little better, that the pause was intended as a signal. Perhaps Zhou and the other leaders in Beijing thought that we would stop advancing toward their frontier if they stopped attacking our troops; maybe they thought that we would now ask them what their true intentions were, or tell them ours. If so, the enemy was too subtle for us and we were too obdurate for them. As Almond explained over and over again on his rounds of the command, the X Corps scheme of maneuver was to attack to the northwest until it reached the Yalu River.

On the day after the Seventeenth Infantry did so, President Rhee, with General Almond at his side, addressed large crowds in Hamhung and Hungnam, telling them that they had nothing to fear and to work for a united Korea. Almond received Rhee and his wife at the Japanese-style villa I had requisitioned as his residence. Under orders to redecorate the house, I had hired Korean artisans to build a magnificent sunken bathtub of mosaic tiles (although there was no running water), and I adorned the reception rooms with handsome hand-painted vases I had discovered in the Hamhung marketplace.

Almond was pleased with the bathtub, but he also seemed to like the effect created by the vases. On the day the Rhees arrived, many of these receptacles were filled with flowers, and, while pointing them out proudly to Mrs. Rhee, Almond actually gave me credit for having found such beautiful objects in a war-torn city. Mrs. Rhee, a brusque and outspoken woman who was an Austrian by birth, fixed the general with a disdainful stare. "Then your aide should know for future reference," she said, "that in Korea vases of this kind are used as chamber pots."

The next day, November 23, was Thanksgiving, and Almond felt comfortable enough about the safety of his troops to invite most of the divisional and regimental commanders to return from the front and dine with him at Hamhung.[20] According to Almond's war diary, there followed three days of routine activity, conferring with commanders and awarding decorations. On November 24, with General MacArthur observing the opening attacks from the battlefield,[21] Eighth Army commenced a major offensive in the west, designed to reach the Yalu River. X Corps' assignment was to support this advance by sending the First Marine Division and a combat team from the Seventh Division in a westward thrust along the shores of the Chosin Reservoir, designed to cut the enemy's lines of supply and place X Corps in a position to envelop enemy forces from the rear.

Their first objective was Mupyongni, a village situated on a road leading into Eighth Army's zone of operations. Their final objective was the Yalu, where they would take up positions protecting Eighth Army's right. This X Corps offensive was to begin on November 27.[22] Despite many attempts to link up—in early November Almond had ordered a whole battalion of the Sixty-fifth Infantry of the Third Division to move west, after he had personally inspected the roads from his L-5 while I trailed him in another light plane[23]—X Corps and Eighth Army never made contact with each other in anything larger than patrol strength.

On November 26, Almond flew from east to west along the Yalu to

Hyesanjin. He saw no sign of enemy activity in that sector. On the way back, however, he stopped at Chosin Reservoir and found the First Battalion of the Thirty-second Infantry engaging the enemy on the eastern side of the lake while on the western side the Marines called for napalm attacks on other enemy formations that were attacking them.[24] Early the next day, Almond visited the command post of the Seventh Marines, about fifteen miles northwest of Hagaru-ri, alongside Chosin Reservoir. Enemy activity had intensified. Ever the perfectionist, Almond pointed out to the colonel commanding the Marines that the drivers of the trucks carrying troops and supplies for the advance on Mupyongni were jamming the road north and "were not practicing convoy discipline."[25]

What I remember is men wrapped up in every last scrap of clothing and blanket that they owned, and still suffering in the winter weather; if you touched your steel helmet or your weapon with an ungloved hand, skin and metal froze together in an instant. "The Seventh [Marine] Regiment had made strong contact with the enemy (Chinese) to the north, west and south," I wrote in the war diary for November 27. "The weather was bitterly cold throughout the day, particularly in the mountains and on the plateau surrounding CHOSEN Lake [sic]."

Newly captured prisoners of war had reported that same day that three Chinese divisions of the Twentieth Army were poised nearby for an attack on this very road.[26] Almond was still thinking in terms of attack, not defense. I had been by his side almost constantly, and I remained very concerned.

> When darkness fell . . . they heard a sudden frightening uproar of noise. Bugles, whistles . . . cymbals . . . drums . . . the crowing of cocks . . . shouting, laughing, chattering . . . human voices. When the noise stopped, [they] were struck by sudden attacks. These had the intense quality described by the Chinese as sang-men kung-tso or "the three fierce actions"—"fierce fires, fierce assaults, fierce pursuits."[27]

That is a description of an attack on a South Korean unit of the Eighth Army on November 25, but it accurately recalls the sounds heard by X Corps units that were attacked in late November and early December. Out of the swirling snow, the Chinese came in great numbers, and, despite taking staggering casualties when they ran into American fire-power, they kept on coming. The popular impression that they employed "human wave" tactics is mistaken; in fact, they usually attacked on a very narrow front with many small units one after the other, hurling platoon after platoon against our defenses until they broke through or were slaughtered. Slaughter was the more usual result. Nevertheless, they halted the advance of the United Nations forces and forced them into a retreat that in some cases more closely resembled a rout.

On the night of November 27, the Chinese IX Army Group attacked Marine and Army units near the Chosin Reservoir, halting the Marines' advance toward Mupyongni. The following night, MacArthur summoned Walker and Almond to Tokyo for an overnight conference. Their reports confirmed what was already apparent—that Eighth Army was in greater peril than X Corps. The Supreme Commander ordered Eighth Army to fall back forthwith to the Imjin River line, north of Seoul, or as far as necessary to escape envelopment by Chinese forces, and instructed Almond to recall X Corps from its advance positions to a defensive position at Hungnam.[28]

Many on Almond's staff, including myself, doubted that X Corps, scattered all the way to the Yalu over hundreds of square miles of broken terrain along a four-hundred-mile front in independently operating units of regimental and battalion size, could be extricated. Intelligence had many reports of large bodies of Chinese troops crossing the Yalu to the east, and it was feared that they might turn on isolated units of the Seventh and Third divisions holding blocking and other positions along the roads and in the mountains and destroy them piecemeal. But the Chinese had other plans farther south, and most of the northernmost X Corps units reached Hungnam with little opposition.

Meanwhile, the Chinese poured into the battle zone along the Chosin Reservoir, concentrating their attack on the First Marine Division and the Seventh Division combat team. Lt. Col. Don C. Faith, Jr.'s battalion, still isolated, came under heavy attack on the night of November 27 but maintained its position. But by the 29th, it had used most of its ammunition and was ordered to move south to link up with the Thirty-first Infantry; after a bloody fight on the ice of the reservoir in which Col. Allan D. MacLean, the task-force commander, was wounded four times before apparently being captured by the Chinese, the linkup was accomplished. With the loss of MacLean, Faith took command of the entire task force.[29] However, he was now surrounded by Chinese troops; ammunition and other supplies were air-dropped while Marine aircraft constantly attacked the enemy in the hills all around.

On November 30, Almond flew to the front again. After hearing the reports of his commanders, he ordered the urgent withdrawal of the

Marine and Army regiments around Chosin to Hagaru-ri. An airlift was improvised, and four days later six hundred wounded or otherwise disabled men were flown out of Hagaru-ri.[30] Reaching Hagaru-ri from outlying positions involved hard fighting through Chinese divisions deployed on the heights above the winding roads; out of more than a thousand men who attempted to fight their way out of Koto-ri, for example, only about three hundred reached Hagaru-ri, ten miles away.

Additional Chinese divisions came continually into action. Some of our units were outnumbered ten to one, or even more. Enemy attacks on X Corps positions were incessant, with both sides fighting with scarcely believable courage. On December 4, Almond visited Koto-ri and awarded two Distinguished Service Crosses and ten Silver Stars to soldiers and Marines benumbed by the cold and combat. On the evidence of my own eyes, I knew that he could as easily have decorated a hundred men who behaved with comparable valor but were not detected in their heroism. This operation was not always, in its first stages, the admirably orderly thing that it subsequently became under Almond's unceasing inspiration, tutelage, and badgering. But it was certainly not the rout it was sometimes described as having been.

On December 4, the force commanded by Lieutenant Colonel Faith, renamed Task Force Faith, was still surrounded. Almond ordered Maj. Gen. O. P. Smith, commanding the First Marine Division, and Maj. Gen. David G. Barr, commanding the Seventh Division, to find a way to rescue Faith. This proved to be impossible, and Faith was ordered to fight his way out under close air support. He and his men did so in an epic of courage and improvisation against overwhelming odds, skirmishing with the swarming enemy across open ice and along precipitous mountain roads. Only three officers and seventy-three men of Faith's battalion survived. Faith was not among them: He died of wounds sustained while leading his men in an assault on a hill from which heavy Chinese fire was sweeping the road below. Altogether, about 1,000 men survived out of the original combined force of 2,500, and only 385 of these were fit for duty.[31] Almond was at first frustrated and then increasingly enraged by the failure to break through and rescue these men. He was never reconciled to our inability to come to their aid. Nor was I.

The First Marine Division and numerous Army units fought their way out from December 8 to 11 in a series of sharp actions along winding mountain roads, capturing the high ground from the enemy as they went. Temperatures sometimes dropped below minus forty degrees Fahrenheit, and much of the action took place in swirling snowstorms in which the opposing troops often could not see one another until they made physical contact. Weapons and human flesh froze in these conditions. The Chinese suffered terrible losses from frostbite; like the first prisoners we had seen, they had no gloves or overcoats, and their goose-down garments were useless when wet. Their rubber shoes, even when worn with several layers of woolen socks, were little protection against the extreme cold. Moreover, they tended to sweat inside their quilted clothes when moving at the double and then to chill disastrously when they took up static positions.

One platoon from the Seventh Marines found some fifty Chinese soldiers sitting in a snowstorm like statues, bolt upright in foxholes, still alive but so close to being frozen in their own sweat after a long run to get into position that they were unable to move. The Marines picked up their rigid bodies like so much furniture and placed them on the road for following units to find; the ungloved hands of some of the Chinese were frozen to their weapons, and in order to disarm them the Marines had to bend and twist their fingers, sometimes breaking them in the process.[32]

Enemy losses to American firepower were very great. Navy and Marine close air support, massed artillery, small-arms fire, and the devastating effect of quad (four machine guns on a single mount) .50-caliber and dual 40-mm antiaircraft weapons, used against Chinese troops in the absence of enemy aircraft, inflicted staggering casualties. It was assumed that most seriously wounded Chinese died because their army provided only the most primitive battlefield medical care and lacked both field hospitals and facilities for evacuation. Postwar estimates indicated that the Chinese may have lost two-thirds of the strength of the nine or more divisions of their attacking force (about 72,000 men) to a combination of wounds and frostbite.[33]

In its fighting withdrawal to Hungnam, X Corps suffered total casualties of 5,638; in its withdrawal to the Imjin River, the Eighth Army lost 7,337 killed, wounded, or captured. Said MacArthur, "This was about half the losses at Iwo Jima, less than one-fifth of that at Okinawa, and even less in comparison with the Battle of the Bulge."[34] These words were written much later; I doubt that optimistic comparisons of this kind occurred to MacArthur at the time, any more than they occurred to the rest of us.

At Hungnam, Almond devised a twenty-mile perimeter, manned by men of the Third and Seventh divisions. A combination of air, artillery, naval guns on warships in the harbor, and antiaircraft weapons converted for use against ground targets, plus the small arms of the defending troops, gave the Chinese no option but to attack and die. This they proved themselves willing to do in truly sickening numbers. Almond reported to MacArthur that we could hold this perimeter indefinitely, and I myself believe that X Corps could still be in Hungnam today had we chosen to remain. Instead, following a brilliant plan drawn up by Marine Col. Edward H. Forney, the architect of Inchon, X Corps embarked on ships, and by Christmas Eve was en route to southern ports to join Eighth Army in the next stage of the war.

However orderly this withdrawal, it was a retreat, and the men felt it. So would the unfortunate civilians we left behind. Almond made sure that any North Korean civilians who had cooperated with us were transported to South Korea if they wished to leave, as they all did. They were not the only ones. Masses of refugees carrying their meager belongings had intermingled with our troops during the withdrawal. It was clear to every soldier and Marine that these people were desperate to escape the returning Communist regime. Just how desperate became unforgettably apparent near the end when, on looking down from our small plane while flying over the harbor at Hungnam, we saw tens of thousands of civilians wading through the freezing surf toward American ships lying at anchor in the harbor.

"We can't leave those people," Almond said. "Take care of that, Haig."

I passed the word, and somehow Colonel Forney found the ships to transport some 100,000 of them to freedom. On Almond's orders, X Corps did not sail until every refugee was embarked. My young friend whose teachers had been massacred was among them, stowed away in great luxury in Almond's command van in the hold of a Liberty ship.

As we left Hungnam, Almond had abruptly asked what had happened to his mosaic bathtub. I replied that nothing had happened to it—it was still in the villa in all its glory. "What the hell is wrong with you, Haig?" he roared. "Go back and blow it up—no damn Russian is going to use *my* bathtub." I returned to the villa and wearily dropped a thermal grenade into the tub. And with this final detail taken care of, Almond boarded the *Mount McKinley* at Hungnam to observe the final out-loading of troops and equipment under a furious covering bombardment from the big guns of the battleship *Missouri*, the cruiser *St. Paul*, and other warships in the harbor. According to Almond's watch, the last soldier was embarked at 1436 hours on Sunday, December 24, meeting the deadline he had set for this event.[35]

During the ensuing campaign, in which the United Nations forces pushed the Chinese back to the 38th parallel, Almond remained in command of

X Corps and, despite many appeals for transfer to a combat command, I stayed as his aide. Finally, he heeded my pleas, and I was posted in May 1951 to Task Force Yoke, which had been given the assignment of seizing the road junction at Habae-jae on the eastern front. At the end of this operation, I was recommended for promotion to major and offered a job in a line outfit. Destiny intervened. My replacement as Almond's aide was killed in action, and I was ordered back to my old job. After a few days, I noticed certain symptoms and casually asked a doctor about them. Because Task Force Yoke had been operating far from any base of supply, we drank river water "purified" with Halazone tablets. The doctor took the proverbial one look at me and diagnosed infectious hepatitis; the disease was well advanced.

Though I protested that I would be all right in a day or two, I was evacuated to the rear and then to Japan. In the next bed was a strapping, cheerful, healthy-looking fellow about my age. I asked him what was wrong with him.

"Hepatitis, the same as you," he replied happily. "You're going to love it here—they feed you milk shakes and steaks to build up your liver."

"Sounds okay," I said, thinking that I'd be out of the hospital and back at the front in a few days.

The next morning, my neighbor's bed was empty; he had died in the night. Of all the ways in which the war might have ended for me, being laid low by hepatitis after spending all that time by Almond's side was the last one I might have imagined.

Sometime during this period, General MacArthur was relieved of command and made his hero's return to the United States. I received the news while in the field with Task Force Yoke, and, like everyone around me, I was saddened but not surprised. More than most, I was of two minds about the event. I thought that MacArthur was right on the military and strategic issues but that Truman was correct to dismiss him in order to preserve the principle of civilian authority over the military. I thought, too, that MacArthur's sycophants had helped to bring him down by making it impossible for the President to ignore the public case they made for MacArthur's views. Even then, I thought, though I did not say this to many people, that MacArthur may have welcomed the opportunity to be relieved of the management of a stalemate and to argue his case to the American people, who loved him for what he was, a great soldier and leader of men, but could not imagine him as the elected leader of the whole people.

* * *

Under new commanders who contrived brilliant victories with strictly limited means, the war dragged on until 1953, when President Eisenhower brought it to an end by letting Moscow know, in John Foster Dulles's words, that the aggressor faced "the possibility that fighting might, to his own great peril, soon spread beyond the limits and methods which he had selected."[36] In other words, the United States was prepared to use nuclear weapons to break the stalemate, and their use might not be confined to the Korean peninsula. The Soviets believed that Eisenhower was capable of carrying out the threat, and all my experience since tells me that they would have been just as intimidated by the same promise of dire U.S. retaliation in June 1950.

With the exception of World War II, Korea may have been the most difficult and harrowing foreign war the United States ever fought. Our troops operated in extremes of weather over difficult terrain, often in the midst of a human flood of destitute and terrified refugees into which the enemy routinely infiltrated snipers, saboteurs, and spies. The American citizen-soldier never acquitted himself with greater valor than in these nearly unbearable conditions. Our young men overcame two formidable enemies in a single year, and, given the necessary support and reinforcement, could likely have defeated the Chinese armies in North Korea and driven them from the country. It is not necessary to suggest what might have been; what actually was accomplished by these brave men and their allies, particularly the South Koreans, merits higher praise than has yet been bestowed.

No one who fought against the PLA in Korea would speak of the courage and fighting qualities of the Chinese soldier with anything but admiration and respect. These were veteran troops, most of whom had fought in the Chinese civil war or against the Japanese in World War II. The force that the Chinese sent into Korea was not, however, a modern army. They were mostly infantry with little artillery, no armor or air forces, and primitive supply arrangements. In some units, two men out of three had no personal weapons.[37] The Chinese ate the food they carried with them, and when captured by our side they commonly complained that they had not eaten for two or three days. The enemy generals have been given more credit than was their due. There can have been few more callous and wasteful exercises in generalship in military history than those of the North Korean and Chinese commands in this war.

In the first year alone, American casualties in Korea were at least

77,000,[38] and for the entire war, with 3 million fewer troops engaged, the number of American deaths sustained in three years of combat (54,246 from all causes) was only 3,905 below the number recorded in the eight and a half years of the Vietnam War.[39] The actual total of North Korean and Chinese casualties will probably never be known, but I do not think they could have been fewer than 1 million. South Korean losses, not counting the enormous toll in civilian dead and wounded, were around a quarter of a million.[40]

In some American units, the carnage was appalling. After the capture of Pyongyang in October 1950, MacArthur talked to members of F Company, Fifth Cavalry Regiment, First Cavalry Division, which had been the first unit to enter the city. "He asked all men in the company who had landed with it in Korea ninety-six days earlier, when it numbered nearly 200 men, to step forward," says the official history. "Only five men stepped forward; three of them had been wounded."[41] Americans captured by the enemy were subjected to barbarous treatment by the North Koreans, and by the Chinese to a form of political indoctrination, or "brainwashing," which was so cruel that few would care to distinguish it from torture.

Any human being finding himself in the midst of such events naturally believes that the world is just as affected by them as he is. On returning home in the summer of 1951, I discovered that this is not always the case. The atmosphere of business as usual and the cool disinterest in the war that I encountered among Americans made an impression on my mind and spirit that was at least as deep and lasting as those imprinted by the experience of combat and by the pathetic condition to which the war reduced the Koreans. At the time, it seemed to me impossible that my fellow Americans, who had behaved with such patriotism and harmony in World War II only a few years before, could be so detached from the fate of their soldiers in the field or so indifferent to the misery of another nation. No doubt the psychic fatigue produced by fighting a war for survival, coming on the heels of the Great Depression, had something to do with this.

No doubt the future will balance the book of memory. In the meantime, like U. S. Grant in regard to the Civil War, "I would not have the anniversaries of our victories celebrated, nor those of our defeats made fast days and spent in humiliation and prayer; but I would like to see truthful history written."[42]

As Richard Nixon was to remark twenty years later in another context, this depends on who writes the history. Our army in Korea was not a cross section of America, as the armed services had been in earlier wars. At first, because they were members of an all-volunteer Army, and later, due to the inequities of a draft that facilitated the exemption of members of the more educated classes, the Korean War was fought almost entirely by enlisted men whose families lacked influence in their communities. This cynical method of selecting young men for dangerous military service was an affront to democracy that would be repeated in the Vietnam War, and it may well have been one of the important reasons why the whole nation's emotions and convictions were never fully engaged in either conflict. Gradually, I came to think that my countrymen had not taken the war in Korea fully to heart because their government had not given them a convincing reason to do so. Korea was the first, though not the last, case in my lifetime in which we chose to believe that American troops could fight a major conflict while large sectors of the home front made no material sacrifices or moral commitment to the struggle. In this delusion lay the source of many of our country's deep social, moral, and psychological difficulties with regard to Korea and, later, to Vietnam.

Our leaders complicated the difficulties by failing to define the reasons for fighting the war in terms of the national interest, by omitting to declare clear military and political goals and then sticking by them, and by placing voluntary limits on our own power without expecting the other side to restrain itself in any way. Also, through a failure of intelligence, in all senses of that word, we made a profound strategic miscalculation by linking the Formosa question to the Korean conflict when they had essentially nothing to do with each other. This led directly to Chinese intervention, prolongation of the war, the renewed division of Korea in defiance of history, logic, and justice, and the infinitely dangerous worldwide perception that the United States was weaker than in fact it was.

Domestic politics intruded into a situation in which the national interest ought to have been the paramount factor. The President was advised by good and experienced men who, out of fear and loathing of the opposition and its policies, turned their backs on their own expertise in order to join the political battle in a situation that cried out for immunization from politics. Dean Acheson captured the deeply distrustful mood of Truman's inner circle when he wrote, in regard to the Republican right, that "their attachment to Constitutional procedures was a veneer at best."[43] From the other side, eight Republican members of the joint committee that conducted the MacArthur hearings concluded that "it is unfortunate, but true, that the State Department has been affected by a group who have interpreted Asiatic problems to the advantage of the Soviet Union rather than that of the United States."[44]

This breakdown in the postwar bipartisanship that had produced the United Nations Charter, the Truman Doctrine, the Marshall Plan, and the Japanese Peace Treaty instilled in the administration a fear of frankness that sorely handicapped the United States in the conduct of its foreign policy. The purpose of diplomacy, after all, is to communicate truthfully with friend and adversary alike—to explain, to reassure, to warn, and, in the last resort, to make credible threats in the hope of preventing one catastrophe by reminding an antagonist that worse ones are possible. American diplomacy of the period displayed few of these qualities, and our lack of consistency created fears and contradictions in the minds of other governments.

The fundamental task of diplomacy is to strip policy of its ambiguity. The Acheson State Department failed to do this. The situation, murky in the beginning, became more so as inconsistent American behavior cast shadows on our real purposes. Our friends did not understand our intentions, and this raised questions about our will to lead and protect the free world. As to our enemies, the administration's failure to communicate real American goals and intentions, epitomized by Secretary Acheson's speech declaring Korea and Taiwan outside our Pacific line of defense, gave them wrong ideas that were even more dangerous than the questions implanted in the minds of our friends. In his memoirs, Dean Rusk quoted Andrei Vyshinsky's answer to an American businessman who asked why the Soviet leadership thought that the United States would attack the U.S.S.R. Vyshinsky replied, " 'Look at Korea. You did everything you could to tell us you were not interested in Korea, and when the North Koreans went in there, you put your troops in. We can't trust you Americans.' "[45]

Our mistakes in Korea became the model for the practice of American diplomacy for the remainder of my time in government, and the habits we acquired in that bitter struggle influenced our policy and actions in ways that prolonged the Cold War well beyond the strict limits of Soviet power to sustain it.

II

VERSIONS OF PEACE

The ultimate objective of all military operations is the destruction of the enemy's armed forces in battle. Decisive defeat breaks the enemy's will to war and forces him to sue for peace which is the national aim.

U.S. Army Field Service Regulations (FM 100.5), 1939

5

Army Life

Gen. Alfred M. Gruenther, who possessed one of the most brilliant minds in the annals of the Army, waited twenty-one years between the world wars to make major. He went on to become Eisenhower's wartime deputy chief of staff and, after World War II, Supreme Commander of allied forces in Europe. He took advantage of this long vacation from the full employment of his talents by becoming a world-class bridge player. I have never liked card games, so I used what little spare time I had to improve my tennis (for which my gift was far more modest than Gruenther's for bridge), while devoting the six years I spent as a captain to the deep satisfactions of Army and family life.

Our sons Alexander and Brian were born eleven months apart at Fort Knox, Kentucky, my next duty station after Korea. They were lively little boys who kept their mother very busy, and it was as much a matter of domestic necessity as any subconscious desire to make up for the absence of a father figure in my own childhood that I became what would now be called a "hands-on" father. Pat and I certainly could not afford a nurse or governess; neither could anyone else we knew in military life. Fortunately, officers and their wives had each other to rely upon; wives baby-sat for each other and helped out when new babies arrived. If a young mother or her children became ill, she could count on help from other young women who knew that they might someday need the same sort of neighborly kindness. I don't remember what a captain's pay amounted to in the early 1950s, but, whatever it was, it provided no surplus for luxuries, and I often regretted the bout of hepatitis that had sent me home before my field promotion to major had come through.

My mother found new reason to wonder about my choice of a career when she visited us at Fort Knox and saw for herself the extremely simple circumstances of our lives—the impersonal family quarters, the sparse furnishings, the lack of material possessions, the transitory atmosphere of a world in which friends were always arriving and departing and family was usually a long way away. But Pat and I were happy in the Army: it was the only life she had ever known, and the only one I had ever wanted. It is very difficult to explain to outsiders, especially to a loving and anxious parent, how good it is to live within a system that provides the security, the positive reinforcement, and many of the rewards and pleasures of extended family life with few of its disadvantages. A career officer and his spouse are surrounded by other men and women who understand their ambitions, their motivations, and their circumstances perfectly because these are usually very similar to their own. Someone wrote of the Navy that it is a system invented by geniuses to be run by ordinary people. That may be, though I doubt it. The Army certainly was not invented by anyone; it evolved over centuries, the product of its own collective wisdom, on which it has constantly been taking diligent notes ever since it came into existence. When a bad practice is noted, it is eliminated; good ones are written into a great body of regulations that are designed to explain everything—which may be why the Army way of doing things is called "the book" and its method of fighting a war is called "doctrine." This style of management, theological and dynamic at the same time, provides a basis of tradition and a fundamental certainty of purpose. There are no large areas of doubt in Army life. It is a system designed to eliminate doubt because, on the battlefield, doubt is the advance guard of defeat. Nevertheless, as the careers of Grant, Custer, Patton, MacArthur and countless other gifted eccentrics testify, the Army is an excellent place for the individualist: It values honorable performance above everything else, and performance is the essence of individualism. Although this fact is little understood in the outside world, life within the Army offers intense personal fulfillment and a measure of freedom to be oneself.

The Army is also a vastly rewarding and amusing school of human nature. My first assignment at Fort Knox, which is the headquarters of the armor branch, was as commanding officer of a headquarters company in a National Guard tank battalion from Alabama. I was delighted by the assignment. First of all, it meant that I would be leading troops again: Throughout my career, beginning with Almond, I had to fight my superiors to give me such postings instead of the staff jobs they usually seemed to have in mind for me. The fact that I was the first Regular Army officer most of these men had ever seen, and they were the first National Guardsmen I had ever encountered, seemed to be as much an advantage as otherwise; this was the "real Army" where all elements of American life mixed; we would learn from one another.

As I soon discovered, what these untamed civilians in uniform had to teach me was not included in the West Point syllabus. This battalion was a microcosm of a citizen Army, and whatever it lacked in traditional military virtue it made up in a rich mixture of soldierly aptitude, field craft, and small-town ideas dating back to the Civil War and beyond. Its members accepted the formalities of rank and precedence that the circumstance of being federalized imposed upon them, but as a practical matter they brought their community and its structure with them and abided by its rules. The most powerful and influential man in the battalion was a warrant officer who was also the richest, most powerful, and most influential man back home; many of the battalion's officers and men worked for him or were otherwise beholden to him in civilian life, and it seemed only natural that they should defer to him now that they were all temporarily in the Army together. There was nothing overt about this, nothing that would offend the decorum of the unit or cause the colonel any embarrassment; it was just understood as a matter of healthy realism. These men had grown up with one another, played football together, roamed the woods and the honky-tonks together. Everybody's real rank had long ago been established by common consent: They knew who was smart, who was brave, who was otherwise. They were, without any exception I ever discovered, fun-loving, down-home fellows who took payday and weekend passes seriously, and it was a rare Monday morning, at first, when at least 10 percent of the company's strength did not report unfit for duty as a result of strenuous off-post activity. Gradually, we worked this problem and most others out among us, and I'm proud to say that the first company I commanded presently became an efficient, well-turned-out unit.

It did not, however, give up its folkways altogether. The Army takes its custody of the taxpayers' property very seriously. When assuming command of a unit, an officer is required by regulations to take an inventory of the unit's property. Every rifle, every bayonet, every uniform, every blanket, sheet, pair of boots, kettle, spoon, and canteen is counted and written down, with surpluses and shortages duly noted. This was the first thing I did, and I was pleased to note that the shortages were few and minor. During a surprise inspection of the supply room soon afterward, however, I noticed that many of the items that had been there during inventory were now missing. On further investigation, I discovered that the Alabamians' traditional way of dealing with a company inventory was to borrow the property of all the other companies in the battalion on inspection day, returning the loaned items after the inspection was over.

Where were the missing items, which included tools to repair the tanks, engine, and gearbox parts, and many other useful things? "Hell, Captain, you know how it is," said the supply sergeant. "Some ol' boy takes a bunch of tools home to work on his truck and just forgets to bring 'em back, then pretty soon he loans 'em to his cousin and his cousin can't find 'em. That ain't stealing, that's just forgetfulness."

Later, it was discovered that an M-4 tank belonging to a company I happened to be commanding had disappeared somewhere between Anniston, Alabama, and Fort Knox. I had not yet joined the company when the tank vanished, and the fact that it was gone had been covered up when I took over. Nevertheless, I was the unit's commander when the Army discovered that it was missing. Therefore, I was legally responsible for its full value to the nation, and the Army duly mailed me a bill for $325,000. Opening the envelope was a memorable moment for Pat. After reassuring her (none too confidently), I told higher headquarters, using the terms prescribed by military courtesy, that I'd be damned if I'd pay for it. Fortunately, my superiors saw the logic and justice in my position. But we never found the tank.

After completing the advanced course at the Armor School at Fort Knox in the early summer of 1953, I was sent back to West Point as an instructor in armor. I had never expected to return except as a visitor, and I was greatly moved once again to see the battlements above the Hudson where I had learned so much despite my own best efforts to slow down the process. If, as I had often been assured, Fort Knox represented the "real Army," the Military Academy embodied the ideal, with its majestic stone buildings instead of rickety wooden barracks, its unselfconscious striving for excellence hour by hour, and the spick-and-span model it achieved in everything from the lawns to the last chin strap on the last shako. At first, I was assigned to the school troops, the Army unit charged with training cadets in the military arts, but midway through the summer the

Commandant of Cadets, Brig. Gen. John H. ("Mike") Michaelis, asked me to accept a position as cadet company tactical officer.

In those days, the companies of the Corps of Cadets were filled according to physical stature. The cadets of A Company, "flankers," as they were called, were the tallest at the Academy and were famous for their easy confidence, laid-back manner, and good-humored laziness. I was given command of M Company, composed of the shortest men at the Point—the "runt company" in time-honored cadet parlance. The runts by tradition were the meanest, shrewdest, most aggressive, most rebellious of the companies, as well as being the most imaginative and relentless hazers. I knew that it was important to establish immediately not merely my authority over these diminutive terrors but also to wring from them the grudging respect that their breed only grants to someone who has beaten them at their own game.

My chance came when, as if some bizarre revolving karma was in operation, I, who had been one of the chief smugglers of my time, was put in charge of finding out how the cadets were sneaking contraband into their rooms. Fortunately, one of my classmates and partners in crime had been a runt, and I knew there was a hinged panel under the sink in his old room that, when kicked in a certain way, would spring open, revealing a concealed hiding place. On my first inspection, I went directly to this room, strode to the sink, and kicked the panel. It popped open, revealing jars of jam and peanut butter and boxes of cookies hidden within. Contraband! I sympathized with the culprits but did my duty, relieved that nothing more potent had been uncovered. The cadets in that room were sufficiently impressed by this display of omniscience to nickname me "Captain Gunter Haig," or "Gunter the Wonder," after my near-namesake, the Olympic runner Gunter Haag, a grudging tribute to my ability (surreptitiously clocked by the runts) to get up the stairs from the first floor to the fourth in less than fifty seconds.

My serious purpose as a tactical officer was not to keep the cadets from snacking between meals but to discover the misfits and, insofar as possible, to do for them what Red Reeder had done for me. It was an energizing experience. The underlying idealism of these young men, their high intelligence, and their tough determination to overcome the system, seemed to me to incarnate the military history of the nation. This impression was all the more stirring because the war in Korea, including the part played by so many similar youngsters, was still fresh in my memory. Although my methods were admittedly unscientific—leadership is much more a matter of instinct than of intellect—I learned things I had not known before. I discovered that some boys mature sooner than others, and that those from my own ethnic and social background often came into their own later than some of their fellows. I observed, too, that the Army brats at West Point were either the best or the worst of their classes. The best were the way they were because their parents' lives of frequent movement had forced them to adjust to a variety of experiences and develop a knack for understanding and adapting to new situations. The worst were nearly always youngsters who had developed negative tendencies because, conversely, they had never stayed in one place long enough to have their weaknesses discovered and knocked out of them. When the latter finally happened, hidden strengths sometimes asserted themselves.

In the fifties, the Academy still believed that it could judge, grade, and categorize every cadet and, from this blurry snapshot of a youngster's four years under the stress of West Point life, predict his career potential. I was as skeptical of this proposition as an officer as I had been as a cadet, and more than once found vivid human evidence that the system had overlooked to reinforce my point of view. One outstanding case was that of Ben Schemmer, the cadet who kidnapped the Navy goat before the Army-Navy football game in 1953. Because of the droll publicity this stunt generated, prolonged because Schemmer and his coconspirators sequestered the goat and no one could find it, the administration wanted to kick him out. I opposed this, arguing that anyone who could penetrate the tight security surrounding this most symbolic of all American goats, and then outwit the entire Brigade of Midshipmen and the authorities at Annapolis by abducting the animal and then frustrating the best combined efforts of the investigative arms of the Army, Navy, and several cooperating police forces to find it, was exactly the type of military leader the nation needed. After much theatrical throat clearing on the part of our mutual superiors, Ben stayed at the Academy and graduated, although I am sorry to say he did not make a career of the Army; I would have been very glad to have had such a resourceful and daring officer in any unit I commanded.

As I was soon to learn by firsthand experience, the Army's will to win the annual football game between the academies paled in comparison to the do-or-die attitude of the Navy in this regard. In 1955, my last year as a tactical officer at West Point, I was transferred to the the Naval Academy at Annapolis, where people in my job were called "executive officers." Compared to West Point, Annapolis is a very loose and informally run post, although the curriculum is more technical and, in some ways, more rigorous. My immediate predecessor as exchange officer, an unfortunate captain named Boyd, had made a bet: in case Army lost the game, he would sing "Anchors Away" in the mess hall while dressed in a Navy gob's "whiteworks," or summer uniform. Army lost and Boyd paid the bet.[1] That would have been all right, painful though it was, but the Navy ran a trick play by tipping off the television networks, and the poor fellow found himself warbling on TV screens all across the nation while dressed in bell-bottoms and sailor cap. This caused great displeasure among many men with stars on their shoulders throughout the Army.

Soon after my arrival at Annapolis, I was offered the same bet and accepted it in all innocence. A few days later, I was called to the telephone and found myself speaking to Gen. George Decker, soon to become the chief of staff of the Army. He said, "Captain, last year the Army was humiliated by an Army officer who lost a bet while on loan to the Navy. Maybe you saw his picture on television. I hope you haven't made the same bet on this year's game, because if you have, and if we lose, you will be transferred to the most distant outpost on the entire inventory of Army installations to await your retirement in your present rank." With my life passing before my eyes—a bet is a bet—I replied, "I understand, sir." Navy was heavily favored to win. The days passed slowly until the fateful Saturday in Philadelphia finally arrived. I remember the game as if it had been played yesterday. Army did not complete a single forward pass in the entire game and trailed Navy 6 to 0 throughout the first half. But Pat Uebel and Pete Lash scored for Army in the third and fourth quarters. Final score: Army 14, Navy 6.

That victory was not the only unexpected pleasure that came my way at Annapolis. I had been given the company of midshipmen that had been rated last in efficiency in the brigade the year before. This year, they won the colors as the best company in the brigade—the first time this had happened to a unit commanded by a visiting Army officer. The United States Navy does not take losing lightly, in athletics or anything else. "You may have the distinction, mister, of being the first brownie to win the colors," said the chief of Naval Personnel, Adm. William R. Smedberg, when he handed me the prize. "But I guarantee you'll be the last." And as far as I know, I was.

Our daughter, Barbara, was born while Pat and I were stationed at Annapolis. This joyful addition to the family, combined with the long wait for promotion, other professional disappointments, and an uncertainty about my next assignment, which created the unhappy prospect of leaving my wife all alone in Annapolis, without benefit of the Army support system, with three small children, caused me seriously to question my future in the service. While serving at West Point, I had been commuting to New York City on my own time to take graduate courses in business administration at Columbia University, and I liked the course content. I was approached by representatives of the Martin Marietta Corporation, and in due course was offered a vice presidency at a salary five times greater than my Army pay. The temptation to resign my commission was great, and I was close to accepting the offer when West Point intervened in my life again. Col. Michael S. Davison, who had been my regimental commander at the Academy, somehow got wind of the situation and sent an emissary to advise me to persevere; better days were coming.

Soon afterward, I found myself in West Germany, still a captain but doing a major's job as operations officer of the 899th Tank Battalion, stationed near Hanau. This was real soldiering, and after about a year, the battalion was selected to run the Seventh Army tank gunnery school on the British army base on the north German plain near the former Nazi extermination camp at Bergen-Belsen. It was an eerie place, gray and rainy, and, when weather conditions were correct, the stench of the ovens wafted on the damp wind. Something supernatural trembled in the atmosphere of that place where so much murder had been done in the name of ideology. Whatever doubts I may have had about the relevance of the profession of arms in a democracy were dispelled by the realization that the armies of democracy had defeated the regime that had committed these crimes against humanity.

Our opponents in maneuvers were the members of the Devon Regiment of the British army. The ground was sandy and therefore excellent for maneuvering tanks. Facing our battalion was the Irish battalion of the Devons. Both sides fought the mock battle with enthusiasm. The British gave themselves a slight advantage in infantry actions by firing rubber bullets, which stung the flesh like major-league fastballs, while the Americans sportingly fired back with blanks. The exchange became so heated as the Americans charged forward during the final stage of the war game that the Irish battalion dropped their rifles and put up their dukes. The free-for-all that followed was enjoyed by all; when ordered to break it up, we officers did our duty with regret. I had never before worked side by side with the British or been a guest in a British mess. It was an eye-opening cross-cultural experience. Her Majesty's officers wore beautifully tailored uniforms and behaved, before dinner, with impeccable etiquette. After dinner, everyone played rowdy games—steeplechases over the dining room furniture and other mysterious pastimes that were part of the regimental tradition—that could hardly be distinguished from a riot. One night, a group of junior officers blew up the fireplace with dynamite. Everyone present had a hearty laugh while inspecting the gaping hole left by the explosion. The next morning, the colonel commanding the regiment surveyed the damage. "What happened here?" "Officers blew out the fireplace with dynamite, sir." "Very well. See that it's repaired at the expense of the mess within one week." That was all. In the United States Army, courts-martial would have been convened, and the explosive combination of distilled spirits and boyish high spirits would not have been regarded as an acceptable defense.

Soon after I had reported to the 899th, the Hungarian revolution erupted. The East German border was not far away, and we went on alert. Many in the battalion expected the United States to intervene on the side of the freedom fighters, which meant that we ourselves would be fighting the Russians very soon. Back at the base, our families (Pat and the children had just arrived) were briefed on evacuation procedures: In case of a Soviet attack, dependents were to get into their cars and drive to French ports for evacuation. In the end, of course, the United States stood back and did nothing. Later on, I witnessed firsthand the Army's extensive responsibilities in connection with handling the flow of refugees who had fled Hungary in the wake of the uprising. I had observed this sad affair burdened, for the first time, with the thought that my country had somehow retreated from promises it had made to another people. The Hungarians had interpreted statements made on American propaganda broadcasts to the East as a call to revolt against the Russians. They did so in the expectation that the United States would intervene. Our government has always maintained that this was a tragic misunderstanding, and so it was, in the sense that when Russian tanks rolled into Budapest the freedom fighters were offered no American help of any kind.

Many died; thousands fled. I met hundreds of refugees from all levels of society in the course of my duties, recording their stories and helping them to find housing, food, and some of the other basics of life. Some of the young men were integrated into the U.S. Army, earning citizenship with their honorable discharges at the end of their enlistments. Most of the Hungarians I encountered asked why they had been encouraged to risk their lives and fortunes and then abandoned to their fate. It was

impossible for me to answer their question on the basis of what I knew
of U.S. policy, and it would have been improper for me to have expressed
the strong sympathy I felt for them in their disillusionment.

But the experience of dealing with the consequences of their desperate
hope of nationhood and personal freedom pressed home a moral I have
tried never to forget: When the powerful drop hints to the hopeless, they
must either accept the obligation to rescue them if they mistake these
hints for promises or be prepared to watch them die.

Still later, when the Eisenhower administration intervened so decisively
in Lebanon, there were hours when it seemed that the 899th Tank
Battalion would be deployed to the Middle East, but in the end another
battalion, the 510th, was chosen to go. I was sorry not to be a part of this
operation, which was a textbook case of successful crisis management, in
which President Eisenhower acted rapidly and unambiguously and put
an end to a situation that could easily have gotten out of control.

It was interesting to be stationed on the front line of the Cold War,
and I enjoyed being in the field with troops again, but this assignment
continued the pattern of my early Army career, in which I usually filled
a slot calling for an officer one or two ranks higher than the one I held;
this was intellectually stimulating, of course, and it also instilled personal
habits of frugality and thrift that Pat and I recall with a certain perverse
nostalgia, now that they are behind us. At all events, I was finally promoted to major in the spring of 1957 and was then posted as a staff officer
at Headquarters, United States Army in Europe, in Heidelberg. Pat loved
this handsome, narrow old city on the Neckar River with its many cultural
advantages and its lovely surrounding countryside, and so did I. We made
a number of German and French friends when, quite unexpectedly, this
assignment opened the door to my first diplomatic experience. I was
placed in charge of negotiating the status of Army installations with the
French and West German governments. I thrived on this work, and the
way in which I did it gave my superiors an idea that I had an aptitude for
it that should be exploited. My career from this point onward, for better
or worse, was strongly influenced by this conception.

Pat and I returned to the United States from Germany in 1959, just as
the Eisenhower administration was entering its Indian summer. Although
we were unable to vote in the 1960 election because we had been moving
around too much to meet the residency requirement, we paid close
attention to the presidential campaign. I completed the regular course of
studies at the Naval War College in Newport, Rhode Island, and then

went on to earn a master's degree in international studies at Georgetown University in Washington, D.C. During most of this period, it was generally believed, though many resisted the idea, that Richard M. Nixon, who was far ahead of all Democrats in the public-opinion polls, would be the next President of the United States. Although I wondered about the soundness of Kennedy's assertions concerning the so-called missile gap and the decline of American prestige abroad and, especially, some of his ideas about "flexible response" by the military to political crises in faraway places, I might have been tempted to vote for him, but I failed to arrange for an absentee ballot. Despite my lifelong Republican convictions, I was disappointed in some aspects of the Eisenhower administration. The President's lukewarm public loyalty to his own Vice President might have been more forgivable in a civilian than in a fellow West Pointer. Hungary, the Suez crisis, the awkward lie about the U-2 flights over the U.S.S.R., the loss of Cuba, the Sherman Adams scandal, and, not least, Eisenhower's sharp reductions in the military budget combined to persuade me that it was time for a change in what was just beginning to be called presidential "style." Kennedy's youthful appearance, his energetic speaking style, and his quick mind suggested that he might be able to deliver on his promise of a New Frontier. Although I found it impossible to root against my own party, I was not dismayed on election night when the networks declared Kennedy the winner by a fraction of a single percentage point in the popular vote.

The last thing I imagined was that the inauguration of a new Commander in Chief would have the slightest direct effect on my life and career. In the event, for better or worse, it changed both forever.

6

A Trip to Iran

In the late summer of 1961, having completed work on my master's degree at Georgetown University, I was posted to the Pentagon as a plans officer assigned to the International Plans and Policy Division. This was regarded as a plum assignment for a young major interested in strategy and geopolitics. The Pentagon is well known for its ethic of workaholism, and Pat and I knew that fifteen-hour days and weekends at the office lay ahead of me, but we agreed that the job would offer a once-in-a-career opportunity to learn more about the policy-making process firsthand. In that estimate, we were in no way mistaken or disappointed. I was assigned to the Middle East desk under the deputy chief of staff for military operations, and before very long I was helping, in a modest way, to manage a crisis precipitated by the President of the United States himself.

The first two years of the Kennedy administration were a period of trouble and misunderstanding in United States relations with Iran. The shah, only a couple of years older than John F. Kennedy, had ruled his country since the age of twenty-two. In 1953, he had been forced to flee the country by supporters of the leftist premier, Mohammed Mossadeq, returning a year later when Mossadeq was overthrown in a coup in which the U.S. Central Intelligence Agency was deeply involved. This experience left the shah with an abiding mistrust of the urban middle class that had formed the core of Mossadeq's constituency. Like his father before him, he based his rule on the loyalty of the armed forces, and he had used troops to break up demonstrations. Most of the political opposition was in exile. SAVAK, the shah's secret police, harassed what remained, and was widely (and accurately) accused of torturing and murdering political prisoners.

A State Department report ordered by President Kennedy in February 1961 stated that recent elections in Iran had been "rigged," that the political opposition had been suppressed, and that "the Shah, though highly intelligent, is emotionally insecure" and "is capable of making . . . a switch [to neutralism]."[1] The CIA, meanwhile, reported to the President that any reduction in support for the shah would increase "the chances of his working out an accommodation with the U.S.S.R. [including] substantial economic aid, and conceivably even military aid.[2]

The shah lived in splendor while all but a few of his people existed in medieval conditions of poverty and ignorance. The Eisenhower administration had urged reform in the direction of democracy; the Iranian government had not responded in a fashion likely to satisfy its critics in the West, and many in the United States questioned the wisdom, even the morality, of continued support for a regime that showed such limited regard for human rights and social justice.*

During his campaign for the presidency, Kennedy had referred to the possibility of revolution in Iran if the shah did not undertake reforms to control corruption and improve the life of the people. American newspapers had already reported that the United States was planning to strengthen its ties to Iranian opposition groups in case the shah was overthrown. The State Department denied this, but the stories made a deep impression on all parties in Tehran, where, in the words of another State Department report, "an amazing political mythology [prevails] whereby almost all political developments are viewed in terms of foreign influence, usually selfish and malignant."[3] After Kennedy's inauguration, the new administration suggested to the shah that future American aid would be linked to policy changes designed to fight corruption, shrink the size of the armed forces, encourage economic growth, and bring a dramatically larger measure of social justice to the Iranian people. Meanwhile, civilian officials at the Defense Department in charge of reviewing military assis-

---

* Had they been able to look into the future, they might have concluded that the shah's way of ruling his people was preferable to the methods of the religious fanatic who replaced him: In thirty years, SAVAK was said to have murdered about fifteen hundred people, whereas the Khomeini regime killed almost that many in a single four-month period in 1981. (See Robin Wright, *In the Name of God: The Khomeini Decade* [New York: Simon & Schuster, 1989], pp. 24–25, 224–232.)

tance to Iran cut from its budget items that were essential to secure the continued support of the shah by certain elements of the armed forces. The Iranian navy was particularly upset that two new frigates for the Persian Gulf patrol had been eliminated. Unless the frigates were reinstated, no one could guarantee the loyalty of the admirals to the shah. These American words and actions struck at the heart of the shah's primal conviction that a strong army, unswervingly loyal to himself, was the chief, if not only, hope of surviving the plots and combinations of powerful and ruthless domestic enemies. Was the new President naïve about the realities of the Iranian situation or was he antagonistic? The shah remarked to one confidant that he regarded Kennedy's advice as "more or less an American coup directed against him."[4]

The new administration was genuinely fearful of losing Iran to the Soviet Union by subversion or conquest, and this had been a subject for discussion in the inner circle from the earliest days in office. At the Vienna summit in June 1961, Khrushchev had predicted to Kennedy that Iran would sooner or later collapse politically and "fall like a ripe fruit" into the lap of the Soviet Union.[5] The State Department concluded that there was no realistic alternative to the shah and recommended to the President that the United States "continue its present policy of reassurance to the shah," including an expedited payment of $20 million in military assistance.[6]

Against this background, the Kremlin beamed an anti-American propaganda barrage to Iran over Radio Moscow and privately suggested to the shah that he could expect economic and military aid from the U.S.S.R. if he would abandon his pro-American foreign policy in favor of a neutralist course. The shah responded by ordering his foreign minister on a goodwill visit to Moscow.[7] In April 1962, the shah visited Washington for talks with President Kennedy and was sufficiently displeased by what he heard to return to Tehran and fire his prime minister, Ali Amini, a popular former ambassador to Washington and proponent of sweeping land reform whom he had appointed in an attempt to please the White House.

Out of the consternation that ensued, an interdepartmental group, or presidential task force on Iran, was formed to study the long-term economic and military needs of that country and the means by which the United States could help in meeting them. This led to the creation of a Pentagon team charged with devising a plan for the military defense of Iran. I was appointed to the team, which was made up of officers drawn from all relevant branches of the services, as the representative of the Plans and Policy Division. Its commander was Brig. Gen. Hamilton

Twitchell, a renowned perfectionist who spared neither himself nor his staff in the hectic weeks that followed.

Of the fourteen permanent members of the team, only two, Lt. Col. Richard T. Kenedy of the Army and Col. Eddie J. Broussard of the Air Force, had any specialized knowledge of Iran; both were experts. As the representative of Plans and Policy, strategic considerations were my baili-wick. Needless to say, I was somewhat out of my depth. What little I knew about Iran, I learned by cramming before arriving there and by listening to the American ambassador in Tehran, J. C. Holmes, and picking Dick Kenedy's brain. The basic facts were understandable enough. Civilian officials at the Defense Department in charge of reviewing military assis-tance to Iran had cut from its budget items that were essential to ensure the continued support of the shah by certain elements of the armed forces. This time-honored view of loyalty as a commodity to be purchased by favors reminded me of the practices of Chiang Kai-shek's army on For-mosa, but it was an idea difficult for the American mind to grasp.

The shah and his envoys had often complained that American military aid to Iran was inadequate and, because of the American budgetary process, unpredictable. American officials argued in return that Iran's growing oil revenues should enable Tehran to underwrite a larger percent-age of the cost of its own defense. In this game of geopolitical poker, however, the shah held the trump card: The strategic importance of Iran, whose large population, natural resources, and geographical blocking position between the Soviet Union and the oil fields and warm-water ports of the Persian Gulf—and of Afghanistan and Pakistan and India beyond—made it unique in the Middle East in terms of the vital interests of the West and the historic ambitions of the Kremlin. Although the afterglow of British power in the Middle East was still an important stabilizing factor, Iran could not defend itself without outside help, and effective help could come only from the United States. The Central Treaty Organization (CENTO), or "Baghdad Pact" of Middle East states, was in the process of collapsing, owing in no small part to the apparently incurable inability of the Arab states to act in a spirit of mutuality. Since the end of World War II, Iran had persistently sought an American guarantee to come to its aid in the event of *any* attack upon it, no matter by what aggressor. The United States had confined itself to promising that it would support the Iranians in defending their country against a Soviet attack.

This produced an interesting psychological effect. I was not in Iran for very long before I realized that most Iranian officials and military officers were far more worried about being invaded by Iraq than by the U.S.S.R. This was a constant theme in all our conversations with our hosts. Standing on Iran's northeastern frontier, gazing at Soviet watchtowers across a bleak landscape scraped clean of vegetation for miles in all directions by Red Army engineers, I saw the reality of the Soviet threat to American strategic interests. This was a place where we might have to fight.

However, the Iranians made it plain in private conversations that they preferred to concentrate their strength at the western end of the Soviet frontier, where the Iraqis were present in force, rather than in the eastern sector, which was a far more likely Soviet invasion route because of the terrain and other militarily favorable factors. They were far more interested in showing us mountain passes along the border with Iraq; Iraqi and Iranian troops had invariably skirmished only hours or days before in these very places as part of an undeclared but busy frontier war between the two Muslim states. The shah, receiving General Twitchell and the rest of us in his large, elegantly furnished, sun-filled office, let us know on first meeting that he shared fully in this attitude. "Any Soviet attempt to take over Iran," he told our team, "is far more likely to come in the form of the manipulation of puppets, such as the Iraqis or domestic enemies, than by an invasion by Soviet troops. The Soviets know any such attack would immediately provoke a superpower confrontation with the United States, and they wish to avoid that because they are weaker than you are."

Insightful words. The shah spoke softly, as was his habit, but with evident sincerity. No one present contradicted him; in fact, the Iranians listened with unfeigned admiration to his every word. He clearly regarded himself as an expert on the Russian mentality, and with some reason. The Soviets and the British had put him on the throne and occupied Iran for most of World War II after deposing his pro-German father, Reza Shah Pahlavi, in 1941. This emotionally disorienting experience, combined with the long and checkered history of Russo-Iranian relations, had instilled in him a deep distrust of the Soviet Union.

Soon we were back in the field. The Iraqis and Iranians were not the only combatants in the informal war along the western frontier; the Kurds, under General Mustafa al-Barzani, were engaged in a guerrilla war against Iraq for an independent Kurdistan. We let it be known that a delegation from our team would like to meet General Barzani. The word went out into the mountains, and a day or two later some of us drove into the Kurdish leader's mountain stronghold in a caravan of Jeeps. As our vehicles labored up a primitive mountain track, we were accosted by a band of Barzani's horsemen who suddenly rose up out of the rocks beside the road. Seen through the cloud of dust stirred up by our Jeeps, these guerrillas with their big, loosely wound turbans, baggy clothes, crossed bandoliers, and obsolete rifles were reminiscent of an illustration in a Victorian book for boys. In fact, they were battle-hardened fighting men who lived in an all-too-real world of ancient hatreds and almost incessant warfare. The Kurds are a comely and impressive people, and I felt an immediate kinship with them. This feeling intensified when we entered their encampment and were greeted by a smiling crowd of elders, wives, and children. Many of the youngsters were fair-haired and blue-eyed.

General Barzani awaited us inside the rude two-story stone dwelling that served as his field headquarters. Inside his headquarters, in which the savory aroma of cooking and the greasy metallic smell of weapons mingled incongruously, we were served sweetened tea in glasses hot to the touch. We offered cigarettes in return. Barzani was a romantic figure, a man of medium stature but extraordinary presence who exuded confidence, physical fitness, toughness, and cunning. His conversation, though lengthy and subtle, contained nothing that surprised. He described his campaigns against the Iraqis with military precision, explained his cause with passion, and asked for American recognition, arms, and money with the confident insistence of an idealist. It was not in our power to promise or deliver any of these things, though arms and money, at least, seem to have been provided later on by other agencies of the United States government during the fierce and ultimately indecisive war fought throughout the 1960s by Barzani (who was killed in 1979) and his men.

In its five or six weeks in Iran, our team covered most of the strategic points of the country from the northern mountain passes to the Shatt-al-Arab waterway on the Persian Gulf and the deserts in the far south. Traveling in open Jeeps over some of the wildest landscapes on earth and encountering an astonishing variety of singular peoples, it seemed to me little short of a miracle that the shah's father had been able to subdue them into anything resembling a nation. Iran had been unified under its present name for less than thirty years. The shah probably understood better than anyone the extraordinary difficulties of holding the conglomerate together. Later on, he may have become something like the embodiment of the state, but in 1961 he was only the second ruler in a dynasty whose founder, his father, had been a lowly sergeant in the army before seizing power and declaring his own royalty. Many influential forces, including large factions of the religious community and the traditional ruling classes, questioned not only the shah's right to rule but also his capability to do so. According to one widely repeated rumor, his own mother had been suspected of plotting during the Mossadeq crisis to replace him with his younger and supposedly tougher brother, Ali, who was killed in an airplane crash in 1954.[8]

Physically, the shah was not an imposing figure who immediately engaged the imagination, as did Barzani of the Kurds. But from my vantage point during royal audiences as a junior (and appropriately silent) member of our team, the shah seemed impressive enough. In those days, as I have said, he was young—scarcely five years older than I. He was dignified, even at times imperious, invariably dressed in a resplendent uniform complete with shoulder boards, choke collar, gold braid, and rows of orders and decorations. He treated all in his presence with courtesy and respect, and, when speaking to another person, had the Middle Eastern habit of locking eyes. His own eyes were large, brown, liquid, and suspicious. Seldom smiling, always attentive to detail, he was reserved almost to the point of melancholy. Like most others who met him, I was struck by the shah's high intelligence, the accuracy and even the eloquence of his speech in English, and the unapologetic realism of his strategic and political thinking. In later years, when I saw him often in private and grew to know him better, these impressions were reinforced.

If, as some of his enemies claimed, he was a despot, then he was an enlightened despot. I thought in 1961, and I still think, that he was as close to being a natural and sincere democrat as anyone I ever met in his part of the world. Certainly he had the courage of his convictions. Even thirty years ago, when such ideas exposed him to real political and there-fore personal risk, he did not trouble to dissemble the instinct for Westernization that was later to become the hallmark of his reign. He saw land reform and the desecularization of the country as the means of breaking the hold of the past on the Iranian people. All of these ideas were shortly afterward transformed into concrete programs under the development program that he called "the White Revolution."

In the end, he was criticized for driving reform too hard and too fast, and the same forces that had wished to remove him a quarter of a century before because he was not doing enough to modernize his country applauded his downfall because they perceived that he had done too much. In the beginning, he asked the United States to understand that he was not yet strong enough to ignore or overcome those who opposed his ideas for modernization. The Kennedy administration was reluctant to make him stronger unless he took more chances in the name of an ideal of individual liberty that had scarcely been heard of in his country and to which the strongest elements in its national life across the whole political spectrum were opposed. The pressure from America to do immediately what he already intended to do with all deliberate speed baffled him, and what was described by the State Department report to President Kennedy as "emotional insecurity"[9] may actually have been bewilderment with foreigners who wished to redesign his society without fully understanding how the existing mechanism worked.

In drafting our team's final report, the fundamental question of how to defend Iran from a Soviet invasion became a point of contention. From a purely military point of view, it made excellent sense to fall back from the northern frontier and hold a much shorter line in the mountains south of Tehran. If this had been our only objective, there would have been no need to question those who wished to base our plans on purely military considerations. My role, however, was to argue strategic factors. We had seen the north of Iran, with its fertile agricultural lands and its teeming centers of population and production, and it was my strong belief that the shah could not concede half of his territory and most of his people and wealth to an invader and expect to hold on to the rest. It was doubtful, given the transport capabilities of the time, that American fighting divisions could reach Iran in time to reverse a Soviet invasion, no matter which line of defense was selected.

Discussions were lengthy and heated, but, in the end, the strategic view prevailed, and, as in the Fox mission to Formosa a decade before, our team drafted a report that formed the basis of the strategic defense of Iran and United States defense policy and military aid for many years afterward. It called for the addition of 10,500 troops above the 150,000 already authorized. In the words of the report, the extra men would "provide, on an austere basis, a visible defense of the northern border area." The report also called for the construction of new bases and airfields, the construction of early-warning radar stations along the Soviet frontier, enhanced training for the Iranian armed forces—and, emphatically, the restoration of those two frigates to the assistance budget for the Iranian navy. All this (except the frigates) was budgeted to cost the United States Treasury $298.6 million over a five-year period.[10]

General Twitchell justified his reputation for perfectionism many times over, demanding draft after draft from Dick Kenedy, who had the misfortune of being the best writer on the team. Even though my suffering was nothing compared to Kenedy's, I felt the exasperation of a victim under this nitpicking when it had the effect, as it often did, of suppressing truths that our superiors might not want to hear. Dick Kenedy and I wanted to tell the White House and the Pentagon the unvarnished truth as we had observed and understood it; Twitchell, shaking a much older and wiser head, understood that an important part of our mission was to tell our masters what they wanted to hear, insofar as this did no damage to the fundamental facts of the situation. The President's skeptical views on the shah and the situation in Iran were well known, and Secretary of Defense Robert S. McNamara had been a leading proponent of reducing military assistance to Iran; telling these men and their loyalists that they were mistaken would not necessarily have caused them to change their minds or revise their policies. It would merely have discredited our report. Twitchell had been given the assignment of discovering the objective facts about the military situation in Iran and drawing the proper conclusions from them for the benefit of the policymakers. That is what he did; and if some important truths were omitted in the name of bureaucratic discretion, the report as approved was perfectly accurate in all the remaining particulars.

In a sense, this process was especially instructive precisely because it fell short of the ideal of reporting the whole truth that had been instilled in me at West Point. With regard to Iran, I was impelled to think about the realities of its situation in a way that engraved these on my memory. The more I understood, the more I believed that Iran would be America's friend only so long as America was the shah's friend. In that, I may have been correct, but, as we shall see later in this narrative, I was sadly mistaken in my youthful belief that no United States administration would so far disregard those realities as to forsake that friendship.

The more important lesson of the experience, that the suppression of candor in the name of political tact when dealing with Presidents contains the seeds of disaster, would be demonstrated in the months ahead in a chain of strategic consequences to American policy in another part of the world. These events, rising from a method of operation that omitted candor almost entirely, culminated in one of the most shocking tragedies in the history of the United States.

7

Missiles and Mythology

Soon after my return to Washington and the completion of the Twitchell Report on Iran, I received orders from my superiors in the Plans and Policy division to take over the Berlin-NATO desk. In light of my recent rocking of the boat, I was somewhat surprised to be chosen. Berlin-NATO was the "hottest" desk in the division. The accepted measure of a desk's importance was the number of papers it sent into the "the tank," the secure conference room located in the subbasement of the Pentagon's "E" ring where the Joint Chiefs of Staff make their decisions. A typical desk might send one or two papers into the tank each month. The Berlin-NATO desk delivered two or three every day. I looked forward to going to the office. The intellectual stimulation of the job and the sense of doing work that was useful to my country made the hours fly by. Gradually, I began to understand how the United States government really works. This learning process was full of surprises, and sometimes these were amusing, as in the case of a peremptory memorandum I was called upon to handle somewhat later in my Pentagon tour. The memo, paper-clipped to a copy of one of William Faulkner's novels, was marked for immediate action—under the Kennedys, there was no other kind of action. The writer had learned that Faulkner's novels were on the required reading list at the U.S. Military Academy, and, inasmuch as Faulkner's work was "unquestionably racist," these volumes were to be removed from the West

Point curriculum and library forthwith. The memo was initialed by the Attorney General of the United States, Robert F. Kennedy.

Not knowing quite how to seize this nettle, I asked my immediate civilian superior, Joseph A. Califano, Jr., for guidance. Califano is as near to being unflappable as anyone I have ever known, but it was clear that he was as nonplussed by Kennedy's order as I was. Neither one of us had read the book in question. "Take it home with you and read it tonight," Califano said. "Then draft a reply to Bobby in the morning." I did as I was ordered and in the process discovered what Faulkner's readers already knew, that this great novelist was the opposite of a racist. My reply stated this fact and added the opinion that denying the cadets Faulkner's books, or those of any other author, for that matter, would be a mistake in principle and practice and would almost certainly lead to an uproar in the press, in which the administration would be subjected to reproach, if not ridicule. I do not remember receiving an acknowledgment, but the subject was dropped and Faulkner remained on the West Point reading list.

I certainly was not penalized for my frankness, and I mention this episode because it illustrates, in a harmless incident, two important characteristics of the Kennedy administration, a sense of idealism and a penchant for impulsive action. A third characteristic, a preference for covert action and secretive maneuver over the candid expression of policy and the open exercise of principle backed by the nation's real power, was the major theme of the administration's foreign policy, and its unfortunate effects were already apparent by the autumn of President Kennedy's first year in office.

By then, the two great foreign policy events of that period, the debacle at the Bay of Pigs in April 1961 and the erection of the Berlin Wall in August of the same year, had already taken place. In the sense that nearly every crisis of the Cold War was related in some way to Berlin, because that was the one place where the United States was weaker than the Soviet Union, the two events were related. In the final hours before the invasion of Cuba, President Kennedy had approved changing the landing site from Trinidad, which offered good military advantages, to the Bay of Pigs, locked in by swamps and thus offering neither the possibility of advance in case of victory nor the chance for escape into the mountains in case of unbreakable resistance. At the last minute, he had canceled a rebel air strike against Castro's air force, apparently on grounds that it would expose the U.S. role in the invasion. Gen. Lyman Lemnitzer, then chairman of the Joint Chiefs of Staff, later called the reversal of the air strike "absolutely reprehensible, almost criminal."[1]

The invading force of some fourteen hundred Cuban exiles, recruited in secrecy by U.S. agents, were inadequately trained and equipped with obsolete weapons. They had been abandoned on the beach when President Kennedy decided not to protect, reinforce, or rescue them, although the carrier *Essex* was lying just over the horizon and U.S. destroyers steamed within sight of the abandoned men as they fought for their lives against hopeless odds. The brigade lost 114 killed in action; a small number escaped in small boats or swam out to sea and were rescued by frogmen; others drowned. After the U.S. destroyers steamed away, 1,189 were captured, interrogated, humiliated, and imprisoned as criminals.[2] Those who lived and had families in Cuba bore the additional burden of knowing that they were responsible for the persecution of their parents, siblings, and more remote relations. (Several thousand relatives were later allowed to leave Cuba with the prisoners.)

It is difficult to avoid the inference that Khrushchev believed that the young President who had wavered so catastrophically at the Bay of Pigs, where he had enjoyed every military and strategic advantage, would waver again in Berlin, where he had practically no advantages. As the Soviet leader later put it in his inimitable way, "Berlin is the testicles of the West. Every time I give them a yank they holler."[3] At their summit meeting in Vienna, less than sixty days after the Bay of Pigs, Khrushchev had told Kennedy that the Soviet Union would sign a peace treaty with East Germany by the end of 1961. After that, all of Berlin would become part of East Germany, Western access to the city would cease, and if the Western garrisons did not leave voluntarily they would be forced to do so. "I want peace," he told Kennedy, "but if you want war, that is your problem."[4]

Khrushchev faced genuine problems of his own in Berlin. East Germans were pouring across the checkpoints into the West at the rate of ten thousand a week;[5] four thousand crossed in a single day, August 12.[6] This exodus imposed such a severe manpower drain on the Communist regime that its chief, Walter Ulbricht, asked the Kremlin to provide a labor force from within the U.S.S.R. Khrushchev refused, with characteristic imagery. "Imagine how a Soviet worker would feel," he said to Ulbricht. "We won the war and now he has to clean your toilets."[7] According to Khrushchev, the idea of the Wall was conceived by the Soviet military commander in Berlin, Marshal Ivan I. Yakubovsky,[8] after President Ken-

nedy made a speech on July 25 itemizing America's vital interests in
Berlin. It was a defiant speech, in which the President called for a $3.2
billion increase in the defense budget and gave notice of his intention to
triple draft calls and to order some National Guard and reserve units to
active service—and, in an especially somber note, called on American
families to build fallout shelters in their backyards. He said that the United
States was prepared to defend its rights in Berlin "at all costs."

However, the right of unhindered passage between East and West
Berlin—the prime concern of the Soviets and East Germans—was not
included on Kennedy's list of American vital interests. This omission gave
the other side what it wanted, and on August 13 East German police
closed many of the border checkpoints, tearing up pavement on the
eastern side of the demarcation line and stringing barbed-wire barricades.
When no Western protest or countermeasures materialized over the next
few days, laborers started to build the Wall. No formal American protest
reached Moscow until four days after construction had begun; by then, the
Wall was an accomplished fact.[9] President Kennedy sent Vice President
Lyndon B. Johnson to Berlin to deliver his reply to a critical letter from
Mayor Willy Brandt of West Berlin. Kennedy wrote that the division of
Berlin could be reversed only by war with the Soviet Union, and no one
thought that was the correct course of action.[10] A token American force,
the fifteen-hundred-man First Battle Group, tested Khrushchev's threat
to seal off Western access to Berlin by traveling by convoy across 110
miles of East German territory. The Russians, who had what they wanted,
did not interfere. Soviet pressure on Berlin intensified over the next
couple of months, culminating in a confrontation between some of their
tanks and some of ours at a border checkpoint, but, once again, the game
being over, the Soviets backed off.

Even as a young officer, I was appalled that my government did not
act more decisively. A crisis must be resolved at the earliest possible stage
in the most decisive possible manner. If not nipped in the bud, a crisis
not only blooms in its own right but pollinates new crises. Months after
the Wall went up, an atmosphere of crisis still prevailed in Washington.
The Wall had not altered the twin realities of Berlin: The United States
could neither defend it nor abandon it. The city, or half city, as it had
now become, was essentially indefensible in military terms, lying as it
did more than one hundred miles inside Communist territory with its
tiny Western garrisons surrounded by scores of Soviet and East German
divisions. Hovering over Berlin was the perpetual question, What next?
and my work on the desk was almost entirely devoted to attempts to guess

the answer and in planning military exercises for the defense of an outpost that was even more isolated and exposed than before. These plans, based on the newly fashionable idea of escalation, in which theoretical American responses to equally theoretical Soviet threats were exquisitely matched to the provocation, were called "the poodle blanket" around the Plans and Policy Division because the initial U.S. reaction to a Soviet move was usually so small in scale, and so tentative, that it left important parts of the anatomy exposed. Instead of making a show of overwhelming force that might frighten or surprise the enemy, the doctrine called for subtle escalation in the form of Western probes designed to show the U.S.S.R. our determination to stand firm against further Soviet challenges while avoiding countermeasures that would risk conflict. In theory, this permitted the superpowers to control any confrontation by limiting it or ending it at any point on the scale of escalation. Actually, because it takes two to de-escalate, this process more closely resembled the intellectual conceit that it was than the viable military procedure that it was represented to be.

I referred to this extreme variation on the theory as "incrementalism." Even in the gaming stage, it soon became clear that, in practice, incremental increases in force tended to intensify the risk rather than control it; as in a schoolyard scuffle, the possibility of either party backing away decreased with every shove and expletive, with the world press acting out the role of the crowd of taunting children. These ideas from the ivory tower contradicted the centuries of military wisdom embodied in Gen. Nathan Bedford Forrest's famous formula for victory, "Get there first with the most men." It seemed to me that any doctrine based on the notion of maximizing the enemy's strength while placing voluntary restraints on one's own freedom of action risked provoking the very outcome it sought to avoid. If combined with a tendency to withhold the whole truth from the men at the top out of a misplaced conception of loyalty, incrementalism was likely to lead to dangerous and unpredictable results. This is exactly what happened not long afterward in Vietnam, where our policy of acting in a laboriously measured, and therefore easily predictable, way permitted the enemy to answer every American military action with a provocative riposte that contributed to escalation rather than deterring it.

The tendency to tell the White House what it wanted to hear about Vietnam was, from the beginning, an integral part of this sad process, and, by the latter stages of the Johnson administration, it had corrupted the reporting process almost totally. The pattern was clear early on. Even then, I was not alone in my foreboding, but little can be done in any administration to control an intellectual fashion to which the President himself subscribes, and President Kennedy believed wholeheartedly in the new concept of crisis management and in its dubious companions, incrementalism and covert action.

Despite my misgivings about incrementalism, I thought in 1961, and still think, that the doctrine of flexible response itself is correct. Moreover, I believe that covert action is sometimes a good and necessary thing, so long as it remains a supplement to policy and not a substitute for it. The chief danger of covert action is that it provides an irresolute President with the illusion that he can resort to unpopular actions without paying the political consequences—that he can act on policies without actually standing up for them. But the price to be paid for playing the American people false is always, in the end, many times greater than keeping faith with them. With regard to flexible response, it is clear that the United States must have the military means to back up its diplomacy in any situation, and to win an unequivocal victory if it becomes necessary to fight, no matter what the level of conflict. But even limited wars should be fought with the object of achieving complete local victory. Any lesser result wastes the lives of American troops and creates an impression of weakness that invites more war, including total war. The doctrine of massive retaliation practiced by the Eisenhower administration dealt with the question of limited war by refusing in most cases to consider it as an option.

Massive retaliation, it should be remembered, grew out of budgetary considerations; President Eisenhower, among many others in his time, sincerely believed that the Kremlin hoped to bankrupt the West by forcing it to fight an endless succession of small and indecisive conflicts. Eisenhower's Secretary of Defense, Charles E. Wilson, had this in mind when he said, "We can't afford to fight limited wars. We can only afford to fight a big war, and if there is one, that is the kind it will be."[11] This philosophy was simplified by Eisenhower's critics to suggest that any Soviet aggression, no matter how limited, created the risk of all-out nuclear attack on the Russian homeland by the United States. The Eisenhower policy worked well for nearly a decade because the United States possessed overwhelming nuclear superiority during most of that period and the Soviets genuinely feared that Eisenhower might use it to temper the inherent adventurism of their foreign policy.

By the end of the fifties, however, the Soviet Union had accumulated an effective nuclear arsenal of its own, while the conventional military power of the United States had declined. This combination of factors gave the Kremlin greater freedom of action to incite or engage in small, localized "wars of liberation" along the perimeter of the free world. The policy of flexible response was based on the principle that the United States should have the capability to fight limited wars while maintaining a powerful strategic force capable of deterring or answering a Soviet nuclear attack on the United States or NATO. This policy was first enunciated in official circles in a 1950 National Security Council paper (NSC-68) drafted by a team working under Paul Nitze, then head of the policy-planning staff at the State Department. In the waning months of the Truman administration, Ambassador George F. Kennan, in a long dispatch from Moscow, called into question the whole idea of containing the U.S.S.R. by means of NATO-style military alliances alone. "Large numbers of people, both in Western Europe and in the United States," Kennan wrote, "were incapable of understanding the Russian technique of penetration and 'partial war' or of thinking in terms of this technique. . . . [As in Korea] Moscow had considered the successful instigation of civil war in a third country as a perfectly fair and acceptable political expedient. . . ."[12]

Kennan's idea germinated among academics and others advising potential Democratic candidates for the presidency, as his ideas had a way of doing, and by 1958 Senator John F. Kennedy was saying that the real threat to Western security was not nuclear attack but "limited brushfire wars, indirect non-overt aggression, intimidation and subversion, internal revolution."[13] Two Army chiefs of staff, Matthew B. Ridgway and Maxwell D. Taylor, were proponents of flexible response, and, while there can be no reasonable doubt that these men believed in a greater role for ground forces as a matter of sound principle, it is also true that the Army felt somewhat left out of the strategic picture and the budgetary process in the Eisenhower era. The new doctrine meant new funding and new importance for the Army after a period when most big-ticket items, especially strategic missiles, went to the Air Force and the Navy. "If we are to assure that the disastrous big war never occurs," wrote Gen. Maxwell D. Taylor in his influential book on flexible response, *The Uncertain Trumpet*, "we must have the means to deter or win small wars."[14] Kennedy agreed: The United States must be prepared to confront all forms of Communist aggression with a level of force appropriate to the situation, but "responsible leaders of the West will not and should not deal with limited aggression by unlimited weapons."[15]

After the Bay of Pigs, the new President appointed General Taylor to be chairman of the Joint Chiefs of Staff. Lyman Lemnitzer, who was chairman when Kennedy assumed office, had departed before the normal expiration of his term, at least in part because he had regarded some of the President's decisions during the crisis as militarily unsound. The signal was clear: Get on the team or get off the field. As an intimate of President Kennedy, Taylor knew the true proportions of the fiasco of the Bay of Pigs and was more familiar than any other high-ranking military leader with the President's thinking on military matters. Early in the administration, Taylor had presided over a White House study of counterinsurgency, an aspect of flexible response that proposed using specially trained American troops in small-scale actions against Communist insurgents in such places as Indochina.

The result was a greatly expanded role for counterinsurgency by the U.S. Army. President Kennedy was intrigued by the idea of twentieth-century American soldiers fighting Communists in Asian jungles with the same stealthy tactics American backwoodsmen had employed against the British in the Revolutionary War—so much so that in the administration's first defense budget McNamara proposed a total increase in manpower of 13,000 for all three services, of whom 3,000 were earmarked for the Special Forces.[16] Kennedy advised the military to read the writings of Mao Zedong and Castro's revolutionary theorist, Ché Guevara, on guerrilla warfare.[17] The Bay of Pigs can, in fact, be described as the first attempt by the administration to apply the principles of counterinsurgency against an aggressive Communist regime.

With regard to Cuba, the Kennedy administration resembled a rash young terrier that attacks a porcupine, suffers the agonizing consequences, and takes its revenge by biting the pesky creature every time they meet thereafter. In geopolitical terms, the Cuban situation was strictly a hemispheric problem when John F. Kennedy entered the White House. The ways in which his administration attempted to solve the problem, and then failed to do so, transformed it into a global problem by involving Soviet prestige and providing Khrushchev, the supreme strategic gambler of his time, a means of getting into the game. The result was the Cuban Missile Crisis of October 1962. The underlying causes of this episode, even some of its circumstances, predated the Kennedy administration. In July 1960, six months before John F. Kennedy took the oath of office, Khrushchev had threatened to use rockets to protect Cuba from a military attack by the United States. Eisenhower and his advisers, confident of U.S. nuclear superiority, dismissed the warning as empty rhetoric. That same month, however, the CIA reported that a number of very large crated items had lately been brought into Cuba by ship from the U.S.S.R., and a military base had been placed off limits. Allen Dulles speculated to Eisenhower that the Soviets might be building a missile base in Cuba, but U.S. intelligence was unable to find hard evidence that this was so.[18]

The hard evidence was finally obtained on October 14, 1962, when American U-2 reconnaissance planes photographed missile sites under construction near San Cristobal in western Cuba.[19] Over the previous few months, the Soviets had introduced tens of thousands of soldiers and technicians into Cuba, together with 42 of the latest MIG-21 fighter-bombers, 42 unassembled Ilyushin-28 bombers, 350 tanks, 1,300 pieces of artillery, SAM (surface to air) missiles, and 700 modern antiaircraft guns.[20] President Kennedy, whose spokesmen had consistently described this Russian military buildup in Cuba as defensive in nature, had ordered the entire island to be photographed from the air after Senator Kenneth Keating, Republican of New York, charged on the Senate floor on August 31 that Soviet missiles were being installed in Cuba. By the time President Kennedy described the evidence collected by the U-2s to the American people in a television address on October 22, the Soviets had put in place or were assembling approximately forty medium-range ballistic missiles (IRBMs). If discovery had been delayed for another ten days, the Soviet missiles would have been operational.

Those missiles, when equipped with thermonuclear warheads, were sufficient to destroy most strategic military bases in the United States, and, if directed at civilian targets, of killing many millions of Americans. The United States had no effective warning radar along its southern coasts and borders, and, even if it had, warning time in regard to the IRBMs, which had an accuracy rate of about 70 percent, would have been less than five minutes.[21] This was a sobering prospect, but there was no need to yield to blackmail. President Kennedy had known for a long time that his campaign rhetoric concerning the existence of a missile gap had no basis in fact. Public opinion had been prepared for this misrepresentation of the true situation by Moscow's success in launching *Sputnik*, the first earth-orbiting satellite, in October 1957. This, combined with a series of embarrassing American failures to duplicate the Soviet feat, had produced an exaggerated notion of the excellence of Soviet missile technology. But U-2 photography had suggested even in 1960 that no missile gap existed.[22] A month after Kennedy's inauguration, Secretary of Defense Robert S. McNamara told the press that the so-called missile gap was "an illusion," and, in August of the same year, the CIA produced an intelligence estimate based on evidence collected by a new tool, space satellites capable of photographing objects on earth, demonstrating that the United States still possessed, and had always possessed, a considerable advantage in missiles and warheads over the Soviet Union.[23]

At the time of the Cuban Missile Crisis, the United States had roughly 250 land-based ICBMs, in addition to 144 nuclear missiles aboard Polaris submarines, and had stockpiled about 5,000 nuclear warheads. The Soviet total was then thought to be no more than seventy-five intercontinental missiles, all of them outdated liquid-fuel rockets that required many hours to recycle, and three hundred warheads.[24] (In 1989, Soviet authorities revealed that they had actually possessed only sixty operational missiles; two-thirds of these were in Cuba during the crisis.[25]) In October 1972, the U.S. Strategic Air Command could deploy some six hundred intercontinental bombers, the Soviet air forces only about two hundred.[26] The American potential to mobilize, equip, and transport conventional forces in concert with its allies was at least as great as that of the U.S.S.R. After the Berlin Wall crisis, the strength of the United States Army had been increased from 875,000 to a million men, with sixteen instead of eleven combat-ready divisions.[27] "Our unswerving objective," President Kennedy told the nation, ". . . must be to prevent the use of these missiles against this or any other country and to secure their withdrawal or elimination from the Western Hemisphere."[28]

Obviously, the United States was in an excellent position to achieve this objective. Our ability to compel a favorable outcome was enhanced by the fact that some of the Ilyushin-28 bombers, and most of the Soviet missiles (the warheads were still at sea[29]), were not yet operational and could not be made so without our U-2s discovering that this was happening. The question was, Would Khrushchev believe in the administration's resolve after it had given him so much reason to doubt it in the cases of the Bay of Pigs and the Berlin Wall? That was the administration's dilemma, and it produced one of the most exhaustively described episodes in the history of the United States. Dramatic account after dramatic account of the deliberations of Kennedy's inner circle, based on interviews with the participants, appeared in the newspapers soon after the crisis. Many of these sources subsequently wrote fuller accounts in their memoirs. All agreed on this essential point: Kennedy had faced down Khrushchev and forced him to withdraw Soviet missiles without making any important concessions in return except for a pledge not to invade Cuba— a pledge that was justified at the time as being essentially meaningless because the United States had no intention of invading the island in the first place. This version of events is, however, flawed by the omission of two essential facts:

First, no rational Soviet leader, and Nikita Khrushchev was eminently rational for all his studied boorishness and bluster, would have contemplated a nuclear exchange with the United States. As Khrushchev himself put it in later years, "To tell the truth, if the United States had started a war at that time we were not adequately prepared to attack the United States."[30]

Second, the crisis was resolved not as folklore would have it, by a steely display of presidential will and courage, but by a secret deal between Kennedy and Khrushchev in which the United States gave up at least as much as it gained.

I stubbed my toe on these facts immediately after the Cuban Missile Crisis while serving as action officer on a Pentagon team detailed to write an analytical study of the crisis from the military point of view. The study was destined for White House consumption, and once again we ran into the difficult problem of producing a paper that would accurately reflect the facts and also support the administration's version of events and the public perception of the outcome. Not only had there been very little chance of a nuclear confrontation between the superpowers over Cuba but in the wake of the crisis fifteen[31] U.S. intermediate-range Jupiter missiles were being removed, in secrecy, from Turkey. More Jupiters were being dismantled in Italy. The Jupiters had been targeted on the Soviet Union and on Soviet installations inside the Iron Curtain and had been regarded as an important element in the Western deterrent. There were no plans to replace them with comparable weapons. It certainly looked as though there had been a secret deal—Soviet missiles out of Cuba in return for the removal of American missiles from Turkey and Italy.

The Turkish government, which had exposed its country to nuclear retaliation by agreeing to the emplacement of the missiles, was bewildered by their abrupt removal. Loss of the Jupiters represented a significant reduction in Turkish national security—not only in terms of the missiles themselves but because their disassembly symbolized a loss of American will to defend a NATO ally. The removal of the Jupiters was already sending a shudder through the whole Western alliance, particularly since the United States had agreed to take out its Jupiters without consulting its allies. If we would not defend Turkey, would we defend West Germany or France? The Europeans had always feared that the United States would abandon its European allies if it came to a choice between the destruction of European cities or American cities. The removal of the Jupiters, which protected Europe, in return for the removal of Soviet missiles in Cuba, which threatened the United States, would certainly be seen as proof that Washington did, in fact, put the safety of its own people above that of its allies. General de Gaulle might even use the episode as a pretext to take France out of NATO, and, if he remained, to strengthen his argument against trusting the Americans to make defense policy—especially in matters nuclear—for the sovereign nations of Western Europe.

When I made these unwelcome but obvious points, I was told that the Jupiters were being withdrawn (the words stuck in my mind) "in an unconnected action justified in its own right." This left our team with the problem of explaining the favorable outcome of the crisis without mentioning the odd coincidence of the hasty removal of our missiles from two strategically vital NATO countries. The problem proved intractable, and the paper we sent into the tank for approval by the Joint Chiefs of Staff mentioned the possibility that what was being described as a coincidence could easily be interpreted as a secret arrangement—and undoubtedly would be if the true facts came to light. When General Taylor read our paper, he flushed angrily, slammed it down on the table, and said that he would never approve it for transmittal to the President. Our paper disappeared.

The fact of the matter is, the United States *did* remove its Jupiter missiles from Turkey and Italy as an inducement to the Kremlin to take the Soviet missiles out of Cuba in full view of American television cameras, and this secret deal was the key to the settlement of the crisis. On October 27, in a letter to President Kennedy broadcast over Radio Moscow, Khrushchev said, "I make this proposal: we agree to remove those weapons from Cuba which you regard as offensive weapons [if] the United States . . . will evacuate its analogous weapons from Turkey."[32] Accounts of the crisis written at the time and afterward by President Kennedy's advisers portray the President as rejecting this proposal out of hand. He is pictured as angrily suggesting that the problem would not have existed in the first place if his orders had been followed: "He distinctly remembered having given instructions, long before the Cuban missiles crisis, that the Jupiters must be removed from Turkey. Now he was confronted with . . . [the] risk [of] thermonuclear war over some near-obsolete missiles the United States had long since written off as militarily worthless."[33] But according to the transcripts of the discussion, Kennedy's immediate reaction to

Khrushchev's letter was to say, "We're going to have to take our weapons out of Turkey."[34]

It was the Kennedy administration that had installed the Jupiters in Turkey, and these missiles had been operational only since July, or about three months.[35] "I did not accept the explanation that the [Jupiter missiles] had become obsolete," said Gen. Curtis E. LeMay after the crisis was over, "nor did any other military man I know."[36]

In fact, President Kennedy secretly accepted Khrushchev's offer on the day it was made. So that there could be no doubt that the President's own word was being pledged, Robert Kennedy summoned Ambassador Anatoly F. Dobrynin to his office at the Department of Justice and told him that the American missiles in Turkey and Italy would come out.[37] Robert Kennedy clung to the pretext that no exchange under pressure was involved, but he insisted on absolute secrecy nevertheless: "If you [the Soviets] should publish any document indicating a deal then it is off."[38]

The Russians guarded the secret well. "I didn't tell Castro that Kennedy promised to remove the missiles from Turkey and Italy, since that agreement was just between the two of us," Khrushchev said in later years. "Kennedy asked me to keep it secret. He believed that if it became known to the American public it might bring unpleasant consequences."[39] The cover story was maintained for more than a quarter of a century.

In political terms, the Cuban Missile Crisis and the legend of eyeball-to-eyeball confrontation invented by Kennedy's men paid a handsome dividend. In the midterm elections of November 1962, which took place only ten days after the end of the crisis, the Democrats gained four seats in the Senate and sustained a net loss of only two in the House. According to Kennedy's biographer, this was the best midterm showing by a party occupying the White House since 1934, when Franklin D. Roosevelt was in his first term.[40]

8

Covert Actions

One of the consequences of the resolution of the Cuban Missile Crisis was the release of more than eleven hundred surviving members of the brigade of Cuban exiles who had gone ashore at the Bay of Pigs. Just before Christmas 1962, they were ransomed by the United States from Castro's prisons, where they had been languishing for some twenty months. The price paid to Castro was about $53 million in goods and cash. As I was soon to learn, that was only the down payment on the moral debt incurred by the administration at the Bay of Pigs.

In February 1963, I was appointed military assistant to Secretary of the Army Cyrus R. Vance. The job included the duty of acting in loco parentis to the rescued Cubans. Vance's hard-driving and gifted right-hand man, Joe Califano, let me know early in our first meeting on the subject that the President himself and, even more to the point, his brother Robert were taking a close personal interest in the rescued Cubans. Apparently, one Kennedy or the other called Califano nearly every day to inquire about their welfare. It was their wish that every veteran be given a new start in life in the United States. My job was to make sure they got it. Few limits were placed on my ingenuity. I realized why when I was introduced, soon afterward, to the brigade's liaison with the Pentagon, Erneido Oliva. He was a very impressive man, physically powerful, quick-witted, and utterly frank and truthful. A former commander of the brigade's armored forces, he had taken over the front on the morning after the landing and commanded the invaders' last stand. Rallying the disorganized and disheartened remnants of the brigade, he had led a counterattack against a superior force until his men ran out of ammunition. He had then attempted to lead a smaller group across the eighty miles of swamps that lay between the beach and the mountains to fight on as guerrillas. There were no roads in the swamp. Unable to find the snakes, insects, and nourishing plants and roots their American trainers had told them would sustain them in the wilderness, and reduced to drinking their own urine, Oliva and his band were captured after a few days and imprisoned, eventually, on the Isle of Pines. A pre-Castro graduate of the Cuban corps of cadets and a former officer of the regular army under both Batista and Castro, Oliva was a soldier to the bone and one of the most fiercely honorable men I have ever known. I have said that he was candid; when it came to the needs of his men, this was an understatement. He did not conceal his belief that the United States of America owed the Cubans who had fought at the Bay of Pigs a debt that could never be repaid, and he understood that the conscience of the President was the exiles' greatest asset.

It was no simple task to integrate some of the veterans into American life. All were embittered by their experience, and some had suffered wounds to body and mind that would handicap them for the remainder of their lives. The brigade had constituted a cross section of the Cuban nation, including in its ranks nearly every social type—idealistic blue bloods, sons of the black proletariat like Oliva, members of the learned professions, university students, and also a certain number of patriotic felons.

Those with genuine qualifications for employment posed no problem. Some of the brigade's officers were commissioned in the United States armed services, with no stretching of the rules required; Oliva, for example, eventually became a brigadier general in the U.S. Army Reserve. A few years later, I encountered some of these officers in Vietnam, where they were well regarded by their superiors and by the troops they commanded. Other brigade officers, however, had won their rank because of the social position of their families or for other militarily irrelevant reasons, and Pentagon personnel officers objected strenuously (and properly) to the idea of offering them commissions for which they were clearly not qualified. It was my job to explain that the Commander in Chief had waived the rules. Many were commissioned despite their lack of professional credentials. Some of the lower ranks were integrated into our armed services as enlisted men. Those who wished to continue their education were usually admitted to colleges and universities; many were awarded scholarships that relieved them of financial anxiety. Some were helped to start a business or find employment. Even the problem cases, and some were problem cases indeed, found places in U.S. society.

Whatever satisfaction I felt in carrying out my mission was colored by a certain rueful awareness that the ethics of the situation were thoroughly mixed. I agreed with Oliva that whatever we did for these men was small payment for the moral debt we owed them, and in that sense what we did was a credit to all concerned. But a sense of moral obligation was not the only factor involved. The operation also achieved the valuable political purpose of keeping the veterans of the brigade quiet about the deep sense of outrage and betrayal that most of them felt in the aftermath of the debacle. As with so much else that happened in this period, the essential truth was obscured by stage management designed to divert public attention from the embarrassing facts of the situation. The President displayed considerable élan in dealing with the Cubans, as when he received the colors of the brigade into his care in a post-Christmas ceremony in the Orange Bowl at Miami and cried out, "I can assure you that this flag will be returned to this brigade in a free Havana!"[1]

This was an extraordinary statement, coming from the man who had left the brigade to its fate when he alone had had the power to save it. No doubt he meant what he said at the moment. In the immediate aftermath of the missile crisis, he was already considering a new secret war against Cuba, designed to remove Castro from power. An earlier secret CIA operation, called Operation Mongoose, authorized by President Kennedy in the wake of the Bay of Pigs and costing as much as $50 million a year, had failed to do the job even though his brother Robert had been in command. Inasmuch as Operation Mongoose had employed some two thousand Cuban agents, most of whom lived in the Miami area, many in the Orange Bowl that night must have been aware of its existence.[2] The American people knew nothing about it. Neither did I until a long time afterward, although, as we shall see, I later played a role in a second campaign of secret military action against Cuba.

John F. Kennedy stoutly took full public responsibility for the failure at the Bay of Pigs but at the same time made it plain that he had inherited the invasion plan from Eisenhower and had been misled by the CIA and others who advised him that the landing would ignite a successful popular uprising against Castro.[3] With repetition over time, this became the accepted rationale for the disaster. Whatever weight President Kennedy may or may not have given to the advice he received before making his decision to invade with a proxy force that could not possibly have succeeded militarily on its own resources, the Bay of Pigs was a very good example of the sort of enterprise that sets the law of unintended consequences in motion with a vengeance.

The chief consequence was its effect on what might be called the geopolitical psychology of the Kennedy administration. At the crucial moment, the President had chosen "plausible deniability" over the forthright exercise of American power to save the situation, thus turning a covert-action project into a devastating public failure. Thereafter, for reasons that defy logical explanation, the administration appeared to believe that covert action was the only sort of action open to it in regard to Cuba. From this misconception flowed many momentous consequences, including, if Khrushchev is to be believed, the Cuban Missile Crisis. According to him, U.S.–backed covert-action operations had so unnerved Castro that he feared the destruction of his regime. "We knew," Khrushchev later explained, "that the American monopolists would not rest until they crushed the revolutionary forces and ruled again in Cuba. The only way out was to put in missiles with nuclear warheads . . . for deterring those who would attack Cuba."[4]

On June 19, 1963, President Kennedy approved a new covert-action program designed "to nourish a spirit of resistance and disaffection which could lead to significant defections and other byproducts of unrest [in Cuba]."[5] An interdepartmental planning group was set up under the overall command and control of Robert Kennedy, who, in the post–Bay of Pigs period, had also been in charge of Operation Mongoose. In this new phase, the President designated the Secretary of the Army, Cyrus Vance, as the executive agent for the entire federal government in dealing with Cuba and the threat that Castro's regime posed to the Western Hemisphere. This included responsibility for coordinating a secret war against Cuba that encompassed sabotage, commando raids, and propaganda and other clandestine operations.

The choice of the Secretary of the Army to coordinate an operation that had little or no relevance to his office in traditional practice was a typical example of management in the Kennedy administration. Both the President and his brother disliked and distrusted the bureaucracy, and by reaching down into the government and setting up ad hoc operations they were able to make certain that projects that were important to them were administered by one or more of the Kennedy loyalists who had been stationed at nearly every junction box in the government. This assured close political control of operations and, as I had discovered in connection with the report on Iran, it also created a system that tended to tell the leadership what it wanted to hear.

In this case, the junction box was the office in which I worked under Vance and Califano, who were honest reporters as well as enthusiastic loyalists, and it was clear that neither was entirely comfortable with the task at hand. Vance, an eastern Establishment liberal of the old school, had an innate horror of violence and a disdain for clandestine behavior, and he displayed little enthusiasm for the secret components of the activity. The taking of human life under any circumstances was abhorrent to him, and to do so as part of a secret operation was even more repulsive. There was never any suggestion or intention of assassination in our planning of these operations; I am quite sure that Vance and Califano would have resigned rather than be part of any such scheme, whether it concerned a private soldier in Castro's army or Castro himself; I would have done the same. But everyone knew that the risk of killing an innocent bystander was a factor that could not be ignored when you blew up a bridge or a factory or a power station. Though Vance carried on dutifully in planning sessions for these potentially lethal activities with McNamara, Califano, and representatives of the CIA, his feelings showed so plainly that somebody remarked, "Vance has got no business being in this business." For that matter, neither did the rest of us; certainly this was no work for a soldier.

Nevertheless, under the impatient prodding of Robert Kennedy and the frequent invocation of the President's name, the clandestine work went forward. The CIA men brought us proposals for acts of sabotage and commando raids inside Cuba and for secret landings on the coast. Fast boats, small weapons, and the necessary explosives were provided; operatives were trained in the necessary skills by U.S. military personnel. The targets were always economic. The approval process was excruciating. After an operation had been subjected by our group to an agonizing examination of all its ramifications, and above all for its deniability if anything went wrong, it went up to Robert Kennedy's group for final approval. Only after that did the CIA's operatives go into action inside Cuba. Typically, there were three or four major operations a month, and this pace was maintained to the end. Thirteen raids into Cuba, including the sabotage of an electric generating plant, an oil refinery, and a sugar mill, were approved for the three-month period beginning in November 1963, the last month of the Kennedy presidency.[6]

With the authorization of Vance and the advice of Erneido Oliva, among others, I processed the decisions, handing them on to representatives of the CIA for execution by their operatives in the field. By no means did I know everything; I was too junior to be included among those who attended the planning sessions in Robert Kennedy's office. I had the impression that the success rate of the operations was reasonably high despite the inherent inefficiency of clandestine work and the growing size and efficiency of Castro's police and military forces.

Some of the CIA's irregulars were Cubans and some were soldiers of fortune of other nationalities. American military personnel were not authorized to engage in operations inside Cuba, but some were engaged in training operations, and the military was an important source of supply for the commandos. Even so limited a role involved contamination of traditional military standards of behavior, even though the orders came, in effect, from the Commander in Chief. Above all, its secrecy was corrupting. Although small in scale and negligible in its final results, this clandestine operation against Cuba was, in fact, indistinguishable from a war except that all knowledge that it was being fought was kept from those who were paying for it and who were liable for its consequences, the American people.

Although it looms large in the foregoing passage, the fact is that the secret war was not an important factor in my own official life. On a day-to-day basis, it took up little of my time and attention—no more than an hour or two a day. When I was not working on it, I forgot it, and I never believed that it could be an important factor in creating a long-term solution to the Cuban problem. That could come about only in Cuba, and in the region, through the wishes and efforts of the people involved. Most of any given day was devoted to the open program aimed at countering Castroite activities and influence in Latin America. This aspect of the effort was enormous in scale, and there was little question among democratic elements in Latin America that such activity was justified. The no-invasion pledge made by the United States in settlement of the Cuban Missile Crisis, a deplorable error that has resulted in political havoc and human suffering throughout Central America, had given Castro, the greatest political-action asset the Soviets have ever had in the Americas, an inviolable sanctuary and base of supply from which to subvert, infiltrate, and terrorize his neighbors. Soon after seizing power, Castro had mounted abortive guerrilla landings in the Dominican Republic, Nicaragua, and Haiti. Now he was setting up revolutionary cadres in several other countries in Central and South America, including Guatemala and Bolivia. Nicaragua and El Salvador were on the brink of bloody civil wars in which leftist rebels were incited and supplied by Cuba with matériel furnished by the Soviet Union and other Communist states.

The United States assistance program sought to counter Cuban-inspired subversion with information, education, economic aid, and with extensive programs to retrain and reequip the police in countries likely to be threatened with subversion. Boats carrying arms from Cuba were intercepted along the coastlines. Although counterinsurgency and other forms of military aid (especially counterinsurgency training) were offered, the administration was reluctant for appearances' sake to work with the military in Central America and the Caribbean. This troubled me. I did not see how strengthening the capability of the police to carry out secret surveillance of citizens and political opponents could in the end strengthen democratic tendencies in these countries. By now, I was a lieutenant colonel. This is not a lofty rank by Pentagon standards. I had little success in my attempts to argue that the Latin "romantic tradition" of regarding the army as the protector of the people's rights and safety offered a promising opportunity to foster democratic values by working sympathetically with younger officers. They were no less idealistic than their contemporaries in the radical political movements of the day—and, if Latin American history was any guide, were somewhat more likely to be running their governments in the future.

In the end, however, it was the covert aspects of the confrontation with Castro that changed history. Although I had no inkling of this at the time, U.S. action against Cuba had included plans to assassinate Fidel Castro and other members of the Cuban leadership. Under the personal leadership of Robert Kennedy, at least eight efforts were made to eliminate Castro himself, the earliest involving Mafia figures recruited by the CIA soon after the inauguration. These attempts continued until the day President Kennedy was himself assassinated in Dallas.[7] The secret of this deadly enterprise was so closely held that not even John A. McCone, Director of Central Intelligence from 1962 to 1965, knew that some of his men were involved until he read about it in a newspaper story. On hearing the truth, McCone, a devout Catholic, is reported to have demanded, "But what about our immortal souls?" Few others paused to ask this question in the atmosphere of ardent activism then prevailing.

It is now clear from the public record that the attempts to assassinate Castro were carried out at the official instigation of the United States, using taxpayers' money and a variety of weapons and other deadly devices, such as poison, provided by officials of the United States government.[8]

No government in Washington had ever before attempted to murder a foreign leader.[9] After the plot against Castro was brought to light in the mid-1970s, such practices were formally prohibited by presidential order. They were, of course, already forbidden by the common law and by the fundamental rules and ideals according to which the nation had always before operated, but no one seems to have raised those points in an effective way, if at all, at the time.

Castro himself was certainly aware that he was a target of assassins activated by the United States government. According to the 1975 report of the Senate's Church committee, *Alleged Assassination Plots Involving Foreign Leaders*, one of the would-be assassins was a member of the Cuban intelligence service who may have been a double agent reporting directly to Castro. During the months before the assassination in Dallas, a number of warnings of the "you'd better watch your step" variety were received in Washington by various means from Havana. Some of these passed routinely over my desk. At the time, in my ignorance of the existence of assassination plots, I assumed that these referred to the commando operations—as indeed some of them may have done. Finally, in September 1963, only a couple of months before President Kennedy was shot, Castro took reporter Daniel Harken of the Associated Press aside at a reception in Havana and told him, "We are prepared to . . . answer in kind. United States leaders should think that if they are aiding terrorist plans to eliminate Cuban leaders, they themselves will not be safe."[10]

The assassination of John F. Kennedy on November 22, 1963, must have been the most shocking event in American history, not excepting the murder of Abraham Lincoln. In 1865, the Civil War had just ended; it caused profound sorrow, but no great surprise, that one of Lincoln's defeated foes should strike him down, and in a sense he was the last soldier to fall in a conflict in which hundreds of thousands had earlier been killed. A century later, in John F. Kennedy's case, the United States was ostensibly at peace with itself and with all nations, and it seemed that none but a madman could hate the popular young President enough to kill him. Grief was near universal, involving not only Kennedy's multitude of admirers but also his doubters and adversaries. Americans mourned not only for the fallen President but also, paradoxically, for the destruction of a certain idea of their nation. Most had believed that the American democracy had progressed beyond the point where it could be tainted by so primitive an act as assassination. It is the supreme irony in regard to what followed that our own government had revived this atavistic practice.

I was assigned the duty of helping with the preparations for the President's funeral. November 22, 1963, the day Kennedy died, was a Friday, and I spent Saturday in the cavernous building, handling details concerning the burial site. These included a telephone call demonstrating that grief was not universal. The call came from a deeply vexed military widow who was now the chief executive of an important national women's organization. She had been told that she, like the spouses of others buried at Arlington National Cemetery, would be sharing her husband's grave. She demanded to know the exact size of the presidential burial plot. I quoted the dimensions and she said, "Haig, how come Kennedy gets 3.2 acres and I have to double-deck with my husband?"

The most difficult technical problems concerned the perpetual flame that Jacqueline Kennedy wished to have situated on her husband's grave. There were few American experts on this subject. The Army Corps of Engineers consulted technicians in Paris responsible for the one that burns beneath the Arc de Triomphe in an attempt to answer such basic questions as to how to make certain that the flame would keep burning in all weather conditions. It was impossible to install permanent gas lines in the time available before the funeral, so a temporary supply was provided for. This and other time-consuming chores were a welcome diversion from the melancholy atmosphere of the day. I was glad that the building was deserted; not many people had the composure to come into the office on that weekend unless ordered to do so. I worked far into the night and came in again early on Sunday morning.

At first, I was alone except for some Army engineers with whom I was discussing technical matters dealing with the grave. A little later in the morning, I became aware of a subdued atmosphere of bustle and expectation. Soon President Johnson arrived with a small retinue, and he, McNamara, Vance, and a few others met in McNamara's office. Busy with my own concerns, I paid little attention to this. Later on, however, I learned that Johnson had expressed deep concern over the circumstances of President Kennedy's death and the effect it might have on the future of the Democratic party.

The fact of the matter is that Lyndon Johnson believed then, and believed until the day he died, that Fidel Castro was behind the assassination of John F. Kennedy, and that the murder of the President resulted from Robert Kennedy's "obsessive desire to eliminate the Cuban leader." As Johnson put it to Califano, among others, "Kennedy tried to get Castro, but Castro got Kennedy first."[11] If the Kennedy administration's plots against Castro's life became public knowledge, the logical conclusion of any investigation would be that President Kennedy's assassination had been carried out by persons who had an interest in preserving Fidel Castro's life.[12] The implication that the KGB was involved was inescapable; it exercised proprietary control over the Cuban intelligence service and must have regarded Castro as a unique Soviet asset to be protected by the most extreme measures. (Lee Harvey Oswald, the suspected assassin, had defected to the Soviet Union in 1959 and lived there until 1962,[13] having married the niece of an official of the KGB before returning to the United States.) Should the background to the crime be exposed, it could be devastating to Democratic prospects for retaining control of the White House in the 1964 presidential election. Johnson believed that any finding that an assassin activated by a Communist government had killed the President of the United States would set off a reaction among the American people, in their fervent patriotism and what he described as their "natural conservatism," that would sweep the Democrats from office and probably deny them power for many years to come. I did not fully understand this argument, but of course I am not a politician.

In any case, the key fact that a secret group headed by the President's brother had been plotting to kill Castro was kept from the Warren Commission and from the American people. That was the seed of the real cover-up, which was designed to protect the reputation of the dead President, and that of his grief-stricken brother, against the terrible suggestion that Castro had acted in self-defense. Although many in the government knew that a motive for the assassination existed, no witness volunteered theories or facts that would lead the Warren Commission in the direction of concluding that Castro's life may have been preserved at the cost of John F. Kennedy's. No questions of any kind likely to harm the memory of John F. Kennedy were asked, and, after a protracted investigation into the known facts and many hearings, the commission concluded on September 24, 1964, that Lee Harvey Oswald had acted alone. That finding was gratefully accepted by many but doubted by many others— including, ironically, Lyndon Johnson, who considered reopening the investigation a couple of years later but desisted, according to Califano, because he did not believe it was in the interests of the country and he did not want to inflict any additional pain on the Kennedy family.[14]

Over the years, innumerable conspiracy theories and charges of cover-up have challenged the conclusion of the Warren Commission, but the judgment it delivered could be based only on the evidence that was vouchsafed to it, and that evidence excluded elements that might have led to a more believable, if far more painful, conclusion.

For reasons of my own, I think that President Johnson's suspicions in regard to Castro's role were amply justified. Very soon after President Kennedy's death, an intelligence report crossed my desk. In circumstantial detail, it stated that Oswald had been seen in Havana in the company of Cuban intelligence officers several days before the events in Dallas, and that he had traveled there by way of Mexico City, where, as the Warren Commission later established, he had been received at the Soviet embassy. The detail—locale, precise notations of time, and more—was very persuasive. I was aware that it would not have reached so high a level if others had not judged it plausible enough to merit the consideration of high officials. As I read the report, I felt a sense of physical shock, a rising of the hair on the back of my neck. I walked it over to my superiors, some of whom had attended that Sunday-morning meeting with President Johnson. Reading it caused their faces to go ashen.

"Al," said one of them, "you will forget, as from this moment, that you ever read this piece of paper, or that it ever existed." The report was destroyed. Notwithstanding the order I was given, I have found it impossible, over the course of the last thirty years, to forget the report as I was ordered to do or to banish from my mind the many unanswered— and now, perhaps, unanswerable—questions that it raised.

9

The Gulf of Tonkin

Around 9:20 Washington time, on the morning on August 4, 1964, an intelligence source reported to the White House and the Pentagon that the North Vietnamese had directed two Soviet-made Swatow gunboats and a P-4 torpedo boat to attack the American destroyers *Maddox* and *Turner Joy* in the Gulf of Tonkin. This was galvanizing news. The *Maddox* had been engaged by North Vietnamese torpedo boats in the Gulf of Tonkin only two days before and President Johnson had warned Hanoi, in an official note of protest, of "the grave consequences which would inevitably result from any further unprovoked offensive military action against U.S. forces."[1]

Within seconds after this new report was received, McNamara and President Johnson spoke to each other on the secure telephone. The President asked how long it would take to conduct a bombing raid on a strategic North Vietnamese target. McNamara consulted the Joint Chiefs of Staff (the chairman, Gen. Earle Wheeler, was in New York that morning), who estimated that planes from the carrier *Ticonderoga*, which was operating off the Vietnamese coast, could hit any target north of the 17th parallel by 6:00 P.M. Washington time (6:00 A.M., Saigon time). This estimate was passed to the President; after that, there was never any realistic doubt that the air raid would take place. The White House press office informed the networks that the President would appear before the television cameras to issue a statement of major importance about Vietnam in time for the seven o'clock news.

In any international crisis, the command post is the office of the Secretary of Defense, where I was working on the day in question as a deputy special assistant to Secretary McNamara and his deputy, Cyrus Vance. What I report to the reader here is what I recall seeing and hearing that day when the nature of American involvement in Vietnam underwent its fateful change. My account will differ somewhat from earlier versions, and no doubt from reports yet to be rendered. I think it better to rely on what I myself saw and heard.

The political reasons for the raid were clear enough. Since the overthrow and assassination of President Ngo Dinh Diem, scarcely three weeks before the death of President Kennedy, South Vietnam had had no effective national government. The weakness of the central authority and the military inefficiency that the coup d'état was supposed to cure had, in fact, been made worse. The temptation to deal with the deteriorating situation in South Vietnam by placing the war under American management and fighting it with American troops had been a powerful one all during the Kennedy and Johnson years; it had intensified in recent months with the near-collapse of the authority of the South Vietnamese government, and many who knew President Johnson's mood believed that massive intervention was inevitable. An attack on American ships on the high seas clearly provided the justification for him to act on his conviction. Apart from any other considerations, President Johnson, never confident of his own popularity, was engaged in a presidential election campaign in which his conservative Republican opponent, Senator Barry M. Goldwater of Arizona, was insistently calling for a tougher American war policy against the Vietnamese Communists.

Naval officers familiar with carrier operations shook their heads in disbelief. The *Ticonderoga*'s primary mission (the *Constellation* was still en route to the Gulf of Tonkin) was defensive—specifically, to protect American surface ships from enemy attack. Carrier aircraft in the Gulf of Tonkin were rigged for air-to-air or air-to-ship combat. It would take hours to remove the weaponry and other equipment they now carried and reload them with the ordnance needed for a bombing raid. More time still would be needed to brief the pilots on the targets assigned to them. Few who were experienced in operations aboard a carrier at sea thought that it would be possible to hit the target in time for the President's speech at seven o'clock. As one harried naval officer put it to me with prophetic accuracy, "We'll be lucky if we can get the order to the fleet in time for the evening news."

The report of an imminent attack had been flashed to our ships. Almost immediately, flash reports began to come in from the *Maddox* describing radar sightings of two unidentified aircraft and of fast boats shadowing the destroyers with the apparent intention of attacking them. The night was moonless and overcast, producing conditions of exceptional darkness. The two destroyers nevertheless opened fire on the *Maddox*'s radar targets with their five-inch and three-inch guns. The *Maddox* reported sonar contact with enemy torpedoes; although the *Turner Joy*'s sonar registered no torpedo contacts then or at any other time, both ships carried out evasive maneuvers. The *Maddox*'s sonarman reported hearing more than twenty enemy torpedoes in the water.[2]

No one on either ship actually saw the enemy boats for certain, although men aboard the *Turner Joy* reported that they had observed two torpedoes running close to the ship. Others on both destroyers described seeing what they believed to be the silhouettes and cockpit lights of enemy boats, the flicker of a searchlight, and other evidence of the presence of an enemy engaged in an attack on their vessels. However, pilots of aircraft from the *Ticonderoga* after the *Maddox* reported sighting aircraft and small boats were unable to confirm these sightings on their own radars or by visual search for the wakes of enemy boats.

However, further intelligence reports seemed to confirm that an attack had been carried out by the enemy; one of these reports referred to the loss of two torpedo boats. From his headquarters in Hawaii, Adm. U. S. Grant Sharp, the commander in chief of U.S. forces in the Pacific, twice assured McNamara that he believed, on the basis of the evidence in hand, that an attack on the destroyers had, in fact, occurred.[3]

All of this information was being conveyed, more or less instantaneously, to the President by the White House Situation Room and by McNamara in a series of telephone calls. The details were discussed during high-level meetings throughout the day. At 6:00 P.M., President Johnson called a National Security Council meeting, followed a few minutes later by a meeting with congressional leaders, and announced that he had authorized an air strike against North Vietnam. Seven minutes later, McNamara telephoned Admiral Sharp and ordered him to execute attacks on an oil refinery in the city of Vinh, near the border with South Vietnam, and five North Vietnamese patrol-boat bases.[4] As already noted, Johnson's speech was scheduled for delivery at 7:00 P.M., to coincide with the networks' evening news shows. He read part of it aloud to the congressional leaders gathered at the White House, telling them that he intended to deliver it before television cameras set up in the Roosevelt Room as soon as their meeting was over.[5]

However, as anticipated by my naval colleague, the carriers were not yet ready to launch their planes at seven o'clock. Pilots were not briefed on the details of their targets until after the attack order was radioed to the fleet.[6] The crews, working to reconfigure some fifty-nine aircraft,[7] had not finished that enormous job by eight o'clock, or by nine o'clock, or even by ten o'clock. It began to look as though the President's announcement, having missed the seven o'clock news, might also miss the eleven o'clock program (as well as the final deadline for the great East Coast morning newspapers). President Johnson was faced with the prospect of delivering his statement while the nation slept. Seething with impatience, he phoned McNamara at frequent intervals and demanded repeatedly to know when, exactly, he could go on the air. The television crew was standing by; the networks were waiting; prime time was dwindling away.

By eleven o'clock, the President's impatience could no longer be contained. "Bob," he roared in a final phone call to McNamara, "I'm *exposed* here! I've got to make my speech *right now*." He went before the cameras at 11:37 P.M.,[8] while some of the planes still awaited takeoff on the deck of the carrier and others were en route to their assigned targets. Aircraft from the *Ticonderoga*, attacking in broad daylight, dropped the first bombs on the patrol-boat base at Quang Khe one hour and thirty-eight minutes later. Ten minutes after that, the crew of the *Maddox* observed smoke rising from direct hits on storage tanks at the refinery at Vinh.[9]

One by one, during the early-morning hours in Washington (late afternoon in the Gulf of Tonkin), our planes came back to the carrier. Despite the advance warning provided to North Vietnamese air defense by the President's speech, only two of our aircraft were shot down. One pilot was killed; the other was captured and spent more than eight years in North Vietnamese prisons.

At the same time, elsewhere in Southeast Asia, other American military aircraft, piloted by officers of the armed forces of the United States, were carrying out a secret bombing raid against enemy infiltration routes. We received a flash message from the war theater informing us that one of these planes had also been shot down. The pilot had parachuted into the jungle. He was alive, and he had turned on his personal radio beacon to provide a homing signal to guide rescue helicopters and air cover to his location. For reasons I still do not understand—perhaps because someone in the pilot's headquarters was overly concerned with preserving the secrecy of the mission, perhaps because someone else yielded to the temptations inherent in state-of-the-art communications—the Pentagon was asked for permission to rescue the pilot.

The answer was obvious: Rescue him at once. What else would we do? However, McNamara had retired for the night. No military officer present was senior enough to issue the necessary order. The question proved agonizing to the civilians McNamara had left in charge. They procrastinated, asking hypothetical questions to which there were no ready answers. Would rescuing the pilot be regarded by Hanoi as a violation of the territory of a sovereign foreign state? Suppose North Vietnamese forces intervened? Were we authorized to engage and destroy them? If we did, might that give the Chinese a pretext for intervening in Vietnam? What if the rescue helicopter, a very costly machine, was shot down? Would a rescue provoke an international incident?

The overriding consideration was the secrecy of the operation. I thought such a consideration insane when the life of the pilot hung in the balance. According to another officer who was present and with whom I compared my recollections when writing this account, I lost my temper and began shouting. That is how I remember it, too, and I will record what I said in the exact words I used in the heat of the moment: "The U.S. Navy has just bombed the shit out of an oil refinery and five other targets in North Vietnam, and it's no secret to the enemy that this pilot dropped bombs on them, too. He's where he is because he loves and trusts his country. It's too late now to worry about international incidents or cover stories. We sent that young man in there and we've got to get him out." Smith and others present supported my position in less disrespectful language.

It was reasonable to suppose that the local enemy commanders knew, or would soon know, of our raids along the coast. They would be in an angry and vengeful mood; our pilot could be captured at any moment, with all that implied. Still, no order went out to execute the rescue. Conversations took place over secure telephones; high officials equivocated; the young pilot remained on the ground, his beacon pinpointing his location, confidently awaiting the arrival of his fellow Americans. They did not come. More time passed. Rescue helicopters orbited over the jungle, awaiting orders from Washington to carry out their mission. The discussion continued. No order was issued.

Finally, time ran out. The word came: "The pilot's beacon has stopped transmitting." A deep, unbroken silence filled the impressive, flag-bedecked office where we were gathered. No one present trusted himself to speak. I am sure that my brother officers shared the feelings of shame and anger and impotence that overwhelmed me at that moment. I went home as dawn was breaking, not knowing the pilot's name or fate. I have never known who he was or what happened to him, but in my mind he symbolizes all Americans who fell in battle in Indochina. Before the conflict ended, more than 200,000 other young Americans would give up life or limb or personal liberty for their country, just as the unknown pilot and the two young aviators, one killed and one captured, in the Tonkin Gulf raids had done, because their government could not make up its mind to behave like a nation at war.

In terms of the future of American involvement in Vietnam, the die was cast. Later in August 1964, after further American deaths in Vietnam, the House voted 416 to 0 and the Senate 88 to 2 to pass the Gulf of Tonkin Resolution, giving the President extraordinary authority to use American military power to defend South Vietnam against Communist aggression. This was not a startling departure from earlier policies. The impulse to fight the war with American troops had been present, as we shall see, from the first days of the Kennedy administration, and it has been my belief, based on what I remember of the atmosphere and mindset of the period and those parts of the official record that I know to be accurate reflections of what really happened, that the Gulf of Tonkin incident merely provided the pretext for the larger and more active American presence that two successive administrations had long considered desirable.

The foregoing proposition is the mother of many painful ironies, the greatest of which is the long-concealed reality that the North Vietnamese almost certainly did not attack the *Maddox* and the *Turner Joy*, or any other United States naval vessel, on the day in question. This fact was known without reasonable doubt to the Johnson administration within weeks after the incident, but it continued to defend the genuineness of the naval action to the end. An internal investigation of the incident by the Pentagon soon after it took place established that the noises identified by the *Maddox*'s sonarman as enemy torpedoes were, in fact, the sounds of the destroyer's own wake, and that while some North Vietnamese craft may have sortied from their bases on August 4, they never attacked or threatened to attack the destroyers.

Analysts later concluded that the original intelligence report probably referred to the action of August 2 rather than to anything that happened on August 4. Although these facts were quickly established and described in an official report, they have never, to my knowledge, been fully confided to the public or to Congress. As I understand it, only two copies of the report existed in original form; whether either copy survives is a matter of speculation. If so, prompt publication should be authorized to clarify the historical record.

Most of the facts cited in the suppressed report could probably have been established, or at least persuasively argued, on the day of the episode. When, for example, the *Maddox* reported twenty or more enemy torpedoes in the water, I can recall no one asking how this could be, when the Swatow gunboats were armed only with light machine guns and carried no torpedoes and the third, the P-4 torpedo boat accompanying them, was equipped with only two torpedoes. Only half an hour before President Johnson went on the air to announce the air raids, Captain Herrick reported that there were strong reasons to doubt that any attack had actually taken place. Herrick's message, radioed from the *Maddox* to Pacific Fleet headquarters at 1:25 P.M. Washington time but not received by the Pentagon until 10:59 P.M., read: "Review of action makes many recorded contacts and torpedoes fired appear doubtful. Freak weather effects and overeager sonarman may have accounted for many reports. No actual visual sightings by *Maddox*. Suggest complete evaluation before any further action."[10]

If the doubts expressed in Herrick's message had been placed before the President earlier in the day, supported by the data already at hand, he would have had little or no reason to order the American attack on the refinery and the torpedo-boat bases. By 10:59 P.M., when Herrick's message arrived, it was too late. President Johnson was hardly in a mood to be approached with information that contradicted the decision he was finally on the point of announcing to the nation on live television. And the probability is that if he had not made the decision then, he would have done so at the very next opportunity.

Another factor was involved. It is entirely possible that Captain Herrick's personal assessment, even if it had come in time to be considered, would have been overruled by the electronic "evidence" transmitted earlier by the *Maddox* and the *Turner Joy*. In McNamara's Pentagon, human intelligence—that is to say, information collected by human eyes and ears and processed by the most sophisticated of all computers, the human brain—was suspect. Conversely, data produced by technological devices was seldom questioned. Any dispute on a factual matter between a human source and an electronic apparatus would normally be decided in favor of the apparatus, which was assumed to be free of the weaknesses that flesh is heir to. This concept spread throughout the intelligence community, and, in some cases, as with photography and other types of data collection by earth satellite, it was triumphantly vindicated. In other instances, it was markedly less effective. A celebrated example was the "McNamara Line," a row of sophisticated sensing and listening devices erected along the demilitarized zone between North and South Vietnam. This electronic screen was supposed to detect the footfall, voices, and other noises made by infiltrating troops from the North and flash their location to waiting troops, who would pounce on the intruders and kill or capture them. Sometimes this happened, but the system was better known for detecting the calls of barking deer—and, on one occasion, the sounds made by two intensely verbal Viet Cong guerrillas, one male and the other female, who chose to consummate their passion on top of a hidden microphone.

It never occurred to anyone, as far as I know, to question the accuracy of the intelligence report that had set the whole sequence of events in the Gulf of Tonkin in motion, or to subject it to a thoroughgoing human examination and analysis. Everyone on duty wanted to make it possible for the President to do what he wanted to do. It was not until weeks later, when the true facts began to seep through the wall of secrecy surrounding them, that I myself examined the evidence more coolly and began to realize that the crisis was born of human error, first on the high seas and then in high places. Endless attempts were made on the day of the Tonkin Gulf incident to verify that an attack had in fact taken place. But there were no devil's advocates on duty; the purpose of every inquiry was to verify the attack on the *Maddox* and the *Turner Joy*, not to question whether it had actually happened.

Those involved were impelled by loyalty, and by doctrinal conviction, to tell the President what he wanted to hear. This infection of the policy-making process, carried into Lyndon Johnson's councils by the same zealous and patriotic men who had injected it into the Kennedy administration, was already systemic. The malady was not new to history, or even to American democracy, but few recognized its early symptoms or guessed at its future ravages.

10

Vietnam: The Illusion

In Vietnam, the United States lost a war in the name of a chimera that it should and could have won in the name of morality. This grotesque outcome produced the deepest political and moral divisions in the American nation since the Civil War, shook the world's confidence in the leadership of the United States to its foundations, and delivered the unfortunate peoples we had set out to preserve from communism into the hands of a merciless tyranny. How could we have done this to ourselves?

No generally acceptable answer to that question is likely to be furnished by those who fought the war or opposed it. Emotions run too deep, memories linger too vividly, and perceptions of the experience differ in fundamental ways. Perhaps some Gibbon or Macaulay as yet unborn will sort it all out after passions have cooled and consequences have faded away. If this historian of the future happens to be Chinese, he may well describe the American experience in Vietnam as the "Disaster of the Three Mistakes." American policymakers subscribed to the fantasy that the Vietnam War was a civil war, a local event isolated from global issues of ideology and superpower competition; that was the first mistake. They were haunted by the fear that the People's Republic of China, an important supplier of munitions to the Vietnamese Communists, wanted the United States to lose in Vietnam and would even intervene with masses of troops, as in Korea, to guarantee a victory for Hanoi; that was the second mistake. Thirdly, the Presidents who made the war, Kennedy and Johnson, faced with the choice of destroying the enemy or getting out of Vietnam, chose to do neither because they feared that either course would lose them the affection of the American people; that was the greatest mistake of all.

I lived within the conflict quite literally from beginning to end. In the early sixties, as a staff officer in the Pentagon, I witnessed the birth of the Kennedy administration's quixotic delusion that the Communist tide could be turned in Indochina by a combination of covert action, limited unconventional warfare, and the public chastisement and transformation of an embattled and fiercely nationalistic South Vietnamese government into an American-style democracy that would win the hearts and minds of the people. In the Johnson administration, as deputy special assistant to the Secretary of Defense and his deputy, I attended briefings and meetings in which the new President expanded his predecessor's theatrical testing of the theory of counterinsurgency into a calamitous war in which more than 57,000 American military personnel, out of nearly 9 million in uniform, lost their lives. Later on in the Johnson years, from 1966 to 1967, I experienced combat duty, first as divisional operations officer and then as a battalion and brigade commander in the First Infantry Division, operating against main force North Vietnamese and Viet Cong units from the Cambodian border to Saigon. As a member of President Nixon's staff for national security affairs, and afterward as vice chief of staff of the Army and White House Chief of Staff, I witnessed the agonizing process of American withdrawal. Finally, it was my duty to carry the messages from Nixon that notified the last president of independent South Vietnam, Nguyen Van Thieu, that the United States had sealed his country's fate by deciding to sign a peace treaty with the North Vietnamese that everyone suspected Hanoi would never honor—and that depended for its credibility not only on massive American aid to Saigon but also, ultimately, on the fantasy that the United States would, if necessary, go back into Vietnam in force to uphold it.

All of these experiences, when I remember them, bring back the intellectual misery, the moral ambiguity, and the painful sense of loss and betrayal that typified the period. It is not my purpose to dwell on those factors but, rather, to suggest what produced them in my own case by describing what I observed as a young Army officer of middling rank who was plunged by chance into the company of Presidents, Cabinet officers, and other high-ranking civilians who made the decisions to embark upon the war and then to prosecute it in the bizarre way in which it was prosecuted. I did not question the fundamental rightness of fighting the war while it was going on, and I will not question it now. I thought that American forces in Vietnam were fighting for freedom against our country's greatest and most dangerous enemy, the U.S.S.R. I believed that Vietnam was the right war to fight, against the right enemy, in the right place, at the right time. The problem was that we did not fight it in the right way, by striking hard at its causes rather than attacking its symptoms. The Vietnam War was prosecuted on the basis of a fallacious strategic theory—incrementalism—that gave the advantage to a weaker enemy by imposing irrational limits on the use of our own power. The enemy perceived this for what it was, moral weakness and military folly, and, by pursuing primitive aims by primitive methods, entangled us Gulliver-like in the threads of our own arrogant sophistication. War is no place for the dilettante; however limited, it is by definition an event that threatens the life of the nation, by disillusionment if not by military defeat, and it had better be fought according to the wisdom of the ages instead of intellectual fashion.

For the Soviet leaders, Indochina was a convenient geopolitical point at which to test the idea of using leftist insurrections as mechanisms for turning former colonies and other developing countries into Marxist-Leninist client states. As early as September 1947, scarcely two years after the end of World War II, the Kremlin theoretician A. A. Zhdanov announced Moscow's policy of supporting armed struggle by Communist or proto-Communist revolutionary movements wherever these occurred, and without regard to legalities of any kind.[1] Zhdanov's scenario envisaged a world divided into two camps, with many small wars being fought by surrogates along the peripheries; it was not until later that these struggles to impose models of the repressive Soviet state upon the people of poor and backward countries were given a name worthy of Orwell, "wars of liberation." Theory notwithstanding, the reality of multiple and simultaneous wars of liberation financed and catechized from Moscow proved to be too expensive for the Kremlin as Communist insurgencies in the Philippines, Singapore, and Malaya were defeated. In the case of the Philippines, the guerrillas were put down (with significant assistance from the United States) by a determined popular government, and in the other two cases by resolute British colonial authorities.

In the aftermath of these experiences, the Kremlin modified its line. Rather than scatter its resources in support of uprisings that were doomed to failure, it chose to concentrate its military assistance and ideological encouragement in a place, French Indochina, where a complete military victory was a realistic possibility; such a victory would provide a model for all future wars of liberation. The so-called objective conditions for revolutionary success in Vietnam were more favorable than in most other places. These included the Viet Minh, a large, battle-tested, well-equipped military force already under Communist discipline; a long and remote border with a Communist power, China, providing secure routes of supply and convenient sanctuary; and a weakened and demoralized central authority in France, which was attempting to hold on to a vast and restive colonial empire while lacking the military and economic means and the political cohesion to do so.

By 1954, when France conceded defeat following a prolonged and exceptionally savage guerrilla war, the United States was covering 80 percent of the cost of the conflict.[2] The funds were not advanced out of any American conviction that Indochina was important to the United States, but because Dean Acheson, always the Eurocentric, decided that granting French requests for military hardware was an acceptable price to pay in return for French acquiescence in the American policy of integrating West Germany into the Western alliance and economic community. Two new states came into being as a result of accords between the combatants. These were Ho Chi Minh's Democratic Republic of Vietnam, north of the 17th parallel, and the non-Communist Republic of Vietnam in the south, headed at first by the last emperor of Vietnam, Bao Dai, whom the French had installed as a puppet president, and then by Bao Dai's former prime minister, Ngo Dinh Diem, who gained power with the help, both open and covert, of the United States. Although little in history before World War II connected the United States to Indochina in any way (the State Department did not even have a section wholly devoted to the region until after World War II), a clandestine struggle for postwar political influence in the newly created South Vietnam took place, with Vietnamese agents of the French on one side and clients of the United States on the other. The contest included lethal clashes between private armies of the contending factions and religious sects in the streets of Saigon, as well as incidents of harassment of Americans by French extremists that included a series of bombings and other acts of intimidation.[3]

In the end, with considerable funding and advice from the CIA's redoubtable Col. Edward G. Lansdale, the pro-U.S. coalition, headed by Ngo Dinh Diem, triumphed. Diem, a Roman Catholic refugee from the North who belonged to the mandarin (civil servant) class, was elected president of South Vietnam on October 23, 1955, winning a national election with 5,721,735 votes to 63,017 for his opponent, Bao Dai. These figures generated some skepticism, but it must be remembered that Bao Dai, who was almost universally regarded as corrupt and incompetent, had been installed as a puppet head of state not only by the French but also by the hated Japanese during the wartime occupation, and that he had been exercising the duties of his office as president from a villa on the French Riviera. The people voted by placing ballots bearing the picture of their candidate in ballot boxes; according to Colonel Lansdale, who paid the printer's bill, Diem's was red, the color of happiness in Vietnamese folklore, while Bao Dai's was "an uninspired shade of green,"[4] the color of a cuckold.

The United States formally assumed responsibility for South Vietnam's security and future as an independent state when, on October 23, 1954, President Eisenhower wrote to President Diem offering "to assist the government of Vietnam in developing and maintaining a strong viable state, capable of resisting attempted subversion or aggression through military means."[5] Secretary of State John Foster Dulles laid down the fundamental rule of American policy toward Saigon: "One can only hold free Vietnam with a government that is nationalistic and has a purpose of its own, and is responsive to the will of its own people."[6]

By 1960, the Republic of Vietnam was perceived by some American observers to be on the point of collapse into chaos. To many Americans, Dulles's dictum encapsulated the reason why. President Eisenhower's last ambassador to Saigon, Elbridge Durbrow, reported in the late summer of 1960 that Diem, a brilliant but aloof and xenophobic leader who ruled largely through an educated urban elite, was losing support in the countryside and even in Saigon, and urged Washington to put pressure on him to introduce reforms.[7] An abortive military coup on November 11 underscored Durbrow's warnings. The perception that Diem (like Syngman Rhee of South Korea before him) was fundamentally undemocratic and repressive toward those who opposed his regime, whatever their politics, became an article of faith in the Kennedy administration and the leitmotiv of American media commentary about him over the three years of life that were left to him. More than any other factor, Washington's refusal to see that Diem's political legitimacy was more important in a war situation than his style of leadership led the United States into the delusion that it could run this strange and contradictory country, whose nationhood was still so painfully new, better than it could run itself.

*   *   *

The Republic of Vietnam was an organism, not a machine; it required patient husbandry. During the Eisenhower administration, which poured $1.4 billion in aid into South Vietnam between 1955 and 1960,[8] the emphasis was on the encouragement of progress in the direction of democracy and the just and efficient administration of a brand-new state that was burdened by the traditions and practices of the ancient civilizations, Vietnamese and Chinese, and the French colonial administration from which it sprang. Progress toward modernity, the goal of American policy toward Vietnam under all administrations, was a slow and expensive process and it involved accepting many small failures as a means of sustaining the only important success, the continuation of South Vietnam as an independent, non-Communist state. American policy changed dramatically in 1961. The Kennedy administration was run by social mechanics and engineers, not by gardeners. Its impulse was to fix things or redesign them, or both, rather than to nurture their growth.

At the end of the Eisenhower administration, the United States military presence in South Vietnam consisted of 692 advisers, 350 of whom were scheduled to be withdrawn by the end of 1960.[9] President Kennedy took the position that the North's infiltration of guerrillas into the South in flagrant violation of the Geneva accords released the United States from the obligation to limit the number of military advisers it sent into the country. Diem, who did not recognize the validity of the Geneva accords, raised no legal objections. By the end of Kennedy's first year in office, 2,600 American military personnel were present in South Vietnam; by the end of his administration, there were 16,000 American troops on duty there.[10]

Almost immediately after his inauguration in January 1961, Kennedy had considered the possibility of sending ten thousand American troops to Vietnam to fight the guerrillas.[11] In May 1961, Kennedy sent Vice President Johnson to Saigon to confer with Diem, who agreed to a list of proposals for increased American military assistance. What this could mean in the long run was clear to all; the Vice President, on his return, told President Kennedy that "at some point we may be faced with the further decision of whether we commit major U.S. forces to the area or cut our losses and withdraw should our other efforts fail."[12]

By autumn, the Joint Chiefs of Staff were arguing that "outside" intervention would probably be needed to control the situation;[13] everyone in the military establishment understood that euphemism to mean American troops. In mid-October, Gen. Maxwell D. Taylor, then working in the

White House as chairman of the President's Counterinsurgency Committee, and Walt W. Rostow, the deputy assistant for national security affairs, both proponents of counterinsurgency as a solution to increased Communist military activity in South Vietnam, were sent to Saigon by President Kennedy. Taylor and Rostow hammered out an agreement under which the South Vietnamese government accepted American counterinsurgency experts as military advisers. On their return to Washington, Taylor and Rostow recommended to President Kennedy that eight thousand American troops be introduced into South Vietnam under the guise of flood-relief workers. This pointless attempt to fictionalize policy was an early sign of the administration's tendency to choose pretext over open behavior in regard to Vietnam. In early November, Secretary of State Rusk and Secretary of Defense McNamara signed a joint memorandum telling the President (though they advised him to delay his decision) that he might soon be faced with the necessity of introducing American combat forces into South Vietnam in order to save it and the rest of Indochina from falling to the Communists.[14] In 1962 and 1963, U.S. Army Special Forces (on direct orders from the President, the Special Forces grew from fifteen hundred men to nine thousand in a single year[15]) established fire bases, mainly in the Central Highlands, and engaged in combat operations against Viet Cong units.[16] Although they fought bravely and effectively and did good work in improving the efficiency and fighting spirit of the South Vietnamese with whom they came into contact, these troops were irrelevant, in the sense that their efforts, however heroic, did nothing to attack the source of the problem, which was the armed interference of North Vietnam supported by Moscow and Beijing.

There can be little doubt, on the basis of the record, that President Kennedy's motivations for ordering direct American involvement in the conflict in South Vietnam included the desire to counteract the impression of weakness created by his behavior during the Bay of Pigs, the erection of the Berlin Wall, and the Cuban Missile Crisis. True, the last of these episodes was being portrayed as a triumph of the President's toughness and spirit. But he knew better than anyone else that the facts did not support this conclusion—and that the Soviets knew this. Three times he had been tested by Khrushchev and three times he had faltered. He needed to demonstrate American determination at a new point of crisis.

At the Vienna summit, Khrushchev had told Kennedy that the worst thing the United States could do was to carry out guerrilla warfare against regimes it did not like.[17] No doubt the Soviet leader had Cuba in mind when he uttered these cautionary words, but Vietnam was a convenient place to challenge the warning. The President's determination to do so was reinforced by his reading of a report by Edward Landsdale, the architect of the victory over the Communist guerrillas in the Philippines. He regarded Vietnam as an ideal theater in which to inflict a defeat on communism through counterinsurgency. The Lansdale report reinforced the President's romantic fascination with the idea of counterinsurgency as a low-cost, low-profile, and, in domestic political terms, low-risk solution to the problem of Communist guerrilla tactics.[18]

As a military solution, however, it had virtually nothing to recommend it. It suffered from the historical handicap described by Robert E. Osgood, author of the first book by an American on limited war: "The real strategic question facing the nation has never been whether or not to adhere to containment, for we have consistently rejected every alternative, but rather by what means to implement containment so as to be able to avoid total wars, to keep wars limited, and to fight limited wars successfully. Unfortunately, this problem has always been obscured by our profound distaste for the very notion of containment and limited war."[19]

In fairness to the advocates of counterinsurgency, it must be said that this was not so obvious before the war was fought as it was afterward. During Eisenhower's presidency, American advice to the Army of the Republic of South Vietnam (ARVN) had emphasized creating the ability to repel a conventional attack from the North similar to the one launched by the North Koreans ten years before. But except for some early battles in which the Viet Minh had made the costly error of trying to fight like a conventional army, the rebel forces had defeated the French by the brilliant application of guerrilla tactics on a massive scale. If the Viet Minh guerrillas had defeated the French army, how could a South Vietnamese army hope to survive by repeating French mistakes? Naturally, this argument reinforced President Kennedy's belief in counterinsurgency, in which (to state the doctrine in its simplest form) Communist guerrillas would be hunted down in the jungles or the mountains and killed by democratic counterguerrillas. An unbroken series of small victories would shatter the mystique of the Viet Cong, and this, combined with visible reform of the Saigon government into a truly humanitarian regime, would win the hearts and minds of the people. President Kennedy quoted Mao's no doubt unconscious paraphrase of Dulles's dictum that revolution (as Mao put it) will surely fail "if its political objectives do not coincide with the aspirations of the people and their sympathy, cooperation and assistance cannot be gained."[20]

A President's enthusiasms are contagious, and plans to save Vietnam by a broad program of counterinsurgency, including not only the Special Forces fire bases in the highlands but also the establishment of what were later called "strategic hamlets" capable of defending themselves against Viet Cong attack, and the training of South Vietnamese regular forces and militia in the techniques of jungle warfare, set the Pentagon and the news media abuzz.

This was a modest beginning, but it was unmistakably a beginning. As late as February 1962, Secretary of State Dean Rusk stated publicly that "the United States has no national requirements in [Southeast Asia]." Evidently, this was intended to reassure the Russians, who had gone along with the neutralization of Laos in 1961, and whom "Rusk thought [to be] . . . eager to stabilize Southeast Asia and sincere in their efforts to end the fighting in the region."[21] But the President, for his own reasons, was in the process of making Southeast Asia the focal point of American strategic interests for a decade to come. He regarded it as a target of opportunity, a place where American credibility could be redeemed at nominal cost by defeating a few bands of guerrillas sponsored not by the Soviets but by the Chinese. The experience of Chinese intervention in Korea only a decade earlier was still fresh in nearly every mind in Washington. "China is so large, looms so high just beyond the frontiers," Kennedy told an NBC interviewer in September 1963, "that if South Vietnam went, it would not only give them an improved geographic position for the guerrilla assault on Malaya but would also give the impression that the wave of the future in Southeast Asia was China and the Communists."[22]

This view of the matter derived in part from the strident anti-imperialist rhetoric coming out of Beijing during this period, but, in fact, the Chinese consistently advised Hanoi against carrying out an armed struggle in the South until well into 1960. In December of that year, a new agreement with Moscow for economic aid and technical assistance made war in the South possible, and China soon afterward increased its own aid to Hanoi as a consequence of the Sino-Soviet rivalry for leadership of Communist movements in Asia and Africa.

We do not know what message the Chinese might have delivered to us in 1959 or 1960 with regard to Vietnam, but, by 1972, when I went to China in preparation for President Nixon's visit, their advice was unambiguous. Zhou Enlai said to me, "Do not lose in Vietnam." I was startled by his frankness. How could a Communist want the United States to defeat a Communist insurgency? Chou explained the reasons for it, which should have been obvious in Washington all along: The last thing China wanted was an armed and militant Soviet client state on its southern frontier. This was not understood in Washington in the 1960s—how could it have been understood when our government had no meaningful contact with the Chinese government? President Kennedy was not alone in believing that China, which apparently never sent a single soldier into combat in Vietnam even as a "volunteer,"[23] was prepared to launch the People's Liberation Army across the border to ensure the success of a revolution of which it did not approve. The consequences of this ill-informed and superficial judgment would be devastating.

The future of American policy in South Vietnam was deeply, if not fatally compromised on November 2, 1963, only twenty days before President's Kennedy's own assassination, when Ngo Dinh Diem was murdered, along with his brother Ngo Dinh Nhu, in a military coup set in motion by the United States government. For many months, Nhu, the head of the South Vietnamese security apparatus, had been the object of criticism by Washington over questions of human rights. On May 8, during a celebration of Buddha's birthday in Hue, troops controlled by Nhu had fired on the crowd, killing nine and wounding fourteen; some in the crowd had been carrying Buddhist flags in violation of laws prohibiting the display of religious banners. A general Buddhist uprising followed, with several monks setting themselves on fire in public places as a form of protest. Nhu's outspoken and politically militant wife, Lê Xuan, charged that the Buddhist movement was infiltrated by Communist agents, and outraged Western opinion by sardonically offering to furnish "mustard" for the Buddhist "barbecue." On August 21, Nhu ordered raids on Buddhist pagodas throughout South Vietnam; some fourteen hundred monks were arrested and about thirty injured.[24]

These events created an uproar in the American media, which had been increasingly critical of the Diem regime. Supporters viewed criticism of the regime's methods as disproportionate to the actual instances of repression, especially in view of the fact that the Viet Cong, among other acts of terror and subversion, were systematically assassinating Diem's village and regional officials at a rate of about two thousand a year, often by public disembowelment in the village squares.[25]

Another factor came into play in August, when reports reached Washington that the Ngos were carrying on secret negotiations with Hanoi with the objective of ending the war and expelling United States forces from South Vietnam. Diem had already, in May, suggested that the United States begin to withdraw its troops, and for a long time before that had made plain his displeasure with increasing American interference in matters he considered to be the exclusive concern of his own government. Diem's detractors in the administration "saw the secret negotiations . . . as a threat to victory."[26]

On August 24, the State Department sent a cable to the American ambassador in Saigon, Henry Cabot Lodge, which read in part:

> We must . . . tell key military leaders that US would find it impossible to continue support GVN [South Vietnamese government] militarily and economically unless . . . steps are taken immediately which we recognize requires removal of the Nhus from the scene. We wish give Diem reasonable opportunity to remove Nhus but if he remains obdurate, then we are prepared to accept the obvious implication that we can no longer support Diem. You may also tell appropriate military commanders we will give them direct support in any interim period of breakdown central government mechanism. . . . Concurrently with above, Ambassador and country teams should urgently examine all possible alternative leadership and make detailed plans as to how we might bring about Diem's replacement if this should become necessary.

Both sides knew that these demands could not possibly be met. But if they were not, the embassy was instructed to tell a group of disloyal South Vietnamese generals, who had long been plotting a coup d'état with the full knowledge of the Americans, that Washington could no longer support Diem and would recognize any government they set up after overthrowing the existing regime. These secret actions had the approval of President Kennedy, who personally approved the cable before it was sent, although it was later said by others that he misunderstood the degree of support it enjoyed among his advisers. His state of mind and intentions are, however, evident enough in a cable he sent to Ambassador Lodge on August 29: "I have approved all the messages you are receiving from others today, and I emphasize that everything in these messages has my full support. We will do all that we can to help you conclude this operation successfully. Until the very moment of the go signal for operation by the Generals, I must reserve a contingent right to change course and reverse previous instructions." Lodge replied, prophetically, "You may not be able to control it, i.e. the 'go signal' may be given by the generals [themselves]."[27]

Approval from Washington was the word the conspirators had been waiting for and they acted on it on November 1 by attacking the Presidential Palace. Diem and Nhu, although they were offered sanctuary in the American embassy after they had gone into hiding, took refuge in a Roman Catholic church in Cholon. They were shot to death on November 2, apparently by the soldiers who had taken them prisoner. Apologists for the American role in this dark event suggested afterward that the murder of Diem and his brother (and the subsequent execution of another brother) could not have been foreseen. The argument is disingenuous; those who overthrew Diem could not possibly have let him live because, whatever else he may or may not have been, he was the only legal head of state that South Vietnam ever had. The legitimacy of the South Vietnamese government died with him. The political chaos and military disarray that followed, with one inept junta replacing another, produced the specters of humiliation and defeat that led the United States, seizing upon the Gulf of Tonkin incident as the necessary pretext, to take over the prosecution of the war.

By the time Lyndon B. Johnson succeeded to the presidency, the combination of Soviet supplies, the effectiveness of irregular forces infiltrated into South Vietnam by the government in Hanoi, and the collapse of political authority in Saigon had produced a situation so grave that Secretary McNamara, after visiting the war zone in December, told the President that "current trends, unless reversed in the next two or three months, will lead to neutralization [of South Vietnam] at best and more likely to a Communist-controlled state."[28] The administration decided to send Gen. Harold K. Johnson, the chief of staff of the Army, to Vietnam to survey the war situation and make recommendations for the use of American military power there. Like others who have climbed the ladder to the office of chief of staff, General Johnson was blessed with exceptional political skills, and he was keenly attuned to the thoughts and goals of the President and the Secretary of Defense. In many ways, his mission provided the model for most future ones, in the sense that the facts that he found in Vietnam supported the actions the administration in Washington wanted to undertake.

It was General Johnson, in connection with his preparations for this mission, who brought me into the topsy-turvy world of Vietnam policy. It was decidedly a back-door entrance. General Johnson asked DeWitt Smith and me to work up a list of every possible action open to the United States in Vietnam—based on what the traffic would bear in the highest civilian circles in the Department of Defense. He made it plain that the task he was giving us was confidential. We were to think and write on our own time, keeping what we were doing to ourselves, and deliver our paper to General Johnson in person.

Now there were plenty of experts on Vietnam in the Pentagon at that time, but I was not among them. Although I was increasingly concerned with Vietnamese matters after the Gulf of Tonkin episode, my duties before that had been concerned with other areas, including the day-to-day monitoring of McNamara's famous Project List, a comprehensive inventory of scores of things to be done in the military establishment to carry out the administration's overall defense policy. It was, of course, impossible after President Kennedy took office for any officer posted to Army headquarters to be unaware of Vietnam and its increasing importance to United States policy. But I had experienced it as a commotion in the next room rather than as something that was happening on my own turf. DeWitt Smith, a capable and articulate officer whose interests were wide-ranging, may have been somewhat better versed in Southeast Asian matters than I. But it is fair to say, I think, that the two of us shared a sense of puzzlement that the chief of staff of the Army would be interested in the input of a couple of lieutenant colonels he hardly knew in regard to a mission of such import.

We set to work immediately. Our task was to make a list, not to philosophize. Make a list is what we did, starting out, as was the style of the Pentagon in those days, with the actions least likely to rock the boat. These were mostly recommendations to shore up the existing effort in the South. Farther down the page, we listed measures to introduce a larger American presence into South Vietnam. These filled the top half of a sheet of paper. The lower half listed possible actions based entirely on the military and strategic realities of the situation. These included full mobilization; the movement of several ready fighting divisions on full alert to the West Coast of the United States and to strategic bases in the Pacific; the creation of an amphibious force capable of invading North Vietnam; the deployment of major naval and air units capable of carrying out a sustained bombing campaign against the North, including the mining of harbors and the interdiction of supplies through attacks on shipping.

The purpose of these maneuvers was to demonstrate the capability of the United States to take military action against North Vietnam, including a readiness to invade its territory and seek out and destroy its armies. Finally, we listed the delivery of an ultimatum to Hanoi and Moscow calling for the immediate cessation of military activity by their surrogates operating in South Vietnam. Such an ultimatum carried the clear implication that the U.S.S.R., as the power behind the war, would not be immune from American action if it did not stop encouraging its client's violent and criminal behavior.

These were strong measures, requiring that certain risks be run, but it is difficult to demonstrate the strength of a great nation's principles and its determination to uphold them without running risks. The objective was not to provoke escalation but to stop the war. The only effective argument against such a demonstration of strength and purpose in 1964 was that it ran counter to the conventional intellectual fashion that argued that many small actions, coming one after the other, controlled or even eliminated risk, while large gestures, such as those associated with the doctrine of massive retaliation, multiplied it beyond the limits of safety.

The balance of military power was such in the early 1960s that the United States might well have prevented a massive American involvement in Vietnam altogether by going to the source of the problem at the outset. Confronting the Kremlin and demanding an end to Soviet aid and instigation with regard to North Vietnam would have answered the concentration of Soviet resources in Southeast Asia with a concentration of American resources at the same strategic point. We were, after all, under no obligation to reinforce the fiction that Soviet meddling did not exist simply because the Soviets chose to act in secret; we knew well enough what was going on. The desired outcome (and in terms of the military realities, the probable one) would have been a Soviet retreat followed by a period of Soviet restraint in Vietnam and, no doubt, the usual threatening gestures toward Berlin. Another possible outcome, of course, was Soviet outrage and defiance, including the possibility of a nuclear confrontation, but this requires the supposition that the U.S.S.R. could be so indifferent to its own survival as to start a world war that it could not win in order to establish a Communist regime in a place such as Vietnam.

The third possibility, a conventional war against North Vietnam in which the United States committed its vastly superior resources, as in the Persian Gulf War thirty years later, startling though it seemed at the time, would almost certainly have been preferable to the war our country actually fought in Indochina. We did not list the fourth possibility— United States withdrawal; at the time, this was a most unfashionable option and I myself did not consider it a viable one, although I now realize that a very good case could have been made for it. The time period in which the events I am describing took place constituted almost the last possible moment to cut our losses and get out.

General Johnson went out to Vietnam, made his survey, and returned to Washington to make recommendations that omitted all but the mildest actions on the list. The bottom of the page, on which all the tough actions were written, was scissored off. General Johnson's mission and the timorous pattern of action that grew out of it had the effect of causing the Johnson administration to concentrate its effort in South Vietnam instead of fighting the war on American terms, from American strengths. This meant accepting conditions that favored the enemy by fighting the war on his chosen ground. All the lessons of Korea notwithstanding, it also meant conceding sanctuary to the North Vietnamese in their own territory and in Cambodia. The pattern of American self-denial was established. We would deal not with causes but with symptoms, not with realities but with illusions, not from strength but from doctrine.

It would be wrong to leave the impression that President Johnson invented these conditions. He inherited them, along with the tendencies that brought them into being, with the advisers from the Kennedy administration he asked to stay on as the core of his own government. They devised a policy based on military tactics that were incapable of producing the unequivocal victory that had always before, except in Korea, been the final justification of U.S. governments that chose to risk the lives of their young citizens in foreign war. In their philosophy, war's object was not victory but something else that they never clearly defined and that, therefore, was not clearly understood either by the people or by the military. Certainly the new dogma contradicted the *Army Field Service Regulations* (Field Manual 100–5) whose graphic words had guided American military operations throughout the life of the republic: "The ultimate objective of all military operations is the destruction of the enemy's armed forces in battle. Decisive defeat breaks the enemy's will to war and forces him to sue for peace which is the national aim."[29]

After he returned from his mission to Vietnam, General Johnson, confessing that he himself did not know the answer, began asking the officers under his command to provide him with a definition of the word *win* as this related to American policy in Southeast Asia. Though many tried to explain to Johnson what the word meant in connection with Vietnam, no one was ever able to do so—except, in the last resort, the enemy.

11

Vietnam: The Chemistry

Not long before Lyndon Johnson's death in 1973, President Nixon sent me to the LBJ Ranch to brief the former President on the progress of the war. It was one of several similar trips—Nixon was conscientious about keeping his predecessor informed on Vietnam and other foreign-policy questions—and after hearing what I had to tell him about the situation overseas, Johnson invited me, as he usually did, to stay for a chat. The weather was good, and we sat in a semicircle of empty chairs on the lawn, where the former President had set up an outdoor command center with telephones and other communications equipment. The view looked out over the hill country across an expanse of lawns and fields dappled by wildflowers. Johnson was in an elegiac mood; he knew that Nixon, like himself, lacked the support in Congress and the empathy in the news media to allow him to end the war through the decisive exercise of American strength. The new administration had no choice but to get out of the war on which Johnson had staked his place in history.

It was a somber moment. At the time of which I speak, Johnson was dying and he knew it, and though his old boisterous humor and commanding mentality sometimes broke through, he seemed to chafe against his reduced circumstances. This great figure, famous for his guile, was in some ways a very open man. He took no more trouble to hide the low spirits induced by retirement than he had taken to conceal his exuberance when at the height of his power and popularity. As we talked, Mrs. Johnson brought him an assortment of pills and capsules and a glass of water, uttering a wifely injunction to take them all. With a crafty smile of acquiescence, Johnson poured the many-colored pills into the palm of his hand, as if to toss them into his mouth; then, after watching his wife retreat into the house, flung them into a nearby shrub. "I'm dying and I want to get it over with," he said to me. "People think I didn't run again because I thought I'd lose, but that wasn't the reason. The doctors told me I wouldn't live out a four-year term, and I didn't want Hubert Humphrey to be President of the United States."

In an earlier book, I have mentioned how Johnson allotted his garrulous Vice President five minutes in which to address a White House meeting: " 'Five minutes by the clock, Hubert, and then the hook comes out! Do you understand what I'm saying?' " Humphrey nodded and began talking in his headlong way; Johnson studied his watch. When the five minutes was up, Johnson thrust Humphrey, still talking, out of the room and shut the door in his face while four rows of congressmen, several members of the Cabinet, and assorted aides looked on.

Something more than a distaste for volubility seemed to be at work in this later revelation, however: Johnson, the most partisan of Democrats, had preferred to see the Democrats' greatest nemesis in the White House because he thought that Richard Nixon was more likely to end the war on honorable terms than his own party's candidate. Johnson felt that Humphrey had joined his political enemies first by questioning the administration's Vietnam policy and then, in the campaign against Nixon in 1968, by repudiating it altogether. Humphrey was not alone in his apostasy, of course. In the end, many subordinates whose advice and moral encouragement led Johnson into the labyrinth of Vietnam had renounced the embattled President and his policies. These wounds were still raw.

On becoming President, Johnson had kept the Kennedy team intact, telling these men, in a much-quoted phrase, that he needed them more than Kennedy had needed them. This was an unfortunate choice of words because it reinforced the general belief among New Frontiersmen that Johnson was in all respects the lesser of the two Presidents. Even after he reappointed them in the wake of his own landslide victory at the polls in 1964, the Cabinet and staff found it impossible to transfer the boundless affection and respect they still felt for the urbane, handsome, and cosmopolitan Kennedy to the uncouth, homely, and quintessentially American Johnson. Like Harry S Truman, whom he greatly resembled in his unapologetic provincialism and his plebeian looks, Johnson was haunted by invidious comparisons to the aristocrat from whom he inherited the presidency. And like Truman, at least in the beginning, he was regarded as slow but teachable by some of the men who worked for him; Dean Acheson's oft-repeated admiration of the posttutorial Truman probably included a certain secret pride of authorship.

"The worst mistake I ever made was to ask the Kennedy people to stay, and then listening to them," Johnson told me in the course of a long commentary on Vietnam. "I should have listened to my own guts. I knew it at the time." He went on to say that his instincts had told him to settle the Vietnam question, and the whole issue of wars of liberation, by using the leverage of superior American power to challenge Soviet adventurism throughout the world and forestall the bloody wars it was designed to produce. This was an exercise for which no man has ever been better suited by temperament and experience than Lyndon Johnson—one smiles merely to imagine him twisting Russian arms, breathing into Russian faces, and beating tattoos on Russian breastbones with a horny forefinger. It was also a confrontation he knew he could have won without bloodshed because of the overwhelming nuclear superiority then enjoyed by the United States. But, he concluded, it was too much of a departure from the policy, and, even more perhaps, from the style of his revered predecessor.

It would be incorrect to give the impression that Johnson was the supine agent of his advisers. On the contrary, he was indubitably the commanding figure in White House meetings. The impression his back-slapping, biceps-kneading, and lapel-grasping made on me, even as one who was not important enough to be subjected to it, was strong and lasting. I never encountered another human being like him. Everything about him—the insistent voice with its Texas twang, the mobile face with its transparent expressions, even the earthy imagery of his speech— accentuated his already-impressive physical presence. So also with his intellect, which was as sinewy as his big hands; when he spoke to a group he wished to convince and motivate and drive toward some objective of his own choosing, it was as though his brain grasped theirs in much the same way that his fingers grasped an elbow while grinding a thumb into the soft muscle of the biceps. His brilliance in summing up the elements of a McNamara briefing, the remarks made about that briefing by those present, and his own view of the question at hand was a wonder to behold, and I have certainly never witnessed anything to compare with it.

If Johnson had not chosen to be a politician, he might have been a great evangelist—but in tent meetings, not on television. To me, then and now, the most perplexing thing about him was that a man who was a virtuoso in his ability to sway, convert, and convince individuals and small numbers of people should have been so nearly incapable of communicating with the American people through the instruments of mass information. His gifts were elsewhere. His performances on television were the despair of his advisers, especially his method of reading a speech, which gave the impression, when he lifted his crafty eyes from the page and looked into the camera, that he was reading from the pedigree of a spavined horse. A TelePrompTer was suggested, by me among others, to cure this problem, but Johnson could never get used to it. I came upon him one day as technicians attempted to rehearse him in the use of the device, which was then a relative novelty. He looked shiftily at the wrong screens, misread his lines, got lost in the text, meanwhile registering on camera a range of anger and outrage worthy of a great Shakespearean actor, except that in Johnson's case the emotions were genuine. Finally, he bellowed, "Get this f———g thing out of here!" and strode from the room, looking as if he would have liked to have smashed the pesky machine to smithereens with a sledgehammer.

Our conversation at the ranch was so cheerless that I did not have the heart to ask Johnson why he had kept the Kennedy men by his side after he had ceased to respect their advice, and I am not sure that Johnson would or could have answered the question even if I had put it to him. It seemed to me at the time that the combination of their love of activism and his constitutional impatience produced a chemistry that propelled them into an impasse that in their mutual intellectual and patriotic excitement neither was able to perceive. This was not a proposition I was prepared to suggest to the already-mournful Johnson. Maybe he had continued to listen to Kennedy's former advisers even after he no longer believed in their wisdom because, as he had said at the outset, he thought he needed them. Like most other American Presidents, he was not an expert in foreign policy on assuming the presidency. He was a rough-and-tumble backwoods politician and consummate legislative compromiser whose primary interests had always looked inward to the improvement of American society through social engineering rather than outward to the world through the projection of American power and ideals. On Capitol Hill, he had been exposed to foreign-policy questions as part of the constitutional process of appropriation, advice, and consent, but his views on the great international questions served political utility rather than a comprehensive idea of a world order. He thought, not altogether incorrectly, that foreign nations, at bottom, were pretty much like American special-interest groups. He knew how to deal with such people. But he was not closely acquainted with the academics and other intellectuals who constitute the priesthood of the foreign-policy establishment; he knew who these people were, but he did not yet know how they thought or talked or promoted their agendas.

The fact is, Johnson thought that the Kennedy men, with their gift of gab and their recondite ideas, could teach him what he needed to know about foreign policy better and faster than anyone else in the Democratic party. Unfortunately, this turned out to be a process of learning by doing what these men advised because Johnson was not operating from a philosophical basis of his own. If he had been doing so, he might have detected error before he fell into it—before Vietnam, after all, no one had ever tried to prosecute a war by reassuring the enemy. During the presidential campaign, William P. Bundy, the Assistant Secretary of State for Far Eastern affairs, carried this tendency into a new dimension by stating that the United States had no intention of overthrowing the regime in Hanoi but only sought to influence it to end the war "it directs and supports in South Vietnam."[1] McNamara and McGeorge Bundy (William's brother), President Johnson's special assistant for national security, were by this time advocating selective bombing of tactical military targets in the North (but not strategic targets such as harbors, docks, petroleum stockpiles, power stations, communications facilities, and government centers in the Hanoi-Haiphong area) together with greater American involvement on the ground in the South, but in accordance with the doctrine of gradual escalation.

The objective of these actions, remember, was not to destroy North Vietnam's war-making capability but to damage it by degrees just enough to force negotiations. McNamara told the President that the "strategy for 'victory,' over time, is to break the will of the [North Vietnamese and the Viet Cong] *by denying them victory.*" Ambassador [to Saigon Maxwell D.] Taylor put it in terms of a demonstration of Communist impotence, *"which will lead eventually to a political solution. . . ."* (emphases added), and, after a two-day visit to Vietnam McNamara suggested "we should give [North Vietnam] a face-saving chance to stop the aggression."[2]

By the time Johnson realized that these abstruse ideas could not be expressed in terms of an American victory, or any lesser outcome consistent with the national interest, it was too late. His presidency, founded on humanitarian purposes and marked by singular accomplishments, was a shambles, the nation was in an uproar that banished logic and the ancient etiquette of mutual respect from political debate, and his own party, except for the right wing, seemed to believe that he would lose the election if he tried to win the war by attacking the enemy with sufficient force to destroy it.

The first time I saw Johnson in action at close quarters, shortly after the Gulf of Tonkin incident, I would have thought it inconceivable that he could have let any situation get away from him. The meeting room in the White House was packed with the leaders of the House and Senate, members of the Cabinet, and the President's aides and advisers. Although I had spent a good deal of time in the White House on various errands (during one of which, the reorganization of the West Wing communications system, we made the interesting discovery that the telephone lines to McNamara's home passed directly beneath the Soviet embassy on 16th Street Northwest), this was a new scene to me.

McNamara had brought me along to handle the charts while he gave one of his masterly briefings on Vietnam. I was wearing civilian clothes and trying to be inconspicuous when President Johnson caught sight of me. Waiters were passing trays of appetizers. Johnson reached a long arm around a couple of senators and took a handful of cocktail sausages wrapped in baked dough ("puppies in a blanket," as they were called). Popping these into his mouth, he chewed and swallowed as he reached out with his other long arm for another handful and gobbled them. All the while, he sent suspicious glances in my direction. No feat of mind reading was required to guess his thoughts. Who was I? How the hell had I got in here? Glowering fiercely, he grabbed and swallowed a third and fourth handful of sausages. By now, I was as fascinated by his amazing appetite as by the cunning light in his eyes. Obviously, he had concluded that I was a gate-crasher up to no good, and I had the feeling that he might at any moment wipe his lips on his sleeve and personally throw me out into the hall. Fortunately, my presence was explained when McNamara gestured me to his side, and Johnson immediately lost interest in me.

Much has been said and written about the intellectual brilliance of McNamara, little of it exaggerated. As a briefer, he was in a class by himself, able to reduce the most complicated situation to a few simple statements connecting a line of thought that often resembled music in its harmonic arrangement of themes. He was a master of bureaucratic ingenuity. When, for example, the White House ruled that no written communication longer than a single page might be sent to President

Johnson, McNamara complied by transmitting memoranda that filled the page with the smallest available type, eliminating margins and leaving a white space at the end of the last line just large enough for a minute signature.

Where statistics were concerned, he was a genius, seeing meanings and patterns in groups of numbers that were invisible to ordinary men until he pointed them out and explained their significance. To watch and hear him at the top of his form in these White House meetings, which were designed to explain policy to important members of Congress and other influential Americans, was to be reminded of Acheson's remark to the effect that he who sets out to educate the public sometimes has to express himself in a way that is "clearer than the truth."[3] In that connection, it was said by Pentagon wiseacres that McNamara could make 2 plus 2 equal 386 any day of the week, but the fact is that his numbers were usually accurate on their own terms. He himself believed in them. The problem was that they were irrelevant because, generally speaking, they confined themselves to a description of the situation in the South (even when they alluded to activities of the North), and thus omitted important elements of the whole equation.

McNamara and his charts were the main bearings on which the policy machine turned in the fateful first years of the Johnson administration, and McNamara regarded the war as a management case study involving a competition between the Republic of South Vietnam and the Viet Cong in which the survival of the former and the frustration of the latter could be achieved by the right "mix" of U.S. money, manpower, technology, and motivational reinforcement. In those early days, before the weight of error became so noticeable in the results achieved in Vietnam, men who had been listening to testimony all their lives listened to McNamara's briefings with the rapt faces of religious converts. Standing behind McNamara as I placed the charts on the easel, I saw that Lyndon Johnson was one of them.

In the opening days of his presidency, he had depended, out of necessity, on McNamara because he was the man who could do the most for him. It is usually so in periods of crisis, because the Secretary of Defense, alone among Cabinet officers, is in control of the aircraft, ships, manpower, and logistical apparatus necessary to carry out the Chief Executive's wishes. When Johnson needed something done, McNamara did it loyally and efficiently. This created a bond between the two men and implanted in Johnson's mind the habit of trusting McNamara's judgment.

Secondly, as we have seen, Johnson was in immediate need of a data base with regard to Vietnam, and no one was better qualified to provide it than McNamara, who was not only the supreme theoretician of incrementalism within the government but who was also the person who had, in an extraordinarily short period of time, created the military means to carry out Kennedy's Arthurian ideas about fighting communism. Kennedy's defense policy envisaged, but never came near to achieving, an American capability to fight two and a half conventional wars all at the same time—that is to say, one full-scale war in Europe, a second full-scale war somewhere else in the world, and a half war in what was not yet known as the Third World. The "half war" was Vietnam, and the unchallenged belief in Johnson's inner circle was that it could be fought and won without drawing upon funds or political support for the unprecedented social programs of the Great Society, and without disturbing the harmony of everyday American life.

A third, and no less important element in the relationship, was McNamara's persona. Kennedy had often referred to McNamara's powerful intellect during his own presidency, and indeed he was a formidable individual by birth and resume. The somewhat contrived plainness of his appearance (slicked-back hair, rimless glasses) reinforced the impression that he cared for nothing but facts, and infallibly knew the facts when he saw them. He usually saw them, moreover, with the aid of a computer, at that time a new and mysterious instrument that not many ordinary people had ever seen, much less mastered. He was working with artificial intelligence while others were still working with pencils and paper.

During the presidential campaign, Johnson had stated that he would not send American boys to fight a war in Vietnam "just for the moment."[4] He made similar statements regarding the bombing of the North before actually bombing it in retaliation for the supposed attack on the *Maddox* and the *Turner Joy*. Apart from the bombing raids on North Vietnam following the Gulf of Tonkin episode, American activities in Vietnam during 1964—that is to say, before the election—continued to follow the largely surreptitious pattern established during the Kennedy administration. We organized the secret irregular naval raids along the North Vietnamese coast in the Gulf of Tonkin, secretly bombed the Ho Chi Minh trail in Laos, and secretly provided pilots who did the actual flying in South Vietnamese air operations while unqualified Vietnamese airmen, known as "sandbags," rode inertly in the extra seat. McNamara and his supporters pressed in secret for bombing of the North on a highly selective basis—that is, far away from Hanoi, and against minor military targets; in secret, the President agreed, and he waited for the enemy to provide him with a plausible reason to launch the planes.

On February 7, 1965, Viet Cong terrorists bombed a U.S. barracks at Camp Holloway at Pleiku in South Vietnam, killing 8 Americans and injuring 126; enemy sappers also destroyed nine helicopters and a cargo plane and damaged other equipment.[5] Hours later, President Johnson launched Operation Flaming Dart, "a program of measured and limited air action . . . against selected military targets in [North Vietnam], remaining south of [the] 19th parallel until further notice."[6] On February 10, the Viet Cong blew up another U.S. barracks at Quinhon. Twenty-three Americans were killed; more retaliatory air strikes were launched.[7] The U.S. Air Force launched Operation Rolling Thunder, which turned out to be, in the words of one historian of the war, "too big for the Communist powers to ignore, yet too small to achieve a major impact on Hanoi."[8] Although some raids were carried out against installations in the vicinity of Hanoi, the bombing generally was confined to tactical targets such as ammunition dumps, barracks and staging areas, bridges and ferries, and transport in the southern part of the country and on some offshore islands.[9] Strategic targets that were vital to the North's war effort were not seriously affected.

The Joint Chiefs of Staff, urging strikes farther north against targets of higher value, regarded Rolling Thunder as the opening phase of the systematic destruction of North Vietnam's capacity to make war, and said that the time had come to send in large formations of American troops to wipe out the Viet Cong. On Saturday, March 6, two battalions of U.S. Marines, the first organized units of American combat forces to enter Vietnam, waded ashore at Da Nang. Next day, Secretary of State Rusk, during an interview on a television talk show, stated that the Marines were in South Vietnam to protect the U.S. base at Da Nang, not to fight the Viet Cong.[10] On April 6, President Johnson authorized the use of U.S. combat forces for offensive operations in Vietnam, and, on the following day, in a speech at Johns Hopkins University, he offered American aid to North Vietnam in exchange for an end to the war; Hanoi declined.[11] Before the Marines went ashore at Da Nang, there were about 23,000 American troops in Vietnam. By the end of the year, there would be eight times that many.[12]

The fear that China would intervene in Vietnam as it had done in Korea, sending masses of troops across the frontier to defend North Vietnam, continued to haunt the President's councils. Although I was in no position to influence the President's thinking, I argued with fellow officers that there was little basis for Sinophobia apart from the freshness of the American experience in Korea. But the situation in Vietnam was not the same as in Korea with regard to the details of Chinese behavior. The Chinese had not furnished volunteers for Vietnam, much less made the war possible by creating a new Vietnamese regular army out of the ranks of the People's Liberation Army, as they had done in Korea; they had not issued warnings of intervention in specific circumstances, as in Korea; they had not moved enormous numbers of troops and matériel into staging areas near the frontier, as in Korea. This is not to say that there was nothing whatever to worry about. The Beijing newspaper *Jen-Min Jih Pao* stated on March 25, 1965, that China was "ready to send [its] own men *whenever the South Vietnamese people want them*" (emphasis added), and the foreign minister, Chen Yi, repeated this formula three days later.[13] The North Vietnamese played upon American anxieties in their own propaganda. "What we should do in the South today," said Hanoi's Gen. Nguyen Van Vinh at a party meeting in the spring of 1966, "is to try restraining the enemy and make him bog down, waiting until China has built strong forces to launch an all-out offensive."[14]

The Soviets, meanwhile, were openly engaged in the large-scale supply of war materials to the Viet Cong through Hanoi. They had secretly sent troops into North Vietnam to operate SAM-2 antiaircraft missile batteries firing on American aircraft; the first of these sites (two in operation, two others under construction) discovered by U.S. reconnaissance planes in the Hanoi-Haiphong area during the first week of July 1965 closely resembled SAM-2 batteries set up by the Russians in Cuba during the missile crisis.* On July 24, the first American plane, a Phantom F-4C fighter flying fifty-five miles northwest of Hanoi, was downed by a Soviet missile apparently fired from a previously undiscovered battery.[15]

Applying the devil theory to China had a benevolent effect on the way in which Washington perceived the Soviet role in Vietnam. When, in July 1965, George Ball suggested to the President "diplomatic feelers" leading to peace talks, he recommended "approaching Hanoi rather than any of the other probable parties." He did not even list Moscow among the alternatives.[16] Nevertheless Moscow became the principal channel through which the United States attempted to communicate with the government in Hanoi.[17] The previous January, Secretary of State Rusk

---

* In 1991, Soviet veterans who had manned such missile sites in North Vietnam demanded the same benefits as those being given to veterans of the Soviet war in Afghanistan.

had told the Senate Foreign Relations Committee that defeating the Viet Cong would show the world that the militant Chinese approach had failed and that the Soviet line of peaceful coexistence was the correct one. If the insurgency succeeded, Rusk suggested, the U.S.S.R., which did not want a war in Indochina, might be forced to adopt the aggressive Chinese line.[18] By November 1967, Rusk was telling V. V. Kuznetov, the Soviet deputy foreign minister, that he, Rusk, "saw no need for a conflict of interest between the United States and the Soviet Union" in Vietnam, and suggesting that the two countries "put aside ideological differences and concentrate on our national interests and see what progress we can make."[19]

All this suggested that the Soviets were bystanders with regard to Vietnam. In reality, it was the Chinese who did not want, could not afford, and were far too busy with the burgeoning Cultural Revolution within China to be able to manage a major struggle in Indochina even if the Vietnamese Communists had been willing to let themselves be managed. One of the reasons for the militancy of Chinese rhetoric was the poverty of Chinese resources, and the primary geopolitical reason for Beijing's assistance to Hanoi was competition with the Soviet Union for postwar influence in the Communist Indochina that Ho Chi Minh hoped to bring into being. *Jen-Min Jih Pao* argued in late 1965 that the Soviet Union had "switched to the policy of involvement, that is, of getting their hand in," only after it became obvious that the Communist side was winning in South Vietnam.[20] As we have seen, the last thing the Zhou Enlai faction wanted to see was a Soviet client state on its southern frontier. Few in the Johnson era, when the walls of silence and suspicion still separated China from the United States, could have imagined that such thoughts existed in the mind of a Chinese leader—or would have believed them to be genuine even if Zhou had found a way to express them to an American listener.

The administration's anxiety that the authority of the revolving South Vietnamese government would collapse altogether before the United States was present in sufficient force to save it from itself was great. "Our deepest worry at that time," Johnson wrote, "was not the military threat of the Communists, but the prospect of another major political crisis in South Vietnam."[21] By early 1966, the President had before him a plan to commit 425,000 troops to Vietnam by mid-1967, and he was disposed to approve it. The number actually on the ground was 184,000 (as against an estimated enemy strength of 221,000).[22]

These Americans had been sent into the war zone, as Johnson wrote later, without making "threatening noises to the Chinese or the Russians by calling up reserves in large numbers."[23] That was precisely the problem. The administration was getting itself into trouble by inches; the details were overwhelming the objective; the fascination of the game had all but driven reality out of the frame of reference.

The most notable expression of this intellectual and political disorder was the policy of the bombing halt. There were eight of them altogether between 1965 and the beginning of 1968. Those who urged these interruptions of the bombing campaign on President Johnson saw them as demonstrations of American altruism and rationality that would persuade Hanoi to negotiate the end of the war. However, as Carl von Clausewitz observed, "war is such a dangerous business that the mistakes which come from kindness are the very worst."[24] Hanoi saw the bombing pauses as symptoms of folly and weakness. So did Moscow. "The net result," in Johnson's words, ". . . was zero. Indeed, it was less than zero for us, because the enemy used every pause to strengthen its position."[25]

During this period, no one in the inner circle, not even the professional military, was advocating the sudden assault in overwhelming force that was clearly dictated by military logic based on the facts of the situation; it was understood that any troops sent to Vietnam would fight according to the terms of the doctrine—that is, in the South, in measured doses of force, as counterinsurgency forces employing small arms and small units in the rain forest of the uplands—in short, on the enemy's terms. This plan was, as we have seen, contrary to the entire tradition of U.S. military tactics, and few senior men in uniform believed in their hearts that it would work. The rule of thumb in fighting guerrillas is that the defending force must have ten men for every guerrilla; even using the low estimates of enemy strength from which the U.S. was working in 1965, this would have meant sending more than a million Americans to South Vietnam. (In July 1965, McNamara estimated that the South Vietnamese armed forces were outnumbered by the Viet Cong two to one in combat battalions.[26]) Of course, it was the military's job to make the plan work if the Commander in Chief ordered it to be carried out, but the stress of preparing for a ground war that the Army and the Marines were not designed to fight produced a professional schizophrenia that deeply affected the conduct of the war then and afterward.

In my own case, the tension was acute. I lived every day with the inner conviction that the policy was wrong and that the United States was inventing its own ultimate humiliation in Vietnam. Nothing I heard on my daily rounds at the elbow of the Secretary of Defense and his chief civilian assistants modified this view.

In those days, I believed that it was better for the United States to get into the Vietnam conflict on the terms defined by the administration than to stay out of it and live with the moral consequences of handing the Indochinese over to totalitarianism. At the back of my mind was the reassuring thought that we Americans would see the error of our ways in time to retrieve the situation. Yet I feared, even as I listened to the supremely confident men around the President state and restate the doctrine of incrementalism with the competitive brilliance of an Ivy League seminar, that something was deeply and maybe irretrievably amiss. The logic of our policy was full of holes through which my erstwhile Alabamian tankers could have driven a whole column of stolen armored vehicles, but no one was pointing this out. The government's capacity, never great, for self-criticism had been paralyzed by consensus, the catchword of the day; by any name, it was Washington's old established nemesis, groupthink.

The Army realized that the war could not be fought and won under the terms laid down by the doctrine of incrementalism, but no senior general, to my knowledge, was telling the civilian leadership this. As a young officer, I had seen fighting generals of the era just before this one— Ridgway, Gavin—lay down their careers for principles they would not compromise. Many generals of the Kennedy and Johnson years were remote from that tradition. Few had been tested in battle as leaders of large formations of troops in World War II and Korea. They had risen to the top during the Cold War in a new environment, the Pentagon, which placed greater value on the political skills needed to get an optimum share of the appropriations pie than the old system, under which the armed services lived under different roofs according to different tribal rules and customs and fought each other for money as hard as they fought the enemy for ground. Like Speaker Sam Rayburn's servile young congressmen, the new breed had learned to "go along to get along." Few who have worked in the Pentagon would, I think, disagree with the idea that the longer an officer spends there, the more of a safe-sider he becomes, the more sympathetic to the political theology of the day, the more likely to tell his civilian superiors what they want to hear.

The difference between doing one's duty and letting oneself be used is a subtle one. By the middle of 1965, I had begun to realize that I, too, was beginning to be affected by this process. Though I resisted it, I felt myself in danger of being politicized. During the 1964 campaign, for example, I was asked to help handle the product of a Democratic spy in the Goldwater camp, and refused on grounds that this was the wrong job for a military officer, as well as being forbidden by the Hatch Act. The man to whom I was expressing these reservations gave me a look of mild surprise. Was I on the team or not? This was not the only time I had said no to similar ethical end runs. Each such experience was disturbing: *No* is not a word that soldiers are trained to utter when presented with an order from a superior officer. On another level, memories of Korea crowded my thoughts, reminding me what it meant to soldiers at the front when political delusion was overtaken by military reality.

I saw taking shape in Vietnam the same errors that had produced such suffering and needless loss in Korea. The enemy sanctuaries were in North Vietnam and Cambodia rather than in Manchuria; the terrain in which the real enemy was hiding and gathering his strength was a tropical jungle instead of broken mountain country covered with snow. But the illusions were the same: that the enemy was in some indefinable way morally superior to the reactionary government the United States was seeking to preserve; that the objective of American military action was not to win the war but to compel negotiations to restore the status quo *ante bellum*; and that this objective could best be achieved by killing large numbers of Asian surrogates of the Soviets while taking care not to provoke the real author of the conflict, the Union of Soviet Socialist Republics.

We were entering upon another limited war on the basis of limited explanations to the American people and to the world of our reasons for doing so, without clearly defining our military and political objectives, and in the expectation of fighting it with an Army drafted almost entirely from the poorest and most disadvantaged classes. I did not see how the administration's illusions could be sustained by these methods.

In June 1965, I received orders to attend the Army War College in Carlisle Barracks, Pennsylvania. Having already delayed my attendance by a year at the request of my civilian superiors, I resisted inducements to remain in Washington for yet another year and set out for Pennsylvania with a sense of relief. After three years in an environment where reaction to events abolished reflection, I looked forward to the luxury of having time to think. I confidently expected to be sent to Vietnam in command of troops after completing the course at the War College, and I welcomed the prospect. The only place to test my misgivings against the doctrine, it seemed to me, was on the battlefield. And in a way that was by no means vague to me, I felt that by soldiering in Vietnam, I might be able to discharge whatever moral debt I owed the country, the Army, and my family for having been part of the process that produced a war whose purposes and aims our government refused to define, and that I deeply feared contained the seeds of disaster.

12

Vietnam: The Reality

On arrival at the war college, I embarked on a program of physical conditioning in preparation for assignment to Vietnam—lifting weights, playing tennis, doing daily calisthenics, and riding horseback through the rugged Pennsylvania countryside. This regimen of fresh air, simple food, and strenuous exercise gradually banished the lethargy induced by three years of bureaucratic life—*mens sana in corpore sano.* My tennis and riding partners were among the brightest officers of my age group, some of them old friends or acquaintances, and no one could have hoped for better company. If the memory of Pentagon service did not exactly fade, it began, at least, to assume its proper proportions.

Late in the academic year, student committees are formed and charged with the task of analyzing relevant topics in written reports. One of these reports is selected by the faculty for presentation to visiting dignitaries during the War College's annual National Strategy Seminar in June. I was appointed chairman of Committee 8, and steered its discussions toward an analysis of the use of force. Our historical research and analysis, which excluded Vietnam, brought us to the conclusion that the lesson of history was that the gradual, as opposed to the overwhelming, application of military power, tended to produce the very outcome it was designed to avoid. In nearly every instance we studied, incrementalism had presented the enemy with opportunities to meet or exceed the measure of force applied, leading to localized military defeats, prolonged conflict, and a greater expense in lives and money than had been forecast by those who had made the policy. We suggested that senior military officers had a duty to point out these military realities to civilian policymakers in the same way they would point out any other danger or anomaly. Our paper was selected by the faculty for presentation and discussion at the National Strategy Seminar. When the day came, my committee scrupulously avoided any reference to current policy and results in Vietnam. But evidently we argued the historical case with sufficient ardor to prompt one of our highest-ranking guests, Gen. Maxwell Taylor, to walk out of the auditorium.

That was not the only occasion on which I affronted higher authority during my year at the War College. Midway through the term, I had received orders to report after graduation not to Vietnam for combat duty as I had so confidently expected but to a staff job in Germany. I was stunned by this change in assignments. By then, the early months of 1966, nearly 200,000 U.S. military personnel had been deployed to South Vietnam and hundreds had been killed in action. Additional fighting divisions and other units were being rushed to the war zone.[1] However incremental and veiled the process, the main burden of combat against the Communist forces was being assumed by Americans. I was more than ever convinced that the only place for me, or any other professional Army officer of that time, was with the troops in Vietnam. I protested my orders through channels and attempted to have them changed, but the Army would not budge: It had no slot in Vietnam for an armor officer of my rank and experience. I said I would serve with any combat arm; I was answered with stony silence. As a last resort, I phoned Cyrus Vance and told him that I would either go to Vietnam or resign my commission. Vance intervened, and, because he was the Deputy Secretary of Defense, my orders were changed.

The Army bureaucracy expressed its displeasure over this failure to play the game by dropping me into the pool of casual officers who would be assigned willy-nilly as replacements on arrival in Vietnam, rather than sending me directly to a specific billet as is usually the case with regular officers. However, as all old soldiers know, the Army takes away with one hand and gives back with the other. When I arrived at the replacement depot in Saigon, I was greeted by Brig. Gen. (soon afterward Maj. Gen.) William E. DePuy (pronounced deh-PEW), who had taken over command of the First Infantry Division in March.[2] By his side was his assistant commander and my old friend, Brig. Gen. James F. ("Holly")

Hollingsworth. DePuy informed me that I was now the G-3 (operations officer) of the Big Red One. The two generals led me to a waiting vehicle, and before the sun went down I had taken off my armor badges and pinned on the crossed rifles of the infantry.

Holly Hollingsworth, a much-decorated, greatly liked veteran of Patton's Third Army, had been the coach of the Fort Riley, Kansas, football team, for which I played while attending the Ground General School the year after graduating from West Point. We met again after the Korean War, when Hollingsworth was in command of the armor contingent of school troops at the U.S. Military Academy during my first tour of duty there. He was a man's man and a born soldier who lived his life on an all-out, try-anything basis and then, over a drink of the best available bourbon whiskey, recounted its funniest moments in a repertoire of war stories that had few if any equals in the Army.

During summer training at Camp Buckner, cadets would gather around Holly, pop-eyed as he described his reason for keeping a round in the chamber of his .45-caliber automatic pistol as well as a full clip of seven cartridges: "Sometimes you need that eighth round. One day in Germany, I popped the hatch of my tank, stuck my head out, and found myself looking at eight angry members of the Wehrmacht. Every one of them was pointing a rifle at me. There was no time to fool around with the machine gun. I drew my .45, shot all eight Germans dead, and drove on." Hearing this tale for the first time, I hid a smile, thinking that the sardonic old tanker was having a little fun with his audience of hero-worshiping kids. Soon afterward, I learned from an eyewitness that the story was perfectly true; so were all of Holly's stories, including some arising from off-duty operations that he didn't usually tell about himself.

When I arrived in Vietnam in July 1966, the First Infantry Division had been operating for about eight months in War Zone C, a wedge of guerrilla-infested territory between the Cambodian border and Saigon. The terrain, traversed by the primitive narrow highways and murky rivers that were the strategic keys to its control, was largely covered with rain forest, interspersed with broad areas filled with tall, coarse grass and the powdery reddish cultivated soil and rice paddies lying near the hundreds of villages that were the targets of Viet Cong activity. Five of the division's seven major engagements between November 1965 and the following April had been fought in the vicinity of the guerrilla stronghold known as the Iron Triangle. The Iron Triangle, often described in the press as "a dagger pointing at Saigon," was a tract of dense jungle roughly forty square miles in extent, bounded on the southwest by the Saigon River, on the east by the Thi Tinh River, and on the north by an imaginary line between the towns of Ben Suc in the west and Ben Cat in the east. The enemy strength in the vicinity included such main force units as the Ninth Viet Cong Division, reinforced by the 101st Regiment of the regular North Vietnamese Army (NVA), and numerous local Viet Cong formations, including the renowned Phu Loi Local Force Battalion, a ruthless and seemingly indestructible outfit that had been terrorizing Binh Duong province for years.[3]

After Bill DePuy took command, the division became even more aggressive. So did the rest of the U.S. Army in Vietnam. By then, the U.S. command had decided, as was inevitable, that aggressive operations would be carried out almost exclusively by Americans, while ARVN, with the exception of certain elite units, provided security for villages and other areas that had already been pacified—that is, cleared of Viet Cong and placed under government control and ARVN protection. As General Wheeler, the chairman of the Joint Chiefs of Staff, put it to a journalist, "Primarily, American units are engaged in search-and-destroy operations . . . to engage the Viet Cong main force units and the North Vietnamese Army units and defeat them."[4]

The principal method of accomplishing this mission was to locate enemy base camps with infantry, provoke them into committing large forces that could be destroyed with artillery and bombing from the air, and then send our infantry back in to mop up. The measure of results was the body count. Like most senior American commanders in Vietnam, Bill DePuy had come to the conclusion that the only way to deal with the Communist insurgency was to wipe it out utterly: As long as it had any life in it at all, it would go on.*

On DePuy's list of "Big Red One Battle Principles," the first principle was this: "The commander who attacks or defends with infantry weapons alone commits an unpardonable tactical error."[5] The first words DePuy spoke to me as my commanding officer were these: "I want you to remember that the United States of America is a very rich country. We have lots of ammunition. Use it on the enemy, and to hell with anybody who doesn't like it. The motto of this division is, 'Waste ordnance, not American lives.' " That was a motto I could live by—and did.

---

*During the year I served with the First Infantry Division, it killed approximately 4,400 enemy soldiers, according to the body count. The actual number of enemy dead probably was a good deal higher. After every battle, we found, in addition to the dead on the ground, innumerable blood trails where the killed or wounded had been dragged or carried away. Large numbers of the wounded, who certainly amounted to several times the number of enemy killed, must have died as a result of inadequate medical facilities.

When it came to the tactics of small units, DePuy was a genius—the best squad leader, platoon commander, and company commander in the division, if not in the entire U.S. Army in Vietnam. His "Big Red One Battle Principles" was the shortest (one page) and best military directive of the war. He invented a new kind of infantry tactics called "the clover-leaf." This permitted aggressive searches ("saturation searches" in DePuy's phrase) in heavy cover by infantry without massing troops in any one spot and thereby inviting large-scale ambush. As soon as contact occurred, massive artillery and close air support were called in and directed by command helicopters flying overhead; additional troops were quickly inserted into the fight by helicopters. DePuy's cloverleaf concept was adopted as tactical doctrine throughout the Army in Vietnam.

He designed an improved foxhole, the DePuy Fighting Bunker, that was as much responsible for saving American lives and enhancing combat effectiveness as any single factor in our military effort in Vietnam. The bunker was a hole in the ground deep enough for two soldiers to stand up in while wearing their helmets and just wide enough to accommodate the pair with their weapons and equipment. It was surrounded on all four sides by a packed berm of excavated dirt three feet high at the lip of the hole, sloping outward to one foot at the base. Overhead cover was pro-vided by a roof of logs covered with a layer of sandbags, covered in turn by a thick layer of dirt. Two firing ports were placed at the corners of the position facing the enemy, and the holes themselves were sited so as to provide interlocking fields of automatic M-16 rifle and M-60 machine-gun fire enfilading the attacking enemy at angles of forty-five degrees. This fire was not aimed directly at the advancing enemy but laid across his path in a lethal hail of bullets low enough to the ground to stop a crawling man. The bunker was heavily camouflaged, and the firing ports were designed to hide the muzzle flashes of our weapons while keeping fire as close to the ground as possible (there is a natural tendency to fire high at night, when many Viet Cong attacks took place). When con-structed according to specifications (as it seldom was in a firefight), the DePuy bunker would absorb almost any amount of the machine-gun fire, mortar barrages, 57-mm recoilless rifle fire, rifle and hand grenades, claymore mines, and pack howitzer attacks that were features of enemy tactics. These bunkers were the basis of First Infantry Division defense, and later were adopted throughout the Army.

I liked DePuy from the start. Short in stature (a characteristic that produced the inevitable comparisons to Napoleon), gruff and taciturn, driven by his love of the soldier, he could, and did, display strong emotion when he lost men in battle. I needed no other reason to admire him. Where his officers were concerned, he was interested in competence, performance, coolness under fire, and, above all, in preserving the lives of the troops. Within the division, he was called "77" (voiced "Seven-seven"), after his radio call sign. Seven-seven liked to talk by radiotele-phone directly to platoon leaders and company commanders in the heat of battle while circling overhead in his helicopter. He was on fatherly terms with nearly every radioman in the division. Often the advice he gave to inexperienced officers under fire saved lives and situations.

In one of the first major battles I observed as divisional G-3, a fierce engagement between three battalions of the First Brigade of the First Infantry Division and the Phu Loi battalion, the disadvantages of tradi-tional infantry tactics became apparent. This action took place on August 25 to 26, 1966, near Bong Trang, in a densely wooded area along National Highway 16, about twenty-five miles from Saigon. This patch of jungle was a well-known enemy refuge from which the Viet Cong regularly emerged to mine roads, conduct ambushes, and generally terrorize the surrounding countryside, which included rubber plantations that were critical to the South Vietnamese economy.

Around 8:00 A.M. on August 25, a fifteen-man reconnaissance patrol from C Company of the First Battalion, Second Infantry found the enemy in battalion force and immediately came under heavy fire. The men of the patrol took cover in a network of Viet Cong trenches and, after reporting that the Viet Cong were in the trenches with them, called in artillery fire on their own position. Two companies of the First Battalion, Twenty-sixth Infantry were sent in as reinforcements, but they made slow progress even though they were accompanied by special tree-felling bulldozers designed to clear a path through the dense jungle growth. Another battalion was airlifted into a landing zone blasted out of the jungle by artillery and air strikes, and a third battalion was moved into a blocking position to the north.

The result was a confused, bloody, touch-and-go battle. Our troops fought with exemplary courage. Of the original fifteen-man patrol, only seven men survived, all but one of them wounded. One isolated unit, B Company of the First Battalion, Sixteenth Infantry, made a series of assaults against heavy automatic weapons and mortar fire that were so punishing that only fourteen men were left to make the final attempt; it, too, was repelled. Elsewhere, our forces reversed this situation. The Viet Cong broke contact all along the line as darkness fell and then vanished into the foliage. They had lost about half their strength, including an estimated 171 dead; our losses, unusually and unacceptably high, were 30 killed and 183 wounded.[6] Only a lenient judge of military results would have regarded the engagement as a victory for either side. Certainly it demonstrated the truth of DePuy's Big Red One Battle Principles No. 3: "Complicated schemes of maneuver have no place in jungle warfare."[7]

Everyone now knows that Vietnam was a new kind of war, but this was not fully understood even by the American military command in 1966. Our objective was not to reduce fortifications, cut lines of communication and supply by capturing highway crossroads, railroad junctions, and airports, taking hilltops or investing strategic towns while driving the enemy before us until he was cornered. This is what Washington and Rochambeau had done at Yorktown, Grant and Sherman had done in the South, Pershing and Eisenhower had done in Europe, and MacArthur and Ridgway had done only a decade earlier in Korea. Our entirely novel objective was to regain control of an entire country whose topography was strange to us and largely inaccessible to a motorized Army, by landing within it, establishing bases surrounded by the enemy, and striking out in all directions against hidden forces whose numbers, weaponry, and exact location were unknown. In Vietnam, strategic factors hardly applied. Tactics was all, and the name of the game was not chess but a demented and bloody form of hide-and-seek.

After the battle of Bong Trang, DePuy discussed these matters in terms of a tactical approach better suited to the volatile nature of the novel war in which we were engaged. Thanks largely to his great abilities as a leader and tactician, the confusion and losses of Bong Trang were not repeated. The division adopted new tactics, new training methods, a new spirit. My job as G-3 was, of course, a great opportunity to grow in military knowledge and self-knowledge. DePuy was a memorable teacher. Like all great soldiers, he believed that the key to success in war was, in the words of the Duke of Wellington, "attention to detail."[8] In lulls between action, DePuy was almost constantly on the move, visiting the troops and talking to them, checking the readiness and morale of every unit. No detail relating to the well-being of the troops was unimportant to him; if any escaped his notice, I was not aware of it. We planned continually and scrupulously for battles to come. When fighting was in progress, the general and I flew above the action in the same helicopter, with DePuy totally in command but having delegated to me such details regarding the movement of troops, the coordination of artillery and air support, and other matters as were the proper responsibility of an operations officer. Never once in the months that I held the job did he second-guess my decisions. This was typical of his character and method: Having decided to give me a certain responsibility (he himself was a former J-3 under the commander of all U.S. troops in Vietnam, Gen. William C. Westmoreland), he let me exercise it as long as I did the job right, in his eyes.

If he had not been satisfied, he most certainly would have fired me. DePuy, the personification of a fighting general, was known to have little use for officers who came to Vietnam from soft billets at the Pentagon with the idea of getting their tickets punched for future promotion by spending a few months in the war zone before going back to another desk job. Before I arrived, he had fired no fewer than thirteen lieutenant colonels from the First Infantry Division. Many who left under the cloud of DePuy's stern judgment were officers straight from the Pentagon whose political skills were greater than their leadership ability. Many had been marked for future stardom. Some had been the protégés of very important generals back home who believed, and openly said, that DePuy was ruthlessly destroying the reputations and careers of some of the most promising young officers in the service. These considerations meant little or nothing to DePuy; the battlefield was his only concern, and he believed that a leader who had wasted the lives of his men in one war through callousness or incompetence should not have the opportunity of doing so again in some future conflict. After Vietnam, DePuy became head of Army Field Forces, a post for which he might have been born, and instituted the new tactical doctrine and training methods that laid the basis for the brilliant performance of the U.S. Army in Operation Desert Storm in 1991.

As the reader has seen, it took only a short time to discover that fighting that enemy in the real world of the Vietnamese backcountry bore little resemblance to the stealthy woodland combat between good and evil guerrillas envisioned by the early enthusiasts of counterinsurgency. President Kennedy had believed that "if [a typical U.S.] division . . . found itself in the jungles of Laos or Vietnam, it would have been like Braddock's army at the Battle of the Wilderness. . . ."[9] In fact, it was the Vietnamese Communists, employing human-wave tactics, who very often marched like eighteenth-century British infantry into the withering fire laid down by American soldiers shooting from concealed positions. In most major infantry battles in the Vietnam War, one side or the other was entrenched. Yet both sides were highly mobile, the enemy moving stealthily along a chain of base camps concealed in the jungle, the Americans lifting soldiers into combat aboard helicopters. This machine (which operated with near-impunity in the early days before the enemy was equipped by the Soviets with modern antiaircraft weapons) opened up a new world of tactics by enabling U.S. infantry to descend on enemy strongholds that were inaccessible to troops tied to the terrain. When we engaged the enemy in this fashion, fixing him with infantry and then destroying him with artillery and air attack, we usually won, inflicting upon him staggering losses in men and matériel.

During my time in Vietnam, American intelligence believed that the equivalent of twelve divisions of North Vietnamese Army regulars were operating in South Vietnam in addition to the local-force guerrilla units; the total rose to fifteen divisions after the Americans left and the Communists took advantage of the cease-fire to overrun the country. The administration, Army headquarters, and the press talked of the two wars America was fighting in Vietnam—one to defeat the Communists and the other to win the hearts and minds of the people of South Vietnam. In his forthright way, Holly Hollingsworth expressed a view generally held by American commanders in the field in Vietnam when he said, "Grab the enemy by the balls and the hearts and minds will follow."

This was unfashionable language. Even now, after all that has been revealed about the appalling facts of life in Communist societies by those who had the misfortune to live in them, I have no doubt that his choice of words will offend some readers. Nevertheless, the principle underlying Hollingsworth's aphorism was sound. The U.S. offensives of the mid-1960s cost the enemy enormous losses (291,000 killed in 1968, probably the peak year), and if continued over a period of years could, conceivably, have defeated him by destroying his manpower reserves. But such an outcome would have taken years to achieve and would have required much higher U.S. force levels in Vietnam.

The day after Richard Nixon was inaugurated as President in 1969, he was presented with a National Security Council memorandum estimating that there were 1.8 million physically fit males between the ages of fourteen and thirty-four in North Vietnam, of whom 875,000 were already serving in military or paramilitary units. Hanoi was committing men to the war in South Vietnam at a rate of 300,000 annually. To counteract this level of reinforcement, "the Allies [would have to] inflict losses of 25,000 KIA per month, or 7,000 more than the current rate. . . . We are not attriting [the enemy's] forces faster than he can recruit or infiltrate."[10]

The moral consequences of carrying out a prolonged war of attrition against a technologically backward but dogged enemy of a different race were less calculable. Kill ratios and body counts are one thing when laid out on a chart in an air-conditioned room in Washington, another when you actually see the enemy dead scattered over the ground and the remains of American kids wrapped in ponchos lying nearby.

Wars are not fought by angels, and combat is a brutal and disorienting experience; if it goes on long enough, it can lead to loathsome acts of cruelty. Landing at a battalion command post after a fierce firefight while I was operations officer, I heard the battalion commander, a man known for his toughness, ask permission from a general officer present to take the bodies of slain Viet Cong up in helicopters and drop them on their fleeing comrades as a grisly propaganda measure. In the heat of the moment, the general seemed to think that this might be a good idea. I was revolted. "No way!" I protested. "The United States Army doesn't fight with dead bodies." The general refused to authorize the operation, and the enemy dead were given the decent burial they had earned by the sacrifice of their lives. Such barbarities, and worse, are commonplace in war, perhaps especially so in wars between soldiers of very different cultures and races. They occurred on both sides in Vietnam—on the Communist side, which began as a terrorist movement and remained one until the end, as a matter of routine practice. Americans who engaged in such behavior were exceptions and ought to have been separated from the service. It is the duty of an American soldier to say, "Not in our outfit!"

As in any other field of endeavor, experience of war is a great teacher, but it seldom repeats itself exactly. In Korea, for reasons I have never entirely understood, considering that General Almond was my constant companion, I was not wounded in action. In Vietnam, General DePuy habitually exposed himself and his helicopter to enemy fire, and, because I was usually sitting beside him, there were occasions when bullets flew quite nearby. One such case occurred when William Beecher, a veteran reporter on military affairs, accompanied us in DePuy's command helicopter during an operation a couple of weeks before the battle of Bong Trang. Some of our men on the ground had come under fire from enemy soldiers dug in on a hill above them. DePuy, with characteristic sangfroid, brought our helicopter into heavy ground fire in order to mark the enemy position with a smoke grenade for the benefit of our artillery. (The general dropped the grenade himself, leaning out the door while shouting orders to the pilot: "Lower! Lower! A little to the left! More! That's it!")

We came through this episode, routine for DePuy, with no apparent damage. But moments later, as we made another low pass over the landing zone, we encountered more enemy ground fire, and a round came up through the deck of the helicopter, nicked the sole of my boot and that of the general's aide, who was sitting next to me. The spent round continued upward, struck the inside of my steel helmet, spun around the rim like a roulette ball, and finally fell harmlessly onto my lap. Bill Beecher said, "You guys *sign up* for stuff like this?" In his otherwise admirable account of this episode, Bill paid me the compliment of writing that the round scratched the skin on my face, near the eye, and that I stoically refused medical treatment. In fact, the bullet never touched me, and, though I needed a new left boot and the aide needed a right one, no blood was shed.[11]

A few weeks after this, DePuy and I were flying over the watery paddy country along the Saigon River south and east of Saigon during a joint search-and-destroy action. The operation was in its waning moments, and, because we had a critical need for fresh intelligence, we were on the lookout for Viet Cong who might be taken prisoners. Below us, lying on the bank of a rice paddy, we spotted a guerrilla. He appeared to be slightly wounded, and he was floundering across the slippery mud, using his rifle as a crutch, in an attempt to get away from us. We landed and I leapt out with the intention of taking the man prisoner. As I drew my pistol, the barrel fell off and dropped into the mud—the result of a careless cleaning that morning in which the pin fastening the barrel to the receiver had not been properly replaced. Uttering an expletive that the reader will have no trouble imagining, I reached out to grab the Viet Cong, who was now lying on the muddy bank, fumbling with something he had taken from his clothing. I suspected that this was a grenade, and was soon proved correct as I saw, in rapid succession, the red Coca-Cola can filled with explosive and metal odds and ends such as screws and nails and bottle caps from which the grenade had been homemade, followed by the brilliant sunlike flash it made when it detonated, and then, blackness. I realized through sense of touch and smell that the guerrilla had killed himself. For a moment, leaning over what remained of his body, I was stunned by the noise and impact of the explosion, and by its probable meaning, which was immediately clear to me. Then I felt DePuy's arms around my shoulders. "Come on, Al," he said. "Let's go." He helped me back into the helicopter. Both my eyes seemed to be bleeding profusely; I could feel the blood streaming down my face and running off my chin, and of course I smelled and tasted it, too. I tried to wipe it away, but still I could see nothing. As the shock wore off, the pain became noticeable, as happens in any injury to the eye. My first coherent thought was this: "I'm going to be blind. That's the end of Army life."

Meanwhile, DePuy was bandaging my wound and talking to me like a father. I was touched by his concern. He was not a man who went out of his way to be likable, but, as I have remarked, I had developed great admiration and affection for him. I was not sure until after the grenade went off beside that rice paddy how he felt about me. DePuy left the battle, an act so contrary to his stern sense of the duty that it continues to astonish me to this day (I just assumed we'd wait until after the fighting was over), and flew me to the Army hospital in Saigon. In a matter of minutes, I was on an operating table, hearing the surgeon say, "It's a miracle. It missed the optic nerve. It missed everything." Later, I learned that a wire about the size of a short piece of spaghetti had passed through the lid and underside of my right eyeball, miraculously missing the optic nerve. My eyes were swollen shut and I had some minor cuts and bruises, but that was all.

Wearing the bandages for several days made me realize how fortunate I was to have been spared a life of blindness. I looked forward with joy to the removal of the bandages. But when this happened, I found myself in a ward with the men most seriously wounded in battle. The first sight I saw was their injuries. These were so terrible to behold that any happiness I might have felt in regaining the sight I thought I had lost instantly turned into other emotions. As every American knows, General Sherman said that war is hell. I disagree. In hell, sinners are punished; in war, it is usually the innocent who suffer.

After leaving the hospital, I was back on full duty at First Infantry Division headquarters in less than a week. Sometimes we had distinguished guests, as when the Israeli general and politician Moshe Dayan visited the division. I was sufficiently caught up in the spirit of the time and place that I felt deep resentment and anger when he told me that the United States would lose the war in Vietnam. His argument was my own, that we were fighting a proxy rather than the real enemy, but I did not want to hear it or believe it after seeing the sacrifices our soldiers had made.

My job as G-3 was tremendously rewarding when there was a battle in progress or a battle to be planned, but the bureaucratic aspects of the post could be frustrating. On November 24, 1966, I wrote a tongue-in-cheek job description for the record that captures the seriocomic flavor of the situation. Here it is, in shortened but otherwise unaltered form ("77," the reader will remember, is General DePuy):

> To decide what should be done; to receive guidance from 77 on exactly what will be done; to mission somebody to work on it; to listen to reasons why it should not be done, why it should be done by somebody else, or why it should be done in a different way. To see if the thing has been done; to discover the horror that it has not been done; to listen to excuses from the person who should have done it but did not do it; to think up something that will pacify 77. To follow up a second time; to discover that the thing has been done but done in a completely unacceptable manner; to reflect that the officer at fault has a wife and seven children, and that in all probability any replacement would be as bad or worse; to think up something that will pacify 77. To consider how much better and simpler the thing would have been done if he had done it himself in the first place; to find out how the thing got so incredibly screwed up. To hope that 77 will not ask how the thing got so incredibly screwed up; to think up ways of pacifying him if he does ask.

I kept on badgering DePuy to give me command of a battalion in the division or let me transfer to another division where such a command was open. I made no progress; the general wanted me to remain where I was. I understood this and was even gratified by it, but I did not give up, any more than DePuy had stopped arguing until Westmoreland let *him* go to a combat command. The issue was finally settled by pure serendipity. The phone rang while DePuy and I were engaged in a lively discussion on this very subject. The commander of II Field Force (the equivalent of corps headquarters) was at the other end of the line. He told DePuy that he wanted me to report to him immediately as *his* G-3. Glaring at me across the desk, DePuy shouted, "Well, you can't have him! I just gave him a battalion."

Soon afterward, in November 1966, I reported as commanding officer of the First Battalion, Twenty-sixth Infantry, nicknamed the "Blue Spaders" after their unit badge. Its fine commander, Paul Gorman, afterward a four-star general, became division G-3 in a swap of assignments. Gorman had brought the battalion to a high state of efficiency, and no unit in Vietnam had a more valiant record in combat. I kept the wise rules he had introduced: No cigarette packages, lighters, or anything else in the helmet-cover rubber; no signs or mottos on the helmet cover itself; no belts of machine-gun ammunition draped across the chest as the troopers had seen it done in movies before they came over. All ammo was carried in the original unopened boxes; otherwise the rounds got dirty and knocked out of line, causing weapons to jam and costing lives. I added one more rule that I knew would be more unpopular than all the rest combined. I banned the drinking of beer on combat operations. It was the Army's practice to fly a hot meal to men in the field and to include two cans of cold beer per man. Two cans of beer usually is not enough to intoxicate, but that was not the problem. Every outfit had its drunkards. They bought or traded for other men's beer and often obtained enough to become intoxicated. A drunk in combat is a source of mortal danger to every man in his unit.

Because he respected the First of the Twenty-sixth for its splendid combat record under Gorman, and because he knew me well, DePuy made it the shock battalion of the division, putting it in the lead in most operations in the months that followed. The officers and men of the battalion always did the job. In no small measure, this was due to the work of the battalion S-3, Capt. (afterward Gen.) George A. Joulwan, a former West Point varsity football center[12] whose combination of intellectual brilliance, shrewd military imagination, backbone, and physical fitness made him equal to any situation. He understood DePuy's methods in his bones and found ways to make them succeed even beyond our expectations. On one occasion, for example, DePuy ordered three or four battalions to undertake a night march in an attempt to envelop and destroy an enemy force. The march took place in pitch-darkness over jungle trails we knew to be mined. Under a plan developed by Joulwan and myself, we roped the whole battalion together, each man tied to the one in front of him. Total silence was maintained as we navigated by compass, following pathfinders who crawled ahead, probing the powdery laterite soil for mines. Although we encountered and disarmed several mines, not a single man was lost on this surrealistic march, and the battalion was first by a long measure of time to reach the rendezvous.

The "winter" of 1966 to 1967 was a period of almost constant action, often against the hydralike Phu Loi battalion of the Viet Cong. Time and again, we lopped off a large part of the strength of this unit, but after a couple of months it would reappear, replenished by cadres from North Vietnam and cannon fodder impressed into service from the countryside. After taking months of punishment, it was still capable of surprise attacks of great violence, as when John Marsh, a Republican congressman from Virginia (later counselor to President Ford and Secretary of the Army under President Reagan), visited my battalion command post during Tet, the Vietnamese lunar New Year, in February 1967.

Although a cease-fire was theoretically in effect in observation of the holiday, my CP was located in a notoriously bad area where the Phu Loi battalion had long been active. I advised against the visit, but Jack Marsh, an old friend from Pentagon days, dismissed the danger. He arrived in a Huey helicopter, escorted by an Air Force lieutenant colonel carrying a bottle of champagne to celebrate the Vietnamese New Year. I showed the visitors into my tent, pitched over a bunker and heavily sandbagged up the sides. The Air Force man seated himself on a bunk and went to work on the champagne bottle. Just as he popped the cork, a claymore mine detonated by the Viet Cong went off, removing the entire top of the tent. Fortunately, the blast passed above our heads and no one was injured. An enemy mortar barrage commenced at the same time, and we dodged through this to a nearby bunker, where Marsh and I spent the next four hours as Viet Cong attackers ran through the camp, firing Kalashnikov assault rifles and hurling grenades. After they had been driven off, we went looking for the Air Force lieutenant colonel across ground littered with the enemy dead. The unfortunate fellow had dived into a slit-trench latrine, an act that saved his life (who would think of looking for him there?) but that must have left him with pungent memories of Army hospitality.

Next morning, we choppered to a rendezvous point near a supposedly pacified village so that Marsh, a firm believer in winning hearts and minds, could study the results of this program firsthand. We landed in a field about half a mile from the tree line. A Jeep driven by the man detailed to escort Marsh, Maj. Robert L. Schweitzer, the commander of the division's Revolutionary Development Task Force, emerged from the tree line and approached the helicopter at top speed. The *pop-pop-pop* of enemy automatic fire was audible; enemy rounds followed the Jeep, kicking up the dust. Schweitzer skidded the Jeep to a stop beside the helicopter, saluted smartly, and shouted in a military manner, "Schweitzer reporting as ordered, sir! Jump in, Congressman!" The Jeep's windshield had been shot out and its body dented in many places by machine-gun rounds. Running such gauntlets was all in a day's work to Schweitzer, who was in the midst of his third voluntary tour of duty in Vietnam. But Marsh, who had seen more action in a few short hours than most other visitors from Capitol Hill experienced in the entire war, wisely decided to pass up the scheduled visit to a pacified village and to return to Saigon.

On January 8, 1967, about a month before Congressman Marsh's rude introduction to the Phu Loi Battalion, the U.S. command launched Operation Cedar Falls, a "seal-and-search" operation designed to seize the community of Ben Suc, a Viet Cong stronghold located in a loop of the Saigon River on the northwest corner of the Iron Triangle. The plan called for troops of the First Infantry Division to surround Ben Suc in a surprise airmobile attack, trap the resident Viet Cong inside, and then clear the Iron Triangle of the enemy forces thought to be hiding there in concealed installations, including the headquarters of Military Region IV, which controlled Viet Cong military, political, and terrorist activities for the entire region surrounding Saigon.

Ben Suc, with a population of about 3,500 (another 2,500 people lived in three nearby villages also targeted by Operation Cedar Falls), had been under Viet Cong control since 1964, when the ARVN battalion stationed in the village was driven out by the guerrillas. The Viet Cong had then executed the village chief, among others, and systematically recruited and trained the remainder of the population as soldiers, laborers, and quartermasters supporting the insurgency. It was believed by allied intelligence that everyone in the village was a member of the Viet Cong, or (willingly or unwillingly) a worker for the cause. All paid "taxes" to the guerrillas.

According to our sources, Ben Suc's people were organized into support units. Some transported rice and other supplies in sampans along the Saigon River. Others unloaded this material and backpacked it to the village, where it was secreted in the villager's houses and in a large network of tunnels and underground storehouses.[13] Others worked in Viet Cong field hospitals as nurses, or helped to recover the dead and wounded from the battlefield, or assisted with booby traps, or performed other chores. The Iron Triangle and most of the countryside surrounding it was honeycombed with tunnels housing hospitals, dumps of ammunition and supplies, and living quarters for thousands of guerrillas. The North Vietnamese had perfected the art of tunnel building during the war with the French; when they moved the war south, they brought their mining expertise with them. The tunnels, entrances, and air shafts cunningly concealed by jungle growth were very difficult to find. In 1966, the U.S. Twenty-fifth Division built its fifteen hundred-acre headquarters at Cu Chi, about twenty-five miles northwest of Saigon, right on top of a large tunnel complex.[14] Once discovered, the tunnels usually could be cleared only by soldiers, working in the dark, who crawled along passageways, killing the enemy, or being killed, as they went along. Tunnels were extensively booby-trapped, and among the devices used by the Viet Cong for their psychological effect were poisonous snakes or pythons suspended in bamboo traps from the ceiling. One species was dubbed a "half-step snake" by the tunnel rats, as American and South Vietnamese cave fighters were called, because its poison killed the man it had bitten before he could complete a step.[15] One of these tunnels was said to be twelve miles long, traversing the entire Iron Triangle from north to south.[16]

Just as the Iron Triangle was the key to Viet Cong activity in the Saigon region, Ben Suc was the key to the Iron Triangle. Operation Cedar Falls, the largest operation of the war up to that time, was designed to deny Ben Suc to the enemy literally by removing it from the face of the earth and to control the Iron Triangle by cutting broad avenues through the jungle with special Rome bulldozers that the troops called "hogs." After the village was secured, its entire population was to be evacuated with all their livestock and possessions to another part of South Vietnam, where they would be given new land for farming and a cash indemnity. After the people left, the village would be razed by bulldozers and its tunnels and underground storehouses would be demolished.

My battalion was chosen to surround and occupy the village, sealing it to prevent the escape of any Viet Cong who might be in residence, and deal with any enemy resistance we might encounter. The second phase of the operation, which included the identification and arrest of Viet Cong soldiers and sympathizers and the evacuation of the rest of the people, was the responsibility of pacification teams that would follow us in as soon as the objective was secured.

Our part of the operation was accomplished with clockwork efficiency—in the literal sense of the word. The entire First Battalion of the Twenty-sixth Infantry, transported in sixty helicopters, accompanied by ten gunships, took off at dawn from Dau Tieng airstrip, nineteen miles from Ben Suc. Minutes later, the flight, one of the largest seen in those parts up to that time, appeared over the village at treetop level. Under the umbrella provided by the gunships, the familiar thick-waisted troop-carrying Huey helicopters called "slicks" by our soldiers, touched down simultaneously at exactly 8:00 A.M. in landing zones to the west, north, and east. Each chopper had been allotted ten seconds to unload its complement of nine or ten soldiers. The entire battalion, 420 men, was on the ground in less than one and a half minutes, and the village was secured by 10:30 A.M.[17]

We encountered only light resistance. Most of the Viet Cong of Ben Suc scampered into the tunnels and escaped. Only 688 men remained in the village. Of these, twenty-eight were classified as Viet Cong after interrogation by intelligence teams, and seventy-eight others were detained for further questioning. Nearly all were low-ranking local guerrillas who could provide little useful information. Forty Vietnamese presumed to be Viet Cong were killed, many by fire from helicopters. Our casualties were light but included two of my men killed moments after landing by a large booby trap located in a tree. Enemy wounded were flown by helicopter to the Army general hospital in Saigon.

A number of North Vietnamese were taken prisoner, including some cadre members from Hanoi, who were noticeable because they were better dressed than the peasants. One of these was an English-speaking professor of mathematics who told us, after he was captured while attempting to escape across a paddy field, that he had been educated at the University of Peking.[18] The search of the village's underground storehouses, some of them three levels deep, revealed 3,294 tons of rice; large caches of medical supplies, including 800,000 vials of penicillin; 447 weapons; 1,087 grenades; and 7,622 Viet Cong uniforms.[19]

With Major Schweitzer in command of the operation, a total of 582 men, 1,651 women, and 3,754 children were evacuated before sundown to a relocation center near Phu Cuong, the provincial capital. Most made the trip in huge double-rotor Chinook helicopters and aboard U.S. Navy riverboats, taking with them 247 water buffalo, 225 head of cattle, innumerable pigs ("I want that sow and her brood reunited by 1700 hours!" DePuy ordered Schweitzer on hearing the frantic squealing of a mother pig that had been separated from its young[20]), 158 ox carts, and 60 tons of rice from the recent harvest. The processing of these people at the relocation center, handled by the Vietnamese provincial authorities under the supervision of the U.S. Office of Civil Operations for Region III (headed by the famous John Paul Vann), was less efficiently managed than the evacuation. In the words of General Westmoreland, "For the first several days, the families suffered unnecessary hardships." To alleviate this situation, a team from the First Infantry Division moved in, pitching dozens of large tents, providing wood and potable water, digging latrines and a buffalo wallow, constructing a cattle pen, and providing food and medical attention.[21]

After my battalion left Ben Suc, the village was obliterated. The tunnels were cleared by the tunnel rats of the 242nd Chemical Detachment. Explosive charges were placed throughout the subterranean complex, the entrances were sealed, and acetylene gas was pumped in with the aid of portable compressors. The charges were then set off, igniting the acetylene and presumably destroying everything inside. Bulldozers razed the village to the ground. Ten thousand pounds of explosives were buried in a shallow cavity at its center and exploded, on the theory that the concussion would collapse any undiscovered tunnels beneath the village.[22] The place was later intensively bombed from the air with the same purpose in mind. The "hog" bulldozers subsequently cleared great swaths of jungle in the Iron Triangle, opening broad passages through which the enemy had to pass in order to move from one part of the forest to the other and clearing helicopter landing zones for future use by our side.

The entire operation was an impressive demonstration of the fighting efficiency and technological expertise of the U.S. Army in Vietnam (no South Vietnamese took part in the assault phase, and indeed the entire operation had been kept a secret from them to prevent the intelligence leaks that had bedeviled earlier joint endeavors cleared with province authorities). Probably no other army that ever existed could have conceived of such an undertaking, much less have carried it off with near-perfect success. It symbolized a certain splendid innocence central to the American character, as expressed in the rueful World War II story about the New Guinea tribesman who, when asked to rate the jungle-fighting capabilities of the troops engaged, said that the Japanese were best and the Australians next. "What about the Americans?" he was asked. "Americans," he replied, "remove jungle."

In Vietnam, the herculean was not enough. Three weeks after my battalion landed at Ben Suc, the Viet Cong were back in the Iron Triangle in force. Many of them, of course, had never left, merely having gone to ground in tunnels and concealed base camps. As soon as the Americans left, they emerged once more into the light of day. On January 28, two days after the end of Operation Cedar Falls, Brig. Gen. Bernard W. Rogers, an assistant commander of the First Infantry Division, looked down from his helicopter above the Iron Triangle and saw "many persons who appeared to be Viet Cong riding bicycles or wandering around on foot. . . . During the cease-fire for Tet, 8–12 February, the Iron Triangle was again literally crawling with what appeared to be Viet Cong." The reason was not difficult to grasp. As Rogers wrote after the war, "We had insufficient forces to . . . prevent the Viet Cong from returning."[23]

* * *

Mounting U.S. casualties, though they represented a tiny fraction of the losses suffered by the enemy, had by this time begun to generate political consequences back home. Word of the administration's concern was brought to us by General Johnson, the chief of staff of the Army, and the feeling grew that the day of large-scale search-and-destroy missions was drawing to a close. In early February 1967, after eleven months in command of the division he had made into the finest in Vietnam, Bill DePuy was rotated home to a Pentagon job. His successor was a veteran of World War II combat in Italy and a former commander of the Berlin Brigade, Maj. Gen. John H. Hay, who arrived in time to command the largest operation of the war up to that point, Operation Junction City. This operation, designed to find and destroy COSVN, the main Viet Cong headquarters in South Vietnam, and to find and destroy North Vietnamese and Viet Cong forces operating in War Zone C, commenced on February 22 and lasted until April 15.[24] My battalion was destined to fight the largest, bloodiest engagement of what proved to be the last of the First Infantry Division's aggressive search-and-destroy operations during my tour in Vietnam.

The mission of the First Battalion of the Twenty-sixth Infantry was to find COSVN headquarters, thought to be located near the bend in the Cambodian border Americans called the Fishhook. Here, in the virtually roadless country west of An Loc and north of Highway 13, we were tasked to engage the Viet Cong and the NVA regulars protecting it. That is the military way of saying that we were the bait with which the U.S. command hoped to entice an enemy force many times our size to come out of the jungle and attack us so that it could be destroyed in the open by American firepower.

My battalion landed in the early afternoon of March 30 near the village of Ap Gu. Like the plan of battle, the terrain was classically Vietnamese: coarse, knee-high wild grass growing in sparse jungle, surrounded by lofty, heavy jungle. As soon as the helicopters touched down, cloverleaf patrols began probing the jungle. No contact with the enemy was made that day, but the patrols did find fortified positions in and around the landing zone. Instinct plays a strong role in combat, and I was sure that we were in for a fight. I chose a site in a grove of widely spaced, stunted, and defoliated trees for our defensive perimeter and ordered the battalion to dig in. I told the company commanders to make sure that their DePuy bunkers were properly dug and sited, and especially that the roofs of logs, sandbags, and dirt were extrastrong. My belief in this bunker, always strong, had been reinforced a few days before when a shell from an enemy mortar landed on my own bunker while Joulwan and I were inside, blasting a depression the size and shape of a vegetable bowl in a sandbag but doing no other damage. When the North Vietnamese attacked, they would hit us with the biggest mortar barrage they could organize. It was not a night for sleep. After darkness fell, ambush patrols were sent out and listening posts established all around our perimeter.

The next morning, our patrols into the jungle resumed. This time, our reconnaissance platoon found signs in English fluttering from the low branches just inside the tree line: GO BACK OR DIE, AMERICANS! At about 1:00 P.M., at a spot in the jungle about three miles south of the Cambodian border, the platoon ran into an ambush. Its leader, 1st Lt. Richard A. Hill, informed me, moments before he was killed, that his unit was being hit from all sides by heavy enemy small-arms and machine-gun fire, and by mortars and grenades. It was apparent that the platoon had only minutes to live unless it was extracted.

Divisional and corps artillery had been prepositioned on roads behind us up to thirty-two kilometers away, and I immediately called for howitzer fire and air strikes. Hill's radio operator stayed on the air, coolly describing the fight and marking the friendly artillery rounds as they fell around his position. I jumped into a two-man bubble Loach helicopter and flew to the scene of the fight. Soon after becoming airborne, I learned that the commander of B Company had bravely but impulsively led his unit to the rescue of the recon platoon without awaiting orders. Now his company, like the recon platoon, had been ambushed and was pinned down by fire from light and heavy machine guns as well as rockets, mortars, and recoilless rifles.

B Company commander reported that the enemy force he was engaging was at least a battalion in size. Our men were running low on ammunition. There was not a moment to lose. I ordered A Company to enter the jungle, pass through B Company, engage the enemy, and extract both recon platoon and B Company. Meanwhile, from the helicopter, I was calling down ever-heavier artillery and close air support with the assistance of the recon platoon radio operator, who was my eyes and ears on the ground.

After several minutes of this, my helicopter, which had been flying just above the treetops, was hit by a round that disabled the engine. The ship hit the ground just at the edge of the tree line, a few yards from A Company's position. The Plexiglas bubble was cracked open like an eggshell by the impact. The pilot and I scrambled out and made a run for the A Company position through the heaviest enemy automatic fire I have ever experienced. Such moments often impose a kind of slow-motion acuity on those involved in them. Rounds passed between my legs, mowing down the grass as I ran through it, and between my arms and my body, tugging at my fatigues. Bullets breaking the sound barrier in the vicinity of my helmet sounded like strings of firecrackers going off on the Fourth of July; mortar shells and grenades exploded behind us, ahead of us, and to either side of us. As I arrived inside the A Company position and dove headlong toward a large tree for safety, an enemy rocket grenade struck the trunk and exploded in front of my face in a shower of splinters. I was untouched. I was raised to respect miracles, and I do not use the word lightly. But it seemed to me that night, when at last I had time to reflect on this experience, that only a miracle could explain my coming through all that without a scratch.

After my helicopter crashed, George Joulwan, as battalion operations officer, took over command and control of artillery and close air support from another chopper. I remained where I was, directing the ground fight (the commander of B Company and several others had been wounded) until the enemy broke contact. Then I returned to the battalion command post and surveyed the broader situation. It was obvious from the volume and nature of the enemy fire that we had found and provoked a large main-force unit. I called for reinforcements, and at 3:55 P.M. two companies of the First Battalion of the Sixteenth Infantry landed and took up positions on our northern flank, beyond a pad of grassy meadow. As soon as darkness fell, I visited every bunker, ordering that they be improved if they were not already properly dug and sandbagged, that the firing ports be correctly aligned, that the claymore mines in front of each position, at least one for each American, be properly emplaced. I told each man to be alert and ready, because I was sure that we were in for a big fight. In some cases, the men may not have dug perfect bunkers despite my orders. They were tired. They had been in a hard fight, the temperature even at night was sweltering (it had been around 110 degrees Fahrenheit during the ambush and firefight that afternoon), and the soil was a sun-baked, concretelike amalgam of clay and laterite. But as I went along the line in the darkness, I heard the sound of entrenching tools, and I believe that improvements were made.

Our listening posts, deployed in the heavier jungle surrounding our positions, reported the sound of enemy movement all around the battalion perimeter. We responded with mortar fire. At 4:55 A.M., a single enemy mortar round exploded to our front. Recognizing this as a registration round, used to find the range for his other mortars, I immediately ordered a full alert at every position and called for artillery fire to the east of our position. Standard enemy tactics dictated a mortar barrage, followed by a heavy diversionary attack, before the real attack, much stronger than the first, was launched from another direction. The enemy mortarmen had crawled so close to our perimeter that our men could hear the shells sliding down the tubes and their fuses popping. When they detonated inside our perimeter, the explosions were so numerous and so evenly spaced that they sounded like a very loud and heavy machine gun. About three hundred mortar rounds fell.[25] The barrage lasted for twenty minutes and then the enemy sappers and infantrymen hit our northeast perimeter. They came as they always did, in human waves, firing AK-47 automatic rifles, hurling grenades, and dropping satchel charges in our bunkers. (After the battle, we found many unexploded satchel charges, actually chunks of plastic explosives with grenadelike fuses, trampled into the dirt at the bottom of our bunkers. They had failed to go off.) Later, we also heard the unfamiliar noise of pack howitzer shells exploding among our positions; this was one of the first times the enemy used them against U.S. troops.

The enemy broke through C Company's perimeter. In fact, many were already inside the perimeter, having followed our men in when they returned from the listening posts. In the words of one of the company commanders I spoke to on the radio at this moment, "The bastards are in the holes with us!" I had stationed the reconnaissance platoon close to my command post as the battalion reserve. Getting out of my own bunker, I got them up and led them through the darkness to C Company's lines. They made the difference as C Company's commander, Capt. Brian H. Cundiff, rallied his men; after some tough hand-to-hand combat, he held his position, personally killing six of the enemy. Cundiff, though wounded three times, refused medical treatment and remained at the head of his men.

Soon after the enemy was driven off, the units involved in this fight asked permission to evacuate their wounded by helicopter. Knowing that at least one able-bodied rifleman would leave with every wounded man, I refused. I could feel the disapproval of my staff at this seemingly cold-hearted order, but the battalion had been understrength when it arrived and was now further depleted. If it was to live, it needed every man who could fire a weapon.

Our artillery barrage, directed by General Hollingsworth from his helicopter directly above the battle, was now very intense. The air was filled with the unmistakable hoarse sound of American 105-mm, 155-mm, and 8-inch shells piercing the air before exploding on the enemy. A flare ship prowled overhead, fitfully lighting up the field of battle. Helicopter gunships and slicks flew along the tree line, firing rockets and machine guns. An airplane equipped with miniguns sent a devastating downpour of bullets into the enemy. A flight of B-52 bombers from Guam, diverted from some other target, dropped its bombs a kilometer or two away and although we could not see the explosions the ground undulated beneath our feet. The enemy attacked steadily, with their usual bravery, for almost three hours. Whole platoons disappeared in fountains of shrapnel thrown up by American shells. The survivors pressed steadily forward. Despite nearly unbelievable losses, they kept on coming, an unmistakable sign that they were part of a very large force.

Low cloud cover, and the darkness, made it impossible to call in air strikes until dawn broke. The enemy attack from the northeast was being held right at the perimeter, and I was convinced that an even larger force was concealed only thirty or forty yards from our northern flank, ready to launch a final attack. The skies were clearing somewhat, but the pilots were unwilling to come in unless they could see our perimeter, for fear they might bomb our own troops. I ordered our mortars to mark the perimeter with phosphorous rounds, and for the planes to lay napalm on top of the phosphorus. Over the radio, I told Holly, "I don't care how you do it, but I want cluster bombs right on top of the napalm—now. Bring them right up to the perimeter."

At precisely 7:00 A.M. (the battalion's air-operations officer, Capt. John M. Buck, crouching in the open behind my bunker while handling the radios, took a photograph that shows the time on Joulwan's watch), Air Force jets struck, dropping napalm and then loads of cluster bombs thirty meters from the perimeter and right on top of the hundreds of enemy soldiers who had been lying in the grass exactly where I suspected they would be. This was followed by strafing runs by F-4 Phantom jets equipped with miniguns, which fire so rapidly that they sound like an enormously loud chain saw biting into a tree trunk. The effect on the target is suggested by this image, and the air attacks (114 sorties in all)[26] broke the spine of the enemy assault. Those attackers who remained alive turned and ran; the retreat turned into a rout as our aircraft and troops pursued what remained of the enemy into the jungle.

After the perimeter was finally cleared at 8:00 A.M., the battalion found 491 enemy dead in the immediate vicinity, including one group of 29 lying in a row where they had been caught by the cluster-bomb strike.[27]

Lieutenant Colonel Haig, chairman (*third from left, first row*), with other members of Committee 8 and faculty of U.S. Army War College, Carlisle Barracks, PA, 1966. Dr. Fritz Kraemer is at far right in first row. (*U.S. Army photo*)

Deputy Secretary of Defense Cyrus R. Vance awards the Legion of Merit to Lieutenant Colonel Haig as Mrs. Haig looks on, June 1965. (*Defense Department photo*)

Conferring with Brig. Gen. James Hollingsworth (*far right*), assistant commander of the First Infantry Division, and another officer after the battle of Ap Gu, Vietnam, April 1967. (*U.S. Army photo*)

After Ap Gu, receiving the Distinguished Service Cross from
Gen. William C. Westmoreland. (*U.S. Army photo*)

Maj. Gen. William
DePuy, commander of
the First Infantry Division,
transfers the colors as
Lieutenant Colonel Haig
takes command of the
division's Twenty-sixth
Infantry Battalion,
Vietnam, January 1967.
(*U.S. Army photo*)

The Haigs with their children (*left to right*) Barbara, Brian, and Alex, in August 1973. (*White House photo*)

Thirty-four dead Viet Cong were collected inside the perimeter.[28] We learned from the handful of prisoners we took and from searches of the enemy dead that we had been attacked by three enemy regiments, including all three battalions of the 271st Viet Cong Regiment, reinforced by the 70th NVA Guards Regiment and by another NVA regiment, so that we had been outnumbered by at least six to one. Total verified enemy losses at the Battle of Ap Gu were 609 killed and 5 captured; judging by the blood trails and other evidence, the actual toll was higher than that. The First Battalion of the Twenty-sixth Infantry, with fewer than four hundred soldiers present for duty, lost nine men killed and thirty-two wounded.[29]

While the battle of Ap Gu was in progress, the commanding officer of the Second Brigade of the First Infantry Division, Col. James A. Grimsley, was seriously wounded during a rocket and mortar attack on his headquarters and evacuated. I was named to replace him. I flew from the battlefield to take up my new command.

There would be no more battles like Ap Gu and no more grand operations like Junction City. The Second Brigade, regarded by many as the finest fighting force in the Army, was given responsibility, during the months remaining in my tour of duty, for the divisional pacification program, which involved clearing the Viet Cong from the villages and their environs and heartening, training, and equipping the inhabitants to defend themselves, with the help of ARVN troops, in case the guerrillas came back, as they often did, to execute village leaders or extort taxes or impress youths into their forces. This meant that the idealistic, much-wounded, uncommonly brave, and boundlessly enthusiastic Maj. Robert Schweitzer, whom the reader already knows, came under my command. Bobby Schweitzer was an inspirational figure, deeply involved in the lives of the villagers he was trying to protect and sincerely committed to the philosophy of pacification. Not only the Viet Cong stood in his way. The ARVN corps commander in War Zone C was not cut from the same bolt of cloth as Schweitzer. The general's field headquarters, located well back from the fighting, was richly furnished with every luxury, animate and inanimate. Visiting there one day we asked him why he had never attacked and cut the road to the Cambodian border regularly used by the enemy to infiltrate troops and supplies into the region. He took a long drag on a reeking French cigarette, held Hollywood villain–style between his thumb and forefinger, before replying with a wink and a smile. "One million dollars U.S.—yearly." We took it that this represented the annual value of the bribes he received from the drug smugglers who also used the road (and who were also undoubtedly part of the Viet Cong apparatus).

In spite of (or maybe because of) such obstacles, Schweitzer made pacification work as well as it possibly could work while a dozen North Vietnamese regular divisions and innumerable Viet Cong units, also by this time largely manned by North Vietnamese, were roaming the South Vietnamese countryside without serious opposition. Inevitably, the Viet Cong filtered back into War Zone C; the North Vietnamese increased their strength in the region; the headquarters and main-force units we had sought to find and destroy were moved across the border into "neutral" Cambodia, out of our reach, and from there planned and executed hostile operations that took many American lives.

Schweitzer knew that I had doubts about the value of the pacification effort. He had none, and openly planned to convert me by showing me results I did not believe could be achieved. "Al," he said with the ebullient enthusiasm that was the hallmark of his character, "I am going to make you happy."

Not long after that, Bobby Schweitzer walked up to the gates of a supposedly pacified village, carrying in his pocket copies of a new manual on pacification. A Viet Cong lurking inside threw a grenade at him. It wounded Bobby so badly that he was evacuated to the United States for treatment. He recovered, and eventually became a lieutenant general. This was far less reward than he deserved. Like so many other Americans who went to Vietnam out of a sense of duty and a belief in the cause of freedom, Schweitzer was a national treasure. But there was no hope by the time Bobby won his sixth Purple Heart for wounds suffered in the cause of winning the hearts and minds of the people of South Vietnam that the idealism and gallantry he personified could possibly make a difference.

III

NIXON'S WORLD

The greatest honor history can bestow is the title of peace-maker.

RICHARD M. NIXON,
first inaugural address

13

Homecoming

Reunited with my wife and children, promoted to full colonel, set free from the Pentagon, I was assigned once again to West Point, this time as commanding officer of the Third Regiment of the Corps of Cadets. With a strong sense of homecoming, we settled into handsome quarters overlooking the placid waters of Lusk Reservoir. No landscape or climate could have presented a greater contrast to the tropical green foliage, red soil, and glaring sun of Vietnam than the Hudson River valley as the oaks and maples and birches subtly changed color in the gentle sunshine of Indian summer.

Thanks to the news media, there was no escape from images of the war, or from the tantrumlike antiwar demonstrations that shook the cities and campuses, or from the self-satisfaction of those Americans who were living their lives as usual, indifferent to the sacrifices of our troops in Vietnam or to the fate of the Vietnamese people. As on my return from Korea sixteen years earlier, I found myself in an America that seemed divided between people who did not want to hear anything about the war and others who wanted only to have their misconceptions about it reinforced. This was a stern test of the returning soldier's self-control. Lately, I had watched brave young men bleed for their country in battle; now I was thrown into the company of other youngsters who would soon be doing the same. The cadets understood what lay ahead of them even if they could not yet imagine the all but incomprehensible reality. Scarcely a day went by at the Academy without a report that last year's first classmen as well as older West Pointers I had known in my previous tours of duty here had been killed or wounded in action. It seemed inevitable that most members of the four classes then in attendance would also go to war, and of course this turned out to be the case.

As commander of the Third Regiment during the 1967 to 1968 academic year, and the next year as deputy commandant of cadets under then Brig. Gen. Bernard W. Rogers, with whom I had served in Vietnam, I dealt every day with the questions and doubts in the minds of the cadets with regard to the war. I described its realities as I had observed them in the field and did my best to motivate the young men whom I counseled to fight the enemy, when their turn came to do so, according to the professional standards of the U.S. Army. In human terms, this was no simple undertaking, believing as I did, in my heart of hearts, that our policy and military strategy in Vietnam were deeply mistaken and were breeding incalculable consequences that would torment the nation for generations to come. What would be the effect of a bungled war on the Army of the future that would be led by these very cadets? Already the Army's honor, along with that of the other armed services, was being defamed and the sacrifices of its soldiers contemptuously demeaned. Students on civilian campuses were marching against the war; the cadets, many of whom doubted that the war was vital to the national interest, were marching away to fight in it.

Keeping up morale in such circumstances was an entirely new challenge for the Academy. Never before in living memory had Americans spat upon the uniforms of soldiers returning from the front or burned the flag as a gesture of sympathy for the enemy. Needless to say I regarded as misguided, or worse, those political hysterics in the antiwar movement who waved Viet Cong flags, shouted anti-American slogans, and openly wanted the other side to win. At the same time, I sensed that doubts about the wisdom of fighting this war as it was being fought ran deep and sincere all across the nation for reasons that were based on patriotism, common sense, and a pervasive suspicion that something had gone very wrong in Washington.

As much as any single institution can be, the United States Military Academy is a consciously contrived cross section of America in which all races, classes, and conditions except low intelligence, old age, and poor health (and, at the time of which I write, healthy intelligent young females) are represented. My duties as deputy commandant—in effect, dean of men—brought me into close contact with cadets from every background, and for that reason carried home to me the most troubling of the many anomalies attached to the war. I had observed in Vietnam that the war was largely being fought, as the Korean War had also been fought, by young people from the lower end of the socioeconomic scale. The sons of what was then just beginning to be called "the white upper-middle class" were effectively exempted from the dangers of combat by a draft system based on the unspoken assumption that their lives were somehow more valuable than those of other young Americans who were less well educated and less well-to-do. Those who could afford to go to college or otherwise exploit the system's loopholes to obtain deferments did not go into the Army; those who could not come up with the cash went in their places. Of the 29,701 men who were registered as undergraduates at Harvard University, the Massachusetts Institute of Technology, and Princeton University between 1962 and 1972, a total of 20 were killed in action or died of other causes in the Vietnam War. By contrast, South Boston, Massachusetts, High School lost twenty-five of approximately two thousand former students, or proportionately nineteen times as many as all three elite colleges, in the same period.*

Evasion of the draft was represented by some as a virtuous, even patriotic act of protest against an unjust war. No doubt this claim was sometimes sincere. Seldom mentioned, however, was its chief moral complication. Draft quotas did not change simply because a selectee refused or evaded service. Somebody else, nearly always a poorer and less educated man, was inducted in the evader's place, and many such involuntary substitutes were killed or wounded in action. The truth of the matter is that the war in Vietnam might never have been fought at all if the children of doctors, lawyers, college professors, business executives, government officials, and other members of the American elite had been subject to a fair and inescapable draft. Those influential parents would have done everything in their considerable power to deflect the Kennedy and Johnson administrations from a policy that threatened to squander the lives of their offspring. As it was, the war was fought, with few exceptions, by the sons of parents whose chief instrument of influence was the vote for President they could cast once every four years. In the

---

*I am indebted for these interesting statistics to former Secretary of the Navy James H. Webb, Jr., who served in combat in Vietnam as a Marine officer. The breakdown by university: Harvard, 12,595 undergraduates, with 12 killed in action; MIT, 8,998, with 2 killed; Princeton, 8,108, with 6 killed. A separate inquiry to Yale University revealed that of 47,691 male undergraduates registered from 1962 to 1973, 14 were killed in Vietnam.

long run, the worst consequence of the Vietnam War may turn out to be the animosity between social and economic classes generated by the appalling inequity of the draft and the hypocritical message this cynical double standard sent to both the privileged and the poor in a democracy whose most cherished principles are the equality of all persons before the law and the obligation of every citizen to do his duty to his country.

It was obvious to everyone in the United States that the future of the country turned on the outcome of the 1968 election. I observed it on television, read about it in the newspapers, and discussed it with my friends with a peculiar mixture of emotions. On the one hand, I knew that nothing could change unless the Democrats were defeated. On the other hand, although I was a Republican by conviction and inheritance, I was personally acquainted with many of the most prominent Democrats, including President Johnson. It is difficult to wish for the defeat of friends who have been good to you, no matter how wrong you believe them to be in their philosophy and actions.

For Lyndon Johnson in particular, I felt a strong bond of sympathy. There was something of the old soldier about him in his profane tempers, his lusty appetites, his pride of profession that had become first nature to him, his air of being far away from home among people who looked down on him even as they went through the motions of obeying him. In my ignorance of the real reason for his decision, I was disappointed when he announced that he would not seek reelection. On the basis of what I had seen of their eccentric relationship, I had expected him to replace Hubert Humphrey on the ticket with some other figure acceptable to the left wing of his party, and then fight out the issues toe-to-toe with Richard M. Nixon. The nation had never more sorely needed a scathing debate of its policies, and no two men have ever been better qualified by nature and party allegiance to conduct it. Johnson and Nixon, so different in their political philosophies, were much alike in background, political instinct, and in their peculiar fate of being maladroit outsiders who had achieved the pinnacles of success in a trade dominated by the clubbable.

The choice between Humphrey and Nixon, as opposed to the choice between parties and philosophies, did not arouse strong feelings in me one way or the other. Having seen Humphrey in action in those White House meetings, I thought that he would make a poor President. His liberal orthodoxy was distasteful to me. The way in which he damned President Johnson's Vietnam policy by faint praise, and later by outright desertion, raised the most serious question that can be raised about a candidate—that is, Will he defend his principles or desert them in the name of popularity? He was one of the more likable men in American politics, but likability, next to intellectualism, may be the most irrelevant quality a President can have.

As to Nixon, the impression of him that overwhelmed all others in my mind was the image of his face—the dark jowls, the guarded eyes, the sweat glistening on the upper lip—during his Checkers speech in 1952. Pat and I had watched him on the flickering eight-inch television set in our quarters at Fort Knox, and I, at least, had not been favorably impressed. I thought his performance maudlin, calculated, and insincere. Some of the incidents in his later political career, such as his "last press conference" after losing the California gubernatorial election to Pat Brown, reinforced this early impression. But on the basis of substance, I was convinced that he had won the debate over Kennedy in 1960. The contest of television images was another matter altogether. Once again, as in the Checkers speech, his appearance was a liability, especially in contrast to the telegenic Kennedy.

These were surface considerations. How a man sounds and looks, as the example of Abraham Lincoln illustrates, are not reliable guides to character and ability. After all was said and done, Nixon was a great politician; he had to be to overcome the disadvantages nature had imposed on him in the form of the physical demeanor and tone of voice that made me, and millions of others, so uneasy. He was also, as I knew from reading his books, articles, and speeches, a powerful and original thinker on foreign affairs and a writer possessed of a prose style that compares in its clearheaded lucidity with those of Benjamin Franklin and U. S. Grant. A computer programmed by the Department of Speech Communication at the University of Texas in Austin examined the writings and speeches of seven Presidents (Truman through Carter) for realism, complexity, variety, and familiarity of language. Nixon surpassed all the others in the three categories associated with clarity of expression. According to the study, "No president even approached the amount of Realism to be found in Nixon's speeches. . . . His Familiarity score was the highest of the seven chief executives . . . his language was also the least Embellished; he did not mince his words but called things as they were. . . . It was the political implications of this style that caused Nixon to be pilloried by the press throughout his career and vilified by every college professor worth his AAUP card."[1]

That brings us to what I regarded as the greatest argument in Nixon's favor: He had the right enemies. The Left had hated, slandered, and ridiculed him ever since, as a freshman congressman in 1948, he led the investigation that resulted in the conviction of Alger Hiss on a charge of perjury. Probably no one in American history has done his nation so much good and himself so much political harm by a single official action. On Hiss's conviction, Herbert Hoover telegrammed somewhat hyperbolically to Nixon, "At last the stream of treason that has existed in our government has been exposed in a fashion that all may believe."[2] However, many could not bring themselves to believe it and were determined that others should not believe it, either. Alger Hiss, the ideal product of the Ivy League, had been the very model of the liberal man of conscience. The Left, with its fundamental disdain for the intelligence and good judgment of the people, could not bring itself to trust Americans to come to the conclusion that not everyone who resembled Hiss politically was also a traitor. The shock of Hiss's treason was all the more unbearable to the liberal intelligentsia because it had been detected and unmasked by a man from Whittier College, Duke University Law School, and a family grocery store in rural California—that is to say, from nowhere.

In regard to the Hiss case, parallels to Greek drama are irrelevant; this act of giant killing could only have happened in America. But it sealed Nixon's fate; the Left would not rest until the man who had discredited Hiss was himself discredited. Attacks on Nixon's character began at once and culminated a quarter of a century later in his resignation of the presidency. No doubt the onslaught will continue long after he is dead. Undaunted, he went on after the Hiss case to win a Senate race in California against a liberal heroine, Congresswoman Helen Gahagan Douglas. Mrs. Douglas, who coined the nickname "Tricky Dick," suggested in her campaign that Nixon was both a fascist and a pro-Communist, and then ascribed her defeat to her opponent's ruthless smear tactics.[3] Her campaign became the model for subsequent anti-Nixon campaigns.

In 1968, I did not think that Humphrey could end the war in Vietnam on honorable terms. It seemed to me that Nixon could do so, and might even win it outright, if he seized the first opportunity presented to him to bring the war home to Hanoi and to warn the Soviet Union to stay out of the situation or deal with the consequences. I thought that he would do just that as a matter of character and conviction, and so I voted for him, thinking that casting my ballot in his favor would be my closest connection to his presidency.

When Nixon won his slim victory over Humphrey and the formidable third-party candidate, Governor George Wallace of Alabama, my tour at

West Point was past the midway point. I was already thinking in terms of another command, probably in Vietnam; certainly I had no intention of going back to the Pentagon. Then, just before Christmas, I was ordered through channels to report to the Hotel Pierre in New York to be interviewed for the post of military assistant to Professor Henry A. Kissinger of Harvard University, whom the President-elect had appointed as his Assistant for National Security Affairs. I knew that my name was far down on the list of candidates drawn up by the Army, and, while obviously I was prepared to report as ordered, I thought it about as likely that he would hire me as that I would be named chairman of the Joint Chiefs of Staff.

I had never met Henry Kissinger, but I had read most of his books and had attended several of his lectures, in which the brilliance of the speaker's ideas combined with his relentlessly ponderous delivery produced the puzzling impression that the subject matter was intensely interesting and oppressively boring at the same time. I mentioned this recollection of Kissinger's speaking style to a former colleague in the Army Plans and Policy Division, Dr. Fritz Kraemer, whom I knew to be a friend of his. He forcefully assured me that Kissinger possessed one of the most brilliant minds he had ever encountered. Kraemer, a German-born intellectual who sometimes enlivened his own lectures by whipping a stiletto from his coat sleeve and waving it about to underscore important points, had served in World War II with Kissinger in the G-2 (intelligence) section of the Eighty-fourth Infantry Division. "Even at age nineteen when he knew absolutely nothing," Kraemer said, "Henry understood everything."

At my first meeting with Kissinger, the many-sided public figure he was later to become—diplomatist, social lion, companion and philosopher to the mighty—had not yet been created by the news media's enthusiastic accounts of his truly remarkable accomplishments. Only the owlish, rumpled Harvard professor was present. This elemental Kissinger was noticeably plump, impressively learned, transparently ill at ease with a stranger—and very funny. Wisecracks and satirical bons mots, directed mostly at himself, tumbled from his lips. This stream of self-deprecating humor came as a happy surprise. After a moment or two, I realized that his jokes had a purpose. It made Kissinger, who was supremely confident in regard to his intellect but painfully shy and unsure of himself in social situations, instantaneously likable. My own insecurity was such that the jovial atmosphere made me think, at first, that my suspicion that I was not a serious candidate was correct. I was only listed at all, as I later discovered, because Fritz Kraemer, Joe Califano, and Robert McNamara had all recommended me to Kissinger outside of military channels. The fact that Kraemer was a fervent conservative, while Califano and McNamara were equally impassioned liberals, struck a chord in Kissinger, who, as he explained almost at once, was bent on introducing all tendencies of opinion and advice into the new President's councils. He said cheerfully that this would probably involve hiring people who disagreed with Nixon or even detested him; nearly all academics, he said, despised the President-elect as a matter of political orthodoxy.

The Pierre is a grand hotel of the old luxurious style that was already well past its best days in 1968. The small room in which Kissinger received me was crowded with reproductions of French furniture, overheated, underlighted, and more than a little shabby. After the pleasantries ran their course, Kissinger asked me his first serious question: "Are you a military intellectual?" I replied that I had never considered myself an intellectual of any kind. Well, then, what *was* I? I said that I was a career Army officer, a combat commander by intention, training, and instinct who had often been deflected into staff jobs against my wishes. It was clear that this was the answer for which he was hoping. As he wrote later, he was looking for "a more rough-cut type, someone with combat experience and therefore familiar with the practical complexities of operational planning."[4] Of course, Kissinger knew all about my background, including my recent tour of duty in Southeast Asia and the preceding stint in the Pentagon. He asked me what I thought about Vietnam. I answered by telling him many of the same things I have told the reader about my experience and opinions on this subject. Kissinger listened intently, then joined in, and the interview became an extended and warmly outspoken exchange of views about foreign policy, strategy, and the nature and intentions of America's friends and enemies. We seemed to agree on nearly everything.

When we finally ran out of breath (there seemed to be no time limit), Kissinger described the duties of his military assistant. The picture he painted seemed to me, on the basis of my previous experience in Washington, to be somewhat rosier than the reality was likely to sustain. His military assistant, he said, would monitor the many streams of foreign intelligence flowing into the White House from the CIA, NSA, the Defense Intelligence Agency (DIA), and other organisms, sort out the wheat from the chaff, and brief the President first thing every morning on the state of the world. He would also advise Kissinger on questions involving military considerations, consult with other NSC staffers, and help to produce policy memoranda and other papers on foreign affairs to be placed before the President for his decision. Kissinger made it plain that Nixon had decided to restore the NSC, which had fallen into disuse under Kennedy and into disrepute under Johnson because the latter suspected it of being the source of leaks, to its former status under Eisenhower as the President's chief instrument of foreign policy. Nixon did not trust the State Department; he was going to be his own Secretary of State, running foreign policy out of the White House.

What did I think of the job Kissinger had described? I replied that it seemed, to put it mildly, the sort of position about which you dreamed. Even after our friendly conversation, I had no idea that I was in the running for it, and I did not really want it. Kissinger nodded, beamed, shook my hand, and told me to report for duty immediately.

14

Nixon and Kissinger

Whatever his true feelings about Hubert Humphrey may have been, Lyndon Johnson came close to winning the presidency for the Democratic candidate in 1968 when, five days before the election, he announced the cessation of all air, naval, and artillery bombardment of North Vietnam. In a television speech on October 31, Johnson said that he had been informed by American negotiators in Paris that a breakthrough had occurred in talks with the North Vietnamese, who had accepted that the South Vietnamese government, previously excluded from the peace talks on the insistence of Hanoi, could now take part. The President said he believed that this development, coupled to the halt in the bombing, "can lead to progress toward a peaceful settlement of the Vietnamese war."[1]

Nixon regarded Johnson's dramatic gesture at the eleventh hour as the one action the incumbent President could have taken to influence the outcome of the election in a decisive way.[2] As the results showed (Nixon won by seven-tenths of 1 percent of the popular vote), it came within a whisker of succeeding, although it became apparent even before the election that Johnson had been wrong in his expectations. On November 2, President Thieu announced that South Vietnam would not participate in the talks, and the North Vietnamese, as usual, took advantage of the pause in the air war to infiltrate more men and supplies into the South.

Believing that "Johnson would not have gone out of his way to help

Humphrey" in the campaign in the absence of a larger objective,[3] Nixon suspected that his predecessor had been misled by his own people into playing politics with the war. It was his belief, based in part on confidential information supplied by Henry Kissinger, who had "entrée into the administration's foreign policy inner circles," that the supposed breakthrough was contrived, in the absence of sufficiently clear assurances from Hanoi, by some of Johnson's people in an effort to salvage the election for Humphrey.[4]

Nixon's suspicions, of course, had serious implications with regard to the future of the peace effort, quite apart from whatever they might mean in connection with the Democrats' campaign tactics. He set out to test his theory as one of the first orders of business of his new administration. This was no easy task. The White House files were virtually empty, the Johnson staff having packed up and carried away nearly every scrap of paper generated by the outgoing administration. No complete file of the understanding reached in Paris could be found. The State Department, never regarded by the new President as a gathering place for loyal Republicans, also professed itself to be without conclusive documentation with regard to the episode in question. In terms of normal State Department archival procedures designed to preserve, with regard to every negotiation with a foreign government, every briefing paper, every memorandum, every copy of talking points, every summary of conversation, every dispatch and cable, this omission struck the President as incredible. Fortunately, the absence of evidence was not total. Some tantalizing telegrams were discovered, and, at a meeting of the National Security Council on January 25, Nixon used these documents as the starting point of an interrogation of Philip Habib, a high-ranking Foreign Service officer who had been familiar with the negotiations.

It is nerve-racking to be cross-examined by the President of the United States before a roomful of Cabinet officers and other lofty figures of the government. Since the interrogator was Richard Nixon, whose prosecutorial skills are the stuff of legend, the experience must have been even more agonizing. Although Nixon was in no way abusive, Habib clearly wished that he was somewhere else as the new President peppered him with questions. Habib, the only person in the room who was on his feet, stood at the end of the long conference table during the cross-examination. Speaking without notes, but with great fluency, he loaded his narrative with anecdote and diverting detail. Did the other side agree to halt infiltration of troops and supplies and rocket attacks on South Vietnamese cities in return for the bombing halt? Well, in a manner of speaking, yes—they had not actually said no to American demands that they do so; therefore, it was considered that they had offered "silent assent."

By means of such responses, afterward jocularly known around the NSC staff as "the dance of the seven veils on the head of a pin," Habib managed to arouse Nixon's curiosity about the incident to fever pitch without satisfying it in any way. Nixon's line of questioning made this possible, because the President gave the misleading impression that he was interested in the answers, and in the atmospherics, for policy reasons. In reality, he was interested in finding evidence that the Paris delegation had misled President Johnson on the details of the agreement for political reasons. One could hardly fault Habib for not answering questions he was not asked. His performance was the most agile by a natural-born bureaucrat that I had witnessed up to that point, and only Habib, with whom I had many subsequent dealings in my capacity as a member of the White House staff and as Secretary of State, ever equaled it afterward. It is no wonder he was one of the most loved and admired figures in the annals of the Foreign Service.

For years afterward, Nixon chased the elusive truth of the matter. ("We've got to get those cables and memcoms. They exist, but where are they? We know there were backchannels.") But owing to this absence of documentation and to the impenetrable discretion of those involved, he never caught up to it. Observing Nixon in his encounter with Habib made a great impression on me, partly because I had never before seen the President in action, but mostly because he was so different in real life from his media image. The image suggested that his intellectual equipment consisted of a combination of political cunning and an instinct for the jugular. In fact, he was brilliantly intelligent. No one could observe him in his element without realizing that he possessed a powerful mind quick to grasp facts and understand their nuances. Moreover, he was equipped with a memory that was remarkable not only for the huge amount of data it contained but for the astonishing speed and accuracy with which Nixon was able to retrieve the facts he wanted. Each fact seemed to be pertinent to some aspect of the presidency. He was wise in the ways of government, knew everyone on Capitol Hill and all their proclivities, and understood the uses, biases, and limits of the bureaucracy. He knew nearly every important foreign leader on a personal basis and had memorized all the pertinent biographical facts about those whom he had not yet encountered in the flesh. He was a living data bank regarding the history, culture, economy, aspirations, secret agenda, and current news and gossip about every important country in the world. In this first meeting, as in all subsequent ones until his concentration was overwhelmed by the agonies of Watergate, he was the best-informed, best-prepared, most articulate, and least predictable person present. It was clear from the earliest moment that this was a man who did not respond to the system, but dominated it.

However, there was another and ultimately more telling aspect of Nixon, and it, too, surfaced in this first encounter. He was shy. You could see it in his eyes and body language and hear it in the tone of his voice. As we shall see, he had an almost pathological distaste for confrontation. Others, both associates and enemies, took advantage of this unfortunate and apparently incurable characteristic throughout his presidency, and, in my opinion, it was the chief reason for his downfall. None of this, of course, was obvious to me at the early stage of which I am speaking. But I went away from the interrogation of Habib somewhat bothered by the feeling that Nixon had let him off the hook. I wondered why. Another President, Johnson being the most picturesque example, would have bullied, threatened, badgered, and, if necessary, humiliated the man until he had the answers that he wanted. Nixon stopped short of that outcome when Habib became visibly agitated; at that point, Nixon himself was rendered ill at ease, as if by infection, and he dropped the subject. It was clear that he could not bring himself to require Habib to fulfill the most elemental duty a diplomat owes to his President, namely to report to him the whole truth as far as he knows it. For all I know, Habib did tell Nixon everything he knew that day; the point is, Nixon stopped short of asking him whether he had done so. This was a puzzling failure; but needless to say I had not yet even begun to understand that it arose from a fatal flaw.

I had never met Nixon before going to work for him, and in those early days in the White House I saw little of him. It did not take long to discover that Kissinger, notwithstanding his rosy description of my duties when we met at the Pierre Hotel, was not going to permit an unknown Army colonel to brief the President when he was in a position to perform this intimate task himself. In terms of palace politics, access to the monarch is power, and no one understood such matters better than Kissinger. Accordingly, I prepared the daily intelligence briefing, arriving in my office in the Executive Office Building at 6 A.M. to sift through the snowdrift of secret dispatches and estimates that had blown in during the night and add them to the three-page summary I had drafted the night before. Kissinger himself presented the finished product to Nixon, standing by while he read to provide whatever additional information the President requested. Interpretation of the facts was rarely necessary.

Deciding what secret material this polymath in the Oval Office should read to begin his day was a daunting task. My first assignment from Kissinger had been to draw up a plan for keeping the President informed of what the intelligence was producing without overwhelming him with trivia, gossip, and ephemera. Kissinger was enthusiastic about the paper I produced and gave it to Nixon, who also liked it and ordered us to put it into effect.

This is not to suggest that Kissinger liked everything I did. He was, at first, highly critical of my writing, denouncing it as turgid, bureaucratic, and overloaded with Pentagonese. (As for myself, I was not a wholehearted admirer of Kissinger's own style, which in my opinion sacrificed clarity of expression for mannerisms designed to draw the attention of the reader to the cleverness of the author; but I was not correcting his papers.) Each morning, Kissinger would read what I had so painfully produced (the task of compressing such intrinsically ambiguous material as intelligence reports into a useful briefing document was not easy); then he would slash it, rewrite it, and redictate it in my presence, crying out as he went along against what he deemed to be grammatical errors and solecisms.

This was not the first time I had been subjected to such criticisms (nor would it be the last), and I was able to bear them with fortitude while striving to do better. I knew that his behavior had as much to do with establishing his authority in his lofty new position as with improving my prose style. Working for Joe Califano, in whose opinion nothing was trivial, no draft was ever quite right the first, second, or third time it was submitted, and no thought was so gemlike that it could not be recut and repolished, was good preparation for employment by Kissinger. The two men were alike in other ways. Both were perfectionists, both were highly intelligent in a narrow intellectual corridor, and both focused on the task at hand to the exclusion of almost everything else. On matters such as hours of work and family considerations short of outright tragedy, both were almost wholly insensitive to the needs of others. Both were given to sudden, and in Kissinger's case quite amusing, fits of temper. Both came from self-consciously elite milieux—Califano from a famous law firm, Kissinger from the Harvard faculty—whose initiates regarded the quaint, slow-footed folkways of the permanent government establishment with a mixture of disdain and exasperation. I liked and admired them both tremendously.

Gradually, Kissinger and I developed a close rapport, based as all such relationships must be on frank talk and a meeting of the minds. Achieving a perfect state of candor with my new superior was no simple matter. We sometimes had sharp differences of opinion that neither of us was content to leave unexpressed. We had only recently met. We came from entirely different personal and professional backgrounds. Although I may have impressed him as a good-enough example of my type, he certainly did not consider me (or anyone else) his intellectual equal. This disparity did not apply across the board. He appreciated my bureaucratic experience and considered that I could be helpful in the inevitable infighting with State, Defense, and other agencies involved in foreign policy.

Beyond that, Kissinger was sure of his intellectual gifts to the point of arrogance, but, as I have already suggested, he was less sure of himself in other ways. He was especially uncomfortable, at this stage of his life, in unfamiliar social situations. He was, so to speak, still in tweeds while all around him were dressed in pinstripes. Although Nixon did not like the idea (most Georgetown socialites who seek out the transient celebrities of successive administrations are liberal Democrats), Kissinger felt obliged to accept the invitations sent to him by the President's old antagonists. But which ones? Essentially European and bourgeois in his sense of rank and its relationship to wealth and family background, he was on unfamiliar ground in Washington. Eventually, of course, he became adept in these arcane matters, and the titillating indiscretions of his table talk, together with his mordant wit, made him welcome in nearly all the great houses in town even after he left the government.

Kissinger was unusually sensitive to criticism and too easily hurt by it. A scrap of gossip in which he was unfairly demeaned or a casual snub by a stranger could cost him hours, and sometimes days, of brooding and resentment. The usual obverse of this devalued psychological coin is a fondness for flattery, and more enthusiastically than most he welcomed praise and reassurance. It follows from this that he was sensitive to the news media. This attitude was, and is, in no way unusual in Washington. In Kissinger, it was so transparent that it could even have been called endearing. There are dangers in this all-too-human reaction to the published word. Kissinger came from an honorable family and he was the beneficiary of an old-fashioned old-world upbringing. He was outraged by duplicity and moral cowardice in others and was himself incapable of telling a spontaneous lie. When he was obliged to prevaricate for reasons of state, the results were usually either comical or disastrous, because

mendacity was so unnatural to him that he couldn't bring up the reinforcements—that is to say, invent more lies—fast enough to wriggle out
of the situation.

Although he was by no means a neophyte—he had been in the public
eye in a minor way for years—Kissinger did not know the Washington
press corps, a strange and mysterious guild of moody misanthropes. Its
members are, above all, a solemn lot. Because Kissinger's sense of humor
was so active, I feared that he might entrap himself with witticisms.
Because he admired intelligence in others, I was apprehensive that he
would be attracted to the brightest members of the news media, who are
usually the most dangerous. Kissinger, who knew as well as I did that the
media were capable of turning on their benefactors and eating them alive,
may have sensed my anxiety. In any case, he asked my advice quite early
about the way in which he should conduct himself with journalists. I
smile even now as I remember my answer. My grave counsel to Henry
Kissinger was to avoid reporters altogether except in news conferences
and other open encounters. I remember my exact words: "The best thing
you can do is stay away from the press altogether. If you want to be
effective, be a faceless servant of the presidency. Let the results of your
work speak for you."

As the world knows, Kissinger did not heed my advice. As he became
ever more deeply involved with journalists, I found myself drawn into
the process, usually in the capacity of fireman. His wit, as I had feared,
was sometimes mistaken for mendacity. When he tripped over this weakness, he needed help: "Al, Joe Kraft is not speaking to me! He says I lied
to him about ————. Please call him up and straighten this out!" I would
dial the famous columnist's number; Kraft would register his outrage,
usually at length. The basis of the misunderstanding would emerge. I
would say, "Joe, that's not what Henry meant," and then I would do my
best to explain what Henry *had* meant.

When, later in my career, I was required to deal with the press as a
matter of duty, I did my best to stick scrupulously to the facts. At the
same time, the necessity of safeguarding confidences was never far from
my mind. "Haigspeak," a discursive form of expression of which I was
publicly accused by reporters during that period (no one has ever charged
me with not coming to the point in private), was a way of putting my
friends from the media on hold while I went through a mental card file
in search of some scrap of the truth that it was safe and proper to tell
them.

*   *   *

At first, Kissinger traveled a good deal with his deputy, Lawrence S. Eagleburger, interviewing candidates for the NSC staff. True to his stated intention, Kissinger brought aboard a number of people who would not ordinarily have associated themselves with a Republican administration, let alone with a government headed by Nixon. Many came because they thought that Kissinger was, in his political soul, one of them; if this was ever true, they soon learned that it was true no longer and that Kissinger was a wholehearted believer in the President's foreign policy. Most of the people Kissinger hired were bright, competent, and honest; others held views that were antithetical to the President's; still others had hated Nixon as an expression of political virtue for the greater part of their adult lives.

Some of the professors Kissinger hired were his seniors in terms of academic tenure and reputation, and it is fair to say (they tended to be outspoken about Kissinger in his absence) that most of them, whatever their rank in academia, felt that they surpassed him in terms of knowledge, scholarly distinction, and sheer brainpower. Some clearly believed that their superior brilliance would be noticed by the President if only they could get closer to him, and that he would then come to rely more upon their advice than on that of their friend Henry. They were given plush offices across the street in the Executive Office Building.

Kissinger occupied the only office space allotted to the NSC staff in the White House proper, a suite of cells and cubbyholes adjoining the Situation Room, plus one good-sized office whose small barred windows looked up and out on a parade of disembodied shoes and stockings hurrying by along a sidewalk. Larry Eagleburger occupied the most spacious cubbyhole, adjoining Kissinger's office. In that subterranean place, inaccessible to most of the rest of the staff, everything important happened and all interesting papers were kept in safes. Some NSC staffers may have imagined that these arrangements were Kissinger's way of isolating them from the heart of power, but the fact of the matter was, and is, that mere Assistants for National Security Affairs have no control over such supremely important matters as the assignment of office space. That is the purview of the White House Chief of Staff and a vigilant bureaucracy that decides who sits where.

Kissinger was, in fact, the dominant intellectual on the staff. He was, however, less at home as an administrator, and the weakness of the unstructured apparatus he had created, in which most members of the staff were left like dons to their own devices and eccentricities, became apparent less than a month into the administration, when Nixon was preparing to visit Europe to pay his respects to President Charles de Gaulle of France and our NATO allies. The briefing papers requested from the State Department and the NSC staff were late, lengthy, and in some cases pompously condescending to the President. When I say *late*, I mean that the last of them came in two hours before the departure for Paris. Kissinger threw the whole jumble onto the floor, where Eagleburger and I crawled about, reading, discarding, and cutting and pasting like the Marx Brothers with the camera speeded up, in order to have something to put into Nixon's hands once he was airborne.

Kissinger's mood was stormy. Pacing the floor among the scattered documents, he pronounced the nautical homily to which he often resorted in such situations: "When the ship sails onto the rocks, the captain is relieved!" His tone left no doubt that Eagleburger and I were the cocaptains; Henry was the admiral. We steered the vessel safely into port. Much of the recobbled briefing book we produced was typed aboard *Air Force One* by those infinitely efficient, infinitely patient White House secretaries without whom the United States government would grind to a halt.

Through all of this, Kissinger had understandably been venting his feelings about prima donnas, and as he left, tousled and flushed, with bulging briefcase in hand and Eagleburger by his side, he instructed me to bring order out of chaos: "Al, I never want to go through this again! Reorganize this place while I'm gone and have it running right by the time I get back!" That gave me eight days to bring order to Henry's universe. All I could do was try. I had already seen enough of my colleagues to guess how cordially they were going to respond to a mere colonel with a lowly master's degree when he began telling them how to run their professional lives. Somehow, however, the thing got done. I drafted a plan to reorganize the staff along geographical and functional lines, instituted channels for reporting, guidelines for the length and content of reports, a system of deadlines, and other bothersome but indispensable mechanisms and structures.

Kissinger approved the scheme without significant changes and told me to move into the basement cubbyhole adjacent to the Situation Room. This space, resembling the inside of a diving bell (without the portholes) and providing about the same level of ventilation, was just large enough to hold a desk and chair, and I left my roomy office in the EOB with mixed feelings. Despite a certain amount of muttering about the military mind and the ways of martinets, the new system worked. Because I was still Kissinger's military assistant in addition to being the administrator of the reorganization and an involuntary man of all work, this required spending fourteen to sixteen hours at the office, seven days a week.*

Sometimes, when deadline pressure was acute, days could be longer. Often they seemed so even when they were not. Kissinger was the hardest worker I had encountered up to that time. His powers of concentration were truly amazing. On one occasion, after many hours of uninterrupted work, Kissinger asked Eagleburger to get him a certain document. Larry stood up, turned deathly pale, swayed, and then crashed to the floor unconscious. Kissinger stepped over his prostrate body and shouted, "Where is the paper?" Fearing that Eagleburger had suffered a heart attack or a stroke, I called the White House medical services, who soon arrived with their emergency gear and revived him. On further examination, it turned out that nothing serious was the matter. The eventual diagnosis was exhaustion, and soon after that Eagleburger moved on to a more tranquil job. Nixon, who always took an anxious interest in the health problems and other personal difficulties of those who worked for him, made sure that Eagleburger got the job he wanted and then wrote a letter to his young son, telling him what a fine man his father was. It should be noted that Kissinger, once his concentration was broken and he realized that his friend and alter ego was lying on the floor because he was in distress, was more concerned and solicitous than anyone else.

I deputized when both Kissinger and Eagleburger were gone, reading through the huge stacks of paper that came across Kissinger's desk, taking whatever routine action seemed necessary, and consulting him by secure telephone before acting on larger matters or deferring them until his return if time permitted. I became expert in reproducing Kissinger's initials as a means of returning all but the most important of the documents to the senders with appropriate comments appended. If he ever suspected that forgery was the reason why he found a tidy desk instead of a mountain

---

*Among other assignments, I was delegated by Nixon and Kissinger to act as liaison with a Texas billionaire named Ross Perot, who was interested in our prisoners of war and Americans listed as missing in action in Southeast Asia. Perot, a graduate of Annapolis who had made a fortune in electronics, was possessed of one of the most fertile minds I have ever encountered, and the two of us spent much time on the telephone sorting out the many initiatives that he conceived. Some of his ideas were unworkable for policy reasons or because they conflicted with other programs already in motion, but nothing he suggested was uninteresting. With enthusiastic White House support, he formed an effective advocacy group called United We Stand. He and I worked together, for example, in organizing his trip to Southeast Asia at Christmas 1969, when he and other volunteers attempted to deliver two planeloads of gifts, including fourteen hundred canned Christmas dinners, to U.S. POWs. This mission of mercy got as far as Bangkok, but the North Vietnamese refused permission to land in Hanoi. Among many other activities, Perot also sponsored a trip to Paris for 152 wives and children of POWs. The North Vietnamese delegation to the Paris peace talks refused to receive them.

of memorandums on his return from his labors overseas, he condoned the offense by never mentioning it.

As Kissinger's man in charge of staff assignment and morale, I spent a good deal of my time counseling or fending off unhappy souls who felt that they had not received their due. They had come to the White House in the expectation that they would know things that would advance their knowledge of foreign policy and impress their friends, and in most cases they knew only what they needed to know in order to do their jobs. One man used to linger in front of my desk in my tiny office for long periods, making small talk or delivering petty complaints. It was difficult to interrupt him because I could never catch his eye. I wondered why he was wasting our time until I read some material from my files in a newspaper article and realized that he had developed an ability to read upside down and was scanning the documents on my desk preparatory to dropping juicy excerpts into his luncheon conversation with a journalist.

Sometimes, late at night, I would hear my name spoken in a familiar hearty baritone and would then look up and see Nixon standing in the doorway. No matter how late the hour, he was always well groomed, always dressed in one of his neat ready-made suits with snowy white shirt and sober tie; at his most casual, he substituted a cardigan for the suit jacket. He would ask me a question in his plainspoken, clearheaded fashion, listen intently while I answered, nod, thank me, and disappear back upstairs. Sometimes he would give me a brief order before departing. Although he always addressed me formally, by my military rank, he was always perfectly cordial in demeanor and confiding in tone, as if speaking to someone he had known for years. But there was never any small talk apart from an occasional "How's Pat? And the kids?" (Nixon never said *your wife*; he called her by name.) There was something touching in his formality, his stiffness. I had the impression that he kept our conversations short not because he didn't want to waste his time but because he didn't want to waste mine. The less said, the sooner I could clear my desk and go home to the late supper Pat was waiting to share with me.

Nixon, like Eisenhower, proposed to make decisions relating to foreign affairs on the basis of "options," or differing and sometimes conflicting recommendations supported by the arguments in their favor. This way of doing things reflected his desire to be his own Secretary of State; he appointed William P. Rogers, who had no diplomatic experience whatever, to head a State Department that was systematically isolated from the policy-making process. Not surprisingly, this led to an atmosphere of rivalry between Kissinger and Rogers, and also between Kissinger and Melvin R. Laird, the Secretary of Defense. The rivalry descended into bitter personal feelings with which Nixon, in his abhorrence of confrontation, was unable to deal. He was seldom able to talk to Rogers at all, even though he was one of Nixon's earliest advisers and assistants and among his most trusted friends.

As the administration wore on, I became the messenger between Nixon and Rogers, a function whose acute discomforts I will describe later on in this narrative. Very early on, I was called upon to take notes of conversations between Nixon and visiting heads of state because both Kissinger and Rogers wanted the job and the President could not decide between them. In typical fashion, he solved this vexing personnel dilemma by not addressing it directly: "Al, they can't both do it. You do it. Just explain matters to both of them." I tried, but when Kissinger wanted to take notes of a particularly interesting session, he found a way to do so. Subsequently, the note-taker's job was offered to Brig. Gen. Vernon ("Dick") Walters, a polyglot with a photographic memory who had been Nixon's interpreter on some of his vice presidential travels. Walters, then stationed in Paris as military attaché, turned the job down. His refusal was accepted because he was performing extraordinary duty as secret liaison to the North Vietnamese delegation to the peace talks.

Nixon was a masterly host in dealing with foreign leaders, informed but attentive, tactful yet firm. He invariably understood his visitor's problems; if he could do anything to help, he did it. With no exceptions that I know about, the kings, presidents, and prime ministers came, made their case, listened, and went away impressed with the man and encouraged about United States leadership of the free world. He was, however, often ill at ease with females who held top positions in their own countries. Indira Gandhi made him uncomfortable with her intellectual arrogance and transparent anti-Americanism. Imelda Marcos, whose approach combined clouds of perfume with startling claims on the patience and generosity of the United States, filled him with apprehension. "Don't leave me alone with that woman!" he would say, wagging a finger, before she was ushered in.

The concentration of foreign policy in the White House represented a conscious effort on Nixon's part to avoid the groupthink of the Kennedy administration and the consensus of the Johnson administration that had led the country, among other costly mistakes, into the impasse of Vietnam. It should be said at the outset that the impression created in the news media that Nixon was the subordinate partner in his relationship with Kissinger is entirely mistaken. Nixon was a strategic thinker of historic dimensions; Kissinger's brilliant gifts as a diplomatic tactician carried Nixon's ideas forward to success. But most of the ideas were Nixon's, and, as the reader will discover, he was sometimes alone even in the White House in his confidence in them. In at least one case, the opening to China, and arguably in several others, his ideas changed the world.

The first test of Nixon's decision-making system in a crisis came on April 15, 1969, after North Korean MIGs shot down a U.S. Navy EC-121 intelligence-gathering aircraft with thirty-one men aboard in international airspace off the North Korean coast. The action came as a shock because similar reconnaissance flights along this coast, using similar aircraft, had been routine for about twenty years. Nixon regarded the incident as a test of his resolve, and his first reaction was that "force must be met with force."[5] In practical terms, this meant retaliating by bombing a North Korean installation, probably a military airfield, and moving naval forces closer to Korea. Kissinger began by supporting this view. However, at an NSC meeting soon after the crisis broke, Secretary of State Rogers and Secretary of Defense Laird counseled extreme caution, arguing that the shoot-down might turn out to be an isolated incident, another proof, like the capture of the USS *Pueblo* fifteen months before, of the essential recklessness and uncontrollability of the North Koreans. Both Rogers and Laird, and especially Laird, were finely attuned to the probable domestic political effects of what they apparently regarded as presidential overreaction. Any American attack on North Korea, they warned, would almost certainly result in politically inconvenient street demonstrations by the antiwar movement in the United States. The danger, not very great but still worth thinking about, that such an attack might provoke an invasion of South Korea from the North was also mentioned. Faced with this split among his advisers, Nixon agreed to stay his hand until all the discoverable facts were known (as they probably never could be), and—this is significant—ordered Laird to move elements of the Seventh Fleet into Korean waters. He also asked for options from the NSC staff on a crash basis. Kissinger immediately set up two teams to produce them. One was structured to provide a hard option with supporting rationale; the other, a soft option.

The reader will not be surprised to learn that I had not concealed my strong opinion that this was a matchless opportunity for the United States government under a new President not only to solve the North Korean problem once and for all but to place relations with North Vietnam and the U.S.S.R. on a more realistic footing through a forceful show of resolve. Kissinger assigned me to the hard-option team, which included one of Kissinger's recruits from the ranks of the liberal Democrats, Morton Halperin, a think-tank intellectual. Intelligence analyses to the contrary notwithstanding (the CIA pointed out that April 14 was Kim Il-sung's birthday, and the destruction of the plane with the loss of thirty-one American lives might have been intended as a birthday present to the North Korean dictator), it seemed to me unlikely that the attack on the EC-121 had been an isolated incident.

It was, just as Nixon perceived it to be, a test of the new President's will and resolve, and if he met it forcefully, as his experience and intuition were telling him to do, I was sure that the other side would back off and the way to an honorable peace in Vietnam would be made easier. If he responded weakly or not at all, the war would escalate, the enemy would be more recalcitrant at the bargaining table, and, beyond that, other tests of his character would come in rapid succession, as had happened when President Kennedy faltered in his early opportunities to put the nation's strength at the service of the nation's interests.

The question was how to make these points to Nixon in such a way that he would be persuaded to do what he wanted to do. One of the best ways to capture a President's attention is to present him with the draft of a speech. Our team set out to do just that, in addition to presenting him with the raw option we had been asked to produce. In Nixon's case, different from that of every other President I have served, there was no question of writing a speech that he would simply approve and deliver. Although he paid attention to drafts and suggestions from his staff, he wrote his own speeches. One of my most vivid memories of him is the way in which he would slide down in a chair onto his spine, put his feet up on an ottoman, and write on a lined yellow legal tablet braced against his legs, crossing out, inserting, rephrasing, and revising until he had what he wanted. He took the English language, as he took most things, very seriously.

We knew that the NSC meeting had been theater. Nixon's unvarying practice in situations of this kind was to listen to the discussion in the meeting, read the options, collude with Kissinger, and then keep his decision to himself until he was ready to announce it, usually not confiding his intentions even to Kissinger. In this case, State and Defense were opposed to strong action, but if the President ordered such action to be taken, they would carry out his instructions. That, at least, was what we on the NSC staff assumed at the time, before we learned better.

The real issue was, Were we, at the inception of the Nixon administration, going to draw the line on the Soviet Union and its proxies or let them carry out brutal and illegal actions that were costing the lives of young Americans and trampling on the honor of the United States? There was no question that the President saw the matter in precisely these terms. As Nixon said over and over at the time, and subsequently wrote in an axiomatic passage in his memoirs, ". . . experience bolstered my instinctive belief that the only way to deal with Communists is to stand up to them. Otherwise, they will exploit your politeness as weakness. They will try to make you afraid and then take advantage of your fears."[6]

The President's convictions and wishes were not, as it turned out, the only factor involved. Even as we worked on the options, we began to receive indications that carrier groups of the Seventh Fleet were not carrying out the swift movement into North Korean waters that the President had ordered. Nixon was puzzled and angered by this failure when we reported it to him. On his orders, Kissinger checked with Laird and received no straight answer to the plain question of whether the Navy was doing as the President desired. As Kissinger described it to me at the time, he was left with a discomfiting impression of "dissembling and foot-dragging." Kissinger told me to call Col. Robert Pursley, Laird's military assistant, to see what I could find out. Speaking in the name of the President, I did so more than once, and each time was treated to answers that seemed to me to be evasive and incomplete. ("Bob, where are the carriers?" "I'll have to call you back on that, Al." "Can you tell me which carriers and other fleet elements are involved?" "Al, I'll have to check that out, too." "Bob, what the hell is going on over there?" Silence.)

Finally, by going outside channels, we confirmed the scarcely believable truth that Laird had not passed the orders of the Commander in Chief on to the Joint Chiefs of Staff. On hearing this, Nixon exploded. His instructions were signaled to the Navy. By now, however, it was April 17, nearly three days after the EC-121 had been shot down. The element of secrecy and the shock value of the carriers' deployment were lost. The slow public progress of the U.S. Navy task force, photographed off the shores of Japan by boatloads of television cameramen, incited the ridicule of the American news media and political counterculture. Predictably, it also aroused a flutter of anxiety in the State Department and elsewhere in the U.S. government that there might be a lot of drowned journalists to explain to a hostile world press if the fleet was forced to defend itself.

Meanwhile, the options had been delivered to Nixon. My team produced an option that called for the destruction by bombing of a North Korean military airfield, accompanied by a strong and unequivocal warning to Moscow to stay out of the situation and a presidential statement drawing a clear line on the limits of American tolerance in Vietnam. This was no time for politeness or for extending the benefit of the doubt. Any suggestion that the United States would be doing wrong by retaliating against the North Koreans was disingenuous. Even if the CIA's "birthday present" scenario was correct, that was hardly an excuse for the premeditated murder of thirty-one Americans. If, in fact, this ruthless act of war had been inspired for such frivolous reasons, that only compounded the outrage.

The soft option recommended that future reconnaissance flights in the vicinity of North Korea be defended by U.S. fighter aircraft; that was all. Nixon regarded this recommendation as feeble. On his own, he added a secret component that the soft-liners had not mentioned and did not support—a B-52 strike against North Vietnamese and Viet Cong staging areas, headquarters, and supply bases inside Cambodia along the border with South Vietnam. This was not so much of a departure from caution as it may seem. One secret bombing raid against these same targets had already been carried out with the acquiescence of the Cambodian government of Prince Sihanouk, who wanted the Vietnamese Communists driven out of his country before they took it over entirely. More would follow.

Among the soft-liners there was great nervousness that these raids might be exploited, as eventually they were by polemical journalists who misconstrued every important point about them. They feared that exposure of the Cambodian bombing would produce an escalation in antiwar demonstrations in the United States and that this, added to the effect of bombing an airfield in far-off North Korea, might escalate the protests beyond the power of the government to control them. Retaliation against North Korea, they argued, provided the North Vietnamese or the Soviets with a golden opportunity to make public the Cambodian bombing and brand Nixon as a warmonger. In fact, the enemy never referred to their existence; to do so would have meant abandoning the fiction, devoutly endorsed by Hanoi's sympathizers in the West, that there were no Vietnamese Communist troops in Cambodia. This was yet another example, in yet another administration, of the way in which choosing to act in secret in the hope of avoiding adverse political consequences raises the paralyzing specter of political blackmail.

On April 18, Nixon appeared before a press conference and revealed that he had selected the soft option. No mention was made of the B-52 raids, of course. I listened to the President's words with a sinking heart, believing that we had cut the moral ground from beneath our own feet and missed a compelling opportunity to save lives in Vietnam by shortening the war. In later years, Nixon told me that he considered the decision to adopt the soft option in response to the EC-121 shoot-down the worst mistake of his administration in the field of foreign policy. Kissinger echoed this estimate in his memoirs. It was cold comfort, when it was too late to do anything about it, to be reassured that my first instincts had been correct.

Nixon's decision was by no means the end of the story even with regard to North Korea. It was, rather, the beginning of another long-running drama. Even the soft option turned out to be impossible to implement. We discovered after the President had appeared before the cameras that the Secretary of Defense had taken another very surprising unilateral action. Hours after the EC-121 was shot down, without bothering to inform Nixon, Laird had ordered the suspension not only of all reconnaissance flights over North Korea or along its coasts but of all such flights throughout the world. This could have no other effect than to lead Moscow and all its clients to believe that Kim Il-sung had scared Nixon off.

The White House learned about Laird's unfathomable action only by breaking down, with great difficulty, a Pentagon stone wall composed of delays, excuses, and obfuscation. Finally, we learned the truth. Nixon ordered the immediate resumption of the flights, but three weeks elapsed before the EC-121s were flying again. A vivid and probably ineradicable impression of presidential indecision and vacillation had been planted in the minds of our adversaries. As in the case of the capture of the *Pueblo* and its crew during the Johnson administration, the United States appeared once again to be the "pitiful, helpless giant" Nixon had promised in his presidential campaign to arouse and reform. No more embarrassing outcome could have been imagined.

Laird's actions were incomprehensible in terms of the traditional relationship between the Commander in Chief and the Secretary of Defense. The latter is supposed to obey the former. Maybe Laird wanted to save Nixon from himself and the Republican party from any suggestion that it was a war party. This may be explained as political wisdom or as an arrogant and dangerous conceit, but there is no reason to think that Laird did not have the best interests of the President and the Republican party at heart. There is no question that a bombing raid on North Korea, occurring while half a million American troops were fighting a war in Vietnam, would have produced dramatic political effects at home. Domestic politics was Laird's specialty; he had until recently been one of the most influential members of Congress, and he understood Capitol Hill and the limits of its political courage better than most, though not better than Nixon.

In the heat of the discovery of this undermining of policy, Nixon wanted to fire Laird and Bill Rogers along with him. He realized, however, that his hands were tied. Laird was so highly regarded by his former colleagues on Capitol Hill that he would take with him, if he went, much of Nixon's congressional support for his Vietnam policy. Furthermore, once the reason for Laird's dismissal was made public, he would almost certainly become an idol of the antiwar movement, whose propagandists would doubtless portray him as the man who had kept Nixon from starting another war in Asia. Even if these factors had not applied, it is very difficult for a President to fire his Secretaries of State and Defense in the third month of his presidency without bringing his own good judgment into question.

Kissinger was even more furious than Nixon, because he understood that Laird's actions signaled the beginning of a power struggle that had profound implications for the NSC system. Nixon might have contained the damage by calling in Laird and reading him the riot act. At least this would have put Laird on notice that the President was angry with him while firmly placing him under direct orders to execute presidential orders in the future or face the consequences. Many men, treated to such an expression of displeasure and lack of confidence by the Chief Executive, would have resigned as a matter of honor or chagrin.

It was suggested to Nixon that he bring Laird in for such a confrontation. But the President, with his ingrained distaste for unpleasant personal contacts, could not contemplate this prospect. "No," he said, shaking his head and averting his eyes. "I don't want to see Laird. *You* talk to him. Tell him there'll be no more of this."

Kissinger did as the President wished, and so perhaps did the White House Chief of Staff, Bob Haldeman, Nixon's long-suffering proxy in such matters. But Laird was a worldly man, and he knew who had won this round and who had lost, and he knew that he did not have to listen to mere messengers.

15

National Security

All Presidents have been bedeviled and exasperated by leaks to the news media. Jefferson started his own newspaper to defend himself against them. Eisenhower regarded them as treason. Reagan turned the carnivores of the Washington press corps into house cats by filling innumerable saucers with inside dope and setting them out on the White House doorstep. Others, including Lyndon Johnson and eventually Richard Nixon, were driven to the brink of mania by leaks; according to Nixon, Johnson left office believing that the only man in Washington a President could trust was J. Edgar Hoover.[1]

Nixon made it plain at the outset of his presidency that he wanted a leakproof NSC. He was not so artless as to think he could actually have such a thing. But even *he* was surprised by the speed with which his councils were penetrated, and by the scale of the breach. The very first National Security Council Memorandum was leaked to the *New York Times* less than forty-eight hours after the President had signed it.

After that, the hemorrhage began: By the end of May, at least nineteen stories based on highly classified information from the NSC files had appeared in just two newspapers, the *Washington Post* and the *New York Times*. In no case was the leaked information trivial or inaccurate. It made public advance details on the position of United States with regard to Middle East peace negotiations; particulars of the President's options on Vietnam, including discussions of unilateral troop withdrawals; details of a secret study on U.S. military bases overseas; particulars of Soviet missile deployments obtained by U.S. reconnaissance satellites; discussion of the President's options and personal views in regard to the EC-121 shoot-down; and an exact summary of a secret study of U.S. nuclear forces.

Among other things, these stories represented an intelligence bonanza that might have saved a thriftier superpower than the U.S.S.R. many millions of rubles in the cost of running its espionage service. Taking the price of a metropolitan newspaper in 1969 to be fifteen cents, the whole expense to the KGB of reading this sequence from the White House's innermost files was $2.85.

The President was infuriated; so was Kissinger. The spillage of secrets called into question Nixon's ability to settle the war in Vietnam, a matter of life and death to countless Americans and Vietnamese, and undermined his hopes for certain other historic breakthroughs in foreign relations, such as the opening to China, that had so far remained secret precisely because only a minute circle knew about them. Some of these leaks endangered the lives of American troops in Vietnam and elsewhere, others compromised our intelligence sources and methods of collection, still others compromised sensitive secret negotiations with foreign powers, and the stories about withdrawal from Vietnam deeply upset Saigon, while giving aid and comfort to Hanoi.

The leaks were, of course, acutely troubling to Kissinger because most of them could have originated only from a source that had access to papers and meetings in which the most sensitive national security matters were discussed—in other words, a member of the NSC staff. Suspicion fell immediately on some of the ideological outsiders Kissinger had hired. These appointments had been opposed during the transition period on grounds of security by General Wheeler, the chairman of the Joint Chiefs of Staff, and by J. Edgar Hoover, the Director of the Federal Bureau of Investigation. These men now reminded the President and Kissinger that their advice had been rejected, and they called for the removal of the man they regarded as the prime suspect, together with two others. No actual evidence had been gathered linking any of the three to the leaks, but inasmuch as they had been handling the information that leaked, the suspicions about them were not altogether unreasonable, nor did they seem so to the President. Although, as was his style, he had not confronted Kissinger on the issue, Nixon had never been comfortable with the idea of admitting those he viewed as his political enemies into his inner councils. Of all Presidents, he had the least reason to give those who despised him the benefit of the doubt.

The obvious solution was to get rid of the three suspects. During the transition period before the administration actually took office, it would not have been necessary to do anything so dramatic as firing them. Hoover, among others, had suggested at that time that they simply be denied security clearances, an action that would have disqualified them for employment that involved handling classified information. This was a peremptory way to deal with the matter, but a security clearance is a privilege, not a right, and the denial or termination of such a clearance in the name of caution was well within the boundaries of customary practice then as now.

Kissinger, whose career in academia had equipped him with a tolerance for ideological eccentricity that was greater than that of the Director of the FBI and the chairman of the Joint Chiefs of Staff, had resisted this solution. The President had not ordered him to go along with it. This created a situation in which Hoover and those who agreed with him either had to substantiate their suspicions or drop the subject. As everyone knew, it was not Hoover's way to ignore his own suspicions, and in fairness to him it must be said that it would be a very poor FBI director who did so. He was, after all, the head of domestic counterespionage and counterintelligence for the entire United States government, and as such it was his business to be suspicious.

Hoover and Nixon were old friends and confidants. Nevertheless, Nixon was aware that Hoover's FBI had grown old along with him. He was beginning to feel that it was time to bring new blood into the Bureau and modernize its outlook and methods.[2] Hoover knew this. He was not ready to go (he was seventy-four, but he wasn't dead yet). The leaks gave him an opportunity to demonstrate his indispensability to the new President.

On April 25, 1969, Hoover and Attorney General John N. Mitchell came to the Oval Office to discuss with the President a program to investigate the leaks. After the meeting had been in progress for a while, Kissinger was called in. Hoover told him that three members of the NSC staff had been identified by the FBI as possible leakers and that a fourth person, a foreign journalist Hoover evidently suspected of being an espionage agent, was also under suspicion. The suspects had been selected in accordance with three criteria: access to leaked information, indications of security problems in the individual's file, and pertinent information about leaks developed by FBI investigations. All four were going to be investigated by the FBI, and the means of surveillance would include telephone wiretaps.

Hoover and Mitchell assured Kissinger, correctly, that there was nothing unusual or illegal about any of this. All that was required to institute such a wiretap under the law as it then existed was the prior approval of the Attorney General.

After the meeting, Kissinger called me into his office and, after summarizing the discussion in the Oval Office, handed me the files compiled by the FBI on three members of the NSC staff. Clearly shaken by Hoover's thesis and the President's sympathy for it, he wondered aloud whether he had read these files with an untrained, and therefore too tolerant, eye. I was an experienced bureaucrat. Would I read the files in the light of my training and experience and tell him whether I found anything that in my judgment rendered the suspects unfit to be granted a security clearance?

The FBI's method of conducting the background investigation of a candidate for sensitive employment is a simple one. Its agents verify everything about the subject that can be verified from the written record, then talk to as many people who know him or her as possible. They ask certain standard questions, augmented by questions that fit the particular case, and write down with scrupulous accuracy what is said to them. It is this collection of raw information that is presented to the potential employer, and it is up to him, within certain established guidelines, to decide whether he wants to hire the candidate.

The FBI makes no attempt to evaluate the data it collects and expresses no opinion as to the reliability of what its agents have been told. It follows that a typical file on a background investigation is a mixture of biographical detail derived from documentary sources and statements of fact, hearsay, and opinion about the activities, associations, habits, and character of the subject. These can range from the bland to the inflammatory to the scandalous. Because sources are guaranteed anonymity if they request it, they tend to speak frankly, even recklessly, and sometimes with rancor. Unless you are a voyeur by nature, reading the file of a subject who has made vindictive enemies is an uncomfortable, embarrassing experience.

There were passages in some of the files Kissinger gave me that raised doubts about the alleged habits, good judgment, and associations of the American citizens involved. In one case in particular, my purely personal reaction was that the subject had made friends with a good many people with whom I myself would not have wished to be on intimate terms. That was his own business. The FBI had reported nothing, in my judgment, that brought loyalty to the United States or the personal trustworthiness of any member of the trio into serious question. After reading the files, I recommended that all three be retained on the staff in the absence of any hard proof of wrongdoing. This seemed to me to be a matter of simple fairness and, considering that an investigation had been authorized, of letting the system work. Kissinger agreed, with expressions of gratitude, and kept all three suspects as members of the NSC staff.

On May 9, William Beecher of the *New York Times* (whom the reader has already met in Vietnam as a passenger in Bill DePuy's bullet-pierced helicopter) broke the story of bombing raids on enemy installations inside Cambodia. The existence of these air attacks, which went under the tone-deaf Pentagon code name "Menu" (the first raid was called "Breakfast," another "Lunch," and so on), was one of the administration's most closely held secrets. Its publication enraged the President. He told Kissinger to instruct Hoover to take all possible steps to find the source of the leak. Kissinger and Hoover talked to each other by telephone. By late afternoon, Hoover was telling Kissinger that one of the suspects named in the April 25 meeting in the Oval Office was the prime suspect in this case. At 6:20 P.M., the FBI placed a tap on the man's telephone.

Kissinger designated me to act as his liaison with William Sullivan, an assistant director of the FBI who was in charge of the investigation. I did not welcome the assignment. I hoped it would uncover the leaker or leakers and do so quickly, and that the guilty party would be severely punished for what was, to my mind, a very serious crime against the United States. But I just did not think that Kissinger and I, or anyone else on the NSC staff, should be parties to the investigation. We possessed neither the qualifications nor the temperament for it.

Clearly, the liaison with the FBI should be handled by the White House General Counsel, who was responsible for matters pertaining to the law. Later on, I made this point to Kissinger insistently, not to say incessantly, but at this stage he and I had known each other for less than six months. Although our working relationship had grown steadily closer, I did not think that it was proper for me to question a course of action initiated by the President, especially in a matter as sensitive as this one. I suspected that Kissinger was in the same boat with regard to Nixon, especially since the suspects were Kissinger's appointees.

This is not to say that I disapproved of the investigation or had the slightest reservation about the reasons for carrying it out or the methods contemplated. In the armed services, random telephone taps on personnel handling military secrets are one of the routine facts of life. I never questioned their necessity in a military context: After all, a slip of the lip *can* sink a ship. In the case of these civilians, the leaks of strategic information were ample reason to investigate and the methods were entirely legal and correct according to the standards of the day. There was ample precedent for wiretaps of this kind. National security wiretaps, as such, were originated by President Franklin D. Roosevelt in 1940, when he signed a memorandum authorizing Attorney General Robert H. Jackson to approve wiretaps on "persons suspected of subversive activities against the Government of the United States." Roosevelt took this action in the face of two separate rulings by the Supreme Court that information "obtained from the interception of wire and radio communications was inadmissible in court." FDR remarked in his memorandum to Attorney General Jackson that he was "convinced that the Supreme Court never intended any dictum in the particular case which it decided to apply to grave matters involving the defense of the nation."[3] His Justice Department took the position that since interception alone was not illegal, there was no prohibition on national security wiretaps so long as the information obtained from them was not divulged outside the government, and that no warrant was needed so long as each wiretap was duly authorized by the Attorney General.[4] These two principles were applied, with refinements and reaffirmations and sometimes by efforts to broaden the legislative authority of the executive to wiretap, by all subsequent administrations.

On Saturday morning, May 10, I called on Sullivan at his office in the Department of Justice. We already knew each other; my earlier duties at the Pentagon had included liaison on routine matters with the FBI, and Sullivan had often been the man on the other end of the telephone. Bill was not a G-man from central casting. Short, florid, and pugnacious, with a loud rasping voice, he looked a lot more like Popeye the Sailor than a leading man. There was nothing comical about him as a policeman; Sullivan was mentally tough, implacably persistent, and beyond surprise where human nature and behavior were concerned. After a lifetime of service under Hoover, he had the weary air of a man who has been sifting other people's secrets all his life and finding them not particularly interesting.

As Kissinger had instructed me to do, I formally requested in the name of the President that investigations be made of three members of the NSC staff, in addition to a fourth man serving in the Pentagon who had knowledge of the Cambodian bombing. Sullivan, sitting stolidly behind a large desk, heard me out with paternal patience, but I had the impression that I was merely confirming orders that he had already been delivered and probably even acted upon.

It was my impression (and Kissinger's) that the operation would be brief: Wiretaps would be placed, evidence would either be discovered or not in a matter of days or at most a couple of weeks, and that would be the end of the matter. I said this to Sullivan. He did not contradict me. I did not press him for details; police methods are not an interest of mine. I did not tell him what to listen for; enough secrets had been let out of the box. He took it for granted that Kissinger and the President would want to see transcripts of intercepted conversations when these seemed to refer to classified information, and that they would also want to be kept up-to-date on other material produced by the investigation. We arranged that Sullivan would call me when he had something important to show us. I would then go over to his office, read the material, and pass it on verbally to Kissinger. We agreed to keep paper to a minimum.

Later suspicions to the contrary notwithstanding, there was no dark purpose of concealment in this. The supposition that something is conspiratorial and designed to deceive because it is not written down is not necessarily correct. In this case, my intent was to make sure material that might be misinterpreted by future investigators did not find its way into the security files of the people under investigation. Once an item is placed in such a file, it is there forever; keeping it out in the first place preserves the individual from false suspicion and the government from future mistakes in judgment. Then, too, given our recent experiences with sensitive documents, it seemed wise not to have raw transcripts of tapped phone conversations floating around the White House; the only thing worse than having a false accusation in one's FBI file is having it published in the newspapers.

There was another factor. I had learned a lesson during Pentagon days about the sort of paperwork telephone wiretaps can generate. As is well known, the FBI in the 1960s carried out a lengthy and intensive investigation of the Reverend Martin Luther King. The most damaging results of this investigation were circulated throughout the government, under the lowest possible security classification, in a document signed by Hoover. It was one of the most shocking papers I have ever read, not only for the astounding range and invasive nature of its allegations but because it was sent on a wholesale basis to people who had no conceivable reason to know anything about King's private life. Urged on by Califano and me, among others, McNamara had called Hoover and urged him to withdraw the memorandum, and in due course—too late—Hoover did so. It was in nobody's interest that such a breach of due process and simple propriety should occur in this case.

The leaks from the White House continued. Ten days after my meeting with Sullivan, the *Washington Post* published details of Nixon's secret plans for a meeting with President Thieu. Two days later, the *New York Times* carried a story describing secret discussions about testing a new missile warhead before the SALT arms negotiations with the Soviets began. Other revelations based on sensitive NSC memorandums and meetings followed.[5]

The FBI's wiretaps yielded no clue as to who the leaker or leakers might be. Two more people were tapped because they had had access to the compromised information. In this period, I visited Sullivan's office at his invitation and read some transcripts whose contents had nothing to do with leaks. A week or so after that, the President and Kissinger received the first of several letters from Hoover transmitting information produced by the wiretaps. None of these data were relevant to the question of the identity of the leaker or leakers; the FBI clearly was interested in things that were of no interest to us.

At this stage of the operation, some natural law of eavesdropping seemed to spring into being. The wiretaps began to cross-pollinate and multiply. When I remarked on this, Sullivan assured me that "you guys are pikers" compared to the eavesdropping practices of foregoing adminis-trations. * Nevertheless, I was taken aback by the way in which this masked Topsy grew. One of the suspects would call or be called by someone who would say something, usually something ambiguous, that aroused the FBI's curiosity. The second party would then be tapped. Someone would call him and say something else that seemed relevant to the Bureau; the third party would be tapped, also, always with the authorization of the Attorney General. I have no idea how many conversations were overheard in all.

After a time, I began to wonder whether the FBI was tapping people about whom the President, Kissinger, and I didn't even know. Hoover's sudden decision to communicate his findings by letters instead of having

---

* This seems to be the case. According to statistics compiled by the Church committee, the yearly average of warrantless FBI wiretaps in operation during the Nixon administration was 125, compared to a yearly average of 315 for FDR; 352 for Truman; 197 for Eisenhower; 194 for Kennedy; 172 for Johnson. The Roosevelt administration (1940–1945) operated a total of 1,888 warrantless wiretaps; Truman (1946–1952), 2,465; Eisenhower (1953–1960), 1574; Kennedy (1961–1963), 582; Johnson (1964–1968), 862; Nixon (1969–1974), 747. (Church committee report, p. 301.)

Sullivan call me over to read raw transcripts seemed to suggest this, but it is also possible that Hoover simply wanted to take personal credit for the product. Reading the transcripts, which were mostly composed of irrelevant garbage (the word I used to describe it at the time), I wondered why. Some wiretaps were discontinued when they proved to be unproductive or provided strong indications that the subject was loyal and trustworthy. I had no authority to terminate telephone wiretaps, and, in the absence of instructions to the contrary, never made such a request. I thought, and I believed that Kissinger agreed, that this proliferation of eavesdroppers must be a reflection of the Bureau's long-established methods; if they had been tapping telephones for all those years, they must know what they were doing.

By July 8, nothing of interest had been produced. Sullivan suggested that some of the wiretaps be removed, and, on Kissinger's authorization, I agreed that they should be. The discontinued taps were soon replaced by new taps on people who wandered into the net of the surveillance. A White House assistant who had no access to national security information was overheard agreeing to leak the text of a forthcoming presidential speech to a journalist while boasting, inaccurately but in the evident and rather touching hope of being taken seriously, that he was the author of the speech. Although I transmitted no such request to the FBI, and Kissinger never instructed me to do so, this unfortunate fellow was tapped. I was not made aware of this at the time and never saw any more transcripts of his conversations. Other wiretaps revealed even more human moments, as when someone else, until then unsuspected of being a foot soldier in the sexual revolution, was overheard planning an orgy. Ninety-five percent of the monitored conversation consisted of the everyday traffic of ordinary life—chats with relatives and friends, spats with neighbors, conversations with repairmen who had promised to come and failed to show up. The 5 percent that Hoover considered interesting usually had nothing to do with leaks.

More journalists became entangled in this web of crossed lines, either because they were in touch with someone on the growing roster of those already being tapped or, in at least one case, because the reporter published a story based on leaked information. From such coincidences are castles of paranoia built, but it was all, or nearly all, happenstance. The American reporters who got tapped simply blundered into the operation; to my knowledge, no snare was laid for them as individuals. A total of seventeen wiretaps (four of these on journalists) were instituted by the FBI. I was not informed of all of them at the time by the FBI or anyone else. There may have been more about which I was never informed. The FBI installed and removed the wiretaps on Attorney General Mitchell's legal authority, according to their established practice in such matters. Apart from passing along names furnished to me by Kissinger or, in one case, the President, I did not enter into this process, and never ordered wiretaps to be removed, because I had no authority to do so. At least two wiretaps were applied to people who had no connection whatever to the NSC; one was a prominent Republican political worker. I did not learn about these two cases until long after the fact. The suspicion that they were politically motivated does not seem unreasonable to me. Whatever the motive, the action was indefensible in terms of the stated purposes of the investigation.

No shred of evidence linking Hoover's prime suspect to the leaks was ever revealed to me, and, to the best of my knowledge, none of the three original "likely suspects" was ever shown as a result of wiretaps or by any other means to be the source of leaks. A fourth member of the NSC staff was, however, caught red-handed leaking sensitive information to a journalist over his home telephone. Kissinger, who had no more taste for disagreeable personal moments than Nixon, instructed me to fire the man. I called him into my office and did so as gently as possible: "You've been leaking, and you've got to go." The man, a holdover from the Johnson administration and a veteran of the Paris peace talks, did not deny the charge or attempt to defend himself. Nor did he seem to be surprised or ashamed that he had been caught. He simply went quietly.

During the latter stages of the wiretap operation, I became more and more vocal about my feeling that it was inappropriate for Kissinger and me to be involved in the process. He agreed. From the beginning, his hope had been that the wiretaps would exonerate his appointees, and he often said that that had been his purpose in going along with the FBI operation. He discussed the matter with Nixon, and on May 13, 1970, almost exactly a year after the first wiretap was installed, Hoover came to the White House to meet with the President. On that day, Kissinger and I were relieved of all further involvement in the program. It was arranged that future FBI reports would be transmitted to Bob Haldeman.

Nevertheless, Sullivan continued to call me from time to time when the wiretaps turned up something about the NSC that he regarded as noteworthy. According to the FBI, wiretaps on eight NSC employees and one other person who had access to NSC documents and deliberations were removed on February 10, 1971. Around that time, Sullivan asked me to come and see him. "I wanted you to know that we're discontinuing all nine," Sullivan said. "Hoover is going up to the Hill to testify pretty soon, and every time that happens we always remove most of our wiretaps so that he can report a low number to Congress."

What was the end result? More than a year and a half of surveillance had produced very little to support the suspicions with regard to the original trio of likely suspects. One leaker whom no one had suspected in the beginning had been detected and fired. According to the standards applied by Hoover, that single discovery justified the whole operation. No doubt he was disappointed that he did not catch the fish for which he had baited the hook, and he may have felt that everyone, especially the FBI, would have been saved a good deal of trouble, expense, and frustration if Kissinger had only been willing to discharge the suspects instead of presuming their innocence in the absence of proof to the contrary.

Although he authorized every one of them, Kissinger never joined me on my visits to Bill Sullivan's office at the FBI or called on Hoover in the latter's office. The place made him nervous. Finally, Hoover, who called Kissinger fairly frequently, asked him to come and see him. Kissinger demurred on grounds of a busy schedule. Hoover insisted; he had something of the gravest import concerning the security of the Office of the President itself to discuss with him. Kissinger asked me to accompany him, and we were driven over to the Department of Justice in a White House car. On Kissinger's part, it was a nervous journey. Hoover had cultivated the ability to arouse a potent mixture of apprehension and curiosity in the human breast. This is certainly the effect his call produced in Kissinger, who wondered aloud as we drove down the Mall what the matter of import was and why Hoover was so anxious to see him.

The suspense intensified once we entered Hoover's office. This was a large, high-ceilinged suite with a reception room where we were kept waiting, a trophy room filled with what seemed to be hundreds of plaques, loving cups, and other glittering tributes to Hoover, and finally Hoover's spacious inner office, decorated with signed photographs of the mighty and the famous.

All of these connecting rooms were equipped with heavy tables, chairs, sofas, and trophy cases that were noticeably larger in scale than ordinary furniture. As the visitor passed from one room to the next, the furniture became larger and larger. The effect was hypnotic. The closer Henry and I got to the inner sanctum where Hoover waited, the smaller we seemed to be in comparison to the decor. The impression of irreality intensified as we entered the inner sanctum. Here the furnishings dwarfed us. Hoover's desk and chair were elevated on a wooden base, so that a man of ordinary height standing before it and gazing upward at Hoover on his dais had the illusion that he had shrunk to his boyhood height. In fact, it was the Director who was short, and according to Sullivan he was so sensitive about this that he customarily stood on a low box when receiving agents from the field; the latter were instructed on pain of transfer to the backwoods to look into Hoover's eyes, not downward at his box. When Kissinger and I sat down, as the unsmiling Hoover invited us to do without rising from his own chair, our vantage point was even more humble.

Hoover, unsmiling, wanted no time on preliminary niceties. "Doctor," he said to Kissinger in a low, meaningful tone of voice, "here in Washington there lives a foreigner, a woman who works in the embassy of a third country which is friendly to the United States. She is a charming woman. She is a highly intelligent and witty woman. She is a very, very beautiful woman. To the casual observer, she appears to be a perfectly harmless woman." Here Hoover leaned over his desk and fixed Kissinger with a chilly stare. "However, Doctor, in reality this seemingly inoffensive female is a spy in the pay of the Cuban intelligence service! Imagine my shock and surprise, therefore, when I learned this morning that this very beautiful Communist spy had been *inside the White House*, accompanied by a highly important member of the President's staff. Not only that, this woman who is in the pay of Fidel Castro was *escorted into the Oval Office*! She sat *in the President's chair*! It is my personal opinion, Doctor, that this episode should not be repeated, and that this woman should be one hundred percent persona non grata with every single person in the White House. I hope you agree."

Kissinger did agree, heartily. He took several minutes to assure Hoover of this. Hoover's story did not surprise me. Members of the White House staff often bring friends into the West Wing at night to show them the Oval Office, the Roosevelt Room, and other points of interest. It is a harmless perquisite, and it has often been used to impress members of the opposite sex. All papers are locked up in safes after hours and, with guards standing in every doorway, the security risk is close to zero— although I suppose it might be possible, as Hoover's pontifical manner suggested, for some Mata Hari to place a poison thumbtack on the seat of the President's chair or a bug in his desk lamp.

Kissinger thanked Hoover for the information and we departed. He was strangely silent as we threaded our way among the glittering mementos and Brobdingnagian furniture and back to the front door. Kissinger by this time was well known as the escort of glamorous women. In the car,

I asked him, "Tell me, Henry—where did you meet this sinister beauty?" Kissinger erupted. "It was that damn Ziegler! He introduced this glorious creature to me at a cocktail party. She said she had always wanted to see the Oval Office. So I gave her the tour."

The wiretaps, like so much else born in secrecy, eventually became public knowledge. Lawsuits were filed and the Supreme Court eventually affirmed an award of damages.[6] The fact remains that the wiretaps were legal according to the standards applying in 1969 and for many years before. Since 1969, the courts and the Congress have modified the law, and today, in nearly all cases involving domestic groups of individuals, the Attorney General "must submit a detailed application to a federal judge to obtain an order authorizing a wiretap." Before eavesdropping can commence, the judge must determine that probable cause exists that the "proposed subject of the wiretap is committing an offense" under the laws concerning espionage, sabotage, bribery, or kidnapping.[7] In other words, a federal warrant is now required before the government can listen in on the conversations of any citizen or resident of the United States.

As I am not a lawyer, there is no point in my venturing an opinion as to whether the government would have been able in 1969 to persuade a federal judge that probable cause existed to eavesdrop on any of the people whose telephones were in fact tapped. Making the effort to present the evidence in a systematic way instead of relying on instinct and precedent might have clarified the thinking of those responsible in such a way as to produce a more efficient investigation.

It can certainly be argued without referring to legal considerations that a better result might have been produced by a more methodical approach. My own view, then and now, is that the entire exercise, and its many woeful consequences, might have been avoided by calling in the suspects, confronting them with the suspicions about them, and giving them the opportunity to defend themselves in private. The prime suspects need not have been singled out; every member of the staff should have been subjected to the same procedure. If any of the likely suspects had insisted on confronting his accusers, so much the better. It would have given Hoover and Wheeler an opportunity to justify their doubts by bringing forward whatever supporting evidence they may have had. It is better to hurt a man's feelings than to hurt his reputation, or to hurt the country.

The fundamental flaw in the background investigation is its pointless secrecy. It is my belief that every subject of a routine national security background investigation should be provided as a matter of right with a copy of the final report and given the opportunity of replying to allegations and correcting errors of fact. Such access is already provided under the Freedom of Information Act with regard to past government investigations, and is routinely granted as a matter of law to the subjects of private investigations in such matters as credit records. There is no plausible reason why an applicant for a federal job, as opposed to a suspect in a criminal proceeding, should not know what others have told the FBI or other investigative agencies about him or her, so long as sources who wish to remain anonymous are permitted to do so, as is now the practice. Among other effects, this might make the government's files more truthful; inaccuracies would still exist, as in the press, but they would not go unchallenged. There is no argument for continuing the present clumsy system except that it invests the process with the mystery of police methods and encourages hostile testimony whose truthfulness is not routinely put to the test of corroboration as in ordinary police investigations.

The wiretaps of NSC staff members ordered in 1969 were a product of Hoover's instincts and the President's altogether righteous wrath, and they turned out to be largely futile. In my view, it is a great pity that they did not produce evidence incriminating those responsible for the leaks, whoever they were; a public hanging in a case of this kind, early in the administration, would have been a salutary thing. The fact that only one person was shown to be leaking on the basis of the wiretaps does not mean that other leaks did not take place or that other people did not leak. It means only that wiretaps failed to incriminate them.

Although there was no way of guessing this at the time, the most important fact about the telephone-tapping operation is that it was taken over, after Kissinger and I were relieved of oversight, by others in the White House whose subsequent activities led to the burglaries of the office of Dr. Daniel Ellsberg's psychiatrist in California and of Democratic National Committee headquarters at the Watergate office building. These undercover operations by the special investigative group afterward called "the plumbers," whose existence was unknown to me until I read about them in the newspapers in the aftermath of the Watergate break-in, led directly to the resignation of President Nixon. No plainer example of the unpredictable course of clandestine activity exists in history or could be imagined.

16

Steel and Mush

The primary objective of Richard Nixon's first term, overshadowing all others, was to end the Vietnam War. In March 1969, Nixon told the Cabinet that he expected the conflict to be over in a year. He based this estimate not on any belief that the war could be won in the turbulent political circumstances that it had generated in the United States but on his judgment that the combination of the secret bombing of the enemy's military installations in Cambodia and repeated American offers through many channels to negotiate a comprehensive peace would bring the North Vietnamese to the bargaining table.[1]

However, Hanoi stubbornly refused to acknowledge the existence of either component of Nixon's design, and by the beginning of that summer it was clear that peace could not be achieved on so optimistic a timetable. Bombs falling into the Cambodian jungle, even when they struck the military targets at which they were aimed, fell too far away from Hanoi to affect the enemy's fundamental capacity and will to make war. Hanoi clearly believed that if it held on long enough, the pressure of street demonstrations and the casualty lists would lead to a further erosion of political will in Congress and in the administration and that this would force Nixon to get out of Vietnam. The administration itself believed that it lacked the political backing on Capitol Hill and in the news media to achieve a settlement by the only means that Hanoi could not long resist—

that is, by using its overwhelming military power to give the enemy the choice between negotiations and destruction.

There can be little question that North Vietnamese intransigence was to some degree a product of the administration's failure of nerve on the EC-121 shoot-down. As Nixon himself put it, "Communist leaders believe in Lenin's precept: Probe with bayonets. If you encounter mush, proceed; if you encounter steel, withdraw. I had feared that in our handling of the EC-121 incident in 1969 the Communists may have thought they had encountered mush."[2]

They certainly behaved that way all over the world, and nowhere more provocatively than in Indochina. On February 22, one month and two days after Nixon's inauguration, the North Vietnamese and the Viet Cong launched a so-called mini-Tet offensive throughout South Vietnam that resulted in the deaths of 1,140 American and at least 1,500 ARVN troops in the first three weeks of fighting. In the first half of March, the enemy carried out thirty-two rocket attacks against South Vietnamese population centers. North Vietnamese "infiltration" of Cambodian territory along the South Vietnamese border had reached the point of saturation; Prince Norodom Sihanouk, the Cambodian head of state, told a press conference that one of his provinces had been all but taken over by the North Vietnamese Army and another was in the process of being swallowed whole. "In certain areas of Cambodia," he said, in words that would later assume an awful resonance when the Khmer Rouge embarked on a policy of genocide, "there are no Cambodians."[3]

Apart from the secret air raids on the enemy's installations in Cambodia, the United States did not retaliate in any special way against these bloody provocations. Rogers and Laird urged Nixon to avoid even the appearance of escalation. The bombing halt called by President Johnson in November 1968 was still in effect. The fact that it had produced no progress toward peace suggested to me that the enemy had interpreted it as a sign of weakness. In other minds, Hanoi's lack of response apparently reinforced the delusion that further concessions might do the trick.

The Nixon administration began talking about unilateral troop withdrawals at the NSC meeting five days after the inauguration, with Rogers suggesting the rapid extraction of 50,000 men, or about 9 percent of our strength (there were 536,100 American military personnel in Vietnam at the end of 1968). After the meeting, Kissinger reviewed his notes and exploded. "Why did Nixon hire these guys?" he asked, throwing up his hands in mock despair. "Defense is opposed to the use of force; State is obsessed by compromise. They'll sabotage everything the President tells me he wants to do in foreign policy." Events soon confirmed Kissinger's apprehensions. In March, Rogers proposed unconditional private talks with Hanoi through the Soviet ambassador, Anatoly Dobrynin, without telling the President or Kissinger in advance what he was doing. Soon afterward, Laird announced a 10 percent reduction in B-52 strikes for budgetary reasons, also without informing the White House.[4]

Laird coined the term *Vietnamization* as an improvement on *de-Americanization*, the more straightforward word for unilateral withdrawal then in use. Recognizing Laird's invention as a stroke of public-relations genius, Nixon immediately adopted the euphemism as official terminology. Whatever the program was called, it was another expression of the error of confining the war to the enemy's chosen ground, South Vietnam. This principle was not even raised as an issue for discussion, possibly because everyone present understood that Vietnamization was a program designed to mollify American critics of the war, not a policy for the effective defense of South Vietnam.

Obviously, Rogers and Laird were determined to end the war by any means that would result in a second term for Nixon and good prospects for the election of another Republican to succeed him. They were plainly motivated by the entirely defensible conviction that the restoration of the United States to a condition of domestic tranquillity was far more important than the survival of South Vietnam. They realized that Nixon had won the presidency by the narrowest of margins; they knew that Congress and the news media were controlled by his enemies; they were keenly aware that he was only the second Republican President elected since 1928. They were simply behaving in the way that party men behave; Harriman and Vance had acted no differently when they set out to save Lyndon Johnson from himself by circumventing his instincts. Nixon empathized with Rogers and Laird where their political objectives were concerned. He has often been called a partisan in the pejorative sense of the word, but he was also a partisan in the praiseworthy sense that Lincoln and Truman and the two Roosevelts were partisans. I have never known anyone who was remotely as Republican as Nixon was. He believed in his marrow in the principles and policies of his party and thought that it should govern because it was in every way more fit to do so than the Democratic party.

Kissinger, on the other hand, thought that advice based on scholarship was better than advice based on political considerations and that this was a principle worth defending. In another part of his being, Nixon agreed with this proposition, too. It was quite clear to Kissinger, as it would have been even to a far less intelligent man, that he could not prevail over his arch-rival Rogers and his arch-tormentor Laird by opposing Nixon on the issue that would decide the President's own political future and that of his party. Therefore, he adapted himself to reality. Post-Watergate folklore to the contrary notwithstanding, it was not Kissinger's way, then or later, to question the President's orders or oppose his wishes. Instead, he strove to find ways to circumvent not only his rivals but also Nixon himself. He fought off the policy proposals of State and Defense by using his powerful intellect to demolish their arguments and, in the case of the State Department, by unleashing his wicked sense of humor. Nixon, who regarded the Foreign Service as "a bunch of pantywaist left-wing liberals," was as deeply amused by this badinage as he was attracted by Kissinger's profound knowledge of his subject.

In short, the atmosphere was such that the new President was not getting the realistic, balanced advice from his inner circle that he deserved and needed. It was not in Nixon's essentially unassertive character to demand this advice, and it was not in the character of any of the men around him to play devil's advocate, to make him listen, to encourage him to act against a defeatist trend if that was the direction in which his principles or the logic of the situation might lead him. More and more, in any choice of options, the timorous tended to overcome the bold. Kissinger, reflecting the President's bold private opinion in the matter, continued to think tough and to talk tough. Acting tough involved asking the President to play for much higher stakes. Would Nixon, who would not confront his own Cabinet officers when they undermined his policy, take advice from Kissinger that might lead to the greatest domestic political confrontation of the twentieth century?

Kissinger, who was in a better position than anyone to guess what Nixon's answer to this question might be, did not offer such advice. In the first days of April, he presented a memorandum to Nixon recommending that the United States accept a cease-fire and complete American withdrawal and acquiesce in a role for the National Liberation Front (NLF), the political arm of the Viet Cong, in the postwar government of South Vietnam. As Kissinger afterward noted, these concessions exceeded anything the Johnson administration had ever offered, and even went beyond the rejected plank offered to the 1968 Democratic National Convention by the other party's leading doves, Senators Edward Kennedy, George McGovern, and Eugene McCarthy.[5]

I played no role in the preparation of this memorandum; on reading it in draft form, I said to Kissinger, "We are starting out in the wrong way."

I argued that if the President commenced his term with a display of strength in Vietnam, linked to the palpable Soviet desire for a closer relationship with the United States, he would get a settlement of the war. Appeasement could only result in delay and frustration. Kissinger replied with a lofty jest: "You military men! All you think about is bombs. Subtlety is not your strong suit." He attempted to reassure me by predicting that Hanoi would automatically reject any first proposal by the new American administration no matter how generous it was. That, he said, would give the United States justification for stronger military action if such was necessary to bring the enemy to the bargaining table. I thought it very dangerous to mislead the enemy about our real intentions.

American offers to negotiate were communicated to Hanoi through the Soviets (usually by way of the affable Dobrynin); through a confidential courier (Jean Sainteny, a French businessman who was a former delegate-general to Hanoi); through the press (by design as well as by leak); and through other channels. The enemy made no concessions or gestures of any kind in response to this aurora borealis of American signals and continued to insist that the only basis for peace was the total unilateral withdrawal of all U.S. forces from Indochina and the removal from office of the democratically elected president, vice president, and prime minister of the Republic of Vietnam and their replacement by a provisional postwar government dominated by Communists and their sympathizers.

That is why the leaks of secret presidential deliberations about unilateral withdrawal and Vietnamization were so disturbing to President Nguyen Van Thieu in Saigon. He knew that Vietnamization, if it became a program instead of a catchword, meant the end of him and the end of the Republic of South Vietnam because it would make it impossible to win the war on the battlefield or to negotiate terms of peace from a position of strength.

In March, Vietnamization became a program. Laird returned from an official visit to the war zone with his master plan, which envisaged the phased but rapid and total withdrawal of United States forces from Vietnam and their replacement by retrained and reequipped South Vietnamese armed forces. The latter were, as Thieu and everyone else realized, the same forces the United States had been retraining and reequipping for fifteen years, and whose inability to defend their country against the Communists had brought American combat forces to their rescue. Nevertheless, after hearing Laird's cheery report on the prospects of transforming ARVN and its sister services into a force capable of holding off the North, Nixon adopted Vietnamization as national policy.[6] Détente with Moscow would make it work, or so Nixon and Kissinger believed, by trading treaties and agreements with the Soviets in return for a radical reduction in the Soviet arms and supplies that made Hanoi's military activity possible.

On May 14, as a follow-up, the President offered a comprehensive eight-point peace plan, largely inspired by Kissinger's memorandum, that went far beyond anything that had ever been offered before, including a cease-fire, internationally supervised elections, and the simultaneous withdrawal of most foreign troops from South Vietnam. (Until then, the United States had insisted that Hanoi's withdrawal must begin six months before ours.) As Kissinger had predicted, Hanoi did not respond in any substantive way.[7]

Three weeks later, after a meeting with Thieu on Midway Island, Nixon went a step further, announcing the immediate withdrawal of 25,000 American troops. Both Thieu and Gen. Creighton Abrams, the U.S. commander in Vietnam, objected to this reduction in force, but the President went ahead anyway in the apparent hope that Hanoi (or at least the antiwar party in the United States) would read his action as a sign of his flexibility.[8] Once again, there was no response from Hanoi.

In July, the enemy leadership summarized a prescient view of the situation in a secret document captured on the battlefield: "In the process of de-escalating the war, the Americans may suffer increasing losses and encounter greater difficulties; therefore they may be forced to seek an early end to the war through a political solution which they cannot refuse."[9]

Through all this, Nixon knew that Hanoi respected nothing but force and that force was the only practical means of moving the enemy in the direction of peace. He decided to try a somewhat harder line. If he could not use force, he could at least threaten to use it. On July 15, he sent a secret letter to Ho Chi Minh. If there was no breakthrough for peace by November 1, the anniversary of the preelection 1968 bombing halt, Nixon wrote, he would feel obliged to resort to "measures of great consequence and force."[10] To Hanoi, that phrase could only mean resumption of the bombing of North Vietnam.

In a matter of days after the delivery of Nixon's letter containing its veiled threat to Ho Chi Minh, Hanoi proposed a secret meeting between Kissinger and a member of its delegation to the Paris peace talks, Xuan Thuy. Having encountered American steel for the first time in the new administration, it seemed that the enemy was making a tactical withdrawal. In fact, as Kissinger found when he met Xuan Thuy on August 4 in Jean

Sainteny's apartment in Paris, Hanoi was merely stepping back in order to probe once more with the bayonet. Xuan Thuy, an official of the North Vietnamese foreign ministry, had no authority to negotiate. He mechanically repeated the demands Hanoi had been making all along: total, unconditional withdrawal of U.S. and allied forces, and the abandonment of the Saigon government to the Communists.[11] Two days later, enemy forces raided the American base at Cam Ranh Bay, and on August 11 attacked more than a hundred cities, towns, and military bases all across South Vietnam.[12]

In late July, Nixon watched the splashdown of *Apollo XI* in the South Pacific after its crew made the first landing on the moon. He stepped off Air Force One on Guam and, in the course of a news conference, extemporized a new United States policy with regard to wars of liberation. From now on, he said, the United States would furnish arms and matériel and economic assistance to nations under attack, but the latter would have to supply the manpower to defend themselves against aggression from within or without. If, however, a major nuclear power attacked one of our allies or friends, we would respond with nuclear weapons.

This statement represented a dramatic departure from John F. Kennedy's inaugural promise that the United States would "pay any price, bear any burden, meet any hardship, support any friend, oppose any foe to assure the survival and the success of liberty."[13] It was analyzed in the news media, in foreign ministries, and elsewhere as if it had been produced by the most exquisite high-level deliberations, but in fact it sprang fully formed, unrehearsed and spontaneous, from the brow of Nixon. Nobody in the government had any advance warning that he was going to say what he said, and at first not even Kissinger was sure exactly what he meant. No sooner did the President's words come over radio and television than my telephone in the basement of the White House began to ring as anxious officials called in search of explanation and reassurance. Was the President going back on the ringing pledge Kennedy had made to the world on the first day of the New Frontier? It certainly sounded that way, but the main effect of what (after considerable polishing) came to be called the Nixon Doctrine was to prepare the ground for Vietnamization and the total withdrawal of American troops from Southeast Asia. In its classic mixture of the crystal clear (the United States would no longer bear other nations' burdens when they were unwilling to bear them themselves) and the imponderable (in certain undefined cases we might protect the security of other nations with nuclear arms), it was an excellent statement of policy. In domestic terms, it also laid the basis of an effective defense of the affront to its own principles that the United States was planning to commit in Southeast Asia.

On August 25, Nixon received a coldly defiant reply from Ho Chi Minh. The United States, Ho wrote in response to Nixon's six-week-old letter, "must cease the war of aggression and withdraw their troops from South Vietnam, respect the right of the population of the South and of the Vietnamese nation to dispose of themselves, without foreign influence."[14] This message from beyond the looking glass, in which the North Vietnamese Communists became the protectors of the people they had been slaughtering and the defenders of the territory they had been illegally occupying for fifteen years, turned out to be Ho Chi Minh's last such communication to Washington. He died, aged seventy-nine, on September 3.

Six months elapsed between Kissinger's first secret meeting with the North Vietnamese in Paris and the second, which took place on February 21, 1970. On this occasion, Le Duc Tho, a member of the politburo, represented the North Vietnamese side, and so great was the American tendency to look on the bright side that his mere presence was interpreted as a sign that Hanoi might be ready to engage in serious negotiations. No progress was made on issues of substance, but optimism increased when Le Duc Tho suggested another meeting. The fact that the North Vietnamese were in the process of launching an offensive across the Plain of Jars in Laos did little to dampen Washington's hopefulness.[15]

The administration continued to send mixed signals to Hanoi. A policy driven by the antiwar party in the United States was unlikely to produce the honorable escape from the war that Nixon desired, but there was no way the President could ignore the hysteria. Congress, the cockpit of the liberal opposition, was in a state of hyperpopulism, susceptible as always to any militant minority that threatened to turn public opinion against it. The New Left was in an uproar and the old was in a tizzy; the news media had decided that the story was where the commotion was; Republicans looked at the slim margin by which Nixon had been elected in 1968 and nervously remembered their long years in the Rooseveltian wilderness.

It is true that I was impatient with our slow progress toward peace and that the military factor was never far from my thoughts. Although I may not have realized it at the time, I now think that this was a result of having seen the dead of the Vietnam War, our own and the enemy's, at close range. After the experience of combat, the passage of time was connected in my mind to the mounting toll of human life. By the end of 1968, 36,143 Americans had been killed in Vietnam. In the four years and three days it took the Nixon administration to achieve an agreement with the North Vietnamese, an additional 20,108 Americans died.[16] That was a rate of thirteen American lives per day. During that time, approximately 107,500 South Vietnamese, or 73 per day, were killed in action—and no one knows how many civilians, North Vietnamese soldiers, and Viet Cong guerrillas also perished.[17]

Dobrynin let eight months go by without bothering to tell Kissinger (and without Kissinger inquiring) what had happened to his proposal, made in April 1969, for a meeting in Moscow between Cyrus Vance and a North Vietnamese negotiator to settle the terms for negotiations to end the war. Then Dobrynin mentioned casually, in the course of a long conversation about other matters, that Hanoi had refused to talk to us and Moscow had preferred to say nothing rather than transmit a disappointing response.[18]

Those who counseled patience with the North Vietnamese usually did so in terms that suggested that theirs was the moral position, presumably because it was passive, whereas any suggestion that the enemy be coerced toward peace by military means, and especially by the bombing of military targets in the North, was somehow immoral because it was offensive in nature. I could not then, and I cannot now, understand how it was moral to accept the death and wounding of tens of thousands of young men and innocent civilians in protracted combat in the South yet immoral to risk the lives of untargeted civilians by bombing strategic targets made of steel and concrete in the North.

17

Cambodia

On March 18, 1970, Prince Sihanouk was overthrown by his prime minister, General Lon Nol. This bloodless coup took the polite form of a unanimous vote in the Cambodian National Assembly and Council of the Kingdom to remove the prince as head of state. Sihanouk was in Moscow at the time, where he had gone after a lengthy vacation in the French Midi "to ask [the Soviets] to curb the activities of the Viet Cong and Viet Minh in my country."[1] The coup was preceded by demonstrations in the villages against North Vietnamese occupation of Cambodian territory, by anti-Hanoi riots in Phnom Penh, and on March 13 by an order from the foreign ministry expelling all Vietnamese Communist armed forces from Cambodian territory forthwith. Needless to say, the Cambodians lacked the means to enforce this ultimatum.

In Paris, Le Duc Tho harangued Kissinger about what he regarded as the secret American role in Cambodia, and made it plain that Hanoi intended to overthrow the new government in Phnom Penh. Sihanouk had been granted asylum in China, joined his fortunes to Hanoi's, and declared war on the Lon Nol government, whose members he described as "stooges of the American imperialists."[2] It was only natural that Hanoi should perceive the hand of the CIA in the Cambodian developments, but in fact there were no CIA personnel in Cambodia; Mike Mansfield, the Democratic leader of the Senate, had insisted that none be posted

233

there out of respect for Cambodian neutrality. The coup took the U.S. government completely by surprise and left Nixon fuming about "those clowns at Langley" until he was reminded of the Mansfield prohibition. He called in Richard Helms, the Director of Central Intelligence, and ordered him to dispatch an officer and a communications technician to Phnom Penh forthwith. The State Department bureaucracy managed to delay implementation of this instruction for more than three weeks, partly on grounds that the embassy in Phnom Penh was too small to accommodate the pair from the CIA and their radios. Two additional direct presidential orders were required before State reluctantly carried out Nixon's instructions. This did nothing to elevate Nixon's regard for the Foreign Service. "Jerks!" he growled.

Nixon correctly regarded Sihanouk's decision to entrust his future to Hanoi and its sponsors as a permanent defection from neutrality; should Sihanouk be restored to power by the Communists, he would become their puppet and all of Cambodia would become a North Vietnamese sanctuary for operations against South Vietnam. The President immediately began looking for ways to help Lon Nol survive. Rogers and Laird advised him to hold back: Moscow, Beijing, and Hanoi, they warned, might think we had staged the coup. The CIA didn't think Lon Nol could last.[3] Helms suggested that it might be embarrassing for the United States, and limit its future influence in Cambodia, if it rushed to help a government that was overthrown before it was fairly established. When Nixon pronounced himself ready to take this risk, Helms immediately gave his loyal support to the President's policy while continuing to offer characteristically detached and highly intelligent advice.

Soon after the secret Kissinger–Le Duc Tho conversations adjourned in Paris, North Vietnamese troops began attacking Cambodian objectives. In the next three weeks, they moved westward out of the border sanctuaries in force, and by the end of April they had occupied about 25 percent of Cambodian territory and were on the verge of surrounding Phnom Penh. Repeated appeals by the Cambodians to the United Nations for help in repelling the invaders were ignored.

This was a very troubling development. Although the United States had largely fought the war in Southeast Asia as though Vietnam and Cambodia bore no strategic relationship to each other, the two countries were, in fact, geographically and strategically inseparable. The takeover of Cambodia by Hanoi would almost certainly mean the loss of South Vietnam because it would turn the entire country, with a common border six hundred miles long, into a base for invasion and a military sanctuary for North Vietnam. The North Vietnamese had been systematically violating the neutrality of Cambodia for precisely these purposes ever since the beginning of the war. Now even the pretense of Cambodia's neutrality would vanish; so would Cambodia's nationhood.

The full strategic significance of the events in Cambodia were slow to register on Nixon's inner circle. Weeks passed without an American response of any kind, except that on April 20 Nixon announced the withdrawal of 150,000 American troops from South Vietnam over the following twelve months,[4] 115,000 having already been withdrawn.[5] On April 22, the Joint Chiefs of Staff stated that "most lines of communication leading into Phnom Penh from the north, east, and south have been interdicted by enemy forces and the security of Phnom and Penh and the Cambodian government appears to be seriously threatened."[6] U.S. commanders in Vietnam and the Pacific were asked for recommendations for relieving pressure on the Cambodians. Up to this point, our total contribution to the defense of Cambodia consisted of supplying three thousand captured Kalashnikov assault rifles to Lon Nol's army. These weapons were delivered in secret by the South Vietnamese in order to avoid any suggestion that the United States was providing aid to Phnom Penh and thereby "widening the war."[7]

In January, I had led a team of NSC analysts on a mission to study the military situation in South Vietnam. The hope in Washington was that our report would declare Vietnamization an unqualified success, and in fact we were able to report some hopeful signs. At the same time, all ARVN combat units were still understrength by as much as 30 percent as a result of the government's policy of guaranteeing noncombat duty to volunteers while filling up the fighting divisions with draftees, and the chief weakness of the South Vietnamese military, corrupt or incompetent leadership among the highest-ranking officers, was slow in being corrected.[8]

On the other hand, the enemy was not the same fighting force it had been three or four years before. The NVA and the Viet Cong (now almost entirely manned by infiltrators from the North) had been greatly weakened by U.S. search-and-destroy operations before suffering catastrophic losses of cadre and rank and file in the 1968 Tet offensive. According to U.S. calculations, the Saigon government, which had always controlled the cities, now controlled more than half of the countryside, so that more than four-fifths of the population now lived under Saigon's authority. The enemy now controlled less than 10 percent of the countryside outright; the rest, in which some 4 million people lived, was held by the government by day and by the Viet Cong by night.[9]

Unfortunately, these favorable statistics on the internal security situation in South Vietnam meant little even if they were accurate. The chief threat to Saigon came not from within South Vietnam but from the enemy sanctuaries in Cambodia. It was from Cambodia that NVA and Viet Cong operations had always been planned, manned, supplied, and managed. The secret B-52 raids continued, but they were ineffective against widely scattered troop concentrations hidden in the jungle, against headquarters that moved from one place to another on an almost daily basis, and, especially, against the thousands of caches of arms, ammunition, and military supplies buried or otherwise concealed in the dense forest. So long as this infrastructure remained, the danger to Saigon would not abate. Hanoi had merely to infiltrate a sufficient number of troops into the sanctuaries and then fling them across the border in order to threaten the life of the country; Saigon was only a hard day's march away from the two most famous enclaves, called the Parrot's Beak and the Fishhook.

Only infantry with heavy artillery and close air support could clean out these enemy nests. American infantry had been prohibited from doing so; few had believed that ARVN was capable of carrying out the mission alone if the enemy was present in strength. However, the invasion of Cambodia proper by North Vietnamese and Viet Cong combat formations formerly based in the sanctuaries created a military opportunity to clean out the sanctuaries, cut off a large proportion of the enemy's main force from its bases of supply and communication, and, incidentally, preserve Cambodia from conquest.

The principal argument against an attack on the sanctuaries was that it would leave the administration open to the charge by its domestic critics that it was expanding the war. This argument ignored the plain fact that it was Hanoi that was expanding the war by naked aggression against Cambodia and that any action by the United States that prevented the fall of Phnom Penh would tend to limit the dimensions of the conflict. In the early stages, Rogers and Laird opposed any action in Cambodia. When Nixon was determined to go ahead, they opposed the use of American troops. Laird later expressed the opinion that a combined U.S.–ARVN operation against both objectives would result in eight hundred casualties a week.[10] Laird finally suggested an attack on the Parrot's Beak using only South Vietnamese troops.

Both objectives were located on the frontiers of Military Region III, where the First Infantry Division had conducted its operations. The Battle of Ap Gu had been fought on the approaches to the Fishhook. Because I knew the terrain from having fought over it and had so recently been in Vietnam to study the military situation, Nixon asked my opinion. I told him that the Parrot's Beak, although it was only thirty-three miles from Saigon, was a far less important objective than the Fishhook, which constituted the southern terminus of the Ho Chi Minh Trail and was the nerve center of enemy operations in the South. If we attacked the Parrot's Beak and left the Fishhook undisturbed, enemy reinforcements would flow into the Parrot's Beak from the Fishhook.

No lasting military result could be achieved by attacking the Parrot's Beak. The Fishhook, however, was a choke point. Believing that such an operation was beyond the capabilities of the South Vietnamese and that a defeat would undo whatever had been done to mend their morale and build up their fighting strength and spirit, I argued vigorously against sending ARVN in alone. From a military point of view, the thing to do was attack the Parrot's Beak as a diversion, using the large ARVN forces in the vicinity, and to direct the main attack against the Fishhook, using a combined U.S.–South Vietnamese force supported by American air power and artillery. Although Laird continued to urge attacks on secondary targets by a force that excluded American troops, General Abrams gave the President roughly the same advice as I had rendered.

On May 1, a combined U.S.–ARVN force swept into the Fishhook. Over the next three weeks, it attacked twelve enemy bases, locating and disrupting the mobile COSVN headquarters, capturing five and a half tons of enemy documents and enough small arms and other weapons, ammunition, food, and other supplies to equip six or seven enemy infantry divisions. About 12,000 bunkers and other military structures were destroyed. The President had authorized the destruction of all enemy bases, and these numbers would undoubtedly have been much higher if allied troops had stayed longer in Cambodia and continued to search for the enemy; they might even have engaged the main-force enemy units that were attempting to overrun the rest of Cambodia. But Nixon withdrew them after only two months under strident pressure from his own advisers, doves in Congress, and the antiwar movement.

Dissent burst forth in the White House itself. The press reported, on the basis of accurate leaks, that Laird and Rogers had opposed the Cambodia operation. Three of Kissinger's mutinous young protégés on the NSC staff resigned in protest over the President's decision to raid the enemy

sanctuaries. Most of them subscribed to the notion that the way out of
the war for the United States was to accept the historic inevitability of the
result we had hoped to prevent. If Cambodia had not provided them with
an excuse to go away angry, they would no doubt have found another.
As Kissinger has written with admirable understatement, "they had no
great use for Nixon,"[11] and they had made this so evident that they had
long since been cut off from the policy-making process.

The days following the attack on the Fishhook were marked by a wave
of violent campus demonstrations and bombings, culminating on May 4
in the fatal shooting of four young people by the National Guard at Kent
State University. The events at Kent State touched off a new wave of
campus protest. Tens of thousands of demonstrators descended on Washington to protest the Cambodian incursion. A barricade of buses was
formed around the White House and combat-ready troops were brought
inside the grounds to defend it against a possible attack by the mob
(although no machine guns were set up, as in the worst days of the anti-
Johnson hysteria).

The lowing of the crowd could be heard in the Oval Office and even
in my basement cell. From time to time, I went outside to look at the
demonstrators as they passed along Pennsylvania Avenue waving their
Viet Cong flags and shouting their slogans and obscenities. Viewed from
the White House lawn, the scene was a combination of demonic ceremony, class picnic, collective tantrum, and mating ritual. Most of the
marchers seemed to be nice, sincere kids who had come to the capital
from all over the nation because it was the thing to do in that season of
faddish radicalism and—unless youth had changed more than I suspected
since my own college years—because it was a way to meet boys and
girls. The marchers were dressed in the mock military uniform of the
movement—blue jeans, work shirts, and boots, with hair worn at regulation length. The unisex costumes and flowing tresses of both genders
created a curiously androgynous impression. They were a herd. The
thought crossed my mind that they all would have been wearing white
bucks and tweed jackets or saddle shoes and plaid skirts if the march had
taken place in 1950 instead of 1970.

One night just after midnight while the tribal chant drifted through
the West Wing, Nixon appeared in the doorway of my cubbyhole. As
usual, he urged me to remain seated while he stood before my desk.
That was all that was usual about his appearance. He was somewhat
disheveled—tie a little askew, coat unbuttoned, hair slightly tousled.
These signs of disorder were so small that they might have passed unre-

marked in a man less meticulously well-groomed than Nixon. In him, they were very noticeable. He smiled, also a rare event when he was in private. "We've had a tough day, Al," he said. "Things are bad out there. But we've got to stick to our guns. We've done the right thing and we have to go on." He gave me a look of deep sympathy and I realized that he had come downstairs to buck me up; he knew that I was deeply disturbed by his decision to limit the duration and depth of the operation in Cambodia. It was his way of telling me, to whom he owed no explanations of any kind, that he agreed with the advice I had given him even though political considerations had caused him to modify his decision. In the small hours of that same morning, he paid an impulsive visit to the young people camped around the Lincoln Memorial. This adventure made the Secret Service very uneasy; it was entirely possible that he might have been attacked by the mob. As it was, he chatted quietly about his policies and goals with some of the youngsters, saying that he hoped that their "hatred of the war, which I could well understand, would not turn into a bitter hatred of our whole system, our country, and everything that it stood for."[12] When his remarks were reported in the press the next day, he was portrayed as having insulted the idealism of the marchers by discussing sports rather than issues with them. He was stung by the unfairness of this distortion, despite his long experience with ideologues.

Although it ended too soon and did not achieve its full potential in terms of the destruction of enemy resources in the sanctuaries, the Cambodian incursion was a military and strategic success by any rational standard of judgment. The government of Lon Nol and the existence of Cambodia as a nation were preserved, however temporarily. No significant enemy activity was launched out of Cambodia into Vietnam for the next two years, partly because the huge quantity of supplies that had flowed into the Cambodian sanctuaries from the port of Sihanoukville (estimated at 85 percent of the total being used in the war against us) was choked off.[13] The enemy troops remaining in the sanctuaries relied thereafter on supplies carried down the Ho Chi Minh trial through neutral Laos.

As to measurable political effects among the American people, a Gallup poll taken in mid-May reported that 65 percent of those polled approved of the way in which Nixon was handling the presidency. Fifty percent approved of the decision to send troops into Cambodia. When Kissinger next met with Le Duc Tho in Paris, on September 7, he found his opposite number in a mood that approached affability. The North Vietnamese dropped their demand that the United States get out of Vietnam entirely inside of six months, made no mention of the ten points Xuan Thuy had recited to Kissinger, and even suggested that they might reconsider their political proposals. To my military mind, this suggested that we might be witnessing a case of cause and effect; having whacked the creature on the snout instead of cooing into its ear, we had given it the idea that it might be in its interest to be better behaved. Few were as willing as I was to see this connection.

18

Two Confrontations

Around this same time, the Soviets, acting as usual through surrogates, staged a series of tests of American will in places where their influence was strong. In 1970, these included not only the hectic enemy offensive activity in South Vietnam, Cambodia, and Laos but also the attempted establishment of a Soviet naval base in Cienfuegos, Cuba, and the Syrian invasion of Jordan, with Soviet advisers riding the Syrian tanks right up to the frontier. In 1971, came the Indo-Pakistan War, in which the Soviet hand manipulated the Indian pawn in an attempt to destroy an ally of the United States.

Two of these episodes, the Syrian invasion of Jordan and the construction of a Soviet naval base in Cuba, occurred in the same week. Both involved vital strategic interests of the United States. Either might well have escalated into war with the U.S.S.R. but were controlled by the timely deployment of military power in conjunction with plainspoken diplomacy.

The former episode, later memorialized as "Black September" in Palestinian versions of the event, sprang into being on September 1, 1970, when terrorists of the Palestine Liberation Organization (PLO) attempted for the second time in three months to assassinate King Hussein of Jordan. The PLO objective was to take over the government of Jordan with the backing of the Soviet Union's two chief clients in the region, Jordan's neighbors Syria and Iraq. Because this operation could have no other purpose than an eventual attempt to invade and destroy Israel, the fall of Hussein would certainly have meant a preemptive Israeli invasion of Jordan. That, in turn, would likely have sparked a war in the Middle East from which the United States, because of its commitment to the survival of Israel, might not have been able to remain aloof. In Nixon's words, "It was like a ghastly game of dominoes, with a nuclear war waiting at the end."[1]

Like so many other situations involving the fate of mankind during the Cold War, this was not a misunderstanding that could be resolved by an appeal to reason. In fact, American interest in preserving the status quo was based in part on the reality that King Hussein was the only leader in the region who was willing to listen to reason within the limits imposed by his precarious situation. Because the territory he ruled, an expanse of desert slightly larger than Indiana, had formed the portion of Palestine lying east of the Jordan River before the British broke it off in 1922 to create the emirate of Transjordan, Palestinians expelled from Israel regarded Jordan as part of their historic homeland. (Transjordan became the Hashemite kingdom of Jordan in 1946.)

After the 1967 Arab-Israeli War, in which Israel conquered territories surrounding Jerusalem on the West Bank of the Jordan that had been occupied by Jordan during the 1948 War, the PLO had formed in Jordan what amounted to a state within a state. This sad collective of the dispossessed was governed, policed, and symbolized politically by a large army of guerrillas scattered among numerous base camps from which attacks on Israel's territory and citizens were launched. The guerrillas were not the only foreign military presence in Jordan; about 17,000 Iraqi troops left over from the 1967 war were stationed in the eastern part of the country, ostensibly to defend it and the Palestinians against Israel.

Immediately after the second attempt on the king's life on September 1, fighting broke out between the Jordanian army and the Palestinian guerrillas. Jordanian artillery shelled PLO positions. Iraq issued an ultimatum warning that its troops would intervene to protect the Palestinians unless the shelling stopped by 11:00 P.M. Despite appeals from Hussein for U.S. diplomatic and moral support, the State Department temporized. The two sides began to talk.

On September 6, terrorists belonging to the Popular Front for the Liberation of Palestine (PFLP), one of the more homicidal components of the PLO, hijacked a TWA Boeing 707 and a Swissair DC-8 and forced the pilots to fly them and the passengers to a dirt airstrip outside Amman.

A Pan Am 747 was also hijacked and was flown to Cairo, where the passengers were released before the plane was blown up. Three days later, a British VC-10 was hijacked and then landed on the desert airstrip near Amman. The passengers aboard the three remaining airliners, many of them American, were held as hostages. After the United States and Israel rejected an offer by the hijackers to exchange the passengers (except for Israelis and Americans holding both U.S. and Israeli passports) for terrorists held in prisons in Israel and other countries, the hijackers moved their hostages to various undisclosed locations in Amman, and on September 12 they blew up the three hijacked planes. Nixon ordered that a message be sent to Arab governments warning that the killing of hostages could have serious consequences. Arabists in the State Department, ever mindful of how easily feelings are wounded in the Middle East, blocked the message. The Arabists argued (as I understood what they were saying to me over the telephone) that such an insult might incite the terrorists to murder the hostages as a proof of manhood.

By September 16, the hijackings and other calculated Palestinian affronts to Jordanian sovereignty had driven the king's loyal army into a state of retributive anger. Hussein surrounded Amman with loyal troops and declared a military government. Nobody believed that the Palestinians would accept the reestablishment of the king's authority without a fight.

Through all this, Nixon and Kissinger were far stronger than the rest of the administration. Both understood that the preservation of Hussein's government was the key to peace in the Middle East, and that its collapse could result in world war. Despite the domestic political risks involved, Nixon was prepared from the beginning to intervene with United States forces if such action proved to be necessary to save the situation. Kissinger tended to favor Israeli action if the situation got out of hand, because the Israelis, who had no problem in the Knesset where the defense of Israel was concerned, could do what had to be done quickly and efficiently.

On September 17, Hussein ordered his forces into Amman. Fierce fighting with the Palestinian guerrillas broke out in the capital and elsewhere in the country. Before launching his military operation, Hussein had warned the newly arrived American ambassador, Dean Brown, that Syria might intervene on the side of the Palestinians. Brown, a leading State Department expert on the Middle East, told me over the telephone that he did not believe that this was likely.[2] In a matter of hours, however, we learned that Syrian tanks were massed near the border and were apparently on the point of crossing over into Jordan in support of the

Palestinians. This development had not been anticipated, or even mentioned as a possibility, by anyone in the United States government, apparently because it constituted the unthinkable crime of aggression by one Arab state against another.

Nixon, who was in Chicago on a speaking tour as these events unfolded, told the editors of the *Sun-Times* that the United States might have to intervene in Jordan to preserve King Hussein's government if the Syrians or the Iraqis took a hand. This blunt public warning caused consternation in the news media, the State Department, and Congress. (Both Mike Mansfield, the majority leader of the Senate, and Richard Russell, the chairman of the Senate Appropriations Committee, told the administration that they were opposed to the use of American troops in the Middle East.[3]) It even ruffled the composure of Kissinger, who had hoped to avoid such a specific public statement of American resolve and who was somewhat startled when the President jumped off the tracks his advisers were so laboriously laying for him. Kissinger, in his capacity as chairman of the Washington Special Actions Group (WSAG) that was managing the crisis, was in charge of presenting options to the President on the basis of information flowing in from the site of the emergency. Much of the information flowed through me, and I passed it on to Kissinger or the President.

On Nixon's orders, an American naval force of overwhelming strength was moved close to the scene of the crisis. The aircraft carrier *Saratoga* and her escorts, including a cruiser and twelve destroyers already in the eastern Mediterranean, were ordered to join the carrier *Independence* and its task force off the coast of Lebanon. A third aircraft carrier, the *John F. Kennedy*, was dispatched with its supporting warships to the eastern Mediterranean from its station off Puerto Rico, and other naval units, including the helicopter carrier *Guam*, the cruiser *Springfield*, and two amphibious task forces of U.S. Marines, also joined the armada.

An infantry brigade then on maneuvers in West Germany was placed on alert, together with elements of the Eighty-second Airborne Division at Fort Bragg, North Carolina; this brought the number of American troops on alert to twenty thousand. The ostensible reason for alerting the troops was the possible rescue and evacuation of hostages and other American citizens in Jordan; another reason, obvious to all, was the possible reinforcement of Hussein. All military moves connected to the crisis in Jordan were made as openly as possible in order that the Soviets and their collaborators would quickly know from their own intelligence what we were doing and draw the accurate conclusion that we were determined to prevent the fall of Hussein and his government.*

On September 18, Golda Meir, the prime minister of Israel, called on Nixon in the Oval Office. The meeting had been scheduled far in advance, but of course its importance was greatly increased by the circumstances. As I have said, all female heads of government made Nixon uncomfortable. The matriarchal Mrs. Meir was no exception, and on this occasion she followed her usual practice of laying down the law in a stern, motherly tone, to which her patient smile added the impression, familiar to every erring boy, that she was giving her listener a scolding for his own good. The United States, she said, had let the Egyptians get away with violations of the 1967 cease-fire with Israel and had not taken a tough enough line about the heavy flow of Soviet arms, equipment, and military advisers into the Middle East. Soviet troops were operating antiaircraft missile batteries and other advanced weapons supplied to the Egyptians; Soviet pilots were flying Soviet aircraft with Egyptian markings in encounters with Israeli planes along the Suez Canal.

---

*This time, the fleet movements and other military measures ordered by the President were carried out without delay because they were communicated directly to the Joint Chiefs of Staff at the same time that they were passed to the Secretary of Defense. After the EC-121 crisis, Nixon ordered that a military liaison office be set up in the White House to provide a direct channel of communication between himself and the chairman of the Joint Chiefs of Staff. Capt. (afterward Rear Adm.) Rembrandt C. Robinson, USN, was seconded as head of this office during the summer of 1970 by the new chairman, Adm. Thomas H. Moorer. The President's intention, clearly stated, was that the chairman should be kept fully informed through the NSC system not only of all presidential orders affecting the military but that he should also be provided with any other national security information the JCS needed to know. It was, in short, a system set up by the President for the stated purpose of making his decisions and the deliberations that led to those decisions known to the chairman of the Joint Chiefs of Staff on a routine basis. Nixon's order, an example of the lengths to which he would go to avoid confrontation, was carried out with a measure of discretion not because of any clandestine purpose but because of his wish to spare Laird embarrassment. In 1991, a book (*Silent Coup*, by Len Colodny and Robert Gettlin) advanced the bizarre theory that the military liaison office was the center of a "military spy ring" whose sinister and hidden purpose was to drive Nixon from office by stealing the secrets of the presidency on behalf of the Joint Chiefs of Staff. The complete opposite was true: Nixon set up the military liaison office for the very purpose of transmitting sensitive national security information to the chairman of the Joint Chiefs of Staff because he wanted to be sure that the Chiefs knew what he wanted them to do in a crisis and why he wanted them to do it. By turning this subtle example of presidential handling of an obdurate Cabinet member into a fairy tale for conspiracy buffs, the authors missed the real and far more interesting story. Their theory, and the "evidence" on which it is based, is so disconnected from reality that it would not merit mention here except for the attack it makes upon the honor of Rear Admiral Robinson, who, after leaving the White House, was killed in line of duty in Vietnam. Robinson is unable to defend himself from the grave. To the extent that I can perform this service for his memory and his family, I do so now by stating categorically that any suggestion that this officer committed any act of disloyalty whatsoever to the United States or to his Commander in Chief while serving in the White House is totally false. On the contrary, he carried out the orders of the President with the honesty, efficiency, and initiative that were the hallmarks of his character and career.

The Israeli ambassador to Washington, Yitzhak Rabin, crouched before the two heads of government, tracing Egyptian and Soviet infractions on secret maps spread out on the carpet. Soviet meddling, not the Arabs, was the chief danger to Israel, said Mrs. Meir, waving a finger in admonition. Soviet meddling was the reason behind the crisis in Jordan and the reason why the position of the United States had been deteriorating throughout the Middle East. Nixon must do something about this. The way to deal with the problem, she said, was to "go to the Soviets directly and demand an adjustment of the situation."[4]

Though he could not have enjoyed being spoken to in the tone of voice Mrs. Meir was using, Nixon exercised his usual iron self-control in such situations and gave no hint that he was discomfited in any way. He found nothing to disagree with in her discourse; he understood that Moscow was behind our problems in the Middle East as in most other parts of the world (although, in fact, his opinion that the Soviets could be weaned away from bad behavior may have been stronger than his visitor's). He told Mrs. Meir in detail what we had been saying to the Soviets and what they had been saying to us. The Americans were being firm. The Russians were being reassuring; when the Russians behaved in that way, the wise had reason to be cautious.

He then launched into a masterly summary of the dangers and opportunities presented by the crisis in Jordan. America's interest in this particular case was to prevent the overthrow of Hussein in such a way as to leave him stronger after the event than he had been before. This meant avoiding any precipitous military action by Israel, such as a ground invasion of Jordan. Hussein's moderation had already cost him dearly in the Arab world; any appearance that he had been rescued by Israel from defeat by the Palestinians would destroy his credibility and effectiveness forever.

No one understood this better than Mrs. Meir, and when Nixon asked for her assurance that Israel would not move into Jordan with military forces without consulting with the United States, she agreed.[5] He had already assured her that the United States intended to preserve the balance of military power in the Middle East. This was the customary way of saying that Washington would continue to provide the Israelis with the arms, matériel, and diplomatic support they needed to defend themselves against an attack by any combination of Arab states. Few foreign leaders ever left Nixon's presence unimpressed by his candor, knowledge, and good sense; to all appearances, Mrs. Meir was no exception.

The fact that Mrs. Meir had agreed to let the United States know in advance of any Israeli military action against the Syrians or the Iraqis did not mean that Israel had abandoned the idea of taking such action, or that others in the United States government had abandoned the option of Israeli intervention. Kissinger and his WSAG colleagues advised the President that armed Israeli action was preferable to direct American intervention, even though the President took the opposite view. Nixon, as he had explained to Mrs. Meir, believed that an Israeli rescue operation, even if it left Hussein in power, would destroy him as effectively in political terms as a Palestinian takeover. Kissinger argued that the Israelis would be a factor in any case because the only overland supply route for U.S. ground forces in Jordan was by way of Israel.[6] (In fact, American airborne troops would have dropped from the sky and been supplied from the sky once they established an airhead.)

On September 18, the day of Mrs. Meir's visit, more than a hundred Soviet-made tanks of the Syrian army crossed the border into Jordan. Intelligence reports told us that the units involved were composed entirely of Palestinian troops recruited in the refugee camps in Syria. They were led by officers of the Syrian army, and large numbers of Soviet military advisers had ridden the tanks right up to the border before jumping off and sending the Arab crews forward on their own. The latter proceeded only a very short distance into Jordan before halting—about one-fourth of a kilometer. Kissinger delivered a stern note to the Soviets; Rogers made a public statement calling on the Syrians to withdraw. By late afternoon, about half the tanks had turned around and returned to the Syrian side of the frontier.

During these events and throughout the crisis, I was in frequent contact with Ambassador Rabin. It was evident from my conversations with him, which took place over the telephone and in person in the White House and the Israeli embassy, that whatever Mrs. Meir had promised Nixon, Israel wanted to cross into Jordan with ground forces as a matter of self-defense. Naturally, I reported this immediately to the President and Kissinger. They were not surprised to hear what I told them. They instructed me to remind the Israelis of their promise of advance notice and to discourage them in the President's name from invading. I did my best to do this.

Rabin, an expert in tank warfare, was under no illusions as to the probable outcome if a Palestinian armored force out of Syria was to join the Palestinian guerrillas against King Hussein's army. Neither was I. In the absence of enemy armor, Jordanian forces were doing very well; Hussein's forces, originally established by the famous British general John Glubb as the Arab Legion, had a reputation for military efficiency, fighting spirit, and fierce loyalty to their brave and intelligent king. But they were short of armor, and judging from the reports of Ambassador Brown, who was talking to the Jordanian high command and briefing me regularly by telephone from a bunker in embattled Amman, and from other indications (the Palestinians had established a "liberated zone" in the north), the Jordanian army was already in a very difficult situation. In case of a massive armored attack from Syria, Hussein's forces would be in danger of being overwhelmed.

On Sunday, September 20, Syrian tanks crossed the Jordanian border in two columns in the vicinity of Ramtha. Once again, they were manned entirely by Palestinian crews, officered by Syrians, and accompanied by Soviet military advisers until they reached the frontier. King Hussein informed us that his forces had knocked out about thirty tanks and he asked for air reconnaissance by United States aircraft to see whether the Syrians were bringing up reinforcements. Later in the day, two more armored brigades of the Syrian army attacked across the border at several points. There was no possibility that the Jordanians could defeat such a force on their own resources.

The President was at Camp David. Kissinger spent much of the day in meetings with the WSAG and in consultation with Nixon. That left me to handle the telephones. A steady stream of calls came in from Jordan and from Rabin. The Jordanian center was beginning to buckle. I recommended moving the airborne brigade in Germany to its airhead, which reduced its alert time to four hours, and placing the entire Eighty-second Airborne Division on combat alert and all U.S. forces on a lower form of alert. Kissinger agreed with these recommendations and passed them on to the President, who approved them. Kissinger returned from this presidential encounter in a state of high amusement; he had found Nixon in the White House bowling alley, nonchalantly rolling a few lines while wearing highly polished black oxfords. Kissinger, always alert for the comic detail, regarded Nixon's nonregulation shoes as a priceless touch.

At about 10:00 P.M., Kissinger came into the office where I had spent most of the long day alone and telephoned Rabin, who was in New York attending a dinner in honor of Mrs. Meir. Rabin asked whether it would be all right with Washington if the Israeli air force flew some reconnaissance missions over the battle area at dawn (about three hours away in the Middle East time zone) and asked for the acquiescence of the United States government in Israeli air strikes on the Syrian armor. Kissinger approved the reconnaissance but temporized about the air strikes. While

Kissinger was still on the phone with Rabin, Hussein called to say that his forces had been split in two by the Syrian armored assault.

Kissinger descended once again into the bowling alley and the President approved Israeli air strikes. Kissinger called Rabin back and told him that we would not stand in the way of air action against the Syrian armor by the Israelis and that the United States would replace any Israeli equipment or matériel lost or expended in the effort. Moreover, we'd do our best to forestall Soviet interference; thanks to the reinforcement of the Sixth Fleet, we had strong local superiority in sea and air power. Nixon, having finished his game of bowls, strolled into Kissinger's office and listened while Kissinger talked. Then Nixon went upstairs. Kissinger, after more meetings with WSAG and numerous telephone calls, went home to bed at about 2:00 A.M. I stayed a couple of hours longer, then drove myself home.

The phone was ringing as I entered the bedroom, where Pat, inured to the sound of bells in the night, was awakened by my loud groan of weary resignation; I had not slept for at least eighteen hours. I answered the phone. The caller was Ambassador Brown in Amman, describing the sense of desperation that had settled on the capital as a result of reports from the battlefield. For several hours, stretched out on the bedroom floor with the telephone at my ear, I received and made call after call, unable to return to the White House, a twenty-minute ride from our house in the suburbs, for fear that I would be out of touch at the crucial moment. Pat provided me with cups of coffee that helped to keep me awake.

Rabin called to say that Israeli intelligence suggested that Jordanian forces were on the point of breaking in the vicinity of Irbid, Jordan's second-largest city, located about fifteen miles from the border of Israel. Rabin is a man of temperament who speaks his mind when the occasion calls for it. With some heat, he said that air strikes might not be enough to deal with the situation. His government was more than ever of the opinion the Israeli army should go into Jordan on the ground: "If we're going to do this, Al, we should do it right." From a purely military point of view, he was correct; the distances separating Israel from her enemies are in many cases very short, and it was entirely possible that the Syrian tanks, if they broke through the Jordanian line, could be inside Israel in an hour. Rabin asked for the President's approval of a ground attack.

I woke Kissinger at 5:15 A.M. and told him what Rabin had said. Kissinger talked to the President and instructed me to tell Rabin that we

would call him back with the President's decision about Israeli ground
attacks. On balance, the President was still against any such action, as he
had been from the start, and for the same reasons. It occurred to me, so
it must have occurred to Nixon and Kissinger, too, that the mere threat
of such an attack—a movement of troops and tanks—might be enough
to cause the Syrian armor to retreat.

I had no authority to encourage the Israelis to mobilize, but, inasmuch
as we had promised to discourage the Soviets, I ordered a COB aircraft,
a small propeller-driven machine often used by the Navy to transport
high-ranking officers, to fly a command planning team from one of the
U.S. carriers to Tel Aviv, informing Kissinger of my action after the fact.
This was designed to create the impression in Moscow, which monitored
Sixth Fleet radio traffic, that joint U.S.–Israeli operations in Jordan might
be imminent. Meanwhile, the alert status of U.S. ground troops was
stepped up, with two battalions of the Eighty-second Airborne Division
being placed on six-hour alert while the battle-ready brigade in West
Germany was ordered to prepare to enplane. These signals, too, would
be picked up by Soviet listening posts.

The other side shortly responded to all this scurrying about. First, the
Soviets delivered a conciliatory reply to the American note of the day
before. We had demanded the immediate withdrawal of all Syrian forces.
The Soviets replied that they were now urging the Syrians to withdraw
and expressed the hope that we were urging restraint on the Israelis.
Second, the Syrian air force, commanded by a little-known general
named Hafez al-Assad who was to seize power in Syria soon after the
war, grounded itself; not a single Syrian plane took off in support of the
Syrian armored columns, which were by now deep inside Jordan along
a broad front. This was an astonishing departure from tactical doctrine,
especially since the Jordanian air force reported that it was attacking the
Syrian tanks from the air. Despite the threats of intervention issuing from
Baghdad before the fighting began, the Iraqi troops inside Jordan had
remained quiescent, taking no part whatsoever in the conflict.[7]

While these events unfolded, midmorning came and went without
word being passed to the Israelis regarding the President's attitude toward
a ground attack designed to drive the Syrians (and, by implication, the
Iraqis) out of Jordan. Rabin phoned to ask for an explanation of the delay.
I could give him none.

"How much longer must we wait?" asked Rabin.

The Israelis had, of course, already received Nixon's approval in regard to air strikes and this was still in effect. There was no need to consult anyone again on this point.

I said, "You've already got the President's okay on the bombing. Go ahead and do the air."

It was subsequently reported that Israeli fighter-bombers struck the Syrian columns in northern Jordan, destroying many tanks and breaking the back of the invasion. Authorized accounts of the battle, however, omitted mention of the Israeli role and credited the Jordanian air force with the destruction of about 125 Syrian tanks, added to about 30 said to have been destroyed during the first incursion. Israeli kills may have been hidden in these totals, which may themselves be an understatement of Syrian losses.

On the evening of September 22, in a public conversation at a reception at the Egyptian embassy, Kissinger rejected a suggestion by Yuli M. Vorontsov of the Soviet embassy that the Syrians might merely stop where they were inside Jordan instead of recrossing the border. This was, of course, an open admission of Soviet complicity. Kissinger insisted that the invaders must withdraw from Jordan forthwith and to the last man. Vorontsov went on to say, for the benefit of hovering reporters, that Moscow wanted the Syrian intervention ended. This represented the complete Soviet abandonment of the attempt to take over Jordan that Moscow had conceived, encouraged, advised, and equipped.

By 3:00 P.M. on September 23, Washington time, what remained of the Syrian armor had disengaged, reversed direction, and was fleeing back toward the border. The Israeli air strikes, together with strong American diplomacy backed by credible military maneuvers suggesting that overwhelming United States air, sea, and ground power would be committed to the conflict if necessary, preserved King Hussein's regime, and, with it, the frazzled peace of the region. The whole American operation, as conceived by a calm and judicious President and orchestrated by Kissinger, was a textbook example of steady behavior by a superpower in defense of the rule of law, and it contained a great lesson in regard to the central reality of the world situation—namely, that the combination of America's moral and military strength was irresistible when invoked in the right cause.

A second crisis precipitated by a reckless Soviet adventure was in the making even while the crisis in Jordan was in progress. On September 15, four days before Syrian tanks crossed the border into Jordan for the first time, U-2 reconnaissance photographs confirmed that the Soviets were building a naval base on the tiny island of Cayo Alcatraz in the bay of Cienfuegos, located on the southern coast of Cuba roughly 240 miles due south of Miami. We already knew that a considerable Soviet naval force was steaming toward Cuba. The base at Cienfuegos, obviously designed to service nuclear ballistic missile submarines, was practically complete even though construction had begun less than three weeks earlier. Pictures taken by the U-2s' cameras showed barracks and administration buildings onshore and a Soviet submarine tender and support barges moored in the harbor. Submarine nets had been strung across the entrance to the harbor. A few miles down the coast, another base was under construction on the mainland. It included a new dock, fuel-storage tanks, and a powerful new communications installation guarded by radar and antiaircraft missiles.[8]

CIA analysis of the photographs confirmed the obvious—the U.S.S.R. was establishing a base in Cuba for offensive naval operations in the Atlantic and the Caribbean. The Defense Department told the President that the base at Cienfuegos would mean that the Soviet navy could increase the number of ballistic-missile submarines on station off the eastern and southern coasts of the United States by one-third, or increase their patrol time by about one-third. Because nuclear missiles from Soviet submarines were capable of striking every city and military installation in the forty-eight contiguous states and were much more numerous and powerful than the comparatively primitive IRBMs the Soviets had tried to smuggle ashore eight years before, the base at Cienfuegos was a far more serious threat than the missile bases that had precipitated the Cuban Missile Crisis.

The construction of this installation was a flagrant violation of the 1962 Soviet–U.S. understandings on Cuba, under which the Soviets had guaranteed the Kennedy administration that they would in the future build no offensive military facilities in Cuba. Its construction in such obvious haste could only be regarded as evidence of the Soviet's intention to present Nixon with a strategic fait accompli on the eve of midterm elections, just as they had nearly succeeded in doing when they installed their rockets in Cuba during the second autumn of John F. Kennedy's presidency.

Nixon, however, was an entirely different kind of adversary. His first reaction was to ask what measures, overt or covert, the United States could take to put American missiles back in Turkey or build an American submarine base in the Black Sea—"anything," as he put it, "which will give us some trading stock." His directive was to keep the matter quiet in the hope he could avoid turning negotiations into the sort of media extravaganza that had accompanied the Cuban Missile Crisis. He believed that the Soviets were more likely to dismantle the base if they could do so without making a worldwide show of backing down in the face of U.S. power.[9] The public-relations fable that Khrushchev had quailed before Kennedy in 1962 had contributed to the Russian's downfall. That lesson still lingered in the Kremlin and rankled in the Soviet armed forces, making any show of Soviet abjectness unlikely in this case.

The Joint Chiefs of Staff recommended removing the Cienfuegos base by whatever means necessary. If it remained, it would not only increase the military threat to the United States and its people beyond tolerable limits but also represent a humiliation of the United States that would certainly result in an intensification of Cuban subversion and terror in the southern hemisphere. At the NSC meeting of September 23, Secretary of State Rogers took the adamant position that the United States should do nothing about the Cienfuegos base in the short term, and that its very existence should be kept a secret from the American people until after the November elections.[10] Evidently someone present disagreed with this approach. On the twenty-fifth, C. L. Sulzberger of the *New York Times* broke the story of the Cienfuegos construction, and that afternoon the Pentagon confirmed the existence of the Soviet submarine base in what was described as an inadvertent admission by a spokesman during a routine press briefing.

That afternoon, Kissinger met Dobrynin (just back from lengthy consultations in Moscow) in the White House Map Room. He told him that we knew about the base and would "view it with the utmost gravity if construction continue[d] and the base remain[ed]."[11] Dobrynin asked whether we considered that the understanding of 1962 had been violated. Kissinger said yes, we did, and that the deceptive way in which the Soviets had gone about building the base reinforced our concern. Dobrynin, registering grave concern, replied that he would communicate what Kissinger had just told him to the Kremlin. In the face of this relatively mild expression of U.S. displeasure, construction activity at Cienfuegos, as monitored by our U-2 flights, slowed down somewhat. But it did not cease.

In a quixotic moment, Nixon ordered that all leaks to the press on this matter should stop. Somehow, for the most part they did. Those that had already taken place proved to be less damaging than the President had feared. The last thing the Democrats in Congress and their sympathizers in the news media wanted on the eve of the congressional elections was a successful display of Nixonian machismo. Press reports generally minimized the importance of the base, echoing the line of Democrats on Capitol Hill that Cienfuegos was a trumped-up crisis invented by a devious President for the purpose of swelling the defense budget and increasing Republican vote totals. James Reston and some others in the press understood the gravity of the situation, but their judicious comments were obscured by their more doctrinaire colleagues who thought that Nixon was crying wolf.

Nixon himself, half-amused and half-vexed as usual by the tenor of the coverage, knew that he could have obliterated this argument by showing the evidence gathered by the U-2s on television, as Kennedy had done in 1962. Later on, he told me he was never tempted to do so; he had been appalled by the theatricality of Kennedy's management of the Cuban Missile Crisis.

Nixon left on September 27 for a long-scheduled trip to the Mediterranean, taking Kissinger, Rogers, and Laird with him. No reply to Kissinger's warning had arrived from Moscow before the President departed. Additional evidence was subsequently received that the construction activity was continuing. Kissinger phoned me from *Air Force One* and told me to call on Dobrynin at the Soviet embassy and deliver the message again. I said, "In the same terms as before?" Kissinger replied, "No. Take a stronger line."

Immediately after Kissinger disconnected, I called the Soviet embassy and arranged for a meeting with the ambassador, stating that I had a message from the President to deliver to the Soviet government. Dobrynin, who served as Soviet ambassador in Washington for twenty-four years, long enough to become dean or the most senior member of the diplomatic corps, was renowned as few envoys ever have been for his ability to push the right buttons in Washington. His charm was legendary. In his dimly lighted office (the Soviets covered all windows with drapes and steel shutters to discourage American eavesdroppers and Peeping Toms), he greeted me with his usual effusiveness.

"Mr. Ambassador," I said, "I am instructed to say the following. You are putting offensive weapons into Cuba. This is an intolerable violation of the 1962 understanding between our two countries. Either you take those weapons out and dismantle the base in Cienfuegos Bay or we will do it for you."

The words were no sooner out of my mouth than Dobrynin's charm vanished. The affable Russian was transformed into an angry and threatening man. Flushing angrily, he said in a loud voice, "You are threatening the Soviet Union. *That* is what is intolerable." His demeanor sent an unmistakable signal: If you want trouble, you're going to get it.

I said, "Mr. Ambassador, I have delivered my message. Now I will leave."

On my return to the White House, I sent Kissinger a message describing my encounter with Dobrynin. Soon after that, he phoned from *Air Force One* in an even worse temper than Dobrynin. "I'm furious; the President is furious," he shouted. "You have exceeded your authority. You can't talk to the Russians that way. You may have started a war."

I did not think so. Presently, the Soviets started to withdraw their naval forces from the vicinity of Cuba, and our U-2s began to bring back photographs indicating that the base was in the process of being dismantled. On October 5, the day Nixon returned to Washington, Dobrynin requested an urgent appointment with Kissinger. He handed us a note stating that "the Soviet side has not done and is not doing in Cuba now— that includes the area of the Cienfuegos port—anything . . . that would contradict that [1962] understanding." Nor, said the note, would they do anything of that kind in the future.[12]

As the President had hoped, the Soviets had withdrawn gracefully and privately, papering over their capitulation with the pretense that the base they eventually dismantled completely had never existed. For whatever it is worth, after this incident my own relations with Dobrynin took on a new cordiality that lasted through the many years of diplomatic contact that remained ahead.

19

Mission to China

The secret diplomatic process that led up to Nixon's famous trip to China in February 1972 has been described elsewhere in minute detail by Nixon, Kissinger, and many others. Although I was the keeper of the details, in the sense that I managed the logistics of the negotiations and in the latter stages frequently took part in clandestine meetings with our principal Chinese contact in the United States, UN ambassador Huang Hua, in a seedy CIA safe house in Manhattan,* I will not tell the whole story again. The basic facts are well known: An accumulation of carefully orchestrated small gestures and assurances, passing through many discreet and unlikely channels over a period of two years, resulted in Kissinger's two trips to Beijing and to the negotiations that led to the admission of the People's Republic of China to the United Nations, the cordial meetings between Nixon and Mao Zedong and Zhou Enlai, and the reestablishment of normal relations between the United States and China after twenty-two years of estrangement.

---

*These secret meetings, with Kissinger and me or sometimes myself alone on the American side and Huang Hua and his diplomat wife, Xe Lilang, on the other, were placed in jeopardy when one of the officials of the Chinese delegation to the United Nations suddenly and inexplicably died. The Chinese suspected that he had been murdered by mysterious American agents. After several tense meetings, they agreed to permit an autopsy to determine the cause of death. The results showed that the man had succumbed to food poisoning as a result of eating spoiled food he had bought in a Chinatown grocery store and cooked in his apartment.

256

This process was buttressed by a number of U.S. actions that preserved Chinese interests. When, early in the administration, the Soviets had floated the suggestion that they might destroy the Chinese nuclear capability with a preemptive nuclear strike, Nixon had instructed Kissinger to tell Dobrynin that the United States would not countenance such a wrongful and dangerous act. In December 1971, at a time when China was too weak militarily to decisively influence the situation itself, resolute American diplomacy backed by fleet movements had frustrated a Soviet-Indian conspiracy to conquer both parts of Pakistan and establish a hostile, Soviet-influenced India along China's southern frontiers.

The diplomatic point man in all these events was, of course, Henry Kissinger, but it was Nixon who, in successive flashes of inspiration, conceived the grand design. Nixon had made a public case for reestablishing normal relations with Beijing in a *Foreign Affairs* article published in 1967, and he had referred to the question indirectly in his inaugural address and afterward, but these statements attracted little attention in the United States. Most foreign-policy thinkers, fixated on the Soviet Union as the superpower on the other end of the nuclear seesaw, regarded the quarantine of China as irrevocable, at least by any American initiative. Then, on February 1, 1969, Nixon let Kissinger know in the deepest secrecy that he intended to seek rapprochement.[1]

When Kissinger called me into his office and told me about the President's order, so utterly unexpected, so grand in its conception, and so different from the timid holding actions of the 1960s, I was dazzled by its potential for influencing the Soviets. Kissinger, who reacted to almost any sudden development with a rush of words, gave me no chance to express an opinion. He was the picture of a man taken unawares. He was by no means convinced that the President's policy was capable of fulfillment. "Our Leader has taken leave of reality," he intoned in mock despair. "He thinks this is the moment to establish normal relations with Communist China. He has just ordered me to make this flight of fancy come true." He grasped his head in his hands. "China!"

This mood did not last very long. Soon Kissinger caught up to the President's thinking and I myself began to see that it was more far-reaching than the clever anti-Soviet chess move I had at first thought it to be. (Normal U.S. relations with China, besides being justified by a simple respect for reality, would be good, not bad, for our relations with the U.S.S.R., the rest of the world, and the political opposition in the United States.) Kissinger became at least as enthusiastic about Sino-American reconciliation as Nixon himself. As both he and Nixon have recorded in detail in their memoirs, Kissinger helped execute the President's visionary plan to reunite the Chinese with the other three-quarters of the human race with a brilliance seldom matched in the annals of diplomacy.

In January 1972, after Kissinger had twice conferred with Zhou in Beijing and established the agenda for the summit meeting, it was decided that I would head the team that made the advance arrangements for Nixon's own visit to the Chinese capital. This made administrative sense, inasmuch as I was one of the handful of people in the government who had been involved in the process from the beginning and knew both the details and the larger goals of the enterprise. Although it turned out that there was little to complain about, the two men may also have felt that I was likelier to complain to our hosts about shortcomings than anyone else they could send. Neither Nixon nor Kissinger gave me any special instructions before I left for Beijing. My team from the White House included Press Secretary Ron Ziegler; the chief presidential advance man, Dwight Chapin; my West Point classmate, Brig. Gen. Brent Scowcroft; and my indefatigable and indispensable secretary, Mrs. Muriel Hartley; as well as John Scali of Cuban Missile Crisis fame and specialists from elsewhere in the government. Our task was a straightforward one. We were to make certain that the physical arrangements for the President's trip were appropriate, so as to avert any possible embarrassment to either side and also tie up a few diplomatic loose ends.

As it turned out, the Chinese chose to treat our presence as a dress rehearsal for Nixon's visit, with me as his stand-in. The first signs of this became evident on arrival. We were welcomed at the airport, as Nixon would be in his turn, by a large group of officials from the foreign ministry and an honor guard composed of what appeared to be the tallest, most athletic soldiers in the People's Liberation Army. Kissinger remarked after his return from Beijing that he had never before met any Chinese Communists.[2] I had, and inspecting these impressive troops in a wintry wind out of Manchuria awakened graphic memories of Korea. Formalities over, we were ushered into a fleet of large black Chinese copies of Soviet limousines that appeared to be bolted together by hand rather than factory-assembled. An official of the foreign ministry, sitting in for Zhou Enlai, rode next to me on the plush backseat, while a burly Chinese security guard sat beside an equally burly driver in front. During the bumpy ride into the city over a two-lane road made of badly joined concrete slabs, all windows except the windshield were covered with black curtains.

Somewhere between the airport and the city, my Chinese host pushed aside the curtain on my side of the car, but there was little to be seen of

China in the one-inch strip of empty landscape thus revealed. As we entered Beijing, my host opened the curtains another inch. There were almost no people in view; on entering the wide, utterly empty boulevards of the capital, I realized that the streets had been cleared. Gazing down a deserted side street off Tiananmen Square, I glimpsed the anticipated crowds of pedestrians and bicyclists a couple of blocks away. As the days passed, my host continued to open the curtain wider, apparently as a subtle signal of increasing trust and openness. By the last day, the curtains were wide open, and as the car made its way through a sea of bicycles we were gazing through the windows into the curious and friendly faces of the crowd.

On the evening of our arrival, in the Great Hall of the People, we saw the overscale totalitarian China familiar to all who had ever watched television news—the heroic posters of workers clutching the Red flag, the enormous rooms the size of football fields with fifty-foot ceilings. Our Chinese escorts revealed this colossal building to us with obvious pride, noting that it had been constructed in a remarkably short time by patriotic Chinese workers. Zhou Enlai and all the rest of the party and government leaders except Mao Zedong (whom I never met) were already present in a reception hall. After introductions and refreshments we were ushered into an even vaster banqueting hall. Seated puppetlike in the place of honor, I was called upon to reply to the formal welcoming toast by Zhou Enlai. After this, a large number of exquisitely polite toasts were offered by lesser officials. Each toast was drunk in maotai, a fiery brandy said to be 180 proof, or 90 percent alcohol. Because the Chinese took turns draining their glasses, the visitor was placed in the position of drinking a dozen times to their one. According to someone present, the guest was supposed to empty his glass with every toast and turn it upside down on top of his head to show sincerity. I ignored this custom but still found the toasts an ordeal. I knew that Nixon, whose tolerance for alcohol was very low, would never be able to remain standing if he tried to keep up. In my first message home to Kissinger that night, I included a cautionary note: UNDER NO REPEAT NO CIRCUMSTANCES SHOULD THE PRESIDENT ACTU- ALLY DRINK FROM HIS GLASS IN RESPONSE TO BANQUET TOASTS. In the event, Nixon, perhaps already forewarned by Kissinger, merely touched the maotai glass to his lips.

The banquet broke up early by Western standards, and after drafting my report to Washington I settled gratefully into bed at about 11:30 P.M. I had scarcely closed my eyes when the telephone rang; the prime minister wished see me again, alone, in the Great Hall of the People. I called

Muriel Hartley and the two of us went to meet Zhou Enlai. (We, like Kissinger earlier and Nixon later, took no interpreter of our own, because the President felt that it would flatter the Chinese to use their interpreters; in practice it made no difference which side did the interpreting, since a lie is still a lie and the truth the truth no matter who translates it from one language to another.)

It turned out that Prime Minister Zhou was not alone in the huge meeting room where he awaited us. Instead, he was surrounded by most of the upper leadership of state and party and by what appeared to be the entire Beijing press corps with microphones and television cameras set up to record the scene. The whole company was standing, and as I walked into the brilliant circle of klieg light surrounding Zhou he launched into a harangue about U.S. colonialism and imperialism. His rhetoric, as rendered into flawless American English by his interpreter, Tang Wen-sheng (born in New York and called Nancy Tang by all but the most linguistically correct Americans), was strident; when he began talking about Vietnam, it became inflammatory. The television cameras and tape recorders were turning; strobe lights winked as the still cameras went off. It was apparent that Zhou's performance was a propaganda exercise staged for the cameras and perhaps designed to reassure his domestic opponents.

As such, it was a calculated insult and a bad beginning for a venture that could only succeed on the basis of mutual honesty and respect. What would the President do in this situation? What would he want me to do to preserve him from a similar embarrassment? This was no time for hesitation or equivocation. I said, "With respect, Prime Minister, I did not come to Beijing to hear my country insulted. If that is why I was invited here tonight, I will take my party to the airport and depart at once."

Zhou, who gazed intently into my eyes as I spoke, understood my words without benefit of interpretation. Without hesitation or reply, he clapped his hands—once—and everyone present except Zhou himself, Muriel Hartley, Nancy Tang, a Chinese note-taker, and me hurriedly left the room. As soon as the others were gone, Zhou, with no change in facial expression and no sign that anything untoward had happened, beckoned me to a pair of overstuffed chairs. We sat down side by side and he launched without preamble into a very warm speech of welcome. In my own language, I thanked him just as warmly in return for his hospitality. He leaned toward me and said, "Now that we are alone, I should like to go on with our conversation."

For nearly three hours, while Mrs. Hartley took stenographic notes, he discussed the state of the world with great eloquence and an amazing grasp of fact and detail. Despite the great differences in rank and age between us, there was a good deal of give and take; it was clear that he wanted to know where the hard points in the American position were and that he was interested in the thoughts of an American soldier who had fought against Chinese troops in Korea and now worked closely with Kissinger and the President. When he arrived at the subject of Vietnam, though he never said the unsayable, it was evident, as I have already reported to the reader (and, of course, immediately reported to Nixon and Kissinger), that he regarded an American defeat and withdrawal from Southeast Asia as an outcome that would be dangerous to China and a threat to regional stability and world peace.

An undercurrent of urgency ran through everything he said, but he seemed particularly determined that I understand his meaning regarding the war in Vietnam. I had the impression, later confirmed by Zhou himself in his talks with Nixon, that he realized he was already an old man (seventy-four) and that he was impatient to normalize relations with the United States as the last great political action of his life. The irony was, as Nixon himself has pointed out, that it was the President who had only a short time to live, in the political sense.[3]

There was, of course, an element of the artificial in my encounter with Zhou. The charm of great men is more often calculated than not, and most of what Zhou Enlai said to me that night, including the instructive and amusing anecdotes that made such wise and subtle points about human nature and the state of the world, he had already said to Kissinger and would later repeat to Nixon.

Even though I was aware of this calculated redundancy, having read the memorandums of his talks with Kissinger, I was tremendously impressed by Zhou's words and manner. So was everyone else who ever met this extraordinary man, but I was one of the first Americans of my generation to do so in private, and there was little in my previous experience to prepare me for the powerful effect of his personality. For most of my adult life, Zhou had been one of the most mysterious figures in the world and, according to some of my fellow Americans, one of the most villainous. The experience of meeting such a man, alone and face-to-face, and striving to form a true opinion of his character was daunting, especially since he was so much larger and more complex in life than in popular image.

In that respect, and in the breadth of his knowledge, in the defining nature of his political commitment, and in his dark, rather saturnine physical appearance, he reminded me, incongruously, of Richard Nixon. I thought the two leaders would get along famously when they met, as indeed they did. In those days, Zhou was by far the more relaxed, outspoken, and detached of the two—a mandarin version of the wise and jovial elder statesman Nixon became after his rise from the ashes of Watergate. Indeed, there are times, when Nixon lets himself go over the telephone or during an interview on television, that he reminds me of Zhou.

One of the most surprising and instructive aspects of this conversation with Zhou had nothing to do with its substance. Nancy Tang often interrupted, corrected, and argued ideological points with the prime minister. This sisterly hectoring of a head of government was something new in my experience of interpreters, but Zhou took her interventions calmly, as a normal part of the proceedings. As time went on and I spoke to other Chinese about this encounter, I came to realize that the prime minister's forbearance was an expression of ideological principle: The People's Republic of China was an egalitarian society in theory, and he was doing his part to make it so in practice, at least in the presence of a stranger. The fact that Nancy Tang was an influential member of the party and a favorite of Mao's and of his politically powerful wife, Jiang Qing, may also have influenced Zhou's behavior. (Zhou's consciousness was not raised so high that he approved of Nancy Tang's tendency to offer toasts in maotai; she was the only Chinese woman of her period apart from Jiang Qing to do so, and Zhou criticized her for it.[4] Mao's opinion of her appears to have been a mixture of suspicion and respect: "Never trust an American girl!"[5])

The Chinese behaved in unexpected ways on other matters. Part of my mission was to settle the details for construction by the United States of a satellite communications station that would permit the instantaneous transmission of color television images of Nixon's visit all over the world. The signing of the contract, regarded as routine, was delayed by the other side. When I asked why, experts from the White House Communications Agency reported that the Chinese were dragging their feet over the financial arrangements; they thought we were undercharging them. The Chinese refused to sign the agreement until the price was adjusted upward to a figure that more closely reflected their idea of fair-market value. No one on the delegation had ever before dealt with a foreign power that wanted to pay the United States government more than the asking price for strategic hardware and technical assistance. Nothing in the guidelines provided for upping the price. Where did duty lie? To the troubled bureaucrat in charge of negotiations, I said, "Take the money and thank the Chinese on behalf of the American taxpayer." That broke the impasse to everyone's satisfaction except, one supposes, the unfortunate book-keeper back home who had to find a way to deal with the windfall.

An entire hotel near Tiananmen Square had been emptied for our party, which was by no means large enough to fill it. The large, overfur-nished bedrooms were noticeably chilly; the curtains flapped like laundry on the line when the wind blew through gaps in the rattling windows. We had been cautioned by our security people that our rooms, cars, and telephones would be bugged, as was standard practice in Communist countries. A close observer of the Ceausescu government in Romania, a nation with 1.9 million telephones, told me after the dictator was shot that the secret police had been capable of intercepting 2 million telephone calls at any one time.[6] The Chinese in 1972 were probably not quite so advanced. Until the arrival of Western technology, in fact, eavesdropping in China apparently had been a labor-intensive affair; walking down the hallway of our hotel soon after arrival to call on Ron Ziegler in his room, I looked through an open door and saw what appeared to be a full platoon of uniformed Chinese, all listening to American conversations through World War II–vintage headphones. I smiled and nodded; they all smiled back.

We soon discovered that the most efficient way of communicating with our hosts was to address observations or complaints to the empty air. Our words would immediately be picked up by hidden microphones and in a matter of minutes a Chinese functionary would be at the door to correct the situation. We used this simple procedure to accomplish everything from obtaining more towels to suggesting that a banquet planned for the President was too long. It not only got results, it saved face by eliminating any need to criticize our hosts directly.

Other questions of "face" arose that were not so conveniently disposed of. In Shanghai, at a banquet in another enormous hall, one of our official hosts, a party official named Xu Jingxian, delivered a very offensive anti-American toast. This was annoying, but I thought it best not to make a commotion by replying in kind. At the same time, I wanted to make a point, so I made no reply at all. When I did not rise immediately after Xu's toast and make my way to the microphone as everyone expected, a sort of collective gasp ran through the thousand or more guests present. As course after course was served and I still did not rise, a silence fell over the crowd. By dessert, it would have been possible to hear a pin drop. As soon as the final course had been eaten, a high-ranking party official,

Wang Hugwen, approached me. He was a large man, broad-shouldered and over six feet tall. Looking down at me in my chair, he said, "This dinner is over." Then he turned on his heel and left. The crowd, still locked in deathly silence, departed in minutes. The State Department expert in protocol accompanying our party warned me that I had insulted our hosts and would be lucky if they did not cancel the President's visit as a result.

An immediate chill settled over our relations with the local Chinese. Smiles vanished, relaxation was replaced by stiffness of manner, and the easy working methods we had developed gave way to strict formality. The curtains in my limousine were closed so that not even a chink of light could enter. Next day, while I was touring an industrial fair somewhere in the vast and bitterly cold metropolis, someone came up behind me and tapped me on the shoulder. It was Nancy Tang. She had flown in from Beijing on orders from the prime minister. Her manner, in contrast to her relaxed and cordial behavior in Beijing, was proper but, like that of all the rest of the Chinese, very cool. She led me into a small room where we could speak privately.

"General Haig," she said, "the prime minister is very concerned. He wishes to know if your host insulted you last night."

"Insulted me?" I replied. "How?"

"By the things he said in his toast."

"No, of course not."

"Then why didn't you reply? The prime minister finds this very puzzling."

"Oh," I said earnestly. "Was I *supposed* to reply? I didn't think it was necessary, since I had already replied to the prime minister in Beijing."

Nancy Tang gave me a look that I remember, in all modesty, as one that mingled a certain admiration with broad relief. Face had been saved. Smiling happily, she said, "I will tell the prime minister. I know he will be very glad to hear what you have said."

When I returned to the car, the curtains were wide open. A complete thaw in personal relations followed, as if a thermostat had been turned down and then up again—as indeed it had been. Nothing more was said about the omitted toast during my stay. When Nixon arrived in Shanghai, however, the party official was not present at the banquet in his honor. Some years afterward, I was told by an apologetic Chinese that the towering Wang Hungwen was a hard-line Maoist who was opposed on philosophical grounds to rapprochement with the United States. In 1980, along with Mao's widow, he was sentenced to death as a member of the Gang of Four on charges of attempting to overthrow the regime headed by Zhou's protégé, Deng Xiaoping.

Nixon's visit to China was a triumph on every level. It restored the historic ties between two great peoples who had a history of friendship and no compelling reason to be enemies. At a moment when many in America and elsewhere in the West thought otherwise, it demonstrated that the power and moral authority of the United States was the principal engine of change in the world. It revealed to leaders and peoples in both countries their common humanity; and by sweeping away the mystery that had surrounded China's leaders and the misrepresentations that had obscured Nixon's true character and intent, it caused a quarter of a century of harsh propaganda by both sides to dissipate. It ameliorated the American phobia that China was prepared to intervene with troops in Indochina in order to prevent an American victory over Hanoi, and it eased Chinese fears that the United States would support an invasion of China from Taiwan. This exchange of reassurances, however oblique, made possible a more rational approach to the process of ending the war in Vietnam while unequivocally identifying the Soviet Union as the main obstacle to peace in Indochina as elsewhere in the world.

The Shanghai Communiqué, the official bilateral summary issued at the end of Nixon's visit, departed from usual diplomatic usage by openly listing areas of disagreement between the United States and China. By frankly acknowledging their differences, the United States and China advertised before the world their mutual belief that they could live peacefully with those differences. This included the question of Taiwan, which had been the symbol of their animosity. By conceding the unity of China on both sides of the Taiwan Strait without compromising the future of Taiwan, Nixon and the Chinese leaders cut the Gordian knot of Sino-American relations. This made possible the understanding that neither China nor the United States "should seek hegemony in the Asia Pacific region and each is opposed to efforts by any other country or group of countries to establish such hegemony."[7]

This provision of the Shanghai Communiqué was little understood at the time, but it was its most important result because it wrote "finish" to the notion of a monolithic communism dominated from Moscow, while at the same time binding the most populous Communist state on earth to the world's strongest democracy in a strategic combination designed to neutralize the aggressive designs of the Soviet Union in Asia. It may reasonably be argued that this ambiguous compact, one of the great diplomatic flanking movements of modern times, marked the beginning of the end of the Cold War.

Like all great strokes of diplomacy, the opening of China was as important for what it made possible as for what it actually accomplished. In terms of Nixon's priorities, its chief benefit was to remove China as an obstacle to settlement of the Vietnam War. Many difficulties remained, particularly with regard to Vietnam. By no stretch of the imagination had the Chinese leaders suggested that they would actively help us to end the war in Vietnam on terms favorable to the United States and South Vietnam. On the contrary, Zhou had made a point of telling Nixon that he and Ho Chi Minh had been friends since meeting in France in 1922. "Our position," Zhou told Nixon, "is that so long as you are continuing your Vietnamization . . . policy, and as long as they continue fighting, we can do nothing but to continue to support [Hanoi]." By this time, as Nixon frankly told Zhou, the President was ready to withdraw all American forces from South Vietnam in six months in exchange for a cease-fire and the return of all American prisoners of war. The North Vietnamese had rejected this offer as insufficient, insisting once again that the Thieu-Ky government must be dismantled by the United States as the first step in a political settlement whose unmistakable purpose was the establishment in South Vietnam, without recourse to genuine elections, of a Communist regime controlled by Hanoi.[8]

Ironically, it was the policy of Vietnamization that had produced the curious situation in which the enemy declined to terminate a war the United States had prevented it from winning while the administration, in Nixon's phrase, was "interested in almost any potential peace agreement."[9]

20

The Art of the Possible

The mission to China was not the first I had undertaken on President Nixon's behalf, but it was typical of all the others in the sense that it required a certain willingness to be blunt under delicate circumstances. In an administration of affable politicians who worked by guile and indirection (Laird was so compulsively foxy that one could not help but like and even admire him for it), Nixon found it useful to have a plainspoken soldier in the wings to handle the confrontations. The front line of the innumerable battles resulting from Laird's tendency to substitute his judgment for the President's in moments of crisis was not the Oval Office or even Kissinger's office but, rather, my basement cubbyhole. Outgoing and incoming fire passed through the telephone line connecting my desk with Col. Bob Pursley's in Laird's outer office. On one occasion, Laird told Kissinger he thought it was "great the way Haig and Pursley argue over things." Henry said he thought it was "terrific," too—as well he might, inasmuch as the shouting matches Pursley and I engaged in as surrogates for Kissinger and Laird relieved them of the need of ever being unpleasant to each other, even in memoirs.

Thanks to my military training and status, I could be relied upon to deliver unwelcome messages, as when the President detailed me to tell Secretary of State Rogers, his closest friend in the government, that the entire process of arranging Nixon's visit to China, the most important

267

single diplomatic effort of the Cold War, had been kept secret from him, as well as from the Secretary of Defense. I delivered the news in the office complex in San Clemente while Kissinger was in the air, bringing word of his own successful mission to China. "Al, you'd better tell Bill Rogers what's been going on before Henry lands," Nixon said. I walked across the compound and did so. As I laid out the details one by one, Rogers stared at me in shocked disbelief, as if each fact were a round from a pistol I was firing into the ceiling. I kept talking until Rogers, ever the gentleman, recovered his composure. If there was ever a case in which the temptation to behead the messenger was all but irresistible, this must have been it, but Rogers treated me with great kindness. "I see," he said at last, loudly clearing his throat, "very interesting." Not many men could have taken this galling news as gracefully as he did. The entire episode was vintage Nixon.

As the reader will remember, my own early glimpses of Nixon in action, though vivid, occurred in fits and starts. After being given the title of Deputy Assistant to the President for National Security Affairs in the spring of 1970, I came to know him at closer quarters owing to the necessity of acting in Kissinger's place during the latter's frequent absences. Even then, the relationship remained formal and proper. To a degree, this was my own doing. I was Kissinger's deputy, and as such it was my duty to represent his opinions to the President rather than to advance my own. As a matter of principle, I did not volunteer opinions, but when Nixon asked what I thought, I answered honestly, as was my duty, and afterward told Kissinger what I had said. In the beginning, this worked pretty well, but keeping a proper balance between the needs of a President who was as mistrustful as Nixon and a superior whose ego was as dynamic as Kissinger's was no mean feat.

Nixon's wariness placed severe limits on those spontaneous private moments, which Plutarch regarded as truer indications of a great man's character than victories and other public triumphs.[1] One seldom caught this President unawares, intellectually or otherwise. He displayed no natural gift whatsoever for the harmless, half-sincere gestures and small talk that etiquette substitutes for true feeling. Nor did the cartoon Nixon of Kissinger's verbal comic strip materialize as I drew closer to the flesh-and-blood original. The Nixon I knew was virtually humorless. No doubt that is one of the reasons why Kissinger (himself one of the few droll civilians I ever encountered in close proximity to the Oval Office) found him so amusing.

In his unbending reserve, Nixon reminded me of my Haig relatives, whose Episcopalian diffidence was to some degree a reflection of the influence of Quaker quietism on the culture of Philadelphia. As a boy, I had been impressed by my father's and grandfather's strict code of decorum, and I had passed from their influence to that of the Army, in which self-control is also regarded as a virtue. Nixon's reluctance to put his inner self on display may have struck his enemies as pathological ("old Nixon, new Nixon"); in my eyes it was consistent with his upbringing, and in many ways admirable. His combination of Christian forbearance, ascetic remoteness, and roundabout discipline of those weaker than himself seemed to me far less strange, and a good deal more genuine, than Kennedy's studied insouciance or Lyndon Johnson's theatrical camaraderie and laying on of hands.

All this is not to suggest that Nixon did not have moments when his humanity was exposed. As the reader knows, the criticism of the news media got under his skin when it was ill-informed or mean-spirited, as it often was because so many important journalists disliked him for ideological reasons. On the other hand, the fulminations of politicians generally did not bother him unduly; good old American partisan pointing with alarm (as opposed to populist hypocrisy or the hate-driven invective of the counterculture) was part of the game, and the politicians on the other side whom he liked best, such as Lyndon Johnson, tended to be the ones who were best at it.

Even the wounds inflicted on him by ungrateful advisers did not seem to distract him in any serious way. He had evidently come to the conclusion that there was nothing to be done about human nature, especially in politics. Betrayals of trust usually triggered colorful bursts of temper, though his abhorrence of the unpleasant moment assured that these almost never occurred in the presence of the object of presidential displeasure. When feeling double-crossed, he was capable of vivid profanity and imaginative promises of vengeful action, and when egged on by sycophants he would sometimes, as the world knows and he himself has recorded, act on his worser instincts. This never happened in my presence. When left to his own devices, he would run out of breath, the storm would pass, and he would go on with the business at hand as if nothing had happened. The next day, or even later in the same day, he would seem to have forgotten the outburst; whether he ever forgot the offense that begat it is another question, but then again he had learned to live with enmity and insult on a scale and intensity inflicted on few other politicians in history.

Sometimes I thought that Nixon regarded his tantrums as therapeutic, a way of ridding himself of bad humors. In any case, he was careful to keep these outbursts within limits—possibly, as he himself has suggested, because his father was subject to fits of unbridled temper that were the origin of his lifelong aversion to personal conflict.[2] Certainly he was aware that the consequences of blowing up were more dangerous for a President than for an ordinary mortal; just how much more dangerous was yet to be revealed to him. It was his nature to be circumspect. One day, before we knew each other well, I had to inform him of a particularly deplorable leak to the press. He exploded in anger, uttered a string of curses, and ordered that lie-detector tests be administered forthwith to every member of the White House staff. He looked and sounded like a man who meant what he said, but, knowing that he was simply letting off steam, I had no intention of actually carrying out such an order without asking him to confirm it after he had cooled down. Presently, he recovered his composure and we went on to the next items on the agenda. As I left, he said, "Al, about the polygraphs. That wasn't an order." I nodded and made a show of scratching the lie-detector tests off the list.

Considering later events, the phrase *That wasn't an order* might profitably have been repeated by Nixon to others who apparently did not always know when he was serious and when he was not, and, by pretending to take his exaggerations at face value, reinforced his dark fantasies for their own purposes. It is worth remembering that Nixon was not the first Chief Executive to ponder revenge in the Oval Office or to turn the air blue with expletives. A greatly admired political motto ascribed to the Kennedys was, Don't get mad, get even. In practice, of course, retribution, especially clandestine retribution, is usually the product of anger. From all accounts, Nixon's temper was no more incendiary than Truman's, Eisenhower's, Kennedy's, or Johnson's. But he was less ably protected than they were by advisers and by friends in the press from the blinding emotions and unworthy impulses to which even Presidents sometimes succumb.

Gradually, I came to realize that Nixon valued my services and took a personal interest in my career. This insight was a couple of years in the making, partly because Nixon was not the sort to discomfit a subordinate by showering him with compliments and partly because I did not think there was any reason for him to be inordinately pleased because I was doing the job I had been hired to do. Besides, my duty in the White House was temporary. I was a regular officer of the U.S. Army and it was the Army's function to judge my fitness for promotion. This had already happened once since I had arrived at the White House. In November

1969, before the President came to know me well, I was promoted to brigadier general. Nixon pinned on the stars in an impromptu ceremony in the Oval Office attended by Kissinger's old mentor, Governor Nelson A. Rockefeller, who happened to be visiting the White House that day. "It's all over for Haig now," Kissinger quipped as we walked down the corridor together afterward. Rockefeller asked Kissinger what he meant. He replied, "There are lots of smart colonels in the Army, but as soon as they make general their minds begin to deteriorate." Rockefeller, usually the soul of good humor, was a great defender of the military. He was outraged by this harmless witticism and while I listened with a certain amused satisfaction he gave poor Henry a pointed lecture on the contributions of American generals to the nation's history.

There is never anything automatic about achieving general officer rank in the U.S. Army, but this promotion was based on my military record and probably would have occurred no matter where I was posted. My work in the White House, though generously evaluated by Kissinger in my 1969 efficiency report, was not a determining factor in this promotion or in its timing. Nixon's first written personal recommendation on my behalf came in April 1970, in an endorsement to a special efficiency report requested by the Army for all officers eligible for promotion to major general. Kissinger, as my immediate superior, recommended in glowing terms that I be promoted immediately to two-star rank. In endorsing this recommendation, Nixon wrote, in part:

> During the last two months I have had many direct dealings with General Haig. He is a phenomenal individual with outstanding judgment and leadership ability. . . . He is the type of General that we must have in those jobs that demand the ultimate of a General officer. He is certainly ready to assume the highest responsibilities we can give him in the Defense Establishment, and I wholeheartedly endorse the recommendation that he be rapidly moved to the highest ranks of the Armed Forces.

The President initialed this last sentence to show that he meant what he said, but he did not specify exactly *when* he wanted my elevation to take place, so I was not included in the next group of major generals created by the Army promotion board. A year passed before the next routine efficiency report was due. In April 1971, Nixon endorsed Kissinger's steadfast support ("Another year with General Haig has reaffirmed my earlier conviction that he is the most outstanding flag officer in the Armed Forces") in the following language:

> I increasingly rely on [Haig's] superior judgment and keen assessments. . . . Time and again his wise and independent counsel has proven correct. . . . He is the type of inspiring leader that the Army needs at the top. I not only want him promoted to Major General immediately but feel he should be moved as rapidly as possible to the highest leadership positions in the Army.

Nixon's use of the word *immediately* closed the loophole, and on March 1, 1972, I was advanced to two-star rank. I was proud and happy to be promoted in timely fashion, but I thought I had earned it. I would have preferred to have been promoted while leading troops, but I expected that I would be doing that again before much longer. And if the second star came a bit sooner than expected, that almost made up, as Pat said, for all those years of waiting to make major.

To this day, the origins of Nixon's good opinion of me and my work is something of a mystery to me. Of course, I had a generous advocate in Kissinger. Possibly it also had something to do with the "independent counsel" mentioned in my efficiency report. "Governing a large state is like boiling a small fish," wrote Lao Tzu, the legendary Chinese sage usually identified as the founder of Taoism. Scholars tell us that he meant that such a fish can be spoiled if it is handled by too many cooks.[3] Nixon, possessed of an intensely original vision of the way in which the United States should be governed, refused to impose this vision on his inner circle. Consequently, he worked, as it were, in a kitchen crowded with undercooks, all competing to improve upon his recipe while his attention was elsewhere. I refrained from stirring the pot behind his back, and perhaps he appreciated that.

It was part of my value as a messenger that the President knew I did not leak to the news media or anyone else, and that I spoke my mind when called upon to do so by a superior officer—and sometimes in other circumstances. Despite Kissinger's agitation over my remarks to Dobrynin during the Cienfuegos affair, for example, I never got the impression from Nixon that he thought I had gone too far in light of the results. Thereafter, he often sent me on missions that required forthright speech on the scene and frank reporting on return home. This was especially true in the case of Vietnam, a place and situation that had long frustrated Presidents in search of simple truths and clear explanations.

During the first two years of his presidency, Nixon believed, on the basis of Laird's continual assurances, that Vietnamization was working. In terms of its original purpose, it was, but this had little to do with its military effectiveness. Vietnamization was a success not in Vietnam but in the United States, where, as the Secretary of Defense and his faction had hoped and intended, it had lessened opposition to the war in Congress and the news media by offering a program that promised a definitive end to American casualties. These had indeed fallen dramatically as a result of massive U.S. troop withdrawals and a relatively low level of aggressive enemy operations, but reduced American casualties had little to do with the military effectiveness of the armed forces of South Vietnam.

It was inevitable that ARVN should be tested. No one expected the North, although still recovering from the losses of the 1968 Tet offensive and the supply and other difficulties created by the Cambodian incursion, to remain inactive. In late 1970, it was estimated that Hanoi was infiltrating combat-ready troops into South Vietnam at a rate of about six thousand a month, mostly by way of the Ho Chi Minh Trail through Laos. If infiltration continued at this rate, it could only lead to a large new enemy offensive inside South Vietnam during the 1971 dry season.

Prodded remorselessly by Nixon and Kissinger, the Pentagon finally devised a plan to disrupt this timetable, and on January 18, 1971, in a meeting in the Oval Office attended by Kissinger, Laird, Rogers, Helms, Admiral Moorer, and me, Nixon authorized the operation. Code-named Lam Son 719, it called for ARVN ground troops to strike westward along the strategic east-west Highway 9 from the former U.S. Marine base at Khe Sanh and take Tchepone, an important NVA supply base located about twenty-five miles inside Laos. The ARVN task force was to be supported by U.S. artillery, air power, and logistics. U.S. ground troops would be positioned at Khe Sanh to protect ARVN's rear and reinforce the task force if necessary. Those who briefed the President on this plan were optimistic about its success, and it was understood that the key factor was all-out U.S. military support of ARVN. This included the prompt insertion of American ground forces into Laos in case our ally got into trouble despite congressional restrictions on U.S. military operations there. This approach to the operation was, of course, a classic exercise in incrementalism.

On February 8, a regiment of South Vietnamese infantry (about three thousand men) was airlifted in American helicopters to positions south of Tchepone; meanwhile, an additional two thousand ARVN troops crossed the border by highway and a smaller force established a fire base alongside Highway 9 about ten miles inside Laos. By February 11, the force traveling on the highway (reinforced by now with an additional 15,000 South Vietnamese troops) reached the halfway point to Tchepone. There the advance bogged down because of heavy rains that turned Highway 9 into a mud wallow and made air operations difficult. The floundering task force was attacked by some 36,000 North Vietnamese regulars equipped with the latest Soviet-made tanks, long-range artillery, including 130-mm Russian guns that outranged all U.S. artillery except for a few 175-mm guns, and highly effective antiaircraft weapons. Meanwhile, heavy fighting broke out along the South Vietnamese border to the rear of the task force. The heavily outnumbered ARVN troops fought bravely, but U.S. air and artillery support broke down, and some ARVN units panicked. Only a couple of battalions out of about two dozen were involved in this local breakdown, but American television news footage pictured the South Vietnamese as a demoralized force that was in the process of being routed by a superior enemy.

Kissinger, whose bias against Laird's Pentagon and all its works was by now reflexive, denounced the operation as an exercise in incompetence. "Well, Al, your military finally got what it wanted," he raged, "and they've ——— it up!"

Nixon brooded and waited for the inevitable turning point when American soldiers went to the rescue of their desperate allies. After seventy-two hours, it was clear to all, and especially to Nixon, that the operation had gone wrong. The U.S. command in Vietnam took few of the obvious measures to reverse the tide of battle. Though American troops were positioned nearby for precisely that purpose, none was sent into Laos to stiffen the ARVN's resistance. U.S. artillery was wrongly emplaced to bring maximum firepower to bear on the enemy. Close air support was not properly coordinated to suppress the enemy artillery that was punishing the South Vietnamese or the withering antiaircraft fire that was destroying and damaging American helicopters.

There was no sign, despite requests from the Oval Office for clarification, that any U.S. military action was being planned to correct these deficiencies. The enemy was concentrating his forces; the ARVN forces were isolated and under heavy pressure; the prospect of a humiliating and politically devastating defeat grew more likely by the hour. Nixon's questions to the Pentagon, usually transmitted through me, were answered by obfuscation and worse. Given the stakes, this maddened him even more than might have been expected. He could not understand why the optimistic estimates he had heard from Pentagon briefers before the fact now seemed to be turning into predictions of disaster. Most incomprehensible of all, from Nixon's point of view, were reports that Gen. Creighton W. Abrams, the U.S. theater commander, had not left his headquarters in Saigon to assess the battle zone in person. His deputy, Gen. Fred C. Weyand, was monitoring forward operations from a northern command post located some one and a half hours by helicopter from the scene of the fighting.

On the third day, the President called me to his office. Secretary of the Treasury John B. Connally, the conservative Democrat from Texas on whose advice and moral support Nixon increasingly relied during this period, was present. The President was in a cold rage. Without preamble, he told me that he was relieving General Abrams of command in Vietnam immediately. "Go home and pack a bag," he said. "Then get on the first available plane and fly to Saigon. You're taking command." I stared at Nixon in astonishment. Although I had expected an outburst, I had not expected this, and in my shock I replied, "Good God, Mr. President, you can't do that!" Nixon stared back and said, "Why not? Lincoln fired McClellan for sitting on his ass in 1862. That's what I'm doing now. Abrams is the problem, and in situations like this one it's the President's job to remove the problem—the sooner the better."

The logic was unanswerable. Nixon's reaction was not petty or irrational but precisely the opposite. He was Commander in Chief, the paramount war leader, and if he wanted to relieve a four-star general and make a brigadier general commander of a war theater, he could certainly do so without departing from the traditions of the presidency. As for me, I will not pretend that I was not tempted. I had no doubt that I could do the job; I knew the ground, I knew the enemy, and I knew what the President wanted. It is a very unimaginative soldier who has not dreamed of having supreme command thrust upon him in the hour of crisis.

But I could not accept this command under these circumstances. As a personal matter, Abrams had given me his friendship and trust. As a professional matter, this was a presidential decision that involved the honor and spirit of the Army. Abrams was the most popular man in the Army, a great soldier, a hero of three wars who was held in affection and esteem by the entire officer corps. His dismissal from a combat command in response to charges in the news media that he had been given no opportunity to answer would embitter the Army from top to bottom. It would also create an uproar on Capitol Hill that would plunge the nation's military leadership into a political free-for-all, with generals and admirals lined up to testify before the inevitable congressional investigating committee. Nixon listened to what I told him, but his determination to fire Abrams and replace him with me seemed unshaken. "Mr. President," I said, in a phrase I was to use many times in the future, "I think you should wait until tomorrow on this."

He did so, and in a calmer mood ordered me to go to Vietnam, assess the situation on the ground, and report my findings to him. I left immediately, but Nixon had been right: It was already too late to reverse the situation except by a radical change in tactics. This did not occur. In an intensive tour of the battleground and other areas, I talked to all the key U.S. and ARVN commanders, to as many of the troops as possible, and to President Thieu. On the basis of their statements and other evidence, I reported two main conclusions to Nixon: First, the South Vietnamese troops, though in some cases poorly led by their higher-ranking officers, had fought bravely and performed well. Second, U.S. fire support and close air support had been inadequate, and the number of helicopters, especially gunships, available for the operation had been lower than the norm for U.S. operations of the same type. Our artillery had been positioned too far away from the battleground to give optimum support. Close air support in all but the final stages had also been inadequate. This resulted in casualty rates among South Vietnamese troops that no American commander would have countenanced. As I put it to the President, "This would never have been allowed to happen if American soldiers had been doing the fighting on the ground."

Why, then, had it happened? It is difficult to explain the debacle in terms of military procedure; no commander wants his artillery so far from the battlefield that the shells fall short of the target, nor does he want his helicopters flying over ground that has not been strafed and bombed and shelled to suppress antiaircraft fire. General Abrams was far too loyal and honorable a soldier to put the blame on anyone but himself as the responsible U.S. commander in the theater. But the departures from combat doctrine could not be explained in terms of Abrams's personality or professional competence; he was arguably the best fighting general in the Army. I came away from my discussions with him and other American commanders convinced that they had been powerfully influenced, if not actually ordered, by civilians in the Pentagon to do everything possible to keep American casualties to an absolute minimum. The obvious way to do that was to keep them as far away from the fighting as possible. American ground troops fighting the same engagement would almost certainly have won an unequivocal victory at far less cost in blood, not because they would have fought more skillfully or bravely than the soldiers of the ARVN who went into Laos but because the force of politics back home would have been working for their rescue, not against it. The moral was clear: No matter how bravely they fought, South Vietnamese troops could not prevail over NVA forces without the help of massive U.S. firepower.

Ground fighting continued until March 6, when two thousand South Vietnamese troops took Tchepone in a helicopter assault. By then, the village had been virtually destroyed by U.S. air action. The ARVN forces, having satisfied appearances by gaining their original objective even though they did not attempt to hold it, began a fighting retreat along Highway 9. On March 7 and 8, American air power finally came into full play, with two thousand aircraft including B-52s carrying out widespread attacks on North Vietnamese units and installations.

The last of the ARVN troops crossed back into South Vietnam on March 24 after forty-five days of fighting. On the whole, it was an orderly withdrawal, but television footage showed panicky ARVN soldiers clinging to the skids of American helicopters as the machines lifted out of the battle zone.

By allied count, about 14,000 North Vietnamese troops had been killed and another 5,000 wounded or otherwise taken out of the battle—most, as usual, by U.S. air strikes. The South Vietnamese reported 5,671 casualties, including 1,160 killed in action, or 28 percent of the numbers engaged. The Associated Press reported that ARVN had actually suffered 50 percent casualties, including 3,800 killed; this figure, though unverifiable, became the accepted one in the news media. President Thieu characterized the Lam Son operation as a victory that had disrupted Communist supply lines and would forestall enemy attacks on his country's northern provinces in 1971. Hanoi newspapers claimed a "complete victory . . . a major milestone in the history of the coordinated fight by the Indochinese people."

The tendency in Congress and the news media was to regard North Vietnamese claims of victory as the more believable. A storm of criticism burst over Nixon's head as elements of the opposition lamented or rejoiced, according to their position on the ideological spectrum, over what seemed to be a humiliating defeat for our allies, ourselves, and the fundamental policy of the administration in Vietnam. Attacking the "cruel and inhuman policy of . . . indiscriminate bombing," Senator Edward M. Kennedy, Democrat of Massachusetts, asked, "Can America ever wash its hands of the innocent Asian blood it has spilled?" Senator McGovern said that the operation cast doubt on "the whole credibility of the South Vietnamese force" and promised he would end the war in a matter of weeks if elected President.

On April 7, American pilots reported that NVA truck traffic on the Ho Chi Minh Trail appeared to be back to normal, reinforcing the impression that the operation had accomplished nothing despite heavy loss of life on both sides. The Lam Son operation was designed to ensure the success of Vietnamization and make possible the withdrawal of additional American troops. Instead, it looked as though the first major combat test of Vietnamization was going to destroy everything it had accomplished over the previous two years in terms of building up the strength, confidence, and morale of ARVN.[4]

A year later, by the time Nixon went to China, most American troops had already left South Vietnam. Just before his departure for Beijing, he had authorized the removal of an additional 70,000 by the end of April; this drawdown would leave only 69,000 American military personnel in South Vietnam out of the 536,000 stationed there when he took office three years before.[5] On January 25, Nixon disclosed in a televised speech that Kissinger had been engaged in secret negotiations with the North Vietnamese since August 1969, noting that the enemy had rejected every American proposal to end the war.

In September 1971, in one of the first of many similar missions, I had carried an American proposal for settlement of the war to Saigon and presented it to President Thieu together with a message from Nixon. The provisions of this early draft included a cease-fire; fixed withdrawal date for U.S. and other foreign forces from South Vietnam; return of prisoners of war; elections five months after a formal peace settlement to be supervised by a mixed commission that would include Communists. Thieu would step down one month before elections but would be entitled to run. I told Thieu that the United States considered it very unlikely that the enemy would accept the proposal.*

As a practical matter, Hanoi had little incentive to negotiate. The enemy had achieved his primary objective, the departure of American

---

*In this same meeting, also according to instructions, I suggested to Thieu that he broaden his political base by including members of the opposition in his government. He asked whom we had in mind. I suggested Nguyen Cao Ky, a former prime minister. Thieu said, "Perhaps we could add some responsible Buddhists." I suggested putting Ky in charge of stamping out corruption. Thieu laughed delightedly, the only time in all our meetings I saw him do so.

fighting forces while the outcome of the war was still in doubt, without having to give anything in return. Meanwhile, he was left undisturbed in his sanctuaries in Laos, Cambodia, and above the 17th parallel to train troops, stockpile supplies flowing in from the U.S.S.R., China, and Eastern Europe, and infiltrate new cadres and fighting formations into the South. It was the belief of most U.S. and South Vietnamese military commanders that Hanoi was planning to launch an offensive during the dry season of 1972—that is, almost immediately before Nixon returned from China. I reported to the President that "I believe a test of some sort will come in 1972." The signs were clear. Despite the Lam Son operation and continual air attacks on routes of infiltration, an estimated 71,000 North Vietnamese troops arrived in the South in 1971 out of a total of 106,000 sent by Hanoi, and on the basis of current mobilization figures it was believed that the enemy planned to send about 200,000 south in 1972.

The Saigon government controlled about 70 percent of the countryside, but ARVN was beset by fundamental problems. Nearly all combat units were seriously understrength and many were still commanded by incompetents. During my visit, I urged Thieu to increase combat pay and fill his combat units to at least 90 percent of mandated strength. I also advised the summary removal of inefficient divisional and regimental commanders. Thieu had been slow to do this, and faulty leadership was sapping the spirit of the troops. Few American military leaders—perhaps least of all General Abrams, the man in charge of Vietnamization—believed that ARVN could defend South Vietnam in the face of a massive enemy offensive. Although vast quantities of U.S. arms and matériel had been transferred to ARVN and its discipline and leadership had improved, Lam Son had shown that it was not yet a modern army capable of stopping the NVA with massive firepower and air power and superior tactics or a patriotic force willing to die to the last man for the fatherland.

A more important question was how effectively U.S. forces could support ARVN. Our air power and sea power were capable of striking the enemy hard—in my opinion capable of bringing him to his knees if directed against the right targets in the Hanoi-Haiphong area—but the old reluctance to hit the enemy where he lived was still very much alive. Our intelligence reported large concentrations of NVA troops just north of the demilitarized zone (DMZ). On January 20, Abrams asked Washington for permission to bomb military targets north of the DMZ for the purpose of disrupting the enemy's obvious preparations to invade the South. The bombing halt had been in effect for more than three years, and few in the upper reaches of the foreign-policy bureaucracy wished to run the risks involved in approving Abrams's eminently sensible military recommendation. Laird offered a compromise allowing U.S. aircraft to bomb selected targets in the South while placing more electronic sensors in the DMZ to detect the coming of the enemy troops and vehicles. This plan, designed to preserve the political truce between the White House and Congress, was accepted. Its military weakness was that it permitted the enemy buildup to go on undisturbed. By the time we detected the footfall and jingle of equipment of soldiers marching southward, it would, of course, be too late. Once again, the United States had elected to fight on the enemy's chosen ground, at the enemy's chosen time, according to rules of international behavior that the enemy refused to respect.[6]

21

Biting the Bullet

The invasion came on March 30, 1972, with the first wave of some 120,000 North Vietnamese regulars crossing the DMZ behind a massive artillery barrage and tank assault with the objective of seizing Quang Tri Province in the north. Other NVA units struck ARVN strong points in the Central Highlands with the idea of breaking through to the coast. A third thrust out of Cambodia aimed to capture the provincial capital, An Loc, which controlled Highway 13, thus threatening Saigon through a linkup between invading NVA regulars and main-force units already operating between the frontier and the capital.[1] "This is the decisive moment where the survival or loss of our country is at stake," said President Thieu. The enemy's objective, he said, was to capture Quang Tri and Thua Thien provinces in the north and to establish a capital for the National Liberation Front (NLF) as a prelude to a political settlement "ultimately taking over all our country." Another aim was "to cause the failure of the Vietnamization program so as to create political dissension within the United States."[2]

Nixon was determined to prevent the North Vietnamese from succeeding in their design. On February 2, he had told the NSC that he would not accept failure on the battlefield resulting from a lack of U.S. support for the South Vietnamese—in other words, no more Lam Sons.[3] As usual, it was easier to issue this stern order than to have it carried out.

No one disagreed that the invasion was the decisive test of Vietnamization. But it soon became obvious that this was regarded by the Laird faction as a reason *not* to help the South Vietnamese in any extraordinary way. By now, inner-circle opinion had rediscovered the long-neglected first principle of counterinsurgency—namely, that the South Vietnamese must fight and win the war themselves. The advice the President received from the Secretary of Defense was to do nothing special to turn back the invasion, just keep up the normal level of assistance and supply and let events take their course.

Nixon was not receptive to this counsel. He had always said that he would react to an invasion of the South with all-out bombing of the North, and despite fervent opposition from within the administration he ordered air strikes and naval bombardment of North Vietnam up to the 18th parallel (still more than two hundred miles south of Hanoi). Once again, he was reminded that he could command but that the Defense Department must dispose. Hardly a bomb fell on enemy territory for a week—partly because of bad weather, which made air operations difficult, partly because of confusion in the command structure, but also because Laird, supported by Abrams, wanted all U.S. air power targeted on enemy forces in South Vietnam.[4] Although this approach would have inflicted enormous casualties on the enemy, it was a formula for impasse. Hanoi had shown repeatedly that it was willing to spend almost any number of lives in return for political advantage. What would it be willing to pay for territory that it might be able to use at the bargaining table even if it failed to achieve a complete military victory? On April 6, acting on instructions from Nixon and Kissinger, I prepared a contingency plan calling for the bombing of all military targets in North Vietnam and for the mining of enemy ports. The President ruled that this plan would go into effect on May 8 if ARVN showed signs of breaking under the enemy invasion.

Before the ink was dry on this paper, I was sent to Vietnam to survey the situation on behalf of the President. The NVA, committing the usual horrible atrocities against pro-Saigon civilians as it advanced, had captured territory in the north, was in the process of overrunning Binh Dinh province on the central coast, and shelled and occupied half of An Loc city in the south.

Grim as this combination of enemy successes seemed, the situation I found on the ground was somewhat more encouraging than expected. While it was true that the bulk of ARVN units in Military Region II, which encompassed the rugged central one-third of the country, were tied down in remote and vulnerable positions in the western Highlands, South Vietnamese forces appeared to have stalemated and inflicted heavy losses on NVA units in Cambodia. About half of the ARVN Twenty-second Division had been destroyed after abandoning a string of fire bases in the Highlands, but this was mainly the result of a loss of nerve by its inept commander.

"For each case where they have failed," I reported, "there have been dozens of cases in which ARVN and territorial forces have fought bravely and efficiently." On the other side, the North Vietnamese had suffered heavy casualties. On the basis of my inspection of prisoners and talks with American military advisers and South Vietnamese officers in the field, I told the President that ARVN had not been outclassed or outfought as in the past, and stated the reason why: "The NVA main-force units are unquestionably less capable than in the past, reflecting heavy losses and poor leadership."

Throughout this period, Kissinger went on shadowboxing, as he called it, with the North Vietnamese, suggesting meetings of the Paris peace talks, seeing them brusquely postponed or canceled by the enemy, and sending Hanoi messages through the Soviets (who professed an eager desire to help but failed time after time to do so) and the Chinese (who declined to be enmeshed in the problem) emphasizing U.S. determination to defeat the invasion. On April 15, the North Vietnamese canceled a secret meeting with Kissinger, scheduled for April 24 in Paris, that the Soviets had led us to believe might produce an agreement.

That weekend, Nixon authorized a series of B-52 and fighter-bomber strikes on fuel depots, warehouses, and motor pools around Hanoi and Haiphong. Four Soviet cargo ships anchored in Haiphong harbor were accidentally hit by American bombs. Naturally, the Soviets protested, but in terms empty of any real threat. This was partly because there wasn't much more that Moscow could do to make our position in Vietnam more difficult short of sending in combat divisions, but it also had to do with the strong Soviet desire for a summit. The only real hope of maintaining the independence of the Republic of South Vietnam after the American withdrawal was to induce the Soviet Union to reduce its flow of military supplies and military assistance to the North at the same time that we were getting out of the South. Because the political atmosphere at home tended to exclude any action to bring the war home to Hanoi, an accommodation with Moscow designed to limit the violence of the conflict offered the best hope that something of American goals and South Vietnamese expectations might be preserved. This was the immediate goal of Nixon's policy of détente. However, the Soviets began a massive increase in the flow of military supplies to Hanoi immediately after Nixon's return from China.*

After Hanoi canceled the Paris meeting, Nixon was convinced that the Soviets wanted to take advantage of his difficult domestic political situation to pressure him on the summit. The Soviets fed his suspicions by inviting Kissinger to Moscow for a secret meeting to discuss the summit and perhaps other matters. Nixon was reluctant to let him go; he wanted assurances from the Kremlin that the Soviets would give more effective help on the Vietnamese situation before rewarding them with the propaganda benefits and bilateral agreements such a summit would produce. Kissinger, who believed that it was better to negotiate secondary questions rather than not to negotiate at all, pressed Nixon to let him go to Moscow and see what might happen. On April 20, despite deep misgivings on the President's part, Kissinger went. Nixon wanted him to concentrate in the first instance on questions relating to Vietnam, and to pack his bags and come home if the Soviets refused to cooperate. Kissinger, who did not believe that Moscow was in "direct collusion with Hanoi,"[5] requested, and was reluctantly granted, a more flexible brief.

Not without reason, Nixon was in a melancholy mood during Kissinger's absence. The news media were operating at fever pitch, reflecting the rising political temperature in Washington and across the country. Campuses were in an uproar, with hundreds of arrests being made. On April 13, by a vote of 68 to 16, the Senate had passed a bill to limit the President's power to make war without congressional approval; all four Republican leaders voted with the majority. On April 17, after hearing Roger's stout defense of the bombing, the Senate Foreign Relations Committee voted to terminate funds for U.S. combat operations in Indochina after December 31.[6]

Nixon spoke of "crossing the Rubicon"; the phrase popped up again and again. In my presence, he talked almost exclusively about hard options: blockade, the bombardment of strategic targets in the Hanoi-Haiphong agglomeration, destroying the railroads, mining the harbors, interdicting shipping from whatever source to stop the materials of war

---

*According to CIA estimates, North Vietnam received $505 million in military aid from the U.S.S.R. in 1967 (the year before the Tet Offensive); $70 million in 1970; and $100 million in 1971. In addition, Soviet economic aid to Hanoi for those three years totaled $860 million. In the same years, China provided an additional $305 million in military aid and $204 million in economic aid (Knappman, p. 58).

from getting through to the enemy. Agreeing that this was the minimum necessary under the circumstances, I said that any bombing campaign would have to continue day after day without pause until the enemy yielded, no matter how long that took. Nixon agreed, but he thought that he would have to cancel the summit in Moscow if he did all that we had discussed, or even a substantial part of it. Kissinger, although he supported the bombing, believed that it was impossible to bomb and still have the summit. The bombing Nixon had already ordered had unloosed a stampede of critics at home and abroad. Senator J. W. Fulbright, Democrat of Arkansas, the chairman of the Foreign Relations Committee, captured the tone when he said on April 27 that Nixon's resumption of the bombing had "removed one of the normal human restraints upon the savage cruelty and inhumanity present in all wars."[7] It was not impossible that in a matter of hours Nixon's Soviet policy would collapse or that the situation in South Vietnam might take an irreversible turn for the worse.

In Moscow, the Soviet leader, Leonid Brezhnev, blandly denied to Kissinger that pre-invasion shipments of Soviet war matériel to Hanoi had been in any way out of the ordinary but agreed to consider cutting back; he refused to put any pressure on Hanoi apart from forwarding a message from us suggesting talks designed to negotiate the end of the war. Kissinger did make progress on the agenda for a Soviet–U.S. summit meeting, and he came home convinced that we were on the brink of negotiating and signing a Strategic Arms Limitation Treaty (SALT) with Moscow that would be, as he put it with trademark enthusiasm, the most important document of its kind in history.

Nixon began to talk about saving the situation in Vietnam at the cost of his own reelection if necessary. He mused about stepping aside as a candidate after choosing his successor. Although he listed several names (Reagan, Rockefeller, Chief Justice Warren Burger), it was clear that his real choice was John Connally, the only member of his Cabinet who, along with me, supported his toughest instincts.

Nixon wanted to be strong, but he had so often been warned of the political consequences of behaving strongly that he could not dismiss them from his calculations. I told him about my last conversation with Johnson at the LBJ Ranch, in which he had said that he had gone wrong on Vietnam when he'd listened to his advisers instead of his own instincts. This home truth seemed to make an impression. "Is that what Lyndon told you?" Nixon asked. This was a truism from someone who could truly understand a President's responsibilities or live with a President's mistakes—another President.* A few days later in the Oval Office, he told Kissinger, Haldeman, Connally and me, "As far as I'm concerned, the only real mistakes I've made were the times when I didn't follow my own instincts." He cited his softness after the EC-121 shoot-down, when he had failed to retaliate against an act of war, as the prime instance: "If we had bombed North Korea then, the damned war would be over now."

Forty-eight hours after Kissinger's return from Moscow, Nixon announced that an additional twenty thousand U.S. troops would be withdrawn from Vietnam over the ensuing two months. He felt that this action, taken while the enemy was invading South Vietnam, "would dramatize our desire for peace."[8] On May 1, a secret meeting with Le Duc Tho having been arranged at last, Kissinger left for Paris. On the same day, Brezhnev sent Nixon a letter warning against any U.S. action in Vietnam that might imperil the summit. In Paris, Kissinger was harangued and insulted by the other side and broke off the talks. On his return, he advised Nixon (who had already toyed with the idea) to cancel the Moscow summit before the Russians did so.

My own advice was just the opposite. "The Russians want détente more than they need Hanoi," I told Nixon. "Let *them* cancel the summit if they don't like your policy. The key issue is not to lose the war; every other question is subordinate." The President wrote to Brezhnev pointing out in strong language that Soviet supplies to the North had made the invasion of the South possible, and that determined actions by the United States were only to be expected under the circumstances. Although no suggestion of canceling the summit came back from Moscow, Kissinger and others continued to believe that Nixon could not bomb Hanoi and have the summit, too. Besides myself, only John Connally advised the President otherwise, although Kissinger also came to advocate the bombing.

Meanwhile, the war continued. In the three weeks ending on April 15, ARVN lost 2,109 killed in action, while enemy dead were estimated to be more than 12,000. Thirty-four Americans were killed during this period.[9] The battle for Hue had begun; An Loc was under siege (more

---

* In April, the Nixon administration said that the invasion by North Vietnamese troops was a violation of the 1968 understanding with the Johnson administration that bombing of the North would be halted in return for Hanoi's pledge not to violate the DMZ or bombard civilian population centers. In reply, the North Vietnamese delegation to the Paris peace talks issued a statement claiming that Hanoi had made no such pledge and had always understood that the 1968 bombing halt negotiated by Johnson's men was "unconditional." This reinforced Nixon's belief that no agreement had ever existed.

than two thousand enemy shells fell on the city in a single day); and on May 1, after heavy fighting, the city of Quang Tri in the northern panhandle fell to the Communists, who fulfilled Thieu's prophecy about their intentions by forming a provisional revolutionary government and declaring Quang Tri its capital. Abrams sent home an alarmist message suggesting that ARVN was about to crack; he thought that the South Vietnamese had lost their will to fight and that total capitulation might occur at any moment. Nixon, who had never recovered confidence in Abrams after the Lam Son operation, could not believe that his commander in Vietnam was telling him that South Vietnam might simply choose to cease to exist.

On May 8, during a three-hour session of the NSC, Nixon announced his intention to bomb Hanoi-Haiphong and mine the harbor. Laird opposed this decision for his usual reasons. Rogers argued against it on grounds that it might upset the Soviets and derail détente, but he went on to discuss the options in such equivocal terms that Kissinger slipped me a sardonic note while the Secretary of State was still talking: " 'If it works, I'm for it; if it fails, I'm against it.' "

Nixon informed the leaders of Congress of his decision that evening. He asked for their support if they felt that they could give it. Both Democrats and Republicans received his words in stony silence. It was a chilling and revealing moment. After the meeting, Nixon chewed over this display of cold indifference and asked for opinions as to its cause. I told the President I thought it had been a mistake to ask for support from such a suggestible group; as President in an hour of national crisis he had the right to demand it. "You'll get what you tell them to give you—no more, no less."

Later that evening, he went on television and told the nation what he intended to do and why. "There is only one way to stop the killing," he said. "That is to keep the weapons of war out of the hands of the international outlaws of North Vietnam." The bombing, mining, and interdiction of shipping would continue, he said, until Hanoi was prepared to return all American prisoners of war and accept an internationally supervised cease-fire throughout Indochina.[10]

As soon as he finished speaking, the inevitable electronic storm broke over the White House. The news media were all but unanimous in the prediction that the summit would be canceled forthwith by an outraged Soviet Union. But Nixon had sent a four-page letter to Brezhnev explaining the reasons for his action and arguing that events in Vietnam should not affect the summit. Shortly after the speech, Dobrynin came to the White House and let Kissinger know that the meeting between Nixon and Brezhnev would take place as scheduled.

To quote his own imagery, Nixon had crossed the Rubicon. Predictably, he landed on the opposite shore well in advance of his Secretary of Defense and the foreign-policy bureaucracy. The Pentagon's reaction to the President's call for an all-out air assault on the enemy's base of supply was to schedule two hundred sorties a day against the whole country. Thousands were needed. Nixon wrote a blistering memorandum to Kissinger accusing Defense and State of undermining his policy and demanding "*action* which is very *strong, threatening,* and *effective.*"[11]

Less than a week after these events, Nixon and Kissinger flew to Moscow for the summit meeting.* Kissinger regarded the May 1972 summit as "one of the great diplomatic coups of all time." In Moscow, he and the President endured a shouting match with Brezhnev and other Soviet leaders over Vietnam but completed negotiations on treaties regulating antiballistic missiles (ABM) and establishing temporary limits on the numbers of ICBMs and submarine-launched missiles each side could have until a permanent agreement (SALT I) was concluded. The final draft agreements were cabled to me by Kissinger, and I showed them to the Joint Chiefs of Staff as a matter of routine. They objected strenuously to certain aspects of the section dealing with submarines. Although the provisions in question had already been agreed to in Moscow by both sides, I was obliged to get Kissinger out of bed and explain the situation. It was a colorful conversation. Kissinger, who was under the mistaken

---

* Among other prepatory duties I had been charged with finding out what Brezhnev wanted as a state gift from Nixon. My contact at the Soviet embassy replied, in playful tones, "Can you not guess?" I could; Brezhnev was a collector of automobiles. I ventured the obvious suggestion: "A Cadillac?" The reply was a delighted laugh and the whispered words "El Dorado." I called General Motors and the firm agreed to donate a fully equipped 1973 model as a patriotic gesture. Brezhnev presented Nixon with the model of a Volga Seagoing Model 70 hydrofoil he planned to give him in return. The vessel itself was not delivered until Watergate was in full swing, and it was deemed unwise to ship the Soviet gift to Florida, where the sight of Nixon skimming over the waters might further increase the indignation of the press. Nixon loved the hydrofoil and was determined to take a ride in it. The government authorities in charge of traffic on the Potomac River expressed terror at the idea of the President of the United States weaving among slow-moving craft at speeds above fifty miles an hour, but Nixon was adamant. Finally, the hydrofoil was launched in the Potomac and he took a sedate trip in it, though the crew never revved it up sufficiently to cause it to rise up out of the water as a hydrofoil should. At subsequent summits, Brezhnev received a Lincoln Continental and a silver-gray Chevrolet Monte Carlo, both donated by the manufacturers, in addition to other handsome gifts, including a golf cart and a custom-made Pederson hunting rifle. In return, Nixon received on behalf of the nation such memorabilia as rugs made from the skins of a Siberian wolf and a Russian snow panther, a lugubrious painting of Moscow by night in the Socialist Realism style, and a large quantity of Soviet-made vodka and wine.

impression that the Chiefs had previously agreed to the provisions to which they were now objecting, was embarrassed, outraged, and deeply reluctant to reopen the negotiations. The President, knowing that no treaty opposed by the Joint Chiefs had the slightest chance of being ratified by the Senate, put the matter back on the table and renegotiated it to the Pentagon's satisfaction.

Nixon returned from Moscow on June 1, having signed agreements for a joint U.S.–Soviet space mission and other initiatives, as well as the breakthrough treaties on strategic arms limitation. The summit had not only taken place in the face of conventional diplomatic wisdom that had deemed it impossible, it had achieved concrete results. Not the least of these, Nixon thought, was the impression he had been able to make on the Russians with regard to his intentions in Vietnam. He had left them in no doubt that he intended to deal with Hanoi from a position of superior power, and it may be that Soviet president Nikolai Podgorny told the North Vietnamese that when he visited Hanoi shortly after the summit.

Buoyed by public-opinion polls that showed two-thirds of Americans polled in favor of the mining of Haiphong harbor and three-quarters in favor of the bombing of Hanoi, Nixon recovered his good spirits. By keeping pressure on the Pentagon, he achieved an effective air campaign in the North. In South Vietnam, ARVN retook the occupied portion of An Loc and stiffened all along the line with the help of strong U.S. tactical air support. Although heavy fighting continued on the ground, it gradually became evident that South Vietnam was in no immediate danger of disintegration as long as it could rely on U.S. air power and resupply. Representative Gerald R. Ford of Michigan, the Republican leader in the House, had said earlier that the bombing of the North had been "the right course."[12]

His was a lonely voice, but the corner had been turned. Nixon's foreign policy, carried forward in the face of frenzied opposition at home, had reconfigured the world order, bringing China back into the community of nations, building a structure of dialogue and agreements with the Soviet Union under the rubric of détente that began the process of civilizing that nation's international behavior, and laying the basis for honorable U.S. withdrawal from Vietnam.

In hindsight, it is possible to argue that these great interlocking achievements, each regarded by the conventional wisdom of the time as either unattainable or undesirable, contributed to the ultimate collapse of international communism by opening it up further to the peaceful influence of the rest of the world and thus subjecting it to the irresistible pressures of political evolution. No one would have imagined such a connection at the time, and even now some will question its reality. History must decide this among many other clouded questions relating to Nixon and his presidency. At the very least, the results vindicated the principle that military strength in support of national aims is more effective when applied in sufficient measure to achieve the results desired. Nixon's bombing of the North in response to the invasion marked the first time such an unequivocal standard had been applied in the Vietnam War, and perhaps also marked the first time that the enemy understood our meaning and our determination.

Meanwhile, other events were unfolding. On June 17, 1972, five men on the payroll of the Committee to Re-Elect the President (CRP) were arrested after breaking into the headquarters of the Democratic National Committee in the Watergate Office building for the apparent purpose of tapping a telephone. Six days later, Nixon met in the Oval Office with Haldeman and ordered him to instruct the CIA to block the investigation of this tawdry burglary by falsely telling the FBI that it involved foreign-intelligence operations. The CIA ultimately refused to support the lie, but this base and furtive transaction, taking place in the afterglow of Nixon's grand display of nerve and statesmanship on the world stage, produced the farrago of conspiracy, revelation, and retribution that would destroy his presidency.

22

A Parting of the Ways

From the break-in in June 1972 until I left the White House on January 4, 1973, to return full-time to the Army, the Watergate affair was not a factor in my life or work. After September, when Nixon appointed me Army vice chief of staff, my duties in the White House were connected almost entirely to Vietnam, and I spent as much time as possible at the Pentagon, filling in as best I could for the chief of staff–designate, General Abrams, whose confirmation had been held up in the Senate over allegations of unauthorized bombing missions in Southeast Asia. If Watergate ever came up in conversation at the White House or in the Pentagon, I do not remember the occasion; the President never mentioned it to me and I certainly never brought it up in his presence. It would have seemed inconceivable to me, had the thought even occurred, that attempts were being made in another part of the White House to "manage" the burglary's consequences by cover-up.

As a practical matter, my contacts were few and far between with those who were later shown to be involved, except for Haldeman, who was Nixon's faithful and efficient go-between in nearly all things. I knew Ehrlichman, Charles Colson, John Dean, and most of the others in the way one knows neighbors in the suburbs—they were familiar figures as they went about their lawn mowing and leaf raking, and they sometimes showed up at PTA meetings and barbecues, but I had little idea what they actually did for a living or who their friends were. All were involved in domestic policy, and Nixon never discussed domestic policy with me, except to minimize it as the housekeeping chores he had to do in compensation for the more pleasurable aspects of presidential life: "Al, this country is so big and strong, and has so many smart people in it, that it runs itself; the President's job is to try to keep the government out of it." My respect for Nixon's intelligence, and for his deep natural caution, eliminated any thought that he or anyone close to him could possibly be involved in such a comedy of errors. Looking into the ruddy face of the presidency from close at hand, I did not detect the viruses multiplying within. Such diagnostic skills as I possessed were focused on more obvious threats to the administration's political and strategic health.

On the first of July 1972, when I visited the war theater again, confidence was high among the South Vietnamese. From President Thieu on down, the leadership in Saigon believed that ARVN had not only defeated the enemy invasion but was now stronger in South Vietnam than the NVA and Viet Cong. The quality of enemy infantry had declined sharply; many recently captured NVA troops were young, inexperienced, and poorly trained. Thieu and his generals believed that it would take five to ten years for Hanoi to mount another conventional offensive comparable to the one they had just stopped in its tracks. "These projections may be grossly overoptimistic," I told President Nixon. "But one thing is certain: Saigon has been given a new lease on life."

Actually, the reasons for optimism were limited. South Vietnam's two northern provinces remained under effective control of the tens of thousands of enemy troops who remained in the country. Most of the staggering casualties inflicted on the NVA had been the result of U.S. air strikes. ARVN's organizational problems had not been overcome. Senior leadership was still politically strong but professionally weak; structure and mobility were essentially the same as they had been eight years before. On the other side, enemy air defense was far better than at any time in the past, and this would limit the effectiveness of U.S. air support in any future combat. Meanwhile, in Cambodia, Khmer Rouge strength was estimated to have increased to roughly forty thousand guerrillas armed with Soviet and Chinese weapons and trained and catechized by Hanoi in a more ferocious form of classic Viet Cong terror tactics. As the Cambodian government was incapable of dealing with this threat, the prospect of a Communist Cambodia was real and present.

The American priority remained the same: withdrawal of all U.S. troops from Vietnam and the conclusion of an agreement in Paris that would permit us to depart from Vietnam under color of law and honor. There were two chief obstacles to this result: First, Hanoi's insistence on overthrowing Thieu's government as a precondition to a cease-fire, and second, Thieu's insistence that he would never agree to a cease-fire while enemy troops remained in South Vietnam, or under conditions that would impose a Communist government on his country. In moral terms, Thieu's position was the correct one, and it deeply engaged my own sympathies. In political terms, his position was irrelevant because Nixon lacked the needed support in Congress to impose a strictly moral solution by force of arms. All sides to the negotiations, including Thieu, understood this, and the United States dealt with the dilemma by repeated promises that it would intervene with air and sea power if the cease-fire was violated by the North.

The effect of the bombing became evident later in the summer of 1972 when the diplomatic channel became active, suggesting that Hanoi might be ready at last to engage in serious negotiations. By that time, the enemy had concluded that the Democrats were not going to win the presidency in November (at the end of August, Nixon led McGovern in the Gallup poll by 64 percent to 30 percent and the Harris poll found that majorities still supported the bombing of Hanoi and the mining of Haiphong harbor).[1] Hanoi had begun to think that it would be wiser to negotiate with Nixon before his victory than afterward.

Everyone knew that the chief hope of a breakthrough lay in finding a formula that would provide for some form of participation by the NLF in the postwar government in South Vietnam without betraying and destroying the Thieu government. As an accommodation to the United States, Thieu had already volunteered to step aside sixty days before any legitimate presidential election, but when I spoke to him on July 3 he reiterated his fundamental belief that Hanoi would never agree to a permanent cease-fire unless it got a coalition government.

In Paris, on September 26 and 27, the North Vietnamese handed Kissinger a new ten-point program. This proposal contained no clearly defined provisions for the removal of NVA troops from the South. Hanoi insisted that it had no troops in country but argued at the same time that "a solution of the internal problem in South Vietnam must proceed from the actual situation that there exist in South Vietnam two administrations, two armies, and other political forces." Hanoi's new proposal called for the replacement of Thieu's government with a "provisional government of national concord" composed of equal membership from the existing Saigon government, the Quang Tri "Provisional Revolutionary Government" (whose existence neither Saigon nor Washington acknowledged), and unidentified "neutral" elements.[2]

Blind Homer would have perceived that this was a wooden horse filled with Communists. In a conversation at Camp David, Nixon told the Soviet foreign minister, Andrei Gromyko, who was in town to sign the SALT I treaty, that he would terminate the peace talks and "turn to some other methods after the elections"[3] unless Hanoi was more forthcoming in the next meeting with Kissinger in Paris the following week. Nevertheless, Hanoi's proposal was treated as a basis for negotiations, and we prepared detailed refinements for discussion at the next session in Paris.

On October 2, I met with Thieu in Saigon to explain the U.S. counterproposals that Kissinger planned to table in Paris the following week. I told Thieu that Nixon had asked me to speak to him, soldier to soldier, without regard to diplomatic niceties, so that Thieu would be aware of the President's innermost thinking. The U.S. counterproposals also called for the replacement of the existing government with a transitional body that would write a new constitution and establish a postwar government by means of the election of a Constituent Assembly. The other side was opposed to popular election of a president, but I told Thieu the administration believed that the enemy proposals could be used to keep him in power through manipulation of the process (for example, the Constituent Assembly could elect a national president as a first order of business, then draft a constitution) and control of the membership (according to our calculations, Thieu would control one-third of the provisional government outright and decisively influence one-half of the other two-thirds of the neutral faction, assuming that it was not composed of crypto-Communists).

Thieu wanted to know why we were in such a hurry to negotiate. I assured him that our negotiating strategy was not influenced by election-year considerations and explained that Nixon was upset by the strident language in some of Saigon's communications to us and by its delaying tactics. Thieu heard me out with scarcely concealed skepticism, then adjourned the meeting to consult with his advisers.

On the morning of October 4, he gave Ambassador Ellsworth Bunker and me his answer. The U.S. proposals, he argued, would formalize the existence of two governments in South Vietnam. "Everything will disappear," Thieu said, "the president, the constitution, the general assembly, even the government itself." I tried to reassure him. He was beyond reassurance. Because what we said to each other that day was so typical of our exchanges in the many meetings that followed as we proceeded inexorably toward an accommodation with the enemy, I will quote at length from my notes of the conversation:

> HAIG: We have two fundamental objectives. First, the continuation of your government after a settlement with the power to govern. Second, to be sure that [you] cannot be victimized so long as we do not have a situation of true peace. . . . If I return to the United States and tell President Nixon that we cannot work out a counter-proposal . . . that will protect the Republic of Vietnam, we will be faced with a major crisis with disastrous effect for your government and ours. . . . I realize that you and your people have lost more in this war than we. . . . We want to be able to continue to support this conflict with the funds, the firepower, and the bombing. . . . You should tell us [what] you want. . . . We want to abide by your solution. We need your advice.
>
> THIEU: Dr. Kissinger does not deign to consider what we propose. He just goes his own way. . . . That is my feeling, that is my impression.
>
> HAIG: It is quite obvious that there has been a breakdown in mutual confidence.
>
> THIEU: . . . I have run out of ideas. Sooner or later the government will crumble and President Thieu will have to commit suicide. . . . In 1967 when I was asked by Ambassador Lodge to absorb the NLF I said, "We are a sick man. Please don't give us another spoon of microbes. It will kill us. We must get better first." Now we are willing to take the risk, a great risk, and let the NLF participate [in the postwar transitional government]. . . . All we ask is that the Democratic Republic of Vietnam withdraw [its troops] from South Vietnam. . . . How many more last miles will there be? No one tells [the leaders in Hanoi] to step down. That would be a humiliation for them. I have endured that humiliation for two years. If President Nixon has any drastic measures to take against South Vietnam, he should go ahead. As a soldier, I am not afraid to say such words.

There were tears in his eyes. My own emotional state was deeply unsettled, but feelings on both sides were mild compared to what was yet to come. I assured Thieu that the United States would conclude no agreement with Hanoi without prior consultation, made the usual assurances about U.S. support in case of enemy perfidy, and went back to Washington.

By the autumn of 1972, strong differences regarding the Paris peace talks and a certain discord based on personality issues had grown up between Nixon and Kissinger. The President thought that Kissinger, with his subtle mind and his love of byplay, was in danger of becoming more interested in the process than in the result in Paris. Kissinger's worldwide floating badminton match with the press was also a cause of almost constant aggravation. No real philosophical differences underlay this squabble. Next to Nixon, Kissinger was the most realistic thinker in Washington with regard to North Vietnam. As he put it in his memoirs: "Displays of American strength never failed to be taken seriously by [Hanoi]. . . . Acts of goodwill . . . were treated as signs of moral weakness, even as they scorned them."[4] Kissinger was not usually in favor of displays of strength before other remedies had been exhausted, and this was the source of the friction.

My own mental model of a peace agreement, as both men knew, was the Korean settlement, which removed all Communist troops from South Korea and even banned the Communist party there; established a fortified border between the belligerents; stationed sixty thousand U.S. troops in South Korea; and left President Rhee at the head of an elected government that was founded on democratic principles, even if it was not yet fully democratic by American standards.[5] All this had been achieved, after years of stalemate, through the threat of using overwhelming force against the enemy. This view of cause and effect on an acceptable outcome in Indochina was closer to Nixon's ideas than to Kissinger's. I thought that our lack of confidence in our own power and our apparently incurable reluctance to use it while we perversely overestimated the power and good instincts of the U.S.S.R., North Vietnam, and other Communist states constituted fundamental flaws in the international behavior of the U.S. government. Kissinger continued to regard this opinion as the product of a severely limited military mind.

Although Nixon's own view of the matter was more subtle and complex than either Kissinger's or mine, he sympathized with my point of view. As a matter of human nature, this led the President to seek my opinion more frequently on questions pertaining to Vietnam, and finally to make me his personal messenger to Thieu in matters connected to the peace talks. This created tension. Kissinger's travels were frequent and some-times long, not only because of the negotiations in Paris but because Nixon's system of concentrating foreign-policy operations in the White House made Kissinger the government's primary crisis manager. He had also become a media figure, and tending this public persona consumed a good deal of his time. The issues on which he concentrated usually required his entire attention; while he contended with Le Duc Tho in Paris or roved the world managing the crisis of the hour, I assumed the rest of the NSC portfolio. This inevitably meant that I saw a great deal of the President.

Although I did not regard this propinquity as a threat to my loyalty to Kissinger, or to his own position with Nixon, it troubled him. He began to suspect that I was taking advantage of his absences to influence the President on Vietnam, or at least to reinforce the President's natural preference for a harder line. Kissinger had learned by sad experience at Harvard to be on the lookout for petty treachery, and his sensitivity in this regard had not been blunted as a result of the turf wars with Rogers and Laird and other lurkers whom he detected along the perimeter of his territory. It did not surprise me that he felt as he did, but he need not have worried about attacks from the rear. Kissinger knew where I stood on Vietnam, and I never expressed an opinion to Nixon that I had not previously expressed to Kissinger. Not once during this period did Nixon ever criticize Kissinger in my presence, much less place me in the position of discussing the latter's advice or actions behind his back, even in periods when I knew from the newspapers and White House gossip that the President was furious over some misunderstanding or Kissingerian assig-nation with the press. Nixon understood, I think, that I would resent and confront any attack on Kissinger, and he wished to avoid that. But the real reason for such strict observation of the decencies was the President's own sense of loyalty and fair play toward Kissinger, whom he still greatly liked and admired.

For some time, I had wanted to return to the Army. In the summer of 1972, Kissinger for the first time agreed with my suggestion that this might be a good idea. On September 7, after negotiations between Kissinger and Laird, Nixon appointed me vice chief of staff of the Army, nominating me for promotion to four-star rank over the heads of more than 240 officers with greater seniority; the Senate Armed Services Committee confirmed the nomination on October 6.[6] Although by no means un-precedented (FDR had promoted George C. Marshall from one to four stars and made him chief of staff), this nomination made a stir, though not so great as that created in 1906 when John J. Pershing jumped from captain to brigadier general over the heads of 862 officers senior to himself. Nixon's desire had been to appoint me Army chief of staff in succession to William C. Westmoreland, whose term was coming to an end. Laird demurred, suggesting with some reason that my confirmation hearings would reopen the controversy over the Vietnam policy. The real reason, many thought, was that Laird had promised the post to Creighton Abrams, whose own confirmation would be held up by the Senate from June to October 6. For reasons the reader already knows, the President was not enthusiastic about Abrams, and possibly he envisioned an even higher military post for me as part of his design to make the Joint Chiefs of Staff, along with the rest of the government establishment, more responsive to his policy in the second term. In any case, I had hoped to take up my duties in the Pentagon as soon as I was appointed, but this was not to be.

Nixon directed me, on my return from Saigon after the meeting with Thieu, to accompany Kissinger to Paris for the meeting with Le Duc Tho scheduled for October 8. In the sense that this put the Atlantic Ocean between Nixon and me while the negotiations were in progress, the arrangement probably pleased Kissinger; in the sense that he may have thought (wrongly) that Nixon had sent me along to keep an eye on him, it did not. The President wanted a settlement but not at any cost. By now, it was apparent that he would be returned to office with a large majority a month hence, while he no doubt would have been glad to have peace before Election Day, the President had little interest in concluding the peace talks as a means of gaining political advantage. He did believe, and so did Kissinger, that Hanoi reckoned it could get better terms before the election than after, and he wanted to use that perception to strike hard for a final agreement. Nixon's real objective was to free himself of Vietnam as soon as possible so as to prevent it from poisoning his second term, which he envisaged as a sort of Augustinian autumn in which he would reorganize the government, revitalize the republic, and confound and scatter the domestic enemies who had plagued and undermined him since the beginning of his public life.

Kissinger, who had been subjected to the maddening frustrations of the Paris negotiations for nearly four years, somehow summoned the patience and energy to deal with Le Duc Tho and his colleagues for what everyone hoped would be the last time. In four days of talks, Kissinger achieved an agreement calling for a cease-fire, the return of POWs, and the withdrawal of U.S. forces within sixty days. These provisions satisfied the basic American requirements. As to the future of South Vietnam, the other side dropped its demand that Thieu resign and abandoned its insistence on a coalition government, agreeing instead to the American proposal for a National Council of Reconciliation and Concord composed in equal parts of representatives from Thieu's government, the NLF, and neutral parties. This body would be able to act only on the basis of unanimous vote, which meant that Thieu would never be outvoted but also that each party possessed a veto, so that its ability to make decisions would be doubtful. There was no requirement for the withdrawal of enemy troops from South Vietnam. These now numbered at least 300,000 according to Thieu's calculations (probably slightly less than half that figure by actual count), but North Vietnam insisted on the blatant falsehood that all residual Communist forces were indigenous members of the Viet Cong, who constituted the army of the Provisional Revolutionary Government. Hanoi did agree to close its border sanctuaries in Cambodia and Laos. It was solemnly argued inside the U.S. delegation that this would lead through the cut-off of supplies and infiltration to the "withering" and eventual disappearance of what everyone knew were NVA forces. The cease-fire would begin on October 31.

Kissinger believed that he had achieved the final breakthrough. We returned to Washington on October 12 and went immediately to Nixon's hideaway office in the Executive Office Building. In triumphant tones, Kissinger described the terms to Nixon. He must have known, and the President certainly knew, that this was not the achievement for which we had all hoped. What made it acceptable on the moral level were the underlying, unilateral guarantees to Thieu that we would punish infractions by the North with massive American military power, and the assumption that our influence with Moscow would be sufficient to cut the flow of military supplies to the NVA.

The President, evidently believing that further delay would not produce a better outcome, seized the opportunity to put an end to the matter and approved the terms. Kissinger wanted to stop the bombing of North Vietnam altogether as a gesture of goodwill. My own view, well known to both Kissinger and Nixon, was that we should keep on bombing as the only hope of inducing the enemy to remove his troops from the South. It was too late to argue the self-evident truth that Thieu's regime could not survive if we permitted a huge Communist army to remain inside his country. Eventually, Nixon compromised on a reduction to 150 sorties a day. In a rare display of conviviality, the President had ordered steaks for the three of us to be sent over from the White House mess and called for a bottle of French wine from the family quarters. I had taken little part in the conversation, and in his memoirs Nixon says that he noticed that I was "subdued."[7] A better word might have been *despondent*. The President asked me what I thought Thieu's reaction was going to be. "This agreement may be as much as the traffic will bear," I replied, "but I don't think Thieu will accept it."

Laird, Rogers, Abrams, and others enthusiastically endorsed the draft agreement. Rogers told the President that it represented a "total surrender" by Hanoi on the political points.[8] After stopping in Paris to discuss unresolved questions dealing with the return of enemy POWs and the replacement of war matériel on both sides, Kissinger flew to Saigon on October 18 to confer with Thieu. Under the best of circumstances, this would have been a difficult meeting because Thieu did not trust Kissinger and Kissinger had little patience with Thieu's incurable habit of pointing out the flaws in draft agreements and their unfortunate probable consequences. Under the actual circumstances, in which a fatigued yet enthusiastic Kissinger bore the fate of South Vietnam in his briefcase, it proved to be a disaster. Kissinger's impatience to complete his consultations with Thieu and continue on to Hanoi, where he was scheduled to initial a draft agreement on October 22, did not go unnoticed in the Presidential Palace.

Thieu was convinced that the agreement was a sellout. He pointed out the military dangers of leaving a large enemy army in place on South Vietnamese territory and the acute political perils of condoning the barefaced lie that this was not a foreign army. We had reduced the bombing, Thieu said; we had left the NVA in the South; we had opened the door to legitimization of a puppet provisional revolutionary government supported by that army. The accords would not be respected. Kissinger replied that the people and government of the United States would never stand for violations of an agreement purchased with so much American blood and suffering, and that the enemy force would wither away from lack of supply and reinforcement. He sent a cable home saying that it was his impression that Thieu and his colleagues were "having great psychological difficulty with cutting the American umbilical cord."[9] After discussing Thieu's reaction with me, Nixon told Kissinger to push the South Vietnamese leader, but not to the brink.

Meanwhile Thieu's warnings of enemy duplicity were given point by Pham Van Dong, the North Vietnamese premier, who fed an American journalist visiting Hanoi the mendacious information that the draft agreement provided for a coalition government in Saigon and for the payment of American reparations to the North. (Such compensation had been discussed, and on February 1, 1973, Nixon wrote to Pham Van Dong, offering to commit U.S. funds in the "range of $3.25 billion" for postwar reconstruction in the North. On June 26, the House prohibited the use of any U.S. funds for such purposes unless specifically authorized by Congress.[10])

In Washington, I informed Nixon of new evidence that NVA units were moving on the ground to occupy as much territory in the South, and especially around Saigon, as possible before the cease-fire. He responded by ordering a massive airlift of military supplies to Thieu's government and by cabling Kissinger in Saigon that concluding an agreement before the election was not important; doing the right thing in regard to the future of South Vietnam was. In a reply steaming with the pent-up exasperation produced by his herculean efforts to achieve a cease-fire, Kissinger accused Thieu of stalling and warned that if we did not get an agreement before the election that Hanoi would be tougher afterward. This was no Sunday school picnic, Kissinger said; we had come this far and we had to seal the deal. Nixon told him in return not to go to Hanoi without getting Thieu's agreement to the draft. Hanoi unexpectedly dangled a carrot by conceding the two remaining points having to do with the return of Communist prisoners and arms replacement.[11] Nixon cabled Thieu a warning: If he failed to approve the agreement, the resulting controversy "would have the most serious effects upon my ability to continue to provide support for you and for the government of South Vietnam."[12]

The next day, October 22, Kissinger cabled Nixon that Thieu had accepted the agreement. Reading the smudged top-secret teletype, I could scarcely believe my eyes. A few hours later came a second, final telegram from Kissinger: "Thieu has just rejected the final plan or any modification of it and refuses to discuss any further negotiations on the basis of it."[13] In their final session, Thieu told him, "I see that those whom I regard as friends have failed me."[14] Kissinger canceled his trip to Hanoi and came home. Nixon instructed me to call in Dobrynin and tell him that Hanoi had wrecked the agreement with Pham Van Dong's statement and other acts that undermined Saigon's confidence.

All of this activity was, of course, secret, and in the absence of a final agreement Nixon wanted to keep it that way until after the U.S. presidential elections, which were now only two weeks away. To his dismay, however, a shower of leaks predicting imminent announcement of a peace agreement drenched the news media. For the most part, these emanated from Hanoi through French and other sources, so Nixon should have been relieved of the usual angry suspicion that his most closely held secrets were being betrayed by his inner circle. Unfortunately, this was not to be. After his return from Saigon, Kissinger lunched with Max Frankel of the *New York Times*, and Frankel published a story saying that American officials believed that a cease-fire might soon be announced, "perhaps even before election day, Nov. 7, barring a supreme act of folly in Saigon or Hanoi."[15] Kissinger may not have said this, but it certainly sounded like him. It also sounded like an attempt by the administration to make political hay of the peace process. Soon afterward, Radio Hanoi broadcast a statement accusing the United States of having reneged on a peace agreement.

However, the paranoia lingered, like some noxious influenza that felled one victim, lay dormant for a while, and then was invisibly reborn to infect someone else. In Nixon's eyes, the chief carrier of the germ at this point was Kissinger, whose assiduous cultivation of journalists would have made him vulnerable to the qualms of a far less distrustful President than Nixon. The suspicions ran both ways; at about this time, an exhausted and emotionally drained Kissinger was capable of imagining many forms of presidential abandonment, including the suggestion that Nixon was "setting me up as the fall guy in case anything went wrong [with the peace agreement]."[16]

On October 26, twelve days before the election, Kissinger held a press conference in the White House and uttered these words: "We believe that peace is at hand."[17] It is hardly possible to imagine a phrase, so redolent of Neville Chamberlain and the effete 1930s cult of appeasement, more likely to embarrass Nixon as President and presidential candidate, inflame Thieu's anxieties, or weaken our leverage in Hanoi. The President regarded Kissinger's gaffe as a disaster.

Unfortunately, that wasn't all. Kissinger exacerbated the situation by letting himself be carried away in an interview with Oriana Fallaci of Italy's *L'Europeo*. According to Signorina Fallaci, who had a gift for extracting quotes that her "victims" had trouble remembering on publication, Kissinger made statements that seemed to suggest that one of Nixon's best moves in terms of assuring his place in history had been to appoint him as his National Security adviser. This incensed the President, and so did Kissinger's purported remarks (endearing to anyone who took the trouble to imagine Kissinger wearing six-guns, chaps, and ten-gallon hat while digging his spurs into the flanks of a galloping mustang) to the effect that he, Kissinger, was born to be "the cowboy . . . who rides all alone into the town. . . ."[18]

23

Persuasive Force

Two days after the election, in which Nixon was returned to office by the largest number of popular and electoral-college votes in American history while the Democrats retained control of both Houses of Congress and the Vietnam opposition increased its representation in the Senate by three seats, I returned to Saigon, bearing another letter from Nixon to Thieu. The latter had made a number of speeches and statements to the press since Kissinger's visit, and the President (actually Kissinger, who drafted the letter) wrote that his "continuing distortions of the agreement and attacks upon it are unfair and self-defeating." He followed this with promises to dilute the powers of the National Council of Reconciliation and Concord so as to make plain that it "is in no way a governmental body" and to press for the "de facto unilateral withdrawal of some North Vietnamese divisions."[1] On reading this, Thieu drew a circle around the word *some* and asked for time to consult his advisers.

The next day, in the presence of his entire National Security Council, he rejected all compromise on the revisions he had asked for and sent Nixon a letter stating his point of view in detail. I cabled Kissinger my impression: "[Thieu] will go along only if we at least explore the issue of North Vietnamese troops in the South. . . . He wanted a reference to timing and some means of verification. Like you, I am very uncertain that Hanoi will accept this. On the other hand . . . without Thieu's acquiescence, I'm not sure I know where we are. If he refuses to accept the cease-fire negotiated by us under conditions that are unacceptable to him, have we really settled anything?"

The question was moot. On November 14, Nixon wrote to Thieu again, listing the changes that had been negotiated, in part as a result of Thieu's objections. "You have my absolute assurance that if Hanoi fails to abide by the terms of this agreement it is my intention to take swift and severe retaliatory action" Nixon wrote. However, he added, "If . . . we are unable to agree on the course that I have outlined, it will be difficult for me to see how we will be able to continue our common effort towards securing a just and honorable peace. As General Haig told you I would with great reluctance be forced to consider other alternatives. . . ."[2]

The Paris peace talks resumed on November 20. In the opening session, attended by Kissinger and myself, the United States asked for sixty-nine changes in the text. Many were nitpicks of the Vietnamese text originating with Thieu, but there were also provisions calling for a reduction in the NVA presence and its concentration in specified areas that could be inspected, and for the prohibition of movement across the DMZ. Le Duc Tho received this coldly and responded by reviving the demand for Thieu's resignation and calling for total, accelerated U.S. withdrawal, among other changes he knew we could not grant. Many messages passed between Nixon and Kissinger; by now their relationship was so touchy that Kissinger was negotiating with a maddening adversary while in a state of burning resentment toward his own President. His complaints were vigorous, even for him, and I thought they were directed as much to me, the advocate of strong action, as to Nixon, who was just then vulnerable to my kind of advice. This emotional tug-of-war in no way diminished his skill or attention to detail. Hours of negotiation were devoted to haggling over words, phrases, and punctuation marks. Apart from provoking a statement by Tho that the Democratic Republic of Vietnam had been tricked and deceived by the United States as she never before had been in her dealings with the duplicitous French and other enemies, which Kissinger savored as a mordant compliment, little was accomplished.[3]

After this session, Kissinger and I met in his ornate bedroom in the American embassy residence. Kissinger called Nixon on a scrambler telephone that stood incongruously on a magnificent antique desk and told him that the United States had two options: to break off the talks and escalate the bombing or abandon Thieu and sign the agreement as it stood. Nixon equivocated, first instructing Kissinger to go back to the principles of the October 8 draft and to hell with Thieu (not his exact words). Then he told him to break off the talks.

Soon the phone rang again. It was Nixon, asking whether I agreed with Kissinger's estimate of the situation. I said yes, we should break off the talks. When I reported this conversation to Kissinger, he exploded: Nixon didn't trust him. Before he could develop this hasty reaction into a full-scale tantrum, the President called again and told him to break off the talks and come home. The President was ready to apply force. But by the time we reached Washington, he had changed his mind again.

Laird and others who scouted Capitol Hill for the administration reported that support had evaporated for the administration's Vietnam policy in the new Congress that would convene in January. Both Nixon and Kissinger thought that all funds for the war would probably be cut off by the lame-duck Congress almost as soon as it returned; Kissinger urged this possibility on the President as a reason for concluding an agreement as soon as possible.[4] If the war could not be prolonged to improve the terms, it could be intensified. On November 30, Nixon met with Laird and the Joint Chiefs of Staff in the Oval Office and instructed them in Kissinger's presence and mine to prepare a plan for a resumption of the bombing of Hanoi and for reseeding the Haiphong channel with large magnetic mines. The Joint Chiefs were reluctant to risk pilots and aircraft in a war they considered to be over. Kissinger, who had agreed to meet again with Le Duc Tho in Paris on December 4, thought that this judgment was premature. Nixon, sensing that he had little time left in which to act decisively before Congress tied his hands, told him he was thinking about resuming the bombing before the next session in Paris.[5]

Thieu sent his foreign affairs adviser, Nguyen Phu Duc (a most likable man whom everyone except Nixon called "Ducky"), to Washington; Nixon received him in the Oval Office and told him cold-bloodedly that we were going to settle with Hanoi, but he repeated his bedrock assurance that we would bomb the North intensively if it violated the agreements. Thieu, understandably, was by now in an advanced state of shock and nerves. On the human level, the President seemed to sympathize with his plight and admire his courage; no doubt he felt that Thieu was behaving much as he himself would have behaved under the same circumstances—that is, he was going down fighting. At the same time, Nixon desperately wanted to put Vietnam behind him, and he shared some of Kissinger's volcanic frustration and anger at this stubborn ally who had made himself the chief obstacle to winding up the war.

Thieu's name was often coupled to an expletive in discussions at the highest levels of the administration during this period, but that, and the application of irresistible diplomatic pressure, was as far as things went. At least one sensational account published since suggests that the possible assassination of Thieu was discussed during this period. I was not privy to every foolish conversation that took place in the White House, but this report is certainly false. In any case, it was never even hinted at in my presence, and I do not believe that the President would have considered such a scheme.

Kissinger went back to Paris with instructions from the President to settle the issue or abandon the talks. As a result of his travails in Paris and Washington, Kissinger was in low spirits, saying that he would resign if he could not break the deadlock in two days. The United States being an open society, North Vietnamese intelligence on the attitudes of Congress was at least as good as ours, and Le Duc Tho knew that we had much to gain by settling soon and much to lose by delay. Therefore, he procrastinated, behaving with what Kissinger described to me as "cocksure insolence."[6] Nevertheless, Kissinger made what he regarded as progress on the wording of the sections on the DMZ and the arrangements for establishing a postwar government. Then, to Kissinger's bewilderment, Nixon called Dobrynin on December 10 and told him that he had rejected Kissinger's compromise on the DMZ, and he then told me to instruct Kissinger to offer it to the North Vietnamese again "as the final U.S. concession."

Actually, this was an exercise in Nixonian guile designed to use the Russians to put the North Vietnamese on the wrong scent. As a last resort, the President was prepared simply to cave in, as he put it, and accept the best agreement he could get. If that happened, he would send Vice President Spiro T. Agnew to Saigon, with me as his traveling companion, in a last-ditch effort to bring Thieu around. It would be Agnew's job to explain the situation to Thieu in a climactic "like it or lump it" confrontation in Saigon. In reality, there would have been nothing to explain: Had Nixon broken with Thieu, the action would have deprived the United States of any legitimate power to enforce the agreement, and Thieu would have understood that the life of his nation had come to an end. Le Duc Tho made Agnew's mission unnecessary on December 12 by submitting proposals that Kissinger rightly reported were "outrageous" and "absurd" and by insisting on transparently artful changes in wording previously agreed upon.[7] Kissinger came home without scheduling another meeting.

By now, there was growing sentiment in Washington, in the news media, and throughout the nation simply to get our POWs back and abandon Vietnam to its fate. America was sick of this war, and as a practical matter Nixon had already all but taken us out of it as a belligerent. Our withdrawal of troops had proceeded faster than anyone had imagined possible. (Laird would come into the White House smiling and saying, "We got more out this week than planned!") Fewer than 25,000 U.S. military personnel were still stationed in the war theater.

There were many arguments against a resumption of the bombing, and every one of them was made to the President in the days that followed. Because of bad weather conditions over Indochina in monsoon season, the B-52, which flew above the weather, was the only aircraft in the U.S. arsenal capable of carrying out a sustained attack on Hanoi-Haiphong. Opponents of the bombing argued that the B-52, designed to drop nuclear bombs close enough to a large objective to destroy it, was not a precision instrument and that its use as a delivery system for conventional bombs targeted on smaller installations was bound to produce accidental casualties among civilians. My own experience during the war, in which I had called in B-52 strikes to within one thousand yards of my battalion perimeter (the bombs falling from the invisible aircraft out of a silent sky with a terrifying chorus of witchlike shrieks followed by explosions that caused the topsoil to move like a loose scalp), told me that this argument was not valid. We could hit military targets without terror-bombing civilians. The Air Force expected heavy attrition of its machines and crews by the vastly improved North Vietnamese air-defense system, which included the most advanced SAM batteries, many manned, as we have seen, by Soviet troops.

When Nixon solicited my views about resumption of the bombing and mining, I told him that I was strongly in favor of it as the only course likely to force the North to agree to acceptable terms for a settlement. I told Kissinger that on the evening of December 13, when I met him at Andrews Air Force Base on his return from Paris. If he had reservations about going ahead, he did not denounce the bombing. However, the standard resistance to prosecuting the war by warlike measures was already forming elsewhere within the administration. Laird had announced his opposition to further air raids on the enemy capital in writing, claiming the support of Admiral Moorer. The latter told me that although he had reservations about the operation based on its cost in lives and machines as estimated further down the chain of command, his position had been misunderstood by the Secretary of Defense. He had pointed out the probable costs of the operation, as was his duty; once the decision was made to go ahead, however, he stoutly supported the President.

On the morning of December 14, Kissinger and I met with the President in the Oval Office. No one present believed that there was any alternative to some sort of military action to break the impasse. Kissinger mentioned a number of milder possibilities, such as intensifying the bombing below the 20th parallel. This was incrementalism raising its head again, and I opposed it with all the fervor created within me by a quarter of a century of observing at close hand the ruinous results of timidity. If we were going to strike the enemy, then we should strike hard at its heart and keep on striking until the enemy's will was broken. No matter what the level of bombing, the level of denunciation in Congress and the press would be the same, but the political consequences of a limited effort that did not succeed would be worse than those for an all-out effort that did. No matter how little or how much the President bombed, questions would be raised about the morality of his action. The reality was that any operation that sacrificed lives and did not do the job was morally indefensible.

Nixon ordered the mining and bombing to begin on December 17. At the same time, he ordered me to carry another letter, even more brutally frank than his earlier ones, to Thieu in Saigon. I was a reluctant messenger. The President knew why, but he insisted that I put my feelings aside and go. "No one else can do this, Al. Thieu doesn't trust anyone else," he told me. Nixon's insistence took the decision out of my hands; it did not make the mission any easier.

Thieu was shaken by what he read when I gave him Nixon's letter in the Presidential Palace on December 19. I am not speaking figuratively; a shudder ran through his body. "General Haig's mission," the President wrote (this time entirely in his own voice; he dictated the letter himself), "now represents my final effort to point out to you the necessity for joint action and to convey my irrevocable intention to proceed, preferably with your cooperation, but, if necessary, alone. . . . I have asked General Haig to obtain your answer to this absolutely final offer on my part for us to work together in seeking a settlement along the lines I have approved or to go our separate ways."[8]

That morning, the United States had reseeded the mines in the Haiphong channel and launched a series of air raids against the Hanoi-Haiphong complex with more than 120 B-52 bombers, in addition to F-111 and A-6 fighter-bombers. I briefed Thieu on the operation and what it was designed to achieve. Then, speaking loudly and distinctly, I added, as I had been instructed to do, "Under no circumstances will President Nixon accept a veto from Saigon in regard to a peace agreement."

Thieu received these words in silence. He then asked a series of questions. What about NVA withdrawal from Laos and Cambodia? I replied that both were provided for but that the time factor was not yet refined. Who would supervise the withdrawals? I replied that the International Commission of Control and Supervision (ICCS), a vestige of the 1954 Geneva accords made up of officials from Communist and other nations, would do so. Thieu said that the ICCS had been ineffective before and asked why it should be effective now. I replied that the United States would be allowed to make as many as forty reconnaissance flights a day to verify withdrawal. Thieu asked me to explain again how we would get the NVA to withdraw from South Vietnam if the agreement lacked specific provisions to accomplish this. I replied that the interlocking provisions on infiltration, the use of Laos and Cambodia and base areas, and the demobilization principle were designed to achieve this result. Thieu asked how the shipment of war matériel from North to South could be controlled. I stated that the United States could inspect the infiltration routes unilaterally.

Thieu gazed at me for a long moment. Then he said, "It is very clear to me that there will be no peace as a result of this agreement. . . . After the cease-fire, the enemy will spread out his troops, join the Viet Cong, and use kidnapping and murder with knives and bayonets. Then, after U.S. troops have been withdrawn, they will take up their guns again and resort to guerrilla warfare, but always at a level that does not justify U.S. retaliation." I replied that that was probably true but that South Vietnam had the troops, police, and support to defeat such an insurgency: "In the early 1960s President Diem, with far less political and real power than you yourself possess, was able to contain guerrilla warfare by indigenous forces, and in fact was winning the struggle against subversion when he was killed. That is what brought the NVA into the South."

Thieu nodded. In 1963, as an ARVN colonel, he had participated in the overthrow of Diem, although it was well known that he had sought to protect the president's life against those who murdered him and his brothers. "We can easily stamp out a guerrilla insurgency," Thieu said. But in his view, that was not the problem.

"Given the realities of the situation," he said, "what I am being asked to sign is not a treaty for peace but a treaty for continued U.S. support."

I said, "I agree with your analysis."

The next day, Thieu made the gesture of handing me a letter to Nixon in which he declined to support the agreement unless the NVA withdrew from the South entirely; unless it clearly stated that the Communist Provisional Revolutionary Government was not a government parallel to his own government; and unless the composition and functions of the ICCS "not be those of a supercoalition government in disguise."

Thieu was right on every point, including the wraithlike moral point that had haunted all of our many conversations. Unfortunately, this was irrelevant in light of the political realities. Thieu understood that the President of the United States might be prevented by Congress from keeping any promise he might make to protect South Vietnam against violations of the agreement. He staked out the moral ground anyway and prepared himself and his 19 million people for the inevitable.

Fifteen B-52s were lost in the bombing of Hanoi-Haiphong, most in the first three days; ninety-three American airmen were listed as missing, with thirty-one of these known to be POWs.[9] The Pentagon wavered under the early losses. The admiral commanding U.S. forces in the Pacific, who was in overall command of the air war in Vietnam, recommended an end to the bombing on grounds that we could not tolerate such losses. The Joint Chiefs equivocated, though Moorer remained steady; the commander of the Strategic Air Command, whose planes and pilots were at risk, recommended that the raids continue. In a rare exercise of personal browbeating, Nixon told Moorer to keep on attacking at full strength or he would hold him responsible for the failure. The initial heavy losses turned out to be rooted in faulty tactics—there had been insufficient suppression of the air defenses and the routes flown by the bombers were too predictable—and were reduced to acceptable limits when the Air Force and Navy devised new ways to approach and attack the targets, which would neutralize the enemy's air defenses.

As anticipated, criticism in the news media and in Congress was unrestrained; the more extreme critics, including some Republicans, were divided between those who thought Nixon's action was insane and those who regarded it as evil. Senator Jacob Javits, the dean of liberal Republicans in the Senate, predicted a cutoff in funds for Vietnam within weeks, and no one in the White House disbelieved his forecast. Nixon saw this outcry against his policy as the first counterattack against his election victory by enemies who could not bear to acknowledge the evidence of his overwhelming popularity.[10] He was determined to override them, to prove them wrong, to complete his defeat of their ideas in the eyes of the nation, and to achieve what he regarded as an honorable peace. They were just as determined to stop him or at least to maim him for the rest of his term by discrediting his motives and condemning his methods.

In December 1972, short weeks after his great victory at the polls, Nixon was as alone as ever he had been. With the exception of Connally, Kissinger, and myself, or so he thought, his entire inner circle was opposed to the bombing. Then James Reston of the *New York Times* published a column suggesting that Kissinger had been opposed to the bombing. Three days later, Joe Kraft wrote in his nationally syndicated column that Kissinger's honor had been compromised by Nixon's "twelve days of murder bombing," and suggested that Kissinger would soon resign unless Nixon made him Secretary of State. The President believed that these stories could have come only from Kissinger,[11] and the idea that Kissinger, of all people, should give comfort to his enemies on this issue devastated him. Characteristically, he gave no hint of his anger to Kissinger himself, but instead instructed his counselor, Charles Colson, to order Kissinger to have no further contact with any member of the news media. Questioned by Haldeman, Kissinger said that he had never expressed "a personal opinion different from the President's" and denied that he had given the story to Reston.[12] This did not placate Nixon. According to a report by Colson years afterward, the President instructed him to order the Secret Service to keep a log of all of Kissinger's incoming and outgoing telephone calls and report any conversations with members of the press.[13]

In regard to Vietnam policy, the President was under attack by Congress, under moral examination by the media, isolated from his own Cabinet, estranged from his closet adviser—cut off, in short, from every part of the political estate except the Silent Majority, whose existence had so dramatically been confirmed by his landslide reelection. It was in this period that I first observed him in the almost-mythic loneliness that marked my later experience of him as White House Chief of Staff during Watergate. Those who do not wish to believe that Nixon had redeeming qualities will not care for this simile, but to me he resembled the marlin in Ernest Hemingway's novella, *The Old Man and the Sea*. Like some wounded creature of the deep, he would fight ferociously, dragging his enemies great distances in his wake, then sound to brood awhile in solitude and silence before rising to the surface to fight again. Life did not carry the metaphor as far as Hemingway did. In the end, unlike Hemingway's symbol of misunderstood genius, Nixon slipped the hook and eluded the sharks in their final feeding frenzy.

When, in the midst of this contretemps, Nixon asked me (once again sparing me any hint of his anger with Kissinger) what I thought he should do about the bombing, I replied, "Keep it up." It was the only course of action available to him likely to bring results by the end of his first term. There was no question, based on information from many reliable sources, that the bombing was having the desired effect. Nixon called a Christmas halt, but on December 26 ordered the heaviest raid of the war. The next day, Hanoi asked for a resumption of the talks.

Kissinger went back to Paris and returned on January 13 with a final agreement, which was scheduled for signing by the foreign ministers of the United States and North Vietnam in Paris on January 27. I flew back to Saigon with the English text, no Vietnamese version having yet been produced, and with yet another presidential letter. Thieu pointed out that the agreement met none of the points he had raised concerning the presence of the NVA, the status of the DMZ, and the powers of the transitional political structure. After I reported this, Nixon sent him a cable that included the following language: "Your rejection of the agreement now would irrevocably destroy our ability to assist you. Congress and public opinion would force my hand." In response, Thieu appealed for a toughening of the agreement "in the name of the longstanding and very close friendship of our two nations, sealed in the blood, sweat, and tears of our soldiers and citizens."

However, the race was run, all but the final heat, and Thieu, knowing this, gave the United States government what it insisted on having. The timing almost certainly averted a constitutional crisis. On January 2 the House Democratic caucus voted overwhelmingly to cut off all support to South Vietnam as soon as U.S. troops and POWs were safely out of the country. Although it was bombing that settled the question, bombing that got our prisoners out, bombing that gave Thieu at least a chance for survival with continued U.S. military and economic aid, the President probably could not have continued to pound Hanoi without provoking a showdown with Congress that might well have led to his impeachment. Even Connally did not think that he could go on without making his entire second term hostage to the crisis. My own belief was that he should fight it out to the end because the honor of our country and the lives of millions of people in Indochina were at stake. Though few could then have conceived of such a thing, the irony is that a battle without quarter between the legislative and executive branches on this issue would have been preferable to Watergate, because Nixon had principle on his side in Vietnam and, therefore, every prospect of winning in the end.

On January 23, three days after Richard Nixon's second inauguration, the day after the death of the Vietnam War's most famous political casualty, Lyndon Baines Johnson, the agreement became final. Nixon's approval rating in the Gallup poll rose to 68 percent, the highest point of his presidency.[14] In 1973, Kissinger and Le Duc Tho were jointly awarded the Nobel Peace Prize for having negotiated the settlement in Paris. Nixon (who in early February 1973 had directed that his name be withdrawn from consideration for the prize)[15] was awarded no honors, but it was he who had forced the issues, he who after ten years of exquisitely considered incrementalism had ordered the unflinching application of U.S. power that ended the shedding of American blood and achieved the disengagement of the United States from Vietnam.

24

Aftermath

On January 4, I had left the White House and returned to the Army at last as vice chief of staff. We moved into spacious quarters at Fort McNair, and Pat happily redecorated the house, revamped our social schedule, and in every way possible renewed the bonds of friendship and duty that tied us to the Army. The first night I came home in uniform, Duncan, the family dog, barked at me; he hadn't seen me in anything but civilian clothes for such a long time that he didn't recognize me. For the first time in four years, I found it possible to have dinner at home most nights, to spend evenings around the house or with friends, and to chat with the children and meet their friends. Our son Brian was now a member of the Corps of Cadets at West Point, but Alex, a student at Georgetown University, and Barbara, still in high school, lived at home.

My schedule remained hectic, but I largely controlled it myself. Doing my job left me little time or inclination to think about anything else, or even to read the newspapers. It does not take long for a former insider to become an outsider in Washington, and gradually, as my work carried me farther and farther from the center of events, my association with the White House ebbed. Nixon continued to invite me to meetings having to do with Vietnam, and in April 1973 I visited Saigon again. U.S. military strength in country had been reduced to 220 personnel, including 156 Marine guards at the embassy, although there were thirty-two Air

315

Force, Navy, and Marine Corps aviation strike squadrons offshore or elsewhere in Southeast Asia. At this time, a little more than two months after the cease-fire, more than one hundred armed violations of the cease-fire by the enemy were being reported every day. As Thieu had predicted, the ICCS had proved to be ineffective. Our intelligence reported that the intensity of combat was increasing and estimated that there was a 25 percent chance that the Communists would mount a large-scale offensive in one or more areas of Vietnam that spring. The U.S. bureaucracy's approach to this situation was consistent with the past, as shown in this State Department comment on an NVA attack on a South Vietnamese town:

> While we agree that the deliberate siege of Ton Le Cham by the Communists is a gross violation of the cease-fire, we are concerned that clumsy action . . . in the ICCS by the government of South Vietnam . . . could have counterproductive results.

A month after this, I was recalled to the White House as Chief of Staff in circumstances presently to be discussed. Not long after my arrival, Kissinger came to me with even more alarming reports of cease-fire violations and told me that the President must apply the sanctions we had promised Thieu we would apply if the life of his nation was threatened. That meant bombing Hanoi, but by now Watergate and the action of Congress in reducing military aid to Saigon had made such action simply undoable for the beleaguered Nixon.

Laird had departed as Secretary of Defense, but on my recommendation (I thought it was better to have him inside the administration than running free), Nixon brought him into the White House as Counselor for Domestic Affairs. In June 1973, while in San Clemente, as White House Chief of Staff, I was informed that the House of Representatives was on the verge of passing a bill to call a total halt to all bombing by U.S. aircraft throughout Vietnam, Laos, and Cambodia by August 15. Passage of this bill would render worthless the promises Nixon had made in person and I had so often repeated to Thieu that the United States would punish Hanoi for breaches of the cease-fire.* The level of violence

---

*On April 3, Nixon and Thieu had issued a joint communiqué after a meeting in San Clemente, warning that continued violations of the cease-fire by the North "would call for appropriately vigorous reactions." Elliot Richardson, the new Secretary of Defense, said that the United States would not resume bombing enemy territory in the absence of a "flagrant" violation, such as a full-scale invasion of the South (Gareth Porter, ed., *Vietnam: A History in Documents*, p. 470).

had greatly intensified in South Vietnam, and this measure was tantamount to giving Hanoi a green light to conquer the country.

I phoned the Republican leader of the House, Gerald Ford, and asked him in the name of the President to stop the bill. Ford, as honest as the day is long, made no effort to hide his surprise and dismay. He said he had been led to believe by Mel Laird that this bill was acceptable to the President. I told him that Laird's support was news to the President. Ford was stunned. If he reversed himself now, he might have to resign as Republican leader.

Despite my concern, Nixon could not bring himself to ask Ford to do that: "Al, I can't lose Jerry Ford." The bill passed on June 29 and Nixon signed it into law three days later,[1] thereby sealing the fate of Thieu and his people and writing "finish" to the misbegotten experiment in calculated weakness that began with counterinsurgency and ended with Vietnamization, took the lives of millions of Indochinese and destroyed the hopes of many more, and, as sadly for the world as for the United States, caused Americans to question the honor of their country, which had always before been the very symbol of right behavior in the hearts of its citizens and in the eyes of people everywhere.

In the late winter of 1975, Thieu sent me one last message. By then, Nixon had returned to private life and Gerald Ford, his successor, had named me NATO Commander. Thieu's emissary was my old friend Nguyen Phu Duc. He came to see me at NATO headquarters in Belgium on a gray, bone-chilling northern European morning. As we spoke, South Vietnam, starved of funds and military aid by Congress, was being overrun by Communist armies, and the political bureau, party military committee, and general staff of North Vietnam had officially agreed that "the United States is unlikely to intervene and could not save Thieu even if it did."[2]

"President Thieu has sent me to ask you just one question," Duc said. "It is this: 'If you had it to do over again, would you recommend to President Thieu to accept the terms of the cease-fire?' "

In the two years that had passed since my last meeting with Thieu, I had seldom gone to sleep at night without asking myself that same question. The answer was always the same: Because America had lost the will to use its power, it would have made no difference in the end. That is what I told Duc.

That night, sleepless, I realized that Thieu would never have sent Duc to see me, or asked such a question, if he had not been sure that a collapse of his government and the loss of South Vietnam was near. I called Kissinger, now the Secretary of State, and told him about Thieu's message and expressed my feeling concerning it. Kissinger did not disagree that the end was in sight. When I suggested that President Ford must take some strong action to forestall the final disaster, however, he told me that this was impossible. Isolated from the President by the White House staff, he lacked the influence even to recommend such a course of action.

The next day, I requested an appointment with Ford and flew back to Washington. During an hour-long meeting in the Oval Office, I urged him to call a joint session of Congress and demand that the United States redeem its promises to the people of South Vietnam.

In his good-hearted way, Ford gave me a look of sympathy. "Al," he said, "they'd never support me."

"So what, Mr. President? You would have done the right thing."

We talked for almost an hour. I expressed my belief that keeping America's word to the South Vietnamese was the key issue of his presidency, the moral theme on which he could govern and be reelected. Ford listened patiently. At last he said, "Al, I'm sorry. I just can't put the country through this again."

This was the last of many presidential decisions, made by good men for what seemed to them to be good reasons, against which there can be no appeal except to the judgment of history and to the memory of all who died in that tortured and benighted land and in Cambodia and Laos before and after the cruel peace imposed by the victors.

On April 11, 1975, the Ford administration did ask Congress for an additional $722 million in military aid for South Vietnam; Kissinger explained to journalists that this was necessary to ensure Thieu's cooperation in the evacuation of Americans. Saigon fell on April 30.[3]

IV

WATERGATE

Nothing happens to any man that he is not formed by nature to bear.

MARCUS AURELIUS,
Meditations, V. 18

25

"Deep Throat"

Before proceeding to a description of the climactic stage of the Watergate crisis as I observed it from inside the White House from May 1973 to August 1974, it seems useful to assure the reader that there is no truth whatsoever in the whispering campaign that has attempted to identify me as "Deep Throat," the mysterious, all-knowing informant on whose revelations the journalist Bob Woodward relied in composing the stories about Watergate that he and Carl Bernstein wrote for the *Washington Post* in the latter half of 1972 and the spring of 1973.

This pusillanimous lie was given currency in 1982 by John W. Dean III in his book *Lost Honor*. Dean admits therein that his theory is pure speculation and that he was unable to find a single scrap of actual proof to support his thesis.[1] Dean's accusation was false and defamatory, but lawyers advised me that it was useless to sue. Because I happened to be a former White House Chief of Staff and Secretary of State, I was a public figure who could be libeled with impunity as a result of decisions of the Supreme Court that had, for all practical purposes, stripped people in public life of the traditional right to protect their reputations.

While Dean's titillating fabrication was still hot gossip, I encountered Benjamin C. Bradlee, the editor of the *Washington Post*, in the Montpelier Room of the Madison Hotel in Washington, where we were lunching at different tables, and stopped to have a word with him.

"Ben, is the *Post* still the champion of truth and justice we've all known it to be?"

"Sure it is, Al. That never changes."

"Then don't you think your newspaper, which knows the truth in this matter, has an obligation to tell its readers that Al Haig is not Deep Throat? I'm not suggesting that you reveal who *is*. All I want is for you to nail the lie."

Bradlee shook his head and gave me a rueful grin. "Al," he said, "you know I just can't do that."

Or, as "the English Juvenal," George Crabbe (1754–1832) put it in his poem "The Vicar":

> *Habit with him was all the test of truth,*
> *"It must be right: I've done it from my youth."*[2]

John Dean's pseudodox having taken root in the imagination of conspiracy buffs, I am under no illusion that anything short of the gathering of all souls before the judgment seat promised in Romans 14:10 will persuade them to part with their fantasy. However, I will try.

Three assumptions must apply:

1. Deep Throat had to know the secrets he divulged to Woodward by June 1972.
2. Deep Throat had to be personally acquainted with Woodward.
3. Deep Throat and Woodward had to be in Washington at the same time in order to meet and exchange information as Woodward describes in *All the President's Men*, the book he and Bernstein wrote about the episode.

The facts, which could easily have been ascertained at any point by Dean or by any journalist who cared to call me up and inquire, are as follows:

Knowledge. At the time in question, my job in the Nixon administration was exclusively concerned with foreign affairs, and neither the President nor anyone else ever discussed the Watergate burglary or anything connected to it with me before I returned to the White House on May 4, 1973, as Acting Chief of Staff. By then, the entire story had been public knowledge for months. I had no knowledge of the matters discussed by Woodward and Deep Throat in 1972 and early 1973 until I read about them in the *Washington Post*.

Acquaintance. Woodward and Bernstein and I did not know each other at the time in question. (The authors of the inexhaustibly zany *Silent Coup* state that Woodward, when a Navy lieutenant attached to Admiral Moorer's staff, briefed me in the White House on JCS matters during Nixon's first term. Woodward is quoted on page 81 of that book as denying that this ever happened, or that he even knew me in this period. His statement is consistent with my own memory.) In fact, I met Woodward and Bernstein for the first time in the late summer of 1974, a month or so after Nixon resigned as President. Returning home late at night, I found them sitting on my doorstep and invited them inside. They were looking for confirmation of a report that I had issued orders to the White House medical staff in the closing days of the resignation crisis to keep a close watch on the disheartened President in case he should try to harm himself by taking an overdose of prescription pills.* I told them I could not provide information for their newspaper, but we chatted in a desultory way for an hour or so. It was a civil encounter. Woodward has recently assured me that this conversation was helpful to him and his partner in their effort to understand the Watergate affair. From what I remembered of what was said, I was surprised that this should be so.

Timing. In *All the President's Men*, Woodward and Bernstein identify several dates on which Woodward met Deep Throat late at night in an underground parking garage somewhere in the Washington metropolitan area. These include a four-and-a-half-hour session ending at 6:00 A.M. on October 8, 1972.[3] On that date and for several days afterward, I was in Paris for a session of the peace talks, having just returned from Vietnam. On June 19, 1972, Deep Throat told Woodward that E. Howard Hunt had been involved in the break-in, which had taken place two days earlier;[4] it is not clear whether they actually met on that day or communi-

---

*This detail, which found its way into their second book, *The Final Days*, was accurate. In compiling this book, Woodward and Bernstein benefited from the advice of the late J. Fred Buzhardt, President Nixon's Special Counsel for Watergate. Buzhardt, one of the most honorable and patriotic men ever to have served a President, phoned me after Nixon had left the White House to inform me that he was trying to decide whether to talk to the two journalists, who had approached him to provide background for their book. On the one hand, he was reluctant to breach the confidentiality of his relationship with Nixon. On the other, he felt that it was important, in the interests of history and what was left of the former President's reputation, that Woodward and Bernstein base their account on accurate information from a knowledgeable source. Buzhardt asked me whether I thought it would be wrong for him to cooperate with the writers. I told him that this was a matter for his own judgment but that I could not imagine him saying or doing anything that would harm Nixon or distort the record, whereas many others could be counted upon to do both. He told me that he intended to go ahead with the arrangement, and, on the basis of the unusual level of truthfulness achieved in certain passages of the published work, I have always assumed that he did so.

cated by telephone or some other means. In any case, on June 19, I left Andrews Air Force Base for Pittsburgh at 3:55 P.M. and delivered an after-dinner speech beginning at 8:30 to a group of local business leaders and directors and officers of the Mellon Bank, who had arranged the affair. On January 24, 1973, when Woodward and Deep Throat met to discuss the involvement of Mitchell and Colson in the scandal, I was at Fort Belvoir, Virginia, in my capacity as Army vice chief of staff, addressing an audience from the Army Materiel Command. On April 26, when Woodward and his source discussed Acting FBI Director Pat Gray over the telephone, I was on my way back from Los Angeles, having testified there at the Pentagon Papers trial on April 25. On May 16, when the duo met at 11:00 P.M. and Deep Throat warned Woodward that "everyone's life is in danger,"[5] I was still in my office at the White House, having commenced a meeting with Brent Scowcroft at 10:15. During the first week of November, date unspecified, the pair met to discuss erasures in the tapes; I left for Key Biscayne on November 1, after dining at a private house in Washington with Golda Meir and others, and remained in Florida through November 5; on the evening of November 8, I spoke in Chicago at a dinner honoring Representative Sam Young.

Deep Throat and I do seem to have been in Washington at the same time on some of the dates on which Woodward and Bernstein say they met, but I was not present on any of these occasions (or at any other time, for the benefit of the humorless) to make it a threesome.

Then there is the question of resemblance. In *All the President's Men*, Woodward (apparently Bernstein and Deep Throat never met) records many details about his informant's appearance, habits, beliefs, and personality. The book portrays him as one male individual rather than the composite he is sometimes suspected of being. In summary, Woodward describes his source as being tall, gaunt, careless in his appearance, with a tough beard that he sometimes does not shave. He is a night owl who is either unmarried or wedded to a very unsuspicious wife. He thinks, talks, and acts like a lawyer. He is an expert handler of the press and a superb spotter of journalistic talent—his friendship with Woodward seems to have begun when the latter was an obscure member of the *Post's* metropolitan staff, or even before. His speech is guarded, though fluent and eloquent. He is a clandestine personality, constantly on the alert for unfriendly surveillance, and he takes elaborate precautions against being followed or wiretapped that seem absurd unless his behavior is a result of having been a victim of such practices in the past. Woodward regards him as a kind of guru: "It is enough that Deep Throat would never deal with me falsely. Someday it would be explained."[6] He seems to be a public figure, even a celebrity, who fears being recognized by strangers. He is deeply suspicious of the Establishment and believes that the system is failing, and he seems to have the idea that he can save it (or perhaps expedite its fall) by exposing its ignoble secrets to the *Washington Post*.

In none of these particulars does Deep Throat resemble me. I am about Woodward's size, of medium build and coloration, neat and tidy and clean-shaven, long married and in the habit of going straight home from work. No lawyer, I am famously ineloquent as the originator of Haigspeak, unversed and uninterested in the clandestine arts, an object of brooding mistrust to liberals in the news media and leftists everywhere, and was at the time in question so little known to the public that I cannot remember ever having been recognized by a stranger. I was a believer in the system and never thought during Watergate, or at any other time, that it was in any danger of failing if it was permitted to work as intended by the Constitution.

Although I do not think this is the result of a conspiracy (Dean apparently was just trying to make money), one of the side effects of Dean's fabrication and the subsequent campaign of disinformation directed against me has been to protect the identity of the real Deep Throat. This is a consequence I have been able to bear without excessive difficulty. I care nothing about the real identity of Deep Throat; even if I knew his name, I would not think that I knew much worth knowing (or all there is to know, because I would be very surprised if he acted alone).

I do not believe that I ever saw Bernstein again (except to catch glimpses of him at large Washington social events) after I found him and Woodward on my doorstep in 1974. Some months after that, Woodward approached me in hope of an interview in connection with his book. I declined, just as I refused for many years after the event to talk to any other journalist, or to accept offers, some of them lucrative, to write my own reminiscences.

After I became NATO commander, with headquarters at Mons, Belgium, Woodward called me from London, saying that he had spent his own money on an airline ticket to go there in the hope that I would agree to see him if he continued on to Belgium. I replied that I could not and would not discuss with him or anyone else what I knew about Nixon or Watergate or any other subject connected to my duties in the White House. He persisted. Something in his urgent tone of voice made me think that he might be going to all this trouble to discharge some professional obligation. I told him that I would see him in my office but warned him once again that he could expect to hear nothing of substance from me. "If you want to do it on a pro forma basis, come on over," I said. "But it will be a waste of time for both of us, because there is absolutely nothing I can tell you."

Woodward arrived on February 12, 1975. The meeting was short. After describing some of the topics covered in his book, Woodward earnestly told me, "You can come off as a hero in our book—or not. It's up to you." That ended the discussion. Brig. Gen. Joseph Bratton, who was serving as my executive officer at that time, was present during this encounter.

The fact that Deep Throat's identity remains a conundrum twenty years after the event owes something to the obtuseness of those who have been too incurious to follow up the available clues, but mainly it is a tribute to Woodward's steadfast adherence to the journalist's code of silence in regard to the identification of confidential sources. It is a matter of regret that the United States government is unable to keep its own secrets as effectively as he keeps his.

26

On Virtue

In 1981, during my confirmation hearings before the Senate Foreign Relations Committee for the office of Secretary of State, Senator Paul S. Sarbanes, Democrat of Maryland, kept pressing me to render my "value judgment" on the actions of Richard Nixon in connection with Watergate. I resisted. What Sarbanes actually wanted from me, I thought, was a mea culpa, another obsequious testimonial to the civic virtue of those who had brought Nixon down. My wise lawyer, Joe Califano, urged me to keep my cool, but finally I lost Sarbanes's vote by saying, "Do you think I am going to endorse what was done? In no way, on either side. . . . No one has a monopoly on virtue—not even you, Senator."[1]

The Watergate affair is generally portrayed as a morality play in which the American people and system were rescued from the forces of evil (Nixon and his associates) by the forces of good (the political Left and its collaborators in the news media). Although Nixon clearly did wrong and his enemies on the Left, with the help of certain of his trusted associates, were the instruments of his downfall, it was not so clear-cut and Manichean as that. There were venal people and noble people, and patriotic and ambitious ones, on both sides. The stakes were higher and the circumstances stranger than the world imagines. Viewed from inside a White House under siege, it sometimes more closely resembled a coup d'état or a primitive ritual out of mythology than the high-minded patriotic crusade it was promoted as being.

Watergate was not simply an isolated event in which a President, corrupted by power, was detected in high crimes and misdemeanors and justly punished by being deprived of his office. It was the culmination of a long and bitter struggle for control of the government and the hearts and minds of the American people between Left and Right, between Congress and the Executive Branch, between the intelligentsia and the commonality, and, above all, between Richard Nixon and those who, many years before, had invested their own political validity and self-esteem in the innocence of Alger Hiss. The catalyst that transformed these elements into the great political explosion of Watergate was the Vietnam War, which split the country into two camps and created a confrontation, the most emotional and ungenerous since the Civil War, which tested to the utmost the power of our institutions to preserve the Constitution.

Nixon's errors and crimes were real, as he himself has publicly conceded, and they proceeded directly from his inability to confront an unpleasant situation and overcome it by open, decisive action. If, on first learning of the break-in, he had called in his subordinates, demanded an explanation, and fired the lot of them, the issue would have been resolved except for prosecution of those suspected of criminal acts under due process of law. Instead, he instructed Bob Haldeman to find ways to avoid the issue, and thereby opened a Pandora's box filled with misery and grief.

The methods he chose grew out of his belief that he had been betrayed from within from the beginning of his presidency and that these betrayals had done great harm to the United States. He connected the leaks from the White House with the unsympathetic liberals Kissinger brought into the NSC staff and with natural political enemies embedded in the permanent bureaucracy. The disloyalty of these people, in the form of damaging leaks to the press, exacerbated his belief that his enemies on the Left were engaged in a long-term vendetta against him. He tried to catch the culprits and stop the hemorrhage of secrets by calling on the FBI to investigate under existing legal safeguards, only to discover that FBI wiretaps could not do the job. Out of that disappointment, and the continued spillage of national-security information, came the plumbers, who in their zeal to produce results strayed from legal procedures. It has never been demonstrated that illegality was Nixon's intention, and I, personally, do not believe that it was.

Nixon knew, and frequently said, that he was not judged as other

Presidents had been judged. More often than not even his honest actions would be perceived by those who hated him as mendacious and hypocritical. As Professor Stephen E. Ambrose writes in the meticulously researched but sometimes wrongheaded third volume of his biography of Nixon, ". . . in most areas of his criminal acts [he] only followed where his Democratic predecessors had led . . . [yet he] underwent a pounding from a torrent of criticism such as never before descended upon an American President, not even Andrew Johnson, not even Herbert Hoover."[2] Probably no other President, certainly no Democrat since FDR, would have been called to personal account under comparable circumstances. Examples of such omissions abound. Well-founded suspicions of vote fraud in Chicago and elsewhere that decided the close 1960 presidential election in favor of Kennedy were not prominently reported at the time, let alone permitted to bring the legitimacy of Kennedy's presidency into question. The Kennedy campaign was well known and much admired for playing tricks on the opposite camp; such episodes were regarded as examples of healthy high spirits. Had Republican National Headquarters been burglarized by a Democratic goon squad during the Kennedy administration, chances are that the episode would have been regarded inside Washington as a charming prank, and the controlling impulse in the federal bureaucracy and the news media would have been to prevent it from contaminating the President or anyone close to him. In Nixon's case, it may be argued that the comically mismanaged break-in of June 17, 1972, provided the opportunity for the personal and political annihilation that his enemies had been hoping for ever since Hiss had been convicted of perjury (and, by implication, of espionage and treason) in January 1950.[3]

I am not suggesting that Nixon was innocent of wrongdoing with regard to the cover-up or that his transgressions should have been ignored; I am merely making the point that he was subjected to a different standard of judgment than other Presidents. It has often been said that Nixon was paranoid in regard to his enemies. Less often is it acknowledged that his enemies felt the same about him. Watergate was the child of these twin pathologies.

Even so, things might not have gone as far as they did if Nixon had been reelected in 1972 by a less humiliating margin. For more than twenty years, the liberals had been telling the people not to trust Nixon, not to believe anything he said, not to vote for him. Yet they were alarmed, throughout the fifties and sixties, by the possibility that he might be elected President. I think that Nixon believed that the Democrats had stolen the 1960 election from him through vote frauds in Chicago, Texas, and Pennsylvania.*

After observing him in action as President for four years, during which time he came under unceasing and often hysterical criticism from his detractors, the voters returned him to office by a record margin of 47.2 million popular votes (60.7 percent) and 520 electoral votes (96.8 percent), against 29.2 million popular and 17 electoral votes for his radical Democratic opponent, George McGovern. No Republican had ever been elected President by so large a margin, and only one Democrat, Lyndon Johnson in 1964, had received a higher percentage of the popular vote. Watergate provided to Nixon's ideological foes the means of rescuing the people from their devastating "mistake" in judgment by overturning the results of a national election.

Not all the rancor was on one side. The scope of Nixon's victory convinced him that he had prevailed at last over his enemies—the Left, especially the antiwar coalition, which had insulted and demeaned him; the bureaucracy, which had frustrated and sabotaged him; with Congress, which had become a mechanism dominated by the special interests and hypnotized by the news media; with the functionaries of the Republican National Committee, who had been embarrassed by him. He came out of November believing that the rightness of his position on Vietnam and the righteousness of his underlying political beliefs had been ratified by the people. He set out to exploit this overwhelming popular mandate by doing many of the things the opposition most feared he would do: reducing the size of the government, radically reducing federal spending, maintaining defense at high levels at the expense of social programs, reducing the size of the federal bureaucracy through attrition and taking away much of its power to obstruct and delay by concentrating decision making in a super-Cabinet run by the White House. He also wanted to revitalize the Republican Party by getting rid of all the apparatchiks who were not real Republicans, and, as part of this effort to clear the decks, he asked for the resignation of every presidential appointee in the federal government.

Those whom Nixon intended to smite in his pent-up anger were under no illusions about his intentions, his nerve, or the power of the mandate bestowed on him by the voters. They saw in Watergate a chance to

---

*In his memoirs (p. 334), Nixon writes as follows about Election Night 1968: "Waves of nausea had swept over [Mrs. Nixon] as she feared that we would have to experience a repeat of the outrageous frauds of 1960. . . . She asked emotionally, 'But Dick, are we sure of Illinois? Are we completely sure?' "

save themselves—and, as they saw it in the light of their own political convictions, to save the nation.

Joe Califano, then serving as counsel to the *Washington Post*, among other functions, expressed the mood of the opposition when he called me soon after the news broke that I was being recalled by President Nixon to the White House. "Al, for Christ's sake don't take this job," Califano said. "We've got the goods on Nixon, and we're going to destroy him. If you take the job, you'll go down with him."

I understood what Califano was saying to me, but I also understood that duty, in its unpredictable way, had called me. Therefore, I reported as Acting Chief of Staff in the White House on May 4, 1973, and remained beside the duly elected thirty-seventh President of the United States until the end—or, rather, until Richard Nixon, after resigning the most majestic of all human offices, gave up the political ghost and laid himself down to bleed awhile before rising to fight again.

27

The Worst Happens

The call came on May 2, 1973, while I was attending a working dinner party in the officer's club at Fort Benning, Georgia. The club officer told me that the President wanted to speak to me. I thought (and may have muttered), Oh, my God. Only three days before, in a nationwide television broadcast, Nixon had announced the resignations of his two closest aides, H. R. Haldeman and John D. Ehrlichman, along with those of the White House Counsel, John W. Dean III, and Attorney General Richard G. Kleindienst. Earlier in April, I had received calls from Ron Ziegler saying that Nixon wanted to know whether he should fire Haldeman and Ehrlichman. I told Pat about my conversations with Ziegler, saying that I had managed to avoid offering an opinion. How? she wanted to know. I replied "I just said, 'Why ask me?' " A sixth sense told me why: Nixon was thinking of asking me to come back.

When I picked up the phone in the club office at Fort Benning, Bob Haldeman, not Nixon, was on the line. As was his style, he came directly to the point: "Al, I'm with the President now, and he has asked me to tell you that he wants you to be his Chief of Staff in the White House." It took me a moment to collect myself. It is one thing to imagine a fateful juncture such as this, when your entire life, past and future, is flung into the balance by forces beyond your control; it is another to have it actually happen to you. I knew that this could mean the end of the life I had chosen for my family and myself. Given the poisonously anti-Nixon mood then prevailing in Washington, the personal consequences were incalculable. Nobody, of course, knew that better than Haldeman. I said, "Bob, if this is what the President wants, I'll do it. But I think the worst thing he can do in this situation is appoint a military man." I went on to remind him that I had little experience in the field of domestic policy, few close relationships on Capitol Hill and virtually none in the news media, and no political experience. Most important, I was no expert on Watergate, and there was nothing in my background that would be helpful to the President in managing the crisis that was threatening to demolish his presidency. "It's just totally beyond me," I said, with regard to the Watergate situation. Haldeman heard me out in tactful but heavy silence. Finally, I said, "Please ask the President to reconsider this." Haldeman replied, "All right," and hung up.

I went back to the dinner party and finished my salad. Before the next course was served, I was called to the telephone again. It was Haldeman. He said, "Al, I've told the President what you told me. He understands your reservations, but he wants you to do this."

In other words, this was an order from the Commander in Chief in an hour of distress. "Then of course I must do it," I said.

"The President will be glad to know that you feel that way," Haldeman replied. "He knows that you want to get back to the Army as soon as possible, and he wants you there. The White House job will be an interim appointment, a matter of a short period of time. The President just wants you to get the government organized and up to speed. As soon as he finds a permanent Chief of Staff, you'll go back to your old job in the Army. While you're here, you'll have nothing to do with Watergate. Others will handle that. Your duties will be strictly organizational."

I said, "Okay. When do I start?"

"The President would like you to come in tomorrow. We'll send a plane for you."

"All right. But first I have to talk to my wife and report what you've told me to General Abrams."

"That will be fine. The President will be here when you arrive. Good luck."*

I hung up the phone. Through the plywood door of the bare office, I

---

*I have reconstructed this talk with Haldeman and other conversations in the Oval Office from memory and my own notes and papers. An exact transcript of this and other conversations recorded by the White House taping system before July 18, 1973, when I ordered the removal of the system, will not become available until the rest of the tapes are made public.

could hear music, the murmur of conversation, the occasional burst of laughter after a joke had been told—the homely sounds of Army people relaxing at the end of a routine day. Never had the ordinary seemed more poignant. I picked up the phone again and called Pat. "The worst has happened," I told her. I did not have to explain what I meant or what the assignment would probably do to our lives. She said, "Oh, Al!" This meant the end of the peaceful domestic routine she had waited so long to enjoy; it meant leaving the gracious house she had just finished decorating, leaving her lifelong friends and the Army life that she had loved since childhood, and going back, after only ninety days of normal existence, to the frantic fishbowl way of life we thought we had escaped at last. But good soldier that she is and always has been, she packed our gear without complaint or reproach, and, as always, did more than her part.

I took off from Fort Benning at dawn. The feeling that I was hurtling toward some unknowable destination intensified as the majestic panorama of Washington's monumental buildings and broad lawns appeared beneath the wings of the White House executive jet. It was still very early, and the many flags fluttering over the empty streets gave the city an air of tranquillity and, owing to the classical architecture, a suggestion of Roman virtue. These, I knew, were illusions. After landing at Andrews, I stopped at the Pentagon to tell my boss, Creighton Abrams, that I would be leaving. He listened with an air of sympathy but agreed that I must report as ordered. "It's tough," he said. "But you've got to do what you've got to do. And who knows, maybe you can help the President." From my desk in the Pentagon, I called Henry Kissinger, who immediately let me understand that he had known the news before I did. He told me, in his usual blend of sarcasm and sympathy, that I must accept the job even though it would probably mean the end of my military career. Haldeman is said to have told Nixon that he felt that one of the things that qualified me for his old job was the fact that I had been "diplomatic enough to have served under Henry Kissinger and survived."[1] Nixon has written that one of my strong points, besides "force of personality," was the fact that I "understood Kissinger."[2] Others have recorded that Kissinger, loath to report to a former subordinate, opposed my appointment, even threatening to resign if Nixon went through with it.[3] This rings true; Kissinger's encounters with Haldeman had taught him the power of the White House Chief of Staff, and he knew, like it or not, that he would be taking orders from me. In his memoirs, Kissinger says that he "decided to put the best face on the situation and to make the inevitable easy on everybody."[4] It is typical of Kissinger that nothing that he said to me, and nothing in his behavior toward me before or after I returned to the White House, suggested that he harbored negative feelings of any kind. Certainly my feelings about him did not change with the adjustment in our hierarchical positions.

When I arrived at the White House in the afternoon, I found the offices formerly occupied by Haldeman, Ehrlichman, and Dean guarded by FBI agents. This meant that the agents, embarrassed and uncomfortable but gravely watchful and efficient, loitered within a few steps of the Oval Office. In these dim, windowless spaces, the effect was cinematic, as perhaps it was intended to be. The agents had been ordered into the White House by the new Attorney General, Elliot L. Richardson, who explained that his purpose in inflicting this outrageous insult on the President had been to prevent the removal of evidence by the three suspects who until recently had been the latter's most trusted aides. On my way in, I heard that the President had slammed one of Richardson's guards against the wall on first seeing the men posted in the West Wing. Even though he was said to have apologized to the man afterward, I could scarcely believe that he was capable of committing an act that was so wildly out of character. Nixon knew that the presence of the guards created an indelible impression of a government besieged by itself, of a President who was being denied the presumption of innocence by his own Attorney General, of the White House as a center of criminal activity. But he had not even called Richardson and told him to remove the FBI agents, and this passivity was more like Nixon in his seemingly boundless willingness to let others inconvenience and even abuse him. My first act as Chief of Staff was to call Richardson and demand that he remove the FBI agents at once; he assented without argument.

Greeting me in the Oval Office, Nixon was subdued. Over the days just past (although I did not then know this), he had considered resignation, and the strain of wrestling with this unprecedented choice, combined with the pain of dismissing Haldeman and Ehrlichman, had dispelled the mock toughness that I had observed in earlier crises. Anger and melancholy showed through the shell of his self-possession. Naturally, I studied him closely, and it seemed to me that the ordeal had strengthened him. He had not lost his composure. He emitted an almost palpable determination, as if he had gathered himself for the fight ahead.

Typically, he began with an apology for having inconvenienced me. "Sorry to take you away from the Army like this, Al, but there's a lot to be done," Nixon said. In other circumstances, he added, I might soon

have become Chief of Staff of the Army, even chairman of the Joint
Chiefs of Staff; maybe that would happen yet, but in the meanwhile he
needed me in the White House. "I just want to reinforce what Bob told
you," he continued. "This won't last long—we'll get a permanent Chief
of Staff and let you go back to soldiering as soon as possible. And you
won't be involved in Watergate; your job is to get this government back
on the tracks."

He spoke Haldeman's name with a mixture of affection and regret
usually reserved for the recently dead. Even though it was difficult to see
the President's face—at his invitation, I was seated in Haldeman's chair
to the left of his desk, looking into the light-filled window behind him—
it was evident that he was still suffering from the emotional effects of
having fired this most loyal, discreet, and self-effacing of presidential
assistants. I, too, felt a certain sadness. My dealings with Haldeman had
been limited. He had sometimes sought my help when Nixon didn't like
something Kissinger was doing; this usually involved contacts with the
press, and Haldeman's purpose had always been to resolve the situation
with as little embarrassment as possible to all concerned. On the basis of
what I had seen of him, I had regarded Haldeman as a very admirable
fellow, good at his job to the point of flawlessness, entirely selfless and
devoted to the President. He was in no way intoxicated by power, and
always kept his place, sitting against the wall at Cabinet meetings instead
of taking a place at the table, always taking the least desirable seat in the
presidential helicopter. His purpose in life had been to make things easier
for the President, and he had remained in character up to the last instant.
Even knowing that his own ruin would be the almost certain result of
this unselfish action, he had made the departure of Ehrlichman and
himself as untroubling as possible by suggesting that they should resign
in the interests of the presidency and the country. In effect, he had fired
himself and induced Ehrlichman to do the same. Even so, actually
accepting the resignations had been a job nobody but Nixon himself
could do, and Nixon knew that whatever wrong Haldeman may have
done, he had done out of loyalty. I thought the President was still shaken
by the experience of saying good-bye to this paragon, and it seemed
natural that he should be. Haldeman had been a true friend to him, as
well as a matchless chamberlain.

By now, the first stage of Watergate was over. On August 29, 1972,
Nixon had said, ostensibly on the basis of an investigation carried out by
John Dean, that "no one in the White House staff, no one in this
administration, presently employed, was involved in this very bizarre

incident." He added, "Overzealous people in campaigns do things that are wrong. What really hurts is if you try to cover it up."[5] The burglars and their handlers had either pleaded guilty or been convicted and sentenced to terms in prison. The second stage, in which new crimes connected to the cover-up were being exposed or hypothesized, was unfolding in a bewildering succession of revelations. Now it appeared that Nixon's closest aides may have been among the overzealous. Just since April 20, the press had reported on the part played by the plumbers in the break-in at the office of Daniel Ellsberg's psychiatrist; the acting Director of the FBI, L. Patrick Gray III, had resigned after the *New York Daily News* reported that he had destroyed documents recovered from the safe of the chief Watergate burglar, E. Howard Hunt; the *Washington Post* reported that John Mitchell had told a grand jury that he had approved payments from CRP funds to the seven Watergate conspirators for legal fees; and the *New York Times* reported that Dean had supervised cash payments of $175,000 to the felons.[6] The general impression that a cover-up existed and that it reached into the White House had been established by these and other stories in the press. There was plenty of grist for the media's mills: testimony before three federal grand juries and the House Judiciary Committee, information and allegations provided by the burglars as part of the plea-bargaining process, and, more lately, the apparent decision of Nixon's own legal counsel, John Dean, to tell everything he knew to federal prosecutors in an apparent effort to gain immunity.

In a Harris poll taken April 18 to 23, only 9 percent of the 1,537 households polled felt that the White House had been frank and honest about Watergate, and 61 percent considered Nixon's handling of the case "fair to poor." On the other hand, another Harris survey of 892 persons taken May 1 to 3 found that 48 percent approved of the way Nixon was handling the presidency, 56 percent said they were no less likely to vote for a Republican in the next election despite Watergate, and only 13 percent thought Nixon should resign (thus, 77 percent thought he should not quit).[7]

The President gave the impression, in private as in public, that he was meeting this situation head-on. In his speech on April 30, announcing the resignation of Haldeman and the others, he announced that he had taken personal command of the investigation. He was, he told a nation-wide television and radio audience, "determined that we should get to the bottom of the matter, and that the truth should be fully brought out—no matter who was involved."[8] I did not doubt that this was his actual intention. It seemed inconceivable to me that the President himself was

involved. In the first place, the original crime was stupid and the idea
that it was possible to cover it up was even more so. I thought that Nixon
was just too smart to be involved. The basis of my admiration for him
was my deep respect for his extraordinary intelligence, knowledge, and
intellectual honesty. In the second place, his innocence had not yet been
impugned by the evidence adduced up to that point. Moreover, I had
observed that he was often unfairly judged by his detractors, and that he
was not ideally equipped by nature to fight back by standing up to his
tormentors, or even to his friends. His meek toleration of Richardson's
insufferable arrogance in placing the President's offices under guard was
only the latest example. This passivity was embarrassing to me because
in my own scheme of values it seemed unmanly. But I thought, in one
of the least correct judgments of my life, that Nixon's dread of the personal
encounter was not important so long as he had made the right decisions
and had somebody by his side who was competent to handle the confrontations. The force of circumstances had now decreed that that somebody
should be me.

Despite the President's well-meaning assurances to the contrary, I knew
that I would inevitably be drawn into the day-to-day management of the
Watergate crisis unless he immediately put someone else in charge. Just
dealing with the barrage of allegations in the news media was a full-time
job, and bad publicity was only the dragon's breath. Things could only
get worse. In his speech on April 30, Nixon had authorized Richardson
to appoint a special prosecutor to investigate Watergate; in a fateful choice
of unqualified words, he told the American people that he had given the
new Attorney General "absolute authority to make all decisions bearing
upon the prosecution of the Watergate case and related matters."[9] The
next day, the Senate passed a resolution, introduced by a Republican,
Senator Charles H. Percy of Illinois, and cosponsored by seven Democrats
and eleven Republicans, calling for the appointment of a fully empowered
special prosecutor. On May 17, the Senate Select Committee on Presidential Campaign Activities under the chairmanship of Senator Sam J.
Ervin, Jr., Democrat of North Carolina, was scheduled to open its hearings. The Justice Department was conducting its own probe, the grand
juries in Washington, New York, and Orlando, Florida, continued to
hear testimony, and several congressional committees were looking into
aspects of the scandal. The combined effect of so many official investigations, all of them influenced to some degree by political considerations
and magnified by a hostile and increasingly frenzied press, would inevita-

bly result in the President of the United States being transformed into the prime suspect. If that happened, he would almost surely be impeached.

I believed that Nixon, especially if he was innocent, needed a defense attorney to make sure that his rights were respected. In the absence of legal challenges that were as ingenious as the charges raised against the President, there would be almost no effective restraints on those conducting the investigation. On April 30, Nixon had appointed Leonard Garment, a liberal Democrat with whom he had made friends in the early sixties when both were members of the same Manhattan law firm, to replace Dean as White House Counsel, but it was evident that the President was not entirely comfortable with this arrangement. Neither was Garment. Nixon knew that he needed someone who could devote his entire attention to the legal aspects of Watergate. I thought that finding the right lawyer was the key to saving the presidency, and that "the right lawyer" must by necessity be the best criminal lawyer who was willing to take the case.

In our first business meeting on my first full day on the job, I expressed my view to Nixon that he should go outside the White House to find the best-qualified, best-known lawyer available, and that he should do this immediately and announce his choice to the world without delay. Nixon did not disagree with this basic idea or with my comment that his choice must be someone the opposition trusted. He asked for a name. I replied, "Edward Bennett Williams." Nixon was startled. "But he's a criminal lawyer," he said. So he was, I replied, probably the most famous one in the country. That was precisely what was needed—someone with fighting instincts and the skills and reputation to back them up.

Williams was a stalwart Democrat and no admirer of Nixon on the political level, but he was a patriot and a defender of the Constitution. Although I had not discussed the matter with him (at that time I hardly knew him), I felt that he would take the case, among other reasons that all lawyers would understand, for the opportunity it would provide to defend not just Nixon but the institution of the presidency. Nixon said no. Engaging a criminal lawyer to defend the President of the United States would send the wrong message to the country, and besides, Williams was a Democrat. Did I have anyone else in mind? I named my next choice, Joe Califano. "Why *him?*" a surprised Nixon wanted to know. The arguments against Williams applied to Califano, too (even more forcefully, considering our most recent telephone conversation), but so did what I considered the far more powerful points in his favor. In Califano's case, these included a veneration of the presidency and a keen and knowledgeable sympathy for those who occupied the office, acquired as Lyndon Johnson's closest aide during the harshest hours of the latter's incumbency. Joe also knew and understood every powerful Democrat on Capitol Hill; he would be able to sense their mood and intentions in a way no Republican could. Nixon expressed doubts that Califano would take the job; I said I thought I could persuade him to do so. Nixon gave his familiar jowly head-shake. "Al, both these men are Democrats," he said. "You're right about our needing somebody. But I've suffered too much from people who have mixed loyalties. We've got to have a man who's with us, a man we can trust."

At the time, I thought that Nixon's decision was flawed by his incurable partisanship, and I still believe that Williams and Califano were lawyers first and that they would have put their client's interests above ideology and all other considerations.* On the other hand, it cannot be denied that Nixon had a hardheaded point based on bitter experience, and a few months later, after we got to know Professor Archibald Cox, Richardson's choice as the Watergate Special Prosecutor, I saw what the President had feared come true before my unbelieving eyes.

Although he had rejected my candidates, Nixon had bought my idea in regard to the need for a defense lawyer and had charged me with the task of finding the right one. I soon discovered that there were few great courtroom advocates who were also Republicans, and that there were no qualified volunteers for the job we had in mind. Finally, I turned, without enthusiasm, to J. Fred Buzhardt, the acting general counsel of the Defense Department, whom I had known slightly at West Point (he graduated a year ahead of me) and later in the Pentagon. Buzhardt (pronounced buz-AART) was a former aide to Senator Strom Thurmond, Republican (formerly Democrat) of South Carolina. Fred was virtually unknown to the press, and he had limited experience and no national reputation as an expert in criminal law. However, I knew him to be hardworking, intelligent, rigorously ethical, self-effacing, and discreet, and I recommended him to the President as the best man immediately available for the job. Timing was critical; the President needed a defender now. Buzhardt was named special counsel to the President on May 10, the same day a federal grand jury in New York indicted John Mitchell and Maurice Stans, respectively the former chairman and finance director of the Committee to Re-elect the President, on charges of accepting a $200,000

---

* Years later, Califano told me that he would have taken the case had it been offered to him. I think he would have won it—in part because this would have denied the Democrats the benefit of his advice.

campaign contribution from financier Robert L. Vesco in return for a promise to intercede with the government on his behalf. Vesco, who was also indicted, was under investigation by the Security and Exchange Commission with regard to an alleged mutual-fund swindle. Mitchell, the former Attorney General of the United States, and Stans, Nixon's loyal Secretary of Commerce, each faced fifty years in prison and $85,000 in fines.

One day after these indictments were handed down, Judge W. Matthew Byrne of the U.S. District Court in Los Angeles dismissed all charges against Daniel Ellsberg and his codefendant, Anthony J. Russo, in the Pentagon Papers case, declaring a mistrial because of government misconduct—for example, the burglary of Ellsberg's psychiatrist's office by the plumbers and an FBI wiretap on Ellsberg's telephone.[10] Then, on May 14, a California newspaper published a story charging that Nixon had used a million dollars in campaign funds to purchase his home in San Clemente. Within a month, a House subcommittee was estimating that the government had spent $10 million for improvements on the President's houses in San Clemente and Key Biscayne; the fact that these were largely temporary measures related to security that could be removed at the end of Nixon's term received little notice. Meanwhile, the news media disclosed that Nixon had paid no state or federal income taxes since becoming President and began to question the basis of the exemptions and deductions by which he had avoided doing so.[11]

Buzhardt and Nixon had not known each other until I brought them together, but they became acquainted on a crash basis in the next few days. Nixon's attempts to explain Watergate once and for all in his speech of April 30 and then again on May 9 in a talk before a fund-raising dinner in Washington had raised more questions than they answered. This had happened, I believed, not because Nixon had dissembled but because he himself did not know or remember all the facts. Like others before me, I had suggested very forcefully that Nixon—the President himself, not a speechwriter or other surrogate—should discover the true facts and issue a statement in which he told the American people everything important known to himself about the Watergate affair: "Whatever you did, whatever others did, put it all out, Mr. President. Everything, no matter what, the people will support you." He agreed that this was the only possible course of action and set to work almost immediately, examining files and scribbling on yellow tablets in his EOB hideaway. Buzhardt was his chief collaborator in this project, and he spent hours in seclusion with the President, going over the minutiae. Whether Nixon consulted the tapes,

I do not know. At this point, neither Buzhardt nor I knew that the White House taping system existed.

In his new statement on Watergate, delivered to the press on May 22, Nixon conceded that there had been a cover-up but told the nation that he would not resign the presidency because he himself had not been involved in it. He denied any prior knowledge of the Watergate break-in; denied participation in or knowledge of the cover-up; denied any prior knowledge of funds being provided to the Watergate defendants; denied any personal involvement in attempts to implicate the CIA; denied prior knowledge of the burglary of Ellsberg's psychiatrist's office; denied authorizing or encouraging subordinates to engage in illegal or improper campaign tactics.

Of these seven denials, all but the first would subsequently be shown to be false. Nixon's statement was designed, like the earlier ones, to disarm his enemies by preempting their future accusations; instead, it made him hostage to his own deceptions. The outcome could hardly have been otherwise, because a considerable number of people—John Mitchell, Bob Haldeman, John Ehrlichman, John Dean, Charles Colson, and Jeb Stuart Magruder, among others—knew they were false.[12] All of these men, having been repudiated by Nixon, were in imminent danger of going to prison. His statement came under attack in the news media immediately, in part, no doubt, because the President made a point of referring to "some of the more sensational—and inaccurate—of the charges that have filled the headlines."[13]

On May 28, CBS News reported that federal prosecutors had offered John Dean the opportunity of pleading guilty to one count of obstruction of justice in return for his testimony. The next day, the *Washington Post* reported that prosecutors were considering calling Nixon as a witness before the Watergate grand jury in Washington.[14]

Meanwhile, the administration was faced with burgeoning inflation, a fight over the budget that involved, as Nixon warned with great prescience, the whole future pattern of federal spending, and an energy crisis. The Soviets were arming and goading the Arabs into an attack on Israel that could very well lead to a nuclear confrontation between the superpowers. This dangerous Middle Eastern game was, among other things, an opportunistic response by Moscow to signs of American debility and disorder, and, as we shall see, the spectacle led them into dangerous miscalculations. "How can you Americans do this to your President?" Ambassador Dobrynin asked me, in a mood that resembled moral outrage. "How can he be so weak as to let it happen?"

As a result of Nixon's call for wholesale resignations by his own appointees, more than 185 high-level vacancies existed, including about 60 requiring Senate confirmation. Some of these were Cabinet posts and a large number were sub-Cabinet and senior-executive jobs.[15] In certain agencies, the bureaucracy was running the show without effective policy direction, an undesirable situation under any conditions but a catastrophe for Nixon, who needed sympathizers, or at least fair-minded men and women, at the levers of government as no President had ever needed them before. He knew he was unlikely to find loyalists among career government employees; as he was fond of pointing out, the senior ranks at the Department of Justice included many lawyers appointed by FDR and Truman, and only 5 percent of the Foreign Service was Republican.[16]

Watergate had demolished Nixon's grand plan to reorganize the domestic Cabinet departments and some agencies into four superagencies (Human Resources, Natural Resources, Community Development, and Economic Affairs) under tighter control by the White House staff. It was clearly impossible under present circumstances for Nixon to push a grandiose reorganization of the federal government through a Congress that was on the point of impeaching him. The task at hand was to wake up the administration and reassert the President's authority by a dramatic series of appointments designed to show that Nixon was in charge and the government was proceeding under a full head of steam. Manifestly, this could not be done by concentrating power in a White House that was under siege. What was needed, instead, was decentralization of the decision-making process, a lower profile for the White House staff, and greater independence and visibility for the Cabinet. All that, I discussed and cleared with Nixon. There was no need to tell him that the purpose of this exercise was to create a government that could go on doing the people's business no matter what happened to the President. He understood this better than anyone.

On May 6, two days after assuming my duties as Chief of Staff, I presented Nixon with a plan for reorganization of the Executive Branch, the concept of which was to "dramatically revitalize [the] Cabinet with emphasis on quality and decentralization of power from the White House to the Departments [and] lower profile of White House Staff. . . ." The plan also called for action to establish "immediately an office of Special Counsellor to the President competently staffed and physically located *outside the White House* [emphasis added] which will conduct all activities related to ongoing and pending investigations, hearings and litigation.

The Presidency as an institution and the [Watergate] investigation must be separated immediately in *theory* and *fact.*"

Obviously, these recommendations were sharp departures from the President's plans for the Cabinet and the way in which the Watergate scandal had been handled up until then. A siege mentality gripped the White House staff. Nixon was devoting most of his time to defending himself. In the process, he had become his own lawyer, and it was evident how much truth there is in the aphorism about the man who places himself in this situation. Removing the legal defense process from the White House, I thought, would let the President behave like a President, reduce media pressure on the White House by establishing a new source of answers to journalists' questions, and produce a calmer atmosphere and a more rational, orderly, and effective defense.

My recommendations: Henry Kissinger to replace William Rogers as Secretary of State;* John Connally (now a Republican about to join the White House staff as a special adviser without pay) for Secretary of the Treasury, with the incumbent head of that department, George Shultz, taking over John Ehrlichman's former duties; CIA Director James Schlesinger to become Secretary of Defense in succession to Richardson; Brent Scowcroft to succeed Kissinger as National Security Adviser. Having failed to bring the dynamic Joe Califano aboard as presidential defender, I mentioned him as a second choice for Secretary of Defense, and as first choice for a new position as counselor to the President, charged with drafting legislation to reform political campaign practices, one of Nixon's chief objectives. Again Nixon said no, but I would have preferred to have had Califano inside the perimeter.

However, most of the other recommendations having to do with personnel changes came to pass. The happy effects of replacing Rogers with Kissinger, I thought, would include providing Nixon with the incorruptible Rogers as a moral presence and as a source of legal and political advice. It would also accomplish the early removal of Kissinger to the State Department, where he would be isolated, as he wished to be, from the Sturm and Drang of Watergate. There, his competitive instincts would ensure the revitalization of the State Department and its return to its proper role as a center of policy making, and there he would be insulated from the irritations of working for a former subordinate within

---

*I was not aware, and Nixon did not tell me, that this exchange was already in the works, Rogers having promised Haldeman that he would leave sometime in June.

a system of management that would, insofar as human nature permitted, emphasize orderly procedures, teamwork, and collegiality over stardom and time-consuming competition for access to Nixon. A soothing side effect of Kissinger's confirmation as Secretary of State was that he now outranked me again, at least in theory, and this restored not merely the appearance but also the reality of cordial relations between us. Kissinger felt that he should keep his old job and be Secretary of State, as well. At first, he did wear both hats, giving up the old one to Scowcroft with some reluctance when the doubling of responsibility proved to be unworkable.

I was faced with a doubling in my own work when the President declined to replace Ehrlichman. In the absence of a successor, and according to the President's wishes, I took over most of his former duties as principal adviser for domestic affairs, as well as Haldeman's old job as Chief of Staff. Under the circumstances, my order to the staff to commit nothing to written memorandum that the sender would not wish to see on page one of the *Washington Post* may be regarded as a defensive measure; in fact, it resulted in a truly dramatic reduction in the number of memorandums. No abatement in press activity was likely, and, despite ill-conceived advice to change press secretaries, the long-suffering, utterly loyal, and completely unambitious Ron Ziegler remained as the chief presidential spokesman. One of the most astute political operatives in town, Bryce Harlow, a former aide to Eisenhower and other Presidents, and a longtime confidant of Nixon's, was persuaded to return as a political adviser. Melvin Laird returned at my suggestion, to provide the background in domestic and congressional affairs that I lacked. As expected, he played by the same self-made rules as before, springing jolting surprises, exuding charm, and working hard to advance his own ingenious ideas, which weren't always the same as Nixon's, and seldom the same as mine. Pat Buchanan, a conservative bulldog who genuinely felt for Nixon in his tribulations, and Ray Price, a fine and thoughtful man, more broadminded and less ideological than Buchanan (or the President, for that matter), were the speechwriters.

As my principal assistant, I brought in Maj. George Joulwan, who had occupied the same bunker with me at the Battle of Ap Gu and other firefights as my battalion operations officer in Vietnam and had more lately been my executive assistant during my brief tour as Army vice chief of staff. I needed someone I could trust absolutely, someone who could handle the second echelon of staff who did most of the real work of the presidency. George remained with me until the end, and he did the brilliant job that I had fully expected him to do.*

The procedures Joulwan helped me to institute and administer in the White House included an early-morning daily meeting of the senior staff (with twice-weekly attendance by the Secretaries of State, Defense, and Treasury and sometimes the Attorney General) over which I presided for the purpose of making the President's wishes on all pertinent issues plainly understood; a later meeting of the middle staff in which Joulwan checked on the progress of the tasks and decisions passed on to the senior staff that morning; and various procedures designed to speed production, improve internal communication through a policy of plain speech, and bolster morale by instilling a sense of purpose and an atmosphere of teamwork. "Ignore the scandal, think of the country," I said. This was easier said than done, and I knew it.

Optimum performance was simply too much to hope for under the circumstances. From the first day, I had the strong feeling that a lot of fine young people were being destroyed by the atmosphere of guilt by association. Those who had worked for Haldeman and Ehrlichman and others touched by accusation were in a state of shock and disillusionment. They knew they were vulnerable; their reputations were under the microscope, their expectations were a shambles, and their loyalties were shaken and divided. It is not surprising that this created troublesome problems of morale and efficiency. We were trying to keep the President's schedule focused on the business of the American people, but no sooner would we get into a businesslike mode than some new calamity would land on the doorstep. The morning staff meetings, in which the news stories of the day before were reviewed, quickly became known as "the morning horrors." Leaks, the problem that had spawned Watergate by creating an atmosphere of suspicion and mistrust, continued to sabotage trust and efficiency. Although I chewed many a tail and handed down many a caution, it proved impossible to staunch the flow of indiscretion and disparaging remarks emanating from the staff.

For myself, the experience was like entering into a whole new life. This was not the White House I had known; Nixon was not the President he had been or that I had expected him to be after his triumph at the

---

*At the time, I felt a certain anxiety that Joulwan's association with one of the greatest political debacles of all time would have a negative effect on his future in the Army. As I might have known, George became a four-star general despite this handicap, a development that not only confirms his excellence but demonstrates the ability of the Army selection system to concentrate on essentials and come to a just conclusion.

polls. Days were long, hard, and dispiriting. Because most people thought that Nixon already had enough on his mind, they brought problems to me that they would ordinarily have taken to him. Meanwhile, several members of Congress, among others, questioned the legality of my serving even as Acting White House Chief of Staff while I remained on active duty in the Army. The Pentagon believed on the basis of much precedent that the situation was legal and in no way unusual, and so did I, but this log was thrown onto the bonfire of controversy.[17] My basic pay as a four-star general, $36,000 per annum, worked out to $7.69 an hour before taxes, based on the ninety-hour week I usually worked. To disembarrass the President of a meaningless issue, I announced my retirement from the Army in June; the word *acting* was dropped from my title, and as a civilian Chief of Staff my salary ($42,500 per annum) rose by $1.39 per hour. The great issues seemed worth any amount of trouble and sacrifice, but the burden of petty questions sometimes threatened to buckle the knees.

For the first month or so, I tried hard to act according to Nixon's mandate and separate myself from the issue of Watergate. This was not because I feared contamination. As an Army officer, I had lived by a code of ethics all my adult life. It was in my bloodstream, and no situation was desperate enough to cause me to change. As a practical matter, quarantine was impossible. Watergate had invaded every organ of the presidency. I took what precautions I could, never taking a step until I had discussed the legal implications with Buzhardt or Garment, or both, but the daily outbreak of new revelations was a constant reminder of how bad things were and how little we knew about the true dimensions of the situation.

Two weeks before Nixon announced John Dean's resignation, the latter said, "Some may hope or think that I will become a scapegoat in the Watergate case. Anyone who believes this does not know me, know the true facts nor understand our system of justice."[18] On June 3, the Sunday *New York Times* and *Washington Post* carried front-page stories reporting that Dean had told Senate investigators and federal prosecutors that he had met with Nixon on at least thirty-five occasions to discuss actions designed to cover up White House involvement in the Watergate burglary. The stories said that Nixon had discussed paying a million dollars to Watergate defendants to ensure their silence.

On Monday morning, Nixon called me into the Oval Office. His expression was morose and he sat very still behind his uncluttered desk, in his usual dark suit and immaculate white shirt. He gestured me to my usual chair beside the desk. Normally, he began to talk and issue instructions as soon as I sat down with my lined yellow tablet, but now there was an extended moment of silence, as if he expected me to say something first. Under the circumstances, I did not know what to say, so I waited.

Finally, the President broke the silence. "Al," he said, "this Dean testimony is fatal to me."

It is a very strange thing to hear a President of the United States calmly describe his own doom. Those who had listened to Lincoln describing his dream about his own funeral may have felt some of the things I felt on this occasion—a rush of sympathy for the man, a wish to disbelieve, concern for the nation.

"Mr. President," I said. "I must know in order to serve you. Is Dean telling the truth?"

"No, Al. He's lying. But the damage is done. The question is, Should I resign, put an end to things, save the country the agony of what's coming?"

I was shocked by the notion that he could so easily surrender. He had been elected by the people; he had an obligation to honor their votes. I said, "Mr. President, you don't have the luxury of resigning. It wouldn't serve due process. You just can't do it."

We chatted a little longer. Before I left, I said, "Mr. President, I think you should wait till tomorrow on this."

That night, I went home and reflected on what I knew about the case and what I knew about Nixon and Dean. The reader knows my opinion of the President. I had never had much use for Dean. He was too fashionably dressed and barbered, too glib, too obviously satisfied with himself. * After sleepless hours, I concluded that Nixon was telling me the truth—and, as it turned out when the tapes of his conversation with Dean were released, he was. Dean told him about the crimes of others, but he did not tell him that he, Dean, had attempted to suborn perjury; that he had destroyed evidence from Hunt's safe; that he had given FBI reports to the CRP; that he had raised and passed money to the original defendants. All of these wrongful acts may fairly be said to have been the logical product of Nixon's first significant conversation with Haldeman

---

*While I was still working for Kissinger, Dean, in Ehrlichman's name, had requested that I send a plane from the presidential flight to pick up Robert Vesco somewhere in the Caribbean or Latin America. At the time, I had no idea who Vesco was, but when I asked, and Dean replied that he had no official connection with the government, I said there was no way I could dispatch a U.S. government aircraft to pick up a private citizen.

about Watergate on June 23, 1972, when he decided to treat the break-in as a public-relations problem rather than a legal and moral issue and, in effect, instructed his closest aides to apply damage control. They did so. But they did not always tell Nixon exactly what they were doing. I thought that the President may have been guilty of self-deception, wishful thinking, and of putting his trust in the wrong man, but when it came down to a choice of believing him or a frightened and desperate young man who was clearly trying to save his own skin, I chose Nixon.

The following morning, I went in to see the President and reminded him that the means existed to prove that Dean was not telling the truth. A few days earlier, Nixon had told me in an offhand way that he had the means to tape-record conversations in the Oval Office and over the telephone. This came as no great surprise to me. I had always assumed that some ability to record important presidential conversations existed in the Nixon White House, as it had under earlier Presidents. I did not press him for details.

Now I asked him whether any of his conversations with Dean had been recorded.

"Yes," he said. "Sure they were."

With a great sense of relief, I said, "Mr. President, only you can decide. But I believe it would be wrong to let yourself be driven from office by perjured testimony. Sit down and listen to those tapes and get out the whole truth."

Nixon agreed enthusiastically. I arranged with Steve Bull, Nixon's personal assistant, for a tape recorder and headphones to be delivered along with the tapes to Nixon's hideaway office. He secluded himself and listened. The next time he called me into his presence, he was beaming with confidence.

"Al," he said, "listening to the tapes has confirmed to me that what I told you is true. Dean lied. The details are clear."

I offered a silent prayer of thanks, believing that the truth was finally available and that it would deliver the President and the country from the shame and political disorder that had been threatening them.

28

Shadow of a Coup

In the second week of June 1973, while the Watergate scandal metastasized and pressure mounted for Nixon to resign the presidency, Elliot Richardson told me that Vice President Agnew's name had come up in an investigation of kickbacks connected to public construction projects in Baltimore.

"How serious is this likely to be?" I asked.

The Attorney General said, "They're taking it pretty seriously up in Baltimore, Al. It appears that Agnew received bribes while he was Baltimore County executive and while he was governor, and I'm afraid they think he took money even after he became Vice President." Richardson, who had the heart and instincts of a seventeenth-century Calvinist, delivered this information in a detached, fatalistic manner, as if the discovery that the Vice President of the United States was a common felon confirmed some divine law of probability already known to him.

In my own mind, two words formed: *double impeachment*. I am not subject to visions, but as Richardson left my office a vivid picture grew in my mind of the President and Vice President of the United States, both charged with high crimes and misdemeanors, side by side, on trial together before the Senate. I called Fred Buzhardt and told him what Richardson had just told me and what I feared.

"Oh, shit," said Fred.

"Then it's within the realm of possibility, under the Constitution?"

"Absolutely," Fred replied. "You could have a coup d'état with the Legislative Branch taking over the Executive Branch under the cover of the Constitution. The Speaker of the House would become President."

"But he's a Democrat. That would reverse the results of the election. We've got to find a way to decouple these two situations and deal with them one at a time. Otherwise, they'll go down together and the country will go with them."

Fred said, "Amen, brother."

After my conversation with Buzhardt, I walked down the hall to the Oval Office and told Nixon what Richardson had just told me about Agnew. The President received the news with remarkable composure. Although I did not know this at the time, and Nixon, in typical fashion, did not bother to tell me, the President had known about the situation since April 10, when Agnew had told Haldeman about the investigation. After assuring Haldeman of his own innocence, Agnew apparently asked that the White House contact Senator J. Glenn Beall, Jr., the brother of George Beall, the U.S. Attorney for Maryland, and suggest that the administration did not want Agnew's name dragged into the case. Nixon had declined to intervene on the sensible grounds that doing so would probably make things worse.[1]

I did not learn these details until years afterward, when Nixon published his memoirs. For my own part, I said nothing to him about my fear of double impeachment. It did not seem to me that I could do so without committing the lèse majesté of suggesting in the President's presence that I thought it possible he had committed impeachable offenses. Besides, I was confident that he would grasp the implications as quickly as Buzhardt and I had. (Only a few days before, Clark Clifford, the Democratic wise man, had proposed to resolve the crisis over Watergate in three steps: 1. Agnew resigns. 2. Nixon appoints a new Vice President from a list of three names provided by Congress. 3. Nixon resigns and the Democratic Congress's new Vice President succeeds him.[2])

I was not surprised by the President's composure. The prospect of Agnew being indicted on criminal charges was no more bizarre or threatening than many other daily events in the Nixon White House, and I thought that the President assumed that this was just another way his enemies were trying to get at him.

"When all is said and done, Al," Nixon said, "I suspect this will just turn out to be Maryland politics."

"Elliot doesn't think so, Mr. President."

"I know that. I just want to be sure Agnew is fairly treated."

This case was about bribery. Money had little power or influence in Nixon's life. The rule of a successful political career, he had often told me, was "Never let a dollar touch your hand." That had always been his own rule, and I am quite sure, whatever else he may have done, he never had departed from it. But he knew that greed was the doppelgänger of politics. It did not surprise him that charges of corruption should show up, or be made to appear to show up, in the life of a man such as Agnew, who had spent his days in politics. Leaving him that day, I thought that he was as suspicious of Richardson's puritan righteousness as of Agnew's capacity to resist temptation.

Late in July, Richardson submitted an updated report. "They say, up in Baltimore," he told me, "that they have enough evidence to charge the Vice President with forty felony counts for violations of federal statutes on bribery, tax evasion, and corruption."

"There's no mistake about this?"

Richardson laughed mirthlessly. "Oh, no, Al," he said. "There's no mistake. They've got him—credible witnesses, documents, heaven knows what else. In all my years as a prosecutor, I have never seen such an open-and-shut case." This was a sobering statement: Richardson was a former U.S. Attorney for and Attorney General of Massachusetts.

His tone was one of cold contempt for these crimes—and for all who violate the public trust. I sensed that the Attorney General felt that the Vice President would deserve whatever he got if found guilty, and that there was little doubt in his mind that he would be. The fact that the accused was a member of Richardson's own party and the Vice President of the United States only made things worse. The higher the office, the greater the offense. Richardson's puritanism ran deep. In his confirmation hearings in May, he had told the Senate Judiciary Committee, "I am among the Republicans who feel betrayed by the shoddy standards of morals . . . which have recently come to light. . . ." This sense of betrayal, he added, should negate fears that "as part of the administration I might be tempted to go easy" on Watergate suspects.[3]

Although I was sometimes taken aback by Richardson's sanctimony, I admired his high principles. I even shared them in the abstract. However, I was deeply disturbed by what he had just told me. What could I tell the President? Even more now than the month before, I did not see how the administration could survive both Watergate and the public disgrace of the Vice President. This newest bombshell climaxed a month that had included a life-threatening illness of the President, the disclosure of the existence of the White House taping system, with the resultant blizzard of subpoenas, and the sensational testimony before the Ervin committee of John Dean, John Mitchell, John Ehrlichman, and other leading figures in the Watergate scandal.

As before, I asked Richardson how much time we had before the facts about Agnew were disclosed. He replied that it was hard to tell; the law moved at its own deliberate pace. The investigation was almost complete. In the next stage, a grand jury would be convened, evidence would be presented, and indictments would be handed down. At that point, he said dryly, matters usually became quite noticeably public.

"All right, Elliot, but *how long*?"

He shrugged. "A month, six weeks."

His tone did not suggest that he was much concerned with the implications of this situation for the President. Richardson told me that he had subjected himself to "a lot of soul-searching" with regard to the Watergate scandal. "I am trying," he said, "to behave in a manner that when looked at six months to a year from now will be good for the President. It is very hard."

The Agnew case made it even harder. All month long, Buzhardt and I had been devoting the major part of our efforts to devising a strategy to quarantine the presidency from the scandal that was about to doom the Vice President. The question of Agnew's future had to be decided as quickly as possible. For any number of reasons, including Nixon's waning influence in his own administration, we could not count on the President for effective help. Of course, Agnew, whose instincts for self-preservation matched his superlative skills as a politician, was watching this process carefully. In his book, *Go Quietly . . . Or else*, he writes, "General Haig . . . was the de facto President. . . . Mr. Nixon did not have the stomach to confront me openly, so it is logical to conclude that Haig took over and determined how to force me to get out. . . . Haig did not want me in the line of succession."[4]

In fact, it was not the question of vice presidential succession but the growing likelihood of the simultaneous impeachment of the President and the Vice President that preoccupied, not to say terrified, Fred Buzhardt and me. The expulsion of both from office would mean handing over the presidency to the other party and invalidating the votes of the 47 million Americans who had cast their ballots for Richard Nixon. My own belief was that the people's faith in the democratic process would never recover from such a blow. The mystical basis of power—the result of the quadrennial vote being the American equivalent of the divine right of kings—would be destroyed. Only a President voted into office by all the people had the right to nominate his successor. Therefore, Nixon must last longer than Agnew.

It was Nixon who did not want Agnew in the line of succession. Even before his own political future was engulfed by Watergate, it was John Connally, the former Democratic Governor of Texas, and no other figure in American political life, whom he imagined as the Republican President who would come after him. He had hoped to position Connally for the nomination in 1976. That was the reason for Connally's change of parties. As soon as Agnew's resignation became a possibility, Nixon spoke of replacing him with Connally in a matter of days. My task, as the President's crisis manager, was to do what I could to arrange matters so that Agnew's departure did the least possible damage to the President and to the presidency, and to do what I could to make sure the vacancy was filled as soon as possible by Nixon, who alone in the nation had been voted the authority to appoint a new Vice President.

Soon after Richardson's visit, I called on Agnew to ask him what he thought his options were. Agnew was his usual collected self. If he felt any anxiety, it did not show. Like Nixon, he blamed the situation on Maryland politics. A bunch of eager young prosecutors, he conjectured, were hoping to make a name for themselves by dragging his name into an investigation of small-time crooks. One of the witnesses against him was a man "who had accused everyone in Baltimore of crimes, including his own mother." Crazy slander of this kind was a cross all politicians had to bear. Agnew wasn't worried, nor should I be. He was innocent, and due process of law would soon demonstrate this fact to all the world. Fred Buzhardt and Leonard Garment looked at the evidence available to the Justice Department and affirmed Richardson's opinion that the case against Agnew appeared to be very strong.

On August 1, U.S. Attorney George Beall sent Agnew's lawyer a letter officially informing him that the Vice President was under investigation for possible violation of federal criminal statutes including but not limited to those dealing with extortion, conspiracy, bribery, and taxes.[5] I continued to talk to Richardson and Agnew in the hope of finding some means of making the latter admit the hopelessness of his situation. Richardson was reluctant to tell Agnew or his lawyers more than they already knew about the evidence against the Vice President. He thought that he might already have gone beyond the ordinary limits of what he called "prosecutorial prudence."

Agnew could never have been in any doubt that his resignation was wanted. He played on the fact. The President's desire for him to go was his only real bargaining chip, and he used it with great skill and dogged self-interest. He said he needed time—four or five days at least—to talk to his lawyers and plan his strategy. Maybe, he said, he would think it best to go on leave of absence as Vice President while he defended himself. The situation was a strange mixture of the grand and the petty. Although some of Agnew's concerns were constitutional (I am not being sardonic; among other things, he was a fine lawyer and a patriot), he continued to worry about smaller issues, including his pension. He was concerned about whether his years of federal service in the armed forces and government were sufficient to qualify him for benefits, and at one point he suggested to Nixon that he might be given government employment abroad after his resignation as a means of maximizing his benefits.

Nixon called a meeting with Richardson on August 6. The Attorney General repeated the information he had given me a few days before. Not wishing to breach the confidentiality between the President and the chief lawyer of his administration, I stayed away, but an unoptimistic Nixon told me afterward that the meeting ended with the usual admonitions and assurances that nothing about the case must leak. The *Wall Street Journal* broke the story of Agnew's troubles in its August 7 editions, which went on sale late on August 6, hours after the meeting in the Oval Office. Knight Newspapers reported that Agnew had allegedly received $1,000 a week in illegal payments from contractors while he was Baltimore County executive (1962 to 1966), and governor (1967 to 1968), and a further payment of $50,000 after he became Vice President in 1969.[6]

Nixon warned Agnew, famous for his ability to inflame the press and delight his followers with reckless off-the-cuff remarks, to be careful what he said to the news media. Agnew called a press conference on August 8 and said that he had "no expectation of being indicted" and had "nothing to hide." He denounced statements published by the news media as "damned lies," and added, "I have no intention to be skewered in this fashion."[7] These statements did nothing to reduce the size of the media avalanche that followed.

Fred Buzhardt and I went to the President and told him that the press conference, however comforting it might be to Agnew's supporters in the short term, would be a disaster in the long run. "His denials simply won't hold up," Buzhardt said. "I can't understand how he can make such flat denials in light of the facts that are bound to come out."[8]

There was never the slightest doubt that Agnew would have to go. Nixon thought that Agnew had inflicted mortal damage on himself. "By coming out so flatly and telling the President and the country that he is not guilty," the President told me later, "it [makes] it very difficult for us to let him stay on until the trial." From the President on down, all agreed that the only questions were when Agnew would go and under what conditions. The best solution, Nixon thought, was for Agnew to decide for himself that he must do the honorable thing and depart. He asked me to put this thought in Agnew's mind.

This was easier said than done. Agnew did not see things as Richardson did. He assured Nixon that he had not misused the public trust. His view of reality had been formed by a lifetime in politics. In his eyes, any gifts of money he may have received from contractors were legitimate campaign contributions that had been expended to cover normal political, not personal, costs. He had given the contractors nothing in return; all were well-qualified bidders who had won public construction projects on merit. Arrangements of this kind, he said, were common all across the country, and he was being singled out and destroyed by political opportunists who were misrepresenting normal campaign contributions as bribes. This was contradicted by statements from witnesses that it was Agnew who had solicited payments as a quid pro quo for contracts awarded. He strongly denied having received any money after becoming Vice President, but the prosecutors were prepared to charge that regular payments in cash had been delivered to him through Christmas 1972 in his vice presidential office, in the West Wing of the White House, and in the Sheraton-Park Hotel, where he had once maintained a residence. Fred Buzhardt thought that the best thing for the country, and for Agnew, would be for Richardson to explain all the facts to Agnew in the hope that he would see that his only course was to resign. If he chose to fight it out in the courts, the case could go on for years.

"The President believes that you have to decide what to do," I told Agnew. "He's confident that you will make a statesmanlike decision."

I realized as soon as I had spoken that I had been too subtle. Agnew knew exactly what that meant. But he had not gotten to the top in Maryland politics by doing what other people thought was best for him. "I'll fight it out," he said. For how long? I wondered. "Until the end," he said. He reminded me that he had been elected to a four-year term less than a year earlier. "I just hope and pray," he said, "that they aren't basing this case on the testimony of one witness." He made it plain to me once more that he thought Richardson was out to get him, or, at the very least, that he was being railroaded because of the incompetence of Richardson's Justice Department to protect him from his political enemies. He was infuriated by a story in the *Wall Street Journal* that Special Prosecutor Cox had been kept informed of the process of the case against Agnew. It turned out, when I asked Richardson about this matter on behalf of an almost equally furious Nixon, that the Attorney General himself had mentioned the ongoing investigation to Cox; his purpose, he said, was to prevent Cox from being led inadvertently into the case by a witness who might wander into his office.

However that may have been, the Vice President openly believed that he had some reason to doubt the Attorney General's objectivity in this case. In response to these misgivings, the President had designated Henry Petersen, a civil servant who had risen after twenty-six years as a government lawyer to be head of the Criminal Division at the Department of Justice, to look at the evidence and give him a second opinion. Petersen, who had overseen the Watergate case before Cox's appointment, was a Democrat with a reputation for discretion, scrupulous fairness, and apolitical professional conduct. Richardson the genteel liberal and Agnew the bare-fisted conservative were at opposite ends of the political spectrum within the Republican party and had often been at odds in policy councils. Their relationship, moreover, was strongly influenced by their origins— Agnew, the self-made son of Greek immigrants; Richardson, the Boston Brahmin descended from the Pilgrim fathers. Agnew thought that Richardson wanted to be President and that his behavior was controlled by this ambition. Whatever he may have thought about Agnew's probable guilt or innocence, Nixon did not dismiss these arguments out of hand. "Elliot," the President was fond of saying, "wants to be in the Oval Office."

After my chat with Agnew, Nixon and I talked over the Vice President's obduracy yet again. "Everyone thinks he has to leave," the President said. "Does he think he won't be indicted? Does he think he can fight it out as Vice President?"

"He thinks he can," I replied. "He says, 'I'll fight it out over the next two or three years.' "

"How does that strike you?"

"We would not survive."

Nixon said, "The point is, does he deny the substance?"

"He describes it as a frame-up."

Nixon snorted in frustration. But on August 7, he gave Agnew the five days he said he needed to decide his own future. At the same time, he instructed me to call John Connally and tell him to hold himself in readiness for a meeting with the President. "He wants to be sure," I told Connally on the morning of August 8, "that you aren't going to be traveling, or away, or something, especially around the fourteenth, fifteenth, and sixteenth." Connally replied that he understood and that he would be on hand if needed.

That evening, I spoke to Richardson about Petersen's examination of the case against Agnew. The President was still concerned that Agnew be given a fair deal. According to Richardson, Nixon had called Petersen and told him that "when you're dealing with the Vice President of the United States, you're not dealing with a Boston politician." Richardson said that Petersen would assess the credibility of the witnesses. "If you can believe what they have said, then it is a very strong case, so then the question is, [Can you be sure] they are not lying?" he said, adding that there was more than one witness. "If it was one-on-one, we would not move."

I told Richardson that the President wanted Petersen's report, which was really nothing more than a second opinion on the strength of the evidence and the credibility of the witnesses, delivered to him personally by August 16. "What the President wants," I said, "is the hardest and best assessment." Richardson promised Nixon would have that, though maybe not before the deadline. He suggested that he and Petersen might talk to Agnew if the latter wished to talk to them.

On hearing this, Nixon exploded: "I don't want Elliot to talk to him! Agnew's view is that he's trying his damndest to get the Vice President. Do *you* believe that Elliot feels that Agnew's guilty? What the hell did Agnew do what he did today for?" This was a reference to Agnew's press conference. I had no chance to answer any of the President's questions; they were not designed to be answered.

"By coming out so flatly and telling the President and the country that he's not guilty," Nixon continued, "my view is that in his own mind [Agnew] has crossed the bridge and . . . under no circumstances will he resign. [But] if he really is innocent, then he ought to find a way to resign gracefully and fight it. We want to keep him away from the constitutional route [impeachment]. We'll just say that's out of the question."

This was the first reference Nixon had made in my presence to the possibility of impeachment. But what he said made it obvious that he shared my apprehensions about a possible double impeachment and its consequences to American institutions and American democracy.

*　*　*

I was not in a very cheerful mood as the day ended. Earlier, on Nixon's instructions, I had told Bill Rogers that he must resign as Secretary of State. Although I had recommended his departure, I liked and admired Rogers. Actually, my mission was to deliver a forceful reminder rather than introduce a new idea. He had delayed because he was understandably loath to hand over his office to Kissinger, and also because he did not want to give the impression that he was abandoning a sinking ship.

"There has never been an idea that [Rogers] was not leaving," Nixon told me. "This one baffles me."

He instructed me to resolve the situation. "He has to go, Al. Make him understand that." I strongly supported that judgment.

Typically, the President asked at the last moment whether I thought there was any chance of changing the timing. I gave him the answer I knew he wanted: "No. . . . You have to have this change." This also happened to be the right answer in terms of the national interest; the reorganization of the administration had to go forward as quickly and completely as possible so that it could continue to function even in the midst of the ultimate distraction of impeachment.

"Well," Nixon said, "it's not very pleasant."

Indeed, it was not. Rogers fought like a lion. He warned that Kissinger's confirmation hearings were likely to be stormy and politically damaging. (As indeed they were, owing mainly to the fact that the 1969 FBI wiretaps, of which Rogers had no knowledge, were leaked from the Department of Justice and became an issue.) Circumstances may have clouded his time as Secretary of State, but he had been one of the first in 1948 to advise Nixon to go ahead with his prosecution of Alger Hiss.[9] Ever since, in times of trouble, Rogers had been a man Nixon turned to, and Rogers had always given him his honest and considered opinion. Lately, the two men had been less close. The President had wanted him to take over the Department of Justice after Watergate threatened to run out of control; when Rogers refused that job, he asked him to come into the White House to manage the crisis. Rogers had declined that job, too. His refusal to serve may have been the greatest single lost opportunity of the crisis for Nixon. It is very difficult, for example, to imagine Rogers appointing Archibald Cox, or anyone resembling him, as special prosecutor. Rogers wondered aloud whether the President's decision had anything to do with his refusal to be Attorney General. I told him I didn't think so.

"Bill, we can't go on this way with this split and rivalry between you and Henry. It's dangerous for the country and debilitating to our foreign policy."

"Al, I have to talk to the President about this."

"Of course you do, Bill. But you'd better know that he ordered this and he means it."

When I reported this confrontation to Nixon, he said, "Were you brutal?"

I said, "Yes. [But] I think he hopes to talk you out of it. . . . He . . . said you must be upset because he wouldn't take the Attorney General's job."

"Oh, hell," Nixon said. "He told me not to go into Cambodia and not to go to China."

Thinking to reawaken the President's affection for his old friend, which was never far below the surface, I remarked, "He's a tough SOB."

"Yes," Nixon said. "And that's why it would have been helpful if he had taken this job [Attorney General] when we asked him."

On the morning of Wednesday, August 15, I told the President, on the basis of what Richardson had told me, that Henry Petersen's examination of the evidence had convinced him of Agnew's guilt. Petersen would deliver his report on Friday. Nixon said he wanted it on Thursday morning because he was planning to go to Key Biscayne. That was his only reaction; my report just confirmed what he had been warned to expect, and short of granting Agnew a pardon—an option that was never considered or discussed—there was nothing he could do to influence the situation. He had been reluctant earlier to invest what was left of his own credibility in the lost cause of Agnew's defense. Now he was determined not to get personally involved.

Nixon wanted Buzhardt to read the handwriting on the wall to the Vice President. On September 6, he told me, "I want Agnew to know, without Buzhardt telling him I know, what a very strong case there is, so that my rather limited support will be understood. . . . [Agnew] has not told me everything he should. . . . He has never once mentioned what I mentioned to Eisenhower, that I would get off [the ticket in 1952] if [Eisenhower requested that]. . . ."

I said, "He has said, 'I am fighting for my life.' "

"He has never said," Nixon replied, " 'I want to do what's best for the country.' "

It was certainly true that Agnew felt gravely threatened. He had begun to fear that he might end up in prison. That was certainly among the possibilities if the process was prolonged. His suspicions about Richardson darkened as the Justice Department fell into a silence concerning the case. Agnew complained that no one would talk to him. Richardson assured me that he was simply assembling the facts, but this explanation did not satisfy Agnew. "This is the most bizarre thing I've ever seen," he had told me on September 5. "All we have is what we see in the newspapers. Why can't we be leveled with?" I told him that Fred Buzhardt was meeting with Richardson that very afternoon. "I should know what his timing is," Agnew said. "All I know is we got kicked in the ass. . . ."

Around this time, for reasons I do not understand because the strategy was just the opposite, Agnew developed the belief that Richardson was going to refer his case to the House of Representatives for possible impeachment. He wanted to preempt the Attorney General by asking Congress to decide his case, and he asked whether the President would support him in this maneuver by writing a letter to the House of Representatives. This bit of bravado agitated Nixon but produced no result—at least for the moment. The President, frustrated by Agnew's refusal to resolve the situation by resigning, asked me to call John Connally and tell him that he still regarded him as the next Vice President of the United States, and as his own successor in due course. "The President just wanted to be sure," I told him, "that you just held tight . . . to reassure you that everything is precisely the same in his view." Connally, ever coolheaded, responded, "Okay, Al. I'll be talking to you."

Battered as he was by Watergate, by the Agnew situation, by every sort of public attack on his character and integrity and the policies of his administration, Nixon managed to gain seven points in public approval in the mid-August Gallup poll (up from 31 percent August 3 to 6 to 38 percent). *

"That's a good pop when your figure goes up seven points from thirty-one," an encouraged Nixon said. "It's far better than moving from sixty to sixty-eight percent."

The more negative side of the poll showed that 58 percent of the respondents were dissatisfied with the explanation of Watergate the President had given in a major speech on August 15. A Harris poll reported that 71 percent believed that Nixon had withheld "important information" about Watergate.[10]

On August 20, Nixon was scheduled to address a convention of the Veterans of Foreign Wars in New Orleans. The Secret Service reported the existence of a plot against the President's life. Nixon dismissed the

---

* By way of comparison, President Bush's positive rating in mid-March 1992 was also 38 percent.

threat and stubbornly refused to take any other precautions even after the existence of the plot was leaked to the news media. The Secret Service, deeply concerned, continued to urge preventive measures. Finally, he agreed to a change in the route of the motorcade. "But that's it, Al! You tell them that!" When, in New Orleans, I offered him a bulletproof garment provided by the Secret Service, he exploded. "Al, get that damned thing away from me!" His fury seemed to be directed not toward any would-be assassin but toward a homelier tormentor, the press corps, whose members he suspected of jockeying for the best view of any attempt on his life. Moments later, as he was entering the convention hall trailed by Ron Ziegler and the usual gaggle of reporters, Nixon suddenly turned in anger, giving poor Ziegler a mighty shove and crying out in a loud and furious tone, "I don't want any press with me and you take care of it!" The episode provided a memorable moment on the evening television news and almost completely overshadowed the cursory coverage of Nixon's speech on his Cambodia policy.[11]

During the second week of September, Richardson told me that the prosecutors in Baltimore believed that they could prove that Agnew had received $172,000 in improper payments with his own hands. The Attorney General agreed that the prosecution's case was absolutely solid and that if it came to trial, Agnew would almost certainly be convicted and would probably be sentenced to a prison term and a large fine. Agnew, who seemed to have a sixth sense in regard to such shifts in the wind, called me moments after I had finished listening to Richardson. I told him the substance of our conversation and informed him that the decision on whether to present the case to the grand jury might be taken within the week. "That's awful quick," said Agnew worriedly.

After many exhaustive discussions of the matter with Richardson and a series of sharper exchanges with the President, I told Agnew what was happening and warned him that the President would expect him to resign for the good of the country if the grand jury returned an indictment. This statement shattered his composure. "Resign?" Agnew said, with what seemed to be genuine astonishment. "Don't I get a presumption of innocence? I didn't suggest *he* ought to resign over Watergate. I want to see the President and I want to see him now!"

I arranged an appointment. At this somber meeting, Agnew told Nixon that he would be willing to plead no contest to a tax misdemeanor and resign but would never go voluntarily if he was prosecuted on a charge of bribery or extortion.[12] Although Nixon did not mention this conversation to me, it is clear in retrospect that it provided the basis on which the case was eventually settled, and Agnew's lawyers began negotiating with the Justice Department.

On September 13, Richardson authorized George Beall to present evidence to the federal grand jury in Baltimore when it reconvened two weeks hence. I reported to Nixon that the Justice Department had delivered a proposal for a plea bargain to Agnew's lawyers. Buzhardt thought that this document might provide the basis for a breakthrough. Nixon said, "If that doesn't satisfy him, I may have to play tough." His impatience grew stronger. "I'm ready to move in tonight, I'm ready to strong-arm," he told me a week later. I did not take these words at face value; it was just Nixon's way of telling me to put the pressure on. He had wanted the situation resolved by now; he wanted to nominate John Connally for Vice President and overwhelm the bad press Agnew's situation had generated with a burst of media coverage and commentary about Connally. Above all, he wanted to put the danger of double impeachment behind him.

The *Washington Post* reported that a plea bargain was in progress in the Agnew case, and CBS News said that Henry Petersen had remarked to other Justice Department lawyers, "We've got the evidence. We've got it cold."[13] Agnew was convinced that these stories were leaked from the Justice Department in a deliberate attempt to undermine his defense. The leaks, which might just as well have come from Agnew's office, produced the usual choleric reactions in Nixon, who had at least one suspect, an important member of Richardson's staff, in mind. (Earlier, he had instructed me to order Richardson to "give lie-detector tests to all the members of the staff who had access to the [leaked] information. . . . That order is to be carried out this afternoon. Either that or I will order in the FBI." Although I conveyed Nixon's mood to Richardson and to his deputy, William Ruckelshaus, no lie-detector tests were administered, nor was the FBI brought in to investigate the leaks. Probably Nixon never intended that they should be. A few weeks earlier, when he had instructed me to order polygraphs after the discovery of a different leak, I had demurred. A day or two later, he said, "About those polygraphs, Al. Whenever you're unsure of my statements, speak up. I want to know what you're thinking." Adding the look in his eyes and his body language to these words, I supposed that what he really meant was, "If you're not prepared to carry out a foolish order issued in the heat of the moment, just say so.")

Richardson's objectives, as he explained them to me on September 8, were "to precipitate [Agnew's] resignation, to avoid a move toward the House by the Vice President if this can be done, to obtain the relevant testimony under oath as rapidly as possible, to avoid proceeding in any manner that would cause severe criticism that it was inappropriate or unfair." Agnew's objectives were the opposite in every case.

On Tuesday, September 25, after telling Nixon what he intended to do, Agnew personally delivered a letter to Speaker Albert requesting that the House of Representatives decide his case.[14] Citing the precedent of Vice President John C. Calhoun, who was exonerated in 1827 by a House panel of charges that he had profited from War Department contracts, Agnew argued that the House alone was empowered to hear his case while he remained in office.*

That same day, Richardson issued a statement announcing that the plea-bargaining process had failed.[15] This meant that the case would go to the grand jury unless some new agreement could be reached in the next two days. Richardson's announcement gave Albert an out; after conferring overnight with House Democrats, he issued a statement that read in its entirety: "The Vice President's letter relates to matters before the courts. In view of that fact, I, as Speaker, will not take any action on the letter at this time."[16] The next day, a sympathetic but soberly realistic Gerald Ford told me when I turned to him for advice, "Under these circumstances, [Agnew] has no other alternative but to resign. . . . I am now convinced that he doesn't have a prayer."

Albert's rejection of Agnew's request for a trial by the House meant that the plea-bargaining route had to be reopened, a difficult undertaking inasmuch as Agnew was now convinced that Petersen, as well as Richardson, was out to get him. He had similar suspicions about me, and I asked Bryce Harlow to deal with the Vice President on a day-to-day basis in the hope of reducing the aggravation on all sides. At best, we were faced with further delays. The President asked me to call Connally and reassure him once again. "The results," I told him on September 25, "will not change our discussions in any way."

However, Speaker Albert's action, coupled with indications from

---

*He argued also that "the Constitution bars a criminal proceeding of any kind—federal or state, county or town—against a president or vice president while he holds office." The next day, at Nixon's request, the Justice Department delivered to him an opinion that a Vice President, though not a President, could in fact be indicted while still in office; ironically, this ruling laid the basis for the most damaging public action taken against Nixon, his designation by the Watergate grand jury the following year as an "unindicted co-conspirator in Watergate crimes." Calhoun, incidentally, was the only other Vice President to resign the office; he did so in 1832 to enter the Senate. (See Nixon, RN: The Memoirs of Richard Nixon, p. 917.)

House Democrats that they would accept a caretaker Vice President who was pledged not to run for President in 1976, demonstrated that the opposition was aware of the constitutional situation. If Agnew resigned, Carl Albert would be next in line of succession to the presidency after Richard Nixon; if Nixon went, Albert would be President. The Democrats had nothing to gain by bailing Agnew out. Once the vice presidency was vacant, the Democrats in Congress were in a position to keep it so, if they chose, because they were the majority in both Houses. Although I thought that Connally was the best candidate in every way, I felt in my bones that he would never be approved by the Congress because the Democrats believed he could defeat any candidate their own party might nominate in the next presidential election.

Agnew had been a formidable defender of his own person and interests up to this point. Now, he became ferocious. Speaking before a rally of Republican women in Los Angeles, he proclaimed his innocence again, suggested that he was the victim of character assassination, and cried, "Small and fearful men have been frightened into furnishing evidence against me—they have perjured themselves. . . . I will not resign if indicted! *I will not resign if indicted!*"[17] His lawyers filed suit in federal court in Baltimore to halt the grand-jury inquiry on grounds that it was unconstitutional to indict a serving Vice President, and that the Justice Department had conducted "a deliberate campaign" of news leaks "calculated and intended to deprive [Agnew] of his basic rights to due process and fair hearing."[18] In an unusual move, the court gave Agnew's lawyers subpoena powers to assist them in their efforts to discover the source of leaks in the Justice Department. My experience in such matters suggested that this was an empty gesture, but it bought time for Agnew and created further aggravation for the President.

In private, the Vice President was tough, cold, and aggressive in his demands. Agnew was a large, smooth, bullet-headed man, impeccably groomed and tailored in the Washington style, and when he turned off his considerable charm he was capable of conveying a somewhat menacing impression. The hard and cynical world of politics that had made him showed through. In this period, it was my duty to deliver many unwelcome messages to the Vice President while keeping him away from the President, who did not want to see him. Agnew's dislike for the messages I brought him turned into personal dislike for me. There was nothing I could do about this and still do what the President wanted me to do; Nixon had been telling me for a month to make sure that Agnew was "under no false illusions." I guess I succeeded. Agnew's displeasure with me became so palpable that I told Pat, only half in jest, that in case I disappeared she might want to look inside any recently poured concrete bridge pilings in Maryland.

Meanwhile, Agnew's lawyers and Richardson and Henry Petersen were attempting to move the case toward resolution. This was, as Richardson kept explaining, a delicate and difficult process. The elements of any arrangement acceptable to both sides included resignation and limited admission of wrongdoing in exchange for not going to jail. Many in the Justice Department, even elsewhere in the Executive Branch, thought that Agnew should go to prison. No one believed more deeply in retribution than Richardson. Truly loathing those who betrayed the public trust, he wrestled with this question almost to the point of spiritual exhaustion; he kept telling me how tired he was as a result of his attempts to find a just solution. "These are bad things [Agnew has done]," Richardson told me as late as October 8. "In the case of a governor, we would recommend jail." The metaphysical question was, How much more or less deserving of exemplary punishment was a Vice President?

My conversations with Richardson consumed hours and reinforced my earlier impression that the Attorney General's Calvinist conscience was the thing Agnew had most to fear. On October 9, Richardson phoned to say that he had decided that he could, in good law and conscience, recommend that Agnew not be sent to jail if he resigned and acknowledged the evidence against him.

I had never been so surprised in my life.

Agnew was not out of the woods yet. There was no guarantee, Richardson said, that the judge would go along. (All nine federal judges for Maryland, six Republicans and three Democrats, had disqualified themselves from the Agnew case. Federal Judge Walter E. Hoffman of Virginia was presiding.) Some of Richardson's assistants were not enthusiastic about letting Agnew escape serving a long sentence. "I must say it is kind of an uncomfortable position," Richardson told me. "I am in a lonely spot over here. . . . I am going to make clear to my own people that this is the result of my own prayerful consideration." His physical fatigue and the stress of the moral battle he had waged within himself were apparent. He was anxious that I understand, that everyone understand, that he had reached his decision through an independent process of thought and prayer, and that he had not been influenced by the President's wishes. "There is no question of that here," I reassured him, with more heartfelt sincerity than he knew. "There never has been."

Agnew resigned on October 10 and pleaded no contest to a single charge of income-tax evasion before Judge Hoffman in the federal court at Baltimore. In return, the government dropped all other charges against him and recommended leniency. Richardson, appearing personally on behalf of the United States, said that considering the "historic magnitude of the penalties inherent in the Vice President's resignation from his high office and his acceptance of a judgment of conviction of a felony," a prison sentence was more than he could "recommend or wish."[19] Hoffman reminded Agnew that his plea was "the full equivalent of a plea of guilty," then sentenced him to a fine of ten thousand dollars and three years' unsupervised probation.

Agnew's departure showed how right Nixon had been about the effect of his resignation. He was forgotten instantaneously by the public and the press, and I do not recall ever hearing his name mentioned in the White House again.

Nixon asked me to stand aside from the process of choosing a new Vice President. His reason astounded me. "I think you should be one of the candidates," he said. I did not believe for a moment that he really meant this, but I took no part in the extensive polling the President carried out in the next hours. He sent lists of candidates to Congress, to the Republican governors, to the Republican National Committee, to the Cabinet, to the White House staff, and to others.

The outcome was not encouraging for Nixon's own candidate, John Connally. Nixon's plans for him had been very closely held, and even after Agnew's resignation his name did not figure prominently in public speculation about a successor. However, his high regard for Connally was well known, and warning signals immediately went up in Congress. No one questioned that Connally had presidential stature. That was the problem. Democrats feared his appeal at the polls and resented his desertion of their party; Republicans regarded him as a renegade who would be taking the presidential nomination away from a regular Republican in 1976. There may have been some who believed that he could not be elected as a Republican, but none of them told me that.

Mike Mansfield, the Senate majority leader, told Nixon, "There is one fellow we're going to go over with a fine-tooth comb if his name is sent up." He did not say who the man was, but he could have meant no one but Connally, and his tone suggested that the nomination process could become a donnybrook. Issues existed on which Connally's approval could be delayed for months. Mansfield suggested that Nixon consider a caretaker, such as Senator John Sherman Cooper of Kentucky or Bill Rogers,[20] or even an elderly Democrat. Similar rumblings were being heard from the Republican left; the powerful Senator Percy, who had presidential ambitions of his own, was among the liberal Jeremiahs. Conversations with senators of both parties suggested that it was unlikely that Connally would be able to obtain the necessary majority of votes in the Senate.

On congressional ballots, the winner by a wide margin was Gerald Ford, the minority leader of the House of Representatives. Throughout the selection process, Nixon had based his considerations on two factors: the presidential stature of each candidate and his chances of being approved by Congress. It was obvious by midnight that only Ford possessed both qualifications.

As recently as September 21, Nixon had been determined to fight for Connally's appointment in the face of advice from Harlow and Ziegler that it would face strong opposition in Congress. "We've crossed this bridge," he told me. "We cannot back off. If John Connally is willing to go, we'll go. . . . What's the option—Ford? . . . I'm no damned healer. I want to be, but they won't let me."

I said, "We won't have peace."

"There are worse things than fighting a battle," Nixon replied. "So they turn [Connally] down. If they do, he'll be a national hero. . . . I can't give in."

But it was plain that there was no choice but to give in. On October 11, the morning after Agnew's resignation, I called Connally to deliver a double-edged message from Nixon. "You know," I told him, "that the fundamental consideration of the Boss is that you be the 1976 candidate for the party . . . secondly, that you be Vice President in [the interim]. That is his personal preference."

I mentioned that Nixon had met on the question of Agnew's successor with the Republican leaders of Congress the previous afternoon and had been in touch with many others on the Hill. Connally, who had his own sources of information, said, "I gather they are unenthusiastic about me or anyone else who would be a candidate [for President in 1976]."

"Because you are a winner," I replied.

In the next breath, I had to tell him that he might not be a winner in this particular situation, for reasons beyond his control.

"We are probably going to fire Cox within a week or ten days," I said. "There is a good chance that if your name goes forward Saturday that you will be held up in any event. There could be a merger for impeachment [of both the President and the Vice President]. That is the great danger."

Never before in history had a Vice President been appointed instead of being elected, much less elevated to office in circumstances that suggested that he might at any time succeed to the presidency. We needed a candidate for Vice President who could unquestionably be confirmed in the present circumstances by both Houses of Congress.

I then told Connally that Nixon had determined that the only candidate who fulfilled that requirement was the Republican leader of the House, Gerald R. Ford. "We know the House would run him right through and the Senate would not take him on," I said. "If [you should] lose in the Senate, the President feels [it] would be a disaster for you in '76."

Connally did not leap to agree with this opinion. He did not fear revelations, he said, because his life had been clean.* He told me he thought he would win the votes of all but three or four Republicans, as well as most of the conservative Democrats. He suggested that Ted Kennedy would vote for him. "I think they will try to destroy anyone except someone in their own ranks—Jerry Ford or [Senator] Hugh Scott [Republican of Pennsylvania]," he said.

Our polls of Congress indicated otherwise. I said, "The only viable one is Jerry Ford. He would be a good President."

Connally agreed on the second point. But he was willing to take his chances on the nomination process with all its dangers. He thought he could prevail, and by so doing give Nixon the Vice President he really wanted. It was better, he said, to lose by being strong than to win by compromising. He did not agree that defeat would hurt him as a candidate for election. "If they [reject me] on a partisan basis," he said, "I don't know of any better springboard that I could have."

His case was appealing but impractical, and I knew that the President would not be moved. That evening, Connally called back. I told him that on the basis of our soundings during the day, we believed that the situation had worsened in the Senate and that Democratic opposition to him was building in the House. He could not be approved.

"Al, I don't want to be a hostage," he said. "I don't care what they say they will do [on Capitol Hill] . . . the American people will win out. This decision should not be made on whether I can be confirmed. Because I think I will be confirmed. It may be a bloody battle. . . . If [the President] is not prepared to go all out, we ought not to start it. From the personal

---

*Connally was later indicted in the milk-fund scandal, but he engaged Edward Bennett Williams as his counsel and was acquitted of all charges. Ironically, his appointment as Vice President would almost certainly have created a new possibility of double impeachment.

standpoint, no problem. From the political standpoint, if it's going to be a problem for him, then we ought not to do it. . . . If he wants to appoint a Jerry Ford, I will be the first one to say I think it is a fine appointment."

The matter was decided overnight in further polls of the Hill and Republican governors that showed that Connally could not be confirmed in either House. Neither could any of the other possible candidates except Ford. Any hearings or debate over Connally's candidacy would probably destroy his viability as a presidential candidate in 1976. Nixon still spoke in terms of preserving Connally's candidacy and electing him as his heir. In his memoirs, Ford writes that he assured Nixon on the morning of October 12 that he would not seek the presidency in 1976, and that Nixon told him that his choice for the nomination was Connally.[21] I had no knowledge of this exchange, and labored under the impression even while I spoke to Connally that Ford would not mortgage his own future with such a promise.

To Connally I said, "He will go with Jerry Ford."

"Okay, fine, Al," came the stouthearted reply. "You tell him that's fine."

On the President's instructions, I called Ford and told him that the President would send his name to the Congress. He was the fourth person to know, after Nixon, Connally, and the supernumerary in the drama, myself, that he had been chosen for a role entirely new in American history.

With Premier Zhou Enlai, Peking, January 1972. At left, Haig's secretary, Mrs. Muriel Hartley; in second row, Zhou's interpreter, Nancy Tang, and a note taker.

Receiving presidential commission as Deputy Assistant to the President for National Security Affairs in June 1970. *Right,* Dr. Henry A. Kissinger; *foreground,* Fred Bergston of NSC staff. (*White House photo*)

A White House working dinner early in the Nixon administration.
Left to right: House minority leader Gerald R. Ford, Congressman Les Arends,
GOP national chairman George Bush, Counselor Bryce Harlow, Senator
Hugh Scott, President Nixon, Congressman John Rhodes, presidential assistant
William Timmons, Haig, Senator William Griffin. (*White House photo*)

In the Oval Office. (*White House photo*)

Promotion to major general,
January 4, 1973. *Left to right*,
in the Oval Office: Secretary
of the Army Robert Froelke,
Secretary of State William P.
Rogers, Secretary of Defense
Melvin Laird, Kissinger,
President Nixon, Haig, Army
chief of staff Gen. Creighton W.
Abrams, JCS Chairman Adm.
Thomas Moorer, and Brig. Gen.
Brent Scowcroft, military
aide to the President.
(*White House photo*)

Receiving the Distinguished Service Medal from President Nixon in the presence of Rogers, Kissinger, and Laird. (*White House photo*)

With President Nguyen Van Thieu of South Vietnam during the latter's final visit to Washington after the peace settlement, 1973.

Nixon and General Secretary Brezhnev of the U.S.S.R. chatting aboard Brezhnev's yacht in the Black Sea, July 1974. (*White House photo*)

With Nixon just before his resignation.
(*White House photo*)

With his assistant
Maj. George Joulwan, 1974
(*White House photo*)

With President Ford soon after he assumed office. (*White House photo*)

29

A Question of Innocence

At 5:30 A.M. on Thursday, July 12, 1973, President Nixon awoke with a pain in his chest. Although he later described this pain as "stabbing" and "nearly unbearable," he did not summon help immediately. Two White House physicians examined him early in the working day. One doctor thought the President had an intestinal infection; the other said he had pneumonia.[1]

I learned that the President wasn't feeling well after I came to work around eight o'clock. An hour or so later, Nixon summoned me to his bedroom, as he sometimes did when he had early-morning business to conduct. He was, as usual, shaved and combed, but he was still in bed. I had never before seen the President recumbent; normally he was up and about, wearing his dressing gown, during conferences of this kind. He looked very unwell: His skin was pasty, his eyes bloodshot and feverish, his voice weak, his breathing shallow. He coughed spasmodically, and the pain this caused him showed in his face.

He made no reference to his condition but immediately began talking about a leak by the Senate Watergate committee. The morning news reports had quoted from a letter from Senator Ervin to himself. Ervin's letter was in response to a July 6 letter from Nixon turning down Ervin's request that he testify before the Senate Select Committee on Watergate and to furnish it with presidential papers "relevant to any matters the

371

committee is authorized to investigate." Ervin had replied that Nixon's refusal "presented the very grave possibility of a fundamental constitutional confrontation."[2] Nixon was as much exercised by the leak, which meant that the whole world had read Ervin's letter before it was delivered to the President, as by Ervin's grandiose choice of words.

After a moment, he ran out of breath and was seized by a fit of coughing. He sat up in bed, clutching his chest, and I noticed that his pillowcase was spotted with blood.

This was alarming evidence that Nixon's condition was more serious than had been reported to me. I went back downstairs and made inquiries. The President's temperature was 102 degrees Fahrenheit. Diagnostic tests, including X rays, had been ordered. A rapid and correct diagnosis was imperative. Someone mentioned that the fatality rate for untreated pneumonia was 30 percent. There was little question in my mind, and probably none in Nixon's, that news of a presidential illness would be received with skepticism by much of the press. Nixon was sure to resist any course of action, including hospitalization, that might draw attention to his condition and subject him to yet another public indignity. I alerted Ron Ziegler to the situation and began to rehearse arguments that might persuade Nixon to enter the hospital for treatment if the doctors decided that was necessary.

Later in the morning, Senator Ervin telephoned. The President took this call in his bedroom in the presence of Ziegler and myself. Ervin took the position that executive privilege did not cover criminal or political acts. This language was a calculated insult to Nixon and to the presidency, and Nixon took a tough line, taunting Ervin on the leaks from his committee, refusing the committee staff access to White House files. "There's no question whom you're out to get," he said hotly. Ervin replied in his best country-lawyer manner that he and his committee were not out to get anything but the truth. Nixon laughed derisively. I had never seen him so confrontational. He seemed to surprise even himself. "It must be my fever," he said to Ziegler and me after he hung up. Nixon's exact words to Ervin appeared in the *New York Times* shortly thereafter.

The joust with Ervin seemed to rejuvenate Nixon. He rose from bed around noon, got dressed, and announced that he would carry on as usual with his schedule of appointments. In fact, he spent half an hour with Walter Scheel, the West German foreign minister, took some phone calls, and kept a couple of other appointments.

Nevertheless it was increasingly evident that he was a sick man. By early afternoon, chest X rays and other tests confirmed that he had viral pneumonia. At first, he insisted that he could tough it out at home, but that evening he reluctantly consented to enter Bethesda Naval Hospital for treatment.

Over the weekend, Nixon continued to work the telephones from his hospital room, and I visited him on Friday the thirteenth to discuss routine business. Although he was unable to sleep because of the chest pains associated with pneumonia—"It's like broken ribs, Al"—and he showed no interest in eating, his condition improved steadily under treatment with antibiotics. By Sunday night, when I called to inquire about his progress, his temperature had dropped below 100 degrees for the first time since the onset of his illness.

On Monday, July 16, I drove to Bethesda and spent some time with the President. On my return to the White House in the early afternoon, my assistant, George Joulwan, greeted me with the news that Alexander P. Butterfield, a retired Air Force officer and former assistant to Haldeman, had revealed the existence of a White House taping system in testimony before the Ervin committee. According to Butterfield, all of the President's conversations in the Oval Office and his EOB hideaway, including his telephone conversations, had been recorded by an automatic, voice-activated system installed in the summer of 1970 (actually 1971). The President's telephone in the Aspen Cabin at Camp David was also equipped with an automatic recording device. The Cabinet Room was covered by a manual system that could be switched on and off by using the buttons on the telephone.[3]

This was the first I had heard of the existence of an eavesdropping system that recorded every word uttered in the presence of Nixon, and it came as a total surprise to me. In his memoirs, Nixon writes that I phoned him on the morning of July 16 and forewarned him of the nature of Butterfield's testimony. Perhaps someone else knew what was coming and alerted the President, but I had no foreknowledge of Butterfield's appearance, let alone of the nature of his testimony, and I made no such call.

Of course I knew as a result of my conversation about Dean with Nixon on June 4 that some tapes existed, but I had assumed that Nixon's meetings with Dean had been taped as a precaution by some sort of recording system that could be switched on and off. A long time before, I had heard in-house gossip to the effect that Nixon had ordered the removal of the recording system installed in the Oval Office by President Johnson. I knew that every President since the invention of the microphone and recording apparatus had used the available technology to preserve important conversations, and I had always assumed that Nixon must have some means of taping visitors. It never occurred to me that anyone in his right mind would install anything so Orwellian as a system that never shut off, that preserved every word, every joke, every curse, every tantrum, every flight of presidential paranoia, every bit of flattery and bad advice and tattling by his advisers.

Butterfield's testimony had been recorded on videotape by White House technicians. I watched the entire segment on the television set in my office. Near the end, Fred D. Thompson, the minority counsel of the committee, and Butterfield engaged in the following exchange:

> THOMPSON: . . . From 1970 then until the present time all of the President's conversations in the offices mentioned . . . were recorded as far as you know?
> BUTTERFIELD: That is correct. . . .
> THOMPSON: And as far as you know, those tapes are still available?
> BUTTERFIELD: As far as I know. . . .[4]

The twofold import of this exchange was immediately obvious. First, the means existed to establish the guilt or innocence of the President with regard to the Watergate cover-up. Second, his guilt or innocence had ceased to matter, because no President could survive the verbatim publication of his most intimate conversations, any more than a family could expect its reputation to be the same if everything discussed in the privacy of the home, where special assumptions based on trust and deep acquaintance apply, were to be published in the local newspaper. Ordinary human considerations would not apply in Nixon's case. Those who had argued during the recent antiwar hysteria that the state had no right to defend itself against the righteous mob would now maintain that the President had no right of privacy. The objective of the opposition from the moment the existence of the tapes became public knowledge would be to obtain them and make their contents public as a means of humiliating Nixon.

According to Butterfield's testimony, the system had been installed by the Secret Service, which acted as custodian of the tapes. Immediately after watching the videotape of Butterfield's testimony, I called in my deputy, Maj. Gen. John Bennett (USA, Retired) and issued an order: "Tear it out. Now. Make sure it's done."

I also gave orders that the tapes were to be kept in secure storage and that no one was to have access to them without presidential authority. That evening, Bennett reported that the system had been removed and that the tapes had been placed in a safe inside a locked room in the Executive Office Building. The locked room itself was inside a secure area that was guarded by White House police and could be entered only by special permission. Bennett handed me a sealed envelope that he said contained the keys to the room and the combination of the safe, and I immediately placed the envelope, unopened, in my own safe.[5] At this time, I formally placed Bennett in charge of the safekeeping of the tapes; no one except an agent of the President specifically authorized by Bennett to do so could enter the room where the tapes were kept. I myself never entered this room.

I did not discuss these actions with the President beforehand, and he never questioned them afterward.

The issues raised by Butterfield's testimony were too sensitive to discuss over the telephone, so I went back to Bethesda by car and informed the President what had happened and what I had done about it so far. I asked whether he had any orders. Nixon was not in a talkative mood. Above all things, he hated to be made to appear foolish, and he knew that the first consequence of Butterfield's revelation had been to make him a laughingstock. All over the country, his supporters and his enemies were asking the same question: How could he, of all people, have been so dumb as to install such a system? The same question was in my own mind, but I did not ask it.

"Mr. President," I said, "it seems to me that you have two options. You can either keep the tapes or you can destroy them."

"What do you think would happen in each case?" he asked.

"If you keep the tapes and refuse to make them public, you'll spend the remainder of your presidency beating off the prosecutors, the Congress, and the news media. In the end, you may very well have to give them up."

"And if I destroy them?"

"You will be violently attacked. Some will describe it as an admission of guilt. Others will admire your common sense. You will take a tremendous amount of heat, but, whatever happens, it will be over fairly quickly. The process of disclosure will last forever. It will reach into history."

We continued to talk for several minutes along these lines without approaching a decision.

"Mr. President," I said, "I've been in a good many meetings with you, and we both know how the conversation goes. You set up straw men; you play devil's advocate; you say things you don't mean. Others do the same. There is gossip and profanity. Imagine publishing every word Lyndon Johnson ever said in the Oval Office. No President could survive that."

Nixon nodded thoughtfully. It seemed to me that he was leaning toward destroying the tapes. The awful thought occurred to me that he might even order me to return to the White House and burn the tapes myself. I knew that I could not do this; I would resign first. The tapes were not my property or my responsibility. Only the President could destroy them or order them destroyed by someone who was completely outside his inner circle, such as a member of the Secret Service. What would I reply if he gave me such an order now?

Possibly these contradictory feelings showed on my face. In any event, Nixon put an end to the discussion.

"Al, you're not a lawyer," he said. "This is a legal question. Go back and talk to the lawyers, then bring me their recommendations."

I replied, "All right, sir. But this is not a matter we can let float. There's not much time. Whatever you're going to do, you'll have to do as quickly as possible. Tonight."

He nodded impatiently, not in assent but as a sign that he had heard me and understood the point I was making.

Back at the White House, I asked Buzhardt and Len Garment, the Counsel to the President, to come to my office. I did not expect them to have the same ideas about resolving this question; they seldom gave the same advice. Both brilliant, they were a study in contrasts—Buzhardt, the South Carolinian, was practical, apolitical, down-to-earth, possessed of the judicial temperament; Garment, the New Yorker, was excitable, quixotic, voluble, a Democrat at heart, and ruled by the liberal's preference for the general principle over the particular case.

Buzhardt began by offering me the advice that guided me through the controversy that would surround the issue of the presidential tapes from that day onward. "Al, these tapes can lead to the vindication or the downfall of the President," he said. "You'll have to deal with the issue because that's your job. But I have this to say to you: Serve the President in every proper way. But never, *never* touch one of these tapes, never listen to one of these tapes, and never let yourself be alone in the same room with one of these tapes." In the tumultuous days to come, I followed this wise and far-seeing counsel to the letter.

I asked Buzhardt and Garment about the legal status of the tapes. What were the national-security considerations? Every conversation with a foreign head of state was on the tapes, every decision affecting our policy toward the Soviet Union was on the tapes, and every important military and diplomatic secret had been recorded. Everyone except Nixon and Haldeman, who had arranged for the installation of the system, had been unaware that his words were being recorded. It was a piquant, though unmentioned, fact that this included the three of us. Whose property were the tapes? Were they covered, like presidential papers and conversations, by the doctrine of executive privilege? Were they protected by Nixon's constitutional right to privacy as an individual? For months, the President had been besieged by Cox, by Congress, and by the courts for access to his confidential papers. His claims of executive privilege had been challenged on every side, and he himself had made exceptions in dozens of cases in efforts to cooperate with Congress and the special prosecutor. His adversaries had many times asserted a desire to be given free access to all presidential files. The telephone conversation with Senator Ervin, who in effect had wanted his staffers to be given the freedom of the President's files just to see what they could find, was only the latest example of the inquisitorial atmosphere that enveloped the White House.

The answers from Buzhardt and Garment were completely in character, and they were diametrically opposed. Of course, both men had been thinking and reading law ever since Butterfield stepped in front of the cameras that day.

Without hesitation, Buzhardt said, "Al, the tapes are the President's property. Preserving them would create insuperable legal problems for him and for the Office of the Presidency. I think he should destroy them without delay. But he has to decide whether to do this himself. No one can decide this question for him. Especially not you."

"Destroy them?" Garment said. "No! Those tapes are evidence. If the President were to decide to destroy them—and I agree that no one else could make that decision—I would have to resign and go public with all that I knew about it."

Garment's words angered me, possibly because I had anticipated them. "Len, I am not going to deliver that message to the President," I said. "You're going to have to tell him yourself."

Once again I called for a car. All three of us got in. The drive to Bethesda from downtown Washington takes forty-five minutes or more, depending on the traffic. It was now evening and the streets were relatively clear. We made the trip in virtual silence, arriving at the hospital as darkness was falling. The President was up and about, wearing his dressing gown. Only one small light was burning in the cramped sitting room of his suite.

The four of us sat down around a small table. I had told Nixon over the telephone what we wanted to discuss but not what his lawyers thought. Nixon looked into the solemn faces across the table and called for opinions. Buzhardt spoke first.

"Mr. President, these are your tapes to do with as you wish *until they are subpoenaed*," Fred said. "You will have to make the decision. But I am very concerned."

About what? Nixon wanted to know. Neither Buzhardt nor I nor anyone else had ever suggested that there was the slightest question about the President's innocence of wrongdoing. It would have been impossible to express such doubts, even if one entertained them, and go on working for him.

"I'm not referring to evidentiary questions," Buzhardt said. "I'm just very concerned that your offhand remarks, and those of others, will be misunderstood and misconstrued, and that they will be very damaging if exposed in raw form to the world."

"So what are you advising?"

"Destroy the tapes," Buzhardt said.

Garment seemed even more deeply disturbed by this suggestion than before. His response was to warn his client rather than to advise him. "Mr. President, that would be an intolerable act," he said. "If you were to do such a thing, I must tell you that I would feel obliged to resign in protest and publicly explain the reasons for my resignation."

Garment's words and, perhaps more than that, the air of self-congratulation with which they were tinged ignited Nixon's temper. He heard enough moralizing from his enemies and from the news media without listening to it from his own lawyer. "That's enough!" the President said. "Get out of here, both of you! Al, you stay."

Nixon had a habit of striding about the room as he talked. Now, he paced from one end of the dimly lighted cubicle to the other as we discussed the pros and cons of the situation. Finally, he asked me for an opinion.

"Mr. President," I said, "Fred is right. The tapes are your property to do with as you wish."

Nixon has written that I said it would make him look guilty to destroy the tapes. I did say that, because I believed that this would be one consequence of destroying the tapes. But that was not the issue. The tapes might or might not hold evidence of his guilt on Watergate. But if they were revealed, they would certainly expose him to potentially disastrous ridicule, humiliation, or further scandal—not to speak of damage to American interests abroad. This illustrates the point I was attempting to make to him about the difficulties of translating the shorthand of intimate speech into a text that accurately describes real meaning, because, in fact, I believed that his only recourse was to destroy the tapes at once.

"Al, you're not a lawyer," Nixon said again.

"True, Mr. President. But I shudder to think what the Hill and the press would do with some of the things that have been said in the privacy of the Oval Office—things that you did not really mean, things you said when you were playing devil's advocate."

Nixon interrupted me with a wave of the hand. "I'll have to sleep on this," he said.

"There's very little time, Mr. President. The tapes will be subpoenaed."

Before I left, he signed a letter I had brought with me directing that no member of the Secret Service should testify before congressional committees "concerning matters observed or learned [as a result of] their duties at the White House."[6]

At eight o'clock the following morning, I went back to the hospital. By that time, Buzhardt had received a letter from Special Prosecutor Cox requesting access to tapes of eight separate conversations between Nixon and those of his aides who were thought to have been involved in the cover-up. It was evident that the President had not had much sleep; neither had I. I asked him what he had decided.

"Al, I've thought about this all night long," Nixon replied. "Maybe Alex Butterfield has done us a favor. These tapes will be exculpatory. I know I never said anything to anybody that could be interpreted as encouragement to cover things up. Just the opposite."

Nixon often surprised me. What I felt now went beyond surprise. "Mr. President, that's not the only issue. Remember what Fred told us last night. I think you should think very carefully about this decision."

He had a way of gazing away into the middle distance as if distracted by a thought when hearing advice he did not want to hear. That happened now. He lowered his voice. "Al, we know that Dean lied and the tapes proved that. We don't know what other lies may be told by people who are trying to save themselves. Who knows what Ehrlichman might say, or even Bob Haldeman. The tapes are my best insurance against perjury. I can't destroy them."

The tapes had already saved him once. He had made up his mind that

they could do so again. Looking into his eyes, which were filled with
hope and innocence, I knew he would probably not waver from this
decision even if it destroyed him. Even then, I myself feared that it would
destroy him. But Richard Nixon, because he thought that he was not
guilty, believed otherwise.

On July 17, the Ervin committee had voted unanimously to ask the
President to release the tape recording of all of his conversations relating
to Watergate.

I made one final effort to persuade him to change his mind. On the
pretext that it would demonstrate the continuity of government for the
Vice President to call on him, I persuaded him, with some difficulty, to
see Agnew, whom he was never anxious to receive. I did this because I
knew that Agnew was in favor of destroying the tapes. How much influence he would have in his present circumstances I did not know, but I
believed that Nixon respected his judgment in matters of this kind. Seated
side by side on the small sofa in Nixon's hospital room, the two men
chatted for a moment. Then Agnew gripped Nixon's pajama-clad thigh
and said in a loud, earnest whisper, "Boss, you gotta have a bonfire."
Nixon gazed at a picture on the wall and feigned temporary deafness.

On July 23, Nixon refused to surrender the tapes requested by the
Senate committee and the special prosecutor on grounds of executive
privilege and the separation of powers. In a letter to Ervin, he stated,
"The tapes are entirely consistent with what I know to be the truth and
what I have stated to be the truth . . . to open them at all would begin
an endless process of disclosure and explanation of private Presidential
records totally unrelated to Watergate and highly confidential in nature."[7]

That, of course, is precisely what those in pursuit of Nixon had in
mind, and on July 23 not only the Ervin Committee but also Archibald
Cox issued subpoenas demanding surrender of certain of the tapes. When
Nixon again refused, Cox asked Chief Judge John J. Sirica of the U.S.
District Court in Washington to order the President to "show cause
why there should not be full and prompt compliance" with the special
prosecutor's subpoena. After the twenty members of the Watergate grand
jury, who were present in court, unanimously approved his action, Judge
Sirica issued the order as Cox had requested, giving the President until
August 7 to reply.[8]

Everyone knew that this was only the beginning, that the issue would
have to be decided by the Supreme Court. "We'll win it," Nixon told
me. Fred Buzhardt thought that the decision could go either way. The
President had engaged one of the finest constitutional lawyers in the

country, Professor Charles Alan Wright of the University of Texas, to argue the case before the Supreme Court. He pointed out in a public statement that the fundamental issue was that of the separation of powers.

"Separation of powers from the beginning of history has not disabled a court from issuing orders to the Executive Branch," retorted that other professor of law, Archibald Cox. How right he was on this point the Nixon administration was about to learn.[9]

30

Blindman's Buff

Richard Nixon's belief that the tape recordings of his conversations with the Watergate conspirators would prove his own innocence invested the controversy over the release of the tapes with a deep irony. His objective from the moment the tapes were discovered was to make the relevant exculpatory passages known to the world, and it was the efforts of the special prosecutor and the Ervin committee to obtain the tapes through the courts that prevented him from doing so.

Although he had already voluntarily furnished a great deal of material to both, Nixon resisted Cox's subpoena and the much broader subpoena of the Ervin committee, which asked for all records of any kind pertaining to "alleged criminal acts relating to the Presidential election of 1972" by twenty-five named individuals, because both raised fundamental issues concerning the doctrines of executive privilege and the separation of powers. Even so, he was prepared to compromise. "Executive privilege is being invoked only with regard to documents and recordings that cannot be made public consistent with the confidentiality essential to the functioning of the Office of the President," he wrote to Ervin on July 25. He said that he remained willing to furnish documents "that can properly be made public" in response to specific requests. [1]

It was fashionable at the time to argue that the President seized on the issue of executive privilege after the tapes were discovered and subpoenaed

382

as a means of suppressing evidence against himself under cover of the Constitution. As one who observed at close hand the process that led to his decision, I can only say that it was my conviction that he believed that he owed it to all future Presidents to preserve the confidentiality of presidential communications. "A President's advisers and his foreign visitors have got to be able to speak their minds with confidence that every damn fool memo they write isn't going to turn up in the newspapers," he told me. "Otherwise he'll never get the advice he needs."

It was also said of Nixon that he fired Archibald Cox because the special prosecutor was getting too close to the truth. In reality, he thought that the subpoenas filed by the Ervin committee and Cox were open admissions that months of unrestrained investigation of every corner of his life had produced no evidence of criminal conduct on his part. The subpoenas, as Nixon himself put it, were nothing more than last-ditch applications for a fishing license to troll through the White House files at leisure in the mere hope that something incriminating would somehow be hauled to the surface.

In fact, Cox subpoenaed the wrong tapes; none of the eight recordings demanded by him on July 23 contained any information that suggested, much less established, criminal conduct on the part of the President. Only a single tape, the one containing Nixon's conversation with Haldeman on June 23, 1973, contained any such evidence, and the fact that it existed was not known to anyone in the White House—including, in my opinion, the President himself.

Although Nixon was far less concerned than I was about the damaging effect that publication might have on public opinion, he understood that verbatim transcripts of conversations which ranged from the cryptic to the hyperbolic to the profane might create problems of public perception. However, he searched continually for a method that would permit him to release summaries or extracts from the tapes that would lay to rest rampant speculation in the press that he was the real author of the Watergate burglary and cover-up.

"I could send a sworn statement to the committee and to Cox," Nixon told me on July 27, "[saying] . . . I hereby furnish you all relevant information. I cannot furnish [the remainder of the recorded material] because there are matters of national security on them." He instructed me to discuss this idea with the White House lawyers. Except for Buzhardt and the newly arrived Professor Charles Alan Wright, Nixon felt that his legal staff was not merely outnumbered but outclassed by the opposition.

"If only we had some bright people around!" he lamented. "We need some *minds.*"

Nixon's confidence that the tapes could contain no damaging surprises seemed to me, and to most others in his inner circle, a convincing demonstration of his faith in his own innocence. The trend of public opinion was not entirely against him. A Gallup poll published on June 17, after some of the most damaging testimony had been heard by the Ervin committee, showed that 31 percent of the sample of 1,546 Americans interviewed believed that Nixon had learned about the Watergate burglary after it had occurred and then had tried to cover it up.[2] In the second week of September, Gallup found that 33 percent held that same opinion.[3] The rise of 2 percent over a period of three months was considered statistically insignificant.

Nixon resisted the subpoenas for good legal and historical reasons, and he believed that most people understood this. The principle of executive privilege was embedded in American constitutional practice. No court in the history of the United States had ever enforced a subpoena against a President for his confidential papers. In a hearing before Judge Sirica on August 22, the President argued through his counsel, Charles Alan Wright, that the essence of executive privilege was that the President must "decide what can be given, when it can be given, and to whom it can be given."

Cox's position was that "any blanket claim of privilege to withhold this evidence from a grand jury is without legal foundation."

On July 24, Richardson read me the draft of a commentary he proposed to issue on the questions raised by Cox's action. In the first sentence, Richardson said, "The President's decision to protect the confidentiality of Presidential conversations rests, in my view, on substantial legal and Constitutional foundations . . . particularly . . . with reference to the Ervin Committee." But then he went on to say, "It is also my view that Mr. Cox, in seeking access to the tapes, is acting in full accord with the requirements of his job." The final sentence called for a compromise in the interest of justice that would result in making "material portions available."

I said, "I don't think that will be acceptable."

"Why so?" Richardson asked. "I think [Cox] is just doing his job."

"What you have said in your last sentence is that the President would make the material available, and there's no way he will do that. The President said he would not make any material available."

I could hear Richardson's pen scratching as he redrafted. After a moment he read me a new formulation: ". . . in the interest of justice, it seems to me important to try to work out some practical means of reconciling the competing public interests at stake."

I said that would be fine.

"Okay," Richardson replied. "I said I wasn't going to make a deal, but I'll accept that."

When I reported this result to Nixon, he glowered in displeasure. "Elliot's a good one to talk about making deals," he said.

In his argument before Sirica on August 22, Cox made it plain that the character of the President would be a factor in his strategy when he said, "Happily, ours is a system of government in which no man is above the law," adding that "there is strong reason to believe that the integrity of the Executive Office has been corrupted—although the extent of the rot is not yet clear."[4] In the end, this was the argument that defeated Nixon, because in his case criminality was assumed before it was proven, and this influenced the courts. On this occasion, the New York Times noted that "the judge questioned Mr. Wright for 17 minutes and Mr. Cox for only eight, with the queries addressed to the President's lawyer appearing somewhat sharper as well as longer."[5]

Cox's performance before Judge Sirica and the assembled press confirmed Nixon's long-standing suspicion that the special prosecutor's real purpose was not to search for the truth but to lay the basis for criminal charges against the President, drive him from office, and convict him in the courts. The day after the hearing, in San Clemente, he instructed me to call Richardson and let him know the trend of his thoughts. "He [the President] is talking about moving against Cox," I told the Attorney General. "If Cox has the idea that his role is to attack 'the abuse of power,' then that is unacceptable [and] regardless of the price to the President he is not going to tolerate it."

Richardson answered that Cox had concluded a recent chat with a New York Times columnist by "renouncing any personal antagonism toward the President [and] saying that no one would be more relieved than he if the tape recordings showed the President to be not guilty."

This may have been the case; I hoped so. Cox's language had deeply offended the President as an individual and as the custodian of his office. "He was talking about 'rot in the White House,' " I told Richardson, "but more important . . . Cox was speaking essentially against the President of the United States and he is . . . appointed by the President."

Our lawyers had come away from the hearing before Judge Sirica under the impression that he would rule against the President on the question of surrendering the tapes. On August 29, Judge Sirica, stating that "Executive fiat is not the mode" for resolution of disputes over questions of executive privilege, ordered the President to turn over to him nine tapes for judicial review. "The court is simply unable to decide [whether the tapes were exempted from the doctrine of executive privilege because they contained evidence of criminal acts] without inspecting the tapes."[6]

Cox's office expressed satisfaction with the ruling. Nixon's lawyers filed a petition for its reversal, naming Cox as an interested party. Sirica's order, they wrote, was "clearly erroneous and beyond the power of the judicial branch in that it purports to subject the President of the United States to compulsory process for acts performed in his official capacity."[7]

This courtroom drama was the culmination of the policy of confrontation with the President followed by Cox from the day of his appointment. Although he had never, so far as I knew, met the man, Nixon had always regarded him with deep misgivings. Despite the absence of a personal element, it was an ambiguous relationship. "Special Prosecutor Cox [was] not only the President's adversary," as Alexander M. Bickel later noted in a commentary on the case, "he [was] also the President's subordinate. . . . To the extent, therefore, that the President's adversary [was] Mr. Cox, the President [was] litigating with himself. He [was] suing himself and defending himself against himself. . . ."[8] This Kafkaesque situation might have been tolerable if the special prosecutor had been a Holmes or a Taft, possessed of the gift of neutrality, but, to Nixon, the appointee was the arch-liberal. It distressed Nixon—even disgusted him, I think—that the moral authority of the presidency should be personified by a man he regarded as a natural enemy.

Nixon also believed that Elliot Richardson had set up an irreconcilable conflict between his own loyalty to the President and his obligation to keep his word to the President's adversaries when he ransomed his own confirmation by the Senate Judiciary Committee to the promise that Cox would have complete prosecutorial independence. "Though the committee had no 'advise and consent' responsibility over the actual appointment of the special prosecutor," Richardson subsequently explained, "I offered to bring my nominee before it for questioning and to withdraw any name that the committee failed to approve."[9]

Richardson's promise also raised the issue of separation of powers. The Senate had a constitutional right and duty to confirm Richardson's appointment as Attorney General. But it had no right to dictate or even influence what appointments Richardson might make after he was confirmed. The power of presidential appointment, excepting those in which the Senate is directed by the Constitution to advise and consent, belongs exclusively to the President.

In allowing, indeed inviting, the Senate Judiciary Committee to mandate the appointment of Archibald Cox as special prosecutor, Richardson traded away a presidential prerogative that was not his to barter. Having given away a portion of the President's power, he could not get it back. And, as we will see, this extraconstitutional maneuver entrapped the President in a situation in which his appointee, Cox, was a creature of the Senate who argued that he could not be fired without the consent of the Senate. It was this artificial arrangement that led, in the end, to the fall of the injured party, the President of the United States.

Richardson's foolish gesture to the rancorous mood of Congress virtually guaranteed that Cox would turn into the inquisitorial culture hero he became. "I'll have the whip hand," he told the press after Richardson issued guidelines that precluded his removal except in case of "extraordinary improprieties" and gave him authority to continue his investigations "until such time as, *in his judgment* [emphasis added], he has completed them. . . ."[10]

Cox was the model of a liberal academic—tweedy, learned, avuncular, and a witty, brilliant defender of the political faith. Only two weeks before being appointed special prosecutor, he told the University of California's student newspaper that he "had such sharp 'philosophical and ideological' differences with the administration's Justice Department operation that he could not consider taking a job with the department."[11] Henry Kissinger, who had known Cox for many years as a colleague on the Harvard faculty, warned Nixon against him. "Cox will be a disaster," Kissinger said. "He has been fanatically anti-Nixon all the years I've known him."[12]

Others who knew Cox drew different conclusions from similar assessments. No other government appointment in my experience was greeted with a greater sense of triumph by the liberal coterie. Most Washington journalists were happy to grant the newcomer the respect and credibility that went with being Richard Nixon's nemesis. At last, the Left seemed to feel, one of their own was the prosecutor and Nixon was the suspect. As historian Henry Steele Commager of Amherst College would put it after Cox was fired, Nixon deserved impeachment "not merely for the most recent developments but for a long, unparalleled record of corruption and illegal actions."[13] "Sentence first—verdict afterwards," as the author of *Alice in Wonderland* put it.

After suggesting that the Ervin committee should suspend hearings and leave the investigative field entirely to him (the committee declined), Cox assembled a senior staff of which only one of ten members was a Republican and seven were former Kennedy and Johnson appointees. More than half of the supporting lawyers he hired were graduates of Harvard Law School, not usually regarded as a bastion of pro-Nixon sentiment. "As a generalization," another eminent historian wrote nearly two decades afterward, "it is fair to say that they may have assumed Nixon was guilty."[14]

From the vantage point of the White House, it certainly seemed that way. Richardson says he attempted to reassure the President otherwise at an early stage by telling him, "There is no 'they' out there—nobody trying to destroy you."[15] To cite one of Lord Acton's less familiar observations, "There is no error so monstrous that it fails to find defenders among the ablest men."[16] The suggestion that Nixon was a paranoic railing at imaginary enemies was, of course, the favorite diagnosis by liberals of presidential behavior throughout the Watergate controversy. The truth, as I perceived it from a position at the President's elbow, was that he was remarkably restrained in the face of the storm of hatred and accusation that engulfed him. He *was* encircled by enemies, and it would have been a sign of psychosis if he had not recognized this.

Shortly before Cox's appointment in May, Henry Petersen had testified that the Justice Department investigation of Watergate was 90 percent complete. The President expected that the probe could be wound up in a relatively short time. The Ervin committee would complete its hearings, the courts would try the defendants, and the President would move on to the real business of the nation.

However, on taking office, Cox expanded the investigation beyond the boundaries of Watergate. He seemed to regard the entirety of the President's life and the whole of the Executive Branch as his purview. Direct confrontation with the institution of the Presidency began at once. Less than a week after his appointment, the *Washington Post* quoted federal prosecutors as saying that Nixon's culpability was "the one key question" remaining in the grand jury's investigation of the Watergate case, and that there was "justification" for calling the President before the grand jury as a witness. This ignored all precedents; only one Chief Executive, Thomas Jefferson, had ever before been the subject of a subpoena (to testify at the treason trial of John Burr, in 1807; he did not appear but voluntarily provided a letter requested by Chief Justice John Marshall).[17] The leak to the press was, in itself, a breach of grand-jury secrecy that would have been regarded as shocking in almost any other circumstances, and the White House demanded an investigation of the leak by Richardson and Cox. This request was effectively ignored.[18]

In July, Nixon heard that Cox was investigating loans and other details having to do with the purchase of his houses in San Clemente and Key Biscayne. The President ordered me to order Richardson to order Cox to cease and desist. Cox replied through Richardson that he wasn't investigating Nixon's finances.[19] The investigation was taken up by others. Eventually, the President issued a statement listing the complete details of his real estate transactions, and his pursuers conceded after raising suspicions of fraud and tax evasion that he had done nothing illegal or improper in this regard.

Rumors swirled continually through the White House concerning Cox's inquiries. We heard reports that offers of immunity were being made in exchange for information that might incriminate the President. When details of the 1969 wiretapping of National Security Council staffers and journalists (see chapter 15) was leaked to the press just in time for Kissinger's confirmation hearing as Secretary of State, there were suspicions that the disclosure had come from Cox's people. So it was also with leaks having to do with an investigation of the President's brother, Donald, and many other anonymous disclosures to the press of matters under investigation. The fundamental problem lay in what the President, with excellent reason, perceived as Cox's presumptuousness. There was, as we have seen, anxiety that Cox would blunder into the Agnew investigation. Nixon was outraged at reports that Cox or his people were using the FBI to investigate the CIA. At one point, I was informed that Cox's lawyers were investigating J. Edgar Hoover's funeral; no one could explain why. In connection with these matters and others, I was continually in the position of demanding explanations from Richardson.

The deluge of leaks, in particular, maddened the President, who was, as the reader knows, fixated on such breaches of trust and protocol. He might insist in private, as in public, that he had nothing to fear from investigation, but he understood perfectly that the appearance of guilt created by the prairie fire of suspicion and accusation in the press was destroying his presidency, his personal reputation, and perhaps even his place in history. It used to be a truism that a President's otherwise-incomprehensible actions could be explained by the fact that he had more information on any given question than anyone else. Where Nixon was concerned, this was certainly not the case in matters having to do with his own person and fate. The relationship between Cox and the White House resembled some cosmic game of blindman's buff, with the President wearing the blindfold and the nimble Cox dancing near, then evading his grasp. Isolated from reliable sources of information about the intentions of the investigators, alienated from a press that he regarded as the fifth column of a besieging force, quarantined by his own Department of Justice, Nixon felt nostalgia for the sober and dutiful Henry Petersen and wondered wistfully what the situation might be if the latter was Attorney General instead of Richardson. "Petersen would never tolerate what Cox is doing," he told me in mid-August. "Even though he is a Democrat."

Throughout the summer and early fall of 1973, the impression grew that the investigation was drawing inexorably closer to Nixon. Various federal prosecutors, including Cox's staff and the Ervin committee staff, as well as the news media were looking into the President's personal finances, his income taxes, including the propriety of a deduction he had taken in 1968 in connection with the donation of his prepresidential papers to the National Archives, an allegation of improper influence on behalf of the ITT Corporation in an antitrust matter, the Vesco case, the cost to the taxpayers of installing security equipment such as bulletproof glass in his houses in Florida and California, a $100,000 cash campaign contribution from Howard Hughes that had been held for a while by the President's friend Bebe Rebozo and then returned to Hughes, and an allegation by consumer advocate Ralph Nader that the White House had reversed a decision by the Secretary of Agriculture not to raise milk-price supports after the milk industry promised large contributions to Nixon's reelection campaign.[20] These and other probes made their splash in the press but produced nothing whatever in the way of proof of presidential wrongdoing, despite heavy expenditure of taxpayers' money in investigative costs.

There was little disposition even in Nixon's own party on Capitol Hill to give him the benefit of the doubt. "What did the President know, and when did he know it?" asked Senator Baker repeatedly, in the catchiest phrase produced by the hearings.

The ripple effect in the news media of all these events was time-consuming; I spent hours answering inquiries from reporters checking out improbable leads.

We heard insistent reports that the special prosecutor's people and the staff of the Ervin committee were collaborating in their investigations, and that both were cooperating with sympathetic journalists who had become virtual partners in what many of them regarded as a righteous cause. Woodward and Bernstein, for example, were taken to the mountaintop by no less a personage than Senator Ervin, who invited them to share information even before his committee began its hearings on May 17. They cooperated: "the enormity of what the President's men had done seemed staggering." The pair drew the line at identifying sources, but they suggested lines of inquiry and the name of at least one potential witness, "not necessarily a source." In return, they received Ervin's permission to write that he planned to subpoena some of the President's top aides and challenge the claim of executive privilege—so long as they didn't quote Ervin directly. "By May 17, 1973, when the Senate hearings opened, Bernstein and Woodward had gotten lazy," they wrote of themselves. ". . . They had begun to rely on a relatively easy access to the Senate committee's staff investigators and attorneys." (But the debt was handsomely repaid when Woodward, acting apparently on instinct rather than any hard information, induced the committee staff to interview Alexander Butterfield.)[21]

Charles G. "Bebe" Rebozo, a likable, good-hearted, and honest man who became a target of investigators primarily because he was Nixon's friend, was nearly destroyed by the symbiosis between prosecutors and press. Despite severe pressures on his reputation and livelihood and the brutal invasion of his privacy, he never wavered in his loyalty and affection for Nixon. On the first of August, a team of government lawyers descended on him and his bank in Key Biscayne in a search of evidence concerning what the Associated Press called "huge sums in illegal campaign contributions [that] were 'laundered' through gambling casinos in the Bahamas with the cash routed through Miami."[22]

At first, Rebozo was not even sure who was investigating him. "These guys are all working together," he told me on August 2. "When they first arrived, they told me they were Cox committee lawyers. Later [they] said they were from the Ervin committee. They're all working hand in glove. This guy Cox is something else. . . . There's no such thing as laundered money here."

Nor was any corroborating evidence of this or any other unlawful act by Rebozo or his bank ever found, despite the subpoena of the records of every financial institution and business he had dealt with since 1968.[23]

On Friday, October 12, the U.S. Court of Appeals ruled 5 to 2 against the President in the tapes case, directing him to hand over nine recordings for examination in camera by Judge Sirica. Nixon now had one week in which to appeal to the Supreme Court or arrange a compromise that would satisfy public opinion without disabling the doctrine of executive privilege. This provided him with an opportunity to release the conversations bearing on Watergate in the form of summaries that would make public the essential information without breaching the principle of confidentiality. The facts, as he had always hoped and believed, would disarm his enemies.

The problem was verification; Nixon's credibility had been so severely wounded that he himself could not hope to be believed if he vouched for the accuracy of the material. Unless that which was released was accepted as genuine and complete, disclosure would create more problems than it solved.

It was the unfailingly resourceful Fred Buzhardt who suggested that the White House prepare third-person summaries of all passages relevant to Watergate issues and arrange for them to be certified as accurate by a third party who would verify them by listening to the tapes.

"Whom do you have in mind?" I asked.

Fred's eyes twinkled as he replied, "John Stennis."

Senator John C. Stennis, Democrat of Mississippi, was chairman of the Senate Select Committee on Standards and Conduct, a former judge, a conservative, and a veteran of 26 years as a member of the Senate. There was no more highly respected figure in American political life.

Buzhardt and I discussed the Stennis compromise with the President on the afternoon of Thursday, October 11, the day after Agnew's resignation. He immediately recognized the utility of the Stennis compromise. He authorized Buzhardt and me to discuss it with Stennis and Richardson but instructed us to remember the priorities. "The first order of business is to fire Cox," he said. "Tell Elliot that and make sure he understands what we're going to do. I want to keep Richardson if we can. But if we can't, we'll get rid of [Cox] anyway." Nixon had always intended to rid himself of Cox as soon as Agnew went. "First Agnew, then we can move on the other," he told me again and again.

Over the months, Nixon had reinforced his deep conviction that Cox was a zealot who was out to get him and would stop at nothing in order to do so. The multiple affronts to himself he bore with fortitude, but he could not forgive the false suspicions cast on Bebe Rebozo and other friends, and the embarrassment of members of the presidential family. At length, he developed a state of mind that permitted him to say, "If it costs me the presidency, Cox is going to go."

Nixon had no intention of replacing Cox with another special prosecutor. He planned, instead, to return the Watergate investigation to the

Justice Department under the supervision of the man Cox had displaced, Henry Petersen.

Unfortunately, he did not realize that it was too late to slow the momentum created by Cox's prosecutorial fervor. From June to October, while the special prosecutor created an atmosphere of impending retribution around the presidency, we had concentrated on resolving the crisis of the vice presidency. In so doing, we lost any hope of seizing the initiative. Everyone had agreed that a first-things-first approach was the only one possible, but I now think that these lost months, in which our attention was diverted toward Agnew and away from the main question of Watergate, marked the period in which Nixon's adversaries gained the upper hand.

It need not have been so. Nixon had wanted a quick resignation from Agnew but had been unable to bring himself to demand it. As in so many other cases involving his paralyzing diffidence, the power of the presidency proved insufficient to compel a simple and obvious result.

At 8:28 A.M. on October 12, I phoned Richardson and after an exchange of compliments over the outcome of the Agnew matter told him that the President wanted him to come to the White House at ten o'clock to meet with Buzhardt and me. I did not go into details. "We have another set of [legal] problems . . . of some magnitude," I told him.

In the ten o'clock meeting, attended also by Garment and Wright, Buzhardt laid out the scenario. The President was determined to fire Cox for cause, including his refusal to confine the Watergate investigation to relevant issues, his attempt to undermine the principle of executive privilege although a member of the Executive Branch, through leaks to the media, and undue delay in the investigation. Even if the President followed Buzhardt's plan, this would be done as soon as Stennis had agreed to listen to the tapes and verify the summaries, delivering these to Judge Sirica, who would decide in his wisdom to whom to give them—presumably the Justice Department and the Ervin committee. No more tapes would be released after this.

Previous accounts of Cox's dismissal are based on the premise that Richardson was adamantly opposed to firing him under any circumstances and from the first moment. That is not my recollection. Richardson listened to Buzhardt's plan without objection. Then, as I remember it, he volunteered a modification. Instead of firing Cox out of hand, he suggested, we should arrange things in such a way that Cox would, in effect, fire himself. Break the process down into two steps, said Richardson—first, put the Stennis compromise together and present it to Cox as an accomplished fact. This would put the ball in Cox's court; he could either accept the Stennis compromise and keep his job, or he could reject it, giving the President cause to fire him. If he accepted the compromise, he would be neutralized, at least in regard to the tapes issue. Richardson recommended that Wright, a fellow academic, should act as the White House's interlocutor with Cox.

Even at the time, there was some difference of recollection over the authorship of the plan. A couple of those who attended the meeting believed that I offered this idea and Richardson enthusiastically accepted it. Two others remembered it in the opposite sense. It makes little difference who conceived it. The vital point is that Richardson accepted the plan and promised to support it. After we adopted the plan, our entire approach to the termination of Cox's appointment was based on its two-step structure. In its absence, we would not have proceeded as we did; the President would have fired Cox out of hand, and we would have gone on from there on the basis of the Stennis compromise.

We immediately set about the task of putting the Stennis compromise together. Buzhardt telephoned the senator and told him what we had in mind. Stennis seemed receptive. On Sunday, October 14, Nixon invited him to worship services at the White House and discussed the idea with him afterward. Again Stennis responded in a positive way.

Where Cox was concerned, however, Nixon remained an activist. Earlier, he had ordered a letter to Richardson to be drafted, and he signed it on the fourteenth:

> Dear Elliot,
>
> Both you and the Department of Justice merit commendation for your performance in the difficult matters relating to the Vice President. The Department clearly demonstrated its capacity to administer justice fairly and impartially, under the most difficult and sensitive circumstances, without fear or favor, regardless of the individuals involved.
>
> Today, I have decided that all criminal matters now under investigation should be handled within the institutional framework of the Department of Justice.
>
> Accordingly, you are directed to relieve Special Prosecutor Archibald Cox of all responsibilities previously delegated to him by you, effective at 9:00 A.M. [Monday], October 15, 1973, and to assume within the Department of Justice all responsibilities previously exercised by him. Excepting only those career em-

ployees of the Department of Justice, who were detailed from their regular assignment to work with the Special Prosecutor, you should immediately relieve of all responsibility and, after the period necessary for a speedy and smooth transition, terminate from employment all other personnel of the Special Prosecutor's office.

The lapse of time during which the matters under the Special Prosecutor's jurisdiction have been pending has had an adverse impact upon the administration of justice; justice delayed can be justice denied. I, therefore, expect you to act expeditiously upon these matters.

This letter was never sent. Buzhardt and I, among others, felt that it was too confrontational, that the controversy that would be created by such an abrupt dismissal of Cox would not be manageable in the political sense. We persuaded a reluctant Nixon to delay the radical surgery he was so anxious to perform, and he approved the Stennis compromise in principle. As it turned out, this change in plans had fateful consequences.

Buzhardt and I went to Capitol Hill on Monday to discuss the matter in greater detail with Stennis. The senator told us that he regarded the President's request a patriotic duty, but he was concerned about his own health. So were we. On the previous January 30, Stennis, aged seventy-one, had been accosted by two armed robbers as he got out of his car in front of his Washington residence. They shot him repeatedly, then fled. Removal of the bullets from his leg and torso required six and a half hours of surgery. His recovery had been difficult, and he returned to his duties, to a standing ovation in the Senate chamber, on September 5, some seven months after the assault.[24] Stennis said he wanted to sleep on our proposal, and issued a stern warning about leaks in the meantime. He was adamant that the confidentiality of our talks not be compromised.

As we left, it was my impression that Stennis would go through with the process for verification, which we laid out for him in complete detail. Nothing was concealed from him; any attempt at deception would have been inconceivable in light of his stature, self-defeating in consideration of the stakes involved, and probably impossible in view of his sagacity. Stennis conditioned his own final acceptance of the arrangement on the agreement of Senators Ervin and Baker, and asked to be informed at the first possible moment of Cox's reaction. All three of us knew that the presidency hung in the balance.

The vital first step of consultation with Stennis having been taken, I phoned Elliot Richardson at 1:20 P.M. on Monday, October 15, and asked him whether he thought that Cox would accept the Stennis compromise. At the same time, I was under instructions to convey the President's mood. Key passages:

> HAIG: Let me run [through] a scenario with you which [Nixon] thinks is the best we can do. We will go under the assumption that [Wright] can negotiate with Cox . . . that Stennis listens to the tapes and that he verifies their contents, and that John Stennis alone does this. . . .[The President] wants your assurance that you will stand with him in the dismissal of Cox, should [the compromise] not be acceptable to him.
> RICHARDSON: Give me till midafternoon.

Twenty minutes later, Nixon wondered what Richardson would really do if push came to shove ("You know Elliot"). But he was determined to go ahead with the Stennis compromise even if it meant Richardson's own resignation. Richardson had not suggested in any way that he would resign if Cox rejected the compromise and was fired, but Nixon's antennae apparently picked up the tremor of this intention. His determination to get rid of Cox had not cooled. "If Elliot feels that he has to go with his Harvard boy, then that's it," he said. "Either Cox takes it or Cox is out. . . . There is no negotiation with Cox. Do you agree?"

"Yes, sir," I replied.

At 3:20 P.M. I called Richardson and told him that Stennis was leaning toward acceptance. I suggested that he and Buzhardt and I get together "to be sure that . . . all the ramifications have been considered before the approach is made to Cox, so there will be no misunderstanding."

Richardson was all reassurance. "On the fundamental side," he said, "if Cox refuses, then I would support the President's dismissal of Cox. . . . I do believe that this [the Stennis compromise] is a reasonable proposition and that it ought to be capable of producing a resolution of this matter. I would certainly undertake to do anything I can possibly do to put it over. . . . I think Cox should go along with it."

While we struggled to contain a war in the Middle East that threatened to escalate into a superpower confrontation, awaited the decision of Congress on the nomination of Ford (though this was the one question of the day about which there was then little doubt), the Stennis compromise moved forward. This early progress encouraged me to believe, as I told

Richardson at 11:10 A.M. on Tuesday, October 16, that "I think this is viable with or without Cox." In this conversation, Richardson told me that he was "making an inventory of the difficulties." He gave me no indication that he was backing away from his support of the idea of firing Cox in case the latter rejected the compromise.

That day, Richardson had explained the Stennis compromise to Cox and asked for his reaction. Cox asked for a written proposal on which to base his answer. Richardson prepared one and handed it over to Cox after reading it to Buzhardt, who asked for the deletion of a paragraph specifying that the compromise covered only the tapes Cox had already subpoenaed. This foreclosed future demands for presidential tapes and documents, and turned out to be a sticking point with Cox.

At 7:20 P.M., Richardson told me over the telephone that "Cox is being very deliberate. He does not want to be stampeded. He is looking at everything."

I replied, "He is looking well enough to tell the papers you have talked to him about it. The wires just called us to say Cox and Richardson discussed the tapes."

"Oh, my," Richardson said in a tone of distress. "He asked me yesterday if he could consult anybody. I said, 'Archie, I am not going to tell you you cannot have any advice, but I hope it is clear to you that it is important that this not get out.' "

"The real danger is it will blow Stennis out of the game," I said. "He was very categoric about [leaks]. . . . [Nixon] will fire Cox. He is so damned mad. I hope you understand. . . . We just have to move to hold this thing together. We either have to settle it for the good of the country or make a farce out of it. Why he would run out within forty-eight hours of your discussion with him and leak it, I don't know. . . . I have a boss who is absolutely beside himself."

"Jesus," said Richardson. He then engaged in a long and convoluted discussion of the finer legal points of the compromise and enumerated possible reasons why Cox might question these. Accustomed as I was to his gothic speech patterns, I did not follow all of this.

I said, "Elliot, what is your flat assessment? My view is [that] we are not going to get [Cox] to accept this."

"I am not quite ready to say that. He is nervous about what he considers is his own responsibility and what will be publicly accepted. . . . I will have to give you further assessment of it tomorrow afternoon."

I pressed him again. "What I need is what you feel will be the outcome. I don't want to snooker [the President] and I think we may be on the verge of that. . . . I don't want to lead Stennis down any primrose path. He wants to know if it is acceptable to Cox. If it is not, he may make another set of judgments."

"Part of the problem," Richardson said after a little more back-and-forth discussion, "[is that] you and I, and of course the President, have a strong sense of who Stennis is—his strength of character and sense of justice. This is not as evident to Cox."

I supposed this remark referred to Stennis's status as a southern Democrat and a conservative. To Richardson, I said, "I hope you will be thinking very carefully about the bottom line in the event of an unsatisfactory resolution."

Early Thursday afternoon, Nixon asked me, impatiently, whether we had an answer from Cox. I said we had not. He told me to call Richardson and find out when we were going to get one. He wanted to make his decision on firing Cox before the Cabinet meeting at three o'clock.

I called Richardson at 1:10 P.M. and put the President's question and the reasons behind it to him. Of all our talks, this was possibly the most heartfelt on both sides.

Richardson said he expected to receive Cox's "notes" some time that afternoon and there wasn't much he could do until he got them. Rather stiffly, he added, "I really don't see any evidence of this snookering process."

"This man has already established the premise that he won't trust the President," I said. "The second one would be [if he rejected the compromise] that he won't trust a John Stennis. And that will not sell, Elliot."

"It is a good proposal and it is a reasonable proposal," Richardson replied, "but I think you are kidding yourself that [if] Cox rejects it . . . you have the handle to fire him. . . . You are pushing it too far. . . . If the answer is we will dismantle the Cox operation and give [it] to the Attorney General, then you are in one hell of an uproar."

"I'm not so sure."

"I hope we don't have to find out."

"I do, too, [but] the Boss runs it. . . . He cannot lead this country with this constant diversion to excess. There is not a thing that isn't being gutted. No President can put up with it if he is going to be President. . . . They want to overthrow Richard Nixon."

"God knows, Al, no one could pray more fervently for a favorable result on this than I do. I can understand the President's state of mind and your state of mind. I think you are underestimating the results of firing Cox. . . . I have debated telling Cox just what the story is. I concluded that I shouldn't."

"Well, I don't know what else we can do [except fire Cox]."

"From the President's point of view, from my point of view, from the country's point of view, there's a lot riding on this."

Cox did not deliver his answer in time for the Cabinet meeting. But at 5:50 P.M., Richardson called to tell me that Cox had just given him a written response. He read it while I waited on the line.

Finally, he said, in a voice that sagged with weariness, "The paper amounts in substance to a rejection of the unilateral selection of one person to do this. . . ."

In other words, Cox was rejecting the Stennis compromise and the "unsatisfactory solution" was upon us. I asked Richardson to come to the White House at once for a meeting with me and the lawyers. At that meeting, it was my impression that everyone present agreed that Cox had rejected the Stennis compromise and would not change his mind and that he would not relinquish future access to presidential tapes and documents. In short, he had placed himself in a position that justified his dismissal. No one present disputed this, and no alternative to firing Cox was suggested.

Nevertheless, Wright was assigned the task of responding to Cox, and the two subsequently conferred by telephone. These exchanges produced strong confirmations from Cox that he would not accept only "one man operating in secrecy" (as he had put it to Richardson in his letter) as monitor of the tapes, that he would not accept summaries of relevant passages in lieu of verbatim transcripts, and that he would not forego the right to subpoena other tapes in the future. These objections, Wright wrote to him, "depart so far from [the] proposal and the purpose for which it was made that we could not accede to them in any form."[25]

When I briefed the President on these developments, he erupted. "No more tapes, no more documents, nothing more! I want an order from me to Elliot to Cox to that effect, now."

Buzhardt immediately went to work drafting this instruction; there was no secret about it among those who were working on the problem.

First thing the next morning, Friday, October 19,* I spoke to Buzhardt,

---

*On this date, Cox's last full day in office, John Dean pleaded guilty before Judge Sirica to one count of conspiracy to obstruct justice. Dean agreed to testify for the prosecution in future trials of Watergate defendants in return for Cox's promise of immunity from prosecution on all other Watergate-related crimes.

who had been discussing the situation with Richardson. "[Elliot's] very uptight," he said.

"Quittable uptight?" I asked.

"He's not gone, but he's struggling," Buzhardt replied. "Maybe you ought to call [him]."

Richardson called me five minutes later: "I'm calling to say, Al, that if the result is that Cox won't move, and therefore that no agreement is possible, I would like to see the President just as soon thereafter as possible." I assured him that that could be arranged. Though it was obvious that he was struggling with himself, he made no reference to resignation.

By 10:00 A.M., Wright had received a letter from Cox that effectively confirmed his earlier rejections of the Stennis compromise. Wright replied, "As I read your comments of the 18th and your letter of the 19th, the differences between us remain so great that no purpose would be served by further discussion of what I continue to think was a 'very reasonable'—indeed an unprecedently generous—proposal that the Attorney General put to you in an effort, in the national interest, to resolve our disputes . . . at a time when the country would be particularly well served by such agreement."[26]

I called Richardson to inform him of this development and ask him to come to the White House for another meeting with the lawyers and me. He said he would be right over, adding, "I feel strongly that I ought to see the President as promptly as possible." I replied, "That's easy."

A few minutes later, Richardson and the others met again in my office. Despite what he had said to me on the telephone only a short while before, Richardson left those present with the impression that he supported the Stennis compromise and believed that it should be put into effect. He suggested that Cox be given a "cease-and-desist order" with regard to the tapes. This would mean, in effect, that Cox would be barred from suing for any further presidential tapes or documents. I thought it very unlikely that Cox would accept such an order, and I had the impression that no one present imagined that he could remain as special prosecutor if the compromise went through. The likeliest outcome of Richardson's suggestion, therefore, was that Cox would either resign or make it impossible not to fire him. Richardson was clearly hoping that Cox would go voluntarily, thus relieving him of the necessity of firing him.

Richardson was relaxed enough through all this to mention that he planned to take a few days off as soon as the matter was resolved to go fishing out West for steelhead trout with Caspar Weinberger. He did not ask to see the President. Charles Alan Wright has recently reminded me that Richardson's parting remark to the rest of us when he left the meeting in my office was a jaunty, "Gentlemen, there is a Chinese proverb, 'You are cursed to live in fascinating times [sic].' "[27]

On the basis of the meeting and subsequent phone calls with Richardson, and a new expression of support from Stennis ("[He] is enthusiastic about proceeding," I had told Richardson at 1:05 P.M.), Senators Ervin and Baker were asked to meet with the President. After being collected in New Orleans and Chicago, respectively, by Air Force jets, they arrived in the Oval Office at 5:30 P.M. Nixon told them in detail about the Stennis compromise, and, after asking a series of hard questions, they accepted it. One of the beauties of Buzhardt's plan was that they could hardly do otherwise considering Stennis's stature in the Senate, but I thought they received the idea with relief and approved it in the conviction that they were acting in the national interest. Almost as much as the President, these men wanted to get Watergate behind them as soon as possible and get on with the people's business.

Soon after Ervin and Baker departed, Nixon signed a letter to Richardson confirming that the compromise would go forward and instructing him to "direct [Cox] that he is to make no further attempts by judicial process to obtain tapes, notes, or memoranda of presidential conversations." I had read the text of this letter over the telephone an hour or so earlier to Richardson. Although this was nothing more than the "cease-and-desist order" he himself had suggested, he listened in somber silence; I wondered whether he would carry out the instruction, but I did not ask him what his intentions were. In no way did he suggest that he would not do as ordered.

The President's order was made public at the same time that Nixon announced the Stennis compromise in a press statement released at 8:15 P.M.[28] Soon after that, Melvin Laird dropped in to praise the President's action; he mentioned that he had spoken to Richardson, whom he described as being very supportive of the President's position. A little later, Weinberger was reported to have mentioned that he had spoken to a seemingly unworried Richardson and they had discussed plans for their fishing expedition.

Then the first sign of trouble appeared. Bryce Harlow, who had been calling members of the Cabinet to brief them on the President's statements, found himself connected to Richardson. Around nine o'clock,

Harlow reported to me that Richardson was now expressing doubts about the plan. He had told Harlow that he would not carry out the President's instruction. Harlow said to me, "Elliot said, 'I have never been so shabbily treated in my life.' "

It took me some time to reach Richardson, but I finally got hold of him at home. He told me he had had a drink. The moral and physical stress he was undergoing was detectable in his speech, which was slurred and disjointed. Since our last conversation, he had been talking to Cox. Abruptly, Richardson told me that he had changed his mind. "I cannot fire Cox," he said, "and if I am asked to do so, I myself will have to resign."

I was dumbfounded. I led him through a review of our negotiations. We had accepted his plan; I had sold it to the President with the assurance that he was on board. Everyone involved had the impression that he was on board. We had even released the President's letter to him from the White House so that he did not actually have to deliver the instructions it contained to Cox. Didn't he realize that his defection would demolish the compromise?

Richardson said that he had no recollection of entering into any such agreement as the one I had described.

I said, "Maybe you don't remember, Elliot. But I can assure you that the other four people in that meeting remember it very well indeed. No one present had the slightest question in his mind that you were on board when you left the White House this morning."*

Now, at the end of the day that had begun in such good fellowship, Richardson was unmoved by anything I could say. That evening, Henry Kissinger had departed for Moscow for talks with the Soviets on the Middle East, where the situation remained volatile and extremely dangerous. I asked Richardson whether he had any idea what effect the consequences of his decision might have on the crisis. He did not reply.

---

*On November 15, some three weeks after Richardson et al. had departed, I called him once again in the hope of setting the record straight. He and I went over our conversation again because reports in the press had already begun to distort the picture. "I guess everyone's perception can differ," I told him, "but I want you to know that Charlie Wright, Len Garment, and Fred Buzhardt and I have discussed it in detail and we were all in agreement that you proposed breaking this into two steps and [that] this was a twist on our plan to fire Cox for not going with the Stennis compromise. . . ." In another reference to Eastern wisdom, Richardson replied, "Did you ever see the Japanese movie [Kurosawa's *Rashomon*, presumably] in which the audience is given each of the separate perceptions of the evidence and it is only the audience that could have perceived the thing so differently?" I replied, "Yes, you thought we were going to fire Cox. . . . You have to know, Elliot, that all our perceptions when you left here Friday morning were that we had a deal."

I phoned the President as soon as I hung up on Richardson and told him what I had just learned. He was as surprised as I had been. "How can Elliot walk away now?" he asked. "He can't do this. Get him in here tomorrow morning. I want to talk to him."

It seemed unlikely to me that a meeting with the President would budge Richardson; he had made his choice. The sense of disappointment was intense. In view of what was going on in Washington, it seemed to me little short of a miracle that we had been able to put the compromise together at all. Now it was being destroyed by one of its makers.

The next day was Saturday, October 20. By midmorning, Buzhardt had discussed the probability of Cox's departure with Stennis and Howard Baker. He reported that both felt that the compromise was the important factor and that it could be preserved regardless of what happened to Cox. At 10:20, I spoke to Richardson and told him everything I knew about the situation. "I think the earmarks are all [present] for the dismissal of Cox," I said. "The President can't have him in defiance."

Richardson told me he had come to the White House the day before "thinking I would see the President to make one more pitch. I'd made extensive notes why I couldn't stay [but] your handling of the situation . . . averted [this confrontation]." He carried in his pocket a paper entitled "Why I Should Resign."[29] He had not produced this document in my presence, or even referred to any intention of resigning.

Now he spoke of coming up with another proposal to "buy time." Cox's people were already leaking to the press, and this had had its usual strong effect on Nixon's temper. I replied, "Elliot, the way it's shaping up, the outcome is inevitable."

Fifteen minutes later, I called Richardson again.

> HAIG: Elliot, I just had a funny call, saying you were sending over a letter. I just don't want to be hit with any surprises.
> RICHARDSON: Oh, no, I haven't sent it yet; it isn't finished yet. All it says is what I've said before. . . . It says I hope we can work something out, that's all it is. . . . If Cox has to be fired, I thought I would call him and tell him that this is my position. . . . No need to spill any unnecessary blood.

The letter arrived around one o'clock, just as Cox's press conference was assembling at the National Press Club. It was addressed to the President. After reviewing the terms on which he, Richardson, had appointed

Cox, and reminding the President that he had done what he had done on the basis of the latter's assurances of independence, the Attorney General went on to say:

> Quite obviously . . . the instruction contained in your letter of October 19 gives me serious difficulty. As you know, I regarded as reasonable and constructive the proposal to rely on Senator Stennis to prepare a verified record of the so-called Watergate tapes and I did my best to persuade Mr. Cox of the desirability of this solution of that issue. I did not believe, however, that the price of access to the tapes in this manner should be the renunciation of any further attempt by him to resort to judicial process, and the proposal I submitted to him did not purport to deal with other tapes, notes, or memoranda of Presidential conversations.
>
> In the circumstances I would hope that some further accommodation could be found along the following lines. . . . Any future situation where Mr. Cox seeks judicial process to obtain the record of Presidential conversations would be approached on the basis of the precedent established with respect to the Watergate tapes.

The purpose of the letter was clear. Richardson was declining, for the historical record, to carry out the President's order to Cox unless it was modified in such a way as to give Cox future access to materials the President regarded as being protected by executive privilege. This reversed the intent of Nixon's instruction, ran contrary to Richardson's assurances to me and the White House lawyers, and was, of course, a formula for abject surrender to Cox. The President read it with no show of emotion. He had long ago crossed this bridge. Whatever Richardson suggested or did, or refused to do, Cox would go.

Minutes later, Cox drew a packed house at the National Press Club. It was a bravura performance that left the impression with the assembled journalists that the Stennis compromise was a Nixonian design to hide the truth from the special prosecutor, Congress, the courts, and the American people. As to the President's order to him, Cox said, "I think there is a question whether anyone other than the Attorney General can give me any instructions that I have any legal obligation to obey." A reporter asked, "Are you going to wait for the President to dismiss you?" Cox replied, "I am going to go about my duties on the terms on which

I assumed them."[30] In short, he wasn't going to let Richardson or the President off the hook by resigning, and he apparently did not consider that anyone except the Attorney General had the legal authority to fire him.

Richardson phoned me at 2:30 to ask whether the President had watched Cox's press conference. I told him I hadn't spoken to Nixon since Cox went before the cameras, but I thought we had no alternative but to fire Cox. After a long pause, Richardson said, "I don't see any problem, Al, in [Nixon] firing him. [But] I can't help seeing [Cox] as a guy who was doing the job he was asked to do, on the terms in which I was instructing him. . . ."

This was very confusing. Richardson's words seemed to me to be, at the same time, a withdrawal from and a reprise of our conversation the night before.

I said, "I really believe, Elliot, [that] you're assuming a greater degree of sensitivity to that problem than it merits." And I added, somewhat heavily, "We have a problem of finding people who are willing to execute the duties they were hired to be responsible for."

By this, I meant that the Attorney General was required, as a matter of law and precedent, to discharge anyone who worked for him on orders from the President.

He said, "I suppose it just depends on any order that the President gives, if your own view of what is proper permits you to do. It is my view and I don't see how I can change it."

I guessed that this meant it was all right if Nixon or somebody else in the White House fired Cox, but Richardson wasn't going to do it himself. If he refused, of course, he had no alternative but to resign.

I asked him again, "Can you hold up your resignation until this Mideast crisis is over?"

Richardson replied, "That is what I cannot do."

The President signed a hastily drafted reply to Richardson's letter. Because it was intended as much for the historical record as for the Attorney General, it is reproduced here in its entirety:

October 20, 1973
Dear Mr. Attorney General:
    I have your letter of October 20th. My letter to you yesterday, instructing you to direct Mr. Cox to make no further attempts by judicial process to obtain tapes, notes, or memoranda of Presidential conversations, was the end product of very careful

consideration by me. My willingness to make available the relevant contents of the tapes, verified by Senator Stennis, was only on condition that this would end all further confrontations or questions about tapes or other matters relating to Presidential conversations. For that reason, I am unable to modify my instruction of the 19th. In his press conference today Mr. Cox made it apparent that he will not comply with that direction and that he views himself as a fourth branch of Government, not required to abide by instructions of the President. You, of course, recognize very clearly how intolerable a situation it would be if an employee of the Executive Branch were free to defy in this fashion the instructions of the President. Under the circumstances, I am required to instruct you to discharge Mr. Cox immediately and to return to the Justice Department the functions now being performed by the Watergate Special Prosecution Force.

It is my view, with which I hope you will concur, that you will not think the necessity of taking this action, on my instructions, undermines in any way your position as Attorney General.

When I read this letter to Richardson over the telephone, he told me again that he could not carry out the President's instruction, and he asked for an immediate meeting with Nixon in order to resign. Who, then, I asked, would fire Archibald Cox?

"You will ask me, and I will refuse," Richardson replied. "You will then call Bill Ruckelshaus [the Deputy Attorney General], and he, too, will refuse. You will then call Bob Bork [the Solicitor General and the next man in order of rank], and he will not refuse."

Shortly after 4:30 P.M., I showed Richardson into the Oval Office. The President asked him to do him and the country the favor of delaying his resignation for the few days required to complete the Mideast negotiations. At this very moment in Moscow, Kissinger was negotiating a cease-fire with Brezhnev. Richardson, whom Nixon had appointed to three Cabinet posts, more than any other American in history, refused. The President said, "Elliot, I hope you understand that what you're doing involves questions of war and peace. The last thing we need at this moment is a domestic crisis that makes us look weak and indecisive." Richardson replied in terms that left no doubt that he felt that he could do no other than that which he had done.

After Richardson left, the President did not prolong the discussion about him or the episode that had led to his resignation. He was remote and controlled, unsurprised by what had happened; the resignation and the peculiar reasons for it seemed to confirm all his doubts about Richardson.

I could not help but be aware that what happened must also have shaken Nixon's confidence in me. Although he said nothing about this, I was quite sure that he felt that he had been let down not only by Richardson but by me and everyone else who had urged him to accept the Stennis compromise rather than trusting and acting on his own instincts. In hindsight, I realized—and still believe—that Nixon's way would have been the better way.

Urging him to do otherwise was the greatest mistake I made as Nixon's Chief of Staff. From the emotional point of view, facing the results of my advice was the low point of my time in that job.

Richardson's resignation had turned an exercise of presidential authority into a display of futility that did lasting, possibly fatal, damage to the President's credibility. As I told Richardson a few days later in the conversation described in the footnote to page 402, "I'll tell you this. Had I known that it would end up with your resignation, I would have insisted on whatever changes were necessary." Zealous underlings at Justice immediately began leaking distorted versions of the affair to the press, and little could be done to set the record straight.

The remainder of the story is well known. As soon as Richardson left the White House, I called Ruckelshaus and asked him whether he was prepared to execute the President's directive. He refused on grounds of loyalty to Richardson. Robert Bork, who all along had supported the right of the President to discharge Cox, agreed to carry out the President's instruction. In his new capacity as Acting Attorney General, he did so around six o'clock.

An hour or so later, I spoke to the President for the last time that day. By then, the television news had labeled the firing of Cox and Ruckelshaus, and the resignation of Richardson, "the Saturday Night Massacre." Nixon was being accused of gestapo tactics, of dictatorship, of insanity; NBC News (momentarily forgetting the Civil War) said the events of the day "may be the most serious constitutional crisis in [U.S.] history."

Darkness had long since fallen. Nixon was alone in the Oval Office as usual, and some of the anger he had suppressed in his meeting with Richardson flared. On my recommendation, he had ordered that FBI agents be posted in the special prosecutor's office to make certain that no evidence was removed.

He told me, "You should see carefully to that."

I said that I would. He spoke again.

"If Bork disagrees, we can't do it."

"He agrees."

"Good," Nixon said. "Anything else to report?"

I supplied a few details on Ford's chances in Congress (excellent) and on the Middle East crisis (difficult but hopeful).

As he listened, Nixon's spirits resurfaced; his physical vitality seemed to revive; his voice gained in timber.

"Well, Al, it's going to be tough, but we'll handle it," he said. "It will work out."

I realized that he was reassuring me, letting me know that he still had confidence in me. Deeply touched by his simple kindness in what must have been one of the most difficult hours of his life, I felt a surge of admiration and sympathy for this complex, unpredictable, and indomitable man.

But I wondered whether, in the end, we would be able to navigate the maelstrom into which we seemed to have been drawn.

31

The Middle East Crisis

By the first day of business after the Saturday Night Massacre, Nixon's opponents were fixated on the fate of Archibald Cox. The Middle East crisis, still playing itself out on the battlefield and in the Moscow talks, was portrayed as a propaganda exercise drummed up by a cynical and desperate White House. "A crisis a day keeps impeachment away," said the wiseacres. Congressman John E. Moss, Democrat of California, sounded the liberal pitch pipe, saying that the military alert ordered toward the end of the crisis was "an effort to divert attention from the more damaging disclosures the President feared Archibald Cox was about to make when he fired him."[1]

This was nonsense. There was nothing invented or artificial about the Yom Kippur War or the danger of a U.S.–Soviet military showdown that it produced. Israel was seriously imperiled by the surprise attack by the Soviet-equipped Arab forces, and the peace of the world was gravely threatened before U.S. assistance reversed the tide of battle against Moscow's clients.

No small part of the reason for this emergency was the domestic disorder created by Watergate. The Soviets were behind the events in the Middle East, and I know of no knowledgeable person who does not believe that one of the important reasons the Kremlin put the crisis in motion was its calculation that the President of the United States was so distracted and disabled by his domestic problems that he would be unable to react with adequate force and dispatch to prevent a change in the balance of power at the eastern end of the Mediterranean. In this, as we shall see, the Soviets were sorely mistaken.

The Middle East war of 1973 came as a complete surprise to the United States and to Israel. Hostilities began on Saturday, October 6, the date on which Yom Kippur, the Jewish Day of Atonement, fell that year. Within twenty-four hours Israel lost 1,000 troops killed in action, compared to 697 in the entire Six Day War in 1967, together with hundreds of tanks and scores of aircraft. With her reserves fully mobilized, she could put 270,000 soldiers in the field, as against 760,000 for Egypt and 320,000 for Syria. In armor and combat aircraft, she was outnumbered by her attackers by more than two to one.[2]

In the opening phase of hostilities, Egyptian forces seized most of the East Bank of the Suez Canal and poured armor into the Sinai. A Syrian armored force advanced ten miles into the Golan Heights. The Israeli setbacks were due in some measure to the fact that the country was not mobilized for war when it was attacked, and it took time to bring the reserves into action. But imbalances in the Israeli force structure also played a part. They had equipped their armored forces with fast modern tanks but had failed to provide the latest armored personnel carriers and mobile artillery to keep up with them on the battlefield. This made the Israeli tanks, unprotected by infantry, vulnerable to the deadly shoulder-fired antitank weapons supplied to the Arabs by Moscow. Israel's tactical aircraft, equipped for air-to-air combat or conventional bombing missions, were not configured to suppress the new SAM missiles provided to the Arabs along with the latest Soviet armor, artillery, and aircraft. Massive shipments of the most advanced Soviet weapons had been pouring into Egypt and Syria for many months.[3]

The key element, however, was the surprise achieved by the Arabs. Prime Minister Golda Meir apparently believed U.S. intelligence reports that confidently argued that no Arab attack was imminent despite the enormous buildup of Soviet military aid to Israel's most dangerous enemies. Kissinger, who accepted the accuracy of these estimates, had urged Mrs. Meir to trust them also, despite scattered reports from Israeli intelligence sources of suspicious enemy activity, such as the withdrawal of Soviet dependents from Syria and Egypt and unusually heavy air traffic in and out of Cairo and Damascus. After hostilities began, the fact that the United States had given the Israelis false reassurance magnified the sense of obligation the Nixon administration felt toward Israel in her hour of peril.

It has been stated elsewhere that Nixon, who was in Key Biscayne on Yom Kippur, did not learn of the attacks until hours after they had taken place. This is not true. Within minutes after hostilities began, I was informed by the White House Situation Room, and I informed the President, that the Arab offensive was under way. It was then about 6:00 A.M. He decided within the hour to return to Washington to take personal command of the crisis. There was never the slightest question that he intended to take the strongest actions to preserve Israel. It was he who devised the American response, he who fought it through subordinates in the Defense Department who were reluctant to help Israel, and he who dealt with the Soviets in a series of direct contacts with General Secretary Brezhnev. On occasions when he did not personally convey his instructions, I did so on his behalf. As Kissinger put it in his memoirs, "Only a President could have imposed the complex and tough policy that got us this far and sustained it against a hesitant bureaucracy, vacillating allies, a nervous Soviet Union, and the passionate combatants of the Middle East."[4]

As soon as the scope and pattern of Israeli battle losses emerged, Nixon ordered that all destroyed equipment be made up out of U.S. stockpiles, using the very best weapons America possessed. At the same time, he ordered a massive airlift to deliver the necessary matériel.

"Whatever it takes," he told Kissinger, who needed no prodding, "save Israel."

This command was more easily delivered than carried out, especially when Kissinger was the messenger. Like Laird before him, the new Secretary of Defense, James Schlesinger, had become embroiled in a bitter rivalry with Kissinger; the two men disagreed about nearly everything. And like Laird, Schlesinger had his own policy priorities. It soon became evident that he feared that U.S. intervention on the scale mandated by the President would alienate the Arab nations and might lead to an oil embargo against the West. He found reasons to delay shipments to Israel, citing the military and diplomatic dangers of a massive airlift by U.S. military aircraft and the legal difficulties in using civilian aircraft to transport arms into a war zone. The Defense Department insisted, for example, that the Star of David insignia on the tails of El Al cargo planes landing in the United States be painted over before they were loaded with U.S. military supplies for the return trip to Israel. Kissinger repeatedly complained to me about what he described as "Schlesinger's sabotage."

While such follies wasted time, the Israelis were running out of ammunition. Nixon sent Congress an emergency request for $2.2 billion in aid
for Israel, and there was no doubt that this would be approved. However,
it was obvious after the first couple of days that Israel would either survive
or cease to exist in a very short time, depending on the resupply of
equipment by the United States. By October 12, I had been informed,
and had reported to the President, that the Israelis had already lost five
hundred tanks, or nearly one-third of their inventory. I also briefed the
President on the unacceptable delays in the airlift.

That same day, Nixon called Kissinger and Schlesinger into the Oval
Office, and in a rare, but to me highly gratifying, display of personal
domination, banished all excuses. He asked Kissinger to itemize the arms
and matériel Israel needed, and Kissinger read out the list.

"Double it," Nixon said. "Now get the hell out of here and get the job
done."

That evening, while Nixon was announcing to an enthusiastic audience in the East Room that Gerald Ford was his choice for Vice President,
we received a message from the Soviets, who complained that the United
States was supplying Israel with planes, tanks, and munitions; the message
added ominously that Moscow had heard reports that we were sending
150 U.S. Air Force pilots to Israel disguised as tourists.

By the next afternoon, thirty C-130 transports were en route to Israel;
by early the following week, U.S. Air Force and civilian aircraft were
delivering more than one thousand tons of weapons and supplies a day.
The whole operation, over the next several weeks, was larger in terms of
tonnage delivered than the Berlin airlift.[5] The Soviets, meantime, were
airlifting about four thousand tons of supplies in 280 flights to the Egyptians and Syrians.[6] U.S. fighter-bombers were flown directly to Israel
from U.S. Air Force bases and taken into combat minutes after their
arrival by Israeli pilots. Israeli crews drove American tanks off transport
planes straight to the battlefield.

Reequipped Israeli forces drove the Syrians off the Golan Heights and
knocked out half the Syrian air force. By October 14, Israeli advance
units were shelling Syrian positions within four miles of Damascus. Huge
tank battles were fought in the Sinai and in the vicinity of the Golan
Heights, and by the sixteenth the Israelis had breached the Egyptian line
and crossed the Suez Canal with three hundred tanks,[7] flanking the
Egyptian Third Army and exposing Cairo to capture. Thanks to their
own superb military performance and the American airlift, Israel appeared

to have won the war that only days before they had been in danger of losing.

The day after the Israelis crossed the Suez, Nixon met in the Oval Office with four Arab foreign ministers, who emerged uttering compliments to the press about his potential role as a peacemaker in the Middle East. On October 18, we learned that the Soviets intended to submit a proposal to the UN Security Council for a joint Mideast cease-fire resolution. Because the Russian proposal included a fanciful provision for immediate withdrawal by Israeli forces to their pre-1967 borders, it had no chance whatever of being accepted by Israel.

During these days, I was, of course, also engaged in the matter of Cox's departure, and the Middle East crisis often obtruded into my conversations with Richardson. This occurred not because I was attempting to coax the Attorney General into a mood of patriotic self-sacrifice, as was afterward suggested, but because he knew how serious the situation was and asked me for news about it. (Richardson, who had gone ashore in Normandy on D day and often referred to this character-forming experience, took a close interest in martial matters. He had, of course, been Secretary of Defense, albeit briefly, when Nixon asked him to become Attorney General.)

Some of our conversations captured the mood within the inner circle quite well. One such exchange took place in the early afternoon of Friday, October 19, a few hours before Richardson told me he would not fire Cox. Not long before we spoke, Nixon had received an urgent personal message from Brezhnev. The Soviet leader had referred to the "harm" that might be done to U.S.–Soviet relations by the increasing dangers in the Middle East and asked that Kissinger be sent to Moscow for talks that very day.[8] The dramatic tone of the Soviet leader's message, the sense of impending calamity that it conveyed, was way out of the ordinary. We also knew that nuclear-capable Soviet naval units were moving through the Dardanelles. Richardson and I had the following exchange:

> RICHARDSON: One thing on which I have been thinking and chewing . . . the Mideast. How are we doing over there?
> HAIG: The Soviets have sent us a desperate message. The Arabs are unraveling, there's a massive buildup of [the Soviet] fleet in the Med. Henry will be on his way to Moscow by midnight. It's not good.
> RICHARDSON: Jesus!

HAIG: Very serious. This puts Cuba to shame. If [the Soviets] intervene, that's all she wrote.
RICHARDSON: Won't Israel hold back in light of that prospect [possible Soviet military action]?
HAIG: Hard to say. We'll have to put . . . pressure on the Israelis or we are going to risk Soviet intervention.

Two days later in Moscow, Kissinger and Brezhnev agreed on the draft of a cease-fire agreement that called for a cease-fire in place, the implementation of UN Resolution 242* after the cease-fire, and for negotiations between the parties aimed at establishing peace in the Middle East. This was the first time the Soviets had agreed to any proposal for direct negotiations between Israel and the Arabs without conditions or qualifications. Brezhnev informed the Syrians and Egyptians of its terms, and Kissinger carried the proposal to Tel Aviv. Both sides agreed, and a cease-fire went into effect on October 22.

However, sporadic fighting broke out again and the Israelis took advantage of the situation to complete their encirclement of the Egyptian Third Army. On the twenty-third, the day Charlie Wright appeared before Judge Sirica to offer to surrender the subpoenaed tapes, Brezhnev sent Nixon a message over the hot line, charging the Israelis with violating the cease-fire, possibly with American collusion, and urging the United States to take measures to stop the violations. This was a volatile mixture of false accusation and veiled threat. In a measured reply, Nixon asked Brezhnev to restrain the Egyptians, whom we believed had provoked the Israeli actions by attempting to break out of the encirclement,[9] and to hold fast to the gains for peace that had already been made through mutual U.S.–Soviet efforts.

Another cease-fire was agreed to on the twenty-fourth, but by then there was no effective Egyptian force between the Israelis and Cairo, and the Egyptians and the Russians were understandably nervous. Had the positions been reversed, it is unlikely that they would have advised the Arabs to refrain from taking Tel Aviv and occupying Israel. Later in the day, we received intelligence reports that seven Soviet airborne divisions had been put on alert and that large numbers of Soviet AN-22 transport planes, of the type used in their airlift of weapons and supplies, were landing at Egyptian airports. At the same time, a new Soviet naval force

---

*This resolution, adopted by the Security Council on November 22, 1967, called for a "just and lasting peace" inside "secure and recognized boundaries" but did not define these terms. The Arabs have interpreted the reference to "boundaries" to mean pre-1967 boundaries; the Israelis have not.

of not fewer than eighty-five vessels, including landing craft and helicopter carriers, was assembling in the Mediterranean. This was an all-time high, and the total later exceeded one hundred.[10]

That afternoon, Egyptian President Anwar Sadat requested that the United States join the Soviet Union in sending a joint peacekeeping force to his country, and Moscow backed this up with a new charge that Israel's forces were attacking Egyptian forces on both sides of the Suez Canal.[11] We knew this to be false. It was obvious that the Soviets were getting ready to make a move designed to restore their military presence in the Middle East.

Around 9:35 P.M. (4:35 A.M. Moscow time), Dobrynin called Kissinger and read him an urgent letter for the President from Brezhnev. The Soviet leader again charged that Israel was breaking the cease-fire, and he proposed that the United States and the Soviet Union immediately dispatch military forces to the battle zone, with our troops taking up positions on the Israeli side of the line and Soviet troops on the Egyptian side. "I will say it straight," Brezhnev wrote, "that if you find it impossible to act jointly with us in this matter, we should be faced with the necessity urgently to consider the question of taking appropriate steps unilaterally."[12]

When I took this ultimatum, for that was what it amounted to, to the President, he greeted it with a remark and an order. "We've got a problem, Al," he said. "This is the most serious thing since the Cuban Missile Crisis. Words won't do the job. We've got to act."

Nixon ordered me to convene a meeting with Kissinger and the other members of the Washington Special Action Group for the purpose of formulating a response to the Soviet challenge. I went back to my office and called Kissinger. His strong sense of territory leaping to the fore, he suggested that the meeting be held forthwith at the State Department. I knew that the President, who was reeling from the cacophonous reaction to the Saturday Night Massacre, which included charges that he was losing his grip, could not relinquish the helm to his Secretary of State for the management of this grave crisis. The occasion called for strong public action by a strong President, not for a meeting by a committee of his underlings.

I said, "No way, Henry. This meeting will take place in the President's house, the normal location for interagency meetings of this kind."

When I passed on the substance of this conversation to Nixon, he nodded in approval but expressed no enthusiasm for attending the meeting in person. As usual, he preferred to let others set the options while he made his decision in solitude. Besides, he was tired. In addition to everything else, the House Judiciary Committee had announced that day that it was going ahead with impeachment inquiries and the Senate Republican leadership had suggested that Nixon name a new special prosecutor to replace the one he had just fired.[13] With a wave of the hand, he said, "You know what I want, Al; you handle the meeting."

We all knew what he wanted: a worldwide military alert of United States military forces tied to a strong reply to Brezhnev. Both were needed. As Nixon had said, and as all of his closest advisers knew from experience, mere words would not cause the Soviets to draw back. Only action, the preparation of U.S. forces for intervention and an expression of American will to react forcefully if necessary, would be effective.

After leaving Nixon in the Oval Office I joined Kissinger, Scowcroft, Schlesinger, Admiral Moorer, CIA Director William Colby, Joseph Sisco of the State Department, and others already assembled in the White House Situation Room. We agreed unanimously that the President must place U.S. conventional and nuclear forces on alert. This was by no means a routine bluff or a replay of the Cuban Missile Crisis, when the Soviets lacked the nuclear forces necessary to stand their ground. They now possessed many of the advantages we ourselves had enjoyed in respect to Cuba in 1962: Their weapons of mass destruction were capable of laying waste the territory of the United States and Western Europe, and their conventional forces and lines of supply were much closer to the site of the crisis and in a more advanced state of alert than ours. If we drew the line in the sand and the Soviets stepped over it, the consequences would be incalculable.*

In a message drafted by Helmut Sonnenfeldt during the meeting in the Situation Room, the United States flatly rejected Brezhnev's proposal

---

* On the day President Reagan was shot, Secretary of Defense Weinberger unilaterally ordered U.S. forces into an undetermined state of alert (Weinberger was too new to his job to know one Defcon level from another), and it was after a heated discussion of this extraordinary action with Weinberger in the Situation Room that I rushed upstairs to the pressroom and made an appearance designed to reassure the Soviets that we did not think they were behind the plot to kill Reagan and that we had no plans to escalate a domestic incident into a superpower confrontation. ("There are absolutely no alert measures that are necessary at this time. . . .") In this, according to Soviet sources, I succeeded—but at the cost of being theatricalized for the purposes of the network evening news shows. Skillful editors isolated the anxiety and exasperation that showed on my face, linked these expressions to a phrase also designed to reassure Moscow ("As of now, I am in control here, pending the return of the Vice President"), and created a memorable moment in the history of television coverage, as well as a defining moment in regard to my public image. I was not surprised to see my message to Moscow cooked into entertainment in this way, but I was diverted, if that is the word, to discover that journalistic pundits were also prepared to suggest that I did not know the presidential order of succession; I had lived with it from one minute to the next every day that I served as Richard Nixon's Chief of Staff.

for joint military intervention. We were not going to intervene, the Sonnenfeldt draft said in effect, and neither were the Soviets. Kissinger softened this by adding a clause that offered Brezhnev a way out by suggesting that U.S. and Soviet forces might form part of a UN peacekeeping force in the Sinai.

The alert was ordered and the message was sent to the Kremlin. Very soon, of course, the Soviets began to pick up the signs of our military alert, as we knew they would. We realized that the situation was coming under control when Sadat sent a message informing Nixon that he planned to ask the UN to provide an international peacekeeping force. Brezhnev followed this up with a conciliatory message stating that the Soviets would not, after all, send fifty thousand paratroopers to the Middle East but would, instead, dispatch seventy individual civilian "observers." The Soviet airborne corps stood down from alert; the Soviet flotilla dispersed. Moscow had decided, as was its wont when faced with the reality of American power, that the game was not worth the candle. We signaled that we understood by taking our forces off alert. By a determined display of strength and shrewdly timed diplomacy, Nixon defused a superpower confrontation that might very well have led to nuclear war.

That was not all. The agreement between the combatants achieved by Kissinger on May 29, 1974, after his famous exercise in shuttle diplomacy, was made possible by Nixon's stern insistence that he keep at the negotiations until they produced results. This required thirty-two days of almost inconceivably tough negotiations between adversaries whose interests seemed to them to be beyond compromise. Kissinger was under the most brutal stress in these negotiations; during the week before breakthrough was achieved, he sent a message to the White House that he was going to terminate the talks and return home. When Brent Scowcroft brought me this word, I sent back a message telling Kissinger in the President's name to stay put until he had achieved results.

"Damn right!" said Nixon, approving my action after the fact. Kissinger remained where he was and went the extra mile. The brilliant result he achieved laid the groundwork for the Camp David accords, and will in due course be seen as the cornerstone of any comprehensive Middle East peace structure that may emerge from that region's desperate need for normalization.

Nixon, who was soon to be bombarded with charges of anti-Semitism on the basis of some of his remarks as recorded on the tapes, had saved Israel and brought about a truce that ended wholesale bloodshed and open war between Arabs and Israelis for almost a decade.

32

The Burden of Proof

The firing of Archibald Cox on Saturday, October 20, 1973, marked the turning point of the constitutional crisis over Watergate. By the time the Sunday newspapers were delivered, it was evident to all, and especially to Nixon's inner circle, that while he had succeeded in killing what he called the asp in the bosom of the presidency, he had not managed to do so before the serpent administered its poisonous sting.

We had expected that Cox's dismissal would produce strong reactions; in fact, it created a phantasmagoria in which, with some exceptions, what remained of former standards of good sense and fair play gave way to a collective frenzy to bring Nixon to book. On taking up temporary quarters in the offices of Senator Edward Kennedy, Cox himself established the level of hyperbole in a one-sentence statement on the meaning of his removal: "Whether ours shall continue to be a government of laws and not of men is now for Congress and ultimately the American people [to decide]."[1]

Ralph Nader (Harvard Law School 1958) declared that "every citizen in this land must strive to reclaim the rule of law which this tyrant [Nixon] has been destroying month by month, strand by strand." George Meany, the President of the AFL–CIO, said that the President seemed to be suffering from "dangerous emotional instability." Meany's organization passed a resolution calling for Nixon's resignation or for his impeachment by the House if he failed to go quietly. Senator Harrison A. Williams, Jr., Democrat of New Jersey, compared Nixon to Hitler in the last days in the Berlin bunker.[2]

Nixon was truly taken aback by the pathological nature of the onslaught. Even by the permissive standards that applied to attacks on him, the language used by his enemies and the ferocious emotions that generated it were abnormal. He saw Cox's removal as a legitimate exercise of presidential authority, and he had no sympathy for the moral dilemma attributed to Richardson and Ruckelshaus by worshipful pundits. When I told Nixon that Ruckelshaus preferred to portray his departure as a resignation, he exploded: "We don't owe him anything but a good kick in the ass. Ruckelshaus has to be fired. I don't want him to go back to Indiana and run for the Senate."

By this time, of course, Ruckelshaus, along with Cox and Richardson, had become a hero of Watergate to whom the President's enmity was a political asset. The all but friendless Nixon, on the other hand, had no choice but to do what the meeker side of his nature had constrained him to do all along—namely, yield to the demands of those who were determined to use the other two branches of government and the press to force him to incriminate himself.

On Monday, as things fell apart, the opposition let Nixon know that support for Gerald Ford's appointment as Vice President was linked to surrender of the tapes. House Republican leaders sent word that they would not "go to the wall" with him on impeachment unless Nixon gave the tapes Cox had subpoenaed to Judge Sirica. The next day, 80 percent of House members told pollsters from Congressional Quarterly that they believed that action on Ford's nomination would be delayed.[3]

The Stennis compromise collapsed on Tuesday morning when Sam Dash, the majority counsel of the Ervin committee, informed Wright that he was filing a brief with the U.S. Court of Appeals asking for a reversal of Sirica's judgment that the committee had no authority to sue for the tapes. In other words, the committee had broken its word to the President on the Stennis compromise and would now settle for nothing less than the full verbatim record of his private conversations.

That evening, Senator Baker phoned me to suggest that the President consider "some middle ground on this thing." What Baker had in mind, he said, was for Sirica to furnish the committee with portions of the tapes. I told him that the President would never agree to give the tapes "to a committee that has leaked. There is no way a verbatim transcript can go over to you." The suggestion that Sirica might provide summaries to the committee, as agreed in connection with the Stennis compromise, was of no interest to Baker. "I am talking as a politician," he said. ". . . You have fired your cannon. Don't waste it. Let Sirica excerpt portions to the committee." I promised Baker that I would discuss his idea with Nixon, and I did. He rejected it out of hand on several grounds, including the belief that it conflicted with the confidentiality of the grand-jury process.

On Wednesday, I reported this reaction to Baker. Seasoned compromiser that he was, the senator from Tennessee was not quite ready to drop the issue. "Sirica might say that he'd [provide the committee with verbatim excerpts] in an extrajudicial manner," he said. "Since he's uniquely qualified, he could take on the role we visualized for Stennis."

Other arrangements concerning Sirica were already in train, and I put Baker off as courteously as I knew how.

"You sound weary," Baker said before we hung up.

"Not too bad," I replied.

My reply was not entirely responsive. Although I was working eighteen hours a day, seven days a week, in attempt to keep up with the White House routine and keep ahead of the bad news, the fatigue I felt was not physical but psychic. The presidency seemed to be slipping away, and each day brought new portents that this was so. Having just lived through the Agnew crisis, we were once again facing the situation we thought we had escaped, in which the President might be removed by a Democrat-controlled Congress while the vice presidency was vacant.

On Monday morning, the House Democratic leadership had met, with Speaker Albert, the man next in line of presidential succession, announcing afterward that he and his colleagues had tentatively agreed that the House Judiciary Committee would shortly commence a formal inquiry into the possible impeachment of the President. Around noon, John Connally called me from Texas to report what he had been hearing from his own excellent congressional sources and to advise a strong counterattack from the White House.

He did not understand the administration's quiescence in the face of its critics. "Somebody up there has to say the Democrats are going to hold Ford hostage," he said. "Someone should accuse them of stealing the presidency. If you can stand [up to the situation] for two or three more weeks, I think the American people will understand what's involved."

I agreed. On the other hand, I knew that any statement by Nixon or anyone connected to him that the opposition was attempting to "steal the presidency" would be greeted as the ravings of a madman. Nixon had been maneuvered into a position where his enemies were permitted to say anything they wished about him, while he was foreclosed from questioning their motives or even their actions. An exercise in this Kantian dialectic was to occur at a White House press conference on October 26. In response to a question by Dan Rather of CBS News, Nixon said with an unwise show of emotion that he had "never heard or seen such outrageous, vicious, distorted reporting." Rather's CBS colleague Robert Pierpoint asked what in particular about the media's coverage had made the President so angry. Nixon replied in a voice dripping with contempt. "Don't get the impression you arouse my anger," he said. ". . . You see, one can only be angry with those he respects." Professor Ambrose astutely describes the reaction of the White House press corps in his *Ruin and Recovery*: "Reporters gasped audibly. . . . He had let the reporters get to him, and aroused their wolfpack instincts."[4]

By Tuesday, October 23, eight impeachment resolutions, sponsored by a total of thirty-one Democrats, had been introduced in the House. During the debate, Representative Dan Kuykendall, Republican of Tennessee, was hissed from the chamber and the gallery when he advised his colleagues "don't be part of a lynch mob" and held up a hangman's noose "as a symbol of your action." Next day, the chairman of the House Judiciary Committee, Peter W. Rodino, Jr., Democrat of New Jersey, announced that the committee would proceed "full steam ahead" with its impeachment investigation.[5]

There were, of course, other grounds for an all-out assault on the opposition than speculation that they were trying to steal the presidency. Bork, now the Acting Attorney General, informed me early Tuesday afternoon that the files of the special prosecutor's office contained "paper cases against people . . . that are simply ridiculous." We discussed submitting these travesties of justice to the prosecutorial process and turning the witch-hunt on its head by exposing its questionable methods and standards to the light of day. But doing this in the courts would have been a time-consuming process for an administration unwilling to leak uncorroborated charges involving innocent people to the news media. Instead of counterattacking, Nixon decided, once again, to take the reasonable and judicious course and surrender the nine tapes subpoenaed by Judge Sirica—the intact tapes themselves, not summaries or digests as contemplated under the Stennis compromise.

The President's lawyers were unanimous in their advice that this was the best choice open to him. Though he now had fewer illusions regarding the likely side effects of releasing the verbatim record, Nixon himself thought it was the thing to do. Once again, he pointed out that the contents of the tapes would show that John Dean had lied in his testimony before the Ervin committee and, presumably, in his statements to the special prosecutor. Because the President was the only person besides Bob Haldeman* who had ever listened to the tapes, his judgment could not be questioned on the basis of the record.

Confidence was high that Sirica would interpret the tapes fairly, that what he found on them would exonerate the President, and that the nonrelevant portions would not leak from the chambers of a federal judge. Although I had my doubts about the third point, I did not demur.

Had I done so, I am sure it would have made little difference; since the Cox debacle, my stock with Nixon had fallen as I had expected it would. Although he continued to work with me, our relationship was not what it had been before. Until it could be restored, if that was even possible, my willingness to give candid advice and his to listen to it was limited by the mutual feeling that I had let him down. As one who had frequently urged a more confrontational presidential style, I was especially conscious that I had failed him by advising him to act against his own tougher instincts.

In any case, the President ordered Charles Alan Wright to go into Sirica's court on Tuesday and surrender the tapes. In spite of everything, there were hopes that this would somehow defuse the crisis. When, for example, I informed Bork of this decision at 2:20 P.M. on Tuesday, he uttered words that expressed the hopeful objectives of the administration: "I think it was the best thing. . . . We ought to have a talk about regularizing this matter so that it is handled in some routine way and we don't face any more crises." That was the intention. The reality was something else again.

Nixon's all but unbelievable bad luck intervened again. Soon after Wright had gone into court ("This President does not defy the law"[6]) and informed Sirica that the nine subpoenaed tapes would be delivered, Buzhardt discovered that two of the tapes could not be found. One of these was the conversation between Dean and Nixon on April 15, 1973, which the President had always maintained would establish the truth of his version of events. The other concerned a telephone conversation between Nixon and John Mitchell on June 20, 1972. It turned out that

---

* Although this was not known to me until well after the fact, Steve Bull had checked out tapes in April and May. Nixon had instructed Bull to deliver to Haldeman more than twenty tapes in June. This was, of course, several weeks after Haldeman's resignation. On learning of this transaction, I told Bull that nothing of the kind should ever happen again except with my knowledge. To my knowledge, it never did. Bull, of course, had heard portions of the tapes when assisting Nixon with the apparatus.

the latter had taken place over an instrument in the family quarters that was not connected to the automatic recording system.

But the President's conversation with Dean seemed not to have been recorded at all.

The reader will no doubt be surprised to know this, but I do not recall that this discovery caused any serious anxiety in the White House. Nixon in his sturdy optimism seemed to think that the court and the country would accept his word that the two conversations had simply never been recorded. At this point, he had not begun to understand the degree to which his own word was suspect. He spoke about the untidy way in which the Secret Service had handled, logged, labeled, and stored the tapes; Steve Bull had found that some were mislabeled and some stored out of sequence. The Secret Service had never before been faced with maintaining an eavesdropping system on this scale. It was not surprising that there should be some gaps in the record caused by oversight or other human error. He would have a panel of experts examine the evidence, he would provide his own notes of the April 15 meeting with Dean, as well as the recording of a meeting with Dean on April 16 that appeared to have covered more or less the same ground as the April 15 meeting.

There was another reason why Buzhardt did not panic, at least not at first. He thought there was a backup to the conversation, a Dictabelt account dictated by Nixon from his own notes immediately after the April 15 conversation with Dean. Nixon has explained in his memoirs how Buzhardt came to believe this:

> In April 1973, in a phone conversation with Henry Petersen, I had unthinkingly said that I believed that my April 15 conversation with John Dean had been recorded on tape. Petersen reported my remark to Cox, who later wrote to us requesting this tape for his investigation. In order to avoid revealing the existence of the taping system, I told Buzhardt to write to Cox and tell him that the "tape" I had in mind was actually the Dictabelt I had made after the meeting.[7]

Buzhardt, who had no reason to suspect that the President had misled him on this or any other question, was put in charge of finding the reason why the taping system, which was designed to pick up every word uttered in either of the President's offices, had failed to record this conversation of conversations with Dean. Secret Service technicians told Buzhardt that the system was designed to be loaded with two tapes, each of six hours' duration; when the first one ran out, a timing device automatically started the second. The first one was then replaced with a blank tape—except on weekends, when no one on duty was responsible for tending the tape machine. It was assumed, on the theory that the President used his offices much less on Saturdays and Sundays, that two six-hour tapes would cover the weekend.

The technicians speculated, Buzhardt told me, that the conversation with Dean, which took place on a Sunday evening, probably had not been recorded because the timing device malfunctioned, failing to start the second blank tape after the first one ran out.

Buzhardt appeared before Sirica with this explanation on October 31. The judge did not take the matter lightly. How could it be, he asked, that the White House had had the subpoena for the tapes since July and was only now telling the court that two of them did not exist?

Buzhardt had no ready answer to Sirica's question, but the truth was that the White House had assumed, without checking, that the tape existed because it believed that the taping system was infallible. Unfortunately, many of the President's critics were under the same impression, and this made it very difficult to claim, however truthfully, that the technology had broken down.

The embarrassment was only beginning. After Buzhardt's appearance in court, the technical experts decided that there might be another explanation: Both tapes had run out before the Nixon-Dean conversation began because the President had an unusually large number of visitors in his hideaway office that weekend. Poor Buzhardt returned to court and placed this new explanation before Judge Sirica.[8]

Buzhardt's first explanation was greeted with loud skepticism and the second with derision by Nixon's critics; even the President's friends were stunned. As Senator James L. Buckley, Conservative-Republican of New York, put it, "President Nixon has the clear burden of satisfying the American people that he has been speaking the truth. If he fails in this, we are faced with a political crisis of the most profoundly disturbing proportions."[9]

Sirica ordered a hearing, but testimony from the Secret Service agent in charge of the security of the tapes and others failed to produce any new information or explanation.

The episode, coming on the heels of the Cox firing, was a staggering blow to Nixon's credibility and to his chances for survival—which were, of course, one and the same thing. The news seriously undermined, if it did not destroy, Nixon's oft-repeated assurance that the tapes would support his version of events. How could he continue to maintain that the tapes would prove that he was telling the truth and Dean was lying if one of their conversations had mysteriously escaped being recorded?

The President meanwhile was exercised that the press insisted on referring to the tapes as "missing" when it was clear to him that they had never existed. This may have been true, but it was irrelevant. The *New York Times*, the *Boston Globe*, the *Atlanta Constitution*, and other papers across the country, even including Nixon's staunch defender, the *Detroit News*, called for his resignation; so did *Time* magazine in its first editorial in fifty years.[10] This pummeling on the editorial pages had no discernible effect on public opinion. The President's Gallup approval rating had dropped to 27 percent after Cox's firing (but would rebound to 32 percent in a Harris survey published November 11; the same percentage believed he had taken part in a cover-up).[11]

On November 1, the day after Buzhardt rendered his first explanation of the missing tapes to Sirica, the President flew to Key Biscayne. Buzhardt was left with the job of assembling the subpoenaed tapes together with the Dictabelt, having them transcribed, and delivering them to the court.

Of course, I went with Nixon, and a couple of days after our arrival in Florida the usually imperturbable Buzhardt phoned. His voice was agitated.

"Al, brace yourself," he said. "We can't find the Dictabelt."

This was distressing news, but Fred was so upset that I seriously thought that he might be on the verge of a heart attack. Nothing I could say made him any calmer. Of course, he had reason for the strongest feelings. Nixon, as he himself puts in his memoirs, "had put Buzhardt in an untenable position: first I had had him send a letter to Cox in order to divert him from a tape recording to a Dictabelt; now there was no Dictabelt."[12]

To Buzhardt, I said, "All right, I'll tell the President. We'll go from there."

That did not satisfy Buzhardt. He and Garment, he said, wanted to fly to Florida to discuss the matter with Nixon.

I tried to discourage this. What was the point? Nixon did not file his Dictabelts or anything else personally; others did such things for him without bothering him with the details, and he would be the last person who would know where to find a missing or mislaid item. Nevertheless, Buzhardt said, he and Garment wanted to talk to him. It was clear that nothing would stop them from coming to Key Biscayne, so I did not argue further.

As evening fell, I informed Nixon that the Dictabelt could not be found. Nixon seemed genuinely puzzled by this revelation but, once again, not especially troubled. Had Fred checked with Rose Mary Woods, with Steve, with Marge Acker, his other secretary? I told him I supposed they had checked with everyone. Nixon couldn't understand how the Dictabelt could be missing. He dictated his recollections of key conversations into the machine at the end of every day as a matter of routine, he said, sometimes as a diary entry, sometimes as an aide-mémoire. How could he have departed from habit with regard to what he knew, even then, was likely to be a key conversation?

In the absence of some supernatural explanation for this latest attack of bad luck, I was as much at a loss for an answer as he was. After pausing to shake his head over this inexplicable turn of events, Nixon made a suggestion.

"You know, Al," he said, "as far as the Dictabelt is concerned, all we have to do is create another one."

It took me a long moment to respond to this statement. Nixon's words shocked me, in the literal sense that I felt something like the tingle of an electrical current along my scalp.

"Mr. President, that cannot be done," I said. "It would be wrong; it would be illegal; it would be totally unacceptable. It's just impossible."

Unable to hide the astonishment and distress I was feeling, I gathered up my papers and left before Nixon had a chance to say more. As I walked back to my own bungalow, my mind raced in an attempt to understand the meaning of what the President of the United States had just said to me. Had he been joking, and had I embarrassed us both with my pompous reply? Or was he really suggesting that he create a facsimile and represent to the court that it was the authentic original? Considering his intelligence and experience this seemed unlikely. If he had wanted to do that, I asked myself, why hadn't he just dictated the damned thing and kept quiet about it? Was he really asking my advice on whether to commit what was clearly a serious crime? Or was this just another example, albeit a grotesquely inappropriate one, of his tendency to say outrageous things he did not mean in the expectation of being discouraged or contradicted?

I did not know; I still don't know. He never raised the question again, and he certainly never offered to explain himself. As in most other encounters with Nixon, I could not begin to understand what was really in his mind. But if he did mean what he said, this was the only time he ever suggested an impropriety to me.

Buzhardt and Garment awaited me in another bungalow. Joining them moments after leaving Nixon, I told them what he had just said to me about the Dictabelt. If they were agitated before I confided in them, they were beside themselves afterward. Nixon had put Buzhardt, whose total veracity was the hallmark of his character, in the position of making a false statement to Cox, and he was angry at having been duped into telling what would certainly be regarded as a lie and apprehensive over the possible legal consequences to himself. These included indictment, disbarment, and the certain ruin of his reputation. Because Garment had been relegated to a safer and far more passive role, he was in no such immediate peril. Nevertheless, or so it seemed to me, Garment was in a state of great moral and ethical discomfort over the nonexistent tapes, the vanished Dictabelt, and the cumulative effect of having nearly everything the President touched blow up into a new scandal.

It has been suggested elsewhere that Buzhardt and Garment went to Florida for the purpose of advising Nixon to resign. This may be so, but neither of them said anything about this to me then or afterward. What hung heavy yet unspoken in the air that evening was the possibility that Nixon had known all along that the April 15 tape was missing but had not confided this vital fact to his own counsel. If Nixon had kept this from them, what else had he concealed? What new surprises awaited them? Was the President guilty of crimes that were bound to come out, and, if he was, why should they suffer any longer the humiliation of being lied to by their client?

Both lawyers told me that they wanted to see the President at once. I found myself taking a deep breath, just to muster the patience to go on.

"For what?" I asked.

"To tender our resignations."

"You mean both of you? At this juncture?"

They nodded. Although they were emotional, there could be no doubt that they were serious.

So were the implications for Nixon. The resignation of both of his lawyers at this point would almost certainly finish him. It would be interpreted to mean that those who defended him and knew most about him had decided that he was undefendable. Those who wished to bring him down, already strident, would become hysterical. The news media would magnify the crisis. Nixon would be impeached; Ford would be left high and dry by Congress, and Carl Albert would become President of the United States.

I said, "I've got news. You guys are not going to resign. If you do go, you'll be asked to explain why. What are you going to say—that the

President lied to you? Remember what's at stake. We don't have a Vice President, and if the Boss takes one more kick in the shins, and if the Republicans in Congress sink any lower, Ford may never be approved. If you resign, the President will go down and the other party will take over the presidency."

An embarrassed silence followed this outburst. Buzhardt asked me what I advised.

"It's not a matter of advice," I said. "Fred, you know there's only one thing any of us can do—follow what's right in our consciences to see that the law and the Constitution are upheld in such a way that the President of the United States is not railroaded out of office. You may have a doubt in your minds about his innocence. That's not enough. Doubt is not proof. Whatever this man is, whatever he's done, whatever office he holds, he has the right to due process. If you won't defend him, knowing more about the case than anybody else, who will? If he fails to get due process, this will grievously wound the country and bring down consequences no one can measure or foresee. You may think you can desert him, but you can't desert him without deserting the country."

They still wanted to see Nixon. I told them that they could not. The last thing Nixon needed was to see that his own lawyers doubted his case. They quietly returned to Washington and carried on with their duties.

In a matter of days, there would be another disastrous embarrassment regarding the tapes. This was the revelation of the so-called eighteen-and-a-quarter-minute gap in the tape of a conversation between Nixon and Haldeman recorded on June 20, 1972, Nixon's first day back in Washington after the Watergate break-in.

I had known that this tape was damaged since the early afternoon of October 1, when Nixon called me into his office and told me that his secretary, Rose Mary Woods, believed she had accidentally erased a short portion of the conversation. October 1 was a Monday. The preceding Friday, on my instructions, working from a list provided by Buzhardt, General Bennett had withdrawn the subpoenaed tapes, and some others, from the safe.

The President, who planned to spend the weekend at Camp David with Bebe Rebozo as his guest, wanted to take the tapes with him. His idea was that Rose Mary Woods would listen to and transcribe the subpoenaed portions, and perhaps other parts, on her typewriter and he would refresh his memory of these conversations by reading the transcripts. Steve Bull went along to "cue" the tapes—that is, load them into a tape recorder and find the relevant portions for Miss Woods as he had previously done for the President.

Nixon had hoped that the job of transcription could be accomplished over the weekend. But even though Miss Woods, a very fast typist, was transcribing only portions of the tapes, it turned out to be a far more tedious task than anyone had imagined. On Saturday morning, September 29, I called Camp David to see how it was going. Steve Bull answered the phone and told me that he and Rose Woods were making slow progress. For one thing, he was having trouble finding a conversation on June 20 that had included Nixon, Bob Haldeman, and John Ehrlichman. When I checked with Buzhardt, he told me that the conversation Cox had subpoenaed was one between Nixon and Ehrlichman that had lasted from 10:25 to 11:20 A.M. I called Camp David again and told Rose Woods, who answered the phone on this occasion, what Buzhardt had told me.[13]

Later that day, General Bennett told me that Bull had been having difficulty finding one of the tapes—he did not say which one—but he, Bennett, had located it in the safe where it was stored and would deliver it personally to Camp David.[14]

On Monday morning, Nixon told me that something had gone awry. "Rose is very upset," he said when I walked into the Oval Office. He went on to say that Miss Woods had been transcribing the June 20 tape containing a conversation between Nixon and Haldeman when the telephone rang. After handling the call, she returned to her typing and discovered that a portion of the tape, "four or five minutes," had been erased. Nixon said Miss Woods thought she might have punched the RECORD button instead of the STOP button on the tape recorder when she answered the phone.

Nixon was very concerned—not so much about the erasure, which he regarded as an unfortunate accident about which nothing could be done, as by Rose Mary Woods's distress. She had worked for him for years and he not only trusted her absolutely but was very fond of her as a family friend. She was emotionally devastated, Nixon told me, and was blaming herself for what she regarded as an inexcusable mistake that had the potential of damaging the President. Nixon was looking for a way to relieve her mind. Could I talk the matter over with Buzhardt and let him know Fred's opinion?

I went back to my office and called Buzhardt, who identified the damaged tape and assured me that the material Miss Woods thought she had obliterated had not been subpoenaed. I breathed a sigh of relief and immediately passed the word to the President. "Be sure and have Fred tell Rose it's all right," he said. "She's worried enough about this." Buzhardt told Miss Woods the good news, and for the moment the incident faded away.

We were still working our way through the labyrinth into which we had been led in search of an explanation of the two nonexistent tapes and the vanished Dictabelt when, on the evening of November 14, Fred Buzhardt told me that we had yet another problem with the tapes. I went over to the Executive Office Building, where Buzhardt and his Assistant Counsel, Samuel J. Powers, were preparing the subpoenaed tapes for delivery to Judge Sirica. Both wore earphones connected to a tape recorder. A stopwatch lay on the large round table at which they were working.

As soon as I was inside the room, Buzhardt said, "Al, do you remember the accident Rose described to the President after they had the tapes up at Camp David?" I nodded. "Well," Fred continued in his matter-of-fact manner, "we just put a timer on the gap and instead of the 'four and a half to five minutes' Rose thought she had erased, it runs exactly eighteen minutes and fifteen seconds."

"And we're just finding this out?" I asked. The tapes had been duplicated that day, a Wednesday, by experts at the National Security Agency (NSA) and were scheduled to be delivered to the court the following Tuesday.

"That's not all," Fred said. "Sam and I have looked at the subpoena and the prosecutor's brief again, and we agree that this tape *is* covered by the subpoena. We'll have to deliver it to the court, gap or no gap."

"That's not what you told me to tell the President when he asked about this before," I said. "It's pretty goddamn late in the day to be changing your mind about something as important as this."

He agreed. The subpoena had been ambiguous in regard to this particular tape, Fred explained, but the prosecutor's brief, a separate but supplemental document received later, indicated clearly that the tape with the gap was indeed among those subpoenaed. He showed me this document; after reading it and the subpoena, I saw that he was right.

While this was happening, Nixon was meeting with a delegation from the Senate as part of his campaign to discuss Watergate face-to-face with members of the House and Senate.* It was late in the evening; he was scheduled to give a press conference and a speech the next day. I decided that he needed all the sleep he could get and that I would wait until morning to give him the news about the gap in the tape.

When, finally, I told Nixon the new facts, he erupted. "How in hell could they have made a mistake about what was on the subpoena?" he said. "Goddamn it, Al, lawyers are supposed to be able to read subpoenas—that's why they go to law school!" And so on. He instantaneously became his own lawyer, as he was wont to do at such moments, and began issuing legalistic orders to me. After he had got rid of his anger, I interrupted, suggesting that it would be better for him to discuss this matter directly with the lawyers.

He agreed, and at about four o'clock that afternoon Buzhardt came into the Oval Office, where the President and I were waiting for him, and repeated to Nixon what he had told me the night before. By now, Nixon had calmed down, and he received Buzhardt's report gravely but without uttering any recriminations. I kept absolutely quiet throughout the discussion.

Nixon seemed to be looking for a way to give the court the information that was missing from the tape. "I don't remember what Bob Haldeman and I said to each other that day," he told Buzhardt. "But there's got to be some way of reconstituting the thing."

"I've been thinking about that," Fred said. "What about Haldeman's notes?"

"Good idea, Fred," Nixon said. "Bob always took notes on everything."

He directed Buzhardt to search for the notes. We knew that Haldeman's papers were in secure storage in the White House complex, but no one had the combination to his safe. Before leaving in May, he had told me that he had had the combination changed. I called him at his home in California; after remarking that he didn't recall the specifics of the conversation on June 20, either, he suggested that his former assistant, Lawrence Higby, who still worked in the White House, would be able to find his notes, if they existed.

After considerable searching, Buzhardt and Higby did find Haldeman's

---

*The next day Nixon was asked whether another shoe was going to drop in regard to the Watergate scandal. He replied, "As to the guilt of the President, no." Shortly after this, when the story of the eighteen-and-a-quarter-minute gap broke, Anne Armstrong, an idealistic young member of the staff concerned with women's questions, came into my office with tears in her eyes. "Why didn't somebody tell me the shoes would be dropping off a centipede?" she said.

notes among his papers. These consisted of two pages from a yellow legal pad. Fred immediately compared them to the tape and, though the notes were somewhat cryptic, discovered that the erased portion of the conversation had concerned Watergate. As soon as Fred told me this, I walked into the Oval Office and informed the President, handing him the original of Haldeman's notes (a photocopy having been placed in Haldeman's file).

Nixon heard the news without flinching and, typically, even found a spar of hope to which to cling. "These electronics fellows can do a lot nowadays," he said. "We've got to get the best man there is to see if the tape can be reconstituted. Or don't you agree, Al?"

I agreed wholeheartedly. Buzhardt knew an expert on tape recordings at NSA and we arranged for him to examine the damaged tape. We gained a little time in a most unfortunate way when the very able and seriously overworked Sam Powers developed pneumonia and Buzhardt obtained a postponement of the delivery date from Judge Sirica.

Nixon had a busy weekend ahead, and I left the problem of the eighteen-and-a-quarter-minute gap to Buzhardt in order to help him to prepare for it. The President was scheduled to participate in a ninety-minute question-and-answer session with Associated Press managing editors at Disney World, then deliver a speech in Macon, Georgia, and attend the Republican Governors Conference in Memphis. The NSA man had informed us on Friday, before we left for Florida, that he thought that the possibility of reclaiming the lost conversation was practically nil. Buzhardt continued to work with the tape recorder Rose Mary Woods had used, in an attempt to reproduce the tone that could be heard on the erased portion of the tape.

Asked by one of the AP men at the session at Disney World how he felt about the two nonexistent tapes, Nixon replied, "[The fact that they were not there was a] very great disappointment . . . and I just wish we had had a better system. I frankly wish we hadn't had a system at all. Then I wouldn't have to answer this question."[15]

The questions were only beginning to be asked. On Monday, as we approached Memphis, Buzhardt called me aboard Air Force One to say that he had news. We could not discuss it over the notoriously insecure telephones aboard Air Force One, which could be monitored by anyone on the ground who happened to be turned to the same frequency. After the plane had landed, I called Fred back on a land line.

"I've worked with Rose's tape recorder every way I know how, and there just doesn't seem to be any way her machine could have made the noise we hear on the tape," Buzhardt told me.

I groaned.

"It gets worse," Fred said. "You can hear two different tones on the tape where it was erased. One lasts about five minutes. Then the second tone cuts in, and it lasts until the end of the eighteen-minute gap." After a moment in which neither of us spoke, he said, "Al, you'd better tell the President this is pretty damn serious. On the basis of what we know so far, I don't see how the gap could have been accidental."

There was no opportunity to tell Nixon what Fred had told me until we got back on the plane. When the moment came, he listened stoically. "Get together with the lawyers as soon as we get back," he said.

I did so, and their unanimous recommendation was that the court be informed of our findings with the least possible delay.

I carried this advice into the Oval Office as soon as the meeting was over. It was now quite late in the evening. Nixon would have preferred to deal with the problem the next morning, but I pressed him to understand how urgent the matter was.

"All right," he said, with not the smallest trace of hesitation. "It has to be done. So tell Fred to do it as soon as he can get to Sirica."

Buzhardt notified Sirica in chambers of the gap on November 21, telling him, according to Sirica, that the erasure appeared to be deliberate. The judge, who believed that "charges of obstruction of justice and contempt of court were clearly a possibility," required him to announce it in open court an hour and a half later, and set a hearing for the Monday after Thanksgiving, five days hence.[16] Everyone in the White House who had any knowledge of the eighteen-and-a-quarter-minute gap except the President was questioned at length in open court, but no explanation for its existence, or for its expansion from Rose Woods's short erasure to the longer one, emerged from the testimony.

The federal prosecutor, Richard Ben-Veniste, was a zealous and apparently tireless cross-examiner. Half-amused, half-exasperated by his lengthy and transparent attempt to establish a dark interpretation concerning the gap, I lightheartedly (or light-headedly) suggested, with a wink to Sirica that the press gallery missed, that "perhaps some sinister force" had erased the additional fourteen minutes or so after Rose Woods had accidentally blanked out the initial four and a half to five minutes. "That," I testified, "is what I referred to as a devil theory." As a general principle, irony is unwise, especially in the presence of the press; I was quoted next day as suggesting in a serious way that a sinister force had been at work. Another flippant remark to the effect that Miss Woods was a woman and I had known women to spend an hour on the phone in the belief that the conversation had lasted only five minutes got me into trouble with a large and vocal segment of the female population.

In the absence of a factual explanation, devil theory took over. If Nixon felt any special sense of foreboding over this development, he did not show it. But of course he knew, as we all did, that the revelation that a vital segment in one of his tapes had mysteriously been erased, coming on the heels of announcements that two other key tapes had never existed and a critically important Dictabelt had been lost, would be the straw that broke the back of public opinion.

And so it was. Another media storm lighted up the skies over Washington. Accusations flew; suspicions festered; the mood of the Establishment darkened. And as a practical matter, the burden of proof on the question of the guilt or innocence of the President of the United States for crimes still to be discovered or named had shifted. He was now faced with the necessity of establishing his innocence, a process known by the legal profession to be so far beyond human ingenuity that the Founding Fathers had abolished it from American practice in the Bill of Rights.

33

The Tale of the Tapes

While the melodrama of the nonexistent tapes and then the sequel concerning the eighteen-and-a-quarter-minute gap were playing themselves out in Judge Sirica's courtroom and in the press, President Nixon was attempting to find and appoint a new Attorney General and special prosecutor. As regards the Attorney Generalship, Robert Bork was the sentimental candidate in terms of intellectual capacity, character, qualifications, and the trust and admiration he inspired in the President. A former professor at Yale Law School, Bork had been a favorite of Elliot Richardson, who had been so impressed by his powerful intellect and sound judgment that he made a point of bringing him with him to meetings with the President or putting him on the phone with me when especially difficult issues were to be discussed.

But Bork had fired Cox, and no one imagined that he could be confirmed by the Senate after that. A month or so after the event, I told him, "You have [crossed] the Rubicon. I think you will be glad you did it over the years." Perhaps so, but I did not foresee the implacable enmity and resentment he incurred on the Left by carrying out Nixon's order. Even fifteen years later, when he was nominated to the Supreme Court by President Reagan, his brilliant professional qualifications and unimpeachable personal honor could not overcome this crippling ideological handicap, and his nomination was rejected after bitterly partisan hearings before

435

the Senate Judiciary Committee. This was a great loss to the Supreme Court and the country, as well as a chilling warning to young lawyers who may have thought about emulating Bork's courageous devotion to constitutional duty.

As in the case of the vice presidency, probably no Republican who was not a member of the Senate or the House could have been confirmed as Attorney General in the atmosphere then prevailing. Nixon chose Senator William B. Saxbe, a combative Ohio Republican who had worked his way up the ladder of state politics, serving as speaker of the Ohio House of Representatives and Attorney General before being elected to the Senate in 1969. His independence of mind regarding the Watergate case could hardly be questioned; it was Saxbe who had said, in April 1972, that protestations of ignorance from the White House reminded him of "the guy playing piano downstairs in a bawdy house saying he doesn't know what's going on upstairs."[1] After pro forma hearings in which he promised full independence to the special prosecutor, he was sworn in on January 4, 1974.

The more sensitive appointment was, of course, that of special prosecutor. Within hours of Cox's departure, the House Judiciary Committee began drafting a bill to compel the President to appoint a new man to Cox's old job, effectively killing Nixon's plan to hand the Watergate case back to Henry Petersen and the routine machinery of the Justice Department. I began making inquiries and asking for advice, especially from Bork. He insisted, for a whole string of reasons cogently stated, that the President's idea of handing the Watergate investigation back to Henry Petersen and the Justice Department was impossible to implement. There had to be a new special prosecutor, acceptable to Congress. I said, All right—but let's choose him from among the very best lawyers the country has. We began with the lists of names of potential Supreme Court Justices the Justice Department had compiled under the three most recent administrations.

Working with Bork on this difficult and sensitive undertaking was an unalloyed pleasure. His mind was as ingenious as it was brilliant, and he did not hesitate to broach new concepts. Early on, he mentioned the idea of a three-man bipartisan commission of eminent jurists, rather than a single all-powerful special prosecutor. This was an attractive concept, but the problem of finding not one but three qualified lawyers who were willing to give up their privacy and practice and take the job, and who would all be acceptable to the gallery, boggled the mind. Charles Rhyne, the sagacious Washington lawyer who represented Rose Mary Woods in the hearing on the tape gap, offered the soundest, if most superfluous, guidance of all. "Tell the President," he advised, "never again to put himself in the hands of the Harvards."

Whoever the appointee turned out to be, and whatever his other qualifications were, he had to be a Democrat. This was no problem for Nixon as long as the Democrat was a conservative. He regarded many Southern Democrats of the Stennis mold as being closer to him in their philosophy than most eastern Republicans. A number of famous names in this category were brought forward, and some were sounded out, but all declined the honor of being considered for what was, excepting only the Presidency itself, the most difficult job in public life. One well-known New York lawyer was willing to take the job if he could split his time between his law practice and the job of special prosecutor; we said no to that.

One name, that of Leon Jaworski of Houston, Texas, was included on almost everybody's list. He had been approached by the Justice Department during the original search for a special prosecutor, but he had asked to have his name removed from consideration. Jaworski had received his law degree from Baylor University at the age of nineteen and won his first case, the defense of an alleged moonshiner in Waco, at twenty. As an Army colonel, he had been a prosecutor at the Nuremberg Nazi war crimes trial and had served on two presidential commissions, as well as successfully defending his close friend Lyndon Johnson against Republican lawsuits seeking to enjoin him from running for both the vice presidency and the Senate in the 1960 election.[2] He was a former President of the American Bar Association, but he was not a creature of its liberal wing, even though he was a friend of Cox, with whom he had worked during the Kennedy administration. Under both Republican and Democratic Presidents, the Justice Department had included his name among those considered as potential candidates for appointment to the Supreme Court. He was a political ally of John Connally and, as I put it to Nixon on October 30 in a call to Camp David, "a very, very honest man of the Texas Democrat variety."

"My own view is just *get the man!*" Nixon replied. "If he's a decent fellow, get him."

There was good reason for the President's sense of urgency. Earlier that day, the House Judiciary Committee had voted itself broad subpoena powers. The word from Capitol Hill was that the committee's impeachment investigation would soon involve demands for new tapes that were not related to Watergate. The committee was thought to have licensed itself to investigate, like some many-headed clone of Archibald Cox, not just the Watergate case but every aspect of the administration's dealings with the outside world and every corner of Nixon's life and reputation. As I told the President in this same conversation, some of his adversaries had concluded that the Watergate tapes would contain no evidence of his involvement in the cover-up. They needed new issues, new tapes.

Nixon, incredulous, said, "The House Judiciary Committee wants to subpoena the tapes to see if the President could be impeached [on other grounds than Watergate]?"

"Yes. It's the left-wing liberals."

"I must say," gasped Nixon in pained disbelief that anyone, even his enemies, would go so far. Then, after a pause, he added, "I will turn over the keys to the White House first before I turn over any more tapes. . . . Say we will furnish information relative [to the tapes] *but not the tapes*."

Nixon's choice of words regarding the keys to the White House was more prophetic than either of us knew.

I asked John Connally to call Jaworski and sound him out about the job we had in mind for him. When he expressed an interest in talking about the terms of the appointment, I sent a small Air Force passenger plane to pick him up at Ellington Air Force Base, near Houston, and a White House car and driver to collect him at Andrews. We met for the first time on October 31, 1973, in my office in the White House. Even though Nixon had already, in effect, approved Jaworski's appointment and Jaworski knew we would hardly have flown him to Washington with such ceremony unless we thought we wanted to hire him, he had not actually been offered the job, much less agreed to accept it. In fact, the question had not been settled. It seemed to me important to talk to the candidate in person before making any final offer. I had never met Cox (nor, so far as I know, had Nixon), and I had often wondered whether a simple interview before appointment might not have saved us from an irretrievable mistake, or at least reduced the role that demonology played on both sides of the relationship.

My first impression of Jaworski, which was abundantly confirmed in the punishing months ahead, was that of a worldly man of quiet intelligence, judicial temperament, and innate honesty and fair-mindedness. I told him that his name had first come up because I had asked Bork to give me copies of the Justice Department's wish list for possible appointees to the Supreme Court, and he had appeared on the rosters of both parties. My remark was meant as a pleasantry but was later cited as an attempt to dangle a Supreme Court appointment before Jaworski's eyes in order to buy his soul for Richard Nixon; all I can say is, he'd have to be a lot more naïve than his reputation suggested to be to respond to such a clumsy proposition.

Jaworski's chief concern was a natural one: How much freedom of action would he have? I asked how much he wanted. He said he could settle for nothing less than complete independence and the right to sue Nixon in the courts for evidence. These were, of course, the very prerogatives that had caused the President so much grief when exercised by Cox. I promised Jaworski the powers he asked for without hesitation, partly because the President had no choice and partly because Jaworski so obviously was no zealot. On the contrary, as we talked in the most studiously general terms, it became apparent that he was possessed of a respect for the presidency that amounted to reverence. Nixon had already agreed that he would not fire the special prosecutor without the agreement of a majority of an eight-member group composed of the majority and minority leaders of the Senate and House and the chairmen and ranking minority leaders of the Judiciary committees of both houses of Congress. I told Jaworski about this.

It seemed to me that it would be improper to question Jaworski about his intentions should he be appointed, and I avoided doing so. There could be no question of his diligence; his whole demeanor let you know that he would seek the truth no matter where the search led him. He seemed determined to act with all deliberate speed. He betrayed no trace of prejudice or vindictiveness.

I asked Jaworski whether there was any other assurance he needed. He said no. "In that case," I said, "I think I'd better go in and talk to the President. You're welcome to come along and raise any point you wish."

He declined, saying that he thought it would be better if he and Nixon did not meet. In my report to the President, I confined myself to describing the details of my conversation with Jaworski. This, added to my basic impressions—afterward reinforced a hundred times over—were enough to make the case for his appointment. When I emerged, I formally offered the post of special prosecutor to Jaworski and he accepted it. Bork announced his appointment the next day. A mere twelve days had passed since the Saturday Night Massacre, and Nixon had once again delivered his fate into the hands of a stranger.

The appointment of a new Attorney General and special prosecutor under guarantees of independent action broke the logjam that briefly delayed congressional approval of Gerald R. Ford as the thirty-eighth, and first appointed, Vice President of the United States. On December 6, in a tribute by his congressional colleagues to his popularity and reputation for probity, Ford was approved 92 to 3 in the Senate and 387 to 35 in the House.[3] Because I was testifying that day before Judge Sirica on the question of the tape gap, I heard about the votes during court recesses.[4]

A few days earlier, Ford had told me that the Speaker of the House was insisting on having the swearing-in ceremony at a joint session of Congress in the House chamber, with the President in attendance and Chief Justice Warren E. Burger administering the oath. "This isn't what the President had in mind, I know," Ford told me, "but I don't think we're in a position to antagonize the Speaker at this point."

I reminded Ford that Nixon was determined to hold the ceremony in the East Room at the White House.

Ford gently let me know that there was no graceful way to refuse to permit the House to act as host for the swearing-in of one of its own members as the first Vice President ever approved by the House. He passed me some ammunition for future talks with Nixon on the subject. "If he were to come up [to Capitol Hill, wouldn't] it be a good gesture on his part?" Ford asked, adding, "They will have TV. . . . With him coming up, it adds a luster or glamour that would not otherwise be present."

"That side he likes," I replied. "What he doesn't like is that the House is . . . starting impeachment proceedings against him."

In the end, Nixon made the trip down Pennsylvania Avenue in order to observe rather than preside over the swearing-in of his new Vice President. Some had predicted that there would be an anti-Nixon outburst when he entered in the well of the House, but nothing of the kind occurred. Ford was greeted with long and affectionate applause as he and Nixon walked down the aisle together, and the President managed to smile through this expedition into enemy territory. Striking precisely the right note of humility after taking the oath of office, Ford said, "I am a Ford, not a Lincoln." He added the appropriate sentiment that his swearing-in "demonstrated to the world that our great Republic stands solid, stands strong upon the bedrock of the Constitution."[5]

The atmosphere on Capitol Hill revealed more about the political realities of the day than perhaps had been intended. Ford was treated throughout the ceremony and afterward as a President-in-waiting, especially by Republicans, and there can be little question that Richard Nixon's presidency was over, in their minds, from the moment his successor took the oath. By then, the left wing of his own party, and much of the center, had effectively given up hope that he could be saved.

As Christmas approached, the opposition within the party began to reveal itself more boldly. Senator Edward Brooke of Massachusetts went on national television and became the first Republican to call on Nixon to resign.[6] Senator Robert Packwood of Oregon told the President publicly that "Watergate has destroyed your ability to inspire and lead the country." Congressman Paul McCloskey of California, who had been a strident opponent of Nixon's Vietnam policy, said after a meeting with the President that he had sensed an "air of unreality" because the President was "adopting a posture that the opposition to him is politically and partisanly motivated rather than motivated by a search for the truth."[7]

Melvin Laird, whose mood had ever been a reliable reflection of that of Congress, announced that he was resigning his post as presidential counselor and said he believed that an impeachment vote "would be a healthy thing."[8] Blunt Barry Goldwater, the 1964 GOP Presidential nominee, told the *Christian Science Monitor* that "Mel Laird has quit mainly because the President won't listen to him. Bryce Harlow is reportedly quitting for the same reason." Goldwater remarked that he had never known such a loner as Nixon, adding, "He chose to dibble and dabble and argue on very nebulous grounds like executive privilege and confidentiality when all the American people wanted was the truth."[9] When Nixon invited Goldwater to dinner in the White House in the wake of these remarks, word leaked to the news media that a disoriented Nixon had talked "gibberish" throughout the evening. According to the published account, Goldwater had snapped at him, in the presence of Mrs. Nixon and their daughters and sons-in-law, "Act like a President!"[10] The times were sufficiently upside down that this bit of gossip was thought by many to reflect creditably on Goldwater.

This was one of many stories, apocryphal and otherwise, that fed rumors of a Nixon driven to drink and clinical depression by his troubles. The truth is that Nixon maintained psychological equilibrium under conditions that would have driven a saint around the bend. As to his so-called weakness for drink, this was another invention of backstairs raillery and gossip. Although he enjoyed vintage wines and fine spirits, he had a very low tolerance for alcohol, and this physiological condition severely limited his intake. The legend of Nixon's "drinking problem" was just that, a false exaggeration of a minor aspect of his metabolism that played its part in the generalized assassination of his character.

Although many in his own party—including several powerful governors and senators and Ford himself—stood by the President, the impression was inescapable that a large number of Republicans on Capitol Hill and in the party apparatus could hardly wait to see their friend Gerry Ford in the White House. These men and women wanted Nixon to go, and go quickly, so that there would be time for the embarrassments of Watergate to fade before the 1974 congressional elections, and for Ford to convince the American people to elect him President in his own right in 1976.

In January, the White House heard from several believable sources that a Republican cabal was forming in Grand Rapids, Michigan. This group reportedly included members of the Michigan congressional delegation and people from Ford's staff. It had gone so far as to start to form a shadow Cabinet to serve under Ford after the fall of Nixon, an event that the cabal regarded as imminent. "These guys are absolutely determined that Nixon will be out and Ford will be in right after the Moscow summit in June," said one of our sources.

As far as I could tell, there was never the slightest suspicion in Nixon's mind (there was certainly none in mine) that Ford himself was involved in this intrigue or even aware of it; such devious behavior on his part was unimaginable—which was why, we assumed, the cabal was working behind his back at such a long remove from Washington.

The Grand Rapids group were not alone in believing that Nixon was the sick man of American politics. Scarcely a week went by without some prominent person publicly offering the President an ingenious plan for abandoning his office. In the minds of the political establishment, the question was not whether his wounds would untimely carry him off but when and under what circumstances. No schemes to perpetuate him in power ever made the newspapers; above all, there was no Republican Catesby to cry, as in the last act of Shakespeare's *King Richard the Third*, "Rescue . . . or else the day is lost!"[11]

Alas, for those who wished him under the political sod, Nixon did not accept their diagnosis. He believed he could survive and revive his popular mandate. In his solitude, he fought against the abject surrender that resignation represented in his mind, studying the weaknesses of his enemies, mulling over his chances, counting the number of votes he needed to survive a bill of impeachment in the House, and examining the polls for signs of what the American people thought of him.

By early December, Vice President Ford was calling for a conclusion of the House Judiciary Committee's impeachment investigation by April. Chairman Rodino, after denying that Democrats on the committee were delaying the process for partisan advantage, was saying that he might be able to meet that schedule.[12] Scarcely anyone took this statement seriously.

From the President's point of view, of course, an early decision was desirable. The coalition of conservative Southern Democrats and the Republicans constituted the majority he needed to avert impeachment. So long as this coalition hung together, he could hold on and wait, as he said me and others, for his innocence to be established. But he could not wait forever without losing votes. His popular support was low but steady. After dropping to 27 percent after Cox was fired, his Gallup approval rating rebounded within ten days to 31 percent and maintained that level when Gallup again took the nation's statistical pulse a month later.[13]

In early December, after the Saturday Night Massacre, after all the shocks regarding the nonexistent tapes and the eighteen-and-a-quarter-minute gap, after all of the testimony before the Ervin committee, after five former White House and CRP officials and fourteen others had pleaded guilty or no contest to Watergate-related charges—after the worst public battering any President had ever undergone, the Gallup poll found that 54 percent of its respondents answered no to the question "Should President Nixon be impeached and compelled to leave the Presidency?" A Harris poll published on Christmas Eve showed that 45 percent of those approached rejected the statement that Nixon could "no longer be an effective President and should resign for the good of the country."[14]

There was even some mild encouragement from the courts. On December 19, Judge Sirica upheld Nixon's claim of executive privilege in regard to two of the tapes turned over to him on grounds that they contained nothing relevant to the Watergate investigation. Jaworski's office issued a statement agreeing with Sirica's decision not to provide these tapes to the special prosecutor.

I couldn't let myself believe that Nixon, an elected President who had so far withstood the most thorough investigation of his life and work in the history of the republic, was finished. In spite of everything, he was governing the country. He proposed a health-insurance plan to provide uniform health care, especially for the poor and for children, without raising taxes and without putting the private health-insurance industry at risk, and without creating a new federal bureaucracy. He proposed legislation to end the busing of school children, to increase federal funding but decrease federal control of local schools, and asked for $1.3 billion in grants for college students. He achieved agreements on the prevention of nuclear war and the peaceful uses of atomic energy, as well as progress on strategic arms limitations. He approved appointees for all Cabinet and sub-Cabinet posts; on his behalf, I continued to recruit new people for high positions, and filled a higher percentage of key high-level posts than at any other time since 1969. When the settlement of a murderous truckers' strike involving gunplay and other violence was delayed under the mediation of Governor Milton Shapp of Pennsylvania, I ordered the Assistant Secretary of Labor, W. J. Usery, to reconvene the bargaining session after Shapp had gone to bed. He did so, and, when the governor woke in the morning, the issue was settled. Despite mulish opposition from Congress, Nixon struggled to come to grips with rising inflation and unemployment and address the energy crisis brought on by the OPEC oil embargo, which had created long lines at American gas stations and was driving inflation upward with huge increases in prices. Defeating a panicky proposal from Congress to impose gasoline rationing, he stated that increasing supplies was the answer and launched Kissinger on a negotiating process that brought an end to the embargo and laid the basis for future market surpluses instead of the catastrophic depletion of petroleum reserves that was then the fashionable prediction. Although his bills on education and health insurance were rejected by Congress, many of his programs, including the revolutionary idea of revenue sharing with the states in order to increase their authority over their own problems, continued to win approval in Congress through the steady support of the conservative coalition. * During Watergate, he vetoed $35 billion in budget-busting appropriations voted by Congress[15] and held together a supportive coalition of votes in House and Senate. In the election year 1972, Congress approved automatic cost-of-living increases in Social Security, a measure whose popularity is matched only by its relentless pressure on the budget deficit, as well as a major expansion in food stamps.

In January 1974, Nixon was hissed and booed by Democrats in the

---

* Charges that Nixon was an isolated and inactive President, widespread at the time, are contradicted by figures compiled by David Gergen, the White House communications director. According to Gergen's analysis, Nixon spent 168 hours between September 15, 1972, and April 30, 1973, discussing foreign affairs with Rogers, Kissinger, Scowcroft, and me in person and 25 hours with the four of us on the telephone. In the first seven and a half months of 1974, while the impeachment hearings dominated the front pages, he met with twenty-five heads of state and twenty-three other foreign representatives; conducted eight Cabinet meetings and eighty-three personal meetings with members of the Cabinet; received twenty-nine major congressional groups and thirty individual members of Congress; made sixty public appearances; delivered fourteen major addresses; held five press conferences or announcements to the press; presided over ten major economic meetings and eight major meetings on the energy crisis; participated in a summit in Moscow; and announced the unconditional lifting of the OPEC oil embargo as a result of American diplomacy.

House chamber during the State of the Union message when he announced that he would continue to withhold the tapes from the special prosecutor in defense of the principle of executive privilege. Raising his fist, he told the Joint Session of Congress, "I want you to know that I have no intention whatever of walking away from the job that the people elected me to do for the people of the United States." For me, and for his family, with whom I was sitting in the gallery, this was a moment of considerable emotion.[16]

All suspended judgments inside the White House as to the House Judiciary Committee's methods and purposes came tumbling down in January when the committee announced that it had engaged Albert E. Jenner, Jr., of Chicago as chief minority counsel. As such, his duties would ostensibly include assuring fair play in a case in which the impeachment of a Republican President was being pressed by the Democrats. Jenner was a registered Republican. But he was also said to be a close family friend and fund-raiser for Senator Adlai E. Stevenson III, Democrat of Illinois, who had predicted that Nixon would "not survive three more months in office." Most troubling of all, he had stated on a Chicago television program, during a discussion of impeachment, that the President should be legally responsible for the actions of some of his aides even if he did not know about them in advance. "This," commented Attorney General Saxbe, is a "rather bizarre" notion.[17]

To the White House lawyers who brought me the first news of this appointment, it was more than bizarre. "The impeachment hearings will be nothing but a kangaroo court," Buzhardt told me. "They intend to railroad the President."

These worrisome events notwithstanding, Nixon continued to guide foreign policy with a sure hand and win the admiration of other world leaders who understood his achievements. Some of the latter wondered aloud, in private moments, how he did what he did in the face of the rancorous forces assembled against him at home. So did I.

Early in February, Nixon decided not to release five tapes subpoenaed by the Ervin committee, and he also declined to give Jaworski some papers and tapes he had requested.[18] These maneuvers notwithstanding, the President persisted in the stubborn belief that the tapes contained a cure for the suspicions about him. Nixon may have told me in private, and told Congress and the courts and the world in his news conferences and speeches, that he would surrender no more tapes in response to subpoenas, but at the same time he remained convinced that their publication to a candid American people would remove all questions as to his own wrongdoing. And he still wanted to publish the tapes in some abbreviated form that would uphold his version of events. Knowing my position—I continued to argue for full disclosure short of releasing verbatim material from the tapes—Nixon had long since ceased discussing the matter with me.

During the waning weeks of 1973, without telling me what was afoot, the President started the wheels turning in a scheme to transcribe and publish the parts of the tapes in which Watergate was discussed. A confidential task force of editors, typists, and proofreaders working under Pat Buchanan, who shared Nixon's ingenuous belief that release of the presidential conversations would answer all questions, prepared extensive excerpts. They carried out this heady task right under my nose in such absolute secrecy that it not only did not leak to the press but I had no inkling of its existence until Buchanan mentioned in a staff meeting that the transcripts of the tapes were "almost all typed up" and ready for release to the press.

After registering my surprise in emphatic terms (and also my admiration for the way in which Buchanan and his team had kept their mouths shut), I asked to see the typescript, closed the door of my office, and began to read. This was my first exposure to the contents of the tapes. Nixon and Haldeman, and Steve Bull and Rose Mary Woods in a technical capacity, were still the only people (apart from Buchanan's team) who had ever listened to the tapes. In one sense, what I read was heartening. Just as Nixon had said, the transcripts contained nothing that could reasonably be interpreted as expressing criminal intent or action on his part, and they raised doubts as to the accuracy of Dean's version of events.

However, these points were meaningless compared to the overall impression created by the verbatim record of the presidential conversations. Prurient interest already existed on a grand scale, and the transcripts, to put it mildly, could have no other effect than to make it worse. Even I, who had been present during many such conversations and knew what to expect, was shocked by the flavor of what I read.

I repeat, this had nothing to do with any thought that Nixon could be charged with criminal conduct. It was the political consequences I feared. By this, I did not mean furnishing further ammunition to his enemies. *

---

*The uses to which they might be expected to put the material was suggested after a White House tape containing a conversation relating to the milk-fund case filed by Ralph Nader was turned over as evidence in response to a subpoena. One of the Nader attorneys, William A. Dobrovir, admitted in U.S. District Court that he had played portions of the tape at a party.

The danger was that this naked record of Nixon's private conversations would turn his supporters against him, that it would shock, outrage, and alienate that large segment of the American people who had, until now, given him the benefit of the doubt.

This would happen because the verbatim record was not the full record. Words printed in black ink on white pages could not convey the tones of voice, the facial expressions, the irony, and the other unspoken modifiers that had been a part of the original conversations. These were words spoken by people who had seen no need to watch what they said, because they thought they were speaking to the most powerful man in the world in an atmosphere of unbreakable secrecy. Without the softening effects of the wink, the nudge, the smile, and all the other subtle disclaimers involved, words spoken in such circumstances tend to make those who speak them sound like fools or thugs or worse.

My sense of foreboding was so great after I finished the large stack of pages that I thought it best not to trust my own unsupported reaction. I asked Bryce Harlow and Fred Buzhardt to read the transcripts. After doing so, Harlow came into my office and sat down in a heavy silence. He seemed reluctant to express an opinion; I did not press him. Finally, he said, "What do *you* think?"

I replied, "He will never survive this."

"Amen, brother," said Harlow.

Buzhardt agreed just as wholeheartedly. Armed with these opinions, I went to the Oval Office. By now, of course, Nixon had heard that I was in the know.

There was no point in preamble. I said, "Mr. President, there is no way you can release the transcripts Pat and his people have prepared. If you do, what they contain will destroy you."

Nixon wagged his head, thrust out his jaw, glared at me. "All right," he said in a tone of real anger; and then, with a wave of his hand as if to make the offending transcripts, and me, vanish, he repeated more explosively, "*All right!*"

Two minutes after leaving him, I gave orders that the transcripts be destroyed.

Early in February, Leon Jaworski had made it plain in a public statement that John Dean's testimony, based on his recollection of conversations recorded in the tapes and other transactions, remained the key element in the special prosecutor's case against Watergate figures. "If we believed John Dean's veracity was subject to question," the special prosecutor said in a television interview, "we would not use him as a witness."[19] On March 1, 1974, Mitchell, Haldeman, Ehrlichman, Colson, Gordon Strachan, Robert Mardian, and Kenneth Parkinson, all former White House aides or employees of the Committee to Re-Elect the President, were indicted by the Watergate grand jury on felony charges related to the Watergate cover-up. The crimes with which they were charged included conspiracy, obstruction of justice, and perjury. Six days later, another grand jury handed down indictments against six former White House plumbers who were charged with violating the rights of Daniel Ellsberg's psychiatrist, Dr. Lewis Fielding, by breaking into his office in an effort to obtain confidential information about Ellsberg. In New York, Mitchell and Maurice Stans went on trial on charges of having sought to impede a federal investigation of the financier Robert Vesco in return for an alleged secret cash donation of $200,000 to Nixon's 1972 reelection campaign.

The extraordinary spectacle of the President's closest former aides and associates being herded into court in this way had little shock value even in Washington, where the obsession with Watergate was clinical. Elsewhere in the country, the sense of déjà vu was even stronger. Nixon had told Congress that one year of Watergate was enough, and public opinion seemed to agree. In California, a poll conducted by the League of Women Voters showed that respondents rated energy, inflation, tax reform, and unemployment as being greater concerns than the question of impeachment. A street poll by the New York Daily News found that people were more likely to be interested in the oil shortage and inflation than Watergate.[20]

The reality was that by the early months of 1974 the situation had long since moved beyond questions of the guilt or innocence of Nixon's former associates. The President's embarrassment in this regard had reached the point of diminishing returns. Attention was now focussed almost entirely on Nixon himself, and the objective was impeachment as the House Judiciary Committee gradually moved toward the status of the only game in town. Jaworski was looking into a number of issues in cooperation with the committee. The Ervin committee, before ending its hearings in February so as to avoid any conflict with the Judiciary Committee, had examined the milk-fund case and the $100,000 cash contribution from Hughes.

Clearly, the time had come for Nixon to look more closely to his personal defense. At the turn of the year, Charles Alan Wright, who had shared some of the feelings expressed by Buzhardt and Garment over the issue of the nonexistent tapes and his lack of access to the tapes, returned to his professorship at the University of Texas Law School. Nixon reorganized his legal staff on January 5, naming Fred Buzhardt White House Counsel and restoring Len Garment to nonlegal duties in his former post as assistant to the President concentrating on social issues. As part of this reorganization, and at long last, the President appointed a seasoned trial lawyer, James D. St. Clair of Boston, as head of his Watergate legal team. As a young lawyer in the early 1950s, St. Clair had been a staff assistant to the Army's special counsel, Joseph N. Welch, during the Army-McCarthy hearings. St. Clair was a Harvard man, having graduated from that law school, and he had successfully defended a number of political radicals on the Left, but he was also a registered Republican with a reputation for thorough preparation and a flair for courtroom tactics.[21]

I promised St. Clair a busy life, and he was soon embarked upon it. On January 18, the question of the eighteen-and-a-quarter-minute gap was referred by Sirica to the Watergate grand jury, and everyone knew that this question, like others before it, contained the potential for direct accusation of the President. It could hardly be otherwise, since according to White House records only he and Rose Mary Woods and Steven Bull had touched the tapes during the weekend at Camp David on which the erasure (or erasures) had occurred.

With suspiciousness and foreboding all around me, I had done my best to go on believing that the system would, in the end, produce a fair result even with regard to Richard Nixon. My faith was severely tested when I was summoned to testify before the Watergate grand jury on February 25. Before I took the witness chair, Richard Ben-Veniste, the federal prosecutor I had earlier encountered during the hearing before Judge Sirica made it plain that his target was Richard Nixon.

Ben-Veniste proved to be as tenacious as before, but to no avail. I understood why he was after the President, and that he was prepared to keep me on the stand until he got him (or me). But I had no knowledge of any thought or action on Nixon's part that could possibly provide grounds for criminal charges. Undaunted, Ben-Veniste questioned me with many redundancies for well over an hour (and called me back for two later appearances) while the members of the grand jury sat in various states of consciousness ranging from alertness to deep sleep to a trancelike state that I took to be a symptom of nearly terminal boredom.

Somewhat later, on ABC's "Issues and Answers," I asked a rhetorical question that was almost continually on my mind: "At what point in the review of wrongdoing does the review itself involve injustice, excesses, and distortions which, in effect, result in the cure being worse than the illness itself?"[22]

Alexander Hamilton had warned in 1787, as the Constitution was being drafted, that an impeachment process "in many cases will connect itself with the pre-existing factions, and will enlist all their animosities, partialities, influence, and interest on one side or the other; and . . . there will always be the greatest danger that the decision will be regulated more by the comparative strength of the [political] parties than by the real demonstrations of innocence or guilt."[23] The Nixon case seemed a good bet to fulfill his prophecy, as the proceedings against Andrew Johnson had done in 1868. There was no definition in law of what precisely constituted an impeachable offense. The Constitution specified "treason, bribery, or other high crimes and misdemeanors"; the reference to bribery explained the great interest in the milk-fund, ITT, and Vesco cases. Vice President Ford, a former member of the Judiciary Committee, probably came closest to stating the reality when he said that an impeachable offense was "whatever a majority of the House of Representatives considers it to be at a given moment in history."[24]

The original deadline imposed on itself by the Judiciary Committee for delivering an Article of Impeachment to the full House of Representatives or for recommending against impeachment was the end of April. There was no realistic expectation that this deadline would be met, nor was it. Because the ideological composition of the committee was weighted to the Left, it was widely, if not universally supposed that it would, in the end, vote to recommend impeachment. As a conservative member, Walter Flowers, Democrat of Alabama, put it, "The committee make-up does not really reflect the make-up of the House: the Democrats are more liberal than the Democrats in the House as a whole, the [committee] leadership in particular, and the Republicans are more conservative than Republicans in the House as a whole."[25]

Chairman Rodino and the ranking Republican member, Edward Hutchinson of Michigan, had been in charge only since January 1973; before that, two crusty patriarchs of the old school, Emmanuel Celler, Democrat of New York, and William M. McCulloch, Republican of Ohio, had run the committee between them for more than twenty years. With Celler and McCulloch, both of whom retired in 1972, went traditional procedure and the comity on which "the judicious committee," as it had called itself, had formerly taken pride. There was little or no question of Rodino (who had voted against the approval of Ford as Vice

President)[26] exercising discipline over the Democratic majority, which included some of the most outspoken radicals in the House. Not insignificantly, every one of the committee's thirty-eight members (twenty-one Democrats, seventeen Republicans) was a lawyer.[27]

Like every other investigative entity, the Judiciary Committee's first priority was to obtain the presidential tapes. On April 11, it voted 33 to 3 to subpoena forty-two taped conversations. Five days later, Jaworski petitioned Judge Sirica to order Nixon to release sixty-four taped conversations; on April 18, the subpoena was issued.

In theory, at least, Sirica's subpoena could be appealed, like others before it, on grounds of executive privilege. The Judiciary Committee's demand was another matter. The argument was made that the committee could not be denied whatever evidence it demanded because it was engaged in an inquiry mandated by the Constitution; executive privilege did not apply. This was an intriguing legal argument, but, as a practical matter, the committee could issue an Article of Impeachment forthwith if Nixon failed to surrender the forty-two tapes.

In the abstract, immediate impeachment was not an intolerable option, inasmuch as Nixon believed that he controlled enough votes in the House to prevent the bill from passing. His first instinct was to resist both subpoenas. The advice of the lawyers was to meet the need to make the tapes public without formally acceding to the demands of the Judiciary Committee or the special prosecutor by publishing transcripts—in brief, to do what I had prevented from happening a short time before. Even Buzhardt felt that the moment for disclosure had come; he thought it would dispel the miasma of suspicion, not to say superstition, that hung over the tapes. Nothing had happened to change my belief that disclosure of the verbatim record was unwise, and probably terminally so.

Reviving the Stennis concept, I suggested an arrangement to release certified summaries of the pertinent passages; the Judiciary Committee could designate whomever it wished to verify that the summaries were faithful to the tapes. I knew there was little chance of this idea succeeding in any way except to buy time. It was rejected. The lawyers prevailed, and verbatim transcripts were prepared by batteries of typists. As in the earlier effort under Pat Buchanan, the idea was to expurgate the tapes of national-security matters, confidential exchanges unrelated to Watergate, profanity and vulgarity before setting the censored versions adrift on the sea of public opinion.

Nixon himself made many cuts, eliminating his own rather mild profanity and that of others who spoke more ripely, toning down insults to absent personages, and eliminating confidential exchanges. Although, inevitably, it was charged that he had also removed incriminating matter, his purpose was not to suppress the evidence, which was clearly in his favor, but to spare himself and others embarrassment. Nothing could have been more characteristic of the man; he swore little and relatively mildly, as men of his generation go, and those he was attempting to preserve from embarrassment had in many cases said far worse things about him in public than he had said about them in private. This editing process, willy-nilly, produced the epitaph for Richard Nixon's reputation, the phrase "Expletive deleted" to denote the removal of a cussword. "My mother would turn over in her grave if she knew I used such language," he told me, among others, when I questioned the need to take out even the mildest *hells* and *damns*.

In the midst of this process, John Mitchell and Maurice Stans were acquitted on all fifteen counts against them by a jury that had evidently declined to believe John Dean's testimony against them in the Vesco case.[28] This was the end of the good news for quite a long time to come.*

On April 29, Nixon released twelve hundred pages of transcripts from forty-six presidential conversations. In a nationally televised speech, with the bound transcripts heaped at his elbow in the Oval Office, he told the American people that the transcripts "will, at last, once and for all, show that what I knew and what I did in regard to the Watergate break-in and cover-up were just as I have described them to you from the beginning."[29]

From my own reading of the transcripts, I knew this to be true. But I also knew that few who had believed otherwise were likely to admit their mistake. Watching the speech, I was aware of a struggle between my heartfelt admiration for Nixon's nearly superhuman courage in taking this hideous risk with the presidency—and his own place in history— and the rational part of my being, which told me in a most visceral way that he was finished. And indeed, by morning his long-held hope of exculpation had disappeared.

The reaction to his speech and to the transcripts themselves was far worse than anything that even I had anticipated. His enemies refused to believe him and excoriated him; his sympathizers were disillusioned and turned away from him. The fact that he was justified in saying that the transcripts exonerated him did not matter; what mattered was what always matters in politics, appearances.

*The Nixon campaign committee voted to pay Stans's legal bills, which amounted to about $400,000.

After analyzing the transcripts by scholarly method, Professor William B. Todd of the University of Texas, an expert in the scholarly exegesis of texts, issued a judgment that summarizes a majority of more spontaneous comments from all quarters. "Throughout recorded history," he wrote, "no author has ever produced, albeit unwittingly, a text so systematically debased and corrupt."[30] The Greensburg, Pennsylvania, *Tribune-Review*, owned by Richard Mellon Scaife, who had contributed a million dollars to Nixon's 1972 campaign, published an editorial recommending that Nixon step aside. It said, "He makes us feel, somehow, unclean." Such judgments were harsh and unfair, but they typified the first reactions.

Releasing the transcripts had achieved the opposite of what had been hoped and intended. Little else could have been expected from the efforts of a committee of editors whose primary purpose was to protect the President from himself, or from an editor in chief, namely the President himself, who was trying to protect his office, himself, and, in the expurgation of harmless cusswords, the memory of his mother's teaching.

Claiming that nothing else would resolve the questions of authenticity that had been raised by the omissions in the transcripts, the Judiciary Committee and the courts now wanted the original tapes. It was not possible to doubt that sooner or later they would get them. How much better it would have been, I reflected, to have seen the tapes go up in smoke the previous summer.

After our first meeting, Leon Jaworski and I had kept the lines open between us. We continued to meet in the Map Room, just inside the diplomatic entrance to the White House, and our discussions were always frank and unambiguous. My respect for him grew with acquaintance; he was unequivocally engaged in a search for the truth, and he approached his work without the slightest trace of vindictiveness or petty feeling. He was a shrewd player, and the game had changed from a giddy form of Go Fish! under Cox to old fashioned five-card stud poker with Jaworski. He never played with the joker or wild cards. Had I considered that the President was guilty, that would have made him more dangerous; believing otherwise, I regarded his intellectual and professional incorruptibility as assets.

On May 5, a Sunday, Jaworski called for an appointment and came to see me in the afternoon at the White House. We met alone, as usual, in the Map Room while Jim St. Clair and a couple of Jaworski's assistants waited elsewhere. Jaworski, always grave when discussing his responsibilities, seemed exceptionally solemn that day.

Conflict was in the air. True to the principle he had laid down during our discussion on October 30, Nixon had just told the House Judiciary Committee that he would not furnish the tapes they had subpoenaed. Nor would he surrender the seventy-two tapes Jaworski wanted in the absence of a ruling from the Supreme Court; Jaworski, I knew, was preparing to reply to a motion filed by St. Clair appealing Sirica's ruling that the President must turn over the tapes subpoenaed by the special prosecutor. Arguments were scheduled the following day. Although Jaworski had not told me why he wanted to meet, I assumed it had something to do with the tapes and his court appearance.

"Al, I don't want to surprise you and the President tomorrow," he said. "But I'm afraid I may have to do that if this thing comes down to arguments in open court."

I asked him what sort of surprise he had in mind. His reply took me completely by surprise.

"Well, the fact is," Jaworski said, "the Watergate grand jury wanted to indict the President. I explained that they couldn't do that according to the Constitution. But what they did do, Al, was this—they named Richard M. Nixon an unindicted coconspirator in the Watergate case by a vote of nineteen to nothing. That was two months ago, and we've kept the matter confidential all this time."

Although I had sensed that Jaworski had come to see me for some exceptional purpose, I had expected nothing like this. In fact, I had never before heard of anything like this. None of the President's lawyers had ever offered such a hypothesis. I was in no mood to admire the brilliance of the maneuver.

Jaworski assured me that he had no wish to make the grand jury's action with regard to the President public. "But, of course, in due course of time, it will have to become public," he said, "unless the guilty party comes into court and pleads guilty. What I'd like to do is avoid that by reaching an arrangement. I have no interest whatsoever in trying the President of the United States in open court."

That last assurance caught my attention. Once again, I asked him what he had in mind.

In his most disarming Texas drawl, Jaworski replied, "Just a regular old horse trade, Al. If the President will give me eighteen of the tapes I've asked for, I'll forget about the other forty-six on the subpoena. And I won't release the information about the President being named as an unindicted coconspirator. We can just close this whole thing out."

"Leon, I'm not a lawyer," I said, "but if I were, I'd suspect that you were trying to blackmail me and the President."

"Well, Al," said Jaworski, "all I can tell you is, there's blackmail, and then there's blackmail."

In other words, sometimes the victim is in a position to refuse, and sometimes he isn't. Obviously, he thought that Nixon fell into the first category. I didn't know what to think.

"We'll discuss it and get back to you," I said.

Jaworski handed over a list of the eighteen tapes he wanted, then departed.

After he left, I told St. Clair and Buzhardt what he had proposed. St. Clair's reaction was much like my own, right down to the choice of the operative word. "This is a bad deal," he said. "It's prosecutorial blackmail."

There was very little time to react to Jaworski's bombshell, and almost no room to maneuver. In the absence of some gesture from the White House, Jaworski could go into open court the following day and reveal information that would shatter what was left of the President's credibility.

Nixon understood the situation instantly. But he continued to be adamantly opposed to the release of the tapes. Much discussion followed. Finally, I suggested to the President that he listen to the tapes Jaworski wanted before making a decision. Perhaps some compromise could be worked out; Jaworski, after all, had not made his proposal on a "take it or leave it" basis. Taking it as a matter of faith, bolstered by the experience of releasing the transcripts, that the tapes contained nothing that would incriminate Nixon, I did not see how the tapes could harm him. Jaworski's revelation could destroy him.

Nixon agreed to listen, and on Monday he was set up once again in his hideaway office with tape recorder and earphones. After a while, he called me into his presence.

"There's no need for me to go on listening to those things," he told me. "On this business with Jaworski, the answer is no. No more tapes. We've done enough. We're not going any further, not with Jaworski, not with the Judiciary Committee. We're going to protect the presidency. You tell them that."

I knew that he meant what he said, that there would be no change of mind. I had seldom seen him so disturbed or so determined.

"No one is to listen to these tapes," he said. "No one—understand, Al? No one. Not the lawyers. No one. Lock 'em up."

I told him that his orders would be carried out.

But as I left him, I was overwhelmed by feelings of doubt and apprehension. Something fundamental had changed. There was something bad on the tapes, and Nixon had discovered it. I was sure of this as a matter of instinct, though I had no idea what it might be.

Later on, of course, it all became clear. The tape of Nixon's conversation with Haldeman on June 23, 1973, was included on Jaworski's list. Nixon had heard this tape for the first time and realized that it contained the key to proving his guilt as the author of the Watergate cover-up.

In a meeting in the Map Room, I informed Jaworski of the President's decision.

Jaworski was visibly surprised. It was evident that he, too, believed that Nixon had found something on the tapes that was deeply disturbing to him. "You're telling me," Jaworski said, "that he'd rather have it known to the whole world that he's been named as an unindicted coconspirator than let the contents of the eighteen tapes be revealed?"

"I'm telling you," I replied, "that the President is unwilling to release any tapes at all."

"This is not the way to save the President," Jaworski said.

I replied, "I'm not trying to save the President, Leon. I'm trying to save the presidency."[31]

34

Hail and Farewell

Nixon's status as an unindicted coconspirator to unspecified Watergate crimes, later to be described before the Supreme Court by James St. Clair as an "unsubstantiated, unprecedented, and clearly unconstitutional device,"[1] was leaked to the Los Angeles Times and published on June 6, two days before the President's departure on an official visit to five Middle East countries, including the three belligerents in the recent war.

The news media, fed by leaks from the highest officials of the State Department, denounced the President's trip as a seedy effort to claim credit for the Middle East peace that really belonged to Kissinger. Of course, this was twaddle and both men knew it, but the tension between them as the journey began was noticeable, as indeed it had been ever since the Vietnam peace negotiations.

This uneasiness was made worse by a Washington Post story, published on June 5, alleging that Nixon had suggested to Dean, in a taped conversation, that it was Kissinger who had ordered the wiretaps of the seventeen NSC staffers and newsmen beginning in 1969.[2] The next day, a New York Times editorial implied that Kissinger had not been entirely truthful with regard to the question of the wiretaps during his confirmation hearings before the Senate Foreign Relations Committee. These two arrows in the back created in Kissinger a passion for rebuttal. At our first stop, in Salzburg, Austria, Kissinger told me that he had made up his mind to call a press conference and confront the libel. I realized that this would have the effect of diverting attention from the real purposes of Nixon's trip and cloaking it with a miasma of controversy that would follow us wherever we went. Moreover, it would deeply displease the President, who had looked forward to his trip abroad as an escape from the monotony of Watergate.

Nixon, who understandably regarded Kissinger's public-relations problems as trivial compared to his own, was appalled when I told him of Kissinger's plans to meet with reporters. "Goddamn it, Al," he said, "doesn't Henry see that all he's doing is giving them a Watergate lead for their first story about this trip?"

It seemed possible to me that Kissinger, in his dudgeon, had not considered this question as carefully as he might have done. I sought him out. He was still seething. "Henry," I said, "don't do it. The President doesn't need this, and neither do you." I added that the press conference he proposed would achieve precisely the effect he was always warning the President and me to avoid—that is, mix Watergate with foreign policy.

But Kissinger was in a state of wounded feelings, never a happy augury, and he would not be persuaded to desist. Not only did he take on his domestic critics on foreign soil, he added an emotional threat to resign as Secretary of State unless the false charges against his honor were cleared up. (Later on, the Senate Foreign Relations Committee did just that, after Nixon acceded to Kissinger's entreaty that he send the panel a letter acknowledging his own responsibility for the wiretaps.)[3]

"Wonderful," said Nixon sarcastically when I reported Kissinger's public resignation threat to him. "That's all we need." He ignored Kissinger for the next several days. As Kissinger has stated in his memoirs, some "churlish" members of the White House staff refused to speak to him for a while.[4] Our own relations were as chatty as ever, if not more so.

Even as Kissinger harangued the press, my concern about the damage this might do was replaced by another, far more serious worry. I found the President alone in his bedroom with his bare leg propped up on a chair. "I wanted you to see this, but I want you to keep it to yourself," he said. "The doctors are the only other ones who know." The limb was swollen and discolored, and, despite his efforts to conceal his discomfort, I saw that Nixon was in considerable pain. This was the first indication I had that he was suffering from an attack of phlebitis, or inflammation of the veins. The condition was serious, even life-threatening, because of the danger of a blood clot forming in the vein and being carried to the lungs, where it might cause a fatal embolism, or even to the heart or brain.

Had I realized that he was having an attack of this recurrent disorder, I would have counseled strongly against traveling. No doubt that was why he had not told me that he was sick; he now informed me that he had overruled his doctors in deciding to come. He waved away my questions and my concerns; he was determined to go through with his visits to Egypt, Israel, Jordan, Saudi Arabia, and Syria.

How right he was to persist, in terms of his own psychology and the reputation of the United States of America. He was greeted in Alexandria and in Cairo, and indeed everywhere he went in Egypt, by enormous and tumultuously adoring crowds. Ignoring advice from his anxious doctors not to put weight on his afflicted leg, Nixon stood up beside Sadat in an open railroad car for most of the three-hour trip from Alexandria to Cairo.

A joyous throng that was later estimated to have numbered 7 million souls lined the tracks linking the two cities. Most held red flowers in their hands and waved banners and placards. Their signs in English and Arabic read: THANK YOU NIXON & SADAT FOR PEACE! and WE TRUST NIXON! As we passed by, I read these messages (or heard them translated) with a thrill of pleasure on my President's behalf. It was a wonderful treat to see a man who had been so spitefully used in his own capital receive such a joyful reception by a people who wished to thank him for an act of statesmanship that had preserved the lives of their sons, husbands, and fathers.

Great rapport between Nixon and Sadat developed immediately. Sadat had been deeply disillusioned by his experiences with the Soviets, and after expelling them from Egypt remained hostile to Moscow (and convinced that the U.S.S.R. was plotting to take over all of Africa and the Middle East in a grand strategic design) for the remainder of his life. Sadat, who impressed me as he impressed nearly all who met him with his broad and subtle intellect and his transparent personal virtue, called Nixon "a man of peace," adding, "President Nixon never gave a word and didn't fulfill it. He has fulfilled every word he gave."[5]

After Egypt came a quieter visit to Saudi Arabia, where King Feisal and Nixon seemed to arrive at a meeting of the minds on most matters, including the undesirability of the oil embargo and consequent high petroleum prices. As we entered Syrian air space a few days later, *Air Force One* was greeted by a squadron of MIG interceptors in combat formation. Our captain put the presidential plane into a steep evasive dive, and for a few moments it seemed to me, and to others on board, that it might be possible that the Syrian pilots were going to shoot us down. But they did not, and once on the ground Nixon got on surprisingly well with the tough but highly pragmatic President Assad.

In Israel, we found a country deeply shaken by the war through which it had only recently passed. Although Nixon was the first U.S. President to visit Israel, there was too much sadness in the air for joyful welcoming crowds; the chief impression I received was that the Israelis, particularly the younger generation, had had enough of war. There was too much anxiety and the memories of sacrifice were too fresh for anything beyond routine expressions of gratitude to the visitors. The new Israeli leaders were concerned with American attitudes toward the West Bank and the possibility of future military assistance, and that was what they wanted to talk about. Nixon wanted to talk about negotiations with the Arabs that might eventually lead to a peaceful solution of the Arab-Israeli contest. He pointed out bluntly that a policy based on the ability of the Israeli army to defeat its enemies with arms supplied by the United States was bound to fail in the end. "Time will run out," he said.

The Israelis listened, as it seemed, with half an ear. What Nixon was saying was not what they wanted to hear at that point in their history. It may also have been that the Israelis, who are so closely attuned to the moods of the U.S. Congress, wondered how much longer he would be speaking for the United States. Perhaps, too, they were being careful to make no gesture to Nixon that might suggest that they questioned what Congress was doing to him with regard to Watergate.

Soon after our arrival in Israel, there was a moment with Nixon that mixed sadness and humor. As a mark of remembrance to the 6 million Jews murdered by the Nazis in World War II, he was scheduled to lay a wreath at Yad Vashem, the Holocaust memorial on the western outskirts of Jerusalem. Back in Washington, I had informed the President that it was customary to wear a yarmulke when entering this shrine. He disliked wearing hats of all kinds and adhered strictly to a personal rule against wearing headgear when being photographed; anyone who can imagine Nixon in a sombrero or a war bonnet will appreciate the wisdom of this taboo. He said, "No, Al, I won't wear one of those things—you can just forget it!" Having expected this reaction, I told him that the next most acceptable thing was a black felt fedora. That did not please him, either. After some resistance, however, he agreed to wear a fedora and instructed me to buy him one. I did so, going to the hat store personally to make the selection, and delivered a fine black fedora to Manolo Sanchez, the presidential valet. On the morning of the wreath laying, Nixon greeted me with a crafty smile. "Bad news, Al! Manolo forgot to pack my black fedora." From behind my back, I produced a hatbox. "That's all right, Mr. President—I brought a spare!" He gave me the darkest look I ever received from him, clamped on the twin of the hat he had left in his closet in the White House, and limped out of the room without uttering another word.

At the state dinner for Nixon in the Knesset building, I found myself sitting next to a short, bespectacled, but brilliantly intelligent and witty stranger named Menachem Begin. Nothing that happened in the room seemed to escape his notice; he made excellent jokes and many wise remarks about Israeli-American relations. I was not sure who he was, and on inquiring discovered that he was known mainly as a former terrorist during the independence struggle and as a recalcitrant right-wing politician. It seemed to me, even on the basis of a short conversation, that there was a great deal more to him than that, and I would find that this first impression held up when we met again in the midst of future U.S.–Israeli tribulations.

In one of those spontaneous and touching gestures of which he was capable when in the grip of affection or gratitude, Nixon departed from protocol to offer his first toast of the evening to Golda Meir, who was no longer a member of the government. She blushed in pleasure at his compliments, which were unmistakably heartfelt, and then rose to reply. Everyone in the room knew what a heroine this legendary matriarch had been in the country she had helped to create and preserve.

Golda Meir's reply to Nixon's toast was far warmer than words on the printed page can suggest. "Presidents can do almost anything, and President Nixon has done many things that nobody would have thought of doing," she said. "All I can say, Mr. President, as friends and as an Israeli citizen to a great American President, thank you."[6]

Her tone and manner said much more than the words themselves convey, and to be called a "great President" at this moment in his life by a woman whose own greatness few could doubt affected Nixon deeply.

The toast was drunk with considerable emotion. Nixon then spoke in blunt language about the need for peace between the Israelis and the Arab nations that surrounded them. Repeating in public what he had already said in private, he praised the bravery of the Israeli army in the face of overwhelming odds. Then he said, "It takes courage, a different kind of courage, to wage peace. . . . Continuous war in this area is not a solution to Israel's survival and, above all, it is not right."[7]

The reaction of the audience was proper but not enthusiastic. I could see that Begin did not like what he was hearing. Earlier, he had made a joke of the "what have you done for me lately" variety. Now he remarked on the current of feeling that ran through the room. "Don't worry, my friend," he said. "Golda is not the only one here tonight who knows what Nixon has done for Israel lately."

Nixon returned home to Washington from the Middle East on June 19, but he spent less than a week in the United States before traveling abroad again, this time to Moscow, site of his third summit meeting with Brezhnev. Although there was anxiety among Nixon's adversaries that he would somehow use the summit to rescue his presidency, little was expected of this meeting, primarily because the Pentagon, supported by a burgeoning antidétente movement in the United States, was strongly opposed to the two major proposals on the negotiating table. These were an agreement that would limit the number of nuclear missiles with multiple independently targetable reentry vehicles (MIRVs) to around 2,500 each, and a proposal to limit the size of underground nuclear tests.

Secretary of Defense Schlesinger, whose judgment had not prevailed in the Middle East crisis, had now joined forces with Senator Henry M. ("Scoop") Jackson of Washington, a leading Democratic spokesman on foreign policy, in opposing both proposals. Schlesinger wanted limits on the number of delivery systems (rockets) but no limits on MIRVs. In private, he treated the President with a mixture of condescension and thinly veiled contempt that shocked those who witnessed it; in public, he took the extraordinary measure of releasing a letter disassociating the Defense Department from administration policy on this question. In their maneuvers, Schlesinger and Jackson had the support of Adm. Elmo Zumwalt, the chief of naval operations, who argued for the construction of more missile submarines and eloquently supported a Pentagon memorandum that laid out a scheme that would have permitted the United States to "fulfill all possible American programs while curtailing every Soviet one."[8]

At the NSC meeting on June 20, Nixon rejected a proposal from Schlesinger calling for the maintenance of a huge U.S. advantage in MIRV delivery systems. Nixon rejected it on grounds that there was no chance whatever of the Soviets agreeing to it. In regard to the Threshold

Test Ban (TTB) limiting the size of underground nuclear tests, Schlesinger and his collaborators argued, not altogether unrealistically, that the Soviets (who would permit no onsite verification) would cheat because seismic instruments could not accurately measure the force of underground tests above the limits. Inasmuch as the five thousand warheads allowed under the proposed agreement represented enough megatonnage to destroy all strategic military targets in both countries, the point was regarded in some quarters as moot.[9]

The United States was not the only place where suspicion of détente raised obstacles to SALT II. Kissinger had returned from preparatory talks in Moscow with reports that Brezhnev was experiencing similar opposition to the MIRV and TTB agreements from his own military.

Nixon departed Washington on June 25. The first stop was Brussels for a celebration of the twenty-fifth anniversary of NATO. Reports that he was indifferently received by the Europeans on this occasion are quite untrue. Although some European leaders feared that he had been so weakened at home that he would be unable to negotiate from strength in Moscow, everyone I encountered in his presence, from citizens in the streets to the most eminent politicians and military leaders of the Western Alliance, seemed to be very glad to see him; more than one dignitary used me as a medium to convey private messages of encouragement to him. The President was still suffering from acute phlebitis, but, as in the Middle East earlier in June, he was delighted to find himself in the presence of friendly people and he seized every opportunity to mingle with the crowds in Belgium. He ignored his painfully inflamed leg and, to the dismay of his physicians and the Secret Service, insisted on walking from the American embassy to the royal palace to attend a luncheon. It was a bittersweet experience to observe him during these outings. He had something of the air of a political prisoner on parole, delighted to be out in the sunshine again but knowing that he must soon return to a sterner reality.

Nixon injured Kissinger's feelings, already bruised by the estrangement following the latter's impetuous press conference in Salzburg, by instructing me not to place him in the hotel suite next to his in Moscow. "I don't want Henry walking in on me, Al," he said. "I want a little privacy, a little peace and quiet." Although he denied any discomfort to the press and strode about in public as if he walked on two good legs, his phlebitis was giving him a lot of pain, and this affected his mood.

It seemed to me at the time, and the passage of years has not changed my mind, that Nixon would have done well to treat his domestic adversaries with the same mixture of frankness, open-minded argument, and toughness that he employed when negotiating with the Soviets. Time and again, his bluntness broke the soporific spell of Soviet rhetoric and brought negotiations back on track. The psychological difference, I suppose, was that in the Watergate case he was defending his own person as well as the presidency against opponents whose motives he chose not to question simply because they were Americans, while in foreign-policy matters he was defending the United States against foreigners whose interests were open to question per se. In Moscow, he described the domestic political situation to Brezhnev in very realistic fashion. If détente failed, he told the Soviet leader, the hawks, not the doves, would take over U.S. foreign policy. Watergate had little or nothing to do with this debate, which had achieved feverish intensity, but it severely limited Nixon's power to control it.

Although the plenary sessions in the Kremlin, like most formal talks with Communists, were a grinding bore, the trip had some pleasant interludes. I managed to get away in Moscow for a taxi tour of the city. When I asked the driver to describe his life after hours, he shrugged and said, "Vodka. All we do in the Soviet Union is drink." After the opening session in Moscow, the parties flew to the Crimea, with Brezhnev and the Nixons traveling together in the General Secretary's airplane. Brezhnev had a seaside residence at Yalta (more accurately, at neighboring Oreanda) of which he was extremely proud, and the summit continued there. Nixon could not bring himself to acknowledge that he was meeting a Soviet leader in Yalta, scene of the 1945 conference of Roosevelt, Churchill, and Stalin (with a bright U.S. Foreign Service officer named Alger Hiss helping out with the paperwork) that conservatives believed had led to the postwar division of Europe. White House press releases referred to the site as Oreanda; the literal-minded press, housed in a Yalta hotel, slugged its stories "Yalta."

There were two main villas at Oreanda, a large, formal, rather stuffy one on the clifftop and a more modern one on the beach below. One traveled between them by outdoor elevator. The first had belonged to the Czars, but the other was strictly the creation of socialist architects. Brezhnev loved it, with its huge two-story windows overlooking the water, its enormous staff of scurrying servants and guards, and its glass swimming pool designed to give swimmers the illusion that they were paddling in the Black Sea. The Soviet treasury paid all the bills. "What a scandal this would be back home!" I remarked; Brezhnev lifted his luxuriant black eyebrows and smiled complacently. Political scandal was not a problem in a one-party state.

This portion of the trip had some of the aspects of a vacation, at least for Nixon and Brezhnev. The two leaders took walks together through the lush flowering gardens surrounding the villa and talked privately in a man-made grotto built into rocks above the Black Sea. They went for a sail with some of their staff aboard Brezhnev's impressive oceangoing yacht. A great deal of vodka was drunk by everyone except Nixon, a few of his closest advisers, and the Secret Service men. On disembarking, we were all decorated by unsteady KGB men with badges that made us, or so they said, honorary members of that infamous organization.

Not everything was sweetness and light. Brezhnev complained about a speech critical of the agreements under discussion that Jim Schlesinger had given. Nixon called a conference with Kissinger and myself in the presidential limousine, which had accompanied us from Washington and was the only site available that presumably had not been bugged by the Soviets. As a gesture to Brezhnev, it was agreed that I would call Schlesinger on an open line, which was sure to be monitored by our hosts, and feign a stern reprimand. This exercise in playacting satisfied Soviet pride, as well as giving my own spirits a much-needed boost.

The stay was not without its instructive moments with regard to such conundrums as the functioning of the centralized economy. Driving through one region of the Crimea, I was intrigued to see that nearly every woman we passed had bright red hair. Was this a result of inbreeding or what? "Dye," said my Russian companion. "This month, they're all redheads. Next month, maybe all blondes—depends on what color dye the state sends to the Crimea." Was there no choice of colors? "One month, one dye," said the Russian.

Although Nixon brought home no historic treaties, he accomplished a good deal at the summit, especially as regards the Middle East. His talks with Brezhnev on this subject, coming after his discussions only a couple of weeks earlier with the Israelis and the Arabs, laid the groundwork for future breakthroughs. Perhaps as much good was done by this sort of personal exchange as might have occurred through the signing of agreements.

As to Nixon's advocacy of the emigration of the Soviet Jews, a subject of steady discussion between the two leaders, Brezhnev ended by telling the President, "As far as I am concerned, I say let all the Jews go and let God go with them."[10] That, too, happened in time.

35

The Smoking Gun

After having spent all but a few days of the month of June abroad, Nixon returned to Washington from Moscow on July 3. The sense that time was running out was now acute. The Supreme Court was considering the tapes case on an accelerated basis. The House Judiciary Committee, after months of closed hearings, was moving toward a vote on five separate articles of impeachment.

Nixon had notified Chairman Rodino that he would not produce the tapes demanded by the Judiciary Committee, and it had responded by saying that the President's refusal "might constitute a ground for impeachment."[1] On July 9, the committee published its own verbatim printed version of eight tapes previously surrendered to it, together with a 131-page list of differences between the committee's reading of the tapes and the transcripts issued by the White House. Some of the differences were flashy when taken out of context, but none amounted to new evidence. The committee, staking a claim for the greater accuracy of its version, asserted it had used sophisticated electronic techniques in deciphering its copies of the tapes and had employed staff lawyers rather than secretaries as typists.[2]

Nixon's status as an unindicted coconspirator hung over his head but seemed to do him little harm. No one knew what the phrase meant, or on what basis the jurors had applied it, and Jaworski said that the principle of grand-jury secrecy prevented him from offering an explanation based on the facts. On July 1, St. Clair had argued before the Supreme Court that the naming of an incumbent President as an unindicted coconspirator "would be a mockery of due process." Jaworski replied that there was no reason for the grand jury to make an exception of an incumbent President in discharging its sworn duty to determine "whether a crime has been committed and who committed it."[3] In later arguments, St. Clair would put his finger on the constitutional dangers inherent in treating the President as a criminal without publishing the reasons why: "We should not destroy the privilege [of presidential confidentiality] in anticipation of a later finding of criminality."[4]

Nixon was now more alone than ever. At the end of a day filled with body blows, he sometimes raised the possibility of resignation. As he has recorded, I always advised against this course of action. There were two reasons for this. First, I did not think he really meant it; it was part of Nixon's technique to set up straw men for his advisers to knock down as a gesture of support for an opinion he held but did not wish to express. Second, I believed, until the President's situation changed dramatically in the last part of July 1974, that resignation would be the worst possible outcome.

When I told Leon Jaworski that I was trying to save the presidency, I meant that I was trying to prevent Nixon's future from being decided by any means except due process of law. The precedent that would be created by his downfall as a result of a combination of unproved allegations and the ideological hostility of a manipulative minority was too atrocious to contemplate. The law, and only the law, must settle this question if American democracy was to survive in the form given to it by the Founding Fathers. Otherwise, the mob would be empowered to decide who should govern in the future—or, as in the case of Nixon in the wake of his huge popular majority, who should not.

"Your enemies will advertise your resignation as an admission of guilt," I told the President in my standard reply to talk of quitting. "Worse than that, it would mean that they had overthrown an elected President without due process of law."

Of course, Nixon knew all this. His moments of doubt, when he spoke of the humiliation of his family and of the difficulty of regaining the political support and moral authority needed to run the country, came from another source. He must have known, even as we spoke, what I did not yet know—that the evidence to prove his involvement in the cover-up existed and was almost certain to come out.

The media, titillated by a torrent of rumor and speculation by the investigators and by politicians of both parties, continued to drum on the theme of Nixon's isolation. As we have seen, the picture of an alienated President drawn by the press was not wholly inaccurate. A less wary man than Nixon would long since have concluded that there were few people in town with whom he could enjoy an unguarded chat. One such, Vice President Ford, traveled almost continually, because his staff, in the words of one of them, "was seeking every possible excuse to stay out of Washington"; their objective, of course, was to avoid contaminating the future President through too much exposure to Nixon.[5] Kissinger, who had endeavored from the start to keep his own person as well as U.S. foreign policy clear of the Watergate scandal, was peripatetic also. Laird, Harlow, Secretary of the Treasury George Shultz, and others had either disembarked from the listing vessel that was the Nixon administration or were about to do so.

Fred Buzhardt, on the other hand, climbed back aboard. He had been felled by a heart attack on June 13, while Nixon and I were in the Middle East.[6] Although I knew, just as Buzhardt himself knew, that there was a good chance that his job might kill him, I did not try to dissuade him. We needed him; there was no prospect of finding a replacement who remotely compared to him in terms of knowledge of the case, steady judgment, and the respect he commanded from his client and his adversaries. Even on a temporary basis, the loss of Buzhardt was a serious blow to the legal staff, which was now composed of St. Clair and six other attorneys, some of them part-time. They were hard-pressed to keep up with the demands imposed on them by the 150 lawyers collectively employed by the House Judiciary Committee, the special prosecutor, and the Ervin committee.[7]

In spite of everything, there was some reason for encouragement, if not for optimism. On June 30, the Ervin committee passed out of existence without having established any evidentiary link between Nixon and the Watergate case or any other criminal matter. With regard to the refusal to surrender more tapes to the special prosecutor, St. Clair assured the President (who nevertheless continued to think that the Supreme Court would vote the politics, not the law, in deciding this matter) that he had the stronger case from the legal point of view. Contrary to expectations, Nixon's status as an unindicted coconspirator had no negative effect on his standing in the polls. His Gallup approval rating rose three points, to 28 percent, between the middle of May and the middle of June. In another Gallup poll taken in mid-July, 48 percent of the sample thought that Watergate was "a serious matter because it reveals corruption in the Nixon administration," while 43 percent believed that it was "just politics"; 9 percent didn't know.[8]

On June 3, Charles Colson, special counsel to the President throughout Nixon's first term, pleaded guilty to charges related to the cover-up and the burglary of Ellsberg's psychiatrist's office. Herbert Kalmbach, formerly Nixon's personal lawyer, had also pleaded guilty to charges arising from his fund-raising activities in the 1972 campaign. Each received prison sentences and fines. John Ehrlichman was convicted of perjury on July 12. Other trials and pleas of guilty were imminent. But no important new allegations involving the President had been made since the publication of the tape transcripts in late June. Bryce Harlow and Bill Timmons, the White House liaisons with Congress, assured the President that his support in Congress was standing firm even after Rodino was quoted as saying, before all the evidence was in and before the President's lawyers had presented their case for the defense, that all twenty-one Democrats on the Judiciary Committee were going to vote for impeachment. The White House had reason to believe that at least three southern Democrats, Walter Flowers of Alabama, James Mann of Alabama, and Ray Thornton of Arkansas, would vote the other way.[9]

After a flurry of criticism, Rodino disowned his statement, but signs of a predisposition for impeachment within the committee continued to surface. Minority counsel Jenner formally seconded a recommendation of impeachment by John Doar, the majority counsel, and was removed from his post by a vote of the Republican members. By another stroke of irony, Jenner was replaced by Samuel A. Garrison III, a former member of Spiro Agnew's Senate office staff, who was called upon by one Republican member for the "partisan service" Jenner had so noticeably failed to provide.[10]

What lay ahead was quite clear. The House Judiciary Committee's televised public hearings were scheduled to begin in two days' time. The Supreme Court was expected to rule on the tapes at any hour. On the basis of Rodino's hints, Articles of Impeachment were expected by early August. After that would come the vote of the full House of Representatives, and barring the discovery of what the news media were calling "the smoking gun"—documentary evidence of a crime committed by the President—it was not expected that the President's enemies would have the votes to impeach him.

About a hundred members of both parties were thought to be committed to Nixon no matter what, with seventy-five inalterably opposed to him. The rest, in theory, were undecided. Gerald Ford, who knew the House as intimately as anyone of his political generation, believed that Nixon would enjoy a solid fifty-vote majority in a vote of the full House on any article of impeachment. Nixon's other vote counters agreed. As Bryce Harlow put it to Nixon, "Boss, you've got it won."[11]

Brave talk, but everyone knew the arithmetic was subject to sudden change. Jaworski had ended one of our chats in the Map Room with a warning: "Al, I hope the President understands that his worst enemies on the Judiciary Committee are the Republicans. They want him out." Despite the change in minority counsels, there were other indications that Republican support on the committee was eroding. This made no practical difference in committee votes, however, because it was taken that the Democratic majority, excepting the three Southern conservatives, would vote the party line. The danger was that defecting Republicans on the committee would take other Republicans with them. This raised the prospect of larger defections in the House as a whole.

The Nixons, accompanied by the President's core staff, including myself, flew to San Clemente on July 12. The beautiful weather, the sense of larger reality that came from placing a continent between himself and the city of Washington, and the hiatus in bad news combined to restore Nixon to something like inner tranquillity. His two trips abroad had refreshed him and he had been reassured by contacts with old California friends whose loyalty and support were undiminished by his troubles. On July 18, James St. Clair presented a summary of his defense of the President before the House Judiciary Committee, which was sufficiently impressed by his performance to vote against permitting him to repeat it or any variation of it when televised hearings began the following week.[12] This straw was gleefully seized by all in temporary residence at La Casa Pacifica, even though we realized that St. Clair's brilliant performance had only made the Democratic leadership of the committee more determined to drive through to an article of impeachment.

On the morning of July 23, a Tuesday, a Republican member of the Judiciary Committee, Lawrence Hogan of Maryland, announced that he had decided to vote for impeachment. Timmons called to report that the three Southern Democrats on the committee who had been regarded as committed to Nixon would also vote against him. This was stunning news. All three were close to Governor George Wallace of Alabama, who was regarded as a staunch Nixon supporter in the impeachment issue. Nixon's hopes of averting impeachment were based on holding together the coalition of Republican conservatives and Southern Democrats who controlled a majority in the House of Representatives. Wallace, who had polled nearly 10 million votes in the 1968 election, decisively influenced a bloc of Southern conservative votes large enough to control the outcome. The Wallace bloc had always been the hinge on which the impeachment of Nixon turned.

The daily White House press summary that day carried a scurrilous item out of Montgomery, Alabama. It said that Governor Wallace had been told by unnamed sources that the CIA, acting in concert with Nixon, had been involved in the attempt on his life during the 1968 campaign that left him a paraplegic. Only a day or so before, our curiosity had been aroused by reports that Senator Edward Kennedy had been in touch privately with Wallace. What could those two, so different in ideology, so divided by past history, have to say to each other?

As soon as I finished reading the story, I called Wallace's office in Montgomery. The aide who answered the phone paused for a moment on hearing my voice. Normally, my calls went right through to the governor. But this time, he said, "I don't think the governor will take your call, Al. You'll have to have the President call him personally."

Obviously something very serious was afoot. I walked across the compound to the President's office and told him what had happened.

Nixon immediately put through a call to Wallace. When the governor came on the line, the President said, "George, I'm just calling to ask if you're still with me."

Wallace said, "No, Mr. President, I'm afraid I'm not."

Nixon said, "George, isn't there some way we can work this out?"

"I don't think so, Mr. President," said Wallace.

Nixon did not press Wallace for a reason, nor did he argue his case in any way. He simply replaced the receiver and said to me, "Well, Al, there goes the presidency."

The timbre of the President's voice was normal; there was no unusual expression on his face. In Nixon's mind, the Watergate scandal was always a political contest, not a morality play. Now he was dealing with a political result, and, consummate politician that he was, he kept emotion out of it. He made some additional calls to key Southern Democrats. So did I. The people we talked to confirmed what Wallace had already told Nixon: The defection was complete. Better than anyone, Nixon knew what the loss of the Southern Democrats meant: He would be impeached by the House of Representatives, and, if tried in the Senate, he would be found guilty of high crimes and misdemeanors. It was not a matter of the evidence or the brilliance of lawyers on either side; he simply did not have the votes to survive. From the moment he broke the connection with Wallace, the question became not whether Nixon would become the first President to resign his office but how to arrange this event while remaining true to the Constitution.

At 8:30 A.M. Pacific time, Fred Buzhardt called from the White House to report that the Supreme Court, by a vote of 8 to 0 (Justice William Rehnquist, a Nixon appointee, recusing himself), had rejected the President's contention that he had absolute authority to withhold evidence under the doctrine of executive privilege. The Court affirmed Sirica's order to turn over to him the tapes of sixty-four presidential conversations subpoenaed by Jaworski.[13] I phoned the news to Nixon in his bedroom.

"Unanimous?" he asked, in the tone of a man who had accustomed himself to hearing the worst.

"Yes, Mr. President. Fred says there's no air in it at all."

Although Nixon had never expected to win the case in the Supreme Court, he had counted on a split decision that would have given him the benefit of a minority opinion from which to argue further in defense of executive privilege, and he had hoped that the Court's ruling would provide for a solution, such as the provision of court-certified summaries or transcripts rather than the tapes themselves, that would preserve the principle that a President alone decides who shall see his confidential papers and in what form. Although the Court's decision had upheld the doctrine of executive privilege, it had rendered it vulnerable to attack in the future.

"The real damage," Nixon said, "is to the presidency."

There was no doubt in my mind, then or now, that he believed that; personal considerations were secondary because his own fate had already been decided by the defection of the Southerners.

Full compliance with the Court's order was the only option, and Nixon discussed methods for turning over the sixty-four subpoenaed taped conversations with James St. Clair, who was in San Clemente. St. Clair thought that it would take at least a month to prepare transcripts and deliver them to Sirica.

Nixon maintained an aloof calm throughout this conversation. When I called Buzhardt from the President's telephone to tell him what we proposed to do and ask his advice, Nixon took the instrument out of my hand.

"Fred," he said. "There is one tape in particular that I want your opinion on. It's the one for June 23, 1972. I want you to listen to it right away, then call Al and tell him what you think."

This was the first time Nixon or anyone else had mentioned the June 23 tape in my presence. I went back to my bungalow and waited for Fred's call. Two hours later, it came through.

"This is the smoking gun," Buzhardt said.

"Are you sure?"

"Yes. The words are there. But there are other factors. It's not necessarily fatal."

"Listen to it again and discuss it with St. Clair. Then we'll talk again."

St. Clair did not seem to be alarmed by what Buzhardt told him over the phone about the contents of the tape. When he and I discussed it with Nixon later that day, St. Clair took the position that the language was ambiguous and that whatever suggestions the President may have made were canceled out by his subsequent actions, such as ordering the FBI to go ahead with the investigation of Watergate. He also made the point, significant perhaps from a legal point of view but meaningless in Nixon's situation, that a man cannot be charged or convicted for having discussed a criminal act, only for having committed one. "I think this can be handled, Mr. President," he said.

St. Clair's air was confident, even breezy. Nixon listened with a dubious air, voicing no agreement. This seemed significant to me but not earth-shattering. Obviously, there was something on the tape that bothered Nixon. But how serious could it be, compared to everything else that was happening, if two lawyers thought that it presented no serious problem?[14]

"You'd both better listen to the tape yourselves when we get back to Washington," he said. "Then we'll get together with Fred and talk again. Does that seem all right to you?"

That evening, the House Judiciary Committee opened its televised debates on the impeachment of the President, with the proposed resolution and five articles of impeachment being introduced at 8:06 P.M. Eastern time. Nixon did not watch the proceedings. The first article of impeachment expressed the fundamental case: "Richard M. Nixon, using the powers of his high office, made it his policy, and in furtherance of such policy did act directly and personally through his close subordinates and agents, to delay, impede, and obstruct the investigation of [the Watergate burglary]; and to conceal the existence and scope of other unlawful covert activities."[15]

The Judiciary Committee staff had produced thirty-eight books of evidence, and it was evident from their opening statements that a majority of the committee, including some Republicans, had already decided to vote for impeachment. The rhetoric was heated but predictable. "If we are faithful to our oaths [as lawyers and congressmen]," said William L. Hungate, Democrat of Missouri, "we must find Richard Nixon faithless to his." But Charles W. Sandman, Republican of New Jersey, denounced the evidence before the committee as circumstantial and ambiguous. "Find me clear and direct evidence involving the President of the United States in an impeachable offense," he said, "and I will vote for impeachment."[16]

He did not have long to wait.

On Thursday, July 25, while the Judiciary Committee continued its televised debate, Nixon flew to Los Angeles to give a speech about inflation. He and Ray Price, the speechwriter, had worked on it for months, and it contained ideas, programs, and phrases that would have taken the audience and the news media by storm if delivered in normal circumstances by a President at the top of his powers. It was politely received and largely ignored.

The following day, Friday, July 26, the Judiciary Committee voted the first article of impeachment, charging the President with obstruction of justice "in a manner contrary to his trust as President and subversive of Constitutional government, to the great prejudice of the cause of law and justice and to the manifest injury of the people of the United States."[17] The vote was 27 to 11, with six of the seventeen Republicans joining the Democrats in the majority.[18] The last Harris poll taken before the vote showed 66 percent favoring impeachment, with 27 percent opposed. A week before, the split had been 53 percent in favor, 40 percent opposed.[19]

Nixon had just finished a swim in the Pacific and was getting dressed in the beach trailer when Ron Ziegler called him with the news. Soon after he returned to the compound, I called on him to deliver a more complete report. The President listened in silence but with his usual almost otherworldly composure, as I confirmed what he already knew, that at least two additional articles of impeachment, charging him with abuse of power in the first instance and contempt of Congress in the second, were now certain of passage. Our sources on Capitol Hill believed that a majority of the full House would vote for impeachment on all three articles. Nixon nodded; I was not telling him anything he did not know as a result of his examination of the political arithmetic involved.

Our relationship, as the reader knows, had always been formal. I strove to keep it so in the belief that formality was much more likely than familiarity or sentimentality to get us through this agonizing crisis. Nevertheless, I could not leave Nixon without expressing in some way the admiration I felt for the fortitude and dignity with which he had conducted himself.

"Mr. President, the events unfolding now are the result of irrationality, prejudice, and emotion," I said. "But history will judge these matters by a different light. In the end, you will be seen as one of our country's outstanding Presidents. The facts won't permit any other judgment."

A thought crossed Nixon's face as I spoke, but he did not share it with me. He nodded in his brisk, dismissive way. "Thank you, Al. Let's hope you're right."

We returned to Washington on July 28, a Sunday. On July 29, the second article of impeachment, charging Nixon with abuse of power, in that he, inter alia, "knowingly misused the Executive Branch . . . in violation of his duty to take care that the laws be faithfully executed." Article III, charging contempt of Congress for having failed to produce papers and other items demanded by the committee, passed on July 30.[20]

On my orders, Buzhardt had caused a transcript of the June 23 tape to be made, and I read this as soon as I reached my office on Monday morning, the twenty-ninth. Conversations from three separate meetings on June 23 between Nixon and Haldeman had been recorded. Their talk meandered, and, on the basis of my own experience with Nixon, I had the impression that his mind had not fastened on to the problem in the early stages of the conversation. But near the end of the first encounter, which took place between 10:04 and 11:39 A.M., came this devastating exchange:

> PRESIDENT: When you get in—when you get in . . . say, Look, the problem is that this will open the whole Bay of Pigs thing, and the President just feels that, ah, without going into the details—don't, don't lie to them to the extent to say there's no involvement, but just say this is a comedy of errors, without getting into it, the President believes that this is going to open the whole Bay of Pigs thing up again. And, ah, because these people are plugging for [unintelligible] and that they should call the FBI in and [unintelligible] don't go any further into this case period! . . . Well, can you get it done?
> HALDEMAN: I think so.[21]

Out of this conversation came the attempt to end the FBI investigation of the Watergate burglary by ordering Vernon Walters, Deputy Director of the CIA, to inform FBI Director Patrick Gray that the break-in was a CIA operation justified for reasons of national security. This was a lie, and Walters and Richard Helms ultimately refused to mislead the FBI by repeating it. Their refusal to cooperate smothered the cover-up in its cradle. The FBI investigation continued, ostensibly with the President's blessing, and all the other investigators walked in the furrows plowed by the FBI agents.

After reading this document, I knew that the clock had stopped in Richard Nixon's White House. What the tape showed was that the President had been aware at a very early stage of a disposition among his subordinates to cover up White House involvement in the burglary, that he had shared in this disposition, and that he had given the order that legitimized, in the minds of his underlings, everything that they subsequently did to cover up the Watergate crimes.

My belief, notwithstanding the earlier reassurances of the lawyers, was that Nixon's words on this tape would establish his guilt in the public mind and also in his trial before the Senate, and that he could not possibly survive its release. Fred Buzhardt, on further reflection, agreed with me. St. Clair had gone to Cape Cod for a long weekend. When he returned on Tuesday, July 30, he read the transcript for the first time. The experience changed his perspective entirely. He now believed that the words on the tape would be fatal to the President in any legal proceeding. He urged that Judge Sirica be informed of its contents immediately and that all the tapes be delivered to Sirica, as ordered by the Supreme Court, without delay. The evidence the June 23 tape contained was so significant that he worried that any further delay might result in a charge of obstruction of justice against himself, despite his ignorance of its contents, for having withheld it even so briefly.

That same day, Tuesday, St. Clair and Buzhardt advised Nixon on the legal situation created by the June 23 tape. On Wednesday, Nixon called me in and asked for my opinion. Although I was prepared for his question and knew that there was just one answer to it, I spoke with the greatest reluctance. No military officer in our history had ever been in the position of saying to his Commander in Chief what duty now compelled me to tell Nixon.

"Mr. President," I said, "I just don't see how we can survive this one. We have to face facts, and the facts are that this tape will deal a fatal blow to public opinion, to your supporters on the Hill, and to the party. The

Cabinet won't hold; the Republican party won't hold; your own staff won't hold. Once this tape gets out, it's over."[22]

Nixon nodded almost imperceptibly. This conversation was over.

At the end of this distressing encounter, my first thought was to discuss the matter with the man who had brought Nixon and me together, Henry Kissinger. After phoning ahead to warn him of my coming, I called on him in his office in the State Department and for the first time discussed the President's dilemma with him. Kissinger had taken the new West German foreign minister, Hans-Dietrich Genscher, to meet Nixon in San Clemente a few days before, but the time had not then been right to speak of these matters, as I had not yet read the transcript of the fatal tape or discussed its legal significance with Buzhardt and St. Clair, much less with Nixon.

Now I wanted to rally the people who had most reason to be loyal to Nixon in a final display of human support. Certainly Kissinger owed him everything, in terms of the fame, the honors, and the opportunities for public service and future rewards his high appointments had brought to him. Moreover, Kissinger, as Secretary of State, was the agent of transition in this constitutional situation, the figure to whom the President would deliver his resignation. Given Kissinger's penchant for airplane travel, I wanted to be sure that he would be in town to accept a presidential resignation when and if it was offered. It was vital that the forms of law and practice be observed so that whatever was going to happen should happen with dignity. I told Kissinger about the June 23 tape, quoting Fred Buzhardt's phrase about the smoking gun to underline the significance of its contents.

Then, without alluding to Kissinger's strained relations with Nixon and the distance he had placed between his own image and the President's all during Watergate, I added, "You're going to have to get involved in helping the President through this catastrophe. This situation is terminal, Henry. One way or the other, Nixon's presidency is over. He needs our help. And you have a constitutional role to play."

Kissinger did not utter a single word in reply to what I had said to him. Certainly he did not advise me, as has been written, to nudge the President toward resignation. Kissinger himself was too firmly attached to the proprieties to suggest any such thing, and I would have rejected the idea out of hand. It was not my prerogative to interfere in any way in Nixon's decision, which was certainly the loneliest ever made by a U.S. President. As the first American ever to find himself in his position, he could not even look to history for guidance.

Although I believed, as I had told Nixon, that the staff would break when the tape became public, I knew that some, in their loyalty and their rage at the opposition, would want to fight on to the last possible moment. If Nixon did decide to resign, it was important that his staff understand his reasons for doing so and support him in his judgment. After returning from the State Department, I asked Ron Ziegler, Dean Burch, Ray Price, and Pat Buchanan to read the transcript. All came back to me, some with tears in their eyes, with the same reaction: The tape was damning; the President could not hold on any longer.

My own view was that it would be dangerous for the country, and for Nixon, to go through the entire impeachment process. The Senate trial would almost certainly drag on for months, leaving Gerald Ford in limbo and the nation without a functioning Chief Executive. Partisan passions, already high, would be further elevated by the release of the June 23 tape. After the guilty verdict in the Senate would almost certainly come a criminal trial, raising the awful probability that a former President of the United States would be sentenced to prison. By resigning, Nixon would not eliminate the possibility of criminal prosecution or civil lawsuits. But the tacit admission of guilt and the unique punishment it involved might be enough to satisfy all but his bitterest enemies. By resigning, he might preserve his health, some fragment of his reputation, and the possibility of winning back the good opinion of his fellow citizens.

As the *Washington Post* pointed out in its editions of July 31, there were other considerations. If convicted by the Senate, Nixon would lose the pension, allowances, and perquisites due to a former President. If he resigned, he would retain his presidential pension of $60,000 a year, an allowance of $96,000 a year to cover the salaries and expenses of his staff, free office space in a federal building, and a widow's pension of $20,000 per annum for Mrs. Nixon.[23] For a man who would be virtually unemployable, and who had no personal fortune, these were not insignificant considerations. Nixon never discussed them with me, and I doubt that they ever entered into his calculations; he was too much the Quaker, and too much the fatalist, for material things to become a factor in what was, in spite of everything he had done or omitted to do, a moral decision.

First thing Thursday morning, August 1, Nixon told me that he had decided to resign. His manner and his words were cool, impersonal, matter-of-fact. "Al, it's over," he said. "We've done our best. We haven't got the votes. I can't govern. Impeachment would drag on for six months. For the sake of the country, this process must be ended."

His plan, he said, was to take his family to Camp David for the weekend to prepare them for what he was going to do, resign on Monday night in a speech to the nation, then spend a couple of weeks winding up his affairs before finally departing Washington. The chief result of this schedule would be to keep him in the public eye for two weeks in which little beside humiliation and insult were likely to come his way. He seemed oblivious to this possibility; I was worried about it.

"Obviously, we can make whatever arrangements seem best to you," I said. "But I wonder if waiting until Monday is the best choice open to you, Mr. President. The tape is going to be delivered to Judge Sirica today. A lot of people will know by the end of the day what it contains. It will certainly leak over the weekend, and by Monday it will have created an uproar. Your enemies will try to create the perception that you're resigning in response to the uproar. Your friends will be put in a very difficult position. It might be better to resign tomorrow night [Friday], and leave town immediately. That way, you can control what happens to some degree. There will be a new President. Attention will be focused on Ford over the weekend, so that he, not the tape, will be the center of attention on Monday morning."

Silent and thoughtful, Nixon absorbed my words. He may even have agreed with the reasoning behind them. But he was very reluctant to do as I suggested, and I knew that this was because his duty to explain matters to his wife and daughters and sons-in-law seemed more important to him than any punishment he might have to endure in the press. In recent weeks, he had withdrawn further into the family circle; Mrs. Nixon and their children had been a tremendous source of strength to him. Julie and her husband, David Eisenhower, had carried on a public defense of the President, including many touching encounters with reporters, some of whom looked upon a daughter's love and instinctive loyalty as merely another of her father's tricks. Of course, the family believed that Nixon was innocent, indeed incapable of wrongdoing, and it seemed unlikely that the release of the June 23 tape, which even St. Clair and Buzhardt had at first been inclined to rationalize, would change their minds.

"No," Nixon said. His tone was gentle. "It will be Monday. Get Ray Price started on a resignation speech."

Before I could speak, Nixon added another thought. This time, his tone was gruff, and he waved the cautionary forefinger that meant he was laying down the law.

"This is my decision and mine alone," he said. "I don't want the chairman of the Republican National Committee or a Cabinet delegation or a bunch of Republicans from the Hill or anyone else coming in here telling me what I should or shouldn't do. I've resisted political pressure all my life, and if I get it now, I may change my mind."

"Understood, Mr. President."

Nixon added a final instruction. "Al," he said, "you've got to tell Ford to be ready. Tell him I want absolute secrecy. Tell him what's coming. Explain the reasoning. But don't tell him when."

There was no other message. These are the only words that Nixon ever spoke to me in connection with the transfer of the presidency from himself to Gerald Ford until the time came to inform Ford of the exact time of Nixon's departure. On returning to my office, I called Ford and asked for an immediate appointment to see him alone. It was still early in the day, not yet nine o'clock. On my arrival in the Vice President's office in the Executive Office Building a few minutes later, I was surprised to discover that Ford's chief of staff, a former newspaperman named Robert Hartmann, was with him. Of all the members of Ford's staff, which included my friend former Congressman Jack Marsh (my New Year's visitor, along with the Phu Loi Battalion of the Viet Cong, in Vietnam), Hartmann was the last one I should have chosen to be present at this meeting. I hardly knew him, but the little I knew I did not like. His habitual manner was caustic, aggressive, rude; he seemed never to have gotten over being an outsider, and he appeared to think like one. He was, as Ford has written, "suspicious of everyone."[24]

Ford greeted me with characteristic warmth and led me to a seat on the sofa. I sat down and waited for Hartmann to depart. When it became obvious that he was not going to do so, I came directly to the point. I told the Vice President about the June 23 tape and the expectation that it would soon become public. "When that happens," I said, "it is the consensus of the President's lawyers and advisers, and my own opinion as well, that the President's chances of avoiding impeachment in the House or winning acquittal in the Senate will disappear."

Ford asked me for more details about what was on the tape. Had we been alone, I would have supplied them gladly. Under the circumstances, I said that I would see that a copy of the final transcript, which was in the process of preparation, was delivered to Ford.

Ordinarily, Ford is the most relaxed and open of men. After hearing what I had told him, all trace of casual mannerisms vanished.

"Mr. Vice President," I said, "I think you should prepare yourself for changes in your life. I can't predict what will happen, or when, but I think you should hold yourself in readiness."

I did not want to go further than that in Hartmann's presence, but the meaning was unmistakable. Ford, deeply solemn, nodded. I told him that I would keep him informed of developments, and we parted.

Before meeting with Ford, I had asked Fred Buzhardt for legal guidance, as was my invariable practice. I wanted to be certain that every word I said to the Vice President in this delicate and unprecedented situation was consistent in letter and spirit with the Constitution and the statutes. This presented some difficulties because I was not free to tell anyone other than Ford about the President's decision to resign. Of course Fred knew that resignation was one of the options the President must consider. Although I had not asked for such a thing, Buzhardt and some of his staff prepared a list of alternatives to simple resignation or going through the impeachment process to the end. These were:

1. The President could temporarily step aside under the Twenty-fifth Amendment to defend himself before the Senate, with Ford becoming Acting President until the impeachment question was settled.
2. He could delay resignation, hoping for some turn of events that might save the day.
3. He could try to persuade the House to settle for a vote of censure instead of impeachment.
4. The President could pardon himself, then resign.
5. He could pardon some or all of the Watergate defendants, then pardon himself, then resign.
6. He could resign and hope that his successor would pardon him. [25]

The final item (number 6) was typed on a separate sheet of paper; I don't know why.

I did not show this list to Nixon or discuss it with him then or at any other time. As far as I am aware, he did not know it existed until it was published after he resigned.

Knowing that any sort of leak would produce an unpredictable but very strong reaction in the President, I had been reluctant to discuss the contents of the tape or the President's state of mind in the presence of Hartmann. After receiving the list of options from the lawyers, it seemed to me important to lay everything on the table with Ford. Soon after our first meeting, he and Hartmann and other members of his staff had driven to the Capitol, where the Vice President has a second office as presiding officer of the Senate. I reached Ford there and asked for another meeting, this time with just the two of us present. Although, as I later learned, Ford had a policy of having a witness present at all important meetings, he agreed to see me alone at 3:30.[26]

He received me alone in the spacious office assigned to the Vice President in the Executive Office Building. During Ford's tenancy, the office was modestly furnished with overstuffed chairs and sofas, a plain desk, and Ford's favorite leather chair. A decorated screen stood in one corner of the room. This time, I told Ford the details.

"Mr. Vice President," I said, "the President has made up his mind to resign. I'm sorry to have to tell you that the tape I mentioned earlier contains a conversation that can be interpreted to mean that the President knew about the cover-up six days after the break-in, and that he approved a plan designed to shut off the FBI investigation by falsely representing to the Bureau that the Watergate break-in was a CIA operation connected to national security."

Ford asked a number of lawyerlike questions. I tried to answer them in language as plain as his own. The Vice President's distress was obvious. Although they had not been personal friends by any but Washington standards, he and Nixon had known each other and worked together for a quarter of a century; Ford had defended Nixon on the basis of his repeated assurances that the tapes would confirm his version of events and establish his complete innocence. In Ford's case, the President had repeated these assurances on asking him to accept the vice presidency.

I asked Ford for his assessment of the situation, as one who knew Washington well and the Congress intimately. He agreed with me that the President had little or no chance of escaping impeachment and conviction if he chose to stick it out to the end. Ford agreed, too, that the tapes would outrage public opinion and generate demands for immediate resignation. "One thing is sure," he said, "and that is if anyone tries to tell Dick Nixon to leave, he'll stay and fight it out. That's his nature."

According to the White House lawyers, I said without naming them, there were permutations to the option of resignation. I then handed Ford, at the same time, both sheets of paper that Buzhardt had given me, telling him that I wanted him to be sure to understand that the list of options was just that. I was not recommending or supporting any of the options on the list, or any other solution. The lawyers' list was hypothetical, an inventory of possibilities open to the President under the law. I had played no part in drawing it up and it did not represent my own ideas. Because I wasn't a lawyer, I said, I was in no position to have an opinion of any kind on an interpretation of the law.

After reading the options, Ford asked some questions about the pardon powers of the President, a natural thing to do since three of the five items on the list discussed the subject. He wanted, specifically, to know whether the President really did have the authority to grant a pardon even before an individual had been tried and convicted. I replied that this was my understanding, based on what the lawyers had said. Could the President pardon an individual even before he was indicted? I said I did not know.

All of this was beside the point, or so it seemed to me at the time. There could be only one reason for pardoning Nixon apart from the simple humanity of the act, and that was for the good of the country, to spare it from a trial in the Senate that would divert the government from the real business of the nation and create a destructive heritage of hatred and resentment. Ford, politician and patriot that he was, did not need me to tell him this, nor to point out how much courage it would take to issue such a pardon.* Therefore, I did not presume to instruct him in these matters. Privately, I believed that this was a time for mercy if ever there was one. If Ford divined what was in my mind, however, it was not because I told him my thoughts. As quickly as possible, I came back to the purpose of the meeting.

"I am very confident that the President will resign," I told the Vice President. "For the moment, I can't tell you when, but I think you should hold yourself in readiness to assume the presidency on short notice. Will you do that, sir?"

"If it happens, Al, I'm prepared," Ford said.

Our talk had lasted just under an hour. We agreed to stay in close contact in case of any sudden development. "If you have any questions or problems," I said, "don't hesitate to call me, day or night." Ford nodded. "You do the same," he replied. When we stood up, he threw an arm around my shoulders. Then he walked me to the door, warmly shook my hand, and thanked me for the way in which I had handled my part of our conversations.

These acts of kindness were unnecessary but welcome; my talk with

---

* In testimony before the House Subcommittee on Criminal Justice after he became President, Ford explained the reasons for his decision as follows: "I believed the general view of the American people was to spare the former President from a criminal trial. . . . I became greatly concerned that if Mr. Nixon's prosecution and trial were prolonged, the passions generated over a period of time would seriously disrupt the healing of our country from the wounds of the past. I could see that the new administration could not be effective if it had to operate in the atmosphere of having a former President under prosecution and criminal trial." Jaworski told Philip Buchen in a letter dated September 4, 1974, that in his opinion the "massive publicity," among other factors, surrounding the Nixon situation would "require a delay, before selection of a jury is begun, of a period from nine months to a year" (Hearings, pp. 97, 189).

Ford had made the departure of the President seem real and soon to happen, and my heart was heavy. I could see that Ford understood this, and I did not doubt that he felt the weight of this sad moment as much or more than I did. I had always liked and admired Ford, and his plain, good-hearted, human demeanor in this unique situation made me think that the country would be in good hands under his leadership. It was Thursday afternoon, a cloudy, humid Washington day. I left Gerald Ford's office believing that he would be President of the United States by the following Tuesday.

Meanwhile, the task of preparing for the impact of the June 23 tape remained. Ford's deeply felt, if silent, reaction to the revelation that he may have been deceived by Nixon made it all the more urgent that others who had gone out on a limb for the President be given advance notice of the bombshell that was shortly going to explode. One of the most loyal of these men was Representative Charles Wiggins, Republican of California, who represented Nixon's old district in Congress. He had been described in the press as Nixon's "chief defender" on the Judiciary Committee.[27] The day after my meetings with the Vice President, I invited Wiggins to the White House to read the transcript.

He did so in my presence and St. Clair's, then lifted an ashen face and said, "Holy smoke! It's all over." He made some bitter remarks about having been led down the garden path. Finally, he said, "You understand, Al, that I'll have to make this public."

"The President is going to make it public, Chuck."

We discussed the possible effect on the vote for impeachment in the House and conviction in the Senate. "Al, I've already told you," Wiggins said. "It's all over. The minute this tape comes out, he'll lose all but a few Republicans. He may even lose me. [Later that day, Wiggins called on Nixon to resign and announced that he would vote for impeachment if he did not.[28]] He'll be impeached in the House by a huge majority and convicted in the Senate. It's as simple as that."

I passed on this gloomy but realistic estimate to Nixon, who received it without comment; his mind was elsewhere. That evening, he would tell his family of his plans to resign and give them the transcript of the June 23 tape. The evening before, during dinner aboard the presidential yacht *Sequoia*, Nixon had told Bebe Rebozo of his intentions; Bebe had protested that resignation was the wrong thing to do, that Nixon still had millions of supporters in the country.[29] That was true, but he needed thirty-four votes in the Senate to avoid conviction in case of an impeachment trial. According to Hugh Scott of Pennsylvania, the Republican leader, thirty-six senators were leaning toward acquittal, but eleven of these were "soft."[30] As Wiggins had pointed out, there was no hope that this head count would survive the release of the tape.

At 7:20 P.M., August 1, I received a phone call from Ford. We had chatted briefly the night before, when I had called him at home around bedtime to tell him that there were no new developments. My thought, encouraged no doubt by Ford's great courtesy to me earlier in that long and difficult day, was that the Vice President might sleep better if he knew before retiring that he was not likely to be awakened in the night by a call from the White House.

Now, however, his voice was very formal; afterward, I half-remembered that he called me General instead of Al. Without preamble, he said, "I want you to understand that I have no intention of recommending what the President should do about resigning or not resigning, and nothing we talked about yesterday afternoon should be given any consideration in whatever decision the President may wish to make."[31]

His delivery was so measured that I had the impression (later confirmed by Ford in his memoirs) that he was reading from a prepared text.[32] This puzzled me, and if it had come from anyone but Ford, who doesn't have a mean or crooked bone in his body, I would have been deeply offended. We had trusted each other the day before. What had happened in the meantime?

"You're absolutely right, Mr. Vice President," I said. "But I thought that was understood yesterday. There was never any thought here that you should involve yourself in the President's decision in any way."

After we disconnected, I gazed at the phone for a moment and muttered to myself, "What was *that* all about?" After a moment's reflection, I began to understand what was happening. Ford had made this call on the advice of his staff, who were trying to protect him from any future charge that he had made some sort of deal with me in connection with the President's resignation.

Later, Ford wrote that Hartmann had immediately suspected that our discussion of the option list was a subtle way of telling Ford that Nixon expected him to pardon him if he stepped aside. "That reaction was typical of Bob," Ford wrote in his memoirs. ". . . This time, however, I thought he was overreacting, making a mountain out of a molehill, and I told him so." But Jack Marsh agreed with Hartmann that our discussion of the President's power to pardon, even on a theoretical plane, was "a time bomb" that threatened Ford.[33] According to Hartmann, the Vice

President's old friend Bryce Harlow also concurred, telling him that it was "inconceivable that [Haig] was not carrying out a mission for the President. . . ."[34]

This Machiavellian leap of the imagination had nothing to do with reality. To be blunt, the whole conception of exchanging the presidency for a pardon is witless. The advantages for the President are clear. But what possible motive could a Vice President have for entering into such a pact? Ford was going to become President not because Nixon wanted to sell him the office in return for forgiveness of his crimes but because Nixon had no choice in the matter. He could not remain in office because he could not govern; Ford was his constitutional successor. He did not have to give Nixon anything, under any circumstances, in order to become President. That was going to happen anyway, and Ford knew that it was going to happen because I had told him so on the authority of the President.

As for Nixon, he never knew from anything I told him that the subject of presidential pardons had come up in my conversation with the Vice President. The explanation for this is a simple one: It would have been a cruel insult even to mention such talk to Nixon in his agony, and I never for a moment considered doing so.

In the days ahead, Richard Nixon would resign the presidency for the sake of the country. Gerald Ford would pardon him for the same reason. The only connection between the two acts was that both men put the domestic tranquillity of the United States of America above their personal interests.

36

The Final Paradox

On Friday afternoon, August 2, I spent three hours with Nixon discussing the arrangements for his resignation—how and when the transcripts of the final tapes would be released, what he wanted to say in his speech to the nation, how he wanted to say good-bye to the Cabinet and the staff and his friends in Congress, how we could make the transition as easy as possible for Ford, where the Nixons would go after he left the White House, how his personal property would be handled. It was a rambling session that left all of these matters half-decided or undecided, with the single exception of the resignation itself. On that question, his mind seemed to be made up and he did not waver.

After we parted, he spent the evening with his family and Bebe Rebozo. They read the transcript, decided that the words spoken by Nixon to Haldeman were ambiguous, and urged him to follow his instincts and fight on.[1] Quite late that night, he called me at home and told me that he had changed his mind. He would not resign on Monday, after all.

"Let them impeach me," he said. "We'll fight it out to the end."

His plan now was to issue the transcript of the tapes on Monday together with a statement that argued that, whatever he may have said to Haldeman on June 23, he had approved and vigorously pushed the FBI investigation of the break-in during other conversations recorded on other tapes.

First thing next morning, I passed this word to Ziegler, who accepted in his usual unflinching way the nearly unbearable burden it placed on his shoulders. Afterward, I met with Nixon. The support and encouragement of his family had energized him to follow the instinct that made him what he was and stand up and fight against hopeless odds. He had done it before and won. Chuck Wiggins had asked, scathingly, whether Nixon had another Checkers speech in his pocket. His family, in effect, had asked the same question, but in another tone of voice and in expectation that he might once again snatch vindication from the flames of calumny. For the first time in days, there was some trace of vigor, of uplift in Nixon's demeanor; his blood was up. As the loser cries in *Paradise Lost*,

> *What though the field be lost?*
> *All is not lost—th' unconquerable will,*
> *And study of revenge, immortal hate,*
> *And courage never to submit or yield.*[2]

The sentiments were Nixonian, even in a certain sense noble. The President asked me whether I thought he was making a mistake. I replied that it was not my place to make judgments on such matters. The decision was his and his alone, but whatever he did must have the support and agreement of everyone he loved and respected.

There was no point in telling him that the fight was hopeless; he knew that. His family did not. He felt that he owed it to them not to resign on the assumption that the June 23 tape would destroy him. Maybe his wife and children were right; maybe the impact would be less than we thought. Maybe it could be managed. The least he could do was to make the best case he could and then assess the reaction. He said, "I'm not foreclosing the other course [resignation], Al; it may come to that. But let's see what happens about the tape."

After leaving him, I called Buzhardt, St. Clair, and Ray Price to a meeting in my office and gave them the President's instructions. The lawyers were skeptical but reluctantly resigned to an exercise they knew could change nothing. However, in putting the best possible face on the President's new strategy, I apparently created the impression in Ray Price's mind that I somehow shared the Nixon family's unrealistic hopes of a last-minute reversal of fortune. Ray, in his great decency and intelligence and deep loyalty to Nixon, told me in an impassioned way that resignation was still the only possible course. I knew this; we all knew it; nothing had changed except appearances, and those temporarily. It was not my role to be his conscience and whisper to him in private that he must resign. The President had decided, for reasons having to do with his love for his wife and daughters, to do as they asked and wait for a reaction to the tape. But this was only a diversion.

There is nothing so tiring as unproductive work, and Saturday was a long, hard, frustrating day. My mother had recently been hospitalized with a heart condition, and my brother, the Reverend Francis Haig, S.J., at that time a professor of nuclear physics at Loyola College in Baltimore, came to lunch in the White House to discuss her health and other family matters. Frank, whose serene Jesuitical view of the temporal sphere was a welcome change from the usual stuff of White House conversation, stayed on, chatting, for an hour or so afterward, until I was summoned by Nixon.

The President was in a rage. He had just received a letter from Senator Robert P. ("Bobby") Griffin of Michigan, the Republican whip. Griffin wrote that unless Nixon chose to resign, impeachment in the House was certain, and if the President did not turn over the sixty-four subpoenaed tapes to the Senate as evidence in his trial, then he, Griffin, would "regard that as an impeachable offense and vote accordingly."[3]

"Pompous little jackass!" said the President, who had campaigned for Griffin when he first ran for Congress in 1956 and had done him many political favors since. "Who the hell does he think he is?" The letter had been released to the press at the same time it was delivered to the President—though only to the Michigan papers, a maneuver so hypocritical that it left Nixon speechless. The fact that Griffin was from Ford's home state, and that he had been mentioned as a member of the nebulous Grand Rapids group, invested this communication with more than ordinary meaning. It could be a signal that Ford's friends were going public to force Nixon's resignation.

Late Saturday afternoon, Nixon and his family went to Camp David. That evening, Pat and I went to the Kennedy Center with the Kissingers to see, from the presidential box in the Eisenhower Theater, Eva Marie Saint in Eugene O'Neill's *Desire Under the Elms*. The play made no impression on my memory. No doubt my mind was elsewhere.

Early Sunday afternoon, I boarded a helicopter for Camp David at the Pentagon pad. Also aboard were Ziegler, St. Clair, Price, Buchanan, and Joulwan. St. Clair was accompanied by his wife, and, because I thought this might very well be the last time that either of us would visit Camp David, Pat came along, too.

Our objective was to produce a presidential statement to be released next day with the tapes. By now, the group had been seized by the realization that Nixon must have known what was on the June 23 tape since May 6, the day he listened to it in the wake of Jaworski's revelation that he had been named as an unindicted coconspirator. He had not shared what he knew about his own culpability with us, and had issued orders that no one, not even the lawyers, were to listen to the subpoenaed tapes. The realization that the staff had been cut off from the truth in this way was disturbing to everyone, and especially so to St. Clair, who had based his defense of Nixon on the latter's assurance that nothing in the tapes would harm him.

The confidence St. Clair had expressed at San Clemente when first hearing about the tape the week before had turned to deep pessimism. Now he thought that the tape was fatal, and he was concerned that the delay in providing it to the court, if left unexplained, might lead to charges of obstruction of justice against those who had acted for Nixon in the matter, including himself. The consensus of the group was that Nixon would have to concede in his statement that he had listened to the incriminating tape almost three months before but had kept what he heard to himself. Although I was determined that the President's statement must be perfectly truthful, it seemed to me that this went too far. If the question arose, Nixon could answer it. But why was it necessary for him to volunteer a confession to a crime of which he had not yet been accused?

Nixon wanted the statement to emphasize that he had gone ahead with the FBI investigation as soon as he learned that there was no national-security aspect (that is, CIA involvement) in the Watergate break-in. The group regarded this argument as disingenuous, and, with some threats of resignation, declined to support it. Instead, after many drafts, Ray Price produced a text that included Nixon's argument that he had told the Director of the FBI to go ahead with the investigation, and asserted "the basic truth remains that when all the facts were brought to my attention I insisted on a full investigation and prosecution of those guilty."

But the statement also included the following passage:

> Among the conversations I listened to [in May] were two of those of June 23. Although I recognized that these presented potential problems, I did not inform my staff or my Counsel of it, or those arguing my case, nor did I amend my submission to the Judiciary Committee in order to include and reflect it. At the time, I did not realize the implications which these

conversations might now appear to have. As a result, those arguing my case, as well as those passing judgment on the case, did so with information that was incomplete and in some respects erroneous. This was a serious act of omission for which I take full responsibility and which I deeply regret.[4]

That got everyone except Nixon off the hook. When I showed the draft to Nixon, he understood what had happened. Naturally, he did not like it. Why hadn't the group developed his own idea more fully? Why was he issuing this mea culpa? "Damn it, Al," he said, "this is not what I asked for." He handed me his own handwritten notes, several pages from a yellow legal pad, as the basis for a rewrite.

I said, "It's no use, Mr. President. We've been at it hammer and tongs all afternoon and this is the best we can do. The lawyers will jump ship if I ask them to change it." I explained how St. Clair and the others felt and what a struggle it had been to produce even this draft.

Nixon glowered, expelled his breath in exasperation—and finally just shrugged. "The hell with it. It doesn't really matter. They can put out whatever they want."

It was a sad moment. The President had lost the power to demand the words he wanted on a statement that was going to be issued under his own name.

The President's statement and the sixty-four tapes were released to the press at 4:00 P.M. Monday, August 5. Nixon and his family and Rose Mary Woods dined aboard the *Sequoia*. When asking me to arrange this outing, he had explained that he wanted to spare his wife and daughters the ordeal of watching the evening news broadcasts. By now, the whole staff knew that the last act had begun, and about a hundred White House employees, mostly younger people, turned out to cheer the Nixons as they left for the short drive to the Potomac. In his awkward way, like a man who had taken lessons to overcome his inborn shyness, the President walked among them, shaking hands, smiling his brief smile, calling people by name, trying to cheer them up. He hadn't expected anything like this. It was obvious he was deeply touched, and just as obvious that he knew in every particle of his being that he was rehearsing his political funeral.

At noon that day, Barry Goldwater had told me that Nixon had fewer votes in the Senate every hour. His own vote was no longer automatically pro-Nixon; he'd been told what was in the tapes. "It's hopeless, Al; there have been too many damn lies," Goldwater had said. "Somebody has got to tell the President that." He had come out of the Senate Republican policy lunch to take my call. The overwhelming consensus among senators at the lunch was for resignation now, and the discussion was so frank that Gerald Ford, a regular guest, excused himself on grounds that his presence was improper.[5]

After dinner, Rose Woods called from the *Sequoia* to ask on the President's behalf what the reaction to the statement had been. I told her that it had been pretty much what we had expected and let it go at that.

Nixon had asked me to set up a Cabinet meeting on Tuesday morning. Washington buzzed with rumors of resignation, and the unusually large number who attended clearly expected drama. There was an intake of breath somewhere in the room when Nixon, pale and tired but in complete control of the situation, opened by saying that he wanted to discuss "the most important issue confronting the nation—inflation." He went on to talk about the economy for several minutes longer. This dispelled tension and created it at the same time, and I guessed that the colorless preamble was Nixon's way of asserting his control over the meeting. Quite soon, he came to the topic on everybody's mind.

He had considered resignation, he said, but had rejected it because it would establish a precedent under which the President could stay in office only so long as he could win a vote of confidence in Congress. "I am of the view," he said, "that I should not take the step that changes the Constitution and establishes a precedent for all future Presidents. It would [result in] a parliamentary system with all of its weaknesses but none of its strengths."[6] He added, "If I thought there was an impeachable offense, I wouldn't put the Senate through the agony of trying to prove it." He went on in this vein for several minutes more. Looking around the table from my seat against the wall, I did not see much evidence that the importance of the point he was making was registering on the Cabinet.

When he paused momentarily, Ford asked whether he could make a comment. Nixon was taken aback—Presidents are not usually interrupted in Cabinet meetings—but yielded. That morning Ford had issued a statement saying that "the public interest is no longer served by repetition of my previously expressed belief . . . that the President is not guilty of an impeachable offense."[7] Now, addressing himself directly to Nixon, who sat across the polished table from him with a bright window at his back, Ford said, ". . . had I known what has been disclosed in reference to Watergate in the last twenty-four hours, I would not have made a number of the statements I made either as minority leader or as Vice President. . . . I am sure there will be impeachment in the House. I can't predict the Senate outcome. . . . Mr. President, you have given us the finest foreign policy this country has ever had. . . . Let me assure you I expect to continue to support the administration's foreign policy and the fight against inflation."[8]

Nixon listened with a sad, somewhat absent smile on his face. Then, as he started to discuss the economy again, he became aware of a stir beyond the Cabinet table. It was George Bush, who, as a guest of the President, occupied one of the straight chairs along the wall. He seemed to be asking for the floor. When Nixon failed to recognize him, he spoke anyway. Watergate was the vital question, he said. It was sapping public confidence. Until it was settled, the economy and the country as a whole would suffer. Nixon should resign.

Remembering the blizzard of historic precedents produced by Watergate, this particular snowflake, in which the chairman of the Republican National Committee called on a Republican President to resign in the presence of his Cabinet, stands out in my memory. Everyone present knew that whatever the President might say, he would have to resign. A shocked silence came over the room. Nixon brushed Bush aside, saying that it might be a good idea to call a domestic summit conference on the economy.

Bill Saxbe, the Attorney General, spoke up. "Mr. President, I don't think we ought to have a summit conference," he said. "We ought to be sure you have the ability to govern."

This exceeded even Saxbe's very advanced standards for brutal frankness, and his words produced a silence even deeper than the one Bush's remarks had brought down on the meeting. Had no one intervened— Nixon was too flabbergasted to do so—it is possible that the meeting would have exploded into a shouting match. Kissinger rose to the occasion and, in what was surely his finest moment related to the Watergate crisis, rumbled, "We are here to do the nation's business."[9] This restored decorum.

After the meeting, however, Kissinger followed Nixon back to the Oval Office and told him that the best thing he could do for the country was to resign. An impeachment trial would paralyze foreign policy. Nixon thanked him for his advice and dismissed him.[10]

At 2:15, I went in to see the President. Among the odds and ends of business I had for him was a call from Haldeman, who said that he opposed resignation, but if Nixon did resign he should pardon all the

Watergate defendants as his last act in office and balance this general act of clemency by declaring an amnesty for Vietnam War draft evaders at the same time. Ehrlichman, who had hoped to reach Julie Eisenhower, phoned Rose Mary Woods with his own similar recommendation—a presidential amnesty for all Watergate offenders.[11] Nixon barely listened when I mentioned these suggestions to him; he had already made up his mind that there would be no blanket pardons for his former associates.

By now, the full impact of the tapes and the limited confession of wrongdoing in the President's statement was as obvious as it was immeasurable. The media was saturated by the story. Support for Nixon in the House and in the Republican party as a whole had collapsed, with all ten members of the Judiciary Committee who had voted against impeachment reversing themselves and the House minority leader, John J. Rhodes of Arizona, announcing that he would vote for impeachment. In the Senate, Robert Dole of Kansas said that the number of senators supporting Nixon had been cut in half (from forty to twenty), while John Tower of Texas declared that a majority of Republican senators wanted the President to resign his office. Elsewhere, Governor Ronald Reagan of California called for Nixon's resignation, Bush had told the press that he was sure Nixon would "do what is best for the country," and the ever-quotable Melvin Laird confided to the *Washington Post* that he favored Nelson Rockefeller for Vice President after Nixon resigned and Ford ascended to the presidency. Because opposition to impeachment had practically vanished, the House leadership voted informally to reduce the time allotted to debate to one week instead of two, and the Rules Committee approved live radio and television coverage. Members of both Houses of Congress suggested that Nixon be offered a congressional grant of immunity if he resigned from office, but Mike Mansfield said the Senate should try Nixon even if he did resign.[12]

Taking all this into account and remembering the words spoken to the President in the Cabinet meeting, I did not see how Nixon could do anything except resign, and I took it for granted that he would do so quite soon. In appeasing his family, he had demonstrated to them, and to himself, that there was no hope. Nevertheless, I was tugged in both directions just as Nixon was, and I was not sure which was the patriot's course. If my head told me that resignation was the only practical path to take, my heart insisted that the only honorable way was to fight the thing out to the end. I knew that Nixon may have broken the law, that he had misled me and everyone else, but I also knew that his "crimes" were well within the boundaries of behavior that had been accepted, even praised, in some of his predecessors, and that he was being destroyed less for what he had done than for who he was.* His removal without resort to a popular election was a fateful precedent, and I believed with the more combative part of my nature that Nixon should oppose his own downfall to the end, no matter what the cost to himself or the nation. Better to lose six months now than lose the soul of American democracy. I would gladly have stayed with him through the entire impeachment process.

As we have seen, Nixon's habit was to examine every possible course of action, playing devil's advocate with himself and his listeners, setting up straw men in order to knock them down, treating the outrageous and the rational courses of action as equals until he chose one over the other. That is what he did on this occasion.

"Obviously, I can resign and save everyone a lot of time and trouble," he said. "That's a temptation. On the other hand, Al, I may just run it out, go through the Senate trial, put my defense on the record, accept conviction if that's what's in the cards, go on trial, go to prison, lose everything—but go out with my head held high."

For nearly two hours, while I listened, for the most part in silence, he rambled on, struggling against the obvious, scrutinizing his enemies, embracing false hope, admitting the desperation of his situation. He took himself to the mountaintop, looked down on the temptations spread out over the political desert below, and resolutely turned his back. It was a brilliant, deeply moving, utterly candid performance by a man equipped by nature to rule a great nation and change the course of history by the power of his mind and spirit—but condemned, as it seemed, by the gods to have his petty faults weigh more heavily than his heroic virtues on the scale of fate.

Finally, he told me that he had decided to resign the presidency, effective at noon on Friday, August 9, 1974. He would inform the nation of his decision in a televised speech on Thursday evening, spend one final night in the White House, say good-bye to the staff in the morning, and leave for San Clemente at about ten o'clock.

---

*On September 3, 1974, somewhat less than a month after Nixon's resignation, Henry Ruth, assistant special prosecutor, wrote Leon Jaworski a memorandum listing ten matters (not including the Watergate cover-up) having some direct connection to Nixon that were still under investigation by the Office of the Special Prosecutor. These included allegations of criminal conduct in regard to taxes, misuse of the IRS, wiretaps, the milk fund, ITT, the $100,000 campaign contribution from Howard Hughes, and other questions. "None of these matters at the moment rises to the level of our ability to prove even a probable criminal violation by Mr. Nixon," Ruth wrote. (See Hearings of the House Subcommittee on Criminal Justice of the Committee on the Judiciary, 93rd Congress, 2nd Session, p. 190.)

"That will put me over Chicago as Jerry Ford takes the oath at noon," he said. "Gone."

The act of releasing the arguments and alternatives with which he had wrestled in silence for so long seemed to lift a burden from his psyche, and for a moment he seemed almost buoyant. Then, after a short silence, his mood changed.

"You know, Al, you soldiers have the best way of dealing with a situation like this," he said. "You just leave a man alone in a room with a loaded pistol."

He was speaking figuratively, and I knew this. Nixon was a deeply religious man to whom suicide was simply unthinkable. All the same, it was a chilling moment.

"You just have to go on, Mr. President," I replied. I did not know what else to say to him in his desolation, and we parted in silence.

At 5:15, the President called Ron Ziegler and me over to his office in the Executive Office Building and told us both, formally, of his decision to resign. In the hour since we had parted, he had filled several pages of a long yellow pad with notes for his speech, and he read from these while Ron and I took notes.

"I will do this without rancor and with dignity," he said. "I'll go out gracefully."

"You'll do more than that, sir," I said. "You'll take your leave in a manner that is as worthy of history's praise as those who are against you are unworthy of it."

Nixon seemed to be touched by my words. After more discussion of arrangements, he and Ziegler and I walked back to the White House together. As we entered the Rose Garden, some sign of the strong emotion I was feeling must have shown on my face, because Nixon suddenly threw an arm around my shoulders. He was wan and hollow-eyed.

"Come on, Al," he said in his hearty baritone. "Buck up."

It was the first time he had ever broken our code of formality and made so human a gesture toward me. But how many times before, I thought, had I seen this unfathomable man reach out to others when it was his own troubles that warranted sympathy and human understanding.

Overnight, Dean Burch called me with a disturbing report. Burch, a longtime confidant of Barry Goldwater, told me that senior Republicans from both houses of Congress had been pressuring Goldwater to join them in demanding the President's resignation "for the good of the nation and the party." Goldwater had been vociferous on the issue of Watergate—that was his nature—but he had always kept clear of anti-Nixon cabals. I knew that Burch would never have reported this particular story to me if Goldwater had not been looking for help in extricating himself from the situation. As a former presidential candidate and the leader of the conservative movement, his was the most influential Republican voice on Capitol Hill.

"For God's sake, Dean, Goldwater can't let himself be used in this way," I said.

"Well, I'm just telling you he's feeling the heat," Burch replied.

I said, "I want to talk to Goldwater before he comes over here tomorrow night."

Goldwater, Hugh Scott, the Republican leader of the Senate, and John Rhodes, the Republican leader of the House, were scheduled to call on Nixon on Wednesday evening. It was my fear that they would use the occasion to demand a resignation. Any such initiative would be a serious infringement of the doctrine of the separation of powers—it is no business of American legislators to banish an American President—and I knew that Nixon would recognize any such initiative for what it was, a trespass on the Constitution that must be resisted.

Burch called Goldwater and arranged for the three of us to meet over lunch at Burch's house on Wednesday.

We could not meet sooner because Nixon had instructed me to inform Ford of his decision, and at eight o'clock on Wednesday morning I called on the Vice President in his office in the Executive Office Building. He showed me to the sofa and sat down beside me. There was no small talk, no reference to the events of the day before.

I said, "Mr. Vice President, I am here on the President's instructions to tell you that you should prepare yourself to assume the presidency at noon on Friday."

For a long moment after this, we sat in silence, immobilized by the solemnity of the occasion.

Then Ford said, "Very well. What else can you tell me?"

It was important to be precise. I had scribbled a couple of pages of notes on a tablet, and I took these from my pocket as a guide to the rest of my comments. I told Ford what the timing would be and what the arrangements were for the President's departure.

"I hope you will help us to hold this thing together until tomorrow night," I said.

My fear was that Congress would do something precipitous, creating a constitutional conflict that would make it impossible for the President to carry out his intentions. I told Ford about the Goldwater situation and how I hoped to handle it.

I recommended that the White House staff, with the exception of Ziegler, who had decided to go with the President, and a few personal aides such as Rose Woods and Steve Bull and Manolo and Fina Sanchez, be retained for at least thirty days and that all ambassadors and other Presidential appointees also stay on for a month.

"I assume you will want to make an address to the nation on Friday," I said. "We will help with this in any way we can, and with anything else involved in the transition. Is there anything in particular I can do for you, sir?"

Ford said, "Look after the President, Al."

The rest of the morning was a kaleidoscope of meetings with Ziegler, Ray Price, Fred Buzhardt, Jim St. Clair, and others directly involved in the preparations for the President's announcement. Kissinger spent the morning at the White House in case the President wanted to discuss foreign policy with him. Nixon had been reluctant to see him, but he had agreed during our marathon session the day before that he must do so, inasmuch as Kissinger, as Secretary of State, was the officer of the government empowered to receive a presidential resignation. I told Kissinger, when he stopped in to see me around ten o'clock, that the President might be calling him. We discussed the foreign-policy situation and the ways in which Ford could be briefed and supported on urgent questions.

At noon, I went over to Dean Burch's house to meet Senator Goldwater. The encounter was as cordial, under the circumstances, as Goldwater's great geniality could make it. I told him what I had heard he and his colleagues planned to do.

I said, "Senator, you simply cannot let this happen. This is a banana-republic solution." I went on to say that, in the United States of America, delegations from Congress do not give a President his marching orders. Once that tawdry precedent is established, everything changes forever. Separation of powers goes out the window, the sovereignty of the people is compromised, and all sorts of other results follow, all of them contrary to American tradition.

I concluded, "Things are bad enough already; the Constitution is under enough stress. If the President goes, he must go on his own terms, by due process of law, as the result of his own uncoerced decision. Please be patient a little longer."

I could not betray the confidence of the President by telling Goldwater what Nixon's actual intentions were. In any case, the issue was not Nixon's intention but the intentions of the Founding Fathers.

"You're right on every count," Goldwater said. "Don't worry, Al. We won't say a word about resignation to Nixon or anyone else."

That evening at five o'clock, Goldwater, Scott, and Rhodes arrived to keep their appointment with Nixon. I had not told the President about my conversation with Goldwater, and he received them as though he had summoned them into his presence for advice. It was a brief and melancholy encounter; these men had collaborated and socialized for years, and Watergate was only a fragment of their whole knowledge of one another. As Goldwater had promised me, the subject of resignation did not arise. Nixon asked for the estimates of the Senate. Goldwater repeated what he had told me earlier—he could count only a dozen votes for Nixon. "I've got to be frank," he added. "I'm not sure I'm one of the twelve." Scott said there might be as many as fifteen senators who would stand with the President, but no more than that number, and no prospect of more. Bill Timmons, who was present, confirmed these figures.

"Well, it looks damn bad," said Nixon. "But don't worry, I'm not going to cry. I haven't cried since Eisenhower died."

To the reporters milling anxiously outside the West Wing, Barry Goldwater said with perfect accuracy, "We were fond old friends talking over a very painful situation."[13]

Later that evening, Nixon summoned Kissinger to the Lincoln Sitting Room for a final chat. His intention, I think, was as much to stitch up the wounds in their relationship as to engage in the discussion of foreign policy that both have reported in their memoirs. Afterward, apparently, they prayed together for peace. An embellished account of this intensely private moment appeared with minimal delay in the news media. There was a kind of awful symmetry in the circumstance that their relationship, which had been so troubled by leaks from the outset, should end with one that anguished them both.

It seemed to me that the best way to manage Nixon's last full day as President was on a note of routine. We met at length on Thursday morning and then again in the afternoon. As on many mornings in the past, he had a list of things for my attention. I wrote them all down and told him such news as I had. I myself had written out a long list of matters for decision. Which of his personal staff did he wish to take with him and what arrangements for their transportation to San Clemente should be made? How did he want his household goods and personal belongings, including his papers, handled? How long should Secret Service protection for Julie and Tricia be continued? He approved the choice of Steve Bull as project officer in charge of the move. One of the items, I noticed when I looked at this list again recently, read "RN financial condition." If we discussed this, I do not remember it. As a practical matter, he was broke. On Bryce Harlow's advice, he had asked the Joint Congressional Committee on Internal Revenue and Taxation to decide whether the deductions he had claimed for the donation of his prepresidential papers to the National Archives had been justified. The committee ruled that it had not been, and the amount he paid in back federal taxes as a consequence was greater than his entire reserves of cash.[14]

One matter remained—a final talk with Leon Jaworski. Nixon wanted no one to think that he had bargained with the special prosecutor or anyone else in connection with his resignation. Giving up the presidency was a unique act, and he told Ziegler and me that he would prefer to go to prison than make it the subject of a deal for personal advantage. On the other hand, Nixon's tapes and papers were still the objects of prosecutorial curiosity. If we were going to remove them from the White House, we owed the special prosecutor advance notice and certain assurances.

Leon Jaworski and I agreed over the telephone that any visit to the White House by him would touch off a media scrimmage. We arranged to meet quietly at my house at noon on Thursday, and I drove through the ring of journalists surrounding the White House in my own car in the hope of giving the impression that I was on personal business. Meanwhile, George Joulwan picked up Jaworski on a street corner near his office and drove him to my house. These amateurish subterfuges worked; neither of us was followed.

Over coffee provided by Pat, I told Jaworski that the President would resign that night, and briefed him on the reasons for this decision. I told him that Nixon's tapes and papers were going with him to San Clemente. "There's no hanky-panky involved," I assured him. "Nothing will change in regard to access." Jaworski said he would resort to court action if he was denied access. I told him I understood. That had always been the arrangement. I tried to make the briefing as complete as possible, even telling him what no one else knew, that Nixon had no intention of pardoning Haldeman and Ehrlichman, or any other Watergate defendants, before resigning. Nor did I believe that he would testify against them. Jaworski asked how Nixon thought he could avoid this if summoned. I said, "In my opinion, and this is only my opinion, he'll take the Fifth Amendment if necessary. Nixon is a very strong man, Leon. He can stand up to things that would kill an ordinary human being." Jaworski nodded. "I know," he replied.

We now came to the main purpose of the meeting. "Leon," I said, "the President is doing what he's doing on his own. He hasn't asked for anything from you or anyone else, and I hope you'll agree that that fact should be on the record. Nixon will not ask for even this much, but I'd appreciate it if you can issue a statement saying that there was no deal between the President and the special prosecutor with regard to the resignation. This is history. There should be no lingering questions on this point."

Jaworski said, "I agree."*

We shook hands very firmly. It was a strange experience, I suddenly realized, to be saying good-bye to so many extraordinary people in so short a time. I thanked him for having taken on the job I had offered him nine months before. "I know how tough it's been," I said. Jaworski smiled and gave my hand an even stronger grip. "The experience has been a little strenuous," he replied, "but yours has been even worse."[15]

Although we were adversaries, Leon Jaworski was everything an American should be in every action he took—upright, loyal to the Constitution, plainspoken, and absolutely true to his word. The extraordinarily kind words he spoke and wrote about me in later years meant all the more to me because his was an opinion, rare among Watergate figures, that I respected without reservation. There remained the long afternoon. I tried to keep the President occupied with the public business to the last, and in the course of the day he vetoed the agricultural appropriations bill, which exceeded his budget limitation by $50 million. He saw Ford alone and, according to his memoirs and Ford's, mainly discussed foreign policy, with Nixon recommending that the new President retain Kissinger as Secretary of State and me, at least for now, as de facto White House Chief of Staff.[16]

He worked on his speech. From time to time, his mind fastened on the aspect of his resignation that troubled him most. This was not the prospect of being dragged into the dock, convicted, and imprisoned.

---

*On Nixon's resignation, Jaworski issued a statement saying, "There has been no agreement or understanding of any sort between the President or his representatives and the Special Prosecutor relating in any way to the President's resignation. The Special Prosecutor's Office was not asked for any such agreement or understanding and offered none. . . ." (Leon Jaworski, *The Right and the Power*, p. 219.)

"Lenin and Gandhi did some of their best writing in jail," he joked. His worry was that he would be regarded as a quitter. As a high school athlete, he had run just as hard when he was last in a race, as apparently he often was, as if he was the winner. "I've never quit before in my life," he said. "That's what nobody around here has understood during this whole business. *You don't quit!*"[17]

My schedule for that day shows that I escaped at four o'clock to have a haircut; this hardly seems possible, but maybe such intermingling of the historic and the homely was not unprecedented in the annals of great American events.

Finally evening came, and with it the leaders of the Senate and the House of Representatives to say a ceremonial good-bye. Speaker Carl Albert, who had entered Congress as a freshman in the same year as Nixon, 1947, blurted out, in a non sequitur I am still unable to decipher, that he had had "nothing to do with this whole resignation business." Nixon put him at ease. Nixon's old confidant Senator James Eastland, Democrat of Mississippi, wore a ravaged expression. The others were embarrassed or ill at ease for other reasons. Only Mike Mansfield seemed to be immune to mixed feelings. Always taciturn, the Senate majority leader was cold in manner, snubbing Nixon's rather halting attempt to lighten the moment with a personal remark. Nixon bore himself throughout in a composed and conciliatory manner. The occasion was political, not personal. Although these men wished to see him go, they were not his personal enemies, and most of them were his old friends.

Awaiting him in the Cabinet Room were Nixon's personal friends, the forty-six men in Washington who had been closest to him throughout his political career—the ones, in his words, who had "worked together time and again to form the slim but sturdy coalition that repeatedly beat back the Goliath of liberal Democrats and liberal Republicans in the House and Senate."[18] These men loved Nixon, and they let him know this when he entered the room. In a resonant voice, he reminded them of the political victories they had shared over the years; he spoke movingly of the fires through which they had passed, of the ideals that had held them together, Republicans and Democrats alike.

As he talked, those who had been standing or sitting against the walls moved closer and closer to Nixon, who was seated in his usual chair at the center of the Cabinet table, until they were all crushed together around him like a living wall of protection. It was, of course, too late for such instinctive action. As Nixon spoke, many of these men wept. Some sobbed openly in their grief. Finally, Nixon, to whom emotion had always been an enemy to be kept at bay, was overcome, and he, too, broke down and wept.

"I just hope that I haven't let you down," he said brokenly.

His answer was the spectacle of fifty grown men, all of them toughened by a lifetime in the front line of politics, weeping as unashamedly as small boys.

Bill Timmons accompanied Nixon from the room. Minutes later, I found the President alone in the small office off the Oval Office. His eyes were still wet; when he took a deep breath and let it out, something like a sob escaped. He was already back at work, studying the speech he was scheduled to give only minutes later. I wondered silently whether he could do it, whether he could pull himself together and go through the ordeal of giving the speech that would end his great political career.

Nixon seemed to read my thoughts; I suppose this was not difficult. He said, "Al, don't worry. I'll be all right. I just can't stand it when other people cry. But I'm okay. Don't be concerned about the speech. It will be fine."

He smiled with red-rimmed eyes. I said, "I know it will be, Mr. President. It will be a great speech."

Less than ten minutes later, he uttered the first word in his familiar unwavering voice, and delivered the entire text flawlessly. He explained his actions, but he did not apologize. He spoke with pride of his accomplishments in foreign policy. The part that his enemies found most mawkish was, as might have been expected, the part that came directly from his heart:

> . . . I am confident that the world is a safer place today, not only for the people of America, but for the people of all nations, and that all of our children have a better chance than before of living in peace rather than dying in war. This, more than anything, is what I hoped to achieve when I sought the presidency. This, more than anything, is what I hope will be my legacy to you, to our country, as I leave the presidency.[19]

After the speech, Nixon went straight upstairs to the family quarters. I went with him. In my book *Caveat*, I described the experience in words that I cannot improve upon:

> His long ordeal was over, I did not want to leave him alone. . . .
> All Presidents must be aware of history because they are the

limbs on its body. No President was more keenly aware of it than Nixon; better than anyone, he knew what had happened to him and how this event was likely to be viewed. We went together to the Lincoln Sitting Room, his favorite place. He did not turn on the lamps; the only light came from the flickering flames of a log fire on the hearth. . . . Mrs. Nixon entered and embraced her husband. The President's daughters kissed him. . . . Nixon began to talk. He spoke about his predecessors and the times of doubt and anguish through which nearly all of them had passed. Not a single word did he speak about his own tragedy. He uttered no recriminations. He had lost the thing he had wanted all his life, but he seemed to be at peace. . . . I left him there, sitting alone in the dark. When I returned in the morning . . . Nixon was still in the same chair. *
He had a way of sitting on the small of his back, and that is how he was sitting now. The gray light of morning filled the room. On a table before Nixon lay a stack of books—the memoirs of Presidents. In each, he had inserted a slip of paper, marking the place where he found something of interest. That is how Nixon had spent his last night as President of the United States. He had been seeking solace from the only men who could truly know what he was feeling—his kinsmen in history, the other Presidents.[20]

He had been writing his farewell speech on the familiar yellow pad, referring to the books as he composed. He pushed the pad away when I entered. I had brought his resignation with me, and now I laid it on the table before him. He read it, one typed sentence on a sheet of thick White House stationery, and nodded. I left him.

An hour or so later, Nixon summoned me from a senior staff meeting to the family quarters. He was haggard and ashen. He thanked me for what I had done for him. I thanked him for having given me the opportunity to serve. Nothing of a personal nature was said. Any emotional moment we might have been tempted to have had been overwhelmed by the extraordinary scene in the Cabinet Room the evening before, and by a sense that the occasion was too large for sentimentality. By now, there was not much that could be said that we did not already understand.

A little later, in the East Room, he said good-bye to the staff in an

---

*I was under the impression, later corrected, that he had been there all night.

eloquent but rambling and quintessentially Nixonian speech, sentimental and noble, scholarly and corny, self-conscious and magisterial, and, above all, unabashedly old-fashioned and American. There were no more dry eyes in this audience than there had been the night before in the Cabinet Room.

Nor were there any more good-byes for Nixon and me. As he and Mrs. Nixon and their daughters walked to the waiting helicopter with Gerald and Betty Ford, I kept my distance. Finally, Nixon gave his final salute, the familiar uplifted arms and double V-for-victory sign, from the door of the helicopter. The clattering machine lifted off. I was numb with sorrow for my country, for Nixon, and for myself to see such greatness laid waste by a moment of hubris and a season of folly.

But I think I understood, even at that moment, that the end was not yet for this man who was so like the great figures of the past and so unlike anyone else. No one could then have imagined the full reality of his rise from the ashes to become the only American President of the twentieth century whose voice was more respected in retirement than it had been when he was in power.

Nixon's adversaries, by contrast, have never since his fall been able to elect a President who represents their point of view, and it may justly be said of them by future generations that their chief accomplishment was the negative one of overturning the results of a presidential election. In a passage of events replete with irony, the final paradox is that Nixon's tragedy won him a unique place in history, and that by yielding to his enemies, he overcame them.

V

ABROAD AND AT LARGE

Greatly instructed I shall hence depart.

JOHN MILTON,
Paradise Lost, XII

37

Ford's White House

As Lyndon Johnson's experience abundantly illustrates, a Vice President who succeeds to the presidency is well advised to surround himself with his own people. My own recommendation that President Ford retain the Nixon White House staff for thirty days was intended to provide for an orderly changeover from the old inner circle to the new, but I thought he should and would bring in new blood. Ford's own transition team recommended a grace period of two to six weeks. "The one exception we recommend is Al Haig," they wrote. ". . . You should meet with him as soon as possible and prevail upon him to help you and your transition team."[1] Nixon and others, including Barry Goldwater, had recommended to Ford that he keep me on.

The new President did so, but not under the same terms that had applied under Nixon. Ford believed that the strong Chiefs of Staff of the twentieth century, from Wilson's Colonel House to Nixon's Bob Haldeman, had been bad for the presidency. This perception seemed to be more important to him than his own needs. When asking me to remain, in a meeting shortly after he took the presidential oath, Ford explained that he intended to be his own Chief of Staff, with half a dozen co-equal counselors, each reporting to him on separate areas of authority at regular intervals during the day. My area of competence would be administration of the White House apparatus.

Ford called this organizational concept a "spokes of the wheel" approach. A President may do business as he chooses, and I agreed to remain on the terms laid down by Ford. That is not to say that I did not have private reservations. Only a supreme optimist could have believed that such an arrangement would work in a town in which ambition is mother's milk and every symbol of power from job title to parking space is the subject of fierce intrigue. Ford thought he might contain territoriality by having an "open door" to the Oval Office. He told me that he wanted to see as many people as possible; Nixon, he said, had been far too isolated by his staff. With some amusement, I replied that I would be happy to usher in as many visitors as he wanted to see. The problem with Nixon had not been that his chamberlains had barred the door but that he preferred to be alone; almost anyone who got into the Oval Office during my tenure as Chief of Staff did so because I had ramrodded the visitor into the President's schedule.

In a very short time, it became obvious that Ford's open door, "spokes of the wheel" scheme didn't work. He tells us why in his memoirs: "Because power in Washington is measured by how much access a person has to the President, almost everyone wanted more access than I had to give. . . . My working days grew longer and longer, and the demands on my time were hindering my effectiveness." Having made this analysis, Ford then asked me to take over scheduling his appointments, coordinating paper flow, following up on presidential decisions, and providing status reports on projects and policy development. "I did not like the idea of calling this person chief of staff," Ford wrote, "but that in fact was the role he would fill."[2]

No doubt one of Ford's purposes in delaying this step was to avoid demoting Robert Hartmann. He had been Ford's speech writer, close adviser, and chief of staff when he was Vice President and before, and now, naturally, he wanted to maintain this proximity to Ford, not to mention control over access to the President. Minutes after Ford took the oath of office, Hartmann claimed the office closest to the Oval Office as his own. (He later moved down the hall to another office close to the President's.[3])

Hartmann, on whom Ford bestowed Cabinet rank as well as the title of counselor, was an abrasive man who strongly believed that Ford was too kind and too soft. On the other hand, as he himself was not reluctant to point out, Hartmann was no Jerry Ford. His method of operation was based on confrontation and an opinionated frankness that many mistook for insult. He was decisive to a fault. To Ford's displeasure, Hartmann brusquely fired the White House speech writers almost as soon as he was placed in charge of them.[4] His treatment of subordinates, especially his coarse manner toward his unfortunate secretary, scandalized the West Wing and even generated complaints to me from the Secret Service. Jerald terHorst, a reporter from the *Detroit News* who served briefly as Ford's first press secretary, reported in his newspaper column that Hartmann's "nickname, one he jokingly cultivates, is 'S.O.B.,' meaning 'Sweet Ol' Bob.' "[5]

If Hartmann's interest was to enlarge on his intimacy with Ford, my own aim, as with Nixon, was to keep relations on a formal and businesslike basis. Normally, I saw the President once in the morning and once in the evening—unless summoned into his presence between times—never wasting his time with the inessential, and regulating the flow of others whom he needed to see.

Although I made it a point never to mention Nixon to Ford (or to anyone else in the White House except as a matter of strict necessity), the weeks and months following the former President's resignation were the most difficult of my life. It is an awful thing to witness from close proximity the loss of the most powerful office in the world and to observe the effect that such an event has upon the outcast President and the American people. In private moments, I wondered whether I had somehow failed both my country and Nixon by not finding a way around his difficulties. On the intellectual level, I knew that the outcome had been unavoidable once all the elements that led to Nixon's downfall were introduced into the situation. But intellectual judgments are not usually the ones that rob a human being of sleep and peace of mind.

Hartmann, among others, had urged Ford to fire all Nixon holdovers on grounds that they were still loyal to Nixon and constituted a potential source of embarrassment to Ford in that all were tainted by the former President's sins; some might even turn out to have been accessories or accomplices. In these matters, Ford took the fair-minded course that expressed his character, letting those whom he regarded as liabilities go in the first few days and instructing me that the rest must depart by January 1, 1975.[6]

Meanwhile, the storm gauge filled up with leaks. The news media published stories charging me with having failed to carry out an order from Ford to replace portraits of Theodore Roosevelt and Woodrow Wilson with those of Abraham Lincoln and Harry Truman, pushing Pat Buchanan as ambassador to the Republic of South Africa, failing to tell Ford that there were six dead microphones still buried in the walls of the

Oval Office, and issuing memoranda that "somehow [bypass] veteran Ford aide Robert Hartmann until too late." In regard to the origin of the leaks, "Hartmann," as Ford noted, "seemed to be a likely source."[7]

More troublesome were anonymous charges that Nixon was removing the files of his administration, including the tapes, from the White House with my collusion. In fact, large quantities of his presidential papers were packed and placed in storage in the Executive Office Building (according to Ford, "950 reels of tape and roughly 46 million pieces of paper"[8]), and I played a part in seeing that this was done, in the sense that I put someone in charge of the project and expected expeditious action. Ford wanted to be rid of these papers and the lingering controversy they invoked. He asked the Attorney General for an opinion, and Saxbe ruled that the papers belonged to Nixon according to tradition and precedent and should be shipped to him in San Clemente forthwith.* The plan was that Nixon's papers and tapes would be delivered to the General Services Administration for safekeeping in a building near San Clemente, where they would remain under the former President's control except in cases of subpoena.[9] This arrangement was overturned by the Presidential Recordings and Materials Act of 1974, which mandated custody of Nixon's tapes and papers to the National Archives. Nixon challenged the constitutionality of the act, but the Supreme Court ruled against him in 1977. His papers and tapes are stored in a special National Archives facility in Alexandria, Virginia, where all but a small proportion are available to researchers.

There may be some truth in the suggestion, made by Professor Ambrose among others, that Nixon was attempting to control the sources from which the history of his presidency would be written by earmarking them for his own library. Even that was not out of the ordinary. As Nixon remarked to Kissinger on his last night in office when the latter said that history would treat Nixon better than his contemporaries had done, "That depends, Henry, on who writes the history."[10]

Despite these distractions, Ford moved determinedly on the two major priorities facing him, the appointment of a Vice President and the matter of disposing once and for all of the case of Richard Nixon. When Ford asked for my opinion of vice presidential candidates, I came down strongly

---

* George Washington took his papers with him when he left the presidency, and so did all of his successors. Some sold their papers (a dying Grant auctioned his to help provide for his family, and an impoverished James Madison disposed of his piecemeal). Others, including Martin Van Buren and Lincoln's son Todd, destroyed documents; in Lincoln's case, their release was delayed for eighty-two years after his death. More recent Presidents, including FDR, Truman, Eisenhower, Kennedy, and Lyndon Johnson, had lodged their papers in presidential libraries built with private funds but administered by the National Archives (See Ambrose, *Nixon, Ruin and Recovery*, p. 48).

in favor of Nelson Rockefeller. Of the men mentioned for the job, only he and John Connally were presidential in stature, and Connally had by this time been eliminated from consideration owing to his troubles over the milk fund. When Ford made up his mind, I had the pleasure of making the telephone call summoning Rockefeller to Washington in the President's name.

Where Nixon's pardon was concerned, I played no role at all. Shortly after Ford took office, Len Garment wrote a compassionate memorandum to Ford recommending an immediate pardon for Nixon; this was accompanied by the draft of a presidential statement announcing a pardon. Senator Scott, Governor Rockefeller, and others made statements in favor of a pardon.[11] Sometime during this period, Ford asked me (as he also asked others, including Kissinger, the new White House Counsel, Philip Buchen, Hartmann, and Marsh) for an opinion on the pardon. I laid out the pros and cons as I saw them but declined to make a recommendation.[12] Certainly I never discussed the issue with Nixon, on the telephone or otherwise. Some of Ford's people were putting considerable pressure on Nixon to render some sort of statement of guilt as a condition of pardon. Nixon was resisting. Feeling against Nixon was bitter and retributive in the early Ford White House. Involving myself in this situation would only have made matters worse, so I stood back from it. Besides, I knew that Nixon would go to prison rather than grovel.

Ford formally raised the pardon in a meeting on Friday, August 30, 1974, in the Oval Office, saying that he was inclined to pardon Nixon as quickly as possible as soon as he was certain that he had the legal authority to do so. He clearly believed that delay was a mistake, that he must act quickly while his popularity was high, and that a prolonged controversy over Nixon's fate would incapacitate the government. The others present were Kissinger, Hartmann, Jack Marsh, and Philip Buchen; all had opinions, mostly negative, but I kept quiet until the President interrupted himself to take a telephone call. Then I left the room.[13]

A plan for linking a pardon for Nixon to an amnesty for Vietnam-era draft evaders was conceived by Hartmann and others. The Vietnam component called for granting selective amnesty (each case would be dealt with on its own merits). A presidential proclamation was drafted by Hartmann, who apparently carried the only copy around with him in his pocket.

This scheme, which had been kept secret from me, was revealed on August 19 aboard *Air Force One* as it approached Chicago, where Ford was scheduled to address the national convention of the Veterans of

Foreign Wars. Because I had always believed that some draft evaders were genuine conscientious objectors, I had no argument to make against selective forgiveness. However, it seemed to me that the VFW was a poor choice of audience for such an announcement, and I warned Ford that he could expect an unfriendly reaction. He might even be booed. In his dogged way, he announced the amnesty anyway. If he did not make his listeners like what he had to say, he did make them understand that his motives grew out of Christian charity and a patriotic desire that the nation give a second chance to those young men who had "committed the supreme folly of shirking their duty at the expense of others who were also very young. . . ."[14]

In Ford's mind, I think, the amnesty introduced the idea of decoupling clemency from political considerations (a generous and courageous thing in itself, given the times) and opened for him the opportunity of arguing from the general (the draft evaders) to the particular (Nixon).

On Thursday, September 5, President Ford summoned Hartmann, Marsh, Buchen, and me to the Oval Office and told us in his flat, undemonstrative way that he had made up his mind to grant an unconditional pardon to Nixon. He wanted to announce the pardon the following morning but delayed until Sunday, September 8, to give the lawyers and speech writers time to complete the paperwork.[15] It was clear from his manner that his decision was as much a matter of the heart as the head, but that does not alter the fact that he believed that clemency served the national interest better than any of the alternatives.

"I did it," he told me at the time, "because I knew that I could not govern if the country continued to be preoccupied with Watergate." As he later put it in his memoirs, "No other issue could compete with the drama of a former President trying to stay out of jail. . . . America needed recovery, not revenge."[16]

My reaction on hearing the news was one of overwhelming relief. And because I believe with Thomas Paine that the duties of Presidents, like all the rest of us, "consist in doing justice, loving mercy, and endeavoring to make our fellow-creatures happy,"[17] I thought then, as I think now, that the pardon was a great act of statesmanship as well as a praiseworthy human gesture.

Others did not agree. With no prior notice to Ford, Press Secretary Jerald terHorst resigned in protest after less than a month on the job, saying publicly that no pardon should have been granted to Nixon except in exchange for a signed confession.

The pardon took the news media by surprise, a state of affairs that generated retroactive wisdom in the form of stories quoting anonymous sources to the effect that I had engineered the pardon by playing on Ford's sympathies for a Nixon broken in health and spirit. A seemingly circumstantial but erroneous *New York Times* article based on the statements of a "longtime friend of Mr. Nixon's . . . who is a former member of the Presidential staff [who] is in daily touch with affairs inside the Nixons' heavily guarded Casa Pacifica estate" wove such a web of innuendo that the White House press office took the unusual step of denying that it was true.[18] I told Lou Cannon and Carroll Kilpatrick of the *Washington Post* that the *Times* report was "totally untrue," and went on to say that it was "a terrible disservice to President Ford to suppose that he could be manipulated. . . ."[19]

On several occasions, I had advised Ford to get Hartmann under control. The latter's presumptions, as when he attempted to make himself overseer of the new press secretary, Ron Nessen, sometimes ruffled Ford's composure.[20] The President acknowledged the problem but was reluctant to act. The puerile disorder produced by infighting on the staff and leaks to the press brought Ford to the conclusion that he must take measures to control it. The damage was not yet irreparable (the leaks were petty gossip instead of the betrayal of vital national secrets as in the first weeks of the Nixon administration). And the cure was obvious.

Soon after the Nixon pardon was issued, Ford called me in on a Friday afternoon and asked me to accept a formal and permanent appointment as Chief of Staff in the White House, with all the duties and powers usually associated with the position. I replied that I would take the job but only if he granted me the power to hire and fire the White House staff.

"You have at least one fellow who doesn't belong here," I told him.

Ford understood that I was saying that my first use of the authority I requested would be to dismiss Hartmann. He said that he would have to think about it over the coming weekend.

On Monday morning, the President called me to the Oval Office and agreed to the arrangement I had suggested, with one exception. "You'll have to let me deal with Hartmann myself," he said.

"I understand, Mr. President," I said. "But in the circumstances, I hope you will understand that I cannot continue to serve you. I'm sorry."

Ford nodded. "So am I."

My feelings were decidedly mixed. On the basis of what had already happened, I knew that Hartmann and I could not work together and that I could not stay without becoming the target of further leaks and innuendo of the kind that had already damaged Ford's presidency.

Nevertheless, I was sorry to go because I admired Ford and wanted to help him. The President's answer filled me with a sense of release. I had had enough of the White House, and now I could go back to the Army for one last tour with the troops. When my departure was announced, "dope pieces" predictably appeared in the press, suggesting that Hartmann would now take over as first among equals under the revived system of a five- or six-person team of counselors. But Ford quickly and wisely appointed Donald Rumsfeld, the American ambassador to NATO, as Chief of Staff. Rumsfeld, known as a strong personality and a fine administrator, had been a member of Ford's transition team.

Army chief of staff Gen. Creighton Abrams had died on September 4. Although Jim Schlesinger had reservations and there was some opposition within the Army to such an appointment, Ford wanted to make me his successor.[21] My entire military career, despite its many twists and turns, had been spent in preparation for this post. Yet for the second time in less than two years, I found myself in the peculiar position of advising a President to refrain from appointing me to the only job I had ever really wanted. The moment was wrong. Ford had just disposed of the Watergate question by pardoning Nixon. My confirmation hearings, if I were appointed Army chief of staff, would certainly open the whole fetid question again, as well as the issue of the pardon.

Nevertheless, I wanted to return to the Army. Although I had retired in 1973 to spare Nixon embarrassment, full generals are always subject to recall to active duty. It was Henry Kissinger who came up with the idea of naming me NATO commander, an appointment that carries with it a second post, that of commander in chief of all U.S. forces in Europe. Senate confirmation is not required for either of these posts. Ford announced my appointment on September 15.

Because all three of my promotions to general officer rank had come during my time in the Nixon White House, I was regarded by some, including a certain number of my fellow officers, as a political general. Questions were raised about my command experience and military qualifications. One newspaper columnist, a retired U.S. Marine Corps colonel, drew an invidious comparison between "that grim, battle-hardened senior soldier, Marshal Grechko, and young General Haig."[22] I found it interesting that many of those who said I was unqualified to run NATO were the same people who solemnly identified me as having secretly run the United States as de facto President during Nixon's last months in office.

Doubts were not universal. General Lemnitzer, the former chairman of the Joint Chiefs of Staff and NATO commander, said, "I consider it a fine appointment."[23] I myself thought that I was as much a combat soldier as anyone who had held the job before me and, with the exception of Eisenhower, somewhat more of a diplomat.

There was a predictable outcry for congressional hearings from those who wanted to air the issue of Nixon's pardon as a means of reopening the Watergate affair, but Ford announced that he would not send my name to the Hill for approval, and Senator Stennis, the chairman of the Armed Services Committee, decided after speaking to Leon Jaworski and receiving a letter from him not to insist that I appear. It read as follows:

> Dear Senator Stennis,
>   In confirmation of my verbal statement to you, this office does not contemplate the taking of any action involving General Alexander Haig, either as a result of our wiretap investigation or in any other area.
>
>   [*signed*] Leon Jaworski*

After a brief vacation in the sun, I returned to Washington, to discover that my departure from the White House had not, as I had hoped, ended the bickering and enmity on the staff. Already, Rockefeller and Kissinger were being systematically isolated, and they told me then and afterward of their frustration, discontent, and bewilderment that the President's men should be so insensitive to his needs as to hurt him in this way. I listened, but knew that the best thing I could do—in fact the only thing I could do as a military officer back on duty with the Army—was stay out of the situation. Soon I would be in Europe; I looked forward to having three thousand miles of ocean between me and palace politics.

Then Fred Buzhardt, who had remained with Ford during the transi-

---

* In the January 1981 issue of *Armed Forces Journal International*, Jaworski (who made a point of saying that he was among those who insisted on believing that I had briefly been, in his phrase, "our 37½ President"), said, ". . . I did not see then or since, any evidence that a bargain of any kind was struck in [regard to the Nixon pardon]. . . . I considered Haig, and still do, as one of the unsung Watergate heroes. . . . I dealt with the general under circumstances that were unique; we were adversaries. At times we engaged in stern and grudging discussions. But I recognized the loyalty of an officer serving his Commander-in-Chief, and I respected him. I do not believe he ever lied to me. . . . He had a goal, to keep his President in office, and he tried. . . ."

tion period, phoned me at home on the Saturday morning before my departure for Europe with alarming news. President Ford had agreed to appear before the Subcommittee on Criminal Justice of the House Judiciary Committee to testify on the Nixon pardon. His appearance would mark the first time a President had ever appeared before a committee of Congress while under oath.

"Al," said Buzhardt, "I think you'd better come over to the White House. These boys have prepared sworn testimony for the President that could very well result in your indictment."*

Angry and bewildered, I got into my car and drove to the White House. There I read the draft of testimony, prepared for Ford by his inner circle, that suggested that I had offered Gerald Ford the presidency in return for a pardon for Nixon. This vicious lie, if repeated by the President under oath, would have consequences far beyond any charges against myself. It would, first of all, falsify history. And, even though the testimony attempted to exonerate Ford, it would raise ineradicable suspicions that two American Presidents had been parties to a conspiracy to trade the nation's highest office for personal advantage.

The two ranking aides present in the White House that morning were Phil Buchen and Jack Marsh. "Whoever wrote this testimony," I said, "is setting the President up to tell a lie. I won't be a part of it."

I demanded to see the President at once. I was told that would not be possible. This was no time for finesse.

"I will either see Ford immediately," I answered, "or I will call a press conference right now, right here in the White House pressroom, and describe the role people around the Vice President played in the Grand Rapids group, Bobby Griffin's letter, the appointment of Jenner as minority counsel to the House Judiciary Committee, and a good many other things we all know occurred as part of a secret effort by Ford people to hurry Nixon out of the presidency behind Jerry Ford's back."

A few minutes later, I was in Ford's presence in the Oval Office. After watching his reaction to what I told him, I was persuaded that he had not read the testimony. With a look that was, at the same time, deeply sympathetic and deeply troubled, Ford asked me, "What do you want?"

"The truth," I replied. "That's all."

---

* About a year after rendering this final act of friendship to me, Fred Buzhardt died of a heart attack. There is not the slightest question in my mind that his life was shortened by the stress of Watergate. He was a hero among government servants, tireless in the performance of his duty, patriotic in his motivation, and unselfish and honest to the core. If ever a man gave his life for his country, Fred did, and young people weighing a career in public service should look to him as a model of what a good man can achieve in the face of almost inconceivable difficulties.

"You'll have it, Al," he replied.

Never for a moment did I doubt that or that he would correct any injustice that was brought before him. And in his testimony, he described what had happened between us with perfect accuracy. Rumors persist. But truthful history, in this case, prevailed.

Days after Ford was defeated in the 1976 presidential election, I called on him in the Oval Office. It was a moving encounter. He had been a good president—the best one possible, I thought—in the worst of times. Even the supposed gaffe that contributed to his defeat, his statement "There is no Soviet domination of Eastern Europe," was an expression of the optimism and good sense that were the hallmarks of his character. He meant that the peoples under Russian domination did not accept Soviet ideology or Soviet propaganda and that they would one day reclaim their nationhood and their human dignity. Time has demonstrated that it was not Ford but, rather, those who ridiculed him who were the unsophisticated ones.

Ford's voice was barely audible as a result of the sore throat he had developed on the campaign trail. But he smiled and talked about old times, and as I left he threw an arm around my shoulders and made one final gesture of generosity.

"You know, Al, you were right about the staff problem," he said. "The reality was, I wasn't ready to be President, and I relied on those I knew. By the time I realized that I really wanted the job, and could do the job, it was too late."

38

The Western Alliance

My nomination as Supreme Allied Commander Europe (SACEUR) encountered some initial difficulty in the alliance from a small element that looked askance at my White House experience and wondered about my military qualifications. These reservations were quickly overcome by the adroit diplomacy of Henry Kissinger and that of his friend and mine, the astute and stoutly pro-NATO chancellor of Germany, Helmut Schmidt. My appointment became effective December 15, 1974. This represented a certain inconvenience for the man I was replacing, Gen. Andrew J. Goodpaster, who had expected to remain in command until he retired from the U.S. Army the following June.[1]

From the beginning, however, I benefited from the cordial cooperation of the deputy NATO commander, Gen. Sir John Mogg of the United Kingdom, who flew to Washington to tell me he would do whatever he could to ease the transition. In that and in all that followed while we served together, his counsel and friendship were invaluable. While waiting for Goodpaster to wind up his affairs and vacate the Château de Gendebien, the Supreme Commander's quarters near Mons, Belgium, I relieved him as Commander in Chief U.S. European Command (CINCEUR) and moved with Pat into temporary quarters in Stuttgart.

Despite the good work of Kissinger and Schmidt within the councils of the alliance, I again found myself labeled a political general by the European press. I advised European journalists to judge me by what I did as NATO commander, not by what they heard from my detractors. Privately, I thought that the allied forces and I could hold our own with Grechko and the Red Army. That was an expression of faith, but I decided that I must determine the realities firsthand. My first decision was to devote my first six months in command inspecting every aspect of NATO. First I would determine the facts; then I would make my recommendations.

The place to begin, obviously, was with the United States forces I commanded personally. In the past, the deputy CINCEUR had commanded the American components of NATO in the field while his superior tended to focus on NATO affairs. I announced that I would visit Stuttgart at least once a week, and meet with U.S. Army, Navy, and Air Force commanders at their own headquarters once a month, even after I moved to NATO headquarters. Meanwhile, I wanted to see the troops close up.

I was appalled by what I found among the American units. Alcoholism and drug abuse were serious and widespread, as they were nearly everywhere else in the armed forces in the early post-Vietnam period. The war in Southeast Asia had drained the armed forces of manpower, morale, and matériel. Our state of readiness was way below acceptable standards. Serious shortcomings existed in our communications and transport. The component U.S. commanders (Army, Navy, Air Force) had seldom talked to one another in a coordinated military manner. Combined military exercises, the rehearsals for actual warfare, were rare. There was little sense of organized purpose imposed from above, little communication among subordinate commands, and almost no esprit de corps generated by a disciplined striving for agreed standards of excellence within individual outfits.

This was not just an Army problem. The liberal-minded Admiral Zumwalt, as chief of naval operations, had introduced innovative standards of discipline into the Navy. On an inspection tour of the Sixth Fleet in the Mediterranean Sea, I found ill-disciplined, ill-trained, sometimes disoriented sailors operating some of the most sensitive and powerful technology in the American arsenal.

When I indicated that I wanted to go belowdecks, a Navy officer advised me against it: "Officers don't go down there, General," he said. "You're liable to get a knife in the ribs."

I replied, "Follow me, Mister." We emerged unscathed after an intensive tour of the lower spaces, but in my case with a determination to correct an intolerable situation.

If the Soviets had attacked, the American force that I found would have been hard-pressed to hold them off. The other partners in the alliance had recognized U.S. neglect and some were prepared to emulate it. I called my subordinate commanders together, shared with them my observations of the U.S. forces' state of readiness in Europe, and explained to them exactly what changes I expected them to make. Pretty soon, we were all getting along fine. During the months I was in Stuttgart, I spent virtually all my time in the field, visiting every unit in the command, talking to every commander down to platoon level, and with as many of the troops as I could see. Like my great teachers, MacArthur, Almond, and DePuy, I concentrated on the details and tried to make everyone in the chain of command not only do the same but understand the vital necessity of doing so.

Little could be done to make an army riddled with alcoholism and drug abuse into a fighting force without amputating the diseased parts. We instituted alcohol and drug counseling and—against vigorous opposition from Jim Schlesinger and others on civil rights grounds—imposed compulsory urinalysis to identify abusers of drugs. This compromised the privacy of the troops, but it was not a civil rights issue, because the Army is not a civil society. Soldiers under oath to defend their country have no right to endanger the lives of their comrades or to compromise the nation's security through the use of illegal substances. The addicts were weeded out; casual drug use was reduced by a combination of efficient policing, stern discipline, and rehabilitation. Alcohol abuse was a tougher problem because drinking has long been part of military culture, but we brought that under control, too. The methods we devised in the European command to deal with these problems were adopted for use throughout the armed services.

On the military side, we got the troops back in the field, carried out exercises, sharpened capabilities, repaired omissions, and in a matter of a year became a first-class fighting force worthy of the American military tradition.

The change-of-command ceremony in which I became the seventh NATO commander in succession to Eisenhower was somewhat muted in tone because it took place indoors on a gray northern European December day instead of in the open air with formations of troops passing in review and warplanes flying overhead. As the SACEUR who wished, for the time being, to be seen and not heard, this suited me fine. Everyone who counted in NATO, uniformed and civilian, was present, and I took advantage of their presence to call a meeting of the command minutes after the ceremony. This meeting and subsequent contacts with subordinate commanders charged with the tricky job of satisfying national pride while carrying out obligations to the alliance revealed that there were difficulties to be overcome.

When I announced that I intended to devote the first months of my command to observing capabilities, during which I would visit the forces of every NATO member in order to make a personal inspection of the troops and carry out meetings with their commanders, a certain surprise was evident. Soon after arrival, for example, I expressed the desire to visit a certain West German unit. I received unmistakable signals that I was not welcome. In response, I asked a single question: "Is the Federal Republic of Germany a member of NATO?" The answer, of course, was yes. I said, "In that case, kindly prepare your troops to receive a visit from the NATO commander, because I will either inspect that unit tomorrow or I will call a press conference tonight to tell the world how I was prevented from doing so."

The Germans welcomed me to their installation (though *welcomed* is perhaps not the mot juste), and the first link was forged in the strong chain of respect, understanding, and mutual support that eventually developed between the Germans, including Chancellor Helmut Schmidt and his successive ministers of defense, and myself. After this, visits by the NATO commander to the troops of all member nations became a matter of routine, and after everyone got used to the idea of an American general walking down a rank of German, British, or Dutch soldiers, and vice versa, they became useful occasions for fostering the exchange of the ideas, the social contact, and the sense of familiarity that makes for human community and multinational unity.

In the case of the Dutch, I was advised almost immediately on my arrival that something had to be done about the unmilitary appearance of the troops in the Dutch NATO contingent. Joseph Luns, the clearheaded secretary-general of NATO, a former longtime foreign minister of the Netherlands, put the problem to me in no uncertain terms.

"You've got to get down to Holland and order these fellows to get haircuts, shave off their beards, and press their uniforms," said Joe. "They're an embarrassment."

Now the youngsters of the Netherlands army were among the best-educated, most intelligent troops in NATO. They were tops in their technological skills, and very efficient.

"I've always heard that you Dutch are a stubborn bunch," I told Luns. "My guess is that they'll *never* cut their hair if ordered to do so by an American general."

On my first inspection of Dutch troops, I arranged for a large press contingent to follow me around, and I made a point of getting a very close haircut and wearing highly starched fatigues with razor-sharp creases. My brass shone like the noonday sun. The resulting photographs on the front pages of most Dutch newspapers showed a sharp NATO commander chatting with some of the most unkempt troops ever to put on a uniform. Over time, the kids were embarrassed into visiting the barber and pressing their clothes, and the Dutch contingent began to look as good as it was.

In my first six months at Supreme Headquarters Allied Powers Europe (SHAPE), I visited every country in NATO, acquainting myself with the troops and the commander's plans and problems as I went. In particular, I paid attention to our Scandinavian members on the northern flank, who had long felt exposed and undermanned, and to the troublesome situation on the southern flank, where the two local members of NATO— Greece and Turkey—were in a such a state of hostility that I was unable to overfly Greek territory in order to visit Turkey.

U.S. units were not the only ones with problems to be overcome. Soon after my arrival, I received a combat-effectiveness report that revealed many long-standing problems. It seemed better to cut the knot with one stroke of the sword than to assign yet another committee to recommend ways to untie it, and so I called a meeting of the major NATO commanders, shut the doors of my office, and announced, "Gentlemen, we are not leaving here until we all agree on this thing." It was a long but useful session.

My objective was to stimulate a discussion of NATO policy on the most fundamental level. The Nixon policy of détente with the Soviet Union had raised questions in American minds about the need for a strong Western defense and in European minds about the determination of the United States to stand by its allies. I wanted to know what the allies were really thinking. Within five months of taking command, I visited every NATO capital except Athens and Reykjavik. I discovered that questions about the structure, cost, and effectiveness of the alliance were being asked by political leaders in every member state. There was great pressure on defense budgets, the future usefulness of the heavy battle tank was being questioned as a result of Israeli losses in the Yom Kippur War, and there were similar questions about the types and numbers of strike aircraft being deployed by NATO.

Above all, Europeans wanted to know whether the United States, demoralized by Watergate and gripped by an antimilitary mood in reaction to the Vietnam War, would still defend Europe as if it were its own territory in case of Soviet attack. Mike Mansfield, among other powerful Americans, had been calling for the withdrawal of American troops from Europe. An amendment initiated by Senator Jackson tied progress on arms reduction to the emigration of Soviet Jews even though some thirty thousand a year were already leaving the U.S.S.R. as a result of the quiet agreements between Nixon and Brezhnev. These congressional initiatives played their part in the increased aggressiveness of Soviet policy that was noticeable in the 1973 Middle East War, the adventurism in Central America and Africa, and the 1979 invasion of Afghanistan. After a speech before the Western European Union in May 1975, I responded to the question of U.S. resolve in these words: "I would not be where I am if I had any doubts about that."[2]

A steadfast America was not the only question. The alliance as a whole was in sad military condition. After a later speech, I was asked whether détente had "put the West to sleep."[3] In my own estimation, the answer was, Not quite, not yet. After six months of listening and learning, I was convinced that NATO was confronted with an unprecedented security problem. To the east, the Warsaw pact still deployed fifty-seven first-echelon divisions, with thirty more in reserve. We needed advanced tanks; in the Middle East War, 80 percent of all tanks lost by both sides were knocked out by other tanks. This was also true with regard to tactical aircraft, armor's indispensable companion.[4] Soviet naval capabilities had increased explosively, threatening not only the Atlantic sea lanes over which more than 90 percent of Allied supplies had flowed in World War II but also the supply of oil from the Middle East on which Europe depended. In World War II, for example, the Hitler regime had deployed fifty submarines in the Atlantic; the Soviets already had one hundred, and they were far more effective than the U-boats of 1940 to 1945.[5]

Clearly NATO needed to maintain its present force levels and continually improve technology and military efficiency if it meant to remain a credible deterrent to a Soviet Union that was not only heavily armed for the purpose of conquering Western Europe but also capable of interfering with the interests of NATO countries on a global basis. The prime example of such interference was, of course, a threat to the Middle East oil fields. The long-term importance of these judgments was demonstrated more than a decade later in the Gulf War, which could not have been fought—much less won in such dramatic fashion—in the absence of the technologically superb armor and aircraft of the United States and its NATO allies and the capability of moving NATO troops quickly to the theater of operations. The decisions to produce those weapons and devise these logistics were taken in the 1970s under Presidents Ford and Carter in the context of the defense of Western Europe, and that is the purpose they served in Operation Desert Storm, though on another continent.

I proposed a program for rejuvenation of the alliance's conventional fighting forces into an integrated force. I called this plan the "Three Rs":

> READINESS: encompassing troop training, strengthening the chain of command, maintaining stock levels of military supplies, and prepositioning supplies for use in case of enemy attack.
>
> RATIONALIZATION: having to do with member forces of many nations planning and training together under common procedures so as to take advantage of every strength while conserving costs through standardized procedures and equipment.
>
> REINFORCEMENT: dealing with the fast movement of troops to points of need; this had to do not just with American troops in the United States earmarked for NATO but also European reserves that must be mobilized and moved into position, and the organization of civilian aircraft and shipping from all NATO nations to help transport these men and women. A whole new level of cooperation began with NATO's Atlantic maritime assets under the Supreme Allied Commander Atlantic (SACLANT).

These military initiatives were backed up during the Carter administration by a commitment by NATO members to the Long-Term Defense Program and to a 3 percent annual increase in national defense budgets.[6] All this had a single objective: to maintain NATO's alertness and readiness to the threat posed by the military machine to the east by continuing to trade on the technological, economic, and political advantages which made the West ultimately stronger than the East. Our security was tied to strategic weapons, but these would be ineffective without a believable conventional deterrent. We needed to bring our forces to a uniform state of readiness under a plan that made maximum use of each member army's capabilities and to maintain the morale of the alliance through mutual trust.

When I conceived the idea of transporting ten American divisions across the Atlantic in ten days, this mammoth undertaking was regarded as undoable. But we did it not so very long afterward by prepositioning equipment and munitions, by rotating brigades of each division between the United States and Europe, and by revolutionizing the methods of transport.

After that, it became routine. U.S. soldiers flooded into Germany every year to take part in NATO–wide exercises in which every national armed force had a role to play as an indispensable part of the whole. We brought the U.S. Marines, who had never played a major role in NATO, into Norway in a massive operation that demonstrated our flexibility in defending the hitherto undermanned northern flank. We moved an American brigade into a permanent new installation, built and paid for by the West Germans, on the north German plain. This country, the site of those long-ago maneuvers with the Devon regiment, was the likeliest route for a Warsaw pact invasion; that part of the defense of the West had hitherto been the responsibility of the British and West German armed forces.

From the day I took command, my concept was, "Drive it to the maximum." My military colleagues responded with enthusiasm; with their help and the spirited cooperation of the alliance's diplomats, we worked hard together to make sure that the military and civilian sides understood each other's problems and, whenever necessary, participated in solutions. With a renewed U.S. and European military potential, a new level of political cooperation emerged, as well.

It was an exciting time for NATO. We became a dynamic alliance, capable of putting up a defense of the West that not only deterred the Soviets but, as we shall see, convinced some of their more violent sympathizers that they were so overmatched that they must remove what they regarded as the cause of their disadvantage.

One of the bulwarks of NATO strength was, of course, the Bundeswehr. Thirty years after the end of World War II, the Federal Republic of Germany was one of the most liberal democracies in the world and, in economic terms, the most powerful state in Europe. Her army was the largest European force in NATO. Yet in terms of command responsibility, as the West German general Gerd Schmückle put it, "In the Alliance,

American generals wore 73 stars, British generals 66, German generals 24."[7]

Under the terms of the original treaty, there were only two full generals in SHAPE—the Supreme Commander, always an American, and his deputy, always a Briton. This arrangement had reflected the realities in 1950; it no longer did so. As a matter of simple fairness, otherwise called political and military realism, I was determined to bring the West Germans into the highest command by creating a second slot for a Deputy Supreme Commander earmarked for a full general of the Bundeswehr. It required four years to achieve this aim, but in January 1978 the alliance approved the appointment of Gerd Schmückle. Although General Schmückle was universally recognized as a splendid soldier, this development was not immediately popular with some of the other allies. However, it was the right thing to do in terms of West German contributions in manpower, money, and matériel to the alliance and of the psychological subtleties of a situation in which a former enemy had become the strongest of the European allies. As one British general put it to me, "It has occurred to some of us, General, that you really *mean* it—you are hell-bent that NATO shall be a true alliance, with an integrated command."

That was, indeed, my hope and intention, but I could not have entertained the first or realized the second without a meeting of the minds with the leadership of the alliance, military and political. It is not for me, of course, to judge the results of my own command, but I will venture to offer the reader the assessment of one historian of the alliance:

> Haig . . . proved an effective advocate of rearmament [and] came across in NATO as a real soldier's general—he was careful to be seen showing concern about the welfare of his troops, and he was soldierly in his bearing, as befitted a West Pointer of the old school. He was determined to overcome the skepticism of his fellow generals . . . and his style and manner soon overcame the cynicism in NATO that had accompanied the announcement of his appointment. By the time of his departure, Haig had won widespread respect throughout NATO. . . .[8]

Being SACEUR was my idea of a wonderful job: I was in command of troops, fully occupied, and if not free from politics at least not entwined by them. I did not lose touch with home. The reader already knows of my conversation with President Ford before the fall of Saigon. I had other contacts with Ford while he remained in office, and visited Washington regularly to confer with the Pentagon leadership. Although he remains subject to U.S. Army orders in purely American matters, the NATO commander occupies a unique position in that he is in the chain of command of several other nations beside his own and is responsible for representing their interests to the United States and vice versa. I will spare the reader the volumes that might be written about the unique diplomatic requirements this places on a soldier accustomed to taking orders rather than negotiating them.

Ford and James Schlesinger were never entirely comfortable with each other. Something about the post of Secretary of Defense seems to attract and amplify intellectual arrogance. Schlesinger, whose abilities I greatly admired, and whom I had recommended to Nixon for a number of posts, including Defense, was no exception. He and Ford clashed in the first days of the latter's presidency when news stories alleged, on the basis of anonymous sources, that Schlesinger, during Nixon's last days, had ordered "a tight watch on the military chain of command to ensure that no extraordinary orders went out from the White House. . . ."[9] Other stories suggested that Schlesinger had actually slept on a cot at the Pentagon to guard against a military coup d'état instigated by Nixon. The suggestion that a military coup was even a possibility was not only a fantasy, it was an insult to the armed forces. Ford called Schlesinger in and asked for an explanation. Schlesinger denied that he was the source of the stories; in any case, after Ford expressed his displeasure, the leaks stopped.

Some months after I went to NATO, Ford invited me to the Oval Office and surprised me greatly by asking, "How would you like your old job back?"

I said, "But Mr. President, I thought Don Rumsfeld was doing a fine job as Chief of Staff."

"He is," said Ford, "but I'm thinking of him for another job."

The job I hoped to be able to do at NATO was just beginning; I asked the president to let me stay where I was, and he agreed to do so. From the flavor of the conversation that followed, even though nothing specific was said by the President, I got the impression that the job Ford had in mind for Rumsfeld was Secretary of Defense. I already had an appointment with Schlesinger, and when I saw him that afternoon I took the occasion to ask him how he was getting along with the President.

"Fine, great," said Schlesinger.

"Like hell you are, Jim," I said. "You'd better get your[self] over to the White House and mend some fences."

But it was too late. The next day, Schlesinger's resignation was announced and Rumsfeld moved to the Pentagon. Rumsfeld was replaced as White House Chief of Staff by a very able future Secretary of Defense, Dick Cheney.

Ford's assurances to Nixon that he would not run for President in 1976 became inoperative, in one of the catchphrases of the era, when John Connally's chances for the nomination went aglimmering in the milk-fund case. Ford understood that no President can govern effectively if he removes himself from consideration for reelection. Therefore, soon after settling into office, he announced that he would be a candidate for a full term in his own right.

It was a loss to the nation when he failed to win the necessary majority. Ford proved to be an effective President under incalculably difficult circumstances. If he had been reaffirmed in office by the people, he might well have accomplished a complete healing of the wounds of Watergate and, by the example of his own homely honesty, reminded Americans how important it is in a democracy to trust one another.

With President and Mrs. Ford and Brian and Alex Haig at White House
farewell dinner, 1974. (*White House photo*)

Arriving in Germany as NATO commander designate,
1974. (*U.S. Army photo*)

On NATO maneuvers
in Norway, 1978.
(*U.S. Army photo*)

Handing over command of
NATO to Gen. Bernard W.
Rogers (*right*) at SHAPE,
June 19, 1979.
(*U.S. Army photo*)

Secretary of State with President Reagan, 1981. (Time Magazine, *David Hume Kennerly*)

39

Carter Abroad

His Democratic opponent, Jimmy Carter, lacked Ford's calm personality, common touch, and shrewd political sense. In 1976, Carter ran not so much against Ford and the Republicans as against the Washington establishment, and this made it inevitable that the Washington establishment would treat him as an antibody to be driven out of the system as quickly as possible. Although it was not usual for a NATO commander to be relieved in midtour, I should not have been surprised if Carter decided to replace me with another man. However, no suggestion came from Washington that I should depart from NATO. Although I had nothing like the familiar contact I had enjoyed in earlier administrations, many of the men Carter appointed to Cabinet and other posts (Vance to State, Califano to HEW, Harold Brown to Defense) were known to me.

With the major exception of Carter's evangelical policy on human rights in friendly countries (abuses by Marxist-Leninist regimes continued largely to be ignored, especially by the American intellectual community), the new President preserved most of the essentials of the bipartisan U.S. foreign policy created by his predecessors. Carter himself was a stranger to me, as he was to most people in Washington. Although I had been only modestly impressed by his public persona or his campaign rhetoric, I was struck on meeting him by his keen intelligence and by the control he exercised over his Cabinet officers. He ran the administration like a nuclear-submarine crew. As far as I could discover, nobody talked back to this smiling, born-again Christian from the American heartland who wore blue jeans on television when making presidential addresses, regarded prayer as a form of conversation with the Almighty, and was said to listen to classical music several hours a day.

My own hope was that Carter would get along well with the Europeans, but as it turned out he never understood them and they never accepted him. To the allies, he was an unknown quantity, a man inexperienced in foreign affairs, a figure from outside the Establishment who lacked personal knowledge of foreign leaders, a populist; when he was elected, they feared the worst. His administration got off on the wrong foot when Vice President Walter Mondale visited Europe in May 1977. In the hope of being helpful, I called the NATO specialist on the NSC staff, a capable and knowledgeable Harvard professor named Henry Owen, and suggested a number of subjects for Mondale's consideration. As a result of further consultations with Cyrus Vance, Carter's Secretary of State, and Zbigniew Brzezinski, his national security adviser, my suggestions, added to those of others, expanded into a list of dont's. When he went to Europe, Mondale ignored every one of them. This confirmed the Europeans' worst fears about the maladroit qualities of the Carter team. The administration never recovered from this first-round blow to its reputation. Some of Carter's "just plain Jimmy" theatrics, as when he got off *Air Force One* in Brussels and greeted King Baudouin while carrying his own ValPac, embarrassed the Europeans. (The ValPac, I was told by a senior official, was empty.)

Carter was certainly the most morally consistent President the nation had known since Wilson, and his ideals inevitably led him into political difficulties, as when he abruptly decided in 1978 to reverse U.S. policy and not produce neutron weapons and deploy them in Europe. In so doing, he ignored the unanimous advice of Vance, Secretary of Defense Harold Brown, and Brzezinski. Moreover, Carter's decision came after the leaders of allied nations, especially Chancellor Schmidt of West Germany, had exposed themselves to great political risks in order to support the former U.S. desire to deploy the bomb. Schmidt was a Social Democrat, and he overcame strident opposition from the left wing of his party only with great difficulty.

Schmidt was deeply upset. Not only was Carter's decision wrong in strategic terms (among other things, he was unilaterally giving away the most potent bargaining chip before Star Wars) but he had already paid the political price of deployment and there was no rational need to withdraw. My conversations with Vance, Brown, Brzezinski, and Owen left me with the impression that political consequences and strategic considerations simply did not matter to the President in this case; his decision seemed to be based on the religious conviction that it was wrong to arm the alliance with a nuclear weapon that killed people but left property intact. Although the weapon was usually termed a "neutron bomb" in news reports that evoked pictures of huge cities in which entire populations died while architecture remained untouched, neutron technology was designed mostly to produce artillery shells and small missiles for battleground use against enemy armor, entrenchments, and artillery. (The Warsaw pact in 1978 had 20,500 tanks; NATO, 7,000.)

Finally, I asked to speak to the President on a secure telephone line. After explaining the situation as Schmidt and other Europeans and I myself saw it, I asked Carter to reconsider. To my astonishment, he replied, "All right, all right! I'll meet you halfway. We'll produce the neutron bomb, but we won't deploy it."

This wise compromise mollified Schmidt and maintained his irreplaceable political influence while preserving the strategic advantage the neutron weapon represented. Carter was a stubborn man, but he seemed to be a man who would listen. That was very heartening to know.

On the other hand, it was quite remarkable in certain cases how closely Carter controlled his administration by the force of his own naïveté. I experienced his peremptory style when, in 1978, I asked him to consider resuming military aid to Turkey. An arms embargo had been imposed by the United States against Turkey as a result of its invasion of Cyprus in 1974, after the elements of the Cypriot National Guard, led by officers of the Greek army, seized control of the Cypriot government.

The ability of the Turks to carry out their NATO obligations and keep order in a country riven by terrorism and subversion (Ankara was reporting thirty terrorist incidents a day) had been dangerously reduced. Within the Turkish military, resentments ran high against the regime that expected it to defend the country with obsolete equipment, insufficient spare parts, and weapons left over from the Korean War. In the absence of effective aid, the country would either degenerate into anarchy or declare martial law—and soon. Because of the human rights factor, any increase in aid from Washington was problematical while the Turkish government was compelled by the violence to take harsh measures against a militant and violent political opposition. When many efforts to communicate the seriousness of the crisis to the administration failed, I asked to see the President in person.

In the Oval Office, I explained the situation as I saw it to Carter. The private man was not always so genial as the public figure, and he gave me a look of deep skepticism when I told him that the Turkish army was an important social vehicle that absorbed much of the educated youth of the country and was a force for political stability. Finally, I said, "If the United States doesn't lift the embargo, Mr. President, there will be martial law in Turkey in a matter of days, and a military coup will inevitably follow."

Carter replied, "General, you don't know what you're talking about."

It was obvious that the President would brook no further argument. To the chagrin of my companion, Secretary Brown, who followed me down the hall and gave me hell for my lack of manners, I got to my feet and walked out of the Oval Office. The following week, martial law was imposed. Later in 1978, the arms embargo was finally lifted, but by then the terrorist situation was so grave that it resulted in a steady increase in military influence, and two years later a military council took over the government. (Turkey returned to civilian government in 1983, after the military council arranged free elections.[1])

Where his human rights policy was concerned, Carter's inner circle might have served him and the country better by speaking up to him in the voice of realism. Virtue is a great quality in a superpower because, as Churchill said of courage in the individual, it guarantees the rest. But as our experiences in Vietnam taught us to our great cost, virtue alone cannot carry the day. Leadership and wisdom, and a willingness to judge another society on the basis of its own national interests, traditions, and codes of conduct, not on some romantic notion of the same, are its necessary companions.[2] Throughout my public career, I was a strong champion of human rights, and as Secretary of State I believed myself to be in the forefront of American efforts to enhance and guarantee them throughout the world. However, a sense of balance is indispensable in this as in other aspects of our activity abroad. A foreign policy that exalts power over principle will offend America's sense of right; a foreign policy that ignores power for ideals will offend America's sense of reality. Only a policy that balances them both will accomplish progress.

We learned this lesson once again in Iran. Iran was not a member of NATO, but during the mid-1970s, when the British withdrew their military presence from the area east of Suez, the shah's forces became an important factor in maintaining stability in the Persian Gulf region. Even at the time, it seemed risky to place upon this developing country, rent by ancient rivalries and religious tensions, the burden of "policeman of the Gulf." But neither the United States nor any combination of Western powers was prepared to fill the void left by the British. Shortly after my arrival in Europe, I went to London to tell Prime Minister James Callaghan that NATO could adjust to the withdrawal of certain British formations from Germany if this would assist in maintaining the British presence east of Suez. Callaghan replied that Britain could no longer afford even the relatively small cost of maintaining a token force there, and the United States had declined to underwrite it.

As commander in chief of U.S. ground, air, and naval forces in Europe, not as NATO commander, I visited Tehran every six months. Iranian forces were a vital element in the defense of NATO's southern flank, and I thought that the United States and the Western Alliance were very fortunate to have in the shah a friend who shared their strategic judgments and paid for his own armaments while defending the most strategically important country in the Middle East. I was aware of charges that his regime was brutal in its treatment of internal opposition, but, on the basis of what I remember observing as a young officer and what I saw and heard now, I did not doubt that the opposition was real.

On the surface, no country in the Third World seemed to have less reason for a revolution. Compared especially to other Muslim countries, Iran was in some ways a progressive regime, and the standard of living of the people, who enjoyed a level of education and a range of government services unusual in the Middle East, was not so very far below that of some Mediterranean members of NATO. In psychological terms, the power vacuum created by the British withdrawal was a fateful turn of events for Iran. A country that takes up the role formerly exercised by a great power will usually, regardless of larger realities, be impelled to behave as a great power and to regard itself as one. That was one of the meanings of the "White Revolution," the crash program of land reform, modernization, and Westernization undertaken by the shah's petroleum-rich Iran in the 1960s and 1970s. It was said of the shah—admiringly before his fall and in terms of vilification afterward—that he had brought about more social progress and foreign influence in his thirty years in power than all the previous kings of the 2,500 years of the Persian monarchy together. Whether this was good or bad depended on the commentator's politics. His enemies said that the shah was a despot who was destroying an ancient culture and corrupting his people by mimicry of the West. He regarded himself, I think, as the stern but loving father to an obstreperous people who would thank him when, in the future, they realized what he had done for them.

Neither of these conceptions amounts to a modern definition of an enlightened ruler, but the shah was clearly preferable to any of the available alternatives. He was, in short, an arrogant but essentially benevolent despot who was a good friend of the United States, an implacable enemy of the Left and an obstacle to the religious Right, and a remarkable administrator and statesman whose essential goal was the establishment of a modern, socially just state ruled by himself and his descendants. As such, he represented the political center in his own country and also in a region in search of a political center of balance.

But he was not perfect in terms of his human rights record, and the Carter administration let him know that unless he corrected the shortcomings in his rule and met a standard acceptable to the United States, our friendship would be withdrawn. Such talk was, of course, reminiscent of calls for reform issued by an earlier American President who emphasized ideals, John F. Kennedy. As in the case of Kennedy's pronouncements, those of the Carter administration sounded to the shah very much like a call for his removal unless he yielded to internal opposition whose purpose was to wipe out the progress toward modernization and detach Iran from the West, and especially from the United States.

My talks with the mature ruler evoked the frustrations with an incomprehensible American policy that the young shah had expressed when I had first met him nearly twenty years before. In the 1970s, I saw, from one visit to another, what progress the shah's enemies were making in their efforts to create disorder, subvert the institutions of the monarchy, discredit the shah's intentions, and overthrow him and his government. The shah, isolated from the advice and support of the administration in Washington and no longer benefiting from the presence and influence of the British, relied more heavily each day on the military and, in accordance with local usage, put himself under greater and greater obligation to supply them with advanced arms. It was the case of the canceled frigates writ large.

On my last visit to Tehran, in the winter before his downfall, I found the shah listless, fatigued, distracted. There were troubles in the streets, intrigues in the government, doubts about the loyalty of the generals. The large, glossy, intelligent eyes, always the shah's most noticeable physical feature, had changed. There was a deadness in them now that couldn't have been produced by a mental state. I feared that he was being ravaged by some serious, secret illness.

After a desultory conversation with the shah, I drove to the airport through a sudden blizzard, deeply worried. The next day, from Mons, I called Cyrus Vance and told him what I had found in Tehran. The shah was a sick, possibly dying man, with enemies who were growing in strength. The United States must assist in any way it could in maintaining stability in Iran and in making sure that the transition of power, when it came, was orderly, lawful, and compatible with our interests. Of course, none of this was done; plans within the administration to encourage the abdication of the shah were already well advanced.

Over the next year, 1978, the situation in Iran deteriorated very badly. A revolutionary theocratic movement of Muslim fundamentalists, deeply influenced if not directed from exile in Paris by a shadowy Shia mullah named Ruhollah Khomeini, was rapidly turning into a revolutionary force. On August 9, 1978, more than four hundred people died in a fire in a movie theater in Abadan; the government accused religious extremists of setting the fire, and Khomeini countered by blaming it on SAVAK, the shah's secret police. After widespread demonstrations, martial law was declared. On September 8 in Tehran, troops fired on a crowd, killing scores of people. Many violent encounters with the army followed; some of these were provoked by extremists seeking political results or religious martyrdom, or both. On December 2, the first day of the Shia holiday Mohorran, a curfew was imposed in all Iranian cities.[3] It was clear that the shah could not survive very much longer. Despite the unmistakable danger signals sent up by Khomeini's activities, the United States was ill-informed about the man or his purposes and had taken little action to counteract his influence; not even so fundamental a step as insisting to the French that they impose limits on Khomeini's political activities had been taken.

Meanwhile, the United States appeared to be throwing its support behind Shapur Bakhtiar, whom the shah had named prime minister on December 29, 1978. Bakhtiar, committed to the United States to form a republic as a replacement for the monarchy, was determined that the shah should go as quickly as possible.[4] His government gave permission for parades on Shia holy days in mid-December, and some 2 million people turned out, bearing portraits of Khomeini as well as antishah and anti-American placards.[5]

The key to the situation was the military, which was still loyal to the shah. It was my belief, undemocratic though this may have seemed to Carter's men, that the Iranian armed forces should put down the disorders and neutralize the revolutionary opposition. There was no question that this would involve loss of life and deepen political divisions in Iran, but it was far more likely that a democratic form of government might evolve out of the monarchy than from the atavistic theocracy that seemed likely to replace it. That alternative, as events amply proved, was far greater loss of life and even greater repression of political opposition.

On January 2, 1979, I received a transatlantic telephone call from General David Jones, the chairman of the Joint Chiefs of Staff. He told me that the President wanted to borrow my able deputy, Lt. Gen. Robert ("Dutch") Huyser, for a special mission to Iran. I asked the purpose of the mission. Jones's reply was a bit murky. I asked for particulars. No plain explanation was forthcoming.

I declined to release Huyser. Subsequent accounts of my conversation with Davy Jones have me saying to him in Haigspeak, "I nonconcur." I doubt that I actually spoke those words, but they certainly convey my state of mind at the time.

In the wake of my conversation with General Jones, Deputy Secretary of Defense Charles Duncan called me. (Secretary Brown was out of town.) Deeply worried and more than a little angry, I asked once again what was going on. Duncan replied that the President himself wanted Huyser to go to Iran to counsel the Iranian military.

Hoping to muster support among those who were in a position to intervene with the President, I made more calls. The State Department, never a hotbed of the shah's admirers, exercised a pregnant discretion. Brzezinski, who seemed to be on the same wavelength as myself, told me that Huyser would be working to establish civil order through use of the military. I then called William Sullivan, our ambassador to Iran, and learned that he, too, was opposed to Huyser's mission.

Clearly, the White House was not going to reassure the shah; it was going to facilitate his departure. Dutch Huyser's real mission, as events were soon to reveal, was to separate the Iranian military from the shah and keep the troops in garrison while unchecked domestic turmoil forced the shah to retire.

To Charlie Duncan, I said, "This is bad policy. It is also just plain wrong, and what you have in mind for Dutch Huyser is no job for a military man. You're sending the wrong man for the wrong purpose."

All this telephoning happened in a single day. Soon after, I talked to Duncan, General Huyser told me that he had received a call from Duncan conveying a direct order from the President and the Joint Chiefs of Staff to report to Tehran forthwith.

"Then you have to do what you have to do, Dutch," I said. "But watch yourself. You may end up destroying the Iranian military. And that would destroy any hope of a good outcome in Iran."

I flew to Washington to express my concerns and to assess the implications of having been overruled by the President. Although it was clear that the administration was split on the question, it was also evident that the moment of decision had passed and what would be in Iran, would be.

Huyser arrived in Tehran on January 3. He was in Iran for several days before the shah knew that he was there. According to the shah's memoirs, Huyser's question to him, when he did call at the palace, accompanied by Ambassador Sullivan, was, "When are you leaving, sir? Have you set a date?"[6]

In the days that followed, many top-ranking officers loyal to the shah were removed by the Bakhtiar government. On January 16, 1979, America's good and loyal friend Shah Mohammad Reza Pahlavi departed, carrying with him a box of Iranian soil as his father had done when going into exile in 1941.

Two weeks later, Khomeini returned to Iran. The army collapsed in shame and disorder. And on February 11, 1979, the Bakhtiar government, which the United States had hoped to put into power by denying the loyalty of the armed forces to the shah, ceased to exist, and the Ayatollah took absolute power.[7]

After this, I felt that I could not continue to serve the Carter administration. I asked to be relieved, and the administration agreed that I could leave at the end of June.

My tour of duty in Europe had coincided with the heyday of radical terrorism there. The IRA in the United Kingdom, the Baader-Meinhoff Gang and the Red Army Faction in Germany, the Basque ETA-Militar in Spain, the Red Brigades in Italy, and a dizzying number of other terrorist groups made up of the bloodthirsty Marxist-Leninist children of the European bourgeoisie went about murdering and kidnapping prominent people and blowing up airliners and public places with bombs in a monstrous parody of student rowdiness. Prime Minister Aldo Moro was shot to death in Italy and many other prominent people were murdered, wounded, or abducted for ransom.

The Western intellectual fashion at the time, widely reflected in the news media, was to consider such people as idealists who had been driven over the edge of some precipice of conscience by the injustices of capitalistic society. It was also an article of faith that the various terrorist organizations were independent, self-sufficient groups that had no connection to one another or to any foreign power. In fact, they were all, to some extent, part of a general, if loose, conspiracy of the lunatic Left.

I always maintained, sometimes in the face of ridicule, that the Soviet secret service played a key role in the international terrorist movement. That this was the case has now been confirmed by the former legal adviser to Russian president Boris Yeltsin, and by other sources within the new Russian government. As the new government of the old U.S.S.R. opens the archives of the KGB, it will become evident that they were often financed, trained, and armed by the Communist intelligence services, which used them to carry out operations against Western interests and individuals, especially Americans and Israelis. Nearly all terrorist organizations had some connection to the Palestine Liberation Organization (PLO).[8]

As NATO commander, and as an American whose name was associated with the frustration of Marxist-Leninist designs, I was the object of several death threats, as was my family. Some of these were taken so seriously by the security people that on occasion I traveled to and from work by helicopter instead of by car. The intelligence services and police forces of the NATO nations kept my security staff well informed, and I took the precautions they recommended, traveling with U.S. Army bodyguards, enjoying round-the-clock protection of my home and office by military police and the excellent Belgian police, and varying my routine so as to make it more difficult for terrorists to time an attack on my car or aircraft. One night while my family was in residence at the Château de Gendebien, someone fired several rounds from a rifle, striking the roof above the room where my daughter, Barbara, happened at the time to be reading a book. We were aware of no other violent incidents.

NATO headquarters could be reached from the château by one of two routes. The first passed through the city of Mons; the other went through the countryside. In either case, the distance was about eleven kilometers, or a little less than seven miles. We varied the route in a random manner, traveling in a three-vehicle convoy, with a lead car about one hundred yards in front of the sedan in which I rode and a chase car one hundred yards behind. The other two cars were occupied by my American military bodyguards and by members of the Belgian security services. In my own car with me were my aide, Maj. Seth Hudgens, and my driver, Sgt. Hans Hooker of the U.S. Army.

Sergeant Hooker was a superb, though somewhat heavy-footed, driver who loved the big Mercedes-Benz 600 that NATO provided as my command car. Hooker preferred the route through the countryside because it provided opportunities to step on the gas. Although he had often been reminded of the importance of observing Belgian speed limits, the presence of a four-star general in the backseat and several Belgian policemen in the convoy was not always enough to cause him to do so. Because the other two cars adjusted their speed to that of the Mercedes, it was Hooker who set the pace for the convoy. If it made sense to vary routes, Hooker may have thought, it made sense to vary speeds. My policy was to let him do the driving.

On June 25, 1979, five days before I was to leave NATO, we took the route through the countryside. We were a few minutes behind schedule that morning because Pat and I had houseguests and I had lingered over breakfast with them. Hooker, pushing the speed limit even more than usual, drove the Mercedes onto a stone and earth bridge over a small culverted stream about halfway to Mons. Just after the car rolled onto the bridge, it accelerated violently forward, as if flung from a catapult. I looked behind us and saw smoke and flame and the weird image of the steel in the trunk expanding like the rubber of some improbable balloon.

That the car had been attacked was obvious. I was not sure whether we had run over a mine or whether we had been hit by a bazooka round. A well-planned operation would have provided for a second ambush farther down the road in case the first one had not worked. I shouted an order to Hooker to stop the car. He did so immediately and we all leapt out. The explosion had been a large one. Rocks and other debris were still falling from the sky, and the bomb had dug a large crater in the roadway. The chase car, although traveling some distance behind, had driven directly into the explosion and was heavily damaged. The security men inside were now out of the car. One of them, staggering and bleeding heavily from a scalp wound, signaled frantically for us to proceed. After surveying both sides of the road for some distance ahead to make sure that no other ambush had been prepared, we proceeded onward to headquarters—in record time, thanks to Hooker.

Subsequent investigation showed that a large bomb, buried in the earth floor of the bridge, had been detonated by remote control from a point about five hundred feet away. Apparently, it had exploded just under the rear bumper of the Mercedes or just behind it, which accounted for the catapult effect and the distortion of the trunk lid. The men in the chase car were injured, one of them seriously, but there were no deaths. Although my ears rang for a long time afterward, causing a temporary hearing loss, I suffered no serious injury, and neither did Hooker or the other two men in our car.

As soon as I had called Pat to tell her I was all right, I put through a call to Adm. Stansfield Turner, then the Director of Central Intelligence, and asked him to identify the likely suspects. After looking into the matter, Turner called back and told me I had probably been hit by "a splinter group of Belgian nihilists." This seemed unlikely to me, since I was not aware that I had ever done anything to offend a Belgian nihilist, so I turned to the West German intelligence service for a second opinion. After investigation, my contact there told me that, judging by the technique and equipment used, the attempt on my life had almost certainly been the work of one of the German terrorist gangs trained by the KGB or one of its Eastern European counterparts.

My old friend Larry Eagleburger, now serving as American ambassador to Yugoslavia, sent me a cable: "I knew you wanted to go out with a bang, but this is ridiculous!" It was a line good enough to steal, and I did so when interviewed by the press about the incident.

Finally, some of the terrorists who had attacked my car eleven years before were arrested by the West German authorities and charged with a variety of violent crimes. They turned out to be members of the ultraleftist Red Army Faction. According to the testimony of a female member of the gang, Susanne Albrecht, she and nine other Red Army Faction members devised their plot to kill me in 1978, while training in a camp for terrorists maintained in Aden by the PLO. They completed the plan while living in apartments in Yugoslavia and later in a suburb of Brussels. Fräulein Albrecht, who stated that she had not taken part in the actual attack, was also charged with the murder of Jürgen Ponto, head of the Dresdener Bank, who was a friend of her family. The Stasi, the former East German secret police and intelligence agency, gave her a new identity and other support after the attempt on my life.[9]

In April 1991, my old colleague Gen. Gerd Schmückle, now retired, called on Werner Lotze, the leader of the terrorist team, in jail. Lotze spoke freely to Schmückle about every aspect of the plan, telling him that he and his friends had watched my movements for days, following my convoy on a motorcycle, stopwatch in hand, because the detonation of the bomb required split-second timing.

In the event, the buried bomb, a very large one, went off a second too late; had it detonated beneath the car as planned, everyone inside would almost certainly have been goners. "My dear Al," wrote Schmückle after his talk with my would-be assassin, "There is no doubt that your life was saved by the fact that Hooker did not stick to the speed limitation on the bridge."

Schmückle went on to say that, according to Lotze, the terrorists had decided to kill me "because [my] activities at SHAPE were so effective that they became more and more dangerous for the socialist camp, because it could not keep step with NATO's improvements."[10]

Neither Sergeant Hooker nor I ever received handsomer compliments.

40

Politics

After Gerald Ford was defeated by Jimmy Carter, there was no heir apparent to the Republican nomination for President. While I was in Europe, a number of people, some of them well known and well connected politically, suggested to me that I should run. On the basis of what I had observed over the past forty years, I knew that the old saying that anyone can be President of the United States was literally true, and I did not dismiss the possibility that I might have a chance to be elected, given the right backing and the right circumstances. All the same, it seemed unlikely that anything could come of the talk, because I saw no way I could possibly be nominated. All I lacked, as I remarked to one man, were a political base, an organization, money, and a constituency.

My feelings about entering politics were very mixed. On a very basic level, the idea repelled me; my father had said contemptuous things about politicians and advised me never to get mixed up with such people. Having got mixed up with them by an accident of fate, I knew what lives of punishment they led and how their families suffered. My Watergate experiences had not left me with an appetite for the job Nixon had won and lost. On the other hand, I thought that I knew as much about the job, and was as capable of doing it, as anyone who was then regarded as a serious candidate.

On my return to the United States in the summer of 1979 I retired from the Army, this time for good. Pat and I moved into an apartment in the Philadelphia area and I occupied my time by teaching at the University of Pennsylvania and working with the Foreign Policy Research Institute in Philadelphia. Without my knowledge or approval, as is traditional, some kind people in Washington started a Haig for President Committee. I still did not think I had a chance. Then Henry Kissinger, who was working on his memoirs while staying at Nelson Rockefeller's country estate in New York, invited Pat and me to visit him and his wife, Nancy, for the weekend.

In issuing this invitation, Henry had said that Rockefeller wanted to see me, and soon after my arrival he and I got together. Rockefeller told me that he thought that I should run for President; it was a question of public service. "If you do run," he said, "I'll throw all my support behind you." Needless to say, I was flattered and tempted; the fact that the offer came from Rockefeller, the most presidential American of my time who failed actually to become President, was a powerful factor in the equation. But I made no commitment.

There were two reasons for this. First, Harry Gray, chairman of United Technologies Corporation, had been talking to me about joining UTC as corporate president, and I owed him consideration. Second, I suspected that I had a health problem; for some time I had noticed distressing physical symptoms while playing tennis. Army doctors dismissed these cramps and twinges as mere signs of aging (I was fifty-five), but I thought they might be wrong. Shortly after this, it was discovered, in the course of an examination for life insurance in connection with my employment by UTC, that two coronary arteries were blocked. This condition was repaired in Dallas by Dr. Denton Cooley, a pioneer in heart bypass surgery, then a relatively new medical technique, and I enjoyed a rapid and full recovery.

If this combination of events convinced me that I was not meant for the presidency, it apparently persuaded people close to Ronald Reagan that I was a political rival to be taken seriously. As Reagan was preparing to make his own primary run, Justin Dart, a member of his kitchen cabinet, called me up and speculated about my opportunities in an interesting way. Assuming that I was not going to run for President and was looking for something useful to do, Dart suggested, I might be in a good position to become a favored candidate for the post of chancellor of the University of California. Someone of my reputation might also have a good chance of taking over Reagan's radio show, newspaper column, and speaking schedule. "It's a pretty remunerative package," Dart told me.

"And it's not much trouble, Al, because other people do all the writing for you." By then, I had promised Harry Gray that I would join UTC, so I thanked Dart for thinking of me and embarked on what I hoped would be a second career as a corporate executive.

As I have related in my earlier book, *Caveat*, written after I resigned following eighteen months as Reagan's first Secretary of State, that possibility went by the boards when I was called back into government service. The main lesson I had drawn from my life experience, by the time I agreed to join President Reagan's Cabinet, was that an American, whether soldier or civilian, owes his first loyalty to the people and to the Constitution, not to his superior, even if that person is the Commander in Chief, and certainly not to any political abstraction.

For better or for worse, that was my conviction, and in my dealings with the Reagan administration I lived by it as best I could. This resulted in my offering advice that was plainer than Reagan, or most other Presidents, are used to hearing. A President has a relatively brief period, immediately after his election, in which to establish his foreign and domestic policies and take initiatives to carry them out. If he does not say what he is going to do and begin to do it pretty damn quickly, he will find that he is being driven by events instead of doing the driving.

My remarks to the President in Cabinet and NSC meetings conveyed the urgency implicit in this idea. The results were decidedly mixed. My style, as the press called it, aroused the territorial apprehensions of the White House chief of staff, James A. Baker III, and of Mrs. Reagan's favorite presidential aide, Michael K. Deaver. It was evident that the media attention I attracted, favorable at first, had the effect of arousing the apprehensions of Mrs. Reagan, who strongly believed that there should only be one star on the White House lot. In regard to the President, as I wrote in *Caveat*, "Because of his habitual cheery courtesy, it is at times difficult to know when [Reagan] is agreeing or disagreeing, approving or disapproving."[1]

Baker and Deaver and their minions, all experts on the manipulation of the news media, thought from Inauguration Day onward almost exclusively in terms of Reagan's election to a second term. In the early days of the administration, they were transfixed by the problem of ending the recession and inflation Reagan had inherited from Carter and in boosting the President's image and popularity through actions, such as the defense buildup, that created jobs and gave the impression of meaningful action. My Catoesque warnings that the level of defense spending, combined with the mandated costs of social programs, would require either raising taxes or creating an enormous budget deficit, fell on uncomprehending ears.

In our first meeting on foreign policy, Reagan and I had agreed on the importance of speaking in a single voice on foreign affairs, and he had decided that I should be that voice. My earlier book recounts the details, but these arrangements were not put into place by presidential order or supported by presidential action. It proved impossible even to obtain Reagan's signature on the fundamental national-security memorandum that assigned responsibility for the various aspects of foreign policy among the departments and agencies responsible for them.

This vacuum of authority, combined with a babble of leaks to the press and palace intrigues, soon produced a dangerous incoherence in our foreign policy. Finally, I decided I could not stay unless the situation was regularized. On June 14, 1982, I told the President that he must formally invoke his original decision or I would depart. President Reagan pondered this ultimatum for eleven days and then, as I put it in *Caveat*, "accept[ed] a letter of resignation that I had not yet submitted."[2]

Although it was preceded by a good deal of discussion, some of it animated indeed, the President's action was uncharacteristically abrupt. He simply asked me to step into the Oval Office after a meeting in the Cabinet Room and handed me a letter accepting a nonexistent resignation. This occurred on June 25, 1982, in the midst of a major crisis touched off by Israel's invasion of Lebanon. Although I did not object to going, I told him I thought he was handling this matter in a "precipitous way." I went back to the State Department to fill in the gap by writing a letter of resignation that would explain that I no longer supported his policies. While I was still drafting this letter, Reagan appeared in the White House pressroom and announced my resignation.[3]

At the time, and for a long while afterward, I was bewildered by this sudden fit of decisiveness in a President who had previously exhibited no marked tendency toward firm and final action. On that day, as on no other in my experience, Reagan behaved very much like a man whose mind is made up and will not change. I assumed that he had been convinced to get rid of me by Baker and Deaver (later joined by my former deputy at the State Department, William Clark). I also assumed that these three had participated in the brilliantly orchestrated symphony of character assassination against me in the news media. After planting their toxic stories, they had, I supposed, convinced the President that I was a liability because I was attracting so much bad publicity. In a way that mixes a certain unworthy admiration with other emotions, I still believe that this was an important factor.

However, there may have been another element involved in Reagan's method of operation that was quite beyond my imagination at that time, as well as being beyond the control of the most Machiavellian member of the staff. Factor A, as it may be called, was the First Lady's astrologer. As Donald Regan revealed in his memoirs of his years as Secretary of the Treasury and White House Chief of Staff, "Virtually every move and decisions the Reagans made . . . was cleared with a woman in San Francisco who drew up horoscopes to make certain that the planets were in favorable alignment for the enterprise."[4] In light of this information, it may well be that June 25, 1982, was my unlucky day in the literal (or horoscopic) sense of the phrase, and that the reason for Reagan's brusque action may literally have been in my stars, not in myself.*

In any case, the incident belongs to the past. Even at the time, I did not take the slanderous press campaign personally, because I understood that it had nothing to do with the reality of my character or my works but, rather, was designed to disable me as a potential presidential threat— not to Reagan, against whom I could not possibly have run even if there were a prayer of defeating him, but to those who hoped to come after him. I returned to private life in Washington and, starting from scratch, founded and built up my own company, Worldwide Associates. After a lifetime of public service, self-employment was my best option; the bad publicity, combined with a certain reluctance to hire a man who was in the administration's bad books, made me less than attractive to the Fortune 500 companies who had been so interested in my services only a couple of years earlier.

It is always a moot question how much difference a single person can make, even if he happens to be Secretary of State, but I think it is fair to say that Reagan would have had strong advice from me in connection with the most damaging event of his presidency, the Iran-Contra crisis. After all, I had been over such dark and bloody ground before; on the day the news of it broke, I called Don Regan, who was then the White House Chief of Staff. My advice to the President was to place all the facts before the public at once and take complete responsibility on himself. He should, I told Regan, immediately fire the people who had created the disaster and then protect them—by a preemptive pardon, if necessary. Had Nixon done this in the first moments of Watergate, while still at the height of his popularity, he might have survived.

---

*June 25 has been a significant date in my life. The Korean War began on that date in 1950, I took command of NATO on that date in 1975, and the Red Army Faction terrorists tried to blow my car up on June 25, 1979. It is also the aniversary of Custer's Last Stand (1876).

Although I know none of the unpublished details, it seems to me more likely than not that those involved were carrying out what they believed, for whatever reasons, to be the President's policy and wishes. It would have been better for Ronald Reagan—better for his future effectiveness, better for his place in history, better for the country—if he had taken the whole brunt on himself, refusing to cooperate in any investigation and challenging the opposition to impeach him. No opponent, however bold, would have called the President's bluff after he threw the enormous sum of his popularity into the pot.

I have had a good deal to say in this book about the dangers and limitations of covert action as a substitute for open foreign policy. How much superior the latter is in a crisis was demonstrated by President Bush in the Gulf War. The problem of Saddam Hussein was one that contained many of the ingredients that have in the past lured Presidents toward a covert solution. Bush rejected this and, by acting in the open, on the basis of clearly stated principles and objectives, built a winning policy. He did this block by block, putting together the allied coalition, winning the support of the United Nations, and rallying popular support to overcome opposition in Congress. Finally, he gave the military everything it needed and let it do the job without second-guessing from the White House. The result was a tremendous victory for the rule of law, with the United States in the vanguard. We had shown that America had not fought the Cold War in order to make the world safe for old-fashioned aggressor-dictators. In my opinion, the President should have continued hostilities until Saddam was taken out of the picture once and for all, because any result that left the aggressor in place represented an incomplete victory. But that is a matter for the American people to judge, together with George Bush's other accomplishments and missed opportunities, in the presidential election.

In regard to covert action under Reagan, I was at least as vociferous in secret councils as I have been in my writings. In 1981, during one of the earliest of our weekly breakfast meetings, William Casey, the Director of Central Intelligence, laid on the table an idea for secret operations designed to bring down the Marxist-Leninist Sandinista regime in Nicaragua. To Bill's considerable surprise, for he and I were natural allies who agreed on most issues, I opposed it vigorously.

"It won't be effective because you won't be able to do enough," I argued, "and it won't work because it will be exposed and discredited." The Nicaraguan situation was not an isolated phenomenon but part of a global problem connected to the Soviet policy of supplying arms and tutors to guerrilla wars. The way to defeat the Sandinistas and the Marxist-Leninist guerrillas they were encouraging elsewhere in Central America, I said, was for the President to stand up publicly against the Soviets and the Cubans who had created them.

Get the Soviets out of the Western Hemisphere by showing them that it was in their interest to go. Castro would be dealt a hard, perhaps fatal blow; the Sandinistas, depending on him, would also be seriously weakened. We should promote this outcome openly, promoting the principle of democracy in the Western Hemisphere by openly pressuring Havana and Managua on the legitimate issues raised by their own repressive actions, and support Nicaraguans who wished to bring about change. Such means included embargo and every other action possible under the rule of law, and if, in the last resort, a Nicaraguan opposition took up arms, and it was deemed in our interest to support it, then we should support it openly, too.

Clearly my counsel did not prevail, and the linkage of the sale of arms to Iran with the hunger of a covert operation for funds produced the Iran-Contra affair. By any reasonable standard of judgment, the secret actions that generated this scandal were as serious as anything Nixon was supposed to have done in connection with Watergate.* But, as in the case of other Presidents before him, Reagan escaped censure.

The Iran-Contra affair was all the more deplorable in that it involved the fate of people who were in sore need of humanitarian rescue—the

---

*On the other hand, the allegation that the release of the American hostages held in Iran was delayed for political purposes by the Reagan administration seems to me to belong to the realm of fantasy. During the transition period between the Carter and Reagan administrations, I was approached by Carter's Secretary of Defense, Harold Brown, and by the outgoing Deputy Secretary of State, Warren Christopher, both of whom requested permission from President-elect Reagan to grant the Algerian government, the main interface with the Iranians, more time to conduct the negotiations. Granting such permission would, obviously, have had the effect of *delaying* the return of the hostages. I told Brown, the first to approach me, that I had not spoken to Reagan on this issue but was sure that the policy of the incoming administration was to obtain the release of the hostages as quickly as possible, and therefore the answer to the Algerians was no. They could have no more time. Soon after this, in a meeting at Blair House, I told Reagan what I had said and he endorsed the position I had taken. When Christopher later approached me, again asking for more time on behalf of the Algerians, I told him, this time with the full authority of the President, that the new administration "wanted the Algerians and the Iranians to know that unless our hostages had been released by Inauguration Day, it would be a whole new ball game." This phraseology was meant to convey the warning that the United States would take military action against Iran, if necessary, to free the hostages. They were returned on Inauguration Day. One more point. As described in *Caveat* (p. 78), Reagan's inner circle suggested on the day after his inauguration that "the agreement with the Iranians for the return of the hostages, negotiated by the Carter administration, be abrogated." This is not the behavior of men who have reason to fear the exposure of a secret agreement, because the course of action they were recommending would certainly have enraged the Iranians and given them reason to seek revenge by exposing any such sub rosa deal.

Nicaraguans in their poverty and political deprivation, the hostages held in Lebanon and elsewhere by terrorist groups supported by Syria and Iran, and the Iranian people themselves, engaged in a grim mutual slaughter with Iraq. The factors affecting the Middle East were matters of deep concern to the principal U.S. ally in the region, Israel.

Israeli motives in the Iran-Contra affair were mixed, to say the least. Relations between Persians and Jews, going back to the Book of Esther and beyond, had always been intense and complex, and in recent times Israel and the shah had worked together in many ways, often clandestinely. After the fall of the shah, the Iranian Jewish community had been the subject of Khomeini's pathological hatred.

The question of the Iranian Jews was raised by the Israeli defense minister, Ariel Sharon, during my visit to Israel as Secretary of State early in the Reagan administration. At a private meeting in the King David Hotel in Jerusalem, Sharon informed me that he wanted U.S. approval of a plan to ship tires and spare parts for American-made F4 fighter-bombers, and perhaps other war materials, from Israel to Iran.

Surprised, I asked him why he wanted to do this.

Sharon replied, "We have tens of thousands of Jews in Iran. We don't want them to be persecuted or killed."

This anxiety was entirely realistic, given the mistrust of Jews revealed in Khomeini's writings[5] and the outrages that the Khomeini regime was known to have committed on religious grounds against members of the Baha'i faith and even against Shia and Sunni Muslims.

Nevertheless, the only possible answer to Sharon's request was no. I said, "I sympathize with you. But you're talking about shipping U.S. weapons and supplies to Iran, and that's against our law. The answer is no."

Sharon, a volatile man under the best of circumstances, exploded. For the Israelis, whose famous intelligence service, the Mossad, was originally organized for the purpose of rescuing endangered Jews, the issue was fundamental and highly emotional.

Nevertheless, I repeated what I had already told him: "What you do to protect Israeli interests on your own is your business. But no U.S. military goods can be part of the equation under any circumstances."

Some months later, I became aware of reports that shipments of military goods had, in fact, been made from Israel to Iran.

The next time I saw Sharon, I told him once again what our position was: "Nothing has changed. It's still against our law to send American-supplied arms to Iran. If you're doing it, you're on your own."

Sharon never gave up in his efforts to win approval of his scheme at many levels of the U.S. government, and U.S. policy accommodated itself after my departure to the idea of supplying arms to the Khomeini regime. From the outset of the Iran-Iraq War, I argued that the United States policy must be one of strict neutrality, and I said repeatedly that we wanted neither side to win. My position on this issue did not change while I was Secretary of State. I never authorized or offered encouragement for the shipment of U.S. arms to Iran from Israel or any other point of supply, nor was it in my power to do so. If any official of the State Department departed from this practice during my tenure as Secretary, I was unaware of it, did not authorize it, and would have fired the person responsible if his defiance of policy had come to my attention.

What happened later on, the world knows. A different group of Israelis, wishing to supply a different inventory of arms to Iran, obtained the approval of the Reagan administration to do so. In return, the Iranians would pay for the arms and also use their good offices to encourage the release of American hostages being held in Lebanon by terrorist groups. In return for the arms, some but not all of the American hostages who were supposed to be released by terrorists controlled by Iran were set free before the scandal broke in November 1986.

Some semblance of a happy ending to this melancholy episode may be read into the fact that Nicaragua did eventually establish a democratic regime as the result of free elections.

Just as happily, though the Israeli government denied reports that the immigration was tied to continued shipments of arms from Israel to Iran, some fifty thousand Iranian Jews managed to leave Iran for Israel and the United States. According to published reports, at least that number, or about three-fifths of the total thought to be living inside Iran at that time, had crossed the Iranian frontier without opposition by the beginning of October 1987. After leaving Iran in the buses that had transported them from many parts of the country, the refugees were flown to Vienna before continuing on to their new homes in Israel.[6]

As the hymnal teaches us, "God moves in a mysterious way/His wonders to perform."[7] To those who set out to serve what we Americans (and many others) believe to be His country, these words are a constant and most necessary reassurance.

41

Afterword:
America, the Future,
the World

Inner Circles is a memoir of the Cold War as one American experienced it from beginning to end, and its chief lesson is that the Cold War, like many hot wars of the past, might have been prevented. At the end of World War II, Churchill envisaged a grand coalition of the United States and the other Western powers, capable of overawing the threadbare but militarily strong Marxist-Leninist mother country and seizing the future for democracy. Others were reluctant to accept that our brave wartime Soviet ally could never be a partner in building a new world based on political freedom and social justice. The opportunity was lost. Quick to disarm, the United States was slow to understand the dangerous strategic reality created by the presence of a heavily armed totalitarian state beyond the Polish plain. Although our rhetoric was robust, our military capabilities were inadequate. Not until the fateful Korean summer of 1950 did we begin serious rearmament and effective organization of the Western Alliance.

Even then, many intelligent people in the United States and abroad did not believe that America and her allies could stay the course. Whittaker Chambers made a lasting impression on Richard Nixon when he told him that he felt, when he quit the Communist party in the late 1930s, that he was leaving the winning side.[1] There were times, as the episode of Vietnam tragically illustrates, when we did not stay the course. But in

the end, the American people surprised the world—and themselves—
with their fortitude. The central lesson here, as in past conflicts with
seemingly invincible totalitarian systems is, Never underestimate the democracies or their people.

The doctrine of containment was in the air I breathed for more than
thirty years as I served as a soldier in two limited wars and as a staff officer
working closely in crisis after crisis with lofty figures from both great
American political parties. Containment was supported throughout the
Cold War by a bipartisan consensus, and no one can deny that it brought
about the desired result. Nevertheless, it had defects as well as virtues. As
a gentleman from Yugoslavia in the audience at one of my public lectures
said to me recently, "The Cold War went on for half a century because
the Americans refused to win and the Russians refused to lose."

The fundamental reason why the issue was not forced is known to all:
the risk of nuclear war. After the American monopoly was broken, both
sides were deeply conscious that miscalculation might lead to the extinc-
tion of civilized life on our planet. For most of the Cold War, the Soviets
were restrained by the fact of overwhelming American superiority in
numbers and quality of nuclear weapons, and in retrospect it is clear that
the other side could have resorted to the use of nuclear weapons only as
an act of insanity. On the American side, the moral argument against
the use of such weapons, or even the threat of their use, took on the force
of religious belief. Nevertheless, as the reader has seen, the mere existence
of our superior power often bailed us out of potential disaster even though
we were determined, in the depths of the national soul, never to use it.

Our greater power was seldom used to win strategic advantage for the
United States. Eisenhower took advantage of it to break the Korean
stalemate. Kennedy, though less adroit, relied on it in the Cuban Missile
Crisis. As Soviet nuclear capabilities burgeoned, later Presidents enjoyed
no such decisive advantage. However, even after the United States grew
comparatively weaker, the destructive capacity of our nuclear weapons
and delivery systems represented the closest thing to absolute power so far
known to history. We can be proud that this power did not, as the epigram
has it, corrupt absolutely, but instead made American leaders prayerfully
conscious of the awful consequences of its misuse.

By 1980, America's strategic nuclear military decline, coupled to the
deep moral crisis that grew out of Vietnam and Watergate, had brought
the doctrine of containment into question. A seemingly buoyant Soviet
Union challenged United States interests all over the world; a seemingly
exhausted United States rose reluctantly to the challenge, or sometimes

rose to it not at all. Yet, within the decade, it was the Soviet Union that laid itself down on the scrap heap of history. Many had believed that this must happen sooner or later; I myself predicted it in many speeches in the 1970s during my years at NATO and subsequently, as during the 1988 campaign for the Republican presidential nomination. However, few, if any, expected the collapse to occur so swiftly and so completely. It is critically important that we seek to understand this surprising event, and that we understand it correctly. Otherwise, we will be unable to shape and influence the new era that is now in the process of being born. Whatever else it may or may not be, this new era is a child of the Cold War.

As a warrior of the Cold War and one of the architects of the Reagan administration's tougher policy with regard to the Soviets, I should like to believe that it was the power of our moral values, backed by the great military buildup and the perceived toughness of the Reagan years, that won the victory. Certainly these factors played a part in the outcome. However, there was no decisive battle in any established sense of the term. Like the Czar's armies in 1917, the Russians simply deserted the trenches and went home. Crippled by corruption, confounded by the essential falseness of Marxism-Leninism, and threatened by an epidemic of desperation among the Soviet and Eastern European peoples, the Soviet imperial system simply collapsed. Its departure was hastened by the ill-advised cure of last-minute reform. As one Soviet economist put it, the physician who had hoped to heal the Soviet organism and preserve it, Mikhail Gorbachev, "accelerated a corpse." This is not to say that Gorbachev is not owed a debt of gratitude by the world. He is—but for what he did *not* do rather than what he did. His finest hour came when he refused to try to hold the Soviet bloc, or even the U.S.S.R. itself, together by force of arms, thus sparing his people and the world a civil war whose consequences would have been incalculably horrible.

Actually the downfall of communism represented the triumph of our system, not our values. Bombarded by television images of Western affluence, the peoples of the East became aware that our system worked as a method for distributing opportunity and wealth and that theirs did not. This point was made by a prominent European statesman who told me the following story: Just before the fall of the Berlin Wall, a man escaped over the top. Asked what had led him to leave home and family, he answered, "I did not come for your drug problem, your pornography, your crime, your poor schools. Our society was better than yours in some respects. I came because I want fair pay for my work, because I want to leave what I earn to my own family, and because I want to say and think what I like."

It behooves us to be humble as we end one epoch and begin another that, with luck and good management, may be far less dramatic. At this early stage, we know too little about the new epoch to characterize it, but, whatever it may be, it is not a new world order. There is no new world order, only new states rising from the old—Russia foremost among them—looking for an order different from the one that failed them. At the simplest level, there remain the old familiar camps of nations—those committed to democracy, the rule of law, and peaceful change and those still in the grip of leaders who practice tyranny, aggression, and terrorism to achieve their regressive ends. Herein lies our opportunity. If we can bring Russia and the other states emerging from the Communist debacle into the camp of democracy, then the prospect is vast and brilliant for lasting peace and social progress.

If we can hold our alliances together and keep our heads clear, we can reduce, if not entirely overcome, the murderous rivalries of the past and lay the groundwork for a future in which wars, fear, and poverty are as rare as the diseases that ravaged humanity in the Middle Ages and, one may hope, the ideological babble that crippled our capacity to reason and communicate in more recent times.

These are big *if*s. They depend, in turn, on another *if*, because the world here envisaged can only come into being if the United States of America is equal to the task of leadership. No other nation possesses the combination of economic and military power, of political and diplomatic relationships, or so enjoys the trust of other peoples and their governments. As Operation Desert Storm demonstrated, only the United States can do in the world at large what we did for so long in Europe and northeast Asia: articulate the common interest and rally a coalition on behalf of freedom and right. In the wake of the Soviet breakdown, we must resist the easy temptation to declare victory and go home, trusting in history and a new world order to do the job for us. Instead, we must look reality in the eye and accept the opportunity and the burden that it presents to us at this juncture in history.

Simultaneously with the fall of the U.S.S.R., the world has been transformed from a bipolar structure dominated by the two nuclear superpowers into a diverse community in which many new centers of economic, political, and military influence have come into existence and are now reaching the stage of lusty adolescence. That is good news. Cultural diversity and economic progress have long been the watchwords of American society, and we have never feared those characteristics in other nations, or envied them the success they bring. Our allies are alive and kicking and we no longer have to carry the burden of the world's troubles alone, nor would such an approach succeed in a multipolar world.

The reality of these developments is demonstrated by the somewhat hesitant progress toward the unification of Europe as a hospitable, outward-looking economic and political community; the emergence of Japan as the second-largest economy in the world; and the consolidation of the "four tigers of the Pacific," South Korea, Hong Kong, Taiwan, and Singapore (soon to be joined by Thailand and Malaysia and eventually by Indonesia) as powerful economic centers on the Pacific rim. China could become a superpower in fifty years or less. India is moving to revise its attachment to outmoded policies based on economic management from the center. In our own hemisphere, Mexico is taking hard-won steps toward a much brighter future, and the United States can certainly encourage and support a broadened free-trade area with Mexico, and, over time, with all of Latin America. Even the Middle East, for so long an exception to political trends elsewhere, could become a dramatic success story if the skills and potential of Arabs and Israelis can somehow be brought together, now that Soviet influence has receded.

Evolution from a bipolar to a multipolar world structure is, together with international interdependence, the controlling reality of the present and the wave of the future. We are moving from a world based on strife toward a dynamic global system based on diversity and new kinds of cooperation that will sustain it. Science and technology—especially communications and computer sciences—are breaking down atavistic tendencies toward national or regional isolation. Instantaneous communications bring about instantaneous reactions in many centers of influence and power all over the world. As the experience of the U.S.S.R. and its former satellites showed after television and telecommunications gained a foothold, no Iron Curtain or Berlin Wall can keep reality at bay. As the old saying has it, information is power; in the new world now building, information belongs to everyone. More and more, we live in a transparent world. Everyone on earth now inhabits the same electronic time zone— we see and hear what happens on the other side of the globe in the instant when it occurs. Although we have learned to take this for granted in a remarkably short period, this way of taking in information and processing it into thought, perception, and action is the most profound change in all of history in the way human beings live. As never before, every nation in the world is accountable to every other nation. The decisions of national leaders, including those of the President of the United States, must take the interwoven interests of the whole world into account.

In the new era that is evolving out of the old, America will play a more subtle role. It can no longer dominate the world or even a discrete portion of it. Our influence can be great, but it can never again be paramount. We must work with others in a more sensitive and collaborative way, sharing responsibilities, costs, and leadership as part of a coalition in which the interests of all parties are not submerged but counted as equals. The model for this sort of international interdependence was demonstrated in the Gulf War, in which President Bush understood that the United States, though first among equals, must act in close collaboration with a wide range of partners, each indispensable to the coalition.

In doing so, he overcame powerful opposition at home, partly through the influence of the United Nations and other international entities. As this experience suggests, the old distinctions between domestic policy and foreign policy no longer apply. Before a government acts at home, it must consider the consequences abroad—and vice versa. The new statecraft cannot act on the basis of a single overriding issue, as happened so often in the past. Rather, it must consider all of its interests in the light of all the global factors that influence them. Domestic economics cannot be separated from world economic factors. Domestic political considerations cannot drive foreign policy in an irrational direction; the question of trade barriers is an obvious example. Another is the continued United States military presence abroad. More than ever, the presence of American forces in Europe and Asia has powerful political, economic, and social implications quite apart from their military value. They are a symbol of American relevance, of American determination to help guarantee peaceful change no less in the future than in the past. If the United States is not seen to be relevant, if it does not lead from its great strengths, it will be ignored by other nations, not only in military but also in economic and political terms. The quality of life of our children and grandchildren will not remain what it has been for us, the standard of the world.

More than any other nation, the United States has benefited from the success of other free societies. Today, our domestic economy relies ever more heavily on free trade, real-time communications, and multilateral arrangements such as the General Agreement on Tariffs and Trade (GATT). An increasing portion of our gross national product is derived from exports, the fastest-growing segment of our economy. Our allies have also grown stronger.

The question is, Are we Americans ready to bring our thinking into harmony with these new realities? I am not so sure that we are. Philosophical confusion across the ideological spectrum has produced some of the strangest political bedfellows ever seen in our country. Old-style liberals and new-style conservatives are rallying around an attitude best described as the new isolationism. Liberals were once the conscience and driving force of U.S. international commitments. It was the liberals, stimulated by the Cold War, who moved this country from its traditional isolationism into an enlightened engagement with the rest of the world. But internationalism is not the force that drives liberals today. After Vietnam and Watergate, many liberals became estranged from the international role of the United States. The ills of American society—social and economic injustice, poor schools, the drug culture, a collapsing urban infrastructure—were blamed on the diversion of resources on behalf of a failed international vision.

While those who used to propel the United States outward now press it inward from the Left, many on the Right have joined in rejecting the realities of the international situation. As long ago as the dawn of the Reagan era, some believed, erroneously, that military buildup and tough rhetoric would enable the United States to reclaim the mantle of superpower from the mythical age of the late 1940s. Today, these conservatives want the United States to go it alone because they do not believe that the interests of the United States can truly be served if watered down or drained by the interests of other nations.

The actions of these unnatural bedfellows from the Left and the Right have been reinforced by the events in the former Soviet Union and by the current economic difficulties of the United States. Many on the Left would back the United States out of international commitments in the name of domestic need. Many on the Right would back the United States out of its alliances the better to go it alone. Nowhere is this more in evidence than in the debates and actions of the Congress of the United States. Americans should make no mistake about where this is leading our country. A sullen unilateralism that bashes our allies and embraces economic protectionism would make of the United States a wrecking force in a world already shaken by uncertainty.

These symptoms of confusion are not confined to the United States. They can be found in Europe, in the concept of the European Community as an exclusive club. The Continent, with its matchless economic and political experience, must be more open to world trade, more helpful and increasingly hospitable to the newly liberated countries of Central and Eastern Europe, and more receptive to the problems of the developing countries. The recent agreement between the European Community and the nations belonging to the European Free Trade Area and the overtures to Eastern Europe are good signs, although the negative vote in Denmark on EC membership suggests that historic reservations persist.

In Asia, especially Japan, many both fear and flirt with the protectionist idea of a world of trading blocs, each unto itself. But in the final analysis, our allies won't be any better than we are. If we encourage protectionism, they will surely not lag behind.

The preoccupations of Left and Right that feed a new American isolationism and economic nationalism are reinforced by a serious misinterpretation of the changes in Russia and the other nations of the old Soviet bloc. Now that they are nations in search of a constructive role once again, their fate is in their own hands. The Russians alone can make a new Russia; the Ukrainians, a new Ukraine; and so on. As events have already shown, the potential for ethnic strife and violence is very great. Power and bad memories are the driving forces and the genuine democrats are few and divided. The former Soviet peoples must invent a future for themselves in a world from which they have been quarantined for centuries, and no one can guess what that future will be. History is not encouraging. Soviet imperialism was preceded by two centuries of Czarist imperialism. Both were based on militarism, and it is not beyond the realm of possibility that a new arrangement of states dominated by Russia would be driven by the paranoia and imperial ambitions that have characterized the past.

These considerations do not relieve us of responsibility to try to help through our knowledge, our example, our moral convictions, and our very carefully controlled aid. Past experience in assisting less fortunate nations will not always be a reliable guide. The situation of the former Soviet republics is quite different, for example, from that of the European countries and Japan at the end of World War II. The operative word in the European Recovery Program (the Marshall Plan's proper name), was *recovery*. Germany and the other states of Europe were attempting to rebuild and improve infrastructures designed to support political and economic systems that had long existed before they were damaged in the war. To a degree, East Germany and Poland, Hungary and Czechoslovakia, and some of the other countries of Eastern Europe can be said to be in a process of recovery, despite the fact that more than fifty years have passed since they last governed themselves according to their national traditions.

This is not the case with the republics of the former Soviet Union. Although these peoples are highly educated by world standards and are the heirs to a remarkable culture, they have only dim memories of pre-Leninist political institutions and economic policies—and those, too, were disastrous in their own time. Our aid beyond the humanitarian must avoid the grandiose "macro" economic plans beloved by the bureaucrats of the International Monetary Fund. It should concentrate, instead, on the building up of true private enterprise, on breaking up the unfeasible state monopolies, on giving as many individuals as possible a personal stake in the economy. Russia's best safeguard against a reversion to tyranny is tyranny's opposite—diversity.

If the United States is going to lead the world into a new epoch of promise, then we had better take a good look at ourselves and make sure that we are worthy of a leader's role. Only Americans can renew America. Unlike other nations, we have always lived without the possibility of rescue in the event we mismanaged ourselves or our affairs. There is no other power on this planet possessed of a greater vision and greater altruism to bring us answers and assistance as happened when Americans appeared in Germany and Japan after 1945. Vision and altruism do, however, exist within ourselves; no nation has ever possessed such wealth in human resources or such an essential belief in the power of the people to set things right. It is time to remember that. But it is also the moment, in Lincoln's phrase, to "think anew."

There exists in the United States a pervasive sense of political crisis at the very moment when our system seems to have triumphed. It is time, and past time, for a redefinition of what we expect from our leaders. Some believe that the most successful President of the twentieth century after FDR was FDR's admirer and sometime-disciple Ronald Reagan. In his concentration on the importance of the ceremonial aspects of the presidency, Reagan resembled Charles de Gaulle of France. Like de Gaulle, whose intellectual gifts belonged to a somewhat higher category, Reagan was a very successful head of state, one of the most effective America had ever had. Acting with great consistency on the basis of a handful of simple principles in which he deeply believed and effectively communicated to others, Reagan used the symbolism of his office to accomplish great things. These included the restoration of patriotism to American life, the creation of an atmosphere of economic confidence that reflected his own sunny personality, and a sense that military primacy and domestic tranquillity had been restored to our country.

Unfortunately, it is not enough for an American President to be a good head of state. He must also be head of government, and in this Reagan was far less successful because he simply was not much interested in government. He distrusted it even when he was at its head, and he managed to detach himself from the doings of his own administration.

This ambivalence had devastating consequences with regard to our fiscal and social policies. Reagan seemed truly to believe that the government had no role to play in domestic social policy, instead of perceiving that it had merely been playing the wrong role. And because he did not seize the opportunity to use his great popularity to substitute a new domestic policy and a new vision of social justice, for the liberal programs that had so clearly failed, he handed over social policy to his worst enemies, the activist radicals who migrated during the 1980s from the campus movement into the law, the academic faculties, the churches, the news media, and, above all, the lobbies of Congress.

Reagan's passivity (followed by a long period in which his successor was almost totally distracted from domestic considerations by the dramatic developments in Russia and the Persian Gulf) hardened the divisions of an American political system that is more and more organized along ideological fault lines. During the Fourth Republic in France, a synonym for political chaos, the French regimented themselves into a myriad of small factions made up of people who agreed with one another absolutely and permitted no departure whatsoever from orthodoxy. Post-Vietnam America is in the process of achieving similar results through the proliferation of pressure groups that are indistinguishable from radical political parties in all respects except their preference for operating behind the scenes through the mechanism of the two great traditional parties.

This development has practically destroyed the Democratic party. It is so paralyzed by orthodoxy that it has been unable since the fall of Lyndon Johnson to express any new ideas or produce from within its traditional apparatus a candidate capable of being elected President. In my last book, I wrote of the Democratic party that "if it does not change it will die— and if it changes, it will die."[2] Democratic control of Congress has turned that body into a mirror image of the enfeebled party itself.

The clearest consequences of these political deformations are to be seen in the federal budget deficit. According to the Office of Management and Budget, this now amounts to $399.7 billion. In 1987, when I engaged in an admittedly hopeless campaign for the Republican nomination for President, I held up the crash of the stock market as an example of the seriousness of the budget deficit and the political deadlock it symbolized.

Most of my opponents and most of the news media, bathed like the rest of the country in the afterglow of the Reagan prosperity, did not want to hear it.

Today we regard the problem in the harsher light of a long recession. Facts:

- In only a few years, interest payments on the national debt will equal defense expenditures.
- In 1965, when the federal budget was $126 billion, 66 percent of spending was "discretionary"—that is, Congress had to vote on it. In fiscal year 1985, when the budget was $994 billion, 58 percent of spending was *not* discretionary—that is, Congress could not vote on it because of interest payments and because the law mandates automatic payments (the so-called "entitlements") to millions of Americans under Social Security, Medicare, Medicaid, and welfare programs. In other words, more than half of the federal budget is now devoted to interest and entitlements, with just over 40 percent left over for all the other expenses of government, including defense, highway construction, the environment, regulation of commerce, and so on. In 1995, when the budget will be approximately $1.6 trillion, it is estimated that we will spend 65 percent of the annual budget, or slightly more than $1 trillion, on mandatory interest and entitlements.[3]

Because Congress has legislated away control of the budget in favor of entitlements and Presidents have permitted this to happen, the government in Washington has largely lost its capability to offset economic cycles by adjustments in federal spending. Instead, the Federal Reserve Board regulates the economy through changes in the interest rate, a slow and uncertain process that has been compared to shaving a man with a battle-ax—you take off the whiskers but a lot more, too.

The Reagan and Bush administrations contributed to these problems by encouraging a very high level of consumer consumption that was supported mostly by borrowed foreign capital, while personal and corporate savings in the United States remained below desirable levels. Regrettably, the willingness of foreign governments and foreign investors to finance our deficit through massive purchases of U.S. Treasury issues has tended to perpetuate abnormal levels of consumption. Our enormous budget deficits have adversely affected our ability to create capital and our productive capacity. This lack of fiscal and monetary discipline has heightened fears among our trading partners that the United States is simply unable to put its own house in order.

A spendthrift Congress shares the responsibility for the unhappy state of fiscal affairs in the United States. But the Executive Branch has also failed to live up to its obligations. President Reagan cut taxes, but he was a practicing populist despite his claim to being a philosophical conservative, and he was loath to influence, if not control, spending by a determined use of the presidential veto. President Bush has used the veto somewhat more aggressively (thirty-one times by July 8, 1992), but his unwise compromise with the congressional leadership on taxes and the budget in 1990 ignored entitlements, the real wrecker of budgets and rational fiscal policy.

The budget deficit is an enormous but, for the time being, manageable problem. Corrective action will be painful but far less so than the consequences of further delay in confronting the problem. The deficit cannot be brought under control by a constitutional amendment or a line-item veto or any other attempt to legislate fiscal responsibility. Solvency is a moral question, as every mortgage holder knows, because its loss has the most profound human consequences.

The first order of business must be to establish the goal of achieving a balanced budget over an eight- to ten-year period. Obviously, this requires that which has so long eluded us—a genuine partnership in responsibility between Congress and the Executive Branch. The manipulation of the budget for political advantage must cease.

Annual economic growth rates will play a vital role in determining precise measures to be taken. Exports will remain in the near term the locomotive of economic growth, and policies that place export growth in jeopardy must be avoided. Our enormous expenditures for defense and social programs—especially, I say again, entitlements—must be brought to reasonable levels. In years of prosperity, the raising of additional revenue will also be in order. Americans do not resist necessary taxation when they believe that their money is being put to good use. They will support these measures because they understand that continued failure to deal with the deficit is a mindless policy that not only erodes our quality of life and our productive capacity but also contributes to a perception of American incompetence that undermines our ability to compete in the global marketplace.

Because we were preoccupied with the Cold War, we tended not to deal with such questions as education and health-care provision in a clearheaded fashion. No nation on earth spends as much on such activities with so little rational return. We have failed to maintain our national infrastructure in a state of complete modernity. Other shortfalls in planning and execution of the national agenda exist, and we must concentrate on them, not only because it is right to do so but because a people that is proud of its country takes satisfaction from the visible manifestations of its underlying principles. The United States should not have people living in the streets, or people who cannot read, or people who have no access to basic medical treatments or catastrophic medical care.

Above all, we must take up the work of establishing real social justice for all. If reducing the budget deficit is the key to economic stability and growth, the key to social change has to do with race relations and poverty—especially as these affect ghetto dwellers. The intent of the Great Society programs was to relieve misery; their effect has been to increase it by concentrating it in ghettos that have become the focal points of substandard housing, unemployment, violent crime, drug trafficking and addiction, the breakdown of the family, and disease. From 1987 to 1989, the rate of fatal shootings of black teenage males in Washington, D.C., was 227 per 100,000, and in 1991 one in every nineteen black men who applied for enlistment in the armed services from the nation's capital tested positive for the AIDS virus.[4] Everyone knows that human wastage of this kind would not be tolerated in the white community.

In what remains of the twentieth century, the United States must come to terms at last with this bedrock dilemma, and it must do so by confronting the question of race in an honest and open discussion based on the realities of the situation. This is not a job for pressure groups. We are, after all, not without a model for a color-blind meritocracy that produces just results. The armed forces of the United States were ordered to eliminate discrimination by President Truman in 1950 and succeeded in doing so to a truly remarkable degree. The military did not eliminate racism, a human prejudice ultimately beyond the reach of government. It did something better—it made it irrelevant by setting up tests of performance that applied to everyone without favor or exception. Unless we revive the basic American concept of excellence as the key to the door of opportunity, we will repeat the failures of the past.

Solutions to the appalling problems spawned by the ghettos have tended to concentrate on improving conditions through tax breaks, nonexistent jobs, restructured welfare, illusory local control, politically correct rhetoric, and other artifices designed to mollify public opinion. The effect has been to entrap the poorest of the poor. Clearly this is a profoundly racist policy.

Social policy should not perpetuate a bad situation by futile attempts to improve it but should focus instead on eliminating the ghettos. There is evidence enough that these wretched slums within our otherwise just and prosperous and peaceful cities destroy human life by denying its value, and that the main hope of most who live in them is to escape. At the same time, it is evident that the central American experience—to climb out of poverty by means of education, hard work, sacrifice by one generation of strong families on behalf of the next, and the broadening of opportunity to embrace one class of immigrants after another—has not applied to the ghetto.

We should work toward establishing conditions that make racism irrelevant. This means establishing a national timetable for breaking up the ghettos, just as we have done in the past with regard to the integration of the armed services, the space program, the construction of the transcontinental railroad, and many other projects. All of these undertakings have had one thing in common besides a deadline and a benefit shared by all: They brought the country closer together.

The greatest of all entitlements is the opportunity to do something useful every day; everything else flows from that. Work and private endeavor must replace the system of bribes and conscience money that created the ghettos in the first place. President Bush rallied the nation in the Gulf War with the promise that Saddam Hussein's aggression "will not stand." The next President can win a greater victory in American cities than our fighting men and women won in the Arabian desert by making the same promise with regard to social injustice at home. But he must be strong, converting the opposition instead of placating it, and he must keep on until the end; this time the villain must not escape to wreak further murder and mayhem.

Finally, we must, as a nation, get back to saying what we mean and meaning what we say. As Secretary of State, I acquired a certain reputation for befuddling rhetoric—Haigspeak—because in diplomacy it sometimes seemed more useful not to be understood than to be misunderstood. But circumlocution is a bad habit when the subject under discussion is the internal problems of the great American democracy. When I was young, Americans said pretty much what was on their minds without fear or favor; when a statement was particularly outrageous, those who found it so would shrug their shoulders and say, "Well, it's a free country!"

That was the homespun equivalent of Voltaire's passionate (and probably apocryphal) "I disapprove of what you say, but I will defend to the death your right to say it."

One of the most important factors in American policy during the Cold War was the pervasive belief among Western intellectuals that Marxist-Leninists were somehow morally superior to democratic capitalists. There was a feeling that the Soviet Union, if given the benefit of every possible doubt, would evolve into the paragon of just and peace-loving states. This perception, which was most noticeable in an exaggerated admiration for the enemy in the Korean and Vietnam wars, seems to have had its origins in the exhilaration idealists all over the world felt as a result of the 1917 Russian Revolution. Coming as it did at a moment of profound worldwide disillusionment with the old order, bolshevism was welcomed by many intellectuals with the uncritical faith of religious converts.

Out of this came a new way of looking at the world politically, in which visible reality played little part. A kind of demented skepticism became fashionable among the educated classes. The United States was described as an imperialist, colonialist power whose technological superiority made her the true enemy of mankind—even of nature itself. This suited the Marxian conception, as George F. Kennan summarized it, that "imperialism, the final phase of capitalism, leads directly to war and revolution."[5] The grotesque companion to this denial of reality was the pretense that the mother country of socialism, which gave every surface indication of being murderous, socially unjust, and economically disastrous, was in fact a model of virtue.

Those who held to these beliefs got into the habit of falsifying not only history but also the facts of daily life, and the most worrisome heritage of the Cold War is this habit of distorting reality. By no means is it any longer confined to the Left. It has implanted itself in American life to an extent that makes the rational discussion of our problems as a nation very difficult.

The loss of candor is grievous, and in my opinion it may yet prove to be mortal, because if we cannot discuss our problems in plain speech that describes reality, it is unlikely that we will be able to solve them.

I have been aware as this narrative was being composed that a memoir is, in a sense, an epitaph, a tale of deeds done and deeds left undone, and also the story of a journey through events and a renewal of acquaintances with the human beings who set them in motion. In my long tour of duty, I saw more than most, and at every stage I was given cause to reflect on the saying that those who do not learn from history are likely to repeat its mistakes. Yet one of America's greatest strengths lies in the fact that she has never been in thrall to history. Our country has made a great and wonderful history for herself and for the things she touched in the world because Americans have always lived in the future and for the future.

Our policy in the Cold War, expressed in the most fundamental terms, was to save the future from destruction. Having done so with the help of God and our allies, we must not think in terms of celebrating a victory but, rather, in terms of building a peace so strong and just that the question of the destruction of civilization may never arise again.

The construction of that peace must begin at home. Social justice, like the justice of laws, must not only be done, it must also be seen to be done. An American true to itself is an example to the world. The work of my own generation of Americans is almost done. Its epitaph, I hope, will be this: They made possible a future that redeemed by its justice the suffering of their own time.

A NOTE ON SOURCES

In the making of this book, I have relied primarily on my own memory of events, checked against the recollections of other participants where possible, and verified by my papers, which are in the custody of the Library of Congress. I also consulted a wide range of books, articles, government documents, and news stories. Nothing herein is based on classified sources, although the verbatim dialogue between President Nguyen Van Thieu and me is drawn from memoranda of conversations that were declassified by the National Security Council staff, which coordinated the clearance of the manuscript for security purposes.

The fact that I am the last senior member of the Nixon White House staff to write about the administration has caused me to bear in mind the extensive record already published by my colleagues. I did not always remember things as they did. In cases where I was present at the event described, I have adhered to my own recollection, and in some cases this has produced contradictions to existing accounts. These will, I hope, be accepted for what they are: an attempt to augment the historical record.

A. M. H.

NOTES

1. HAIGS AND MURPHYS

1. "X" (George F. Kennan), "The Sources of Soviet Conduct," *Foreign Affairs* (June 1947): pp. 566ff.

2. Richard H. Rovere and Arthur M. Schlesinger, Jr., *The General and the President* (New York: Farrar, Straus, and Young, 1951), pp. 183–184.

3. Kennan, p. 569.

2. COUNCILS OF WAR

1. Courtney Whitney, *MacArthur: His Rendezvous with Destiny* (New York: Alfred A. Knopf, 1956), p. 320.

2. Roy E. Appleman, *United States Army in the Korean War; South to the Naktong, North to the Yalu* (Washington, D.C.: U.S. Department of the Army, 1961), p. 8ff.

3. Jerrold L. Schecter et al., *Khrushchev Remembers: The Glasnost Tapes* (Boston: Little, Brown and Company, 1990), p. 146.

4. Dean Acheson, *Present at the Creation* (New York: W. W. Norton & Co., 1969), p. 424.

5. Ibid., pp. 764–765. Acheson claimed to have meant no such thing, but even his own recollection of his words (the speech was made from notes) suggests that the language was ambiguous on the key question of whether the United States would defend South Korea if it were attacked. The words, as cited by Acheson in his book read: "This defensive perimeter runs along the Aleutians to Japan and then goes to the Ryukus . . . to the Philippines . . . so far as the security of the other areas of the Pacific is concerned, it

must be clear that no person can guarantee these areas against military attack. . . . Should such an attack occur . . . the initial reliance must be on the people attacked to resist it and then upon the commitments of the entire civilized world under the Charter of the U. N. which so far has not proved a weak reed to lean on by any people who are determined to protect their independence against outside aggression."

6. Quoted in Richard H. Rovere and Arthur M. Schlesinger, Jr., *The General and the President* (New York: Farrar, Straus, and Young, 1951), p. 187.

7. Douglas A. MacArthur, *Reminiscences* (New York: McGraw-Hill, 1964), p. 386.

8. Acheson, p. 407.

9. Whitney, p. 322.

10. Harry S Truman, *Memoirs*, vol. 2 (Garden City, NY: Doubleday and Company, 1956), p. 334.

11. Whitney, p. 326.

12. Appleman, p. 50.

13. U.S. Senate, Foreign Relations Committee, Senate Document no. 69, 82nd Congress (Washington, D.C.: U.S. Senate, September 5, 1959), p. 19.

14. Appleman, p. 49ff.

15. Ibid., p. 50ff.

16. Robert Dels Heinl, Jr., *Victory at High Tide: The Inchon-Seoul Campaign*, 3d. Ed. (The Nautical and Aviation Publishing Company of America, 1979), p. 42.

17. Whitney, p. 344.

18. Ibid., p. 341.

19. Ibid., p. 343.

20. Ibid.

21. William L. Sebald, *With MacArthur in Japan* (New York: W. W. Norton, 1965), p. 197.

22. MacArthur, p. 422.

23. Ibid., p. 339.

24. Sebald, p. 189.

25. Truman, pp. 342–343.

26. MacArthur Archives, "Command and Staff Visit to Formosa, 31 July–1 August 1950."

27. Ibid.

28. JCS 87860, dated 4 August 1950.

29. Fox Report, pp. 9–20.

30. General Headquarters Far East Command CX 59840, dated 11 August 1950.

31. Heinl, p. 10; and author's recollection of statements by MacArthur.

32. MacArthur, p. 349.

33. R. Ernest Dupuy and Trevor N. Dupuy, *The Encyclopedia of Military History* (New York: Harper & Row, 1986), p. 1241.

34. Heinl, p. 47 ff.

35. Ibid., p. 24.

36. Quoted in Heinl, p. 41.

37. MacArthur, p. 350.

38. Ibid., p. 349.

39. Ibid., p. 350.

3. MEETING THE ENEMY

1. Roy E. Appleman, *United States Army in the Korean War; South to the Naktong, North to the Yalu* (Washington, D.C.: U.S. Department of the Army, 1961), pp. 504–506.

2. Robert Dels Heinl, Jr., *Victory at High Tide: The Inchon-Seoul Campaign*, 3d. ed. (The Nautical and Aviation Publishing Company of America, 1979), p. 93.

3. Ibid., p. 75.

4. "Personal Notes of Lt. Gen. E. M. Almond Covering Military Operations in Korea Sept. 1950–July 1951," entry for 16 September 1950.

5. Ibid.

6. Ibid., entry for 18 September.

7. Douglas A. MacArthur, *Reminiscences* (New York: McGraw-Hill, 1964), pp. 359–360.

8. Ibid., p. 360.

9. Almond, entries for 20–21 September.

10. Appleman, p. 527ff.

11. Almond, entry for 21 September.

12. Ibid., entry for 22 September.

13. Ibid., entry for 25 September.

14. Appleman, p. 541.

15. Heinl, p. 263.

16. Courtney Whitney, *MacArthur: His Rendezvous with Destiny* (New York: Alfred A. Knopf, 1956), p. 401.

17. MacArthur, p. 355ff.

18. Ibid., p. 355.

19. Jerrold L. Schecter et al., *Khrushchev Remembers: The Glasnost Tapes* (Boston: Little, Brown & Company, 1990), p. 147.

20. Ibid.

21. Ibid.

22. Whitney, p. 330.

23. Dean Acheson, *Present at the Creation* (New York: W. W. Norton & Co., 1969), p. 449.

24. *New York Times*, October 2, 1950.

25. Harry S Truman, *Memoirs*, vol. 2 (Garden City, NY: Doubleday and Company, 1956), p. 361ff.

26. Acheson, p. 452.

27. Ironically, Johnson, who resigned a few days before the Inchon landing, had been one of MacArthur's most powerful backers in connection with this operation. At the MacArthur hearings, he testified, "General Collins—maybe the censor will want to strike this out—did not favor Inchon and went over [to Japan] to argue General MacArthur out of it. . . . I back MacArthur. . . ."

28. Whitney, p. 451.

29. Ibid., p. 392.

30. MacArthur, p. 362.

31. Quoted in Heinl, p. 76. The journalist was Howard Handleman of the International News Service.

32. Truman, p. 375.

33. Ibid., p. 382.

34. Whitney, p. 408.

4. "FIERCE ACTIONS"

1. Roy E. Appleman, *United States Army in the Korean War; South to the Naktong, North to the Yalu* (Washington, D.C.: U.S. Department of the Army, 1961), p. 646.

2. "Personal Notes of Lt. Gen. E. M. Almond Covering Military Operations in Korea Sept. 1950–July 1951," entry for 22 October 1950 et seq.

3. Quoted in Richard H. Rovere and Arthur M. Schlesinger, Jr., *The General and the President* (New York: Farrar, Straus, and Young, 1951), p. 189.

4. Almond, entries for 23 and 24 October.

5. Ibid., entry for 24 October.

6. Douglas A. MacArthur, *Reminiscences* (New York: McGraw-Hill, 1964), p. 368.

7. Almond, entry for 28 October.

8. Ibid., entry for 31 October.

9. Appleman, p. 744.

10. Almond, entry for 30 October.

11. Ibid., entry for 18 October.

12. Ibid., entry for 6 November.

13. MacArthur, p. 366.

14. Ibid., p. 362. Truman later wrote that MacArthur "informed me that the Chinese Communists would not attack" (Truman, *Memoirs*, p. 365). MacArthur calls this "a prevarication" (p. 362).

15. Billy C. Mossman, *United States Army in the Korean War: Ebb and Flow, November 1950–July 1951* (Washington, D.C.: Department of the Army, 1990), p. 65.

16. MacArthur, p. 72.

17. Almond, entry for 21 November.

18. MacArthur, p. 72. "We had often dreamed and boasted during the fighting of 'watering our horses in the Rhine,' but now that we were there, the exaltation seemed to have disappeared. In its place came the realization of the inherent dignity and stature of the great German nation."

19. Appleman, p. 737.

20. Almond, entry for 23 November.

21. Mossman, p. 49.

22. Ibid., p. 48.

23. Almond, entry for 10 November.

24. Ibid., entry for 26 November.

25. Ibid., entry for 27 November.

26. Mossman, p. 89.

27. James McGovern, *To the Yalu* (New York: William Morrow & Co., 1972), p. 107.

28. Almond, entry for 29 November.

29. Mossman, p 99.

30. Almond, entry for 4 December.

31. Mossman, pp. 132–136.

32. Roy E. Appleman, *Escaping the Trap* (College Station, TX: Texas A. & M. University Press, 1990), p. 303; and author's recollection. Chinese officers and men taken prisoner reported to X Corps interpreters that as many as half the men in their units were disabled by frostbite.

33. Ibid., p. 352ff.

34. MacArthur, p. 374.

35. Almond, entry for 24 December.

36. John Foster Dulles, speech before Council on Foreign Relations, January 1954.

37. Mossman, p. 56.

38. Ibid., pp. 502–503.

39. 1990 *World Almanac & Book of Facts* (New York: Scripps Howard Books, 1990), p. 792.

40. Mossman, p. 502.

41. Appleman, *United States Army in the Korean War*, p. 653.

42. Ulysses S. Grant, *Personal Memoirs* (New York: The Library of America, 1990), p. 115.

43. Dean Acheson, *Present at the Creation* (New York: W. W. Norton & Co., 1969), p. 521.

44. U.S. Senate, 82nd Congress, 1st session, Document no. 69, *Individual Views of Certain Members of the Joint Committee on Armed Services and Foreign Relations* (Washington, D.C.: U.S. Senate, 1951), p. 40.

45. Dean Rusk, *As I Saw It* (New York, W. W. Norton & Co., 1990), p. 164.

5. ARMY LIFE

1. *The Pointer*, November 25, 1955, p. 10.

6. A TRIP TO IRAN

1. Yonah Alexander and Allen Nanes, eds., *The United States and Iran: A Documentary History* (Frederick, MD: University Publishers of America, 1980), p. 318.

2. Ibid., p. 333.

3. Ibid., p. 324.

4. Mohamed Heikal, *Iran: The Untold Story* (New York: Pantheon Books, 1982), p. 72.

5. Alexander and Nanes, p. 348.

6. Ibid., p. 321.

7. Ibid., 318.

8. William Shawcross, *The Shah's Last Ride* (New York: Simon & Schuster, 1988), p. 84.

9. Alexander and Nanes, p. 318.

10. U.S. Department of Defense, "Iran: Report of the U.S. Military Planning Team" (Washington, D.C.: July 20, 1962), p. 5.

7. MISSILES AND MYTHOLOGY

1. Thomas C. Reeves, *A Question of Character: A Life of John F. Kennedy* (New York: Free Press, 1991), pp. 264, 269.

2. Ibid., p. 271.

3. Quoted in Warren I. Cohen, *Dean Rusk* (Totowa, NJ: Cooper Square Publishers, 1980), p. 137.

4. Arthur M. Schlesinger, Jr., *A Thousand Days* (Boston: Houghton Mifflin, 1965), pp. 370–374. *See also* Reeves, pp. 301–302.

5. Jerrold L. Schecter et al., *Khrushchev Remembers: The Glasnost Tapes* (Boston: Little, Brown & Company, 1990), p. 169n.

6. Cohen, p. 141.

7. Schecter, p. 169.

8. Ibid.

9. Schlesinger, pp. 391, 394–396.

10. Ibid., p. 395–396.

11. Quoted in Schlesinger, p. 308.

12. George F. Kennan, *Memoirs: 1950–1963* (New York: Pantheon, 1972), pp. 337, 343.

13. Schlesinger, p. 311.

14. Quoted in Schlesinger, p. 310.

15. Cohen, p. 195.

16. Russell F. Weigley, *The American Way of War* (New York: Macmillan & Co., 1983), p. 456.

17. Schlesinger, p. 341.

18. Dwight D. Eisenhower, *Waging Peace* (Garden City, NY: Doubleday, 1965), p. 536.

19. Cohen, p. 151.

20. Reeves, p. 369; Schecter, pp. 170–183.

21. Robert D. Crane, "The Cuban Crisis: A Strategic Analysis of American and Soviet Policy," *Orbis* (Winter 1963): p. 537.

22. Weigley, p. 441.

23. Ibid., p. 442.

24. Ibid., p. 453; Reeves, p. 365.

25. *Washington Post*, January 28, 1989, p. 22.

26. Weigley, p. 453.

27. Ibid., p. 448.

28. Quoted in "The Cuban Crisis: A Documentary Record," *Headline Series* no. 157 (January–February 1963): p. 74.

29. Schecter, p. 172.

30. Ibid., p. 182.

31. Reeves, p. 375.

32. Elie Abel, *The Missiles of October* (New York: MacGibbon & Kee, 1966), p. 173.

33. Ibid., p. 176.

34. *Washington Post*, February 5, 1989, p. D7.

35. Reeves, p. 375.

36. Quoted in Arthur M. Schlesinger, Jr., *Robert Kennedy and His Times* (Boston, Houghton-Mifflin, 1978), p. 524.

37. Robert F. Kennedy, *Thirteen Days: A Memoir of the Cuban Missile Crisis* (New York: W. W. Norton, 1971), pp. 86–87.

38. Schlesinger, *Robert Kennedy and His Times*, p. 523.

39. Schecter, p. 182.

40. Schlesinger, A *Thousand Days*, p. 833.

8. COVERT ACTIONS

1. Public Papers of the Presidents of the United States, John F. Kennedy, January 1 to December 31, 1962 (Washington, D.C.: 1963), p. 556.

2. Thomas C. Reeves, A *Question of Character: A Life of John F. Kennedy* (New York: Free Press, 1991), p. 277.

3. Arthur M. Schlesinger, Jr., A *Thousand Days* (Boston: Houghton Mifflin, 1965), pp. 275–276. "By early Tuesday it was clear that the invasion was in trouble. . . . The President asked me to luncheon with James Reston [of the *New York Times*]. In spite of the news, Kennedy was free, calm, and candid; I had rarely seen him more effectively in control. Saying frankly that reports from the beaches were discouraging, he spoke with detachment about the problems he would now face. 'I probably made a mistake in keeping Allen Dulles on,' he said. . . . As for CIA, 'we will have to do something. . . . Bobby should be in CIA. It is a hell of a way to learn things, but I have learned one thing from this business—that is that we will have to deal with CIA. McNamara has dealt with Defense, Rusk has done a lot with State; but no one has dealt with CIA.' " *See also* Allen Dulles, *The Craft of Intelligence* (New York: Harper & Row, 1963), p. 169: "While I have not commented on any details of the 1961 Cuban operation and do not propose to do so here, I repeat now what I have said publicly before: I know of no estimate that a spontaneous uprising of the unarmed population of Cuba would be touched off by the landing. . . . Much of the American press assumed at the time that this action [the Bay of Pigs landing] was predicated on a mistaken intelligence estimate to the effect that a landing would touch off a widespread and popular revolt in Cuba. Those who had worked, as I had, with the anti-Hitler underground behind the Nazi lines in France and Italy and in Germany itself during World War II and those who watched the tragedy of the Hungarian patriots in 1956 would have realized that spontaneous revolutions by unarmed people in this modern age are ineffective and often disastrous."

4. Jerrold L. Schecter et al., *Khrushchev Remembers: The Glasnost Tapes* (Boston: Little, Brown, and Company, 1990), p. 172.

5. *Alleged Assassination Plots Involving Foreign Leaders, An Interim Report of the Select Committee to Study Government Operations with Regard to Intelligence Activities*, U.S. Senate, pp. 217–218. (Facsimile edition, New York: W. W. Norton, 1976, p. 173.)

6. Ibid.

7. Ibid, p. 89: "The [CIA] Inspector General's report noted that 'it is likely that at the very moment President Kennedy was shot, a CIA officer was meeting with a Cuban agent * * * and giving him an assassination device for use against Castro.' "

8. Although he testified before the Select Committee to Study Government Operations with Regard to Intelligence Activities (the Church committee) that he had never discussed the assassination of Castro with President Kennedy or Robert Kennedy, Gen. Edward G. Lansdale, the architect of Operation Mongoose, is quoted as saying, after the death of both Kennedy brothers, that he had no doubts, on the basis of his conversations with Robert Kennedy, that "the project for disposing of Castro envisioned the whole spectrum of plans from overthrowing the Cuban leader to assassinating him" (Victor Lasky, *It Didn't Start with Watergate* [New York: Dial Press, 1977], p. 86). *See also* the *Washington Star-News*, May 31, 1975. In the August 1975 issue of *Harper's Magazine*, Lansdale was

quoted as saying that "both Kennedys wanted 'to bring Castro down. . . . I feel certain that they had that emotion in them until they were both killed. . . . But Bobby felt even more strongly about it than Jack. He was protective of his brother, and he felt his brother had been insulted at the Bay of Pigs. He felt the insult needed to be redressed rather quickly.' " According to testimony before the Church committee, the President himself raised the option of assassination in at least two conversations, one with the journalist Tad Szulc on November 9, 1961, and another in the same year with former Senator George Smathers of Florida. Szulc testified: "President Kennedy asked 'What would you think if I ordered Castro to be assassinated?' " Szulc's notes of this interview read, in part: "JFK said he was under terrific pressure from advisers (think he said intelligence people but not positive) to okay a Castro murder. Sed [sic] he was resisting pressures." Smathers told the committee that during a walk on the White House lawn, "President Kennedy asked me what reaction I thought there would be throughout Latin America if Fidel Castro were assassinated. . . . I disapproved of it, and he completely disapproved of the idea." Richard Helms, afterward Director of Central Intelligence, who was the CIA's Deputy Director of Plans (i.e., clandestine operations) during the period in question, testified: "No member of the Administration . . . ever told me that [assassination] was proscribed [or] ever referred to it in that fashion. . . . Nobody ever said that assassination was ruled out." See *Alleged Assassination Plots*, pp. 138, 123, 149.

9. Allegations that the Eisenhower Administration contemplated the assassination of Patrice Lumumba, the left-wing Congolese leader who was killed by his enemies in the Congo (now Zaire) in 1960, were based on the testimony of Robert H. Johnson, a notetaker at an NSC meeting attended by Eisenhower, who testified before the Church committee as follows: "Eisenhower said something—I can no longer remember his words—that came across to me as an order for the assassination of Lumumba. . . ." Later in his testimony, Johnson said, "I must confess that in thinking about the incident more recently I have had some doubts." See *Alleged Assassination Plots*, p. 55.

10. Lasky, p. 88.

11. Joseph A. Califano, Jr., *The Triumph and Tragedy of Lyndon Johnson; The White House Years* (New York: Simon & Schuster, 1991), p. 295. See also "Letters to the Editor," the *Wall Street Journal*, January 28, 1992.

12. *Alleged Assassination Plots*, p. 180. In his book *The Last Days of the President*, and in testimony before the Church committee, Leo Janis reported that Johnson had told him, in an interview in 1971, that he had discovered, on taking office, that "we had been running a damned Murder, Inc., in the Caribbean."

13. William H. Harris and Judith S. Levey, eds., *The New Columbia Encyclopedia* (New York: Columbia University Press, 1975), p. 2028.

14. Califano, p. 295; *Wall Street Journal*, January 28, 1992.

9. THE GULF OF TONKIN

1. United States Senate, "The Gulf of Tonkin, the 1964 Incidents," Hearing Before the Committee on Foreign Relations, 90th Congress, 2nd Session, February 20, 1968 (Washington, D.C.: U.S. Senate, 1968), p. 10.

2. Joseph C. Goulden, *Truth is the First Casualty: The Gulf of Tonkin Affair—Illusion and Reality* (Chicago: Rand-McNally, 1969), p. 259.

3. Ibid., p. 260.

4. Ibid.

5. *U.S. News & World Report*, July 23, 1984, p. 64ff.

6. United States Senate, p. 73.

7. Ibid.

8. Goulden, p. 261.

9. Ibid., p. 256ff.

10. United States Senate, p. 57.

10. VIETNAM: THE ILLUSION

1. R. B. Smith, *An International History of the Vietnam War*, vol. 1 (New York: St. Martin's Press, 1983), p. 14.

2. Thomas C. Reeves, *A Question of Character: A Life of John F. Kennedy* (New York: Free Press, 1991), p. 285.

3. Smith, p. 40ff.; Edward Geary Lansdale, *In the Midst of Wars* (New York: Harper & Row, 1972), pp. 245–322.

4. Lansdale, p. 334.

5. Smith, p. 35.

6. Ibid.

7. Ibid., p. 193

8. Ibid., p. 190.

9. Ibid., p. 187.

10. R. B. Smith, *An International History of the Vietnam War: The Kennedy Strategy*, vol. 2 (New York: St. Martin's Press, 1985), p. 27; Lyndon Johnson, *The Vantage Point* (New York: Holt, Rinehart and Winston, 1971), p. 42.

11. Arthur M. Schlesinger, Jr., *A Thousand Days* (Boston: Houghton Mifflin, 1965), p. 315.

12. Johnson, p. 54.

13. Warren I. Cohen, *Dean Rusk* (Totowa, NJ: Cooper Square Publishers, 1980), pp. 179–180.

14. Ibid., p. 181.

15. Russell F. Weigley, *The American Way of War* (New York: Macmillan & Co., 1983), p. 456.

16. Smith, vol. 2, p. 171.

17. Schlesinger, p. 363.

18. Ibid., p. 341.

19. Robert E. Osgood, *Limited War: The Challenge to American Strategy*; quoted in Weigley, p. 412.

20. Quoted in Schlesinger, p. 342.

21. Quoted in Cohen, pp. 185–187.

22. Quoted in Johnson, p. 61.

23. Smith, vol. 1, p. 26. (China did station troops in northern Laos in this period, but this action seems to have been unconnected to any intention to move into Vietnam.)

24. *Alleged Assassination Plots Involving Foreign Leaders, An Interim Report of the Select Committee to Study Government Operations with Regard to Intelligence Activities*, U.S. Senate, pp. 217–218. (Facsimile edition, New York: W. W. Norton, 1976.)

25. Johnson, p. 138.

26. Arthur M. Schlesinger, Jr., *Robert Kennedy and His Times* (Boston, Houghton Mifflin, 1978), pp. 718–720.

27. *Alleged Assassination Plots*, pp. 218–219.

28. Johnson, p. 63.

29. Weigley, pp. 221, 467.

11. VIETNAM: THE CHEMISTRY

1. Quoted in Warren I. Cohen, *Dean Rusk* (Totowa, NJ: Cooper Square Publishers, 1980), p. 237.

2. Memorandum to the President from McNamara, dated April 21, 1965, quoted in Gareth Porter, ed., *Vietnam: A History in Documents* (New York: New American Library, 1981); Report by McNamara on visit to South Vietnam, dated November 30, 1965, quoted in Porter, p. 323.

3. Dean Acheson, *Present at the Creation* (New York: W. W. Norton & Co., 1969), p. 489.

4. Cohen, p. 236.

5. Lester A. Sobel, ed., *South Vietnam: U.S.-Communist Confrontation in Southeast Asia, 1961–1965* (New York: Facts on File, 1969), pp. 131–133.

6. Telegram from Rusk to Taylor, dated February 13, 1965; quoted in Porter, p. 301.

7. Sobel, p. 132.

8. R. B. Smith, *An International History of the Vietnam War: The Kennedy Strategy*, vol. 2 (New York: St. Martin's Press, 1985), p. 378.

9. Sobel, pp. 133–134.

10. Cohen, p. 250.

11. Harry G. Summers, Jr., *Vietnam War Almanac* (New York: Facts on File, 1985), p. 34.

12. Lyndon Johnson, *The Vantage Point* (New York: Holt, Rinehart and Winston, 1971), pp. 138, 233.

13. Quoted in Sobel, p. 170.

14. Quoted in Porter, p. 330.

15. Sobel, p. 139.

16. Memorandum from Ball to the President, dated July 1, 1965; quoted in Porter, p. 314.

17. Porter, p. 343ff. passim.

18. Cohen, p. 247.

19. U.S. Department of State Memorandum of Conversation, dated November 3, 1967; quoted in Porter, p. 350.

20. Editorial in *Jen-Min Jih Pao*, November 11, 1965; quoted in Porter, p. 320.

21. Johnson, p. 246.

22. Ibid., pp. 233, 246.

23. Ibid., pp. 148, 149.

24. Carl von Clausewitz, *On War*, ed. and trans. Michael Howard and Peter Paret (Princeton, NJ: Princeton University Press, 1976), p. 75.

25. Johnson, p. 241.

26. Memorandum from McNamara to the President, dated July 20, 1965; quoted in Porter, p. 319.

12. VIETNAM: THE REALITY

1. Harry G. Summers, Jr., *Vietnam War Almanac* (New York: Facts on File, 1985), pp. 33–40.

2. *First Infantry Division in Vietnam*, vol. 1, p. 12.

3. Ibid., pp. 12–13; "Draft Doctrinal Notes," *First Infantry Division*, dated April 17, 1967.

4. Quoted in Jonathan Schell, *The Village of Ben Suc* (New York: Alfred A. Knopf, 1967), p. 19.

5. "Big Red One Battle Principles," May 1, 1967.

6. "Bong Trang," *Danger Forward, The Magazine of the Big Red One, Part Two*, pp. 31–39.

7. "Big Red One Battle Principles."

8. Quoted in Paul Johnson, *The Birth of the Modern: World Society, 1815–1830* (New York: Harper & Row, 1991), p. 64.

9. Arthur M. Schlesinger, Jr., *A Thousand Days* (Boston: Houghton Mifflin, 1965), p. 316.

10. Quoted in Gareth Porter, ed., *Vietnam: A History in Documents* (New York: New American Library, 1981), pp. 374–377.

11. William Beecher, "A Day with the Big Red One," *The National Guardsman* (February 1967): p. 7.

12. *Pacific Stars & Stripes*, April 4, 1967, p. 6.

13. Bernard William Rogers, *Cedar Falls-Junction City: A Turning Point* (Washington, D.C.: Department of the Army, 1974), pp. 31–34.

14. Tom Mangold and John Penycate, *The Tunnels of Cu Chi* (New York: Random House, 1985), p. 132.

15. Ibid., p. 130.

16. Schell, p. 18.

17. Staff Sergeant Frank P. Castro, *The American Traveler*, January 28, 1967; quoted in Rogers, pp. 34–36.

18. *First Infantry Division in Vietnam*, vol. 1, p. 24.

19. Ibid., p. 15.

20. Rogers, p. 39.

21. Rogers, p. 40.

22. Ibid., pp. 40–41.

23. Ibid., p. 158.

24. *First Infantry Division in Vietnam*, vol. 1, p. 15.

25. Diary of Capt. John M. Buck.

26. Ibid.

27. Rogers, pp. 146–147.

28. Diary of Capt. John M. Buck.

29. Rogers, pp. 140–147; U.S. casualties from *Pacific Stars & Stripes*, April 3, 1967, p. 6.

13. HOMECOMING

1. Roderick P. Hart, *Verbal Style and the Presidency: A Computer-Based Analysis* (New York: Harcourt Brace Jovanovich, 1984), pp. 130, 134–135.

2. Quoted in Richard Nixon, *RN: The Memoirs of Richard Nixon* (New York: Touchstone Books, 1990), p. 69.

3. *See* Nixon, pp. 72–78.

4. Henry Kissinger, *Years of Upheaval* (Boston: Little, Brown and Company, 1982), pp. 106–107.

14. NIXON AND KISSINGER

1. Gareth Porter, ed., *Vietnam: A History in Documents* (New York: New American Library, 1981), pp. 372–373.

2. Richard Nixon, *RN: The Memoirs of Richard Nixon* (New York: Touchstone Books, 1990), pp. 322, 328.

3. Ibid., p. 328.

4. Ibid., pp. 322–329.

5. Ibid., p. 383.

6. Ibid., p. 131.

15. NATIONAL SECURITY

1. Richard Nixon, *RN: The Memoirs of Richard Nixon* (New York: Touchstone Books, 1990), p. 358.

2. Nixon, pp. 596–597.

3. Select Committee to Study Government Operations with Regard to Intelligence Activities, Report no. 94–755, Book III (Washington, D.C.: U.S. Senate, 1976), pp. 278–280.

4. Ibid., p. 280.

5. *See* Nixon, p. 389.

6. *New York Times*, June 23, 1981, p. 15.

7. Haig Papers.

16. STEEL AND MUSH

1. Richard Nixon, *RN: The Memoirs of Richard Nixon* (New York: Touchstone Books, 1990), p. 390.

2. Ibid., p. 490.

3. Henry Kissinger, *White House Years* (Boston: Little, Brown and Company, 1979), p. 251.

4. *See* Kissinger, pp. 263–272.

5. Ibid., pp. 266–267.

6. Nixon, p. 392.

7. Kissinger, pp. 270–271.

8. Nixon, p. 392.

9. "COSVN Resolution No. 9," July 1969, quoted in Gareth Porter, ed., *Vietnam: A History in Documents* (New York: New American Library, 1981), p. 384.

10. Nixon, p. 394.

11. Kissinger, pp. 277–278.

12. Ibid., p. 282.

13. *Bartlett's Familiar Quotations*, p. 1072.

14. Nixon, p. 397.

15. *See* Kissinger, pp. 433–438.

16. "Combat Area Casualties Current File as of October 1989, Record Group 330" (Washington, D.C.: Office of the Secretary of Defense).

17. Harry G. Summers, Jr., *Vietnam War Almanac* (New York: Facts on File, 1985), pp. 48, 57.

18. Kissinger, p. 268.

17. CAMBODIA

1. Quoted in Henry Kissinger, *White House Years* (Boston: Little, Brown and Company, 1979), p. 462.

2. Ibid., p. 467.

3. Richard Nixon, *RN: The Memoirs of Richard Nixon* (New York: Touchstone Books, 1990), p. 447.

4. Ibid., p. 448.

5. Kissinger, p. 475.

6. Telegram from the Acting Chairman of the Joint Chiefs of Staff to Abrams and McCain, dated April 22, 1970; quoted in Gareth Porter, ed., *Vietnam: A History in Documents* (New York: New American Library, 1981), pp. 390–392.

7. *See* Kissinger, pp. 472–473.

8. Haig Papers, "Southeast Asia Trip Book."

9. Kissinger, p. 435.

10. Ibid., p. 500.

11. Ibid., p. 493.

12. Nixon, p. 461.

13. Ibid., p. 467.

18. TWO CONFRONTATIONS

1. Richard Nixon, *RN: The Memoirs of Richard Nixon* (New York: Touchstone Books, 1990), p. 483.

2. Henry Kissinger, *The White House Years* (Boston: Little, Brown and Company, 1979), p. 612.

3. Nixon, pp. 483–484.

4. Quoted in Nixon, p. 484.

5. Ibid., p. 484.

6. Kissinger, p. 620.

7. Ibid., pp. 627–628.

8. Ibid., p. 638; Nixon, p. 486.

9. Nixon, pp. 485–487.

10. Ibid., p. 487.

11. Ibid., p. 488.

12. Kissinger, p. 649.

19. MISSION TO CHINA

1. Richard Nixon, *RN: The Memoirs of Richard Nixon* (New York: Touchstone Books, 1990), p. 545.

2. Henry Kissinger, *The White House Years* (Boston: Little, Brown and Company, 1979), p. 741.

3. Nixon, pp. 575–576, 579.

4. Ross Terrill, *White-Boned Demon* (New York: Bantam Books, 1986), p. 342.

5. Ross Terrill, *Mao* (New York: Harper & Row, 1980), p. 394.

6. Number of telephones from *1990 World Almanac & Book of Facts* (New York: Scripps Howard Books, 1990).

7. Shanghai Communiqué, quoted in Nixon, p. 577.

8. Nixon, pp. 568–569.

9. Ibid., p. 585.

20. THE ART OF THE POSSIBLE

1. Plutarch, *Life of Alexander.*

2. Richard Nixon, *RN: The Memoirs of Richard Nixon* (New York: Touchstone Books, 1990), p. 6.

3. Lao Tzu, *Tao Te Ching*, trans. with an introduction by D. C. Lau (London: Penguin Books, 1963), p. 121.

4. Nixon, pp. 498–499; Howard W. Knappman, ed., *U.S.–Communist Confrontation in Southeast Asia*, vol. 7, no. 1 (New York: Facts on File, 1973); Harry G. Summers, Jr., *Vietnam War Almanac* (New York: Facts on File, 1985), p. 224; *Facts on File 1971 Yearbook*, pp. 83–84.

5. Nixon, p. 584.

6. Henry Kissinger, *The White House Years* (Boston: Little, Brown and Company, 1979), pp. 1099–1100.

21. BITING THE BULLET

1. Richard Nixon, *RN: The Memoirs of Richard Nixon* (New York: Touchstone Books, 1990), p. 586.

2. Howard W. Knappman, ed., *South Vietnam: U.S.–Communist Confrontation in Southeast Asia*, vol. 7, no. 1 (New York: Facts on File, 1973), p. 48.

3. Henry Kissinger, *The White House Years* (Boston: Little, Brown and Company, 1979), p. 1100.

4. Ibid., p. 1113.

5. Ibid., p. 1160.

6. Knappman, pp. 54–61.

7. Ibid., p. 67.

8. Nixon, p. 593.

9. Knappman, p. 54.

10. Gareth Porter, ed., *Vietnam: A History in Documents* (New York: New American Library, 1981), pp. 405–406.

11. Nixon, p. 607.

12. Knappman, p. 66.

22. A PARTING OF THE WAYS

1. Richard Nixon, *RN: The Memoirs of Richard Nixon* (New York: Touchstone Books, 1990), pp. 680, 689.

2. *See* Howard W. Knappman, ed., *South Vietnam: U.S.–Communist Confrontation in Southeast Asia*, vol. 7 (New York: Facts on File, 1973); Henry Kissinger, *The White House Years* (Boston: Little, Brown and Company, 1979).

3. Nixon, p. 689.

4. Kissinger, p. 1312.

5. Stephen E. Ambrose, *Nixon, Volume Three: Ruin and Recovery* (New York: Simon & Schuster, 1991), pp. 53–54.

6. *Washington Post*, September 8, 1972, p. 10; October 7, 1972, p. 12.

7. Nixon, p. 693.

8. Kissinger, p. 1365.

9. Ibid., p. 1375.

10. Gareth Porter, ed., *Vietnam: A History in Documents* (New York: New American Library, 1981), pp. 469, 470.

11. *See* Kissinger, p. 1371.

12. Nixon, p. 700.

13. Ibid., p. 702.

14. Kissinger, p. 1385.

15. Ibid., p. 1398.

16. Ibid., p. 1377.

17. Ibid., p. 1399.

18. Ibid., p. 1410.

23. PERSUASIVE FORCE

1. Nguyen Tien Hung and Jerrold L. Schecter, *The Palace File* (New York: Harper & Row, 1986), p. 383.

2. Ibid., pp. 385–386.

3. Henry Kissinger, *The White House Years* (Boston: Little, Brown and Company, 1979), pp. 1415–1427.

4. Ibid., p. 1416.

5. *See* ibid., pp. 1427–1431.

6. Ibid., p. 1440.

7. Ibid., pp. 1442–1443.

8. Richard Nixon, *RN: The Memoirs of Richard Nixon* (New York: Touchstone Books, 1990), p. 737.

9. Stephen E. Ambrose, *Nixon, Volume Three: Ruin and Recovery* (New York: Simon & Schuster, 1991), pp. 735–737.

10. Nixon, p. 738.

11. Charles W. Colson, *Born Again* (Old Tappan, NJ: G. K. Hall, 1976), pp. 79–80.

12. Haldeman's notes, dated December 31, 1972; quoted in Ambrose, p. 43.

13. Colson, p. 80.

14. Ambrose, p. 56.

15. Ibid., p. 58.

24. AFTERMATH

1. Gareth Porter, ed., *Vietnam: A History in Documents* (New York: New American Library, 1981), p. 470.

2. Ibid., p. 471.

3. Ibid., p. 472.

25. "DEEP THROAT"

1. John W. Dean III, *Lost Honor* (Los Angeles: Harper & Row, 1982), p. 353.

2. *Penguin Book of Quotations*, p. 126.

3. Carl Bernstein and Bob Woodward, *All the President's Men* (New York: Simon & Schuster, 1974), pp. 130–135.

4. Ibid., p. 72.

5. Ibid., p. 317.

6. Ibid., p. 271.

26. ON VIRTUE

1. Quoted in Alexander M. Haig, Jr., *Caveat* (New York: Macmillan and Company, 1984), p. 50. The committee's vote was 15 to 2 for confirmation, with Sarbanes and his fellow Democrat Paul E. Tsongas of Massachusetts casting the nays. On January 21, 1981, the Senate voted 93 to 6 to confirm.

2. Stephen E. Ambrose, *Nixon, Volume Three: Ruin and Recovery* (New York: Simon & Schuster, 1991), p. 138

3. Richard Nixon, *RN: The Memoirs of Richard Nixon* (New York: Touchstone Books, 1990), p. 69.

27. THE WORST HAPPENS

1. Stephen E. Ambrose, *Nixon, Volume Three: Ruin and Recovery* (New York: Simon & Schuster, 1991), p. 141.

2. Richard Nixon, *RN: The Memoirs of Richard Nixon* (New York: Touchstone Books, 1990), p. 856.

3. *See* Ambrose, p. 141.

4. Henry Kissinger, *Years of Upheaval* (Boston: Little, Brown and Company, 1982), p. 109.

5. William B. Dickinson, Jr., et al., eds., *Watergate, Chronology of a Crisis*, vol. 1, (Washington, D.C.: Congressional Quarterly, 1973), p. 11.

6. Ibid., p. 20–22.

7. Ibid., pp. 29, 50.

8. Ibid., p. 35.

9. Ibid., p. 35.

10. Ibid., pp. 46, 61.

11. Ambrose, pp. 153–154.

12. Ibid., p. 148.

13. Dickinson et al., p. 91.

14. Ibid., pp. 106–107.

15. Nixon, p. 768.

16. Dickinson et al., p. 130.

17. *St. Louis Post-Dispatch*, June 13, 1973.

18. Dickinson et al., p. 18.

28. SHADOW OF A COUP

1. Richard Nixon, *RN: The Memoirs of Richard Nixon* (New York: Touchstone Books, 1990), p. 816.

2. William B. Dickinson, Jr., et al., eds., *Watergate, Chronology of a Crisis*, vol. 1 (Washington, D.C.: Congressional Quarterly, 1973), p. 175.

3. Ibid., p. 62.

4. Spiro T. Agnew, *Go Quietly . . . Or Else* (New York: William Morrow and Company, 1980), pp. 190–191.

5. Ibid., pp. 93–94; *1973 Facts on File Yearbook*, p. 663–664.

6. *1973 Facts on File Yearbook*, p. 664.

7. Ibid., p. 664.

8. Nixon, p. 914.

9. Richard Nixon, *Six Crises* (New York: Doubleday, 1962), p. 20.

10. *1973 Facts on File Yearbook*, p. 722.

11. Ibid., p. 703.

12. Agnew, p. 158.

13. Nixon, p. 916.

14. Ibid., p. 917.

15. *1973 Facts on File Yearbook*, p. 801.

16. Ibid.

17. Agnew, p. 180.

18. *1973 Facts on File Yearbook*, p. 818.

19. Ibid., p. 841.

20. Nixon, p. 925.

21. *See* Gerald R. Ford, A *Time to Heal* (New York: Harper & Row, 1979), p. 105; Stephen E. Ambrose, *Nixon, Volume Three: Ruin and Recovery* (New York: Simon & Schuster, 1991), p. 238.

29. A QUESTION OF INNOCENCE

1. Richard Nixon, *RN: The Memoirs of Richard Nixon* (New York: Touchstone Books, 1990), p. 898.

2. Ibid.

3. William B. Dickinson, Jr., et al., eds., *Watergate, Chronology of a Crisis*, vol. 1 (Washington, D.C.: Congressional Quarterly, 1973), p. 194.

4. Ibid.

5. Haig Testimony, pp. 1934–1935.

6. Dickinson et al., p. 195.

7. Ibid., p. 224.

8. Ibid., pp. 208–209, 220, 239.

9. Ibid., p. 209.

30. BLINDMAN'S BUFF

1. William B. Dickinson, Jr., et al., eds., *Watergate, Chronology of a Crisis*, vol. 1 (Washington, D.C.: Congressional Quarterly, 1973), p. 220.

2. Ibid., p. 149.

3. Janice Goldstein et al., eds., *Watergate, Chronology of a Crisis*, vol. 2 (Washington, D.C.: Congressional Quarterly, 1974), p. 45.

4. Ibid., p. 9; *Washington Post*, August 23, 1973.

5. *New York Times*, August 23, 1973.

6. Dickinson et al., p. 14.

7. Ibid., p. 20.

8. Alexander M. Bickel, "The Tapes, Cox, Nixon," *The New Republic*, September 29, 1973.

9. Elliot Richardson, *The Creative Balance* (New York: Holt, Rinehart and Winston, 1976), p. 36.

10. Dickinson et al., pp. 96–98.

11. *Daily Californian*, May 21, 1973.

12. Richard Nixon, *RN: The Memoirs of Richard Nixon* (New York: Touchstone Books, 1990), p. 910.

13. *1973 Facts on File Yearbook*, p. 885.

14. Nixon, pp. 910–911; Stephen E. Ambrose, *Nixon, Volume Three: Ruin and Recovery* (New York: Simon & Schuster, 1991), p. 146.

15. "Elliot L. Richardson Recalls Saturday Night Massacre," *Boston Globe*, February 15, 1976.

16. Letter to Mary Gladstone, April 24, 1881; quoted in *Bartlett's Familiar Quotations*, p. 749.

17. Dickinson et al., pp. 208, 209.

18. Ibid., p. 107.

19. *See* Ambrose, pp. 205–206.

20. *1973 Facts on File Yearbook*, p. 805.

21. Carl Bernstein and Bob Woodward, *All the President's Men* (New York: Simon & Schuster, 1974), pp. 248, 249, 330.

22. *New York Times*, August 2, 1973.

23. *1974 Facts on File Yearbook*, p. 533.

24. *New York Times*, February 1, March 1, September 6, 1973.

25. Dickinson et al., pp. 90–91.

26. Ibid.

27. Letter from Charles Alan Wright to Alexander M. Haig, Jr., April 8, 1992.

28. Nixon, p. 932.

29. Bob Woodward and Carl Bernstein, *The Final Days* (New York: Simon & Schuster, 1976), pp. 64–65.

30. White House transcript of Cox press conference, pp. 11, 12.

31. THE MIDDLE EAST CRISIS

1. *1973 Facts on File Yearbook*, p. 889.

2. Ibid., p. 834.

3. Donald Neff, *Warriors Against Israel* (Brattleboro, VT: Amana Books, 1988), pp. 98, 122, 126, 150, 204.

4. Henry Kissinger, *Years of Upheaval* (Boston: Little, Brown and Company, 1982), p. 1124.

5. Richard Nixon, *RN: The Memoirs of Richard Nixon* (New York: Touchstone Books, 1990), pp. 927–928.

6. *1973 Facts on File Yearbook*, p. 859.

7. Kissinger, p. 542.

8. Ibid.

9. Ibid., 576.

10. *See* Nixon, p. 937; Kissinger, p. 584.

11. Kissinger, p. 578.

12. Ibid., 583.

13. *1973 Facts on File Yearbook*, p. 887.

32. THE BURDEN OF PROOF

1. *Washington Post*, October 21, 1973.

2. *1973 Facts on File Yearbook*, pp. 885–887.

3. Janice L Goldstein et al., eds., *Watergate, Chronology of a Crisis*, vol. 2 (Washington, D.C.: Congressional Quarterly, 1974), p. 71.

4. Stephen E. Ambrose, *Nixon, Volume Three: Ruin and Recovery* (New York: Simon & Schuster, 1991), p. 259.

5. *1973 Facts on File Yearbook*, p. 887.

6. Ibid., p. 886.

7. Richard Nixon, *RN: The Memoirs of Richard Nixon* (New York: Touchstone Books, 1990), p. 946.

8. Goldstein et al., pp. 92–93.

9. Ibid., p. 93.

10. Nixon, pp. 944–945; Ambrose, pp. 261–262.

11. William B. Dickinson, Jr., et al., eds., *Watergate, Chronology of a Crisis*, vol. 1 (Washington, D.C., Congressional Quarterly, 1973), pp. 125, 134.

12. Nixon, p. 946.

13. Haig Testimony, pp. 1038, 2031.

14. Ibid., p. 2039.

15. Ambrose, p. 270.

16. John Sirica, *To Set the Record Straight* (New York: W. W. Norton & Company, 1979), pp. 187, 190, 192, 193.

33. THE TALE OF THE TAPES

1. Janice L. Goldstein et al., eds., *Watergate, Chronology of a Crisis*, vol. 2 (Washington, D.C.: Congressional Quarterly, 1974), pp. 109, 110.

2. Ibid., p. 111.

3. Stephen E. Ambrose, *Nixon, Volume Three: Ruin and Recovery* (New York: Simon & Schuster, 1991), p. 280.

4. Goldstein et al., p. 177.

5. Ambrose, p. 280.

6. Goldstein et al., p. 130.

7. *1973 Facts on File Yearbook*, pp. 886, 942.

8. Ambrose, pp. 283–284.

9. Goldstein et al., p. 184.

10. Ambrose, p. 284.

11. The quotation is from act V, scene iv, just before Richard utters his famous line "A horse! a horse! my kingdom for a horse!"

> *The King enacts more wonders that a man,*
> *Daring an opposite to every danger.*
> *His horse is slain, and all on foot he fights,*
> *Seeking for Richmond in the throat of death.*
> *Rescue, fair lord, or else the day is lost.*

12. Goldstein et al., pp. 180, 185.

13. Ibid., pp. 125, 149, 180.

14. Ibid., pp. 185–187.

15. *See* Gerald R. Ford, *A Time to Heal* (New York: Harper & Row, 1979), p. 20.

16. Ambrose, pp. 298–299.

17. *New York Times*, January 15, 16, 17, 1974.

18. Ambrose, p. 300.

19. *1974 Facts on File Yearbook*, p. 24.

20. *U.S. News & World Report*, March 18, 1974, p. 19.

21. Goldstein et al., p. 192.

22. *1974 Facts on File Yearbook*, pp. 139–140.

23. Goldstein et al., p. 215.

24. Ibid.

25. Ibid., p. 216.

26. Ibid., p. 218.

27. Ibid., p. 215.

28. Ibid., p. 333.

29. Ambrose, p. 332.

30. Quoted in Ambrose, p. 327.

31. *See* Leon Jaworski, *The Right and the Power* (New York: Reader's Digest Press, 1976), p. 136.

34. HAIL AND FAREWELL

1. *Watergate, Chronology of a Crisis* (Washington, D.C.: Congressional Quarterly, 1975), p. 673.

2. Ibid., p. 658.

3. Ibid., p. 709; Richard Nixon, *RN: The Memoirs of Richard Nixon* (New York: Touchstone Books, 1990), pp. 1009–1010.

4. Henry Kissinger, *Years of Upheaval* (Boston: Little, Brown and Company, 1982), p. 1120.

5. Ibid., p. 1126; Nixon, p. 1011.

6. Nixon, p. 1016.

7. Kissinger, p. 1120.

8. Ibid., p. 1017.

9. Stephen E. Ambrose, *Nixon, Volume Three: Ruin and Recovery* (New York: Simon & Schuster, 1991), pp. 365–367.

10. Nixon, p. 1034.

35. THE SMOKING GUN

1. Stephen E. Ambrose, *Nixon, Volume Three: Ruin and Recovery* (New York: Simon & Schuster, 1991), p. 343.

2. Janice L. Goldstein, et al., eds., *Watergate, Chronology of a Crisis* (Washington, D.C.: Congressional Quarterly, 1975), pp. 694–695.

3. Ibid., p. 684.

4. Ibid., p. 690.

5. Ambrose, p. 338.

6. Goldstein, et al., p. 670.

7. *Watergate, Chronology of a Crisis*, vol. 2 (Washington, D.C.: Congressional Quarterly, 1974), p. 289.

8. Goldstein, et al., pp. 669, 709.

9. Ambrose, p. 392.

10. Goldstein, et. al., p. 726.

11. Richard Nixon, *RN: The Memoirs of Richard Nixon* (New York: Touchstone Books, 1990), p. 1042.

12. Ibid., p. 1047.

13. Goldstein, et al., pp. 718–719, 728–729.

14. *See* Nixon, p. 1052.

15. Goldstein, et al., p. 712.

16. Ibid., pp. 716–717.

17. Ibid., p. 122A.

18. Ibid., p. 745; Nixon, p. 1052.

19. Ambrose, p. 399.

20. Goldstein, et al., pp. 122A, 123A.

21. Ibid., p. 90A.

22. *See* Nixon, p. 1057.

23. *See* Ambrose, p. 404.

24. Gerald R. Ford, *A Time to Heal* (New York: Harper & Row, 1979), p. 6.

25. See "Pardon of Richard M. Nixon and Related Matters, Hearings Before the Subcommittee on Criminal Justice of the Committee on the Judiciary, U.S. House of Representatives" (Washington, D.C.: September 24 and October 1 and 17, 1984), p. 94.

26. *See* Ford, p. 3.

27. Goldstein, et al., p. 717.

28. Ibid., p. 760.

29. Nixon, p. 1058.

30. Ford, p. 12.

31. Ibid., p. 13.

32. Ibid.

33. Ibid., pp. 6–7, 11.

34. Robert T. Hartmann, *Palace Politics* (New York: McGraw-Hill, 1980), pp. 136–137.

36. THE FINAL PARADOX

1. Richard Nixon, *RN: The Memoirs of Richard Nixon* (New York: Touchstone Books, 1990), pp. 1059–1061.

2. *Complete Poetry and Selected Prose of John Milton* (New York: Modern Library, 1950), p. 94.

3. *See* Bob Woodward and Carl Bernstein, *The Final Days* (New York: Simon & Schuster, 1976), pp. 354–355. Woodward and Bernstein write that Griffin read the letter to Ford over the telephone before sending it to Nixon.

4. *Watergate, Chronology of a Crisis* (Washington, D.C.: Congressional Quarterly, 1975), p. 760.

5. *See* Woodward and Bernstein, pp. 390–393.

6. Gerald R. Ford, A *Time to Heal* (New York: Harper & Row, 1979), p. 20.

7. Ibid., p. 17.

8. *See* Ford, pp. 20–22.

9. Ibid., p. 21; Nixon, p. 1066; Henry Kissinger, *Years of Upheaval* (Boston: Little, Brown and Company, 1982), p. 1203.

10. Kissinger, p. 1205; Nixon, p. 1066.

11. Nixon, p. 1067.

12. *Watergate*, pp. 761, 765–766, 767.

13. Quoted in Stephen E. Ambrose, *Nixon, Volume Three: Ruin and Recovery* (New York: Simon & Schuster, 1991), p. 427.

14. *See* Nixon, p. 959; William B. Dickinson, Jr., et al., eds., *Watergate, Chronology of a Crisis*, vol. 1 (Washington, D.C.: Congressional Quarterly, 1973), pp. 298–299.

15. Leon Jaworski, *The Right and the Power* (New York: Reader's Digest Press, 1976), pp. 217–219.

16. Nixon, pp. 1066, 1078, 1080.

17. *See* Nixon, p. 1080.

18. Nixon, p. 1082.

19. Ibid., p. 1083.

20. Alexander M. Haig, Jr., *Caveat* (New York: Macmillan and Company, 1984), p. 51.

37. FORD'S WHITE HOUSE

1. Robert T. Hartmann, *Palace Politics* (New York: McGraw-Hill, 1980), p. 166; Gerald R. Ford, A *Time to Heal* (New York: Harper & Row, 1979), p. 147.

2. Ford, p. 147.

3. Hartmann, pp. 179, 185n.

4. Ford, p. 148.

5. *Chicago Tribune*, September 22, 1974.

6. Ford, p. 148.

7. Ibid., p. 185.

8. Ibid., p. 164.

9. *See* Stephen E. Ambrose, *Nixon, Volume Three: Ruin and Recovery* (New York: Simon & Schuster, 1991), pp. 457–458.

10. Richard Nixon, *RN: The Memoirs of Richard Nixon* (New York: Touchstone Books, 1990), p. 1084.

11. *See* Ambrose, p. 455.

12. *See* Ford, p. 161.

13. Ibid., p. 161; Hartmann, pp. 257–259.

14. *See* Ford, pp. 141–142; Hartmann, pp. 213–215.

15. *See* Hartmann, p. 262.

16. Ford, p. 161.

17. Thomas Paine, *The Age of Reason*.

18. *New York Times* and *Washington Star-News*, September 17, 1974.

19. *Washington Post*, September 18, 1974.

20. *See* Ford, p. 184.

21. Ibid., p. 185.

22. R. D. Heinl, Jr., in the *Detroit News*, September 12, 1974.

23. Scranton *Tribune*, September 17, 1974.

38. THE WESTERN ALLIANCE

1. Robert S. Jordan, *Generals in International Politics* (Lexington, KY: University of Kentucky Press, 1987), p. 152.

2. Ibid., p. 156.

3. Ibid.

4. Ibid., p. 158.

5. Ibid., pp. 156–157.

6. Ibid., pp. 166–167.

7. Ibid., p. 168.

8. Ibid., p. 184.

9. UPI dispatch in *Washington Post*, August 24, 1974.

39. CARTER ABROAD

1. U.S. Department of State, "Background Notes on Turkey" (Washington, D.C.: 1988).

2. This paragraph is a paraphrase of a passage in my introduction to Robert E. Huyser, *Mission to Tehran* (New York: Harper & Row, 1986).

3. *See* Roy Mottahedeh, *The Mantle of the Prophet* (New York: Simon & Schuster, 1985), pp. 374–376.

4. Mohamed Heikal, *Iran: The Untold Story* (New York: Pantheon Books, 1982), pp. 170, 171.

5. Mottahedeh, p. 376.

6. Quoted in Heikal, pp. 170, 171.

7. *See* Mottahedeh, p. 376.

8. *Los Angeles Times*, May 26, 1992.

9. Associated Press dispatch, May 2, 1991; *Washington Times*, April 26, 1991.

10. Letter from Gen. Gerd Schmückle, dated April 18, 1991.

40. POLITICS

1. Alexander M. Haig, Jr., *Caveat* (New York: Macmillan, 1984), p. 57.

2. Ibid., p. 314.

3. Ibid., p. 315.

4. Donald T. Regan, *For the Record: From Wall Street to Washington* (New York: Harcourt Brace Jovanovich, 1988), p. 3.

5. Mohamed Heikal, *Iran: The Untold Story* (New York: Pantheon Books, 1982), p. 87n.

6. *Washington Post*, October 3, 1987; *Times* (London), November 14, 1987.

7. William Cowper, *Olney Hymns*, no. 1 (1779).

41. AFTERWORD: AMERICA, THE FUTURE, THE WORLD

1. Richard Nixon, *RN: The Memoirs of Richard Nixon* (New York: Touchstone Books, 1990), pp. 53, 344.

2. Alexander M. Haig, Jr., *Caveat*, (New York: Macmillan, 1984) p. 21.

3. Jeffrey A. Eisenach, *America's Fiscal Future: The Federal Budget's Brave New World* (Indianapolis, IN: The Hudson Institute, 1991), pp. 22, 23, 33.

4. *Washington Post*, May 13, 1992.

5. George F. Kennan, "The Sources of Soviet Conduct," *Foreign Affairs*, June 1967, p. 566ff.

INDEX

Abrams, Creighton W., 229, 275–76, 279, 280, 282, 287, 291, 298, 300, 334, 516
Acheson, Dean, 22, 23, 30, 49, 50, 51, 69, 70, 128, 142, 571n.5
Acker, Marge, 426
Acton, Lord, 388
AFL-CIO, 418–19
Agnew, Spiro T., 307, 350–67, 469
Albert, Carl, 364, 365, 420, 427, 440, 502
Albrecht, Susanne, 542
Algeria, 550n.
Alleged Assassination Plots Involving Foreign Leaders (Senate committee report), 113
All the President's Men (Woodward and Bernstein), 322, 323, 324–25
Almond, Edward Mallory (Ned)
    background and personality, 19, 20, 21, 22, 42–44
    and Korean War, 26, 31, 34, 35, 39, 40–46, 49, 52–54, 55, 56, 58–63, 64–66
Ambrose, Stephen E., 329, 421, 512
Amini, Ali, 86
Amnesty
    selective, 513–15
    see also Pardon
An Loc, 281, 282, 286–87, 289
Annapolis. *See* Naval Academy, U.S.
Antiwar movement, 184, 238, 284
Ap Gu, Battle of, 174–79, 237
Apollo XI, 230
Arab-Israeli War. *See* Middle East; Six Day War; Yom Kippur War
Arab Legion, 247
Arabs, 242–43, 342, 557
    See Middle East; specific countries
Arlington National Cemetery, 114
Armed Forces Journal International, 517n.
Armor School, 76
Arms control. *See* Strategic Arms Limitation Treaties

Armstrong, Anne, 431n.
Army, U.S.
    career officer's life-style, 73–74
    military power, 24–25
    racial integration, 43, 565
    style of management, 74–76
    see also Draft; specific aspects, battalions, divisions, wars; as subhead under Haig, Alexander M., Jr.
Army Field Service Regulations, 139
Army-Navy football game, 78–79
Army of the Republic of South Vietnam, 132, 158, 170, 179, 273, 281
    casualties, 276, 277, 286
    fighting, 228, 235, 237, 274, 279, 282–83, 287, 289, 292
ARVN. *See* Army of the Republic of South Vietnam
Asia. *See* Southeast Asia; specific countries
Assad, Hafez al-, 250, 460
Assassination attempts
    against Castro, 112–13, 578nn.7,8
    against Haig, 539–43
    against Hussein, 241
Assassination plots
    against Nguyen Van Thieu, 307
    against Nixon, 361–62
Assassinations
    of Kennedy, John F., 112–16
    of Lumumba, 579n.9
    of Ngo Dinh Diem, 118, 134
Associated Press, 277, 391, 432
Atlanta Constitution, 425

"Baghdad Pact." *See* Central Treaty Organization
Baker, Howard, 390, 395, 401, 403, 419–20
Baker, James A. III, 546, 547
Bakhtiar, Shapur, 537, 539
Ball, George, 149

599

Bao Dai, 128, 129
Bard, John C., 326
Barr, David G., 63
Barzani, Mustafa al-, 88–89
Baudouin, King, 532
Bay of Pigs, 94–95, 100, 106–9, 578n.3
Beall, George, 351, 354, 363
Beall, J. Glenn, Jr., 351
Beecher, William, 164, 165, 214
Begin, Menachem, 461, 462
Bennett, John, 374, 375, 428, 429
Benny Haven's Tavern, 15, 16, 17
Ben Suc, 170–73
Ben-Veniste, Richard, 433, 449
Berlin, 93, 94, 95–96
Berlin Wall, 94, 95–96, 555
Bernstein, Carl, 321, 322, 323, 325, 391
Bickel, Alexander M., 386
Big Red One, 157
"Big Red One Battle Principles," 158–59, 161
Binh Dinh, 282
Black Americans, 43, 565–67
"Black September" (1970), 241–42
Blanchard, Doc, 13
"Blue Spaders," 167
Body counts, 164
Bolivia, 112
Bonesteel, Charles H., 49n.
Bong Trang, Battle of, 160–61
Bork, Robert, 406, 407, 408, 421, 422, 435–36,
    438
Boston Globe, 425
Boyd, Captain, 79
Bradlee, Benjamin C., 321–22
Bradley, Omar N., 34
Brandt, Willy, 96
Brezhnev, Leonid, 285, 286, 287–88, 406, 413,
    414, 415, 416, 417, 462, 463, 464–65
Brooke, Edward, 441
Broussard, Eddie J., 87
Brown, Dean, 243, 248, 249
Brown, Harold, 531, 532, 533, 534, 550n.
Brzezinski, Zbigniew, 532, 533, 538
Buchanan, Pat, 345, 446, 447, 451, 478, 489,
    511
Buchen, Philip, 483n., 513, 514, 518
Buck, John M., 178
Buckley, James L., 424
Buddhist movement, Vietnamese, 134
Budget
    defense, 24
    federal, 562–63, 564
Bull, Steve, 349, 422n., 423, 426, 429, 446, 449,
    498
Bundeswehr, 527–28
Bundy, McGeorge, 144
Bundy, William P., 144
Bunker, Ellsworth, 294
Burch, Dean, 478, 496–97, 498
Burger, Warren E., 285, 440
Bush, George, 493, 549, 562, 564, 567
    administration, 563
Butterfield, Alexander P., 373, 374, 379, 391
Buzhardt, J. Fred, 323n., 340, 347, 380, 383, 397,
    431–32, 445, 447, 448–49, 468, 481, 488, 498,
    517–18
    and Agnew, 350–51, 353, 354, 355, 356, 360,
        361
    and Cox, 393, 395, 399–400, 402n., 403
    Nixon tapes, 341–42, 376–78, 379, 392, 422,
        423, 424, 425, 426–28, 429–30, 432–33,
        447, 451, 455, 472–73, 475, 476, 477,
        479
Byrne, Matthew, 341

Calhoun, John C., 364
Califano, Joseph A., Jr., 94, 106, 110, 114, 115,
    189–90, 196, 216, 327, 331, 339–40, 344, 531,
    533
Callahan, James, 535
Cambodia, 139, 153, 180, 207, 214, 224, 225,
    233–40, 279, 292, 310, 316
Camp Buckner, 16–17, 157
Camp Holloway, 148
Cam Ranh Bay, 230
Candor in government issue, 92, 97–98, 124,
    152–53
Cannon, Lou, 515
Capps, Arlie G., 35
Carter, Jimmy, 526, 531–39
    administration, 526, 532, 533, 536, 539, 550n.
Casa Pacifica, 515
Casey, William, 549
Castro, Fidel, 105, 109, 110, 111, 550
    assassination plots against, 112–13, 578nn.7,8
    and JFK assassination, 114–16
Caveat (Haig), 503–4, 546, 547, 550n.
Cayo Alcatraz, 252
CBS News, 342, 421
Celler, Emmanuel, 450
CENTO. See Central Treaty Organization
Central America, 550
    see also specific country names
Central Intelligence Agency, 50–51, 389, 471, 549
    Cambodia, 233–34
    Cuba, 108–13, 252
        Bay of Pigs, 108, 578n.3
        Castro assassination plot, 112, 578nn.7,8
        missile crisis, 100–101, 101–2
    Iran, 84, 85
    Vietnam, 128–29
    Watergate, 290, 342, 476, 490
Central Treaty Organization, 87
Chambers, Whittaker, 553
Chapin, Dwight, 258
Cheney, Dick, 530
Chen Yi, 149
Chiang Kai-shek, 17–18, 30–31, 31–32, 48
Chiang Kai-shek, Madame, 31
China, 17–18, 557
    Korean War, 30, 32, 48–49, 50–51, 55–66
    normalization of relations, 256–66
    Vietnam, 125–26, 128, 133–34, 148–51, 261,
        279, 283
    see also Taiwan
Chosin Reservoir, 60, 61, 62
Chou Chi-jou, 31
Christian Science Monitor, 441
Christopher, Warren, 550n.
Church committee, 113, 217n., 578n.8, 579n.9
Churchill, Winston, 534, 553
CIA. See Central Intelligence Agency
Cienfuegos, Cuba, Soviet naval base at, 241, 252–55
CINCEUR. See Commander in Chief U.S.
    European Command
Clark, William, 547
Clausewitz, Carl von, 151
Clifford, Clark, 351
Colby, William, 416
Cold War, 82, 94, 152, 242, 266, 549, 553–55, 564
    U.S. policies, 49–50, 69, 70, 97, 567–68
    see also Détente; Marxism-Leninism; specific
        countries and military actions
Collins, J. Lawton, 35–36, 574n.27
Colson, Charles, 291–92, 312, 324, 342, 448, 469
Columbia University, 80
Commager, Henry Steele, 387
Commander in Chief U.S. European Command,
    520, 521

Committee to Re-Elect the President, 290, 337, 340, 348, 448
Computers, 123–24, 147
Congress, U.S., 47, 330, 412, 439, 444, 460, 559, 562, 563, 564
  Nixon relations, 367, 368, 369, 370, 439–41, 445
  see also Ervin committee; Impeachment
  and Vietnam War, 122, 277–78, 287, 306, 311–12, 313, 316–17, 318, 328
  see also Executive privilege; House of Representatives, U.S.; Senate, U.S.
Connally, John B., 275, 285, 286, 312, 313–14, 344, 354, 358, 361, 363, 365, 367–69, 370, 420, 437, 438, 513, 530
Constellation (ship), 118
Containment doctrine, 554–55
Cooley, Denton, 545
Cooper, John Sherman, 367
COSVN, 174, 237
Coulter, Tex, 13
Counterinsurgency, 100, 131, 132, 133, 151, 162, 282
Court of Appeals, U.S., 391, 419
Covert actions, 98, 108–13
  as substitute for foreign policy, 549–50
  see also Central Intelligence Agency
Cox, Archibald, 340, 357, 359, 379, 380, 381, 382, 383, 384, 385, 386, 387–88, 389–90, 391, 437, 438
  dismissal of, 392, 393–405, 406, 409, 418, 419
Cox, Tricia Nixon, 500
Crisis management, 98
Crisis resolution, 96–97
CRP. *See* Committee to Re-Elect the President
Cuba, 100–105, 131
  Bay of Pigs, 94–95, 100, 106–9, 578n.3
  covert actions against, 108–13
  influence in Latin America, 111–12
  missile crisis, 100–105, 109, 111, 253, 254, 416, 554
  Soviet naval base at Cienfuegos, 241, 252–55
  Soviet-U.S. Understandings on, 252, 253, 254, 255
Cu Chi tunnels, 170–72, 173
Cultural Revolution, 150
Cundiff, Brian H., 177
Cypriot National Guard, 535
Cyprus, 533
Czechoslovakia, 560

Dart, Justin, 545–46
Dash, Sam, 419
Davison, Michael S., 80
Dayan, Moshe, 166
De-Americanization (term), 226
Dean, John W. III, 321, 322, 325, 332, 336, 337, 342, 347, 348, 349, 353, 373, 379, 399n., 422, 423, 424, 425, 446, 447–48, 452, 457
Dean, William F., 27
Deaver, Michael K., 546, 547
Decker, George, 79
Deep Throat, 321–26
Defense Department, U.S., 85–86, 87, 137, 227, 252, 411, 462
  budget, 24
  see also Pentagon
Deficit, federal budget, 562–63, 564
De Gaulle, Charles, 104, 200, 561
Demilitarized zone, 124, 279, 280, 281, 305, 307, 313
Democratic National Committee headquarters break-in. *See* Watergate affair
Democratic party, 226, 253–54, 287, 304, 329–30, 365, 367, 420, 444–45, 471–72, 562

Democratic Republic of Vietnam. *See* North Vietnam
Deng Xiaoping, 265
DePuy, William E., 156–57, 158–62, 164–66, 167, 168, 172, 174
DePuy Fighting Bunker, 159, 174–75
Détente, 228–29, 284, 286, 287, 463, 524, 525
Detroit News, 425, 511
Devon Regiment, 80
Dictabelt accounts, Nixon's, 423, 425, 426, 427
Diem, Ngo Dinh. *See* Ngo Dinh Diem
DMZ. *See* Demilitarized zone
Doar, John, 469
Dobrovir, William A., 446n.
Dobrynin, Anatoly, 105, 226, 228, 232, 254–55, 257, 288, 301, 307, 342, 415
Dole, Robert, 494
Dominican Republic, 111
Double impeachment, 350–51, 369n.
Douglas, Helen Gahagan, 188
Doyle, James H., 35, 39, 40, 53
Draft, military, 69, 185–86
  pardons for evaders, 513–14
Drug testing, 522
Duc, Nguyen Phu. *See* Nguyen Phu Duc
Dulles, Allen, 101, 578n.3
Dulles, John Foster, 23, 67, 129, 132
Duncan, Charles, 538–39
Durbrow, Elbridge, 129

Eagleburger, Lawrence S., 199, 200, 201, 542
Eastern Europe, 279, 519, 555, 560
  see also specific countries
East Germany, 95–96, 560
Eastland, James, 502
Eavesdropping, 263
  see also Wiretaps; Tapes, White House
EC-121 incident, 204–9, 225, 286
Economic multipolarity, 557–58
Economic protectionism, 559, 560
Edwards, Idwal H., 35, 36
Egypt, 24, 410, 414, 415, 459
Ehrlichman, John D., 291–92, 332, 336, 342, 353, 429, 448, 469, 494, 500
899th Tank Battalion, 80, 82
Eighteen-and-a-quarter-minute gap, 428–34, 449
Eisenhower, David, 479
Eisenhower, Dwight, 22, 67, 82, 83, 98, 108, 210, 554
  administration, 82, 83, 85, 98, 579n.9
  and missiles in Cuba, 100–101
  Vietnam policy, 129, 130, 132
  wiretaps, 217n.
Eisenhower, Julie Nixon, 479, 494, 500
Ellsberg, Daniel, 223, 337, 341, 342, 448, 469
El Salvador, 112
Entitlements, 563, 564
Ervin, Sam J., Jr., 338, 371–72, 377, 380, 391, 395, 401
Ervin committee, 338, 353, 371–72, 380, 382, 383, 384, 387–88, 390–91, 422, 445, 448, 468
Escalation (U.S. policy), 97
Europe
  terrorism in, 539–43
  see also Eastern Europe; specific country and organization names
European Community, 559–60
European Free Trade Area, 559–60
European Recovery Act, 560
Executive Branch, 328, 343, 393
  see also Presidency; Separation of powers
Executive privilege, 380, 381, 382–83, 384, 386, 391–92, 393, 443, 445, 472
  see also Tapes, White House

Feisal, King (Saudi Arabia), 459
Faith, Don C., Jr., 62
Fallaci, Oriana, 302
Far East Air Force, 51
Faulkner, William, 93–94
FBI. *See* Federal Bureau of Investigation
Federal budget, 563
    deficit, 562–63, 564
Federal Bureau of Investigation, 290, 328, 335, 389,
    475, 476, 487, 490
    see also Wiretaps
Federal Republic of Germany. *See* West Germany
Federal Reserve Board, 563
Fielding, Lewis, 223, 337, 342, 448, 469
Final Days, The (Woodward and Bernstein), 323*n.*
First Battalion, Twenty-sixth Infantry, 167–68, 174
First Infantry Division, 157, 158*n.*, 159, 160, 162,
    166, 170, 172, 173
    Second Brigade, 179
Fishhook, 174, 236, 237, 238
Flexible response, 83, 98, 99, 100
    see also Counterinsurgency
Flowers, Walter, 450, 469
Flying Fish Channel, 35, 38
Ford, Betty, 505
Ford, Gerald R., 169, 289, 317, 318, 364, 396, 442,
    450, 468, 470, 480–86, 492–93, 496, 497–98,
    501, 505
    Nixon pardon, 513–15, 518–19
    presidency, 509–19, 526, 528, 529–30, 531
    selection as Nixon's vice president, 368, 369, 370,
        408, 412, 419, 427, 428, 440
    selection of Rockefeller as vice president, 512–13
Foreign Affairs (publication), 257
Foreign policy, 22–23, 68–70, 91–92, 98–100,
    230–31, 534, 567–68
    covert actions substituting for, 549–50
    domestic politics intrusion into, 69–70
    and economic multipolarity, 558–59
    future directions, 553–68
    see also Cold War; Détente; specific countries,
        policies, presidents
Foreign Policy Research Institute, 545
Foreign Relations Committee. *See* under Senate,
    U.S.
Foreign Service, 194, 227, 234, 343
Formosa question, 23–24, 58
    see also Taiwan
Forney, Edward H., 34, 65
Forrest, Nathan Bedford, 97
Fort Knox, Kentucky, 73–76
Fox, Alonzo P., 31, 33
Fox mission, 31, 32, 33–34, 50
France, 82, 128, 562
Frankel, Max, 302
Freedom of Information Act, 223
French Indochina. *See* Indochina
Fulbright, J. W., 284–85

Gandhi, Indira, 203
Gang of Four, 265
Garment, Leonard, 339, 347, 354, 376–78, 393,
    402*n.*, 425, 426–27, 448–49, 513
Garrison, Samuel A. III, 469
General Agreement on Tariffs and Trade (GATT),
    558
General Services Administration, 500, 512
Genscher, Hans-Dietrich, 477
Georgetown University, 83, 315
Gergen, David, 444*n.*3
Germany. *See* East Germany; West Germany
Ghettos, urban, 566
Glubb, John, 247–48

Goldwater, Barry M., 118, 441, 491–92, 496–97,
    498–99, 509
Goodpaster, Andrew J., 520
Go Quietly . . . Or else (Agnew), 353
Gorbachev, Mikhail, 555
Gorman, Paul, 167, 168
Grand Rapids group, 442, 518
Grant, Ulysses S., 68
Gray, Harry, 545, 546
Gray, L. Patrick III, 324, 337, 476
Great Britain, 535
Great Hall of the People, 259
Great Society, 147, 565
Grechko, Marshal, 516, 521
Greece, 524
Griffin, Robert P. (Bobby), 489, 518
Grimsley, James A., 179
Gromyko, Andrei, 294
Gruenther, Alfred M., 73
Guatemala, 111–12
Guerrilla warfare, 100, 131, 151
Guevara, Ché, 100
Gulf of Tonkin incident, 117–24
Gulf of Tonkin Resolution, 122
Gulf War, 138, 162, 525–26, 549, 556, 558,
    566

Haag, Gunter, 77
Habib, Philip, 193–94, 195
Haig, Alexander Meigs (father), 3, 4–5, 6
Haig, Alexander M., Jr.
    and Agnew's resignation, 350–58, 360–61, 362–67
    ancestors, 6–7
    in Army
        promotions, 73–74, 82, 112, 183, 270–72
        resignation, 347
        retirement, 544–45
    assassination attempt against, 539–43
    assignments
        as Almond's duty officer, 19–66
        Annapolis, 78–79
        Army vice chief of staff, 291–92, 297–98
        Berlin-NATO desk, 93
        Cuban Missile Crisis study, 103
        Fort Knox, 74–76
        Fox mission, 31, 33–34
        Heidelberg, 82
        International Plans and Policy Division, 84,
            86–92
        JFK funeral preparations, 113–14
        as Kissinger's assistant, 189–91, 195–222
        as McNamara's assistant, 118–22, 126
        as Perot liaison, 201*n.*
        as Vance's assistant, 106–8, 110–12, 118
        War College, 153–56
        West Germany, 80–82
        West Point, 183–85
    Chief of Staff appointment, 331, 332–34
    childhood and adolescence, 3–11
    diplomatic experience
        China mission, 258–64
        Dobrynin meeting, 254–55
        first, 82
        Paris peace talks, 298–99
    education, 10, 11–18, 80, 82–83
    and Ford administration, 509–16
    health, 66, 165–66, 545
    Kissinger relationship, 197, 297, 334–35
    as NATO commander, 516–17, 520–29, 531,
        532, 535, 539–43
    Nixon relationship, 202, 268, 270–72, 296–97,
        474–75, 496
    and political campaigns, 544–46, 555, 562–63
    Reagan relationship, 546–48

as Secretary of State, 327, 416n., 534, 546–48, 567
and vice-presidential selections, 367–70, 512–13
and Vietnam
combat duty, 126, 156–80
missions, 235, 276, 278, 282–83, 292, 294–96, 304–5, 309–11, 313, 315–16
policies and options, 125–26, 136–39, 151–53
wounding of, 165–66
and Watergate affair, 291–92, 347–49, 548, 550
on causes of, 327–31
crisis management, 338–47
Nixon pardon, 513–16, 517–19
Nixon resignation, 478–86, 487, 494, 495–505
tapes, 373–80, 382–86, 392–406, 425–28, 430–33, 446–47, 449, 454–56, 472–78
testimony, 433–34, 449
and West Point, 9, 10, 11, 12–18
world view, 553–69
Haig, Alexander (son), 73, 315
Haig, Barbara (daughter), 79, 315, 540
Haig, Brian (son), 73, 315
Haig, Chester (uncle), 7
Haig, Francis (brother), 4, 5, 8, 489
Haig, Grandmother, 3, 6, 7
Haig, Howard (uncle), 7
Haig, Patricia Fox (wife), 19, 73, 74, 76, 79–80, 81, 82, 84, 202, 249, 315, 332, 334, 366, 489, 500, 520, 541, 542, 545
Haig, Regina (sister), 3–4, 5, 8, 10
Haig, Regina Anne Murphy (mother), 4, 5–6, 7–8, 9–10, 489
Haig for President Committee, 545
Haigspeak, 198, 325, 538, 566
Haiphong harbor, mining of. See Hanoi-Haiphong, bombing of
Haiti, 111
Haldeman, H. R., 209, 219, 286, 290, 291, 312, 328, 332–33, 334, 336, 342, 349, 351, 377, 379, 422, 429, 431–32, 446, 448, 456, 475, 487, 493–94, 500, 509
Halperin, Morton, 205
Hamilton, Alexander, 450
Hanoi-Haiphong, bombing of, 144, 283, 284, 287, 289, 293, 306, 308, 310, 311, 312, 313
Han River, 21, 41, 45
Harken, Daniel, 113
Harlow, Bryce, 345, 364, 368, 401–2, 441, 447, 468, 469, 470, 486
Hartley, Muriel, 258, 260, 261
Hartmann, Robert, 480, 481, 485–86, 510–11, 512, 513, 514, 515, 516
Harvard Law School, 388
Harvard University, 185
Hatch Act, 153
Hay, John H., 174
Heidelberg, 82
Helicopters, 163
Helms, Richard, 234, 273, 476
Hemingway, Ernest, 312, 313
Herrick, John, 123
Higby, Lawrence, 431
Higgins, Gerald, 15–16, 17
Hijackings, airplane, 242–43
Hill, Richard A., 175
Hiss, Alger, 188, 328, 329, 359, 464
Ho Chi Minh, 128, 229, 231, 266
Ho Chi Minh Trail, 147, 237, 239, 273, 278
Hoffman, Walter E., 366, 367
Hogan, Lawrence, 470
Hollingsworth, James F. (Holly), 156–57, 163, 177, 178
Holmes, J. C., 87
Hong Kong, 557

Hooker, Hans, 541, 543
Hoover, Herbert, 188
Hoover, J. Edgar, 210, 211, 212–13, 216–17, 217–18, 220–21, 223, 389
Ho Shai-lai, 30
Hostages, 243, 244, 550n., 552
House, Edward, 509
House of Representatives, U.S.
Judiciary Committee, 337, 416, 420, 421, 436, 437–38, 442–43, 445, 448, 450–51, 453, 454, 466, 468, 490, 494, 518
televised hearings, 469, 470, 473–74
Nixon support, 469–70
Vietnam War bombing halt bill, 316–17
see also Congress, U.S.; Senate, U.S.
Huang Hua, 256
Hudgens, Seth, 541
Hue, 286
Hughes, Howard, 390, 448, 495n.
Human rights, 533, 534, 536
Humphrey, Hubert, 141, 186, 188, 192
Hungarian Revolution (1956), 81–82
Hungary, 560
Hungate, William L., 474
Hungnam, 64–65
Hunt, E. Howard, 323, 337
Hussein, King (Jordan), 241, 242, 243, 244, 245, 247, 248
Hussein, Saddam, 549, 567
Hutchinson, Edward, 450
Huyser, Robert (Dutch), 538–39
Hyesanjin, 57, 58, 61

ICCS. See International Commission of Control and Supervision
Impeachment proceedings
for Nixon, 313, 361, 420, 421, 441, 442, 443, 450, 451, 469, 470, 471, 474, 475, 480, 482, 493, 494
for Nixon and Agnew, 350–51, 369n.
Inchon Landing, 28, 34–40, 46
Incrementalism (policy), 97, 98, 127, 147, 152, 155, 273, 309
India, 50, 241, 557
Indochina, 127–28, 131, 284
see also Cambodia; Laos; Vietnam War
Indonesia, 557
Indo-Pakistan War, 241
Inflation, 491, 492
Interdependence, international, 558
International Commission of Control and Supervision, 310, 311, 316
Internationalism, 559
International Monetary Fund, 561
International Plans and Policy Division, 84, 86–92, 93, 97
Iran, 534–39, 551, 552
hostages, 550n.
Kennedy administration policies, 84–92
Iran-Contra affair, 548–49, 550–52
Iran-Iraq War, 552
Iraq, 88, 244, 552
see also Gulf War
Iron Curtain, 49
Iron Triangle (Vietnam), 157–58, 170, 173
Isolationism, 559
Israel, 242, 243–48, 249, 250, 409–17, 459, 460–62, 524, 551, 552, 557
"Issues and Answers" (TV show), 449–50
Italy, 103, 104
ITT Corporation, 390, 450, 495n.

Jackson, Henry M. (Scoop), 462, 525
Jackson, Robert H., 215

Japan, 22, 28, 29–30, 557, 560
Japanese Peace Treaty, 70
Javits, Jacob, 311–12
Jaworski, Leon, 437–39, 443, 445, 447–48, 451, 453–55, 456, 467, 470, 472, 483n., 500–501, 517
Jefferson, Thomas, 210, 388
Jen-Min Jih Pao (Beijing newspaper), 149, 150
Jenner, Albert E., Jr., 445, 469, 518
Jews
  Iranian, 551, 552
  Soviet, 465, 525
  see also Israel
Jiang Qing, 262, 265
Johnson, Andrew, 450
Johnson, Harold K., 136, 139, 174
Johnson, Lady Bird, 141
Johnson, Louis A., 24, 50, 574n.27
Johnson, Lyndon B., 96, 124, 130, 136, 139, 186, 191, 192–93, 195, 210, 269, 285, 314, 437
  administration, 97, 126, 193
    Kennedy team, 141–45
    missing documents, 192–95
    wiretaps, 217n.
  dependence on McNamara, 145–47
  and Kennedy assassination, 114–16
  and Vietnam War, 126, 150–51
    Gulf of Tonkin, 117, 118, 119–20, 123
    reflections on, 140–45
Johnson, Robert H., 579n.9
Joint Chiefs of Staff, 93, 104, 235, 245n., 253, 298, 539
  Hanoi-Haiphong bombing, 306, 311
  Korean War, 47, 51
  SALT agreement, 288–89
  Vietnam War, 117, 130, 148
Joint Congressional Committee on Internal Revenue and Taxation, 500
Jones, David, 538
Jordan, 459
  Syrian invasion of, 241–51
Joulwan, George A., 168, 176, 345–46, 373, 500
Journalists, FBI wiretaps on, 218
Judiciary Committee. See under House of Representatives, U.S.; Senate, U.S.
Jupiter missiles, 103–5
Justice Department, U.S., 338, 343, 359, 360, 363, 365, 388, 392–93, 436, 437

Kalmbach, Herbert, 469
Keating, Kenneth, 101
Kenedy, Richard T., 87, 91–92
Kennan, George F., 11, 18, 99, 568
Kennedy, Edward M., 227, 277–78, 369, 418, 471
Kennedy, Jacqueline, 114
Kennedy, John F., 83, 106, 187, 191, 205, 230, 252, 253, 254, 269, 536, 554
  administration
    characteristics of, 94–95, 109–10
    Vietnam policies, 118, 122, 124, 126, 129, 130–32, 133, 134, 135, 137, 139
    wiretaps, 217n.
  assassination of, 112–16
  and Berlin Wall, 95–96
  and counterinsurgency, 99–100, 162
  Cuban policies
    Bay of Pigs, 94–95, 578n.3
    covert activities, 108–13
    missile crisis, 100–105
  foreign policy, 94, 98, 99–100, 147
  Iran policy, 85, 86, 90–91, 92
  presidential election, 329, 330
Kennedy, Robert F., 94, 105, 106, 108–9, 112, 114, 115, 578n.8

Kent State University, 238
Key Biscayne, 389, 391, 425
KGB, 115, 465, 540, 542
Khe Sanh, 273
Khmer Rouge, 225, 292
Khomeini, Ruhollah, 85n., 537, 539, 551
Khrushchev, Nikita, 86, 131–32
  Berlin Wall, 95–96
  Cuban missile crisis, 100, 102, 103, 104, 105, 109, 253
  Korean War, 21, 47, 48
Kill ratios, 164
Kilpatrick, Carroll, 515
Kim Il-sung, 47, 48, 49, 52, 205, 208
King, Martin Luther, Jr., 216
Kin Men, 31
Kissinger, Henry A., 189–91, 193, 238, 267, 271–72, 273, 387, 406, 444, 468, 493, 501, 512, 516, 517, 520, 545
  China diplomacy, 256, 257–58, 261
  Haig as assistant, 185–91, 195–222
  and Haig's return to White House, 334–35
  and Middle East, 243, 244, 247, 248–49, 249–50, 251, 410, 411, 412, 415, 416, 417
  as National Security assistant, 195–202, 203–4, 205, 206, 209
  and National Security Council leaks, 211, 212–14, 215–16, 219, 220–22, 328, 458
  personality, 196–98, 334
  relationship with Nixon, 203–4, 296–97, 305, 312, 457–58, 463, 477, 498, 499
  as Secretary of State, 344–45, 359, 389
  and Soviet naval base at Cienfuegos, 253, 254, 255
  and summit conference, 284, 285, 286, 287–89
  and Vietnam, 225, 226–30, 231, 232, 274, 318
    peace negotiations, 239–40, 278, 283, 287, 296–97, 298–99, 300–304, 305–6, 307–8, 312, 313, 314
Kissinger, Nancy, 545
Kleindienst, Richard G., 332
Knesset, 243
Knight Newspapers, 355
Korea. See North Korea; South Korea
Korean War, 18, 19–70, 568
  casualties, 46–47, 63–64, 67–68
  horror of, 54–55
  and "limited war" policy, 22–23
  U.S. military strength at onset, 24–25
Koto-ri Plateau, 56, 63
Kraemer, Fritz, 189
Kraft, Joe, 198, 312
Kuomintang, 33
Kurds, 88–89
Kuykendall, Dan, 421
Kuznetov, V. V., 150
Ky, Nguyen Cao. See Nguyen Cao Ky

La Casa Pacifica, 470
Ladd, Fred, 26, 36
Laird, Melvin R., 203, 227, 254, 267, 273, 297, 298, 306, 345, 401, 441, 468, 494
  Cambodia policies, 234, 236, 237
  EC-121 incident, 204, 206, 208–9, 245n.
  Vietnam policies, 225, 226, 228, 282, 300, 308–9, 316, 317
Lansdale, Edward, 128, 129, 132, 578n.8
Laos, 133, 231, 273, 274, 277, 279, 310, 316
Lao Tzu, 272
Lash, Pete, 79
Latin America, 557
  Cuban influence in, 111–12
Lawrence, D. H., 9

Leaks, 228, 511, 547
  Agnew and, 363, 365
  Nixon and, 253, 270, 272, 359, 499
  NSC, 210–23, 328, 389, 457, 458
  presidential responses to, 210
  Vietnam War-related, 237, 302
  Watergate-related, 346, 355, 371–72, 388–89,
    393, 395, 397, 403, 407, 419, 441, 457
  see also Plumbers
Lebanon, 82, 551
Le Duc Tho, 231, 233, 239, 286, 298, 305, 307–8,
  314
Left, the (political philosophy), 187–88, 231, 327,
  328, 330, 387, 450, 536, 540, 559
LeMay, Curtis E., 105
Lemnitzer, Lyman, 94–95, 99–100, 517
Lenin, Nikolai, 225
L'Europeo (publication), 302
Liberals, 329, 438, 559
"Limited war" policy, 22–23, 98, 132
Lincoln, Abraham, 113, 561
Lin Piao, 50
Lodge, Henry Cabot, 135, 295
Lombardo, Tom, 27
Long-Term Defense Program, 526
Lon Nol, 233, 234, 235, 239
Los Angeles Times, 457
Lost Honor (Dean), 321
Lotze, Werner, 542–43
Lower Merion High School, 11
Lumumba, Patrice, 579n.9
Luns, Joseph, 523–24

MacArthur, Arthur, 36
MacArthur, Douglas, 17, 19, 20–31, 34, 35, 36–37,
  39, 41, 43, 47, 49, 50, 51, 52, 56–57, 62, 64,
  66, 68
MacLean, Allan D., 62
Maddox (destroyer), 117, 119, 120, 122, 123, 124,
  147
Mafia, 112
Magruder, Jeb Stuart, 342
Malaya, 127, 133
Malaysia, 557
Malik, Jacob, 23
Manchuria, 58
Mann, James, 469
Mansfield, Mike, 233–34, 244, 367, 494, 502, 525
Mao Zedong, 17–18, 100, 132, 256, 259, 262
Marcos, Imelda, 203
Mardian, Robert, 448
Marsh, John (Jack), 169–70, 480, 485, 513, 514,
  518
Marshall, George Catlett, 21–22, 50, 51, 297–98
Marshall Plan, 70, 560
Martin Marietta Corporation, 80
Marxism-Leninism, 10–11, 127, 531, 539–40,
  549–50, 553, 555, 567
  see also Cold War
Massachusetts Institute of Technology, 185
Massive retaliation, 98, 138
McCarthy, Eugene, 227
McCloskey, Paul, 441
McCone, John A., 112
McCulloch, William M., 450
McGovern, George, 227, 278, 293, 330
McNamara, Robert S., 100, 101, 110, 114, 137,
  189–90, 216–17
  intellect of, 123–24, 145–47
  and Vietnam, 117, 118, 119, 120, 121, 131, 136,
    144, 151
"McNamara Line," 124
M Company, 77

Meany, George, 418
Media. See Leaks; News media; specific publications
Medicare/Medicaid, 563
Meir, Golda, 245–47, 248, 324, 410, 461
"Menu" (code name), 214
Mexico, 557
Michaelis, John H. (Mike), 77
Middle East, 82, 87, 241–51, 342, 396, 402, 406,
  408, 457, 535, 551, 557
  crisis (Yom Kippur War) (1973), 409–17
  Nixon trip, 459–62
  see also Gulf War; Palestine Liberation
    Organization; Persian Gulf; specific countries
Military Academy, U.S. (West Point), 9, 10, 11,
  12–18, 76–78, 93–94, 157, 183, 315
Milk-fund scandal, 369n., 390, 446n., 448, 450,
  495n., 513, 530
MIRV, 462, 463
Missile crisis (1962). See Cuba, missile crisis
Missile gap, 83, 101–2
Missiles, Jupiter, 103–5
Mitchell, John N., 212–13, 324, 337, 340–41, 342,
  353, 422, 448, 452
Mogg, John, 520
Mondale, Walter, 532
Moorer, Thomas H., 245n., 273, 309, 311, 323, 416
Moss, John E., 409
Mossad, 551–52
Mossadeq, Ali, 90
Mossadeq, Mohammed, 84, 90
Muccio, John J., 19, 20
Multipolarity, economic, 557–58
Mupyongni, 60, 62
Murphy, Edward (grandfather), 6–7, 15
Murphy, John (great-uncle), 6
Murphy, Regina Anne. See Haig, Regina Anne
  Murphy (mother)

Nader, Ralph, 390, 418, 446n.
National Archives, 390, 500, 512
National Council of Reconciliation and Concord,
  299, 304
National debt, 562–63, 564
National Guard, 74–75
Nationalist China. See Taiwan
National Liberation Front, 227, 281, 293, 295, 299
National Press Club, 22, 403, 404
National Security Agency, 430, 432
National Security Council, 31, 119, 163, 191, 193,
  199, 209, 304, 462
  flexible response policy paper, 99
  leaks, 210–23, 328, 389, 457, 458
National Strategy Seminar, 155–56
NATO
  Haig at Berlin desk, 93
  Haig as commander, 516–17, 520–29, 531, 532,
    533, 534, 535, 555
  and terrorist threats, 539–43
  twenty-fifth anniversary, 463
  U.S. commitment issue, 103–4
Naval Academy, U.S. (Annapolis), 78–79
Naval War College, U.S., 82
NBC News, 407
Neeson, John H. (uncle), 7–8, 11, 12
Neeson, Mame (aunt), 7–8
Nesses, Ron, 515
Netherlands, 523–24
Neutron weapons. See Nuclear weapons
New Left, 231
  see also Left, the
News media, 183, 218, 253–54, 269, 277, 284, 287,
  311, 327, 344, 390, 427, 441, 457, 469, 499,
  511, 540, 546
  see also Leaks; specific publications or networks

New York Daily News, 337, 448
New York Times, The, 210, 214, 217, 253, 302, 312, 337, 347, 372, 385, 425, 457, 515
Ngo Dinh Diem, 118, 128–29, 130, 134–35, 136, 310
Ngo Dinh Nhu, 134, 136
Ngo Dinh Nhu, Madame, 134
Nguyen Cao Ky, 278n.
Nguyen Phu Duc, 306, 317
Nguyen Van Thieu, 192, 217, 228, 229, 276, 277, 279, 281, 287, 292, 293, 302
 war negotiations and aftermath, 126, 278, 294–96, 299, 300–301, 304–5, 306–7, 309–11, 316, 317–18
Nguyen Van Vinh, 149
Nhu, Madame. *See* Ngo Dinh Nhu, Madame
Nhu, Ngo Dinh. *See* Ngo Dinh Nhu
Nicaragua, 111, 112, 549–51, 552
Ninth Viet Cong Division, 158
Nitze, Paul, 99
Nixon, Donald, 389
Nixon, Pat, 330n., 479
Nixon, Richard M., 69, 83, 126, 140, 141, 163, 186, 187–88, 190–91, 198, 267, 268, 509, 553
 and Agnew, 351–52, 354, 355, 356, 357–58, 362–63
 appointment of vice-presidential replacement, 367–70
 assassination plot against, 361–62
 assessment of, 285–86, 443–44
 and Cox's dismissal, 392, 394–95, 396, 398, 401, 403, 404, 405–6
 domestic policy, 292, 342, 343, 492
 enemies, 187–88, 419, 420–21, 438, 467
 "Expletive deleted" epitaph, 452
 finances, 389, 390, 478, 500
 foreign policy, 289–90, 445
  China normalization, 256, 257–58, 261, 262, 264, 265
  EC-121 incident, 204–9, 225
  Middle East, 242, 243, 244, 247, 248, 249, 250–51, 411, 412, 413, 415–16, 417, 459–62
  Soviet Union, 228–29, 252–55, 284, 285, 286, 463, 524
  summit conferences, 287–88, 289, 462, 464–65
 Haig relationship, 202, 268, 270–72, 296–97, 474–75, 496
 illness, 371–73, 458–59, 463
 impeachment. *See* Impeachment proceedings
 Kissinger relationship, 203–4, 296–97, 305, 312, 457–58, 463, 477, 498, 499
 pardon of, 500, 513–19
 personality, 194–95, 201, 202, 209, 227, 238–39, 246, 259, 268–70, 328, 338, 393, 408, 441, 452, 496, 502–3
 presidential papers, 500, 512
 public's view of, 314, 330, 337, 361, 384, 425, 442, 443, 448, 468–69, 474
 Republican principles, 226
 resignation, 223, 335, 425, 467, 472, 478–87, 493, 494, 495–505
 speech writing, 205
 and Vietnam War, 281–82, 284–85, 286, 289, 290, 308, 309
  attempts to end, 224–32, 294, 299–300, 312, 313, 314
  bombing of the North, 282, 283, 284–85, 287
  Cambodian incursion, 234–35, 236, 237–39
  missing Johnson administration documents, 192–95
  peace, 301–3, 305, 306–7
 Watergate affair. *See* Tapes, White House; Watergate affair
 and women heads of state, 203, 245–46

Nixon Doctrine, 230–31
Nixon family, 441, 479, 484, 487, 488, 489, 491, 504, 505
NLF. *See* National Liberation Front
Nobel Peace Prize, 314
North Atlantic Treaty Organization. *See* NATO
North Korea, 19–20, 21, 24–25, 34, 46, 52, 57
 EC-121 incident, 204–9
 see also Korean War
North Vietnam, 128, 131, 133, 137–38, 139
 bombing halt, 192, 225, 279–80
 bombing of, 119–22, 144, 147–48, 192, 229, 282, 283, 284–85, 287, 289, 290, 293, 306, 308, 310, 311, 312, 313
 Cambodia and, 234–35, 236
 Gulf of Tonkin and, 117, 119, 121, 122
 intransigence of, 224–25
 peace negotiations, 228–32, 278–79, 299, 305
 propaganda, 149
 see also Viet Cong; Vietnam War
North Vietnamese Army, 158, 163, 179, 235, 236, 273, 274, 278, 279, 281, 282, 283, 292, 299, 300, 301, 305, 310, 313
Notre Dame University, 11–12
NSC. *See* National Security Council
Nuclear war, 554
Nuclear weapons
 Carter policy, 532–33
 and Korean war, 28, 67
 U.S. superiority, 98, 100, 554
 see also Strategic Arms Limitation Treaties
NVA. *See* North Vietnamese Army

Office of Management and Budget, 562
Old Man and the Sea, The (Hemingway), 312–13
Oliva, Erneido, 106–7, 108, 111
OPEC, 444
Operations
 Cedar Falls, 170–73
 Desert Storm, 162, 556
 Flaming Dart, 148
 Junction City, 174
 Lam Son 719, 273–78, 279
 Mongoose, 108, 109
 Rolling Thunder, 148
Oreanda, 464–65
Osgood, Robert E., 132
Oswald, Lee Harvey, 115, 116
Owen, Henry, 532, 533

Pacification, 179–80
Packwood, Robert, 441
Pahlavi, Mohammed Reza, 84–85, 86, 88, 89, 90, 534, 535–38, 539
Paine, Thomas, 514
Pakistani-Indian War, 241
Palestine Liberation Organization, 241–42, 540, 542
Palestinians, 242, 243, 246
Panikkar, K. M., 50
Pardon
 of Nixon, 500, 513–19
 powers of the President, 483, 485–86
Paris Peace Talks, 201n., 229, 231, 233, 234, 239–40, 283, 286, 293–94, 296, 298–99, 305, 313
Parkinson, Kenneth, 448
Parrot's Beak, 236–37
Patton, George S., 44, 57
Pentagon, 86, 93, 152, 288, 462
 computers and, 123–24
 International Plans and Policy Division, 84, 86–87, 93, 97
 see also Defense Department, U.S.
People's Liberation Army (China), 56–58, 61–62, 64, 67, 134, 149

People's Republic of China. *See* China
Percy, Charles H., 338, 368
Perot, Ross, 201*n*.
Perpetual flame (Kennedy grave), 114
Persian Gulf, 86, 87, 89, 534–35, 562
    see also Gulf War
Petersen, Henry, 357, 358, 360, 363, 364, 388, 390, 392–93, 423, 436
PFLP. *See* Popular Front for the Liberation of Palestine
Pham Van Dong, 301
Philippines, 127, 132
Phnom Penh, 233, 234, 236
Phu Loi Local Force Battalion, 158, 160, 168–69
Pierpoint, Robert, 421
Pierre Hotel, 189, 190
Plain of Jars, 231
"Plausible deniability," 109
Pleiku, 148
PLO. *See* Palestine Liberation Organization
Plumbers, 223, 328, 337, 341
    see also Leaks
Podgorny, Nikolai, 289
Poland, 560
Pont, Jürgen, 542
"Poodle blanket," 97
Popular Front for the Liberation of Palestine, 242
Powers, Samuel J., 430, 432
POWs, 201*n*., 300, 308, 311, 313
Presidency
    computer analysis of writings, 187
    need for redefinition of, 561–62
    papers, 512*n*.
    see also Executive privilege; Pardon; specific presidents
Presidential Recordings and Materials Act of 1974, 512
Price, Ray, 345, 474, 478, 479, 488, 489, 490, 498
Princeton University, 185
Project List, 137
Protectionism, economic, 559, 560
Provisional Revolutionary Government, 293–94, 299, 311
Pursley, Robert, 206, 267
Pyongyang, 55, 68

Quang Tri, 281, 287
Quemoy. *See* Kin Men

Rabin, Yitzhak, 246, 247, 248, 249–50, 250–51, 460
Racism, 43, 565–67
Radio Hanoi, 302
Rather, Dan, 421
Reagan, Nancy, 546, 548
Reagan, Ronald, 169, 210, 285, 416*n*., 435, 494, 545, 549, 550*n*., 564
    administration, 546, 550*n*., 555, 563
    assessment of, 561–62
    domestic policy, 562
    relationship with Haig, 546–48
Rebozo, Charles G. (Bebe), 390, 392, 428, 484, 487
Red Army Faction, 542
Reeder, Russell T. (Red), 16, 17, 77
Regan, Donald, 548
Rehnquist, William, 472
Reminiscences (MacArthur), 30, 50
Republican Governors Conference, 432
Republican National Committee, 330, 367, 493
Republican party, 69–70, 226, 231, 284, 287, 300, 311, 317, 367, 390, 416, 428, 440–41, 470
Republic of Korea. *See* South Korea
Republic of Vietnam. *See* South Vietnam
Reston, James, 254, 312

Revolutionary Development Task Force, 169
Rhee, Syngman, 47, 60, 129
Rhee, Mrs. Syngman, 60
Rhodes, John J., 494, 497, 499
Rhyne, Charles, 436–37
Richardson, Elliot L., 316*n*., 335, 338, 350, 352–53, 355, 356, 357, 358, 360–61, 362, 363–64, 366, 367, 384–85, 386–87, 388, 389, 435
    and Cox dismissal, 392, 393–95, 396–404, 413–14
    resignation, 405–7, 419
Ridgway, Matthew B., 99
Right, the (political philosophy), 328, 536, 559
Robinson, Rembrandt C., 245*n*.
Rockefeller, Nelson A., 271, 285, 494, 512–13, 517, 545
Rodino, Peter W., Jr., 421, 442–43, 450–51, 466, 469
Rogers, Bernard W., 173, 184
Rogers, William P., 202–3, 204, 209, 225, 226, 227, 234, 236, 237, 247, 253, 254, 267–68, 273, 284, 287, 300, 344, 359–60, 367
ROK. *See* South Korea
Romania, 262
Roosevelt, Franklin D., 105, 215, 297, 561
    administration wiretaps, 217*n*.
Rostow, Walt W., 131
Ruckelshaus, William, 363, 406, 407, 419
Ruin and Recovery (Ambrose), 421
Rumsfeld, Donald, 516, 529, 530
Rusk, Dean, 49*n*., 70, 133, 148, 149–50
Russell, Richard, 244
Russia, 556, 560, 561
    see also Soviet Union
Russian Revolution, 567
Russo, Anthony J., 341
Ruth, Henry, 495*n*.

SACEUR. *See* Supreme Allied Commander Europe
SACLANT. *See* Supreme Allied Commander Atlantic
Sadat, Anwar, 415, 417, 459
St. Clair, James D., 449, 453, 454, 455, 457, 467, 468, 470, 472, 476, 477, 479, 488, 489, 490, 498
Sainteny, Jean, 228, 230
Saint Joseph's Preparatory School, 10
Saint Mathias School, 10
SALT. *See* Strategic Arms Limitation Treaties
Sanchez, Fina, 498
Sanchez, Manolo, 461, 498
San Clemente, 341, 389, 470, 490, 499
Sandinistas, 549, 550
Sandman, Charles W., 474
Sarbanes, Paul S., 327
Saturday Night Massacre, 407, 415, 439
Saudi Arabia, 459
SAVAK, 85, 537
Saxbe, William B., 436, 445, 493
Scaife, Richard Mellon, 453
Scali, John, 258
SCAP. *See* Supreme Command for the Allied Powers in Japan
Scheel, Walter, 372
Schemmer, Ben, 78
Schlesinger, James, 344, 411, 412, 416, 462, 465, 516, 522, 529–30
Schmidt, Helmut, 520, 523, 532–33
Schmückle, Gerd, 527–28, 542–43
Schweitzer, Robert L., 169, 172, 179–80
Scott, Hugh, 369, 485, 497, 499
Scowcroft, Brent, 258, 324, 344, 345, 416, 417
Secret Service, 361–62, 423–24, 500

Selective amnesty, 513–15
Senate, U.S.
  advise and consent powers, 386–87
  Foreign Relations Committee, 150, 284, 285, 327, 457, 458
  Judiciary Committee, 386, 436
  Select Committee on Presidential Campaign Activities (Watergate committee). *See* Ervin committee
  Select Committee to Study Government Operations with Regard to Intelligence Activities. *See* Church committee
  see also Congress, U.S.; House of Representatives, U.S.
Seoul campaign, 41–47
Separation of powers, 380, 381, 386–87
  see also Executive privilege
Shanghai Communiqué, 265–66
SHAPE. *See* Supreme Headquarters Allied Powers Europe
Shapp, Milton, 444
Sharon, Ariel, 551–52
Sharp, Grant, 119
Sherman, Forrest, 35
Shultz, George, 344, 468
Sihanouk, Norodom, 207, 233, 234
Silent Coup (Colodny and Gettlin), 245*n.*, 323
Silent Majority, 312
Singapore, 127, 557
Sirica, John J., 380, 384, 385–86, 391, 393, 419–20, 421, 422, 424, 432, 433, 443, 449, 451, 472, 476, 479
Sisco, Joseph, 416
Six Day War (1967), 242, 410
Smedberg, William R., 79
Smith, DeWitt, 121, 136, 137
Smith, O. P., 41, 45, 63
"Smoking gun," 469, 473, 475–77, 487, 488, 490–91
Social justice, 564–67, 565
Social problems, 559, 564–67
Social Security, 444, 563
Sonnenfeldt, Helmut, 416–17
Southeast Asia, 120, 133, 138, 139, 234–35
  see also Indochina; Vietnam War; specific countries
Southern Democrats, 471–72
South Korea, 19–21, 23, 28, 47, 557
  army, 21, 26, 28, 34, 45, 46, 55
  see also Korean War
South Vietnam, 118, 144, 146, 150, 163, 192, 225, 228, 234–36, 273, 279, 282, 283, 287, 289, 292, 293, 294, 299, 300–301, 310
  inception of U.S. involvement in, 128–39
  war aftermath, 316–18
  see also Army of the Republic of South Vietnam; Vietnam War
Soviet Union, 49, 67, 70, 81, 133, 257, 525, 553, 554–55, 560
  and Cuba
    Cienfuegos naval base, 241, 252–55
    missile crisis, 100–105
    understandings with U.S. on, 252, 253, 254, 255
  détente. *See* Détente
  disintegration of, 555–56
  and East Germany, 95, 96
  former republics, 560, 561
  and Iran, 86, 87–88, 91
  and Kennedy assassination, 115, 116
  Korean War, 21, 48
  life in, 464–65
  and Middle East, 241, 245, 246, 249, 250, 251, 409–10, 412, 413, 414–15, 416–17

and Nicaragua, 549–50
post-World War II, 17, 18
summit. *See* Summit conferences
Vietnam War, 137–38, 149–51, 153, 232, 279, 283–84
and wars of liberation, 98–99, 127–28
see also Cold War; Russia; Strategic Arms Limitation Treaties
Special Counsellor to the President, office of, 343
Special Forces, U.S. Army, 100, 131, 132, 133
Special prosecutor, 338–40, 392–95, 416
  appointment of new, 435–39
Sputnik, 101
Stalin, Josef, 21, 48, 49
Stans, Maurice, 340–41, 448, 452
Stasi, 542
State Department, U.S., 128
  Haig as secretary, 327, 416*n.*, 534, 546–48, 566
  and Iran, 85, 86, 91, 538
  and Kissinger, 227, 344–45, 359, 389
  and MacArthur, 30
  and Nixon, 193, 202–3, 234
  see also names of other State secretaries, e.g., Rogers, William P.
State of the Union message, 445
Stennis, John, 392, 394, 395, 396, 397, 398, 401, 403, 517
Stennis compromise, 392–406, 407, 419
Stevenson, Adlai E. III, 445
Strachan, Gordon, 448
Strategic Air Command, 102, 311
Strategic Arms Limitation Treaties, 285, 288–89, 294, 463
Strategic hamlets, 133
Stratemeyer, George E., 28–29
Sullivan, William (assistant director of FBI), 214, 215–16, 217–18, 219–20, 221
Sullivan, William (U.S. ambassador to Iran), 538, 539
Sulzberger, C. L., 253
Summit conferences, 284, 285, 286, 287–88, 462, 464–65
Supreme Allied Commander Atlantic, 526
Supreme Allied Commander Europe, 520–29
Supreme Command for the Allied Powers in Japan, 19, 20, 22, 30
Supreme Court, 438–39, 457
  Bork nomination, 435–36
  White House tapes, 391–92, 454, 466, 467, 468, 469, 472, 512
  wiretap rulings, 215, 222
Supreme Headquarters Allied Powers Europe, 524, 528, 543
Syria, 410, 412, 414, 459–60, 551
  invasion of Jordan, 241–51
Szulc, Tad, 579*n.8*

Taiwan, 22, 30–33, 48, 70, 265, 557
  see also Formosa question
Tang, Nancy, 260, 262, 264
Tang Wensheng. *See* Tang, Nancy
Tank, the (Pentagon), 93, 104
Tapes, White House, 333*n.*, 341–42, 349, 373–81, 382–408, 421–56, 466–86
  court decisions, 386, 391, 443, 472
  executive privilege, 380, 382–83, 384, 386, 391, 443
  gap in, 428–34, 449
  legal status, 376–79
  missing, 422–27, 432
  revelation of existence of, 373–74
  "smoking gun" tape, 473, 475–77, 487, 488, 490–91
  subpoenas, 379, 380, 383, 384, 437, 451, 453

summaries, 392–406
surrender of, 419, 421–22, 445, 454–56, 472
taping system, 373–74, 423–24
transcripts, 446–47, 451–53, 466
Task Force Faith, 63
Task Force Yoke, 66
Taylor, Maxwell D., 15, 16, 17, 99, 100, 104, 130–31, 144, 156
TerHorst, Jerald, 511, 514
Terrorism
  in Europe, 539–43
  Viet Cong, 134, 164, 170, 292
  see also Assassination headings
Tet offensive (1968), 235, 273
Thailand, 557
Thieu, Nguyen Van. See Nguyen Van Thieu
38th parallel, 19, 21, 46, 49–51, 65
Thompson, Fred D., 374
Thornton, Ray, 469
"Three Rs" plan, 526
Threshold Test Ban, 462–63
Thua Thien Province, 281
Thurmond, Strom, 340
Ticonderoga (carrier), 117, 118, 120
Time magazine, 425
Timmons, Bill, 469, 470, 499, 503
Todd, William B., 453
Tonkin Gulf incident, 117–24
Tower, John, 494
Transjordan, 242
Tribune-Review, 453
Truman, Harry S., 22, 23–24, 27, 30, 31, 57, 66, 141–42
  administration, 18
  wiretaps, 217n.
Truman Doctrine, 70
TTB. See Threshold Test Ban
Turkey, 524, 533–34
  missile removal, 103–5
Turner, Stansfield, 542
Turner Joy (destroyer), 117, 119, 122, 124, 147
Twitchell, Hamilton, 86–87, 88, 91–92

Uebel, Pat, 79
Ulbricht, Walter, 95
Uncertain Trumpet, The (Taylor), 99
Unilateralism, 559
Union of Soviet Socialist Republics. See Soviet Union
United Nations, 49, 50, 57, 62, 65, 234, 558
  Charter, 70
  Resolution, 242, 414
  Security Council, 23, 413, 414n.
United States Military Academy. See Military Academy, U.S.
United Technologies Corporation, 545, 546
United We Stand (orgn.), 201n.
University of California, 545
University of Pennsylvania, 545
University of Texas, 187
Usery, W. J., 444
USSR. See Soviet Union

Vance, Cyrus R., 106, 109, 110, 111, 114, 118, 156, 232, 531, 532, 533, 537
Vann, John Paul, 172
Vesco, Robert L., 341, 348n., 390, 448, 450, 452
Veterans of Foreign Wars, 523–24
Vice-presidential appointments, 367–70, 512–13
Viet Cong, 131, 132, 134, 144, 146, 148, 149, 151, 157, 159, 165, 180, 225, 299, 310
  in Cambodia, 233, 236
  casualties, 178–79, 232, 286
  Cu Chi tunnels, 170–72, 173

Phu Loi battalion, 158, 160, 168–69
  strength, 158, 160–61, 235, 292
  terrorism, 134, 164, 170, 292
Viet Minh, 128, 132, 233
Vietnam. See North Vietnam; South Vietnam; Vietnam War
Vietnamization, 226, 228–29, 230, 235, 266, 273, 278, 279, 281, 308
Vietnam War, 69, 97, 117–80, 183–86, 192, 224–40, 273–318, 567
  aftermath, 315–18
  American military presence, 130, 131, 148, 150, 151, 156, 163, 225, 278, 286
  withdrawal of. See Vietnamization
  antiwar movement, 184, 238, 284
  bombing of North Vietnam. See North Vietnam, bombing of
  and Cambodia, 139, 153, 180, 207, 214, 225, 233–40, 279, 292, 310, 316
  casualties, 122, 126, 148, 163, 174, 178–79, 225, 232, 276, 277, 286
  and China, 125–26, 128, 133–34, 148–51, 261, 279, 283
  consequences, 186
  draft, 185–86, 513–14
  early involvement of U.S., 128–39
  Gulf of Tonkin incident, 117–24
  invasion of South, 281–82
  Johnson's reflections on, 140–45
  and Laos, 231, 273, 274, 277, 279, 310, 316
  in 1964, 147–48
  pacification, 179–80
  peace negotiations. See Paris Peace Talks
  POWs issues, 201n., 300, 308, 311, 313
  and Soviet Union, 137–38, 149–51, 153, 232, 279, 283–84
  as U.S. "Disaster of the Three Mistakes," 125–26
  U.S. policy, 125–26, 136–39, 151–53
  see also Army of the Republic of South Vietnam; North Vietnam; North Vietnamese Army; Paris Peace Talks; South Vietnam; Viet Cong
Virginia Military Institute, 42–43
Voltaire, 567
Vorontsov, Yuli M., 251
Vyshinsky, Andrei, 70

Walker, Walton H. (Johnny), 27, 36, 40–41, 49, 62
Wallace, George, 188, 470–71
Wall Street Journal, 355, 357
Walters, Vernon (Dick), 203, 476
Wang Hugwen, 264–65
War College, U.S. Army, 153–56
Warren Commission, 115, 116
Warsaw Pact, 553
Wars of liberation, 98–99, 127
War Zone C, 157, 174, 179, 180
Washington, D.C., 565
Washington Post, 210, 217, 321, 322, 325, 331, 337, 342, 347, 363, 388, 457, 478, 515
Washington Special Actions Group, 244, 247, 248, 249, 415
Watergate affair, 223, 290, 291, 321–49, 371–408, 418–56, 466–505, 548, 550
  causes of, 327–31
  Dean's testimony, 347–49, 421–22, 447–48
  Deep Throat, 321–26
  early stage, 332–38
  grand jury, 449, 454
  Nixon as unindicted coconspirator, 454, 456, 457, 466–67
  special counsel appointment, 339–40
  special prosecutor appointments, 338–40, 392–95, 416, 435–39
  tapes. See Tapes, White House

Watergate committee. *See* Ervin committee
Webb, James H., Jr., 185*n.*
Weinberger, Caspar, 401, 416*n.*
Welch, Joseph N., 449
West Germany, 80, 82, 128, 527–28, 532, 542
    NATO forces, 523
Westmoreland, William C., 162, 167, 172, 298
West Point. *See* Military Academy, U.S.
Weyand, Fred C., 275
Wheeler, Earle, 117, 158, 211
White House Communications Agency, 262
White House tapes. *See* Tapes, White House
"White Revolution" (Iran), 90, 535
Wiggins, Charles, 484, 488
Williams, Edward Bennett, 339, 369*n.*
Williams, Harrison A., 419
Willoughby, Charles A., 50, 57
Wilson, Charles E., 98
Wiretaps, 213–23, 341, 359, 389, 457, 458, 495*n.*
    Supreme Court rulings, 215, 222
    see also Tapes, White House
Wolmi-do, 39
Wonsan, 52, 53, 54, 56
Woods, Rose Mary, 426, 428–29, 430, 433, 436,
    446, 449, 491, 492, 494, 498
Woodward, Bob, 321, 322, 323, 324–26, 391

World War II, 10, 21, 553, 560
Worldwide Associates, 548
Wright, Charles Alan, 380–81, 383, 384, 385, 393,
    394, 399, 400, 401, 402*n.*, 414, 422, 448–49
WSAG. *See* Washington Special Actions Group

X Corps, 34, 39, 41, 51–65 *passim*
Xe Lilang, 256*n.*
Xuan Thuy, 229–30, 240
Xu Jingxian, 263

Yakubovsky, Ivan I., 95–96
Yale University, 185*n.*
Yalta, 464
Yalu River, 50, 51, 56, 57–58, 59, 60
Yom Kippur War (1973), 409–17, 524
Yongdungpo, 21
Yoshida, Shigeru, 29–30
Young, Sam, 324

Zhdanov, A. A., 127
Zhou Enlai, 48, 50, 133–34, 150, 256, 258, 259,
    260–62, 266
Ziegler, Ron, 222, 258, 263, 332, 345, 362, 368,
    372, 474, 478, 487–88, 489, 496, 500
Zumwalt, Elmo, 462, 521